America Reads   Seventh Edition

Explorations
in Literature

America Reads Seventh Edition

Beginnings in Literature
Alan L. Madsen
Sarah Durand Wood
Philip M. Connors

Discoveries in Literature
Edmund J. Farrell
Ruth S. Cohen
L. Jane Christensen

Explorations in Literature
Ruth S. Cohen
Nancy C. Millett
Raymond J. Rodrigues

Patterns in Literature
Edmund J. Farrell
Ouida H. Clapp
Karen J. Kuehner

Traditions in Literature
James E. Miller, Jr.
Helen McDonnell
Russell J. Hogan

The United States in Literature
The Red Badge of Courage Edition
Three Long Stories Edition
James E. Miller, Jr.
Carlota Cárdenas de Dwyer
Kerry M. Wood

England in Literature
Macbeth Edition
Hamlet Edition
Helen McDonnell
John Pfordresher
Gladys V. Veidemanis

Testbooks

Guidebooks

America Reads Seventh Edition

Explorations
in Literature

Ruth S. Cohen

Nancy C. Millett

Raymond J. Rodrigues

Scott, Foresman and Company

Editorial Offices: Glenview, Illinois
Regional Offices: Palo Alto, California
Tucker, Georgia
Glenview, Illinois
Oakland, New Jersey
Dallas, Texas

Ruth S. Cohen   Free-lance writer and editor of books for young people. Editor-Compiler of *Craft of Detection, The Life Force, Present Imperfect, Edges of Reality,* and *The Fractured Image.*

Nancy C. Millett   Professor of Secondary Education, Wichita State University. Coauthor of *How to Read a Poem* and *How to Read a Short Story.* Coauthor of literature, grammar, and composition textbooks for secondary and elementary schools. Formerly teacher of English at the University of Rochester and Wichita High School East. Consultant on writing.

Raymond J. Rodrigues   Professor of Education and Director of Teacher Education at New Mexico State University. Executive Board member of NCTE Conference on English Education. Formerly high-school teacher of English in Nevada and New Mexico. Past President of the Southern Nevada Teachers of English and the Utah Council of Teachers of English.

Cover: Embroidery worked freehand in wool on canvas by Miss Letitia Neill, circa 1910. BPCC Publishing Corporation/Aldus Archive, courtesy Mr. and Mrs. J. R. Williams.

Pronunciation key and dictionary entries are from *Scott, Foresman Advanced Dictionary* by E. L. Thorndike and Clarence L. Barnhart. Copyright © 1983 Scott, Foresman and Company.

ISBN: 0-673-27002-5

Copyright © 1985
Scott, Foresman and Company, Glenview, Illinois
All Rights Reserved. Printed in the United States of America.

45678910VHJ93929190

Table of Contents

Unit *1*

*T*ake a Chance

Unit *2*

*L*earning to Cope

Unit 3

*P*oetry

Unit 4

*G*enerations

Unit **5**

*T*he Well-Told Tale

Unit *6*

*O*ut of Control

Unit 7

Greek Myths

Unit 8

*T*he Diary of Anne Frank

*H*andbook of Literary Terms

*C*omposition Guide

No matter whether you want to be the first to climb a mountain, or just to escape in some way from poverty; to catch a murderer and win a reward, or simply to defend yourself against thieves; to be the best in the world, or merely to feel you belong; sometime, somehow, you have to take chances.

Take a Chance

My Teacher, the Hawk

Jean McCord

To say he never forgave me is one thing. To say I've never forgiven myself is another.

I live on a small place about five miles out of town with my grandparents. It isn't really a farm; we've only got six acres, but we keep chickens and plant a garden, and there's lots of room to grow up in.

My grandparents are good people. Five Christmases ago, when I was ten years old, my grandfather, whom I've always called Popsie, asked me what I wanted that year.

"I'd sure like a gun," I answered, looking slant-eyed at my grandmother who hated guns and hunting of any sort.

"Larry, you're too young for a gun," my grandmother spoke up. "You could shoot yourself. Or someone else. What would you do with one, anyway?" Her mouth was pursed with disapproval, but she kept her eyes down on her sewing.

"Tin cans," I muttered. "Target practice. Lots of kids my age have guns. Jim Johnson's got a real deer rifle." This was almost a downright lie. All he had was a .22, and I knew it.

On Christmas morning there was a long, skinny package for me beneath the tree. I sucked in my breath. Had my grandmother relented, or was she pacifying me with a toy bow and arrow set? I ripped open the box. Inside was a beautiful Remington .22 rifle and four boxes of shells.

Popsie's face was a smiling circle. "I talked her into it," he nodded his head toward grandmother, "on condition that you use it properly, of course."

"Oh, Gram," I gave her a bear hug around her short little neck. "You know I'm pretty responsible."

"Huh!" she said, grunting through my hug.

That afternoon Popsie and I went out into the cold, brown fields. Popsie had once been a pretty good hunter himself, but now a bad leg kept him from it. And, I imagined, my grandmother.

"You know, don't you," Popsie was saying, "that you never point a gun at anything or anyone unless you intend to kill them. These stories you hear about accidental shootings are all poppycock as far as I'm concerned. Everyone knows a gun is for one thing only and that is . . . to kill. I don't mean you should ever intend to kill anyone. I'm only saying that if you ever point a gun at a person, even in fun, that's more'n likely what's going to happen."

We'd brought along some empty tin cans and Popsie set them up on a fence post. He showed me how to load the gun, how to carry it safely, and even made me practice going through a fence with it. I had to unload every time, set the gun through the wires, then crawl through myself.

When we were potting at the tin cans, Popsie scored a hit every time, but I never even saw where my shots were going.

"It's a matter of relaxing," he kept telling me. "Everything in the world is best

© 1982 George McLean

done relaxed. Believe me. Even work. Most of all, work.''

We shot up all the shells. By the end of the day I knew what Popsie meant. Line up the sights, relax, squeeze the trigger slowly, and no flinching when the gun went off.

I was content with just target practice for a long time, but when I got so I could hit the cans ten times out of ten shots, I began to look around for something a little more exciting. My first chance came when Grandma came raging in from her garden.

''Those blasted jack rabbits,'' she slammed down a puny handful of carrots the size of my fingers. ''They went right down the rows. Ate half the lettuce, all the carrotops, and most of the beetops, too.''

It was Spring now and Grandma worked her garden in the early morning and again in the evenings until the light failed and she looked like a little hunched-over scarecrow out there in the twilight.

I didn't say anything to her, but that evening after she had straightened up and put away her tools, with Popsie's consent I sneaked down to the garden and cleverly concealed myself in a clump of bushes. When the rabbits came, I could see them clearly in the wash of moonlight that lay over the land, and I picked them off one by one. Rabbits are pretty dumb. They kept coming back, and I kept getting them that night and several nights afterward. In a couple of days Grandma's garden was growing in peace. She didn't say a word to me about it. I guess she knew it was either that or lose her entire garden.

One night we were sitting around, Popsie reading his paper, and I was studying. Suddenly we heard a terrible commotion in the hen house. There is nothing in the world noisier than a bunch of frightened chickens, and they had really cut loose this time. Popsie and I jumped up, and I raced to my bedroom for my gun. We got to the hen house just in time to see a big raccoon coming out with two eggs clutched to his chest. His startled face with those black lines on it looking like a masked bandit peered up at us in the light of Popsie's flashlight. The sight of such a bold robber who had braved squawking hens and my gun for the sake of two eggs made me laugh so hard, I fired over his head just to scare him. He dropped his stolen eggs and high-tailed it to another county.

After that I gave up shooting at tin cans. Instead I roamed the countryside taking pot shots at whatever flew or moved beneath my sights. I did in a lot of ground squirrels, and I don't know how many mourning doves because they just sat low on a tree limb giving out with those sad calls of theirs. Something about their mournful cries in the bright warm sunlight and the good smells of summer infuriated me, and I shot every one I could. I popped off all the bluejays, and in the back of my mind, I could hear Popsie vindicating me.

"The bluejays rob other nests, and Larry kills the bluejays. It's a balance of nature that used to be taken care of in other ways."

And, of course, with these minor triumphs, I began to swell with ambition for something really big and thrilling. I could see myself in the future as "the Big White Hunter," going to Africa and bringing down one of everything. A ground squirrel became, in my imagination, a rhinoceros who charged ferociously, and I brought him to his knees just three feet away from myself and some beautiful dame who had been chasing me all over Africa and I had to keep shooting lions and tigers and such that were creeping around her tent and about to eat her up. By the time I was fourteen, I'd just about shot out every animal in Africa, from the scoreboard in my mind.

I was fifteen when the thing happened to me that changed my life forever. I know now that I'll never hunt or kill a living thing again. I'd hung up my gun in my bedroom and hadn't had time for much hunting because now there was always work to be done around the place, fences to be repaired, tinkering with Popsie's old Dodge that should have been retired years ago, and always schoolwork. Some teachers seemed to think a guy had nothing to do except make reports and write essays and study like he was making out to be a Nobel Prize winner or something.

It was a Sunday morning and Grandma had gone off to services, after which she would stand around and yak a lot with other old ladies. I don't know what they found to talk about, but it always seemed to entrance them for hours.

Popsie came in from outside, stomping his big feet at the door to shake the mud. "There's a hawk after the chickens," he announced. "He's been around all week. Got over half of the Banty[1] babies already."

We looked at each other. When a person keeps livestock and animals, it becomes his duty, and his right, to protect them from predators. It's always been that way.

I went into my bedroom and unracked my gun, wondering in the back of my mind if I had lost my skill. I walked out into our orchard of old, gnarled trees and went down to the far end, leaning against one of the trees to load my gun and look around.

I saw him then, floating high on air currents, almost over my head, and looking down at the grass. I saw that the mother hen with the remaining half of her little black chicks had seen him too, and was clucking in a frantic manner. The baby

---

1. *Banty,* Bantam, a variety of chicken.

chicks stooped close to the ground and hid their heads and bright eyes so that only their little black bottoms showed as a smudge against the earth.

I aimed through the branches of the tree as the hawk drifted sideways, riding the wind like he was some child's kite, loose and on its own, and when he was in my sights, I let go. With the crack of the gun and the smell of acrid smoke came a sudden change in the arrogant flight of the hawk. He slipped sideways against the wind, one wing folded under him, and the other spread out like black fingers clawing at the sky. He went into a power dive, headed straight at the ground, and gaining speed every second. He hit somewhere at the bottom of the orchard.

Setting my gun down, I raced to where I had seen him smash, but though I searched every bit of brush and grass clumps, he was nowhere to be found.

When I returned to the house, Popsie raised an eyebrow at me over his Sunday paper.

"Got him," I said. "He won't be eating chicken dinners anymore."

Then I forgot about the hawk as I cleaned and racked my gun and sat down at the dining room table with my books and papers.

The next day it rained. The day after, it not only rained, it poured down water from the sky as if someone had pulled a plug from the bottom of the ocean. Five days later it was still raining and everyone's nerves were rusty and raw. The teachers were getting so snappy no one dared do anything except bend over books and try to study in gloomy light.

On Saturday morning the rain turned itself down into a thin drizzle and I felt as if I had been living underwater for almost a week. I decided to take a short walk just to get out of the house for a while.

Without thinking, because it was simply easier to walk downhill, I sloughed through the dripping grass towards the bottom of the orchard. And it was while I was standing there, looking off into a light mist below our land, that I saw the hawk.

He was standing upright on spindly legs beneath a mesquite bush and he was glaring at me out of red-rimmed eyes as if he wanted to stare me to death. I was shocked. Popsie's teaching words of five years ago hit me in the stomach. "A hunter never lets a wounded animal get away to die a lingering painful death . . . a sportsman . . ."

Yeah! I was some sportsman. I had knocked this animal down out of his territory, the sky, and left him helpless in the pouring rain for a week. I had honestly thought him dead last Sunday, but that didn't excuse me. Standing there with the drizzle falling down my neck, I had to face up to what I really was, and it left me feeling sick and shameful.

I took a step towards the hawk, not knowing quite what I was going to do. He didn't back off: instead he set himself for a fight. He lifted one wing, shifted his weight like a boxer, and stretched his neck towards me with his beak ready like a sword. His other wing was broken at the shoulder, and it dragged on the ground with the pinion feathers all splayed and ragged. Standing tensed that way, I could see better what had happened to him. His body had shrunken in along the breast bone and he looked more like a bundle of wet old rags than the powerful bird he had once been. I knew he was starving. And, with that thought, I also knew I had to help him.

I slipped out of my jacket, spread it wide, and threw it over him. He put up a struggle, but couldn't get at me through the heavy leather which I pulled under and around his knife-edge claws. I picked the whole bundle up carefully. I didn't know what I was going to do with him, and I was too ashamed to ask Popsie. We had a small tool shed used only for storage, so I took him there, and set him on a table, trying to ease my jacket out from him. His claws had hooked into the lining and he clung to it. When I reached it to loosen them, his beak plunged down and split open the back of my hand. Well, I thought, jerking my hand up to my mouth, I guess maybe I deserved that.

"Keep the jacket, Joe Louis,"[2] I said. "I'll fix my hand up, then try to see what you'll eat."

I sneaked into the house, wanting to bandage my hand before my grandparents saw it and asked a lot of questions. I had no stomach for answering questions right then. Fortunately they were somewhere in the front of the house, so I fixed my hand, then went to the refrigerator wondering what a hawk might eat. I took out some hamburger and a slice of bologna.

When I eased myself through the tool shed door, the hawk was stepping disdainfully out of my jacket as if he had killed it good and proper. I tossed the meat towards him, not wanting to lose another hand, and in a flash he pounced on it, ripping the slice of bologna in half and tried to swallow the whole chunk. It stuck halfway in his throat, so he spit it out and tried the hamburger. He could handle this better, and ate it all. Then he swayed towards me, clattering his beak, as if now he was really ready to fight.

We watched each other. When he saw I wasn't going to attack him again, he eased to the back of the table into a corner, and hunched down, letting his eyes film over,

like he couldn't be bothered with me anymore.

I left him then. At least, he was out of the rain, and had eaten, probably the first time in a week.

On Sunday I fed him some more hamburger balls and left a pan of milk beside his dish of water. I was pretty sure he wouldn't know anything about milk, but I was willing to try anything.

Monday noon, at the school cafeteria, I went over to this rather big girl named Janice Allack. I'd never spoken to her before, but I knew her reputation for rescuing and finding homes for all sorts of orphan animals. I'd heard she had about fifty cats and no one knew how many dogs out at her home. She ran a regular animal shelter league, and probably knew more about animals than anyone else around for hundreds of miles.

"Look," I said, sort of low to her, "I've got this hawk out at my home. His wing's busted. I wonder if you could come out and sort of show me what to do? You know, put it in a splint, or something?"

"Why, sure, Larry," she looked up at me over her macaroni and cheese. "I'll ride the bus home with you tonight. OK?"

"OK." I went back to my lunch feeling relieved. If Janice could fix up the hawk, repair his wing so he could fly again, maybe he'd quit hating me so much, and I'd stop feeling like a low-down worm.

We rode home with Janice sitting by my side chatting happily about all the animals she had fixed up. I guess she was doing what made her feel good. I never mentioned all the animals I had killed.

---

2. **Joe Louis,** a well-known boxer, heavyweight champion of the world from 1937 to 1949.

"Where'd you get the hawk?" she asked.

"Oh, I found him out in the field," I said. "My grandparents don't know about him yet. I've got him locked up in the tool shed."

"Well, there's nothing shameful about helping a wounded animal," she said, twisting sideways to look at me.

"No, I guess not," I answered, shrinking down in my seat.

We jumped off the bus and walked up the lane to my home. It had finally stopped raining, but the ground still felt like you were walking on a sodden sponge.

My grandparents were a little surprised at seeing Janice. It was the first time I'd ever brought a girl home. I guess they thought I was never going to get to that stage.

Then Grandma said, "Larry, what do you have locked in the tool shed? It's been screaming in rage all day."

Janice and I looked at each other.

"Give me some hamburger, Gram. I've got to feed it," I said. "It's a hawk."

I took Janice down to the shed and unlocked it. When we came through the door, the hawk was sitting on the highest shelf; somehow he'd managed to climb up there, knocking over everything in his way. He launched himself straight at us and the open door, but he only managed one wing stroke before he fell to the floor and spun around in dusty circles. You could see he wasn't ever going to be a tame bird.

"Oh, the poor thing," Janice knelt down beside him, and before I could yell at her to watch out, she had her hands on him, pinning both wings so he couldn't hurt himself any more. And surprisingly, the hawk held still, craning his neck around to watch Janice examine his broken wing.

When she finished, she set him carefully back up on the shelf. I thought he would strike at her, but he didn't, just ruffling his feathers a bit in indignation.

"I don't think it can be fixed, Larry," she said gravely. "The bones are too shattered; he can't ever fly again. But isn't he a beauty? He's a redtail, isn't he?"

"I guess," I muttered. I really felt bad. She'd been my only hope of fixing up things between me and the hawk. "Here." I tossed his hamburger up beside him, but now he ignored it.

Janice spied a leather glove. She put it on and held the meat under the hawk's beak. She sure did know a lot about things, that girl. But the hawk wouldn't eat for her either.

"I don't think hamburger is exactly what he's used to," she said. "I'd try him on something else. A piece of steak maybe, cut in strips. If he won't eat that, you'd better go out and get him fresh food."

"Like what?" I croaked.

"Oh, I'd say live mice. And probably little frogs." She sounded so offhand, as if it was the easiest thing in the world. "That's what I'd do." She turned to me. "You do want to keep him alive, don't you? Have you named him yet?"

"Sure," I mumbled. "Sure. I call him Joe Louis." I showed her the back of my hand. "He's a real fighter. He might be down, but he isn't out."

"Joey," she said softly. "That's a nice name." She looked up at the hawk in sympathy. "I've got to go now. But maybe I can help you with him. Anyway, I'll come back. That is, if you want me to?" she added shyly.

"Well, sure. Sure I do. Thanks." I'd never noticed before, but Janice Allack was sort of pretty. Her hair was a soft brown, and her eyes were friendly, and she had this nice feeling of confidence about her as if she really knew who she was and what she would make out of her life. She was bigger than I was, but that was just for now. I hadn't gotten all my growth yet, but I knew it would come.

She came home with me again, three days later. The hawk had refused to eat anything, even a lamb chop which I'd wheedled out of Gram. And he screeched all the time, striking out in fury at the cans of paint and tools strewn around him. The day before I'd put him in a large cage for his own sake, and by now he had torn the sides of the cage into splintery shreds.

Janice dug into a big purse she was carrying. "Here," she said, handing me a box. "My cats bring them in, you know." She hurried outside while I opened the box. Inside were two live mice. Wow! I thought. Whew! A girl who'd actually carry mice in her handbag. That was really something.

I tossed the mice in to Joey, being a little queasy about it myself, but Joey hit like a flash of light and the mice were dead quicker than they would have been in a trap.

"That's more like it," I said, going outside. "Only you'd better wait a minute before going back in."

We leaned against the wall, looking over the land which was coming into full bloom, it being spring and all. The grass was very tall and deep green, and the fruit trees were all covered with a pink froth that looked almost good enough to eat. Birds were darting all around, carrying things in their beaks, getting ready to make nests.

Inside, in a cage, Joey sat hunched over and brooding. I was beginning to know what he must have felt, feeling the air of spring, knowing the thin blue sky was still out there and the winds rising strong and somewhere, maybe, a mate still looking for him.

"Larry," Janice said, looking at me, "have you ever read a story by Walter Van Tilburg Clark? It's called 'Hook.' Just 'Hook.' And it's about a hawk who gets shot down out of the sky and has to live on bugs and battle other birds. In the end he has a fight with a dog." She didn't say anything for a while, then, "I think it is really and truly the most beautiful story I've ever read." She smiled, and turned to go in. "Let's see how Joey is doing."

She stood looking at the cage. "He's terribly angry, isn't he? It must be fierce, having a temper like that." She didn't say any more, but she didn't have to. It was all there in the tone of her voice. I knew she had guessed about me being the one who'd shot him. And I also knew, somehow, that she was trying to teach me something.

"Things do happen," she was saying. "Life is never absolutely safe for any of us, man or hawk. One does what one can, and that's all." She was murmuring to the hawk, and I guess because he had finally eaten, he was allowing her to stroke the top of his head very softly. "Joey, Joey," she told him, "you'll have to learn to accept."

She turned to me. "You'd better start hunting again. Things for him to eat. Try frogs. He won't eat any more hamburger, I'm sure.''

So I found myself going out at night, once more the Big White Hunter, only it didn't seem very noble to be sloshing around in swampy places getting covered with muck for the sake of tiny frogs. After a while though, it got to be a pretty good game if I could restrain myself from moving or shining my light until the frogs had all started singing madly in chorus like a High School Glee Club lacking only a Director.

Joey didn't have to eat every day. He wasn't moving around, so his appetite had dwindled down to a mouse and two or three frogs a week. His wing healed after a while, but not so he could raise it and fly with it. He spent a lot of time preening the feathers on it, straightening them out with his beak, as if he still had hopes.

After I'd had him over four months, and managed to feed him and keep him alive, I had thought he might get to know me and be friendlier. Oh, he knew me all right. He knew I was the one to bring him food, clean his cage, put him out in the sun, and inside again. But he also remembered about the other. And he never forgave me. If I gave him the slightest chance, he was ready to rip and tear at me with claws and his wicked beak. Yet, when Janice came over to see him, he allowed her to pick him up and pet him, without once attacking her.

Still, I was getting terribly fond of him. He was a big part of my life. His complete dependability on me for food and care made me realize what it was going to be like to be married and have kids to feed and all that.

And he seemed to be getting much better. His eyes lost their bitter glaze and his feathers smoothed out and the red color came back into them. The white underparts of him were all snowy and his long curved claws seemed to get sharper than ever, if that were possible. His voice had always been loud and screechy, grating across your nerves like a chalk rubbed the wrong way on a blackboard. And, as he got stronger, he screamed more.

If only I could set him free, I thought. Toss him back up there where he'd been floating so arrogantly. What were a few chickens? Popsie and I should have penned them up long ago, I told myself. It was our own fault he came around.

Janice and I were pretty good friends now. We had a common bond. I no longer considered her sort of nutty for having so many animals. In fact, I even talked my Gram into taking a couple of cats off her hands.

I wrote a theme on Joey, submitted it for my English project, and got an "A" on it.

And every day I heard his mad screeches from the tool shed.

Janice came over one day, bringing her usual gifts from her cats. I had to laugh a little wildly. I guess I'd been spending too much time out in the swamps, not getting enough sleep, and the pressure of the last bit of school was telling on me. School would be over for summer vacation in a week. Then I'd have more time.

We walked down to the tool shed, and she went in, while I went to get some fresh water.

She came right out again and over to where I was running a hose.

"Listen," she said, squatting down by me, "Joey's dead."

We stared at each other, and my throat closed itself into a tight knot while the water ran all over my shoes.

"But he was getting better!" I cried angrily.

"He couldn't take it, Larry." She laid her hand on my arm. "It was prison to him, and he knew he had a life sentence. No way out, except one. Don't you see?"

We stood up and looked out over the peaceful countryside. The sky was empty. The chickens, poor dumb things, clucked safely to each other and rolled in the dust with no worries.

We buried him over on the top of a small rocky point where the wind blew around in rising circles, and nothing ever went there.

My life was empty for a long time.

To say he never forgave me is one thing. To say I've never forgiven myself is another. And worse. Joey escaped from his cage, his prison, but he still lives on in the back of my mind, screeching in fury. I don't think I'll ever escape from him.

Discussion

1. (a) How does Larry persuade his grandparents to buy him a gun for Christmas? **(b)** Do you think he is sincere when he assures them that he will use the gun properly?

2. (a) What events give Larry a chance to start hunting? **(b)** Do his grandmother and grandfather approve of his hunting? **(c)** How does Larry justify his hunting in his own mind? **(d)** After he has started hunting, how do Larry's behavior and attitude change? Why?

3. (a) After Larry shoots the hawk, why doesn't he find it until a week later? **(b)** Why does he take the hawk home to care for it?

4. (a) The title suggests that Larry considers the hawk to be his teacher. What other teachers does Larry have in this story? **(b)** What does he learn from each of them? **(c)** Which of his lessons does Larry violate?

5. (a) What does Larry learn from the hawk? **(b)** What evidence is there that Larry will not forget the hawk's lesson?

Composition

Imagine that you are a close friend of Larry's, and that he has just written a letter to you describing what has happened in this story. You can tell that he is upset, and you would like to help him somehow. What can you say to Larry to help ease his pain? Perhaps you have experienced a similar loss that you would like to share with him. Or perhaps you believe that he is reacting too strongly, and you want to advise him to forgive himself and to try to forget.

Write a letter to Larry of no more than one page in length. Use your own return address and today's date. You might begin by thanking him for telling you about what has happened. Then give him your best advice on how to deal with the situation. Sign the letter with your name.

Jean McCord 1924–

Born in Hayward, Wisconsin, Jean Mc-Cord has had a life characterized by moving and change. She completed high school at fifteen after attending sixteen different schools. "When I was a young-ster," she writes, "I didn't know I would pick writing as a career. It apparently picked me. I should have known, though, as all the signs were clear. I read books all the time." During her life she has worked at more than forty-five different occupations and served in the Women's Army Corps. She now lives in California. "My writing endeavors and ambitions fluctuate, from day to day," she says. "Every day I now swear off writing and every day I go back to it." Many of Mc-Cord's stories are based on incidents of her own adolescent years. She comments: "I always hope my stories can give a little courage and a little understanding to teenagers who are going through proba-bly the most difficult time of their lives."

Comment: Caring for Wild Animals

If you came across a wild animal that was injured or sick, or a baby animal that you thought was abandoned, would you be tempted to take it home or try to care for it?

Most animal experts say, "Don't!"

If you can't tell the exact nature of an animal's injuries, moving that animal is unwise. You could make the injury worse. If the animal, not understanding that you're trying to help, tries to defend itself or escape, it could injure itself further. Or, it could injure you—as the hawk Joey tears open Larry's hand when he captures it. Even an animal that knows you, like your own pet, can be dangerous when it's in pain.

Sick animals often know best them-selves what foods and treatments they need to get well. Furthermore, many ani-mals have diseases that humans can catch, such as rabies, or else they may carry disease-causing parasites.

If you are determined to help an animal, however, first contact an expert such as a veterinarian or a local wildlife refuge or humane society.

Some people try to bring home animal babies they think are lost or abandoned. A little animal alone in the woods has not necessarily been deserted. The parents may be searching for food, or they may be hiding and prepared to attack if you at-tempt to touch the baby. Or they may be so frightened by your presence—or even your lingering scent—that they will truly abandon the baby.

If you do take home a wild animal baby, you must be prepared to provide the proper food and shelter for it. Many ani-mals can live only on a certain kind of diet, and caged animals often suffer from lack of space in which to move freely.

Wild animals do not tame easily, if at all, and even animals raised from babies do not make good pets. When frightened or upset they often act wild; when they be-come adults and ready to mate, they can become mean. But you cannot simply re-lease a "pet" back into the wild where you found it. Because it has not learned how to hunt for itself or to fight, it may starve to death or be killed by other ani-mals.

Every Good Boy Does Fine

David Wagoner

I practiced my cornet in a cold garage
Where I could blast it till the oil in drums
Boomed back; tossed free-throws till I couldn't move my thumbs;
Sprinted through tires, tackling a headless dummy.

5 In my first contest, playing a wobbly solo,
I blew up in the coda,[1] alone on stage,
And twisting like my hand-tied necktie, saw the judge
Letting my silence dwindle down his scale.

At my first basketball game, gangling away from home
10 A hundred miles by bus to a dressing room,
Under the showering voice of the coach, I stood in a towel,
Having forgotten shoes, socks, uniform.

---

1. *coda* (kō′də), a final passage of a musical composition, which gives it a satisfactory ending.

In my first football game, the first play under the lights
I intercepted a pass. For seventy yards, I ran
15 Through music and squeals, surging, lifting my cleats,
Only to be brought down by the safety man.

I took my second chances with less care, but in dreams
I saw the bald judge slumped in the front row,
The coach and team at the doorway, the safety man
20 Galloping loud at my heels. They watch me now.

You who have always horned your way through passages,
Sat safe on the bench while some came naked to court,
Slipped out of arms to win in the long run,
Consider this poem a failure, sprawling flat on a page.

Discussion

1. What various things does the speaker practice in the first stanza?

2. (a) What is his first contest? How well does he do? **(b)** Why isn't he a success in his first basketball game? **(c)** What happens in the first football game he plays?

3. Explain the meaning of "I took my second chances with less care" (line 17) and "They watch me now" (line 20).

4. (a) To whom is the speaker talking in the last stanza? **(b)** In each of lines 21-23, the speaker recalls one of his failures while he describes people who do not fail. Does he totally admire their achievements? Explain. **(c)** Why might the people referred to in these lines consider the poem a failure (line 24)?

5. "Every Good Boy Does Fine" is a sentence many music students learn to help them remember the names of certain musical notes: EGBDF. Do you think it is appropriate as a title for this poem? Why or why not?

David Wagoner 1926–

In regard to this poem David Wagoner writes: "I think I started to write 'Every Good Boy Does Fine' in an attempt to keep the incidents described therein from bothering me any more. During the work on the poem, I realized I was still having experiences similar to those I'd had in high school, that they were symbolic of many kinds of failure, and that the act of writing the poem itself was just one more example, however necessary, of asking for disappointment. I have judges, coaches, and safety men inside me, doing their jobs strictly and sometimes badly and sometimes not for my benefit.

"Every good boy does not do fine. In my own terms, I consider the poem a success, but I didn't manage to get it down on paper because I was 'good,' but because I had learned how and was still willing to take a chance at outfoxing whatever there is inside me that says 'I can't.' "

Emma Hu, That's Who
Lensey Namioka

I was seized with a fierce longing to be home. The only problem was, how could I venture out in public like this?

In traditional China, people married early. In a famous narrative poem we learned in school, the heroine marries at the age of fourteen. But until marriage, a well-bred girl has no contact with members of the male sex other than her closest relatives. This was still standard behavior until the beginning of the twentieth century. Things had changed, but much of the old traditions lingered on, even among those of us living in America. In other words, I was supposed to marry young, but in the meantime my contact with boys was to be minimal. Following American custom, we went out on dates, but the dates were supposed to be very circumspect. I had always felt that the Chinese boys who dated me treated me in an impersonal way. To them I was Miss Hu, the daughter of a well-respected family.

But now, facing Kim, a Korean boy who was my mother's most advanced piano student, I found myself in a different situation. I was very conscious of the fact that he was a nice-looking boy of my own age, and very much a real person, not one of the boys lined up for inspection as matrimonial material. What sort of rules did Kim have for behaving toward girls? I didn't have the faintest idea, and this I found rather exciting.

I cleared my throat. "Shall we start with a fox trot?"

"All right," said Kim. His voice was slightly husky. "The fox trot is four-four time, yes?"

I nodded and put the record on. Not having used the machine much, I fumbled a little with the volume control. First the music came out as a thin whine, then it swelled into a loud blare before I managed a reasonable level.

"Uh . . . shall we begin?" I ventured shyly, and held out my hands.

Kim stood looking baffled and alarmed. The books he had been reading had apparently concentrated on footsteps, but not on what went on above them. Finally he reached out and gingerly took my right hand. He had no idea what to do with his other hand.

It was up to me. "Look, you hold me by the waist . . . like this . . . ," I said, showing him where to put his hands.

At that moment the door to my room opened. "Emma!" gasped my mother. "What do you think you're doing?"

Kim and I sprang apart. "I . . . I was j-just teaching Kim to dance," I stammered.

Mother looked shocked. "Kim, this isn't your day for lessons. What are you doing here?"

Kim's grasp of English was less firm than mine, and now it failed him entirely. But I had recovered myself. Since we had done nothing wrong, why should we feel guilty? "Mother, I asked Kim over so I

Adaptation of pp. 111-127 from *Who's Hu?* by Lensey Namioka reprinted by permission of the publisher, The Vanguard Press, Inc. Copyright © 1981 by Lensey Namioka.

could give him some dancing lessons. He's taking me to the prom tomorrow, and he has to learn how to dance.''

Mother's frown did not relax. "Why hide yourselves upstairs like this? Just because we live in America, Emma, you don't have to lose all sense of decency!''

"We couldn't very well practice downstairs, Mother," I pointed out. "You were giving a lesson in the living room and our record player would disturb you. And we weren't doing anything but dancing, really. Not even that, since you interrupted us before we even got started. Why, I go to dances all the time with Chinese boys like Winthrop.''

"That's different," said Mother primly. "This high-school prom is beginning to sound like a remarkably silly idea. I think you should drop the whole thing.''

"Oh, no!'' I cried.

My desperation showed, and Mother relented a little. "All right, you can go to the prom, if you don't make a big thing of it. Kim has better things to do than wasting time on dancing lessons.''

Mother and I had been speaking in Chinese, leaving Kim to shuffle his feet in embarrassment. Now I switched to English. "We'd better stop the lesson, Kim. Do you think you can manage with only your book as a guide?''

Kim nodded. "The music you played sounded quite simple—no syncopation, no bar-line changes. The easiest Haydn sonata[1] is trickier than that.''

As we walked downstairs, a thought struck me. "Kim, do you know how to get hold of a tux?''

"A tux? What is that?''

Oh dear. "A tuxedo is a man's formal evening suit,'' I explained carefully.

"My father has a dark suit, almost black,

that he wears for teaching,'' suggested Kim. "Will that be all right? Of course, he is shorter than I am, but I can get into it—I think.''

I nearly shook my head in despair. Mother was right. Kim had no place at a high-school prom. Maybe *I* had no place at a high-school prom. Then I remembered my friend Katey's happiness on hearing I was going after all. I couldn't disappoint her. This was my chance to show that I was one of them, that I belonged.

But how could I tell Kim that his father's almost black suit, which was too short, would not serve for the prom? What little money his family had to spare was earmarked for music, and the cost of renting a tux was not a burden I could place on him.

Kim must have seen from my expression that his father's suit would not do. "A tux is a very formal suit, isn't it?'' he asked.

"I'm afraid so. Your father's suit would be fine for most dances, but the prom is a very formal affair. I would be wearing a long dress that goes down to my ankles.''

Suddenly Kim's face brightened. "I have a friend whose father is a concert pianist. I'm sure he has a formal black—how do you say it?—tux. He would be willing to lend it to me.''

If I hadn't been so desperately anxious to go to the prom, I would have been more alert and caught the reference to a concert pianist. As it was, I fell in gladly with Kim's suggestion. So that was settled. He would go to the prom in style, and he wouldn't have to pay for tuxedo rental.

I had to buy the prom tickets—I simply

---

1. *Haydn sonata.* Franz Joseph Haydn (hīd′n), 1732-1809, was an Austrian composer. A sonata (sə nä′tə) is a piece of music for one or two instruments.

couldn't ask Kim to put out money for that. After paying for the tickets, I had exactly sixty-eight cents left of my allowance. Somehow I didn't think that would be enough for a decent corsage. I could ask Mother for an advance on my allowance, but she was already so negative about the whole idea of the prom that I didn't want to approach her. Then I thought of my brother, Emerson.

For the last couple of days Emerson had gone to his room almost as soon as he got home, appearing only at mealtimes. During those moments when I found time to think about something other than the prom, I worried about him.

When I went up to his room, however, he looked calm enough. His desk was piled with books and he seemed to be studying hard.

"All right, Emma," he said, when I asked him for a loan. "How much do you need?"

"I'm not sure," I admitted. "Do you know how much a corsage costs?"

Emerson looked surprised. "What do you need a corsage for?"

It was good to have Emerson's sympathetic ear again. I poured out my troubles: the prom, Kim's offer, Katey's insistence on a corsage. At the end, Emerson smiled. He was my protective older brother again. "You poor kid. Don't worry, *meimei*,[2] I'll get you a corsage."

It had been years since Emerson had called me *meimei*—"little sister." We had started calling each other by our English names almost as soon as we came to America. To hear him use the term again gave me a funny kind of wrench.

Emerson was as good as his word, and late Saturday afternoon he came home with a breathtakingly elegant box. Inside was a yellow orchid decorated with gold and silver ribbons. As soon as I saw it, I knew just which dress I was going to wear.

"That's all right, Emma," he said gruffly, when I tried to thank him. "It's the least I can do."

Right after supper I started to get ready for the prom. It took me half an hour. Katey and the rest had talked about spending the whole afternoon bathing, doing their hair, and applying make-up. Personally, I found that hard to believe. By my estimate, even Sue, who was the plumpest of our group, had only 1.8 times my surface area. If I took ten minutes to bathe, it shouldn't take her more than eighteen minutes. Maybe she had to scrub harder.

Of course I didn't spend much time on my hair—I couldn't. It was long and straight, and what can you do with long straight hair except wash and comb it?

Nor did I take long to dress. I went to the closet and took down my flashiest long Chinese dress, a pale yellow brocade *cheongsam*[3] with a design of flowers and birds woven into it in silver with gold threads. The dress was awfully gaudy, but the kids at the prom ought to enjoy it. At the very least the dress should give me a visibility and safety when I crossed the street: it was certain to stop traffic.

By the time I did up all the frog buttons, the dress was molded to me like a second skin. The trouble was that the dress fitted me too well. I had to hold my back ramrod straight all the time. The side slits went up to my knees, so that I could at least dance in a well-bred, sedate sort of way. That was the kind of dancing Winthrop and other

---

2. *meimei* (mä′mä′), little sister. [*Chinese*]
3. *cheongsam* (chông′säm′), a tightly fitting one-piece dress that has long slits on both sides and a high collar. [*Chinese*]

Chinese boys always took me to, and I didn't expect the prom to be different. Katey kept emphasizing how formal the prom was, so I expected the dancing to be formal too.

When the doorbell rang at seven-thirty, I was completely ready. I opened the front door to greet George, a miracle of good grooming in his father's tux. He and Katey were coming over to pick up Kim and me, so all four of us could go to the prom together.

Katey followed George into the house and close behind them was Kim. I was glad he had managed to arrive at the same time.

The Katey who stepped into our house was a stranger. She looked tall and slim in her gray-blue formal, which was stunning in its simplicity. Her blond hair, lacquered and piled on top of her head, added inches to her height. It was her face that looked especially different. Her lips were painted a deep red, and her eyes were penciled to look immense. They had a dazed, fixed expression.

Then Kim followed the others into the light, and I knew that Katey's dazed look was not the result of make-up alone. For a boy whose mind was fixed on becoming a concert pianist, there was only one kind of formal suit: the kind a soloist wears when he appears on stage. Kim was dressed in tails.

Something in my face must have told Kim that his costume was not what I had expected. He looked down at his own resplendent tails, took in George's tuxedo, and froze. To be accurate, all four of us stood in a frozen tableau. Who knows, we might be there yet if my mother hadn't appeared.

"Why, Kim, how elegant you look," she said, coming down the stairs and looking at

him with approval. "You are quite ready for the *Liebeslieder Waltzes*."[4]

I managed to find my voice and perform the proper introductions. Katey had been to our house before, but this was the first time Mother had met George.

Mother could be gracious when she chose, and George, blossoming under her brilliant smile, managed a bow that would have been appropriate in the nineteenth century. For an instant the atmosphere in our little hallway had a touch of Vienna in the days of the Waltz King,[5] and Kim's tails looked completely suitable. Accompanied by Mother's bright chatter, we moved to the door in reasonably good order.

Our cheerfulness lasted until we reached the car. As George headed the car for the Evesham Country Club, where the prom was being held, we fell into an uncomfortable silence. I was sure the others were thinking about the same thing I was: the hush that would fall over the ballroom when we made our entrance.

Finally it was Kim himself who broke the silence. "This formal suit I am wearing, it is wrong for a high-school dance, isn't it?"

While I fumbled for a reply, George, bless his kind heart, answered first. "As Emma's mother said, you're dressed fine for waltzing in a ballroom. But most of us can't get hold of a suit like that, so we wear the shorter jacket."

Whether Kim believed George or not, he nodded. When another awkward silence threatened, Katey said, "Emma, I think your dress is simply divine! I'm dying to go

---

4. *Liebeslieder* (lē′bəs lē dər) **Waltzes,** Love-song Waltzes, a set of waltzes by the German composer Johannes Brahms (brämz), 1833-1897.
5. *Vienna. . .Waltz King.* Vienna (vē en′ə) is the capital of Austria. The Waltz King refers to Johann Strauss (strous), 1825-1899, an Austrian composer of operettas and waltzes.

through your closet and look over all your gorgeous things.''

"They're not all as glittering as this one," I said. "I haven't experimented yet, but I suspect this dress glows in the dark."

Katey laughed. "And your corsage is so beautiful, Emma. It goes perfectly with your dress! Where did you——" She stopped, suddenly seeing the dangers that lay in discussing the corsage.

I hurriedly covered her pause. "*Your* dress is stunning, Katey! Did you have it made for the prom?"

Katey described the little shop in Boston where her formal had been made for her. Between the two of us, we managed to fill in the time until we arrived at the Evesham Country Club.

Our entrance did not produce the sensation I had dreaded. Certainly there were local ripples around us. Sue, dressed in yards and yards of pink taffeta, nearly choked trying to suppress a fit of giggles, but Harry rushed her away to the punch bowl before she could infect anyone else. Fortunately the ballroom was already pretty crowded, and you had to be quite close to us to notice Kim's tails. Anyway, Kim and I, with my splashy yellow dress, already made such an exotic couple that he could equally well have appeared as a flying swordsman of Szechwan.[6] Maybe the others simply accepted us as part of the decor, like the flower arrangement on the refreshment table. I breathed a little more easily. Perhaps the evening would not be a disaster after all.

As George led Katey off to the dance floor, she looked back at me anxiously. "Will you be all right?"

"Don't worry," I assured her. "We'll do fine. You go and enjoy yourselves."

But in spite of what I told Katey, I was in no hurry to dance. How far, really, had Kim got in his book on dance steps? The orchestra was playing a two-step at the moment, nothing spectacular, but you still had to know what to do with your feet.

Nor was Kim in a hurry to dance. He seemed fascinated by the pianist on stage, who was part of the small combo providing the music. "Interesting music," he murmured. "What they are playing?"

To me the music sounded pretty standard. Then I remembered that Kim had probably spent all his time with classical music, and had never heard a live combo before. Watching the flying fingers of the pianist, Kim seemed quite at ease and not in the least nervous. I realized that in spite of his quiet manner, Kim had a healthy amount of self-respect. No one who hoped for a concert career could be a shrinking violet.

Katey danced past in George's arms. "Emma, when are you coming in? The water's fine!"

I took a deep breath. "Shall we try to dance a little, Kim?"

Kim reluctantly turned away from the pianist. "All right." He took hold of my left hand and placed his other hand around my waist. He had not forgotten what I had shown him the day before. Since the couples all around us were holding each other the same way, he was probably less shy about it than he had been the first time. Next, he listened to the music and counted along with it for a few bars.

Suddenly we were off.

I found myself taking enormous backward steps, steps so big that the slits of my dress were extended to their limit. Kim didn't quite grasp the fact that he was much

---

6. *Szechwan* (se′ chwän′), a province in central China.

taller than I, and what were normal steps for him were for me steps requiring seven-league boots.

"Can you take smaller steps?" I gasped.

But Kim didn't hear. He was too busy muttering, "One, two, one, two."

According to Newton's First Law,[7] an object will move in a straight line at a constant speed unless acted upon by an outside force. Kim backed me right across the room in a dead-straight line. Oh, we might have brushed a few couples along the way, but they were glancing encounters—not enough to deflect our relentless progress. I fetched up against the refreshment table with a force that made the punch glasses tinkle.

"Time to stop for a little refreshment," I suggested brightly.

Kim was puzzled. "But we've just started to dance."

Luckily for me, the music stopped at that moment. "Emma!" a voice shrieked behind me. It was Sue, and her face, shiny with exercise, was almost as pink as her dress. "Isn't the prom just fabulous?"

"Yes, isn't it?" I answered, matching her brilliant smile. I introduced Kim to Sue and Harry, who was already making inroads on a huge plate of cookies. We stood around chatting with a bunch of kids I knew in school. The boys agreed that yes siree, the combo was fantastic, and the girls admired one another's dresses.

"Well, Emma, I see you finally made it," said Arthur's voice behind me.

He was escorting Jeanette, who was clutching his arm as if unable to believe her good fortune.

Arthur looked over Kim's costume and smiled his V-shaped smile. "I'm impressed by your boy friend's finery, Emma. Is he going to give us a recital this evening?"

Jeanette was the only one who laughed.

The rest of the kids turned away pointedly. Arthur's cutting tongue had not made him many friends.

"Come on, Jeanette, let's go for a breath of air," said Arthur, shrugging. "It's stale in here."

A couple of girls came over and oohed and ahed over my dress. Frankly, I was beginning to be sorry I had chosen it. The attention it was attracting made me uncomfortable.

I was glad when Katey came over and all the attention turned to her formal instead. Sue whispered to me that Katey was almost certain to be chosen Prom Queen. There was a trace of envy in Sue's voice, but I had no room at all for envy. I was just happy to be included as one of the crowd.

Now that everyone had seen me at the prom, I was content to spend the rest of the evening as a wallflower. More, after my brief exposure to Kim's dancing, I was *eager* to be a wallflower.

But the music started again, and it had a gay, Latin beat. "Oh, oh, I don't think we should try this one," I said to Kim. "It sounds like a rumba."

Kim's eyes were alarmingly bright. "The rumba I like best of all the dances in the book."

Before I could say another word, he grabbed me by the waist and we were off again. You had to say this for Kim: he learned quickly. He knew now that he couldn't just keep going in a straight line until we bumped against something. Therefore he would go halfway across the room in a straight line, then pivot suddenly and go straight in another direction. At least the punch glasses were now safe from us. But

---

7. **Newton's First Law.** Sir Isaac Newton, 1642-1727, was an English mathematician, physicist, and philosopher. His first law of motion states that a body remains at rest or in motion with a constant speed unless an outside force acts on it.

the other couples were not, and shortly I heard the word go around to keep a wary eye out for the flying tails and the yellow brocade dress.

In the end it was the yellow brocade dress that caused my downfall. I tried to tell Kim my dress couldn't keep up with his giant steps, but I doubt that he was listening.

If Kim could enjoy himself, why couldn't I? After weeks of planning, working, and agonizing, I had finally made it to this dance floor. Our progress around the dance floor was more zigzagging than smoothly curving, but at least we moved in perfect time with the music. And the music was pretty good. The combo had worked itself into a white heat. Or, as the kids in school would say, it was cool, real cool.

I might as well abandon myself to the Latin rhythm too. "Abandon" was right. I gave up worrying about the punch glasses and the other dancers. This was the senior prom, the climax of my four years at Evesham High, and I was going to enjoy myself.

And dancing with Kim was unlike anything I had experienced before. Winthrop, Peter, and the other boys from M.I.T.[8] were good dancers, but they purred along like sleek engines, expertly tuned. Dancing with them was like dancing with a precision instrument straight out of an engineering lab. Kim, on the other hand, danced with a recklessness that was exciting. (Years later, Kim still had not lost this reckless quality. But by then he had it under control, and according to critics, it was what made his piano playing so magnetic.)

The prom was a huge success, I told myself. Even Arthur's nasty crack about Kim's tails couldn't spoil it for me.

Then Kim made one of his abrupt, pivoting turns. Just above my left knee I felt my dress go r-r-rip. It was clear what had happened. The thread holding the top of one of the slits gave way, and that slit, liberated, went zinging happily up the side of my dress.

"Oh, oh, I'm in trouble . . ." I began. But Kim was not listening. Caught up in the beat of the music, he took another giant step.

Rip, rip . . . and the slit went up . . . . Imagine to yourself a sausage straining its casing. What would happen if you made a slit halfway up the length of the sausage? The slit would shoot up the rest of the way, that's what would happen.

I took a deep breath in order to tell Kim about my predicament, but filling my lungs was the last thing I should have done, because it greatly increased my volume. Rip, rip . . . the slit shot up to my armpit, and I felt an ominous draft. . . .

It was now essential for me to get off the dance floor and into some shelter before the music stopped and the lights went on. I dug my fingers into Kim's shoulder, hard enough to break the spell of the music. "Kim! I have to leave the dance—right away!" I hissed. "My dress has come apart!"

Kim dragged his eyes from the combo and looked down at my dress.

Another American idiom I had learned was, "His eyes started." Kim's eyes did more than start. They nearly took off.

I tugged Kim toward the exit. "Get me out of here! We'll have to walk close together."

Kim swallowed with an audible gulp. "Yes," he said hoarsely, "I see we must do that."

---

8. **M.I.T.,** Massachusetts Institute of Technology, a technical college in Cambridge, Massachusetts.

Clutching my dress to me, with Kim's arm tight around my waist, I danced cautiously toward the exit. We were barely (pardon the expression) in time. The music came to a stop just as we made it to the lobby. Checking quickly to see that no one was around, I bolted for the ladies' room.

I waited shivering inside one of the cubicles while Kim went to look for Katey. What he had told her must have sounded desperate, because only a couple of minutes later she came rushing in, crying, "Emma, are you sick?"

"No," I wailed, "but my dress split open!" I unlocked the cubicle and opened it a couple of inches.

Katey looked at me and gurgled. "Emma! What happened?"

I explained as well as I could, but explanations were pointless. The question was: What do we do now?

"Maybe we can ask someone for needle and thread," suggested Katey.

The dress was such a tight fit that I knew a makeshift sewing job wasn't going to hold. "No, it's hopeless, Katey. I want to go home."

"Oh, Emma, you can't! You were having such fun!"

That was not quite accurate. To tell the truth, I was seized with a fierce longing to be home. The only problem was, how could I venture out in public like this? The evening wrap I had brought was a short Chinese silk jacket that didn't quite reach my waist. Then I remembered that Katey had worn a long evening coat. "Katey, can I borrow your coat to cover myself on the way home?"

It took a while to convince Katey, who still wanted to salvage my dress somehow. But in the end she had to give up, and she agreed to lend me her coat. George, after hearing what had happened, offered to drive us home, but I asked him to call a taxi instead. It was bad enough for me to fail Katey; it would never do to interrupt the prom for her and George.

On the way home in the cab, Kim broke the silence once to remark that he had enjoyed the music, especially the pianist. Huddled in Katey's voluminous coat, I couldn't summon up the energy to respond. Besides, I had had enough of Latin rhythms for a while.

When we reached my house, I had to ask my mother for money to pay the taxi driver, since neither Kim nor I had enough. She asked me what had happened, and I took off Katey's coat, thinking it was easier to show her than to explain.

Mother took one look and gave a loud squawk.

The racket soon brought Father and Emerson out of their rooms. Eventually my family calmed down sufficiently to listen to my story.

"Poor Kim," murmured Mother. "I'd better apologize to him." She looked around. "Where did he go?"

Sometime during the family debate, Kim had opened the front door and disappeared discreetly into the night.

Discussion

1. Explain how a reader learns the following things about Emma: **(a)** She wants to be part of the group. **(b)** She is sensitive to others' feelings. **(c)** She is willing to take a chance. **(d)** She is liked by the people who know her.

2. **(a)** Why is Emma so desperate to go to the prom? **(b)** Is Emma's attitude to-

ward the prom the same as, or different from, the attitude of her friends? Explain.

3. How do Emma's parents react to her going to the prom? Why?

4. What differences are apparent in this selection between Emma's Chinese upbringing and the American culture in which her family now lives?

5. (a) How well do you think Emma handles the various events leading up to the prom and the prom itself? **(b)** Would you say that Emma is more mature, less mature, or about the same as the other highschool seniors? Explain.

Vocabulary

Context

The setting in which a word appears is known as the *context* of that word. Often, when you encounter an unfamiliar word, other words or ideas that surround it can give you clues to the meaning of the unfamiliar word.

For example, what words in the following sentence tell the meaning of *frogs?*

Her dress fastened with *frogs,* ornamental fasteners with loops and buttons.

Sometimes you can learn the meaning of a word through examples. What examples suggest the meaning of *decor?*

Emma's gown and Kim's tails seemed to blend in with the flower arrangments, the colored streamers, and the thrones for the king and queen. Emma hoped they would be accepted as part of the *decor.*

Context clues can appear before or after a word or even in another sentence or paragraph, as in the previous example.

Words like *but, although,* and *however* often signal that things are different or opposite and can also help you figure out meanings. What words in the following sentence are the opposite of *voluminous?*

Emma's short jacket was too skimpy to hide her damaged dress, but Katey's *voluminous* coat worked perfectly.

Use context clues to figure out the meaning of each italicized word. Write the letter of the best answer on your paper.

1. A well-bred Chinese girl had *minimal* association with boys, seeing none but her closest relatives. **(a)** as little as possible; **(b)** none whatsoever; **(c)** unplanned; **(d)** a great deal.

2. Emma's mother thought she should drop the idea of going to the prom. When Emma protested desperately, however, she *relented,* and Emma went. **(a)** insisted; **(b)** couldn't decide; **(c)** became angry; **(d)** gave in.

3. Emma thought her yellow dress with silver and gold embroidery would give her *visibility* and safety when she crossed the street—and perhaps even stop traffic. **(a)** a kind of disguise; **(b)** the need to move carefully; **(c)** the ability to be clearly seen; **(d)** a formal appearance.

4. Kim danced in a straight line across the room, but suddenly he went off at an angle. Then he changed directions again. These *pivots* alarmed Emma. **(a)** smooth dance steps; **(b)** direct lines; **(c)** abrupt turns; **(d)** different rhythms.

5. Wanting Emma to remain at the prom, Katey offered to *salvage* the dress by mending the split with a needle and thread. **(a)** trade; **(b)** give up on; **(c)** save; **(d)** decorate.

*M*usic Inside My Head   **Gordon Parks**

In this autobiographical selection Parks, a renowned photographer and film maker, tells how he became interested in music as a youth and how he tried to get the world of music interested in him.

It was natural that we hoped for an early spring. But winter was deep in the earth and unwilling to be hurried. So spring would sneak in a bit at a time, breathe upon the cold, and then retreat. It gnawed at the snow, dwindling it with rain and sun, but the cold wind never slept. It roamed the nights, repairing the damage that had been done during the day. It was good when finally the icicles fell and melted into the earth and the smoke left our breath and the frozen Mississippi moved again.

By now the land was stricken with poverty.[1] Every newspaper and magazine I read showed photographs of men queued up at breadlines[2] and employment halls seeking food and work. And this poverty attacked my family wherever it caught us. Yet hunger, I learned, was less frightening in the summer. I could walk slower and give more freely of what energy I had. And it was easier when the moon shone and the stars twinkled over the warm evenings, and love was close at hand.

July brought such evenings and also my first quarrel with Sally.[3] It happened over some minor thing, but it kept us apart for months. And during those hours I worried

and worked at a composition that spoke my feelings. The song was called "No Love," and I wrote it at an upright piano my sister inherited with the house. And now that I had started writing songs again, I worked at it late into the nights and on weekends; music was the one thing that kept me hopeful. A peculiar experience had kindled my love for it long before Casamala[4] decided that I should become a composer.

I was seven at the time. The Kansas day was hot and I was hunting June bugs in our cornfield when I heard a murmuring in the cornstalks. The murmuring grew into music, and I stood there, my mouth full of mulberries, puzzled, looking up at the slow-drifting clouds to see if they were the music's source. The violins, horns, and drums were as true to me as the sunlight, and I had a feeling that the music was trapped in-

---

1. *By now . . . poverty.* The author is referring to the great depression of the 1930s.
2. *breadlines,* lines of people waiting to receive food given as charity or relief.
3. *Sally,* the girl who later became Parks's wife.
4. *Casamala,* a girl of Parks's acquaintance, who encouraged him in his musical studies.

Abridged from pp. 80-90 in *A Choice of Weapons* by Gordon Parks. Copyright © 1965, 1969 by Gordon Parks. Reprinted by permission of Harper & Row, Publishers, Inc. and the author.

side my head, that it would be there even if I had no ears. I covered them with my hands, and the sounds were still there and they continued until all the clouds moved away and there was nothing but pale sky. Then it was gone as mysteriously as it had come, and I ran toward the house a little frightened, a little joyful, eager to tell my experience. But no one was around and I scooted up on the piano stool and started banging our old Kimball upright—trying to reproduce the sounds I had heard. The noise reached my father in another part of the field and he dropped his hoe and rushed to the house. He opened the door and watched me with astonishment; I was screaming as loud as I could.

"Have you gone batty, boy?"

I jumped down and started telling my story, but he only looked at me, at the mulberry stains around my mouth, and shook his head. "I declare, if you don't quit fondin' yourself on those mulberries, you're goin' to be swearin' you saw the devil. Now stop that bangin' and git to your chores."

Perhaps I never forgave my father's reactions to those delirious moments, for never again did we talk about things bordering on fantasy—not even a bedtime story. On that day, however (and to the woe of my good father), I began to play the piano. Several years later, Earl McCray, a music professor at the white school, offered me free music lessons. I was assigned a trombone and placed in our junior-high-school orchestra. But by now I was accustomed to playing by ear, and the slow process of learning to read music seemed unnecessary. I indulged in trickery. Each Saturday morning, before my appointment with Mr. McCray, my sister fingered my lesson on the piano and I memorized it; then I went off to astonish the professor with my "sight read-

ing." He recommended me as soloist at the graduation concert. And everyone said I played "The Rosary" with great feeling that night. Only my sister knew I couldn't read a note.

This was long past. But now at nineteen, five years later, I regretted the tricks I had played upon the professor. I had never learned to read or write music, though I was determined to compose; it seemed the one way to avoid a less-than-ordinary existence. I worked out a notation system of my own by referring to the piano keys as numbers instead of notes—a process that proved more complicated than the conventional way.

The next consideration was a publisher; it was disheartening to discover that all the important ones were in Chicago or farther east. And there were warnings against dishonest publishers who stole songs; but this didn't bother me. It would have been flattering, I thought, to have composed something worthy of a professional's theft. The difficulty would be to get someone to transpose my numbers to notes and then have the final work accepted. But I knew I couldn't depend on music alone. That first winter[5] had taught me that I would have to fight with everything that came to hand. Learning, I knew, would be the most effective weapon against the coming years. So once again I seized upon books. After school I searched the local library shelves for authors who might help me in different ways. I pushed my mind into the foreign worlds of Thomas Mann, Dostoevski, James Joyce[6] and others whom I had never read before. I tried stone sculpture, short-

---

5. *That first winter,* 1928–1929. When his mother died the previous year, Parks had come to live with his sister and her family in St. Paul, Minnesota.
6. *Thomas Mann, Dostoevski* (dos′tə yef′skē), *James Joyce,* important novelists of the 19th and 20th centuries.

story writing, poetry and, when I could hustle the material, painting. I did everything I could to protect myself against another such winter. Somewhere in between I played basketball for the Diplomats[7] and my high school as well.

A collapse was inevitable, and it came during a basketball game in October, 1931. I had dribbled past two guards and arched the ball perfectly, knowing it would swish through the hoop. But a blackness suddenly covered the court and the ball disappeared into it like a balloon into a cloud, and I felt myself falling. The coach had my teammates carry me to the locker room, where I was examined by the school nurse. Her only comment was that I looked awful hungry and thin to be playing such a strenuous game. But at home later that evening a doctor whom my sister called said I was on the verge of a physical breakdown. I had wasted from 165 pounds to 124 in less than three months. If I was to regain my health, he said, I would have to leave school for the remainder of the year and rest.

So at twenty I found myself an invalid. There was no chance of graduating with my class. I was already too far behind. In fact, I knew that I would never go back to school. For the next five months I sat in the dark of my room rejecting time, light, and reason. I never heard from Sally during that time, but my sister helped me through the long convalescence and tried to get me to read, to write, to do anything that would divert my eyes from the blank wall opposite my bed. I finally opened a book one rainy afternoon. And gradually I began to read, think, and hope again. One thing was clear. I couldn't escape my fate by trying to outrun it. I would have to take my time from now on, and grow in the light of my own particular experience—and accept the slowness of things that were meant to be slow. Spring was back again, but I was afraid to look upon its coming with any pleasure. It had deceived me once too often.

By April I had regained my weight and strength. And before long I was hanging out at Jim's pool hall again, for it was a good place to get back into the stream of things. Arguments were always going; they flared, blossomed, and faded by the dozens. Some of them were senseless, some were heated, some were comical.

During one argument, one man claimed that Glen Gray, the band leader, had a mustache. The other denied it. My interest was casual until one of the men, a waiter at the Hotel St. Paul, boasted that he should know since he "rubbed shoulders with Gray every night." He was lying of course about the shoulder rubbing, but he did see the orchestra leader regularly; anyone working there had the same opportunity. I wondered why I hadn't thought of this before. Many of the best orchestras played at the large Twin City hotels;[8] if only I could get one of them to broadcast my songs. The thought grew and I hurried home, sorted out several of my compositions, and set my alarm clock for six o'clock. And by seven-thirty the next morning I was at the Hotel St. Paul servants' entrance, the songs tucked in my pocket, applying for a waiter's job.

The timekeeper, an old gray-haired man, looked me over and asked me to wait around until he saw the day's work schedule. And for the next four hours I paced the corridor, looking expectantly at him now and then. At eleven-thirty, he motioned for me.

"Are you an experienced waiter?"

---

7. **the Diplomats,** a boys' club.
8. **Twin City hotels.** Minneapolis and St. Paul, Minnesota, are known as the Twin Cities.

"Yessir. Yessir." (I had never waited on table in my life.)

"You ever work here before?"

"Not yet, no, sir."

"Where have you worked?"

"The Minnesota Club, the Lowry, the——"

"Okay, okay. There's a Rotary[9] luncheon today, nothing steady. You want to work it?"

"Is that where the orchestra plays?"

"Orchestra? What's the orchestra got to do with it?" he asked.

"Oh nothing, nothing. Just thought I'd ask." My heart thumped like a drum.

"Well, do you want it or not?" he snapped.

"Yessir, I'll take it." I stepped up to his table and signed in.

The banquet captain changed my status from waiter to bus boy the instant he saw me pick up a tray. And as I trudged back and forth between the kitchen and the banquet hall, under the weight of the trays of drinks, I could hear the music coming from the main dining room. It was frustrating to have Glen Gray so close and not to be able to talk with him. But the driving captain kept his eye on me, pointing to tray after tray. And only once, when the dining-room door swung open, did I glimpse the tall, debonair orchestra leader directing his orchestra. And I noticed then that he did have a mustache.

Much later, the Rotarians were enjoying coffee, puffing cigars and asking silly questions of a mind reader they had hired for entertainment. I hung around, clearing dirty dishes from the tables—and listening to the questions and answers.

"Who's going to be the most famous in this room?" someone asked.

"Good question," the mind reader said.

He then covered his eyes and turned his back to the audience. There was snickering as he supposedly searched the future. Whomever he chose was in for a good razzing. The laughter was already building.

"Gentlemen." There was a momentary quiet. "There is a boy in the back of this room in a white uniform" (every eye in the room turned on me). "He will be more widely acclaimed than any——"

That was enough. Bedlam broke loose. "Boy! Boy! Come up here!" It was the mind reader's voice screaming over the others. "Bring him up, somebody!"

Two men started toward me, but I grabbed a tray of dishes, and, fleeing the banquet hall, I tripped and threw the dishes in all directions. But I got to my feet and kept going until I reached the dressing room.

In spite of that fiasco, I was hired three days later as a regular bus boy, and assigned to the main dining room.

Glen Gray left soon after, without my having had a chance to speak to him. But Kay Kyser, Bert Lown, Jack Teagarden and others, who came later, didn't get off so easy. Each of them suffered through my inexhaustible efforts—and they encouraged me. But none of them acted as though Tin Pan Alley[10] was overlooking a great talent.

Late that summer, I was offered the head bus boy job at the Hotel Lowry, by the *maître d'hôtel,*[11] a former wrestler whose name was Gleason. I took it. And for nearly three hours each day, after the luncheon crowd left, I had the main dining room and the huge grand piano all to myself. Once the tables were set for the evening, I played

---

9. *Rotary.* The Rotary Club is a men's service organization.
10. *Tin Pan Alley,* the body of composers and publishers of popular music.
11. *maître d'hôtel* (me′trə dō tel′), headwaiter. [*French*]

away before an imagined audience—using the light-control switches for color combinations that added to the mood. On one such afternoon I was playing and singing ''No Love'' when I felt someone was behind me. Embarrassed, I stopped, turned and looked into the shadows. It was Larry Duncan, the orchestra leader who was currently engaged by the hotel.

''Is that your music?'' he asked.

''Yes.''

''Go ahead. Play it again.''

I played it again and he listened attentively. When I finished he asked me if I would like to have it orchestrated.

''I sure would,'' I said, and it was probably the understatement of my lifetime. The orchestra's arranger spent the rest of that afternoon with me, taking the piece down as I played it. And, as I watched him work, I hoped that my afternoons of fantasy were coming to an end.

This happened on a Wednesday.

During dinner on the following Friday night, Larry motioned me toward the bandstand. ''We're broadcasting 'No Love' on the network show tomorrow night—with your permission, of course,'' he said.

I got Sally on the telephone and, without knowing whether she cared or not, I excitedly spilled out the good news. ''I composed it for you—don't forget to listen.'' Her voice didn't reveal the slightest interest. She said, very casually, that she would listen—but, I found out later, she spent the next two hours telephoning all her friends. And I spent the rest of that evening and the next day drifting about in a trance.

On the night of the broadcast, Abby, the drummer, congratulated me and showed a group of waiters and myself the program. Fate had arranged things. There was my name among those of Irving Berlin, Duke Ellington, Cole Porter and Jerome Kern.[12] Now, in spite of my imagining the worst—a broken microphone, a broken promise, a canceled broadcast—it was going to happen. I knew that Gleason kept a death watch on unfilled water glasses, so I went about filling them to the brim. I wanted to hear every word, every note, without being disturbed.

When at last the moment came, people continued to eat, drink, and talk, as if they were unaware of the miracle taking place. I wanted to shout, to command everyone to listen, to ascend with me—far above ordinary things. But they kept on eating, drinking, laughing, and talking. And, just before the vocalist approached the microphone, I took refuge near the bandstand where I could hear him sing my lyrics. But now, at such a moment, a drunk started rapping his glass with a spoon. He wanted more water. I ignored him. He rapped louder and I hated him for it.

''What is it, sir?'' A shiver went up my back. It was Gleason's voice.

''Water! Water! Tell that boy our party wants water!''

Such was my lot, I thought, and I turned toward the table only to have Gleason wave me away. He was filling the glasses and proudly explaining that the music the orchestra was playing was mine. The drunk whispered the news to his party, and his party whispered the news to the next table, and soon everyone in the entire dining room was looking toward me. When the orchestra finished, a burst of applause filled the air. I smiled nervously, picked up a tray of dirty dishes and left the room amidst the ovation. Then, slipping into an empty room, I telephoned Sally. ''Yes I listened,'' she said,

---

12. *Irving Berlin . . . Jerome Kern,* well-known songwriters.

"and it was beautiful. Would you like to come over sometime, maybe tonight?"

"As soon as I can get out of here," I answered. The sky was overcast and it was chilly when I boarded the street car; but I couldn't accept such a night. There were stars and a moon instead, and a ridiculous hint of spring in the fall air. My heart, in its joy, would have it no other way.

Discussion

1. (a) Under what financial conditions is Parks living when he writes "No Love"? Explain. **(b)** Why does he write the song? **(c)** What causes his physical breakdown?

2. (a) What inspires Parks to look for work at the Hotel St. Paul? **(b)** Are his expectations there fulfilled? Explain. **(c)** How does Parks meet Larry Duncan, the bandleader?

3. What important personal qualities does Gordon Parks reveal in this selection? Illustrate these qualities by referring to passages throughout the selection.

4. What do you think Parks means by his statement: ". . . learning, I knew, would be the most effective weapon against the coming years"?

5. Reread the last paragraph of the selection. **(a)** What does Parks mean when he says, "There were stars and a moon instead, and a ridiculous hint of spring in the fall air"? **(b)** How does this last paragraph contrast with the opening one?

Application
Figurative Language

Gordon Parks uses a number of figurative expressions to describe, for one thing, the weather behaving as humans behave. What kinds of changes of weather are suggested by "spring would sneak in a bit at a time, breathe upon the cold, and then retreat"? How does "the cold wind . . . . roamed the nights, repairing the damage that had been done during the day" describe not only the weather but how Parks *feels* about it?

Explain the literal meaning of these figurative expressions:

1. "Winter was deep in the earth and unwilling to be hurried." (24a, 1)

2. "Poverty attacked my family wherever it caught us." (24a, 2)

3. "I couldn't escape my fate by trying to outrun it." (27a, 2)

Composition

You probably use figurative language every day as you talk about ordinary events. Choose one of the following that you are familiar with: (1) a certain kind of animal; (2) an event in nature, such as high tide; (3) a certain kind of machine. Think about how your subject looks and sounds, and then make up at least three original figurative expressions to describe it. Keep your comparisons brief and try to make them fresh and appropriate to your subject.

Write one paragraph describing your subject *without mentioning what the subject actually is.* Work your three figurative expressions in smoothly with the rest of your description. Share your description with your classmates. Can they guess what your subject is?

*F*ifteen

William Stafford

South of the Bridge on Seventeenth
I found back of the willows one summer
day a motorcycle with engine running
as it lay on its side, ticking over
5   slowly in the high grass. I was fifteen.

I admired all that pulsing gleam, the
shiny flanks, the demure headlights
fringed where it lay; I led it gently
to the road and stood with that
10   companion, ready and friendly. I was fifteen.

We could find the end of a road, meet
the sky on out Seventeenth. I thought about
hills, and patting the handle got back a
confident opinion. On the bridge we indulged
15   a forward feeling, a tremble. I was fifteen.

Thinking, back farther in the grass I found
the owner, just coming to, where he had flipped
over the rail. He had blood on his hand, was pale—
I helped him walk to his machine. He ran his hand
20   over it, called me good man, roared away.

I stood there, fifteen.

"Fifteen" from *Stories That Could Be True* by William Stafford.
Copyright © 1964 by William E. Stafford. Reprinted by
permission of Harper & Row, Publishers, Inc.

Discussion

1. Summarize what the speaker does in each stanza of the poem.

2. Why do you think the line "I was fifteen" is repeated so many times in the poem?

3. **(a)** If you had been the one to find the motorcycle, would you have been tempted to take it for a ride? Why or why not? **(b)** Can you think of an occasion when you, like the speaker in the poem, were inclined to follow a dream but did not? Explain.

The Inspiration of Mr. Budd

Dorothy Sayers

"Are you prepared to die?" The question threw Mr. Budd off balance, so alarmingly did it chime in with his thoughts about murder.

£500 REWARD

The Evening Messenger, *ever anxious to further the ends of justice, has decided to offer the above reward to any person who shall give information leading to the arrest of the man, William Strickland, alias Bolton, who is wanted by the police in connection with the murder of the late Emma Strickland at 59 Acacia Crescent, Manchester.*

DESCRIPTION OF THE WANTED MAN

The following is the official description of William Strickland: Age 43; height 6 ft. 1 or 2; complexion rather dark; hair silver-gray and abundant, may dye same; full gray mustache and beard, may now be clean-shaven; eyes light gray, rather close-set; hawk nose; teeth strong and white, displays them somewhat prominently when laughing, left upper eye-tooth stopped with gold; left thumb-nail disfigured by a recent blow.

Speaks in rather loud voice; quick, decisive manner. Good address.

May be dressed in a gray or dark blue lounge suit, with stand-up collar (size 15) and soft felt hat.

Absconded 5th inst., and may have left, or will endeavor to leave, the country.

Mr. Budd read the description through carefully once again and sighed. It was in the highest degree unlikely that William Strickland should choose his small and unsuccessful saloon, out of all the barbers' shops in London, for a haircut or a shave, still less for "dyeing same"; even if he was in London, which Mr. Budd saw no reason to suppose.

Three weeks had gone by since the murder, and the odds were a hundred to one that William Strickland had already left a

---

country too eager with its offer of free hospitality. Nevertheless, Mr. Budd committed the description, as well as he could, to memory. It was a chance—just as the Great Crossword Tournament had been a chance, just as the Ninth Rainbow Ballot had been a chance, and the Bunko Poster Ballot, and the Monster Treasure Hunt organized by the *Evening Clarion*. Any headline with money in it could attract Mr. Budd's fascinated eye in these lean days, whether it offered a choice between fifty thousand pounds down and ten pounds a week for life, or merely a modest hundred or so.

It may seem strange, in an age of shingling and bingling,[1] Mr. Budd should look enviously at Complete Lists of Prizewinners. Had not the hairdresser across the way, who only last year had eked out his mean ninepences with the yet meaner profits on cheap cigarettes and comic papers, lately bought out the greengrocer next door, and engaged a staff of exquisitely coiffed assistants to adorn his new "Ladies' Hairdressing Department" with its purple and orange curtains, its two rows of gleaming marble basins, and an apparatus like a Victorian chandelier for permanent waving?

Had he not installed a large electric sign surrounded by a scarlet border that ran round and round perpetually, like a kitten chasing its own tail? Was it not his sandwich-man[2] even now patrolling the pavement with a luminous announcement of Treatment and Prices? And was there not at this moment an endless stream of young ladies hastening into those heavily-perfumed parlors in the desperate hope of somehow getting a shampoo and a wave "squeezed in" before closing-time?

If the reception clerk shook a regretful head, they did not think of crossing the road to Mr. Budd's dimly lighted window.

They made an appointment for days ahead and waited patiently, anxiously fingering the bristly growth at the back of the neck and the straggly bits behind the ears that so soon got out of hand.

Day after day Mr. Budd watched them flit in and out of the rival establishment, willing, praying even, in a vague, ill-directed manner, that some of them would come over to him; but they never did.

And yet Mr. Budd knew himself to be the finer artist. He had seen shingles turned out from over the way that he would never have countenanced, let alone charged three shillings and sixpence for. Shingles with an ugly hard line at the nape, shingles which were a slander on the shape of a good head or brutally emphasized the weak points of an ugly one; hurried, conscienceless shingles, botched work, handed over on a crowded afternoon to a girl who had only served a three years' apprenticeship and to whom the final mysteries of "tapering" were a sealed book.

And then there was the "tinting"—his own pet subject, which he had studied *con amore*[3]—if only those too-sprightly matrons would come to him! He would gently dissuade them from that dreadful mahogany dye that made them look like metallic robots—he would warn them against that widely advertised preparation which was so incalculable in its effects; he would use the cunning skill which long experience had matured in him—tint them with the infinitely delicate art which conceals itself.

Yet nobody came to Mr. Budd but the

---

1. ***shingling and bingling,*** methods of cutting women's hair. A shingle is a tapered haircut; a bingle is a somewhat shorter cut.
2. ***sandwich-man,*** a man carrying two advertising boards hung from his shoulders, one in front and one behind.
3. ***con amore*** (kōn ä mōr′ä), an Italian expression meaning "with love, with tenderness."

navvies[4] and the young loungers and the men who plied their trade beneath the naphtha-flares[5] in Wilton Street.

And why could not Mr. Budd also have burst out into marble and electricity and swum to fortune on the rising tide?

The reason is very distressing, and, as it fortunately has no bearing on the story, shall be told with merciful brevity.

Mr. Budd had a younger brother, Richard, whom he had promised his mother to look after. In happier days Mr. Budd had owned a flourishing business in their native town of Northampton, and Richard had been a bank clerk. Richard had got into bad ways (poor Mr. Budd blamed himself dreadfully for this). There had been a sad affair with a girl, and a horrid series of affairs with bookmakers, and then Richard had tried to mend bad with worse by taking money from the bank. You need to be very much more skillful than Richard to juggle successfully with bank ledgers.

The bank manager was a hard man of the old school: he prosecuted. Mr. Budd paid the bank and the bookmakers, and saw the girl through her trouble while Richard was in prison, and paid for their fares to Australia when he came out, and gave them something to start life on.

But it took all the profits of the hairdressing business, and he couldn't face all the people in Northampton any more, who had known him all his life. So he had run to vast London, the refuge of all who shrink from the eyes of their neighbors, and bought this little shop in Pimlico, which had done fairly well, until the new fashion which did so much for other hairdressing businesses killed it for lack of capital.

That is why Mr. Budd's eye was so painfully fascinated by headlines with money in them.

He put the newspaper down, and as he did so, caught sight of his own reflection in the glass and smiled, for he was not without a sense of humor. He did not look quite the man to catch a brutal murderer single-handed. He was well on in the middle forties—a trifle paunchy, with fluffy pale hair, getting a trifle thin on top (partly hereditary, partly worry, that was), five feet six at most, and soft-handed, as a hairdresser must be.

Even razor in hand, he would hardly be a match for William Strickland, height six feet one or two, who had so ferociously battered his old aunt to death, so butcherly hacked her limb from limb, so horribly disposed of her remains in the copper.[6] Shaking his head dubiously, Mr. Budd advanced to the door, to cast a forlorn eye at the busy establishment over the way, and nearly ran into a bulky customer who dived in rather precipitately.

"I beg your pardon, sir," murmured Mr. Budd, fearful of alienating ninepence; "just stepping out for a breath of fresh air, sir. Shave, sir?"

The large man tore off his overcoat without waiting for Mr. Budd's obsequious hands.

"Are you prepared to die?" he demanded abruptly.

The question chimed in so alarmingly with Mr. Budd's thoughts about murder that for a moment it quite threw him off his professional balance.

"I beg your pardon, sir," he stammered, and in the same moment decided that the man must be a preacher of some kind. He

---

4. *navvies* (nav′ēz), unskilled laborers, especially those who work on canals, railways, etc.
5. *naphtha flares,* street lamps fueled by naphtha (naf′thə), a flammable liquid.
6. *copper,* a large kettle used for cooking or for boiling laundry.

looked rather like it, with his odd, light eyes, his bush of fiery hair and short, jutting chinbeard. Perhaps he even wanted a subscription. That would be hard, when Mr. Budd had already set him down as ninepence, or, with tip, possibly even a shilling.

"Do you do dyeing?" said the man impatiently.

"Oh!" said Mr. Budd, relieved, "yes, sir, certainly, sir."

A stroke of luck, this. Dyeing meant quite a big sum—his mind soared to seven-and-sixpence.

"Good," said the man, sitting down and allowing Mr. Budd to put an apron about his neck. (He was safely gathered in now—he could hardly dart away down the street with a couple of yards of white cotton flapping from his shoulders.)

"Fact is," said the man, "my young lady doesn't like red hair. She says it's conspicuous. The other young ladies in her firm make jokes about it. So, as she's a good bit younger than I am, you see, I like to oblige her, and I was thinking perhaps it could be changed into something quieter, what? Dark brown, now—that's the color she has a fancy for. What do you say?"

It occurred to Mr. Budd that the young ladies might consider this abrupt change of coat even funnier than the original color, but in the interests of business he agreed that dark brown would be very becoming and a great deal less noticeable than red. Besides, very likely there was no young lady. A woman, he knew, will say frankly that she wants different colored hair for a change, or just to try, or because she fancies it would suit her, but if a man is going to do a silly thing he prefers, if possible, to shuffle the responsibility on to someone else.

"Very well, then," said the customer, "go ahead. And I'm afraid the beard will have to go. My young lady doesn't like beards."

"A great many young ladies don't, sir," said Mr. Budd. "They're not so fashionable nowadays as they used to be. It's very fortunate that you can stand a clean shave very well, sir. You have just the chin for it."

"Do you think so?" said the man, examining himself a little anxiously. "I'm glad to hear it."

"Will you have the mustache off as well, sir?"

"Well, no—no, I think I'll stick to that as long as I'm allowed to, what?" He laughed loudly, and Mr. Budd approvingly noted well-kept teeth and a gold stopping. The customer was obviously ready to spend money on his personal appearance.

In fancy, Mr. Budd saw this well-off and gentlemanly customer advising all his friends to visit "his man"—"wonderful fellow—wonderful—round at the back of Victoria Station—you'd never find it by yourself—only a little place, but he knows what he's about—I'll write it down for you." It was imperative that there should be no fiasco. Hair-dyes were awkward things—there had been a case in the paper lately.

"I see you have been using a tint before, sir," said Mr. Budd with respect. "Could you tell me——?"

"Eh?" said the man. "Oh, yes—well, fact is, as I said, my fiancée's a good bit younger than I am. As I expect you can see I began to go gray early—my father was just the same—all our family—so I had it touched up—streaky bits restored, you see. But she doesn't take to the color, so I thought, if I have to dye it at all, why not a color she does fancy while we're about it, what?"

It is a common jest among the unthinking that hairdressers are garrulous. This is their wisdom. The hairdresser hears many secrets and very many lies. In his discretion he occupies his unruly tongue with the weather and the political situation, lest, restless with inaction, it plunge unbridled into a mad career of inconvenient candor.

Lightly holding forth upon the caprices of the feminine mind, Mr. Budd subjected his customer's locks to the scrutiny of trained eye and fingers. Never—never in the process of Nature could hair of that texture and quality have been red. It was naturally black hair, prematurely turned, as some black hair will turn, to a silvery gray. However that was none of his business. He elicited the information he really needed—the name of the dye formerly used, and noted that he would have to be careful. Some dyes do not mix kindly with other dyes.

Chatting pleasantly, Mr. Budd lathered his customer, removed the offending beard, and executed a vigorous shampoo, preliminary to the dyeing process. As he wielded the roaring drier, he reviewed Wimbledon, the Silk-tax and the Summer Time Bill—at that moment threatened with sudden strangulation—and passed naturally on to the Manchester murder.

"The police seem to have given it up as a bad job," said the man.

"Perhaps the reward will liven things up a bit," said Mr. Budd, the thought being naturally uppermost in his mind.

"Oh, there's a reward, is there? I hadn't seen that."

"It's in tonight's paper, sir. Maybe you'd like to have a look at it."

"Thanks, I should."

Mr. Budd left the drier to blow the fiery bush of hair at its own wild will for a mo-ment, while he fetched the *Evening Messenger*. The stranger read the paragraph carefully and Mr. Budd, watching him in the glass, after the disquieting manner of his craft, saw him suddenly draw back his left hand, which was resting carelessly on the arm of the chair, and thrust it under the apron.

But not before Mr. Budd had seen it. Not before he had taken conscious note of the horny, misshapen thumbnail. Many people had such an ugly mark, Mr. Budd told himself hurriedly—there was his friend, Bert Webber, who had sliced the top of his thumb right off in a motorcycle chain—his nail looked very much like that. Mr. Budd thought and thought.

The man glanced up, and the eyes of his reflection became fixed on Mr. Budd's face with a penetrating scrutiny—a horrid warning that the real eyes were steadfastly interrogating the reflection of Mr. Budd.

"Not but what," said Mr. Budd, "the man is safe out of the country, I reckon. They've put it off too late."

The man laughed in a pleasant, conversational way.

"I reckon they have," he said. Mr. Budd wondered whether many men with smashed left thumbs showed a gold left upper eye-tooth. Probably there were hundreds of people like that going about the country. Likewise with silver-gray hair ("may dye same") and aged about forty-three. Undoubtedly.

Mr. Budd folded up the drier and turned off the gas. Mechanically he took up a comb and drew it through the hair that never, never in the process of Nature had been that fiery red.

There came back to him, with an accuracy which quite unnerved him, the exact number and extent of the brutal wounds in-

flicted upon the Manchester victim—an elderly lady, rather stout, she had been. Glaring through the door, Mr. Budd noticed that his rival over the way had closed. The streets were full of people. How easy it would be——

"Be as quick as you can, won't you?" said the man, a little impatiently, but pleasantly enough. "It's getting late. I'm afraid it will keep you overtime."

"Not at all, sir," said Mr. Budd. "It's of no consequence—not the least."

No—if he tried to bolt out of the door, his terrible customer would leap upon him, drag him back, throttle his cries, and then with one frightful blow like the one he had smashed in his aunt's skull with——

Yet surely Mr. Budd was in a position of advantage. A decided man would do it. He would be out in the street before the customer could disentangle himself from the chair. Mr. Budd began to edge round towards the door.

"What's the matter?" said the customer.

"Just stepping out to look at the time, sir," said Mr. Budd, meekly pausing. (Yet he might have done it then, if he only had the courage to make the first swift step that would give the game away.)

"It's five-and-twenty past eight," said the man, "by tonight's broadcast. I'll pay extra for the overtime."

"Not on any account," said Mr. Budd. Too late now, he couldn't make another effort. He vividly saw himself tripping on the threshold—falling—the terrible fist lifted to smash him into a pulp. Or, perhaps, under the familiar white apron, the disfigured hand was actually clutching a pistol.

Mr. Budd retreated to the back of the shop, collecting his materials. If only he had been quicker—more like a detective in a book—he would have observed that thumbnail, that tooth, put two and two together, and run out to give the alarm while the man's beard was wet and soapy and his face buried in the towel. Or he could have dabbed lather in his eyes—nobody could possibly commit a murder or even run away down the street with his eyes full of soap.

Even now—Mr. Budd took down a bottle, shook his head and put it back on the shelf—even now, was it really too late? Why could he not take a bold course? He had only to open a razor, go quietly up behind the unsuspecting man and say in a firm, loud, convincing voice: "William Strickland, put up your hands. Your life is at my mercy. Stand up till I take your gun away. Now walk straight out to the nearest policeman." Surely, in his position, that was what Sherlock Holmes would do.

But as Mr. Budd returned with a little trayful of requirements, it was borne in upon him that he was not of the stuff of which great man-hunters are made. For he could not seriously see that attempt "coming off." Because if he held the razor to the man's throat and said: "Put up your hands," the man would probably merely catch him by the wrists and take the razor away. And greatly as Mr. Budd feared his customer unarmed, he felt it would be a perfect crescendo of madness to put a razor in his hands.

Or supposing he said, "Put up your hands," and the man just said, "I won't." What was he to do next? To cut his throat then and there would be murder, even if Mr. Budd could possibly have brought himself to do such a thing. They could not remain there, fixed in one position, till the boy came to do out the shop in the morning.

Perhaps the policeman would notice the light on and the door unfastened and come in? Then he would say, "I congratulate you, Mr. Budd, on having captured a very dangerous criminal." But supposing the policeman didn't happen to notice—and Mr. Budd would have to stand all the time, and he would get exhausted and his attention would relax, and then——

After all, Mr. Budd wasn't called upon to arrest the man himself. "Information leading to arrest"—those were the words. He would be able to tell them the wanted man had been there, that he would now have dark brown hair and mustache and no beard. He might even shadow him when he left—he might——

It was at this moment that the great Inspiration came to Mr. Budd.

As he fetched a bottle from the glass-fronted case he remembered with odd vividness, an old-fashioned wooden paper-knife that had belonged to his mother. Between sprigs of blue forget-me-not, hand-painted, it bore the inscription "Knowledge Is Power."

A strange freedom and confidence were vouchsafed to Mr. Budd; his mind was alert; he removed the razors with an easy, natural movement, and made nonchalant conversation as he skillfully applied the dark-brown tint.

The streets were less crowded when Mr. Budd let his customer out. He watched the tall figure cross Grosvenor Place and climb on to a 24 bus.

"But that was only his artfulness," said Mr. Budd, as he put on his hat and coat and extinguished the lights carefully, "he'll take another at Victoria, like as not, and be making tracks from Charing Cross or Waterloo."[7]

He closed the shop door, shook it, as was his wont, to make sure that the lock had caught properly, and in his turn made his way, by means of a 24, to the top of Whitehall.

The policeman was a little condescending at first when Mr. Budd demanded to see "somebody very high up," but finding the little barber insist so earnestly that he had news of the Manchester murderer, and that there wasn't any time to lose, he consented to pass him through.

Mr. Budd was interviewed first by an important-looking inspector in uniform, who listened very politely to his story and made him repeat very carefully about the gold tooth and the thumbnail and the hair which had been black before it was gray or red and now dark-brown.

The inspector then touched a bell, and said, "Perkins, I think Sir Andrew would like to see this gentleman at once," and he was taken to another room where sat a very shrewd, genial gentleman in mufti,[8] who heard him with even greater attention, and called in another inspector to listen too, and to take down a very exact description of—yes, surely the undoubted William Strickland as he now appeared.

"But there's one thing more," said Mr. Budd— "and I'm sure to goodness," he added, "I hope, sir, it is the right man, because if it isn't it'll be the ruin of me——"

He crushed his soft hat into an agitated ball as he leaned across the table, breathlessly uttering the story of his great betrayal.

"Tzee—z-z-z—tzee—tzee—z-z—tzee—z-z——"

"Dzoo—dz-dz-dz—dzoo—dz—dzoo—dzoo—dz."

"Tzee—z—z."

7. *Charing Cross or Waterloo,* major railroad stations in London.
8. *mufti* (muf′tē), ordinary "civilian" clothes. Sir Andrew was not in uniform.

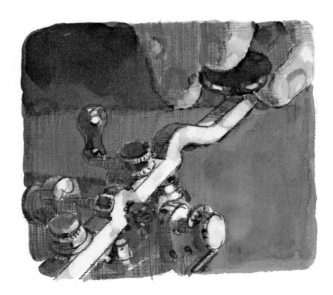

The fingers of the wireless operator on the packet *Miranda* bound for Ostend[9] moved swiftly as they jotted down the messages of the buzzing wireless mosquito-swarms.

One of them made him laugh.

"The Old Man'd better have this, I suppose," he said.

The Old Man scratched his head when he read and rang a little bell for the steward. The steward ran down to the little round office where the purser was counting his money and checking it before he locked it away for the night. On receiving the Old Man's message, the purser put the money quickly into the safe, picked up the passenger list and departed aft. There was a short consultation, and the bell was rung again—this time to summon the head steward.

"Tzee—z-z—tzeez-z-z—tzee—tzee—z—tzee."

All down the Channel, all over the North Sea, up to the Mersey Docks, out into the Atlantic soared the busy mosquito-swarms. In ship after ship the wireless operator sent his message to the captain, the captain sent for the purser, the purser sent for the head steward and the head steward called his staff about him. Huge liners, little packets, destroyers, sumptuous private yachts—every floating thing that carried aerials—every port in England, France, Holland, Germany, Denmark, Norway, every police center that could interpret the mosquito message, heard, between laughter and excitement, the tale of Mr. Budd's betrayal. Two Boy Scouts at Croydon, practicing their Morse with a home-made valve set,[10] decoded it laboriously into an exercise book.

"Cripes," said Jim to George, "what a joke! D'you think they'll get the beggar?"

The *Miranda* docked at Ostend at 7 A.M. A man burst hurriedly into the cabin where the wireless operator was just taking off his headphones.

"Here!" he cried; "this is to go. There's something up and the Old Man's sent over for the police. The Consul's coming on board."

The wireless operator groaned, and switched on his valves.

"Tzee—z—tzee——" a message to the English police.

"Man on board answering to description. Ticket booked name of Watson. Has locked himself in cabin and refuses to come out. Insists on having hairdresser sent out to him. Have communicated Ostend police. Await instructions."

The Old Man with sharp words and au-

---

9. *wireless . . . Ostend,* the wireless telegraph operator on the *Miranda,* a boat carrying mail, passengers, goods, etc., to Ostend (os tend′), a seaport in northwest Belgium.
10. *Morse . . . valve set.* Morse code is a system in which letters, etc., are represented by dots and dashes or short and long sounds. A valve set is a wireless telegraph set that uses vacuum tubes.

thoritative gestures cleared a way through the excited little knot of people gathered about First Class Cabin No. 36. Several passengers had got wind of "something up." Magnificently he herded them away to the gangway with their bags and suitcases. Sternly he bade the stewards and the boy, who stood gaping with his hands full of breakfast dishes, to stand away from the door. Terribly he commanded them to hold their tongues. Four or five sailors stood watchfully at his side. In the restored silence, the passenger in No. 36 could be heard pacing up and down the narrow cabin, moving things, clattering, splashing water.

Presently came steps overhead. Somebody arrived, with a message. The Old Man nodded. Six pairs of Belgian police boots came tip-toeing down the companion. The Old Man glanced at the official paper held out to him and nodded again.

"Ready?"

"Yes."

The Old Man knocked at the door of No. 36.

"Who is it?" cried a harsh, sharp voice.

"The barber is here, sir, that you sent for."

"Ah!" There was relief in the tone. "Send him in alone if you please. I—I have had an accident."

"Yes, sir."

At the sound of the bolt being cautiously withdrawn, the Old Man stepped forward. The door opened a chink, and was slammed to again, but the Old Man's boot was firmly wedged against the jamb. The policemen surged forward. There was a yelp and a shot which smashed harmlessly through the window of the first-class saloon, and the passenger was brought out.

"Strike me pink!" shrieked the boy, "strike me pink if he ain't gone green in the night!"

Green!

Not for nothing had Mr. Budd studied the intricate mutual reactions of chemical dyes. In the pride of his knowledge he had set a mark on his man, to mark him out from the billions of this overpopulated world. Was there a port in all Christendom where a murderer might slip away, with every hair on him green as a parrot—green mustache, green eyebrows, and that thick, springing shock of hair, vivid, flaring midsummer green?

Mr. Budd got his five hundred pounds. The *Evening Messenger* published the full story of his great betrayal. He trembled, fearing this sinister fame. Surely no one would ever come to him again.

On the next morning an enormous blue limousine rolled up to his door, to the immense admiration of Wilton Street. A lady, magnificent in musquash[11] and diamonds, swept into the saloon.

"You are Mr. Budd, aren't you?" she cried. "The great Mr. Budd? Isn't it too wonderful? And now, dear Mr. Budd, you must do me a favor. You must dye my hair green, at once. Now. I want to be able to say I'm the very first to be done by you. I'm the Duchess of Winchester, and that awful Melcaster woman is chasing me down the street—the cat!"

If you want it done, I can give you the number of Mr. Budd's parlors in Bond Street.[12] But I understand it is a terribly expensive process.

---

11. *musquash* (mus′kwosh), a coat made of muskrat fur.
12. *Bond Street.* Mr. Budd's move from Pimlico to the very fashionable Bond Street indicates how much he has come up in the world.

Discussion

1. This story takes place in London, England. **(a)** Which details tell you that it takes place several years ago? **(b)** Does anything happen that would not be likely to happen today? Explain.

2. (a) What is Mr. Budd's opinion of himself as an artist? **(b)** What is Mr. Budd's opinion of himself as a "man to catch a brutal murderer singlehanded"? **(c)** Do the events of the story bear out either of these opinions? Explain.

3. "The hairdresser hears many secrets and very many lies," states the narrator. **(a)** Which of the customer's comments does Mr. Budd think *may* be lies? **(b)** Which statement is certainly a lie, according to Mr. Budd?

4. (a) At what point in the story do you finally realize the nature of Mr. Budd's "inspiration"? **(b)** What details and hints throughout the story prepare readers for the outcome?

5. (a) In what sense is Mr. Budd guilty of "betrayal"? **(b)** How does he feel after he gets the reward? **(c)** What happens that is opposite from what he expects?

6. Mr. Budd recalls the old inscription "Knowledge Is Power." Why might that be an appropriate title for this story?

Application
Plot

1. Describe Mr. Budd's situation at the beginning of the story and why he is so "painfully fascinated" by any offer of a reward. What conflicts does Mr. Budd experience as he reads the newspaper?

2. What internal conflict does Mr. Budd undergo while working on the customer? The point at which Mr. Budd starts to take a decisive action to end that conflict is one climax in the story; locate the paragraphs in which he does so. What determines Mr. Budd finally to act?

3. Trace the events from the time Strickland leaves until he is arrested. What external conflict is there in the story? Does Mr. Budd take part in it? Explain.

4. What events come after the resolution of all conflicts and form the conclusion?

Vocabulary
Combined Skills

A dictionary contains many kinds of information besides definitions. Use your Glossary to answer these questions:

1. Which definition of *capital* best fits the context (34a, 5) in which it appears?

2. The entry word *mean*¹ has a number, telling you to look also at *mean*² and *mean*³. In which entry do you find a definition that fits the context (33a, 1)?

3. Pronunciations are given in parentheses. The pronunciation key at the top of the page tells how to pronounce the sound symbols. What three words from the key represent the vowel sounds in *fiasco*?

4. When more than one syllable in a word is accented, the primary accent mark (′) indicates the most stress or emphasis, while the secondary accent (′) indicates lesser stress. Which syllable of *authoritative* receives the primary stress? Which receives secondary stress?

5. What verb is *borne* a form of?

6. What part of a *shilling* is ninepence?

7. A word's origin is often explained in

brackets at the end of an entry. From what language does *sinister* come? What is the original meaning in that language?

8. Where do you find additional information about what kind of *saloon* Mr. Budd operates? What definition best fits the context (32b, 4)?

9. *Dubiously* does not have an entry of its own, but it is included as a run-on entry at the end of another entry. Under what entry word do you find *dubiously*?

10. Under what entry do you find *artfulness*? Copy the context sentence (39a, 6), substituting the definition. Change words in the context sentence or in the definition in order to make it read smoothly.

Dorothy Sayers 1893-1957

One of the first women ever to receive a degree from Oxford University in England, Dorothy Sayers is best known as a writer of mysteries. Her detective novels are noteworthy not only for their literary style but for their exacting use of background research and for their well-developed characters. In one book, *Murder Must Advertise*, Sayers used her own experiences as copywriter for an advertising agency to provide this background. In her later writing, she abandoned fiction in favor of religious and scholarly topics.

Comment: Hair of Gold—and Other Colors

From earliest times one of the most common beauty treatments used by men and women has been to color their hair. Gold dust was used in many different countries. Powders, such as starch, in white, yellow, and red were widely used. In Greece, some women dyed their hair fashionably blue.

In ancient Rome, people used a lead comb dipped in vinegar to deposit lead salts on the hair that would gradually darken it. In 15th century Italy, both men and women tried to achieve blond hair by using either bleach or saffron (an orange-yellow color, also used in cooking, made from dried flowers), or dye made from onion skins. In Elizabethan England hair was dusted with powder or flour in colors like iris, violet, or white.

For centuries, only natural ingredients were used for coloring, such as powders made from ground minerals or vegetable dyes made from herbs, berries, roots, etc. One of the earliest dyes known, for example, is henna, a reddish-brown dye made from the leaves of a thorny shrub of Asia and Africa, which is still in wide use today.

Then in the late 1800s, it was discovered that hydrogen peroxide will take the color out of hair, turning it a strawlike yellow that can then be dyed any other color. This was followed by a number of other, more sophisticated dyes created not in nature, but in chemical laboratories. It took researchers some time to learn about the ways different chemicals react in combination. The wrong combinations often produced severe effects—from allergic skin rashes to loss of hair to strange colors like the bright green with which Mr. Budd catches his murderer.

The Treasure of Lemon Brown

Walter Dean Myers

He was an eerie sight, a bundle of rags standing at the top of the stairs, his shadow on the wall looming over him.

The dark sky, filled with angry, swirling clouds, reflected Greg Ridley's mood as he sat on the stoop of his building. His father's voice came to him again, first reading the letter the principal had sent to the house, then lecturing endlessly about his poor efforts in math.

"I had to leave school when I was thirteen," his father had said, "that's a year younger than you are now. If I'd had half the chances that you have, I'd . . . ."

Greg had sat in the small, pale green kitchen listening, knowing the lecture would end with his father saying he couldn't play ball with the Scorpions. He had asked his father the week before, and his father had said it depended on his next report card. It wasn't often the Scorpions took on new players, especially fourteen-year-olds, and this was a chance of a lifetime for Greg. He hadn't been allowed to play high-school ball, which he had really wanted to do, but playing for the Community Center team was the next best thing. Report cards were due in a week, and Greg had been hoping for the best. But the principal had ended the suspense early when she sent that letter saying Greg would probably fail math if he didn't spend more time studying.

"And you want to play *basketball*?" His father's brows knitted over deep brown eyes. "That must be some kind of a joke. Now you just get into your room and hit those books."

That had been two nights before. His father's words, like the distant thunder that now echoed through the streets of Harlem, still rumbled softly in his ears.

It was beginning to cool. Gusts of wind made bits of paper dance between the parked cars. There was a flash of nearby lightning, and soon large drops of rain splashed onto his jeans. He stood to go upstairs, thought of the lecture that probably awaited him if he did anything except shut himself in his room with his math book, and started walking down the street instead. Down the block there was an old tenement that had been abandoned for some months. Some of the guys had held an impromptu checker tournament there the week before, and Greg had noticed that the door, once boarded over, had been slightly ajar.

Pulling his collar up as high as he could, he checked for traffic and made a dash across the street. He reached the house just as another flash of lightning changed the night to day for an instant, then returned the graffiti-scarred building to the grim shadows. He vaulted over the outer stairs and pushed tentatively on the door. It was open, and he let himself in.

The inside of the building was dark except for the dim light that filtered through the dirty windows from the streetlamps. There was a room a few feet from the door, and from where he stood at the entrance, Greg could see a squarish patch of light on the floor. He entered the room, frowning at the musty smell. It was a large room that might have been someone's parlor at one time. Squinting, Greg could see an old table on its side against one wall, what looked like a pile of rags or a torn mattress in the corner, and a couch, with one side broken, in front of the window.

He went to the couch. The side that wasn't broken was comfortable enough, though a little creaky. From this spot he could see the blinking neon sign over the bodega[1] on the corner. He sat a while, watching the sign blink first green then red, allowing his mind to drift to the Scorpions, then to his father. His father had been a postal worker for all Greg's life, and was proud of it, often telling Greg how hard he had worked to pass the test. Greg had heard the story too many times to be interested now.

For a moment Greg thought he heard something that sounded like a scraping against the wall. He listened carefully, but it was gone.

Outside the wind had picked up, sending the rain against the window with a force that shook the glass in its frame. A car passed, its tires hissing over the wet street and its red tail lights glowing in the darkness.

Greg thought he heard the noise again. His stomach tightened as he held himself still and listened intently. There weren't any more scraping noises, but he was sure he had heard something in the darkness—something breathing!

He tried to figure out just where the breathing was coming from; he knew it was in the room with him. Slowly he stood, tensing. As he turned, a flash of lightning lit up the room, frightening him with its sudden brilliance. He saw nothing, just the overturned table, the pile of rags and an old newspaper on the floor. Could he have been imagining the sounds? He continued listening, but heard nothing and thought that it might have just been rats. Still, he thought, as soon as the rain let up he would leave. He went to the window and was about to look out when he heard a voice behind him.

"Don't try nothin' 'cause I got a razor here sharp enough to cut a week into nine days!"

Greg, except for an involuntary tremor in his knees, stood stock still. The voice was high and brittle, like dry twigs being broken, surely not one he had ever heard before. There was a shuffling sound as the person who had been speaking moved a step closer. Greg turned, holding his breath, his eyes straining to see in the dark room.

The upper part of the figure before him was still in darkness. The lower half was in the dim rectangle of light that fell unevenly from the window. There were two feet, in cracked, dirty shoes from which rose legs that were wrapped in rags.

"Who are you?" Greg hardly recognized his own voice.

"I'm Lemon Brown," came the answer. "Who're you?"

"Greg Ridley."

"What you doing here?" The figure shuffled forward again, and Greg took a small step backward.

---

1. **bodega** (bō dä′gə), a neighborhood grocery store. [*Spanish*]

"It's raining," Greg said.

"I can see that," the figure said.

The person who called himself Lemon Brown peered forward, and Greg could see him clearly. He was an old man. His black, heavily wrinkled face was surrounded by a halo of crinkly white hair and whiskers that seemed to separate his head from the layers of dirty coats piled on his smallish frame. His pants were bagged to the knee, where they were met with rags that went down to the old shoes. The rags were held on with strings, and there was a rope around his middle. Greg relaxed. He had seen the man before, picking through the trash on the corner and pulling clothes out of a Salvation Army box. There was no sign of the razor that could "cut a week into nine days."

"What are you doing here?" Greg asked.

"This is where I'm staying," Lemon Brown said. "What you here for?"

"Told you it was raining out," Greg said, leaning against the back of the couch until he felt it give slightly.

"Ain't you got no home?"

"I got a home," Greg answered.

"You ain't one of them bad boys looking for my treasure, is you?" Lemon Brown cocked his head to one side and squinted one eye. "Because I told you I got me a razor."

"I'm not looking for your treasure," Greg answered, smiling. "*If* you have one."

"What you mean, *if* I have one," Lemon Brown said. "Every man got a treasure. You don't know that, you must be a fool!"

"Sure," Greg said as he sat on the sofa and put one leg over the back. "What do you have, gold coins?"

"Don't worry none about what I got," Lemon Brown said. "You know who I am?"

"You told me your name was orange or lemon or something like that."

"Lemon Brown," the old man said, pulling back his shoulders as he did so, "they used to call me Sweet Lemon Brown."

"Sweet Lemon?" Greg asked.

"Yessir. Sweet Lemon Brown. They used to say I sung the blues so sweet that if I sang at a funeral, the dead would commence to rocking with the beat. Used to travel all over Mississippi and as far as Monroe, Louisiana, and east on over to Macon, Georgia. You mean you ain't never heard of Sweet Lemon Brown?"

"Afraid not," Greg said. "What . . . what happened to you?"

"Hard times, boy. Hard times always after a poor man. One day I got tired, sat down to rest a spell and felt a tap on my shoulder. Hard times caught up with me."

"Sorry about that."

"What you doing here? How come you didn't go on home when the rain come. Rain don't bother you young folks none."

"Just didn't," Greg looked away.

"I used to have a knotty-headed boy just like you." Lemon Brown had half walked, half shuffled back to the corner and sat down against the wall. "Had them big eyes like you got. I used to call them moon eyes. Look into them moon eyes and see anything you want."

"How come you gave up singing the blues?" Greg asked.

"Didn't give it up," Lemon Brown said. "You don't give up the blues; they give you up. After a while you do good for yourself, and it ain't nothing but foolishness singing about how hard you got it. Ain't that right?"

"I guess so."

"What's that noise?" Lemon Brown asked, suddenly sitting upright.

Greg listened, and he heard a noise outside. He looked at Lemon Brown and saw the old man was pointing toward the window.

Greg went to the window and saw three men, neighborhood thugs, on the stoop. One was carrying a length of pipe. Greg looked back toward Lemon Brown, who moved quietly across the room to the window. The old man looked out, then beckoned frantically for Greg to follow him. For a moment Greg couldn't move. Then he found himself following Lemon Brown into the hallway and up darkened stairs. Greg followed as closely as he could. They reached the top of the stairs, and Greg felt

Lemon Brown's hand first lying on his shoulder, then probing down his arm until he finally took Greg's hand into his own as they crouched in the darkness.

"They's bad men," Lemon Brown whispered. His breath was warm against Greg's skin.

"Hey! Rag man!" A voice called. "We know you in here. What you got up under them rags? You got any money?"

Silence.

"We don't want to have to come in and hurt you, old man, but we don't mind if we have to."

Lemon Brown squeezed Greg's hand in his own hard, gnarled fist.

There was a banging downstairs and a light as the men entered. They banged around noisily, calling for the rag man.

"We heard you talking about your treasure," the voice was slurred. "We just want to see it, that's all."

"You sure he's here?" One voice seemed to come from the room with the sofa.

"Yeah, he stays here every night."

"There's another room over there; I'm going to take a look. You got that flashlight?"

"Yeah, here, take the pipe too."

Greg opened his mouth to quiet the sound of his breath as he sucked it in uneasily. A beam of light hit the wall a few feet opposite him, then went out.

"Ain't nobody in that room," a voice said. "You think he gone or something?"

"I don't know," came the answer. "All I know is that I heard him talking about some kind of treasure. You know they found that shopping bag lady with that money in her bags."

"Yeah. You think he's upstairs?"

"HEY, OLD MAN, ARE YOU UP THERE?"

Silence.

"Watch my back, I'm going up."

There was a footstep on the stairs, and the beam from the flashlight danced crazily along the peeling wallpaper. Greg held his breath. There was another step and a loud crashing noise as the man banged the pipe against the wooden banister. Greg could feel his temples throb as the man slowly neared them. Greg thought about the pipe, wondering what he would do when the man reached them—what he *could* do.

Then Lemon Brown released his hand and moved toward the top of the stairs. Greg looked around and saw stairs going up to the next floor. He tried waving to Lemon Brown, hoping the old man would see him in the dim light and follow him to the next floor. Maybe, Greg thought, the man wouldn't follow them up there. Suddenly, though, Lemon Brown stood at the top of the stairs, both arms raised high above his head.

"There he is!" A voice cried from below.

"Throw down your money, old man, so I won't have to bash your head in!"

Lemon Brown didn't move. Greg felt himself near panic. The steps came closer, and still Lemon Brown didn't move. He was an eerie sight, a bundle of rags standing at the top of the stairs, his shadow on the wall looming over him. Maybe, the thought came to Greg, the scene could be even eerier.

Greg wet his lips, put his hands to his mouth and tried to make a sound. Nothing came out. He swallowed hard, wet his lips once more and howled as evenly as he could.

"What's that?"

As Greg howled, the light moved away from Lemon Brown, but not before Greg saw him hurl his body down the stairs at the men who had come to take his treasure. There was a crashing noise, and then footsteps. A rush of warm air came in as the downstairs door opened, then there was only an ominous silence.

Greg stood on the landing. He listened, and after a while there was another sound on the staircase.

"Mr. Brown?" he called.

"Yeah, it's me," came the answer. "I got their flashlight."

Greg exhaled in relief as Lemon Brown made his way slowly back up the stairs.

"You O.K.?"

"Few bumps and bruises," Lemon Brown said.

"I think I'd better be going," Greg said, his breath returning to normal. "You'd better leave, too, before they come back."

"They may hang around outside for a while," Lemon Brown said, "but they ain't getting their nerve up to come in here again. Not with crazy old rag men and howling spooks. Best you stay awhile till the coast is clear. I'm heading out West tomorrow, out to east St. Louis."

"They were talking about treasures," Greg said. "You *really* have a treasure?"

"What I tell you? Didn't I tell you every man got a treasure?" Lemon Brown said. "You want to see mine?"

"If you want to show it to me," Greg shrugged.

"Let's look out the window first, see what them scoundrels be doing," Lemon Brown said.

They followed the oval beam of the flashlight into one of the rooms and looked out the window. They saw the men who had tried to take the treasure sitting on the curb near the corner. One of them had his pants leg up, looking at his knee.

"You sure you're not hurt?" Greg asked Lemon Brown.

"Nothing that ain't been hurt before," Lemon Brown said. "When you get as old as me all you say when something hurts is, 'Howdy, Mr. Pain, sees you back again.' Then when Mr. Pain see he can't worry you none, he go on mess with somebody else."

Greg smiled.

"Here, you hold this." Lemon Brown gave Greg the flashlight.

He sat on the floor near Greg and carefully untied the strings that held the rags on his right leg. When he took the rags away, Greg saw a piece of plastic. The old man carefully took off the plastic and unfolded it. He revealed some yellowed newspaper clippings and a battered harmonica.

"There it be," he said, nodding his head. "There it be."

Greg looked at the old man, saw the distant look in his eye, then turned to the clippings. They told of Sweet Lemon Brown, a blues singer and harmonica player who was appearing at different theaters in the South. One of the clippings said he had been the hit of the show, although not the headliner. All of the clippings were reviews of shows Lemon Brown had been in more than 50 years ago. Greg looked at the harmonica. It was dented badly on one side, with the reed holes on one end nearly closed.

"I used to travel around and make money for to feed my wife and Jesse— that's my boy's name. Used to feed them good, too. Then his mama died, and he stayed with his mama's sister. He growed up to be a man, and when the war come he saw fit to go off and fight in it. I didn't have nothing to give him except these things that told him who I was, and what he come from. If you know your pappy did something, you know you can do something too.

"Anyway, he went off to war, and I went off still playing and singing. 'Course by then I wasn't as much as I used to be, not without somebody to make it worth the while. You know what I mean?"

"Yeah," Greg nodded, not quite really knowing.

"I traveled around, and one time I come home, and there was this letter saying Jesse got killed in the war. Broke my heart, it truly did.

"They sent back what he had with him over there, and what it was is this old mouth fiddle and these clippings. Him carrying it around with him like that told me it meant something to him. That was my treasure, and when I give it to him he treated it just like that, a treasure. Ain't that something?"

"Yeah, I guess so," Greg said.

"You *guess* so?" Lemon Brown's voice rose an octave as he started to put his treasure back into the plastic. "Well, you got to guess 'cause you sure don't know nothing. Don't know enough to get home when it's raining."

"I guess . . . I mean, you're right."

"You O.K. for a youngster," the old man said as he tied the strings around his leg, "better than those scalawags what come here looking for my treasure. That's for sure."

"You really think that treasure of yours was worth fighting for?" Greg asked. "Against a pipe?"

"What else a man got 'cepting what he can pass on to his son, or his daughter, if she be his oldest?" Lemon Brown said. "For a big-headed boy you sure do ask the foolishest questions."

Lemon Brown got up after patting his rags in place and looked out the window again.

"Looks like they're gone. You get on out of here and get yourself home. I'll be watching from the window so you'll be all right."

Lemon Brown went down the stairs behind Greg. When they reached the front door the old man looked out first, saw the street was clear and told Greg to scoot on home.

"You sure you'll be O.K.?" Greg asked.

"Now didn't I tell you I was going to east St. Louis in the morning?" Lemon Brown asked. "Don't that sound O.K. to you?"

"Sure it does," Greg said. "Sure it does. And you take care of that treasure of yours."

"That I'll do," Lemon said, the wrinkles about his eyes suggesting a smile. "That I'll do."

The night had warmed and the rain had stopped, leaving puddles at the curbs. Greg didn't even want to think how late it was. He thought ahead of what his father would say and wondered if he should tell him about Lemon Brown. He thought about it until he reached his stoop, and decided against it. Lemon Brown would be O.K., Greg thought, with his memories and his treasure.

Greg pushed the button over the bell marked Ridley, thought of the lecture he knew his father would give him, and smiled.

Discussion

1. **(a)** At the beginning of the story, what is Greg upset about? **(b)** Where does he go to think things over?

2. Why do the three thugs come after Lemon Brown? How do Greg and Lemon Brown get rid of them?

3. **(a)** When Greg questions his treasure, Lemon Brown replies, "Every man got a treasure. You don't know that, you must be a fool!" What does he mean? **(b)** What does Lemon Brown's treasure actually consist of? **(c)** Why does he consider it a treasure?

4. At the beginning of the story, Greg is tired of his father's lectures. At the end, he smiles when he thinks of the lecture he will receive when he gets home. What has caused this change in Greg?

Composition

Lemon Brown's treasure might not be something that other people would consider a treasure, but it is important to him. Do you have something that is important to you for personal or sentimental reasons, but that others might not consider important at all? How did you come to have this "treasure"? If someone gave it to you, did that person consider it a treasure, as well? Would you ever pass it on to anyone else? Why or why not?

Write a paragraph describing your treasure and what it means to you. Include answers to any of the above questions that seem appropriate. Can you describe your treasure in such a way that your readers will wish they had one too?

(You may find the article "Getting Started" in the Composition Guide helpful in writing this composition.)

Walter Dean Myers 1937–

Claiming that life is "the best thing I've ever known," Walter Dean Myers has written of life in short stories collected in such anthologies as *We Must See: Young Black Storytellers* and *We Be Word Sorcerers, 25 Stories by Black Americans*. He has written numerous books for young people, including *Mojo and the Russians* and *fast sam, cool clyde, and stuff*. In 1968, his book *Where Does the Day Go?* won the Interracial Council Award for Children's Books.

See **SIMILE** Handbook of Literary Terms

*T*he Base Stealer

Robert Francis

Poised between going on and back, pulled
Both ways taut like a tightrope-walker,
Fingertips pointing the opposites,
Now bouncing tiptoe like a dropped ball
5 Or a kid skipping rope, come on, come on,
Running a scattering of steps sidewise,
How he teeters, skitters, tingles, teases,
Taunts them, hovers like an ecstatic bird,
He's only flirting, crowd him, crowd him,
10 Delicate, delicate, delicate, delicate—now!

Discussion

1. How does the title help explain what is happening in the poem?

2. Does the speaker in the poem seem to be expressing anger, indifference, admiration, or amusement toward the base stealer? How can you tell?

3. (a) The phrases "come on" and "crowd him" are each repeated twice, and the word *delicate* is repeated four times. What effect do these repetitions have on the sense of the poem? **(b)** At the final word *now!* what is happening?

4. If you had never seen a person trying to steal a base in baseball, could you understand the process after reading this poem? Explain.

Application
Simile

Think of a tightrope walker with arms outstretched for balance, delicately "poised between going on and back" and "pulled both ways taut" by being ready to move in any direction at an instant. Now mentally compare the tightrope walker with a baseball player trying to steal a base, "poised" and "pulled" in a similar way. Like most other figurative language, a simile can provide fresh insight into an idea or subject by giving the reader a new way of looking at something—in this case, the base stealer's acrobatic artistry.

1. What two similes in the poem describe the base stealer's bouncing on tiptoe?

2. What kind of movement is suggested by "hovers like an ecstatic bird"?

Robert Francis 1901–

Robert Francis has taught the art of writing poetry for many years. He lives year round in his one-man house, Fort Juniper, in Amherst, Massachusetts, where he has produced essays, poetry, fiction, and an autobiography, *The Trouble with Francis.* In his honor, the University of Massachusetts Press established the Juniper Prize for poetry.

T*op Man*

James Ramsey Ullman

The mountain, to all of us, was no longer a mere giant of ice: it had become a living thing, an enemy, watching us, waiting for us, hostile, relentless.

The gorge bent. The walls fell suddenly away and we came out on the edge of a bleak, boulder-strewn valley. And there it was.

Osborn saw it first. He had been leading the column, threading his way slowly among the huge rock masses of the gorge's mouth. Then he came to the first flat, bare place and stopped. He neither pointed nor cried out, but every man behind him knew instantly what it was. The long file sprang taut, like a jerked rope. As swiftly as we could, but in complete silence, we came out into the open ground where Osborn stood, and raised our eyes with his. In the records of the Indian Topographical Survey it says:

Kalpurtha: a mountain in the Himalayas, altitude 28,900 ft. The highest peak in British India and fourth highest in the world. Also known as K3. A Tertiary formation of sedimentary limestone——

There were men among us who had spent months of their lives—in some cases, years—reading, thinking, planning about what now lay before us, but at that moment statistics and geology, knowledge, thought and plans, were as remote and forgotten as the faraway western cities from which we had come. We were men bereft of everything but eyes, everything but the single, electric perception: There it was!

Before us the valley stretched away into miles of rocky desolation. To right and left it was bounded by low ridges which, as the eye followed them, slowly mounted and drew closer together until the valley was no longer a valley at all, but a narrowing, rising corridor between the cliffs. What happened then I can describe only as a single, stupendous crash of music. At the end of the corridor and above it—so far above it that it shut out half the sky—hung the blinding white mass of K3.

It was like the many pictures I had seen, and at the same time utterly unlike them. The shape was there, and the familiar distinguishing features—the sweeping skirt of

glaciers; the monstrous vertical precipices of the face and the jagged ice line of the east ridge; finally the symmetrical summit pyramid that transfixed the sky. But whereas in the pictures the mountain had always seemed unreal—a dream image of cloud, snow and crystal—it was now no longer an image at all. It was a mass, solid, imminent, appalling. We were still too far away to see the windy whipping of its snow plumes or to hear the cannonading of its avalanches, but in that sudden silent moment every man of us was for the first time aware of it, not as a picture in his mind but as a thing, an antagonist. For all its twenty-eight thousand feet of lofty grandeur, it seemed, somehow, less to tower than to crouch—a white-hooded giant, secret and remote, but living. Living and on guard.

I turned my eyes from the dazzling glare and looked at my companions. Osborn still stood a little in front of the others. He was absolutely motionless, his young face tense and shining, his eyes devouring the mountain as a lover's might devour the face of his beloved. One could feel in the very set of his body the overwhelming desire that swelled in him to act, to come to grips, to conquer. A little behind him were ranged the other men of the expedition: Randolph, our leader, Wittmer and Johns, Doctor Schlapp and Bixler. All were still, their eyes cast upward. Off to one side a little stood Nace, the Englishman, the only one among us who was not staring at K3 for the first time. He had been the last to come up out of the gorge and stood now with arms folded on his chest, squinting at the great peak he had known so long and fought so tirelessly and fiercely. His lean British face, under its mask of stubble and windburn, was expressionless. His lips were a colorless line, and his eyes seemed almost shut.

Behind the sahibs ranged the porters, bent over their staffs, their brown, seamed faces straining upward from beneath their loads.

For a long while no one spoke or moved. The only sounds between earth and sky were the soft hiss of our breathing and the pounding of our hearts.

Through the long afternoon we wound slowly between the great boulders of the valley and at sundown pitched camp in the bed of a dried-up stream. The porters ate their rations in silence, wrapped themselves in their blankets and fell asleep under the stars. The rest of us, as was our custom, sat close about the fire that blazed in the circle of tents, discussing the events of the day and the plans for the next. It was a flawlessly clear Himalayan night and K3 tiered up into the blackness like a monstrous sentinel lighted from within. There was no wind, but a great tide of cold air crept down the valley from the ice fields above, penetrating our clothing, pressing gently against the canvas of the tents.

"Another night or two and we'll be needing the sleeping bags," commented Randolph.

Osborn nodded. "We could use them tonight, would be my guess."

Randolph turned to Nace. "What do you say, Martin?"

The Englishman puffed at his pipe a moment. "Rather think it might be better to wait," he said at last.

"Wait? Why?" Osborn jerked his head up.

"Well, it gets pretty nippy high up, you know. I've seen it thirty below at twenty-five thousand on the east ridge. Longer we wait for the bags, better acclimated we'll get."

Osborn snorted. "A lot of good being acclimated will do if we have frozen feet."

"Easy, Paul, easy," cautioned Randolph. "It seems to me Martin's right."

Osborn bit his lip, but said nothing. The other men entered the conversation, and soon it had veered to other matters: the weather, the porters and pack animals, routes, camps and strategy—the inevitable, inexhaustible topics of the climber's world.

There were all kinds of men among the eight of us, men with a great diversity of background and interest. Sayre Randolph, whom the Alpine Club had named leader of our expedition, had for years been a well-known explorer and lecturer. Now in his middle fifties, he was no longer equal to the grueling physical demands of high climbing, but served as planner and organizer of the enterprise. Wittmer was a Seattle lawyer, who had recently made a name for himself by a series of difficult ascents in the Coast Range of British Columbia. Johns was an Alaskan, a fantastically strong, able sourdough, who had been a ranger in the U.S. Forest Service and had accompanied many famous Alaskan expeditions. Schlapp was a practicing physician from Milwaukee, Bixler a government meteorologist with a talent for photography. I, at the time, was an assistant professor of geology at an eastern university.

Finally, and preeminently, there were Osborn and Nace. I say "preeminently," because even at this time, when we had been together as a party for little more than a month, I believe all of us realized that these were the two key men of our venture. None, to my knowledge, ever expressed it in words, but the conviction was there, nevertheless, that if any of us were eventually to stand on the hitherto unconquered summit of K3, it would be one of them, or both. They were utterly dissimilar men. Osborn was twenty-three and a year out of college,

a compact, buoyant mass of energy and high spirits. He seemed to be wholly unaffected by either the physical or mental hazards of mountaineering and had already, by virtue of many spectacular ascents in the Alps and Rockies, won a reputation as the most skilled and audacious of younger American climbers. Nace was in his forties—lean, taciturn, introspective. An official in the Indian Civil Service, he had explored and climbed in the Himalayas for twenty years. He had been a member of all five of the unsuccessful British expeditions to K3, and in his last attempt had attained to within five hundred feet of the summit, the highest point which any man had reached on the unconquered giant. This had been the famous tragic attempt in which his fellow climber and lifelong friend, Captain Furness, had slipped and fallen ten thousand feet to his death. Nace rarely mentioned his name, but on the steel head of his ice ax were engraved the words: TO MARTIN FROM JOHN. If fate were to grant that the ax of any one of us should be planted upon the summit of K3, I hoped it would be his.

Such were the men who huddled about the fire in the deep, still cold of that Himalayan night. There were many differences among us, in temperament as well as in background. In one or two cases, notably that of Osborn and Nace, there had already been a certain amount of friction, and as the venture continued and the struggles and hardships of the actual ascent began, it would, I knew, increase. But differences were unimportant. What mattered—all that mattered—was that our purpose was one— to conquer the monster of rock and ice that now loomed above us in the night; to stand for a moment where no man, no living thing, had ever stood before. To that end we had come from half a world away, across oceans and continents to the fastnesses of inner Asia. To that end we were prepared to endure cold, exhaustion and danger, even to the very last extremity of human endurance. Why? There is no answer, and at the same time every man among us knew the answer; every man who has ever looked upon a great mountain and felt the fever in his blood to climb and conquer, knows the answer. George Leigh Mallory, greatest of mountaineers, expressed it once and for all when he was asked why he wanted to climb unconquered Everest. "I want to climb it," said Mallory, "because it's there."

Day after day we crept on and upward. The naked desolation of the valley was unrelieved by any motion, color or sound, and, as we progressed, it was like being trapped at the bottom of a deep well or in a sealed court between great skyscrapers. Soon we were thinking of the ascent of the shining mountain not only as an end in itself but as an escape.

In our nightly discussions around the fire, our conversation narrowed more and more to the immediate problems confronting us, and during them I began to realize that the tension between Osborn and Nace went deeper than I had at first surmised. There was rarely any outright argument between them—they were both far too able mountain men to disagree on fundamentals—but I saw that at almost every turn they were rubbing each other the wrong way. It was a matter of personalities chiefly. Osborn was talkative, enthusiastic, optimistic, always chafing to be up and at it, always wanting to take the short, straight line to the given point. Nace, on the other hand, was matter-of-fact, cautious, slow.

He was the apostle of trial-and-error and watchful waiting. Because of his far greater experience and intimate knowledge of K3, Randolph almost invariably followed his advice, rather than Osborn's, when a difference of opinion arose. The younger man usually capitulated with good grace, but I could tell that he was irked.

During the days in the valley I had few occasions to talk privately with either of them, and only once did either mention the other in any but the most casual manner. Even then, the remarks they made seemed unimportant, and I remember them only in view of what happened later.

My conversation with Osborn occurred first. It was while we were on the march, and Osborn, who was directly behind me, came up suddenly to my side.

"You're a geologist, Frank," he began without preamble. "What do you think of Nace's theory about the ridge?"

"What theory?" I asked.

"He believes we should traverse under it from the glacier up. Says the ridge itself is too exposed."

"It looks pretty mean through the telescope."

"But it's been done before. He's done it himself. All right, it's tough—I'll admit that. But a decent climber could make it in half the time the traverse will take."

"Nace knows the traverse is longer," I said, "but he seems certain it will be much easier for us."

"Easier for him is what he means." Osborn paused, looking moodily at the ground. "He was a great climber in his day. It's a shame a man can't be honest enough with himself to know when he's through." He fell silent and a moment later dropped back into his place in line.

It was that same night, I think, that I awoke to find Nace sitting up in his blanket and staring at the mountain.

"How clear it is," I whispered.

The Englishman pointed. "See the ridge?"

I nodded, my eyes fixed on the great, twisting spine of ice that climbed into the sky. I could see now, more clearly than in the blinding sunlight, its huge indentations and jagged, wind-swept pitches.

"It looks impossible," I said.

"No, it can be done. Trouble is, when you've made it, you're too done in for the summit."

"Osborn seems to think its shortness would make up for its difficulty."

Nace was silent a long moment before answering. Then for the first and only time I heard him speak the name of his dead companion. "That's what Furness thought," he said quietly. Then he lay down and wrapped himself in his blanket.

For the next two weeks the uppermost point of the valley was our home and workshop. We established our base camp as close to the mountain as we could, less than half a mile from the tongue of its lowest glacier, and plunged into the arduous tasks of preparation for the ascent. Our food and equipment were unpacked, inspected and sorted, and finally repacked in lighter loads for transportation to more advanced camps. Hours on end were spent poring over maps and charts and studying the monstrous heights above us through telescope and binoculars. Under Nace's supervision, a thorough reconnaissance of the glacier was made and the route across it laid out; then began the backbreaking labor of moving up supplies and establishing the advance stations.

Camps I and II were set up on the glacier itself, in the most sheltered sites we could find. Camp III we built at its upper end, as near as possible to the point where

the great rock spine of K3 thrust itself free of ice and began its precipitous ascent. According to our plans, this would be the advance base of operations during the climb; the camps to be established higher up, on the mountain proper, would be too small and too exposed to serve as anything more than one or two nights' shelter. The total distance between the base camp and Camp III was only fifteen miles, but the utmost daily progress of our porters was five miles, and it was essential that we should never be more than twelve hours' march from food and shelter. Hour after hour, day after day, the long file of men wound up and down among the hummocks and crevasses of the glacier, and finally the time arrived when we were ready to advance.

Leaving Doctor Schlapp in command of eight porters at the base camp, we proceeded easily and on schedule, reaching Camp I the first night, Camp II the second and the advance base the third. No men were left at Camps I and II, inasmuch as they were designed simply as caches for food and equipment; and, furthermore, we knew we would need all the man power available for the establishment of the higher camps on the mountain proper.

For more than three weeks now the weather had held perfectly, but on our first night at the advance base, as if by malignant prearrangement of Nature, we had our first taste of the supernatural fury of a high Himalayan storm. It began with great streamers of lightning that flashed about the mountain like a halo; then heavily through the weird glare snow began to fall. The wind howled about the tents with hurricane frenzy, and the wild flapping of the canvas dinned in our ears like machine-gun fire.

There was no sleep for us that night or the next. For thirty-six hours the storm raged without lull, while we huddled in the icy gloom of the tents. At last, on the third morning, it was over, and we came out into a world transformed by a twelve-foot cloak of snow. No single landmark remained as it had been before, and our supplies and equipment were in the wildest confusion. Fortunately, there had not been a single serious injury, but it was another three days before we had regained our strength and put the camp in order.

Then we waited. The storm did not return, and the sky beyond the ridges gleamed flawlessly clear, but night and day we could hear the roaring thunder of avalanches on the mountain above us. To have ventured so much as one step into that savage, vertical wilderness before the new-fallen snow froze tight would have been suicidal. We chafed or waited patiently, according to our individual temperaments, while the days dragged by.

It was late one afternoon that Osborn returned from a short reconnaissance up the ridge. His eyes were shining and his voice jubilant.

"It's tight!" he cried. "Tight as a drum! We can go!" All of us stopped whatever we were doing. His excitement leaped like an electric spark from one to another. "I went about a thousand feet, and it's sound all the way. What do you say, Sayre? Tomorrow?"

Randolph hesitated a moment, then looked at Nace.

"Better give it another day or two," said the Englishman.

Osborn glared at him. "Why?" he challenged.

"It's generally safer to wait until——"

"Wait! Wait!" Osborn exploded. "Don't you ever think of anything but waiting? The snow's firm, I tell you!"

"It's firm down here," Nace replied quietly, "because the sun hits it only two hours a day. Up above it gets the sun twelve hours. It may not have frozen yet."

"The avalanches have stopped."

"That doesn't necessarily mean it will hold a man's weight."

"It seems to me, Martin's point——" Randolph began.

Osborn wheeled on him. "Sure," he snapped. "I know. Martin's right. The cautious bloody English are always right. Let him have his way, and we'll be sitting here twiddling our thumbs until the mountain falls down on us." His eyes flashed to Nace. "Maybe with a little less of that bloody cautiousness, you English wouldn't have made such a mess of Everest. Maybe your pals Mallory and Furness wouldn't be dead."

"Osborn!" commanded Randolph sharply.

The youngster stared at Nace for another moment, breathing heavily. Then, abruptly, he turned away.

The next two days were clear and windless, but we still waited, following Nace's advice. There were no further brushes between him and Osborn, but an unpleasant air of restlessness and tension hung over the camp. I found myself chafing almost as impatiently as Osborn himself for the moment when we would break out of that maddening inactivity and begin the assault.

At last the day came. With the first paling of the sky, a roped file of men, bent almost double beneath heavy loads, began slowly to climb the ice slope just beneath the jagged line of the great east ridge. In accordance with prearranged plan, we proceeded in relays; this first group consisting of Nace, Johns, myself and eight porters. It was our job to ascend approximately two thousand feet in a day's climbing and establish Camp IV at the most level and sheltered site we could find. We would spend the night there and return to the advance base next day, while the second relay, consisting of Osborn, Wittmer and eight more porters, went up with their loads. This process was to continue until all necessary supplies were at Camp IV, and then the whole thing would be repeated between Camps IV and V, and V and VI. From VI, at an altitude of about 26,000 feet, the ablest and fittest men—presumably Nace and Osborn—would make the direct assault on the summit. Randolph and Bixler were to remain at the advance base throughout the operations, acting as directors and coordinators. We were under the strictest orders that any man, sahib or porter, who suffered illness or injury should be brought down immediately.

How shall I describe those next two weeks beneath the great ice ridge of K3? In a sense, there was no occurrence of importance, and at the same time everything happened that could possibly happen, short of actual disaster. We established Camp IV, came down again, went up again, came down again. Then we crept laboriously higher. The wind increased, and the air grew steadily colder and more difficult to breathe. One morning two of the porters awoke with their feet frozen black; they had to be sent down. A short while later Johns developed an uncontrollable nosebleed and was forced to descend to a lower camp. Wittmer was suffering from splitting headaches and I from a continually dry throat. But providentially, the one enemy we feared the most in that icy, gale-lashed hell did not again attack us—no snow fell. And day by day, foot by foot, we ascended.

It is during ordeals like this that the surface trappings of a man are shed and his secret mettle laid bare. There were no shirkers or quitters among us—I had known that from the beginning—but now, with each passing day, it became more manifest which were the strongest and ablest among us. Beyond all argument, these were Osborn and Nace.

Osborn was magnificent. All the boyish impatience and moodiness which he had exhibited earlier were gone, and, now that he was at last at work in his natural element, he emerged as the peerless mountaineer he was. His energy was inexhaustible, and his speed, both on rock and ice, almost twice that of any other man in the party. He was always discovering new routes and short cuts; and there was such vigor, buoyancy and youth in everything he did that it gave heart to all the rest of us.

In contrast, Nace was slow, methodical, unspectacular. Since he and I worked in the same relay, I was with him almost constantly, and to this day I carry in my mind the clear image of the man—his tall body bent almost double against endless, shimmering slopes of ice; his lean brown face bent in utter concentration on the problem in hand, then raised searchingly to the next; the bright prong of his ax rising, falling, rising, falling with tireless rhythm, until the steps in the glassy incline were so wide and deep that the most clumsy of the porters could not have slipped from them had he tried. Osborn attacked the mountain, head on. Nace studied it, sparred with it, wore it down. His spirit did not flap from his sleeve like a pennon; it was deep inside him, patient, indomitable.

The day came soon when I learned from him what it is to be a great mountaineer. We were making the ascent from Camp IV to V, and an almost perpendicular ice wall had made it necessary for us to come out for a few yards on the exposed crest of the ridge. There were six of us in the party, roped together, with Nace leading, myself second, and four porters bringing up the rear. The ridge at this particular point was free of snow, but razor-thin, and the rocks were covered with a smooth glaze of ice. On either side the mountain dropped away in sheer precipices of five thousand feet.

Suddenly the last porter slipped. In what seemed to be the same instant I heard the ominous scraping of boot nails and, turning, saw a wildly gesticulating figure plunge sideways into the abyss. There was a scream as the next porter followed him. I remember trying frantically to dig into the ridge with my ax, realizing at the same time it would no more hold against the weight of the falling men than a pin stuck in a wall. Then I heard Nace shout, "Jump!" As he said it, the rope went tight about my waist, and I went hurtling after him into space on the opposite side of the ridge. After me came the nearest porter.

What happened then must have happened in five yards and a fifth of a second. I heard myself cry out, and the glacier, a mile below, rushed up at me, spinning. Then both were blotted out in a violent spasm, as the rope jerked taut. I hung for a moment, an inert mass, feeling that my body had been cut in two; then I swung in slowly to the side of the mountain. Above me the rope lay tight and motionless across the crest of the ridge, our weight exactly counterbalancing that of the men who had fallen on the far slope.

Nace's voice came up from below. "You chaps on the other side!" he shouted. "Start climbing slowly! We're climbing too!"

In five minutes we had all regained the ridge. The porters and I crouched panting

on the jagged rocks, our eyes closed, the sweat beading our faces in frozen drops. Nace carefully examined the rope that again hung loosely between us.

"All right, men," he said presently. "Let's get on to camp for a cup of tea."

Above Camp V the whole aspect of the ascent changed. The angle of the ridge eased off, and the ice, which lower down had covered the mountain like a sheath, lay only in scattered patches between the rocks. Fresh enemies, however, instantly appeared to take the place of the old. We were now laboring at an altitude of more than 25,000 feet—well above the summits of the highest surrounding peaks—and day and night, without protection or respite, we were buffeted by the savage fury of the wind. Worse than this was that the atmosphere had become so rarefied it could scarcely support life. Breathing itself was a major physical effort, and our progress upward consisted of two or three painful steps, followed by a long period of rest in which our hearts pounded wildly and our burning lungs gasped for air. Each of us carried a small cylinder of oxygen in our pack, but we used it only in emergencies, and found that, though its immediate effect was salutary, it left us later even worse off than before.

But the great struggle was now mental rather than physical. The lack of air induced a lethargy of mind and spirit; confidence and the powers of thought and decision waned. The mountain, to all of us, was no longer a mere giant of rock and ice; it had become a living thing, an enemy, watching us, waiting for us, hostile, relentless.

On the fifteenth day after we had first left the advance base, we pitched Camp VI at an altitude of 26,500 feet. It was located near the uppermost extremity of the great east ridge, directly beneath the so-called shoulder of the mountain. On the far side of the shoulder the stupendous north face of K3 fell sheer to the glaciers, two miles below. Above it and to the left rose the symmetrical bulk of the summit pyramid. The topmost rocks of its highest pinnacle were clearly visible from the shoulder, and the intervening fifteen hundred feet seemed to offer no insuperable obstacles.

Camp VI, which was in reality no camp at all but a single tent, was large enough to accommodate only three men. Osborn established it with the aid of Wittmer and one porter; then, the following morning, Wittmer and the porter descended to Camp V, and Nace and I went up. It was our plan that Osborn and Nace should launch the final assault—the next day, if the weather held—with myself in support, following their progress through binoculars and going to their aid or summoning help from below if anything went wrong. As the three of us lay in the tent that night, the summit seemed already within arm's reach, victory securely in our grasp.

And then the blow fell. With fiendishly malignant timing, which no power on earth could have made us believe was a simple accident of nature, the mountain hurled at us its last line of defense. It snowed.

For a day and a night the great flakes drove down upon us, swirling and swooping in the wind, blotting out the summit, the shoulder, everything beyond the tiny white-walled radius of our tent. At last, during the morning of the following day, it cleared. The sun came out in a thin blue sky, and the summit pyramid again appeared above us, now whitely robed in fresh snow. But still we waited. Until the snow either froze or was blown away by the wind, it would have been the rashest courting of destruction for us to have ascended a foot beyond the camp. Another day passed. And another.

By the third nightfall our nerves were at the breaking point. For hours on end we had scarcely moved or spoken, and the only sounds in all the world were the endless moaning of the wind outside and the harsh, sucking noise of our breathing. I knew that, one way or another, the end had come. Our meager food supply was running out; even with careful rationing, there was enough left for only two more days.

Presently Nace stirred in his sleeping bag and sat up. "We'll have to go down tomorrow," he said quietly.

For a moment there was silence in the tent. Then Osborn struggled to a sitting position and faced him.

"No," he said.

"There's still too much loose snow above. We can't make it."

"But it's clear. As long as we can see—"

Nace shook his head. "Too dangerous. We'll go down tomorrow and lay in a fresh supply. Then we'll try again."

"Once we go down we're licked. You know it."

Nace shrugged. "Better to be licked than——" The strain of speech was suddenly too much for him and he fell into a violent paroxysm of coughing. When it had passed, there was a long silence.

Then, suddenly, Osborn spoke again. "Look, Nace," he said, "I'm going up tomorrow."

The Englishman shook his head.

"I'm going—understand?"

For the first time since I had known him, I saw Nace's eyes flash in anger. "I'm the senior member of this group," he said. "I forbid you to go!"

With a tremendous effort, Osborn jerked himself to his feet. "You forbid me? This may be your sixth time on this mountain, and all that, but you don't own it! I know what you're up to. You haven't got it in you to make the top yourself, so you don't want anyone else to get the glory. That's it, isn't it? Isn't it?" He sat down again suddenly, gasping for breath.

Nace looked at him with level eyes. "This mountain has licked me five times,"

he said softly. "It killed my best friend. It means more to me to lick it than anything else in the world. Maybe I'll make it and maybe I won't. But if I do, it will be as a rational, intelligent human being, not as a fool throwing my life away——"

He collapsed into another fit of coughing and fell back in his sleeping bag. Osborn, too, was still. They lay there inert, panting, too exhausted for speech.

It was hours later that I awoke from dull, uneasy sleep. In the faint light I saw Nace fumbling with the flap of the tent.

"What is it?" I asked.

"Osborn. He's gone."

The words cut like a blade through my lethargy. I struggled to my feet and followed Nace from the tent.

Outside, the dawn was seeping up the eastern sky. It was very cold, but the wind had fallen and the mountain seemed to hang suspended in a vast stillness. Above us the summit pyramid climbed bleakly into space, like the last outpost of a spent lifeless planet. Raising my binoculars, I swept them over the gray waste. At first I saw nothing but rock and ice; then, suddenly, something moved.

"I've got him," I whispered.

As I spoke, the figure of Osborn sprang into clear focus against a patch of ice. He took three or four slow upward steps, stopped, went on again. I handed the glasses to Nace.

The Englishman squinted through them a moment, returned them to me, and reentered the tent. When I followed, he had already laced his boots and was pulling on his outer gloves.

"He's not far," he said. "Can't have been gone more than half an hour." He seized his ice ax and started out again.

"Wait," I said. "I'm going with you."

Nace shook his head. "Better stay here."

"I'm going with you," I said.

He said nothing further, but waited while I made ready. In a few moments we left the tent, roped up and started off.

Almost immediately we were on the shoulder and confronted with the paralyzing two-mile drop of the north face, but we negotiated the short exposed stretch without mishap and in ten minutes were working up the base of the summit pyramid. Our progress was creepingly slow. There seemed to be literally no air at all to breathe, and after almost every step we were forced to rest.

The minutes crawled into hours, and still we climbed. Presently the sun came up. Its level rays streamed across the clouds far below, and glinted from the summits of distant peaks. But, although the pinnacle of K3 soared a full five thousand feet above anything in the surrounding world, we had scarcely any sense of height. The stupendous wilderness of mountains and glaciers that spread beneath us to the horizon was flattened and remote, an unreal, insubstantial landscape seen in a dream. We had no connection with it, or it with us. All living, all awareness, purpose and will, was concentrated in the last step and the next—to put one foot before the other; to breathe; to ascend. We struggled on in silence.

I do not know how long it was since we had left the camp—it might have been two hours, it might have been six—when we suddenly sighted Osborn. We had not been able to find him again since our first glimpse through the binoculars, but now, unexpectedly and abruptly, as we came up over a jagged outcropping of rock, there he was. He was at a point, only a few yards above us, where the mountain steepened into an almost vertical wall. The smooth surface directly in front of him was obviously unclimbable, but two alternate routes were presented. To the left, a chimney cut obliquely across the wall, forbiddingly steep, but seeming to offer adequate holds. To the right was a gentle slope of snow that curved upward and out of sight behind the rocks. As we watched, Osborn ascended to the edge of the snow, stopped and tested it with his foot; then, apparently satisfied that it would bear his weight, he stepped out on the slope.

I felt Nace's body tense. "Paul!" he cried out.

His voice was too weak and hoarse to carry. Osborn continued his ascent.

Nace cupped his hands and called his name again, and this time Osborn turned. "Wait!" cried the Englishman.

Osborn stood still, watching us, as we struggled up the few yards to the edge of the snow slope. Nace's breath came in shuddering gasps, but he climbed faster than I had ever seen him climb before.

"Come back!" he called. "Come off the snow!"

"It's all right! The crust is firm!" Osborn called back.

"But it's melting! There's"—Nace paused, fighting for air—"there's nothing underneath!"

In a sudden, horrifying flash I saw what he meant. Looked at from directly below, at the point where Osborn had come to it, the slope on which he stood appeared as a harmless covering of snow over the rocks. From where we were now, however, a little to one side, it could be seen that it was in reality no covering at all, but merely a cornice or unsupported platform clinging to the side of the mountain. Below it was not rock, but ten thousand feet of blue air.

"Come back!" I cried. "Come back!"

Osborn hesitated, then took a downward step. But he never took the next. For in that same instant the snow directly in front of him disappeared. It did not seem to fall or to break away. It was just soundlessly and magically no longer there. In the spot where Osborn had been about to set his foot there was now revealed the abysmal drop of the north face of K3.

I shut my eyes, but only for a second, and when I reopened them Osborn was still, miraculously, there.

Nace was shouting, "Don't move! Don't move an inch!"

"The rope," I heard myself saying.

The Englishman shook his head. "We'd have to throw it, and the impact would be too much. Brace yourself and play it out." As we spoke, his eyes were traveling over the rocks that bordered the snow bridge. Then he moved forward.

I wedged myself into a cleft in the wall and let out the rope which extended between us. A few yards away, Osborn stood in the snow, transfixed, one foot a little in front of the other. But my eyes now were on Nace. Cautiously, but with astonishing rapidity, he edged along the rocks beside the cornice. There was a moment when his only support was an inch-wide ledge beneath his feet, another where there was nothing under his feet at all and he supported himself wholly by his elbows and hands. But he advanced steadily, and at last reached a shelf wide enough for him to turn around on. At this point he was perhaps six feet away from Osborn.

"It's wide enough here to hold both of us," he said in a quiet voice. "I'm going to reach out my ax. Don't move until you're sure you have a grip on it. When I pull, jump."

He searched the wall behind him and found a hold for his left hand. Then he slowly extended his ice ax, head foremost, until it was within two feet of Osborn's shoulder.

"Grip it!" he cried suddenly. Osborn's hands shot out and seized the ax. "Jump!"

There was a flash of steel in the sunlight and a hunched figure hurtled inward from the snow to the ledge. Simultaneously another figure hurtled out. The haft of the ax jerked suddenly from Nace's hand, and he lurched forward and downward. A violent, sickening spasm convulsed my body as the rope went taut. Then it was gone. Nace did not seem to hit the snow; he simply disappeared through it, soundlessly. In the same instant the snow itself was gone. The frayed, yellow end of broken rope spun lazily in space.

— Somehow my eyes went to Osborn. He was crouched on the ledge where Nace had been a moment before, staring dully at the ax he held in his hands. Beyond his head, not two hundred feet above, the white, untrodden pinnacle of K3 stabbed the sky.

Perhaps ten minutes passed, perhaps a half hour. I closed my eyes and leaned forward motionless against the rock, my face against my arm. I neither thought nor felt; my body and mind alike were enveloped in a suffocating numbness. Through it at last came the sound of Osborn moving. Looking up, I saw he was standing beside me.

"I'm going to try to make the top," he said tonelessly.

I merely stared at him.

"Will you come?"

I shook my head slowly. Osborn hesitated a moment, then turned and began slowly climbing the steep chimney above us. Halfway up he paused, struggling for breath. Then he resumed his laborious upward progress and presently disappeared beyond the crest.

I stayed where I was, and the hours passed. The sun reached its zenith above the peak and sloped away behind it. And at last I heard above me the sound of Osborn returning. As I looked up, his figure appeared at the top of the chimney and began the descent. His clothing was in tatters, and I could tell from his movements that only the thin flame of his will stood between him and collapse. In another few minutes he was standing beside me.

"Did you get there?" I asked.

He shook his head slowly. "I couldn't make it," he answered. "I didn't have what it takes."

We roped together silently and began the descent to the camp. There is nothing more to be told of the sixth assault on K3—at least not from the experiences of the men who made it. Osborn and I reached Camp V in safety, and three days later the entire expedition gathered at the advance base. It was decided, in view of the appalling tragedy that had occurred, to make no further attempt on the summit, and we began the evacuation of the mountain.

It remained for another year and other men to reveal the epilogue.

The summer following our attempt a combined English-Swiss expedition stormed the peak successfully. After weeks of hardship and struggle, they attained the topmost pinnacle of the giant, only to find that what should have been their great moment of triumph was, instead, a moment of the bitterest disappointment. For when they came out at last upon the summit, they saw that they were not the first. An ax stood there. Its haft was embedded in rock and ice, and on its steel head were the engraved words: TO MARTIN FROM JOHN.

They were sporting men. On their return to civilization they told their story, and the name of the conqueror of K3 was made known to the world.

Discussion

1. Why are these men climbing the mountain?

2. (a) Describe Osborn's personality. (b) How does his personality influence the way he approaches mountain climbing?

3. (a) Describe Nace's personality. (b) How does his personality influence his mountaineering? (c) What incident from Nace's past might help explain his approach to climbing?

4. Often in fiction, external and internal conflicts are mixed. (a) What external conflicts are present in "Top Man"? (b) What internal conflicts are there? (c) Do the external and internal conflicts influence each other? Explain.

5. (a) To what does the title "Top Man" refer? (b) In the final paragraph, "the name of the conqueror of K3 was made known to the world." Whose name is that? (c) When Osborn tells the narrator "I didn't have what it takes," what has he just done? (d) What does he mean by this statement? (e) Who do you think is the "top man" in this story? Explain.

6. Reread the following examples of figurative language in which the mountain is seen as a living creature: 56a, line 15; 64a, 1; 64b, 1. What different feelings toward the mountain are reflected in these examples?

Application
Setting

When do the major events in "Top Man" take place? Where do the events take place?

In this story, the author uses a variety of ways to establish the setting and describe it in detail. Find one or more passages in which the setting is described directly. Find two or more passages in which the setting is suggested through details.

1. To what extent does the setting influence the characters' thoughts and actions?

2. To what extent does the setting influence the events of the plot?

Vocabulary
Affixes, Roots

Many words in English are made up of smaller parts. Recognizing the arrangement and meaning of these parts—the structure of a word—may help you understand the whole word.

The *root* is the main part of a word and carries the word's basic meaning. To the root may be added one or more parts:

prefix	root	suffix
pre-	arrange	-ment

A *prefix* is a word part added to the beginning of a root to change the meaning in some way. The prefix *pre-,* for example, means "before."

A *suffix* is a word part added to the end of a root. Sometimes suffixes change the meaning, but more importantly, they determine the function of the new word. In the example, the suffix *-ment* is added to the verb *arrange* to form the noun *arrangement.*

Now put together the meanings of all the parts to get the meaning of *prearrangement:* "the way or order in which persons or things are arranged beforehand."

The general name for both prefixes and suffixes is *affixes.* A word formed from a root plus one or more affixes is called a *derivative.*

Look closely at the structure of the italicized derivatives in the following material. (If necessary, you may look up the meanings of prefixes, roots, or suffixes in the Glossary.) Then answer the questions on a separate piece of paper.

1. The prefix *dis-* belongs to a group of prefixes—also including *de-, in-, non-,* and *un*—called negative prefixes that mean "not" or have other negative meanings. If something is *dissimilar,* is it the same as or different from something else?

2. What is the root in *inactivity?* How does the negative prefix change the meaning of the root? What part of speech (function) is *inactivity?*

3. If *peerless* means "without a peer, or equal," what does *flawless* mean?

4. When suffixes are added to certain roots, the spelling of the root changes. Common spelling changes are: dropping a final *e,* changing a final *y* to *i,* and doubling a final consonant. What is the root in *supernatural?* What spelling change has taken place?

5. What is the root in *counterbalancing?* What does the prefix *counter-* mean in this word? Use the whole word in a sentence that demonstrates your understanding of the meaning.

Unit 1 Review: *Take a Chance*

Content Review

1. (a) Which of the characters in this unit do you think takes a chance and makes the most of it? Explain your choice. **(b)** Which character makes the least of a chance? Explain.

2. Imagine that the following pairs of characters have gotten together to write books on the topics given. For each pair, explain why the characters are qualified to write on that topic. What might they say about it? **(a)** Emma Hu and the speaker in "Every Good Boy Does Fine": *What to do when things go wrong.* **(b)** Gordon Parks ("Music Inside My Head") and Mr. Budd: *Making your dream come true.* **(c)** Larry ("My Teacher, the Hawk") and Osborn ("Top Man"): *The consequences of hasty actions.*

3. Conflict is an important element in most short stories and dramas, and in some nonfiction and poetry as well. List those selections in which you can find a conflict and explain its nature in each. Is the conflict external or internal, or both?

4. In "Top Man" the setting is not only important, it influences the actions of the characters and contributes largely to the plot. Consider the importance of setting in the following selections. Could the story have taken place anywhere else? Does the setting—either the time or place—influence the events? Explain. **(a)** "My Teacher, the Hawk"; **(b)** "The Inspiration of Mr. Budd"; **(c)** "The Treasure of Lemon Brown."

5. If you had the opportunity to ask any character from this unit to come and talk to your class, which character would you choose? Why? What questions would you ask?

Concept Review: Interpretation of New Material

Read carefully the short story below. Then use the questions that follow to review your understanding of the concepts and literary terms presented in this unit. If you wish, write your answers to the questions on a separate sheet of paper; do not write in your book.

The Drummer Boy of Shiloh[1] · *Ray Bradbury*

In the April night, more than once, blossoms fell from the orchard trees and lighted with rustling taps on the drumhead. At midnight a peach stone left miraculously on a branch through winter, flicked by a bird, fell swift and unseen; it struck once, like panic, and jerked the boy upright. In silence he listened to his own

---

1. Shiloh (shī′lō). Now a national park in S.W. Tennessee, Shiloh was the site in 1862 of a major battle of the Civil War.

heart ruffle away, away—at last gone from his ears and back in his chest again.

After that he turned the drum on its side, where its great lunar face peered at him whenever he opened his eyes.

His face, alert or at rest, was solemn. It was a solemn time and a solemn night for a boy just turned fourteen in the peach orchard near Owl Creek not far from the church at Shiloh.

". . . thirty-one . . . thirty-two . . . thirty-three." Unable to see, he stopped counting.

Beyond the thirty-three familiar shadows forty thousand men, exhausted by nervous expectation and unable to sleep for romantic dreams of battles yet unfought, lay crazily askew in their uniforms. A mile farther on, another army was strewn helterskelter, turning slowly, basting themselves with the thought of what they would do when the time came—a leap, a yell, a blind plunge their strategy, raw youth their protection and benediction.

Now and again the boy heard a vast wind come up that gently stirred the air. But he knew what it was—the army here, the army there, whispering to itself in the dark. Some men talking to others, others murmuring to themselves, and all so quiet it was like a natural element arisen from South or North with the motion of the earth toward dawn.

What the men whispered the boy could only guess and he guessed that it was "Me, I'm the one, I'm the one of all the rest who won't die. I'll live through it. I'll go home. The band will play. And I'll be there to hear it."

Yes, thought the boy, *that's all very well for them, they can give as good as they get!*

For with the careless bones of the young men, harvested by night and bindled around campfires, were the similarly strewn steel bones of their rifles with bayonets fixed like eternal lightning lost in the orchard grass.

Me, thought the boy, *I got only a drum, two sticks to beat it, and no shield.*

There wasn't a man-boy on this ground tonight who did not have a shield he cast, riveted, or carved himself on his way to his first attack, compounded of remote but nonetheless firm and fiery family devotion, flag-blown patriotism, and cocksure immortality strengthened by the touchstone of very real gunpowder, ramrod, Minié ball,[2] and flint. But without these last, the boy felt his family move yet farther off in the dark, as if one of those great prairie-burning trains had chanted them away, never to return—leaving him with this drum which was worse than a toy in the game to be played tomorrow or someday much too soon.

The boy turned on his side. A moth brushed his face, but it was peach blossom. A peach blossom flicked him, but it was a moth. Nothing stayed put. Nothing had a name. Nothing was as it once was.

If he stayed very still, when the dawn came up and the soldiers put on their bravery with their caps, perhaps they might go away, the war with them, and not notice him living small here, no more than a toy himself.

"Well, by thunder now," said a voice. The boy shut his eyes to hide inside himself, but it was too late. Someone, walking by in the night, stood over him. "Well," said the voice quietly, "here's a soldier crying *before* the fight. Good. Get it over. Won't be time once it all starts."

And the voice was about to move on when the boy, startled, touched the drum at his elbow. The man above, hearing this,

2. **Minié** (min′ē) **ball,** a cone-shaped bullet that expands when fired.

stopped. The boy could feel his eyes, sense him slowly bending near. A hand must have come down out of the night, for there was a little *rat-tat* as the fingernails brushed and the man's breath fanned the boy's face.

"Why, it's the drummer boy, isn't it?"

The boy nodded, not knowing if his nod was seen. "Sir, is that you?" he said.

"I assume it is." The man's knees cracked as he bent still closer. He smelled as all fathers should smell, of salt-sweat, tobacco, horse and boot leather, and the earth he walked upon. He had many eyes. No, not eyes, brass buttons that watched the boy.

He could only be, and was, the general. "What's your name, boy?" he asked.

"Joby, sir," whispered the boy, starting to sit up.

"All right, Joby, don't stir." A hand pressed his chest gently, and the boy relaxed. "How long you been with us, Joby?"

"Three weeks, sir."

"Run off from home or join legitimate, boy?"

Silence.

"Fool question," said the general. "Do you shave yet, boy? Even more of a fool. There's your cheek, fell right off the tree overhead. And the others here, not much older. Raw, raw, the lot of you. You ready for tomorrow or the next day, Joby?"

"I think so, sir."

"You want to cry some more, go on ahead. I did the same last night."

"You, sir?"

"It's the truth. Thinking of everything ahead. Both sides figuring the other side will just give up, and soon, and the war done in weeks and us all home. Well, that's not how it's going to be. And maybe that's why I cried."

"Yes, sir," said Joby.

The general must have taken out a cigar now, for the dark was suddenly filled with the Indian smell of tobacco unlighted yet, but chewed as the man thought what next to say.

"It's going to be a crazy time," said the general. "Counting both sides, there's a hundred thousand men—give or take a few thousand—out there tonight, not one as can spit a sparrow off a tree, or knows a horse clod from a Minié ball. Stand up, bare the breast, ask to be a target, thank them and sit down, that's us, that's them. We should turn tail and train four months, they should do the same. But here we are, taken with spring fever and thinking it blood lust, taking our sulphur with cannons instead of with molasses, as it should be—going to be a hero, going to live forever. And I can see all them over there nodding agreement, save the other way around. It's wrong, boy, it's wrong as a head put on hindside front and a man marching backward through life. Sometime this week more innocents will get shot out of pure Cherokee enthusiasm than ever got shot before. Owl Creek was full of boys splashing around in the noonday sun just a few hours ago. I fear it will be full of boys again, just floating, at sundown tomorrow, not caring where the current takes them."

The general stopped and made a little pile of winter leaves and twigs in the dark as if he might at any moment strike fire to them to see his way through the coming days when the sun might not show its face because of what was happening here and just beyond.

The boy watched the hand stirring the leaves and opened his lips to say something, but did not say it. The general heard the boy's breath and spoke himself.

"Why am I telling you this? That's what you wanted to ask, eh? Well, when you got a bunch of wild horses on a loose rein somewhere, somehow you got to bring order, rein them in. These lads, fresh out of the milkshed, don't know what I know; and I can't tell them—men actually die in war. So each is his own army. I got to make one army of them. And for that, boy, I need you."

"Me!" The boy's lips barely twitched.

"You, boy," said the general quietly. "You are the heart of the army. Think about that. You are the heart of the army. Listen to me, now."

And lying there, Joby listened. And the general spoke. If he, Joby, beat slow tomorrow, the heart would beat slow in the men. They would lag by the wayside. They would drowse in the fields on their muskets. They would sleep forever after that—in those same fields, their hearts slowed by a drummer boy and stopped by enemy lead.

But if he beat a sure, steady, ever faster rhythm, then, then, their knees would come up in a long line down over that hill, one knee after the other, like a wave on the ocean shore. Had he seen the ocean ever? Seen the waves rolling in like a well-ordered cavalry charge to the sand? Well, that was it, that's what he wanted, that's what was needed. Joby was his right hand and his left. He gave the orders, but Joby set the pace.

So bring the right knee up and the right foot out and the left knee up and the left foot out, one following the other in good time, in brisk time. Move the blood up the body and make the head proud and the spine stiff and the jaw resolute. Focus the eye and set the teeth, flare the nostril and tighten the hands, put steel armor all over the men, for blood moving fast in them does indeed make men feel as if they'd put on steel. He must keep at it, at it! Long and steady, steady and long! Then, even though shot or torn, those wounds got in hot blood—in blood he'd helped stir—would feel less pain. If their blood was cold, it would be more than slaughter, it would be murderous nightmare and pain best not told and no one to guess.

The general spoke and stopped, letting his breath slack off. Then, after a moment, he said, "So there you are, that's it. Will you do that, boy? Do you know now you're general of the army when the general's left behind?"

The boy nodded mutely.

"You'll run them through for me then, boy?"

"Yes, sir."

"Good. And, maybe, many nights from tonight, many years from now, when you're as old or far much older than me, when they ask you what you did in this awful time, you will tell them—one part humble and one part proud—I was the drummer boy at the battle of Owl Creek or the Tennessee River, or maybe they'll just name it after the church there. I was the drummer boy at Shiloh.

Good grief, that has a beat and sound to it fitting for Mr. Longfellow. 'I was the drummer boy at Shiloh.' Who will ever hear those words and not know you, boy, or what you thought this night, or what you'll think tomorrow or the next day when we must get up on our legs and move."

The general stood up. "Well, then. God bless you, boy. Good night."

"Good night, sir." And tobacco, brass, boot polish, salt-sweat, and leather, the man moved away through the grass.

Joby lay for a moment staring, but unable to see where the man had gone. He swallowed. He wiped his eyes. He cleared his throat. He settled himself. Then, at last, very slowly and firmly he turned the drum so it faced up toward the sky.

He lay next to it, his arm around it, feeling the tremor, the touch, the muted thunder as all the rest of the April night in the year 1862, near the Tennessee River, not far from the Owl Creek, very close to the church named Shiloh, the peach blossoms fell on the drum.

---

1. The place setting is important because (a) there is a church nearby; (b) Owl Creek provides the soldiers a place to swim; (c) Joby is far from home; (d) it is the site of a Civil War battle.

2. Joby's main conflict is between (a) his homesickness and his desire to fight; (b) himself and the other soldiers; (c) his fear and his desire to do his duty; (d) himself and the general.

3. The general's character is revealed mainly through (a) his speech and actions; (b) his thoughts and feelings; (c) physical description; (d) what other characters say.

4. When the general asks Joby whether he has joined the army legitimately or run off from home, Joby is silent (72a, 9). How does the general interpret his silence?

5. When the general tells Joby, "There's your cheek, fell right off the tree overhead" (72a, 10), what is he comparing Joby's cheek to? What does he mean by this?

6. The figurative expression "bunch of wild horses on a loose rein" refers to (a) horses that have escaped; (b) the enemy soldiers; (c) civilians that won't cooperate; (d) untrained soldiers.

7. What makes the following a *simile?* ". . . the waves rolling in like a well-ordered cavalry charge to the sand."

8. The general is upset because he realizes that **(a)** the enemy's army is better trained than his army; **(b)** neither army is well trained; **(c)** Joby is a coward; **(d)** because the general cried, he is not fit to lead.

9. The general says that he wants Joby **(a)** to give spirit to the soldiers; **(b)** to learn how to use a weapon; **(c)** to be his orderly; **(d)** to go back home.

10. Which word best describes Joby's feelings after his talk with the general? **(a)** frightened; **(b)** bitter; **(c)** reassured; **(d)** happy.

Composition Review

Choose one of the following assignments to write about. Unless you are told otherwise, assume that you are writing for your classmates.

1. In "Top Man" James Ramsey Ullman describes the mountain K3 in such detail that it is easy to understand why it seems like a living thing to the climbers. Choose any scene you are familiar with and think of a living creature to compare it to. Create some similes or other figurative language to use in your comparison. (Try to find fresh and original figures of speech.)

Write a paragraph describing your scene in detail and comparing it to the creature you have chosen. Try to use words that will enable your readers mentally to experience the place you are writing about.

2. Which of the selections in this unit do you think would make the best movie or play? Choose one scene from that selection to dramatize. Include a conversation between at least two characters who are in conflict.

Write a script for your scene. First describe the setting and characters; then write dialogue for the characters to speak. (See "The Ugly Duckling" on page 98 for a model.) Also include directions suggesting how and when the characters should move and speak their lines.

3. As in Number 2, choose a selection that would make a good movie or play. Decide which are the main characters (no more than four). Choose a well-known actor or actress who you think would be appropriate to play each character.

Write a brief character description for each main character in your film or play. Then tell whom you have chosen to play that character and why that actor or actress is appropriate for the part.

4. In your opinion, which character in this unit has the most difficult internal conflict? That is, which encounters a problem within himself or herself that is the hardest to solve?

Write a paragraph describing that problem or conflict and explaining how the character handles it. Then, in a second paragraph, tell how you would handle the conflict if you were in the same situation.

unit 2

There are many ways of coping, of struggling
with a problem and reaching a solution for it.
You might build your courage by constantly
testing it, seek ways to succeed in spite
of discouragement, stand up for your beliefs,
yet value the beliefs of others. Making
your way in the world is often a matter of coping.

Learning to Cope

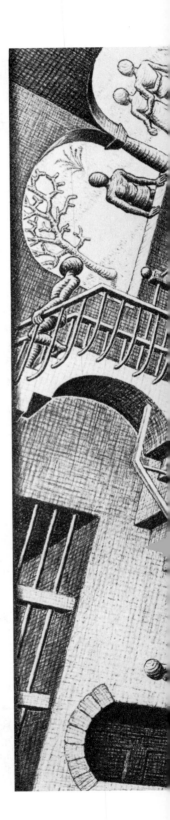

Cress to the Rescue

Jessamyn West

**Did Cress really knock
Edwin down—for fun?**

While her mother and father awaited the arrival of Mr. and Mrs. Kibbler who had called asking to speak to them "about Cress and Edwin Jr.," Mr. Delahanty reminded his wife how wrong she had been about Cress.

"Not two months ago," he said, "in this very room you told me you were worried because Cress wasn't as interested in the boys as a girl her age should be. In this very room. And now look what's happened."

Mrs. Delahanty, worried now by Mrs. Kibbler's message, spoke more sharply than she had intended. "Don't keep repeating, 'in this very room,' " she said, "as if it would have been different if I'd said it in the back porch or out of doors. Besides, what has happened?"

Mr. Delahanty took off his hat, which he'd had on when Mrs. Kibbler phoned, and sailed it out of the living room toward the hall table, which he missed. "Don't ask me what's happened," he said, "I'm not the girl's mother."

Mrs. Delahanty took off her own hat and jabbed the hat pins back into it. "What do you mean, you're not the girl's mother? Of course you're not. No one ever said you were."

Mr. Delahanty picked up his fallen hat, put it on the chair beside the hall table and came back into the living room. "A girl confides in her mother," he told his wife.

"A girl confides in her mother!" Mrs. Delahanty was very scornful. "Who tells you these things, John Delahanty? Not *your* mother. She didn't have any daughter. Not me. Cress doesn't confide in anyone. How do you know these things, anyway, about mothers and daughters?"

John Delahanty seated himself upon the sofa, legs extended, head back, as straight and unrelaxed as a plank.

"Don't catch me up that way, Gertrude," he said. "You know I don't know them." Without giving his wife any opportunity to crow over this victory he went on quickly: "What I'd like to know is why did the Kibblers have to pick a Saturday night for this call? Didn't they know we'd be going into town?"

Like most ranchers, John Delahanty stopped work early on Saturdays so that, after a quick clean-up and supper, he and his wife could drive into town. There they did nothing very important: bought groceries, saw a show, browsed around in hardware stores, visited friends. But after a week of seeing only themselves—the Delahanty ranch was off the main highway—it was pleasant simply to saunter along the sidewalks looking at the cars, the merchan-

dise, the people in their town clothes. This Saturday trip to town was a jaunt they both looked forward to during the week, and tonight's trip, because of February's warmer air and suddenly, it seemed, longer twilight, would have been particularly pleasant.

"Five minutes more," said Mr. Delahanty, "and we'd have been on our way."

"Why didn't you tell Mrs. Kibbler we were just leaving?"

"I did. And she said for anything less important she wouldn't think of keeping us."

Mrs. Delahanty came over to the sofa and stood looking anxiously down at her husband. "John, exactly what did Mrs. Kibbler say?"

"The gist of it," said Mr. Delahanty, "was that . . ."

"I don't care about the gist of it. That's just what you think she said. I want to know what she really said."

Mr. Delahanty let his head fall forward, though he still kept his legs stiffly extended. "What she really said was, 'Is this Mr. John Delahanty?' And I said, 'Yes.' Then she said, 'This is Mrs. Edwin Kibbler, I guess you remember me.'"

"Remember her?" Mrs. Delahanty exclaimed. "I didn't know you even knew her."

"I don't," said Mr. Delahanty, "but I remember her all right. She came before the school board about a month ago to tell us we ought to take those two ollas[1] off the school grounds. She said it was old-fashioned to cool water that way, that the ollas looked messy and were unhygienic."

"Did you take them off?" Mrs. Delahanty asked, without thinking. As a private person John Delahanty was reasonable and untalkative. As clerk of the school board he inclined toward dogmatism and long-windedness. Now he began a defense of the ollas and the school board's action in retaining them.

"Look, John," said Mrs. Delahanty, "I'm not interested in the school board or its water coolers. What I want to know is, what did Mrs. Kibbler say about Cress?"

"Well, she said she wanted to have a little talk with us about Cress—and Edwin Jr."

"I know that." Impatience made Mrs. Delahanty's voice sharp. "But what about them?"

Mr. Delahanty drew his feet up toward the sofa, then bent down and retied a shoelace. "About what Cress did to him—Edwin Jr."

"*Did* to him!" said Mrs. Delahanty aghast.

"That's what his mother said."

Mrs. Delahanty sat down on the hassock at her husband's feet. "Did to him," she repeated again. "Why, what could Cress do to him? He's two or three years older than Cress, fifteen or sixteen anyway. What could she do to him?"

Mr. Delahanty straightened up. "She could hit him, I guess," he ventured.

"Hit him? What would she want to hit him for?"

"I don't know," said Mr. Delahanty. "I don't know that she did hit him. Maybe she kicked him. Anyway, his mother seems to think the boy's been damaged in some way."

"Damaged," repeated Mrs. Delahanty angrily. "Damaged! Why, Cress is too tender-hearted to hurt a fly. She shoos them outside instead of killing them. And you sit there talking of hitting and kicking."

"Well," said Mr. Delahanty mildly, "Ed-

---

1. *ollas.* An olla (ol′ə, ô′yä) is a large earthenware jar, once used chiefly in the Southwest as a container for water.

win's got teeth out. I don't know how else she could get them out, do you?"

"I'm going to call Cress," said Mrs. Delahanty, "and ask her about this. I don't believe it for a minute."

"I don't think calling her will do any good. She left while I was talking to Mrs. Kibbler."

"What do you mean, left?"

"Went for a walk, she said."

"Well, teeth out," repeated Mrs. Delahanty unbelievingly. "Teeth out! I didn't know you could get teeth out except with pliers or a chisel."

"Maybe Edwin's teeth are weak."

"Don't joke about this, John Delahanty. It isn't any joking matter. And I don't believe it. I don't believe Cress did it or that that boy's teeth are out. Anyway I'd have to see them to believe it."

"You're going to," Mr. Delahanty said. "Mrs. Kibbler's bringing Edwin especially so you can."

Mrs. Delahanty sat for some time without saying anything at all. Then she got up and walked back and forth in front of her husband, turning her hat, which she still held, round and round on one finger. "Well, what does Mrs. Kibbler expect us to do now?" she asked. "If they really are out, that is?"

"For one thing," replied Mr. Delahanty, "she expects us to pay for some new ones. And for another . . ." Mr. Delahanty paused to listen. Faintly, in the distance, a car could be heard. "Here she is now," he said.

Mrs. Delahanty stopped her pacing. "Do you think I should make some cocoa for them, John? And maybe some marguerites?"[2]

"No, I don't," said Mr. Delahanty. "I don't think Mrs. Kibbler considers this a social visit."

As the car turned into the long driveway which led between the orange grove on one side and the lemon grove on the other to the Delahanty house, Mrs. Delahanty said, "I still don't see why you think this proves I'm wrong."

Mr. Delahanty had forgotten about his wife's wrongness. "How do you mean wrong?" he asked.

"About Cress's not being interested in the boys."

"Oh," he said. "Well, you've got to be pretty interested in a person—one way or another—before you hit him."

"That's a perfectly silly notion," began Mrs. Delahanty, but before she could finish, the Kibblers had arrived.

Mr. Delahanty went to the door while Mrs. Delahanty stood in the back of the room by the fireplace unwilling to take one step toward meeting her visitors.

Mrs. Kibbler was a small woman with a large, determined nose, prominent blue eyes and almost no chin. Her naturally curly hair—she didn't wear a hat—sprang away from her head in a great cage-shaped pompadour which dwarfed her face.

Behind Mrs. Kibbler was Mr. Kibbler, short, dusty, soft-looking, bald, except for a fringe of hair about his ears so thick that the top of his head, by contrast, seemed more naked than mere lack of hair could make it.

Behind Mr. Kibbler was Edwin Jr. He was as thin as his mother, as mild and soft-looking as his father; and to these qualities he added an unhappiness all of his own. He gave one quick look at the room and the Delahantys through his thick-lensed spectacles, after which he kept his eyes on the floor.

---

2. **marguerites** (mär′gə rēts′), frosted cookies.

Mr. Delahanty closed the door behind the callers, then introduced his wife to Mrs. Kibbler. Mrs. Kibbler in turn introduced her family to the Delahantys. While the Kibblers were seating themselves—Mrs. Kibbler and Edwin Jr. on the sofa, Mr. Kibbler on a straight-backed chair in the room's darkest corner—Mrs. Delahanty, out of nervousness, bent and lit the fire, which was laid in the fireplace, though the evening was not cold enough for it. Then she and Mr. Delahanty seated themselves in the chairs on each side of the fireplace.

Mrs. Kibbler looked at the fire with some surprise. "Do you find it cold this evening, Mrs. Delahanty?" she asked.

"No," said Mrs. Delahanty, "I don't. I don't know why I lit the fire."

To this Mrs. Kibbler made no reply. Instead, without preliminaries, she turned to her son. "Edwin," she said, "show the Delahantys what their daughter did to your teeth."

Mrs. Delahanty wanted to close her eyes, look into the fire, or find, as Edwin Jr. had done, a spot of her own on the floor to examine. There was an almost imperceptible ripple along the length of the boy's face as if he had tried to open his mouth but found he lacked the strength. He momentarily lifted his eyes from the floor to dart a glance into the dark corner where his father sat. But Mr. Kibbler continued to sit in expressionless silence.

"Edwin," said Mrs. Kibbler, "speak to your son."

"Do what your mother says, son," said Mr. Kibbler.

Very slowly, as if it hurt him, Edwin opened his mouth.

His teeth were white, and in his thin face they seemed very large, as well. The two middle teeth, above, had been broken across in a slanting line. The lower incisor appeared to be missing entirely.

"Wider, Edwin," Mrs. Kibbler urged. "I want the Delahantys to see exactly what their daughter is responsible for."

But before Edwin could make any further effort Mrs. Delahanty cried, "No, that's enough."

"I didn't want you to take our word for anything," Mrs. Kibbler said reasonably. "I wanted you to see."

"Oh, we see, all right," said Mrs. Delahanty earnestly.

Mr. Delahanty leaned forward and spoke to Mrs. Kibbler. "While we see the teeth, Mrs. Kibbler, it just isn't a thing we think Crescent would do. Or in fact how she *could* do it. We think Edwin must be mistaken."

"You mean lying?" asked Mrs. Kibbler flatly.

"Mistaken," repeated Mr. Delahanty.

"Tell them, Edwin," said Mrs. Kibbler.

"She knocked me down," said Edwin, very low.

Mrs. Delahanty, although she was already uncomfortably warm, held her hands nearer the fire, even rubbed them together a time or two.

"I simply can't believe that," she said.

"You mean hit you with her fist and knocked you down?" asked Mr. Delahanty.

"No," said Edwin even lower than before. "Ran into me."

"But not on purpose," said Mrs. Delahanty.

Edwin nodded, "Yes," he said. "On purpose."

"But why?" asked Mr. Delahanty. "Why? Cress wouldn't do such a thing, I know—without some cause. Why?"

"Tell them why, Edwin," said his mother.

Edwin's head went even nearer the floor—as if the spot he was watching had diminished or retreated.

"For fun," he said.

It was impossible not to believe the boy as he sat there hunched, head bent, one eyelid visibly twitching. "But Cress would never do such a thing," said Mrs. Delahanty.

Mrs. Kibbler disregarded this. "It would not have been so bad, Mr. Delahanty, except that Edwin was standing by one of those ollas. When your daughter shoved Edwin over she shoved the olla over, too. That's probably what broke his teeth. Heavy as cement and falling down on top of him and breaking up in a thousand pieces. To say nothing of his being doused with water on a cold day. And Providence alone can explain why his glasses weren't broken."

"What had you done, Edwin?" asked Mrs. Delahanty again.

"Nothing," whispered Edwin.

"All we want," said Mrs. Kibbler, "is what's perfectly fair. Pay the dentist's bill. And have that girl of yours apologize to Edwin."

Mrs. Delahanty got up suddenly and walked over to Edwin. She put one hand on his thin shoulder and felt him twitch under her touch like a frightened colt.

"Go on, Edwin," she said. "Tell me the truth. Tell me why."

Edwin slowly lifted his head. "Go on, Edwin," Mrs. Delahanty encouraged him.

"He told you once," said Mrs. Kibbler. "Fun. That girl of yours is a big, boisterous thing from all I hear. She owes my boy an apology."

Edwin's face continued to lift until he was looking directly at Mrs. Delahanty.

He started to speak—but had said only three words, "Nobody ever wants," when Cress walked in from the hall. She had evidently been there for some time, for she went directly to Edwin.

"I apologize for hurting you, Edwin," she said.

Then she turned to Mrs. Kibbler. "I've got twelve seventy-five saved for a bicycle. That can go to help pay for his teeth."

After the Kibblers left, the three Delahantys sat for some time without saying a word. The fire had about died down and outside an owl, hunting finished, flew back toward the hills, softly hooting.

"I guess if we hurried we could just about catch the second show," Mr. Delahanty said.

"I won't be going to shows for a while," said Cress.

The room was very quiet. Mrs. Delahanty traced the outline of one of the bricks in the fireplace.

"I can save twenty-five cents a week that way. Toward his teeth," she explained.

Mrs. Delahanty took the poker and stirred the coals so that for a second there was an upward drift of sparks; but the fire was too far gone to blaze. Because it had not yet been completely dark when the Kibblers came, only one lamp had been turned on. Now that night had arrived the room was only partially lighted; but no one seemed to care. Mr. Delahanty, in Mr. Kibbler's dark corner, was almost invisible. Mrs. Delahanty stood by the fireplace. Cress sat where Edwin had sat, looking downward, perhaps at the same spot at which he had looked.

"One day at school," she said, "Edwin went out in the fields at noon and gathered wild flower bouquets for everyone. A lupine, a poppy, two barley heads, four yellow violets. He tied them together with blades of grass. They were sweet little bouquets. He went without his lunch to get them fixed, and when we came back from eating there was a bouquet on every desk in the study hall. It looked like a flower field when we came in and Edwin did it to surprise us.''

After a while Mr. Delahanty asked, ''Did the kids like that?''

''Yes, they liked it. They tore their bouquets apart,'' said Cress, ''and used the barley beards to tickle each other. Miss Ingols made Edwin gather up every single flower and throw it in the wastepaper basket.''

After a while Cress said, ''Edwin has a collection of bird feathers. The biggest is from a buzzard, the littlest from a hummingbird. They're all different colors. The brightest is from a woodpecker.''

''Does he kill birds,'' Mr. Delahanty asked, ''just to get a feather?''

''Oh no!'' said Cress. ''He just keeps his eyes open to where a bird might drop a feather. It would spoil his collection to get a feather he didn't find that way.''

Mr. Delahanty sighed and stirred in his wooden chair so that it creaked a little.

''Edwin would like to be a missionary to China,'' said Cress. Some particle in the fireplace, as yet unburned, blazed up in a sudden spurt of blue flame. ''Not a preaching missionary,'' she explained.

''A medical missionary?'' asked Mr. Delahanty.

''Oh, no! Edwin says he's had to take too much medicine to ever be willing to make other people take it.''

There was another long silence in the room. Mrs. Delahanty sat down in the chair her husband had vacated and once more held a hand toward the fire. There was just enough life left in the coals to make the tips of her fingers rosy. She didn't turn toward Cress at all or ask a single question. Back in the dusk Cress's voice went on.

''He would like to teach them how to play baseball.''

Mr. Delahanty's voice was matter-of-fact. ''Edwin doesn't look to me like he would be much of a baseball player.''

''Oh, he isn't,'' Cress agreed. ''He isn't even any of a baseball player. But he could be a baseball authority. Know everything and teach by diagram. That's what he'd have to do. And learn from them how they paint. He says some of their pictures look like they have been painted with one kind of bird feather and some with another. He knows they don't really paint with bird feathers,'' she explained. ''That's just a fancy of his.''

The night wind moving in off the Pacific began to stir the eucalyptus trees in the windbreak. Whether the wind blew off sea or desert, didn't matter, the long eucalyptus leaves always lifted and fell with the same watery, surf-like sound.

''I'm sorry Edwin happened to be standing by that olla,'' said Mr. Delahanty. ''That's what did the damage, I suppose.''

''Oh, he had to stand there,'' said Cress. ''He didn't have any choice. That's the mush pot.''

''Mush pot,'' repeated Mr. Delahanty.

''It's a circle round the box the olla stands on,'' said Crescent. ''Edwin spends about his whole time there. While we're waiting for the bus anyway.''

''Crescent,'' asked Mr. Delahanty, ''what is this mush pot?''

''It's prison,'' said Cress, surprise in her voice. ''It's where the prisoners are kept. Only at school we always call it the mush pot.''

"Is this a game?" asked Mr. Delahanty.

"It's dare base," said Crescent. "Didn't you ever play it? You choose up sides. You draw two lines and one side stands in the middle and tries to catch the other side as they run by. Nobody ever chooses Edwin. The last captain to choose just gets him. Because he can't help himself. They call him the handicap. He gets caught first thing and spends the whole game in the mush pot because nobody will waste any time trying to rescue him. He'd just get caught again, they say, and the whole game would be nothing but rescue Edwin."

"How do you rescue anyone, Cress?" asked her father.

"Run from home base to the mush pot without being caught. Then take the prisoner's hand. Then he goes free."

"Were you trying to rescue Edwin, Cress?"

Cress didn't answer her father at once. Finally she said, "It was my duty. I chose him for our side. I chose him first of all and didn't wait just to get him. So it was my duty to rescue him. Only I ran too hard and couldn't stop. And the olla fell down on top of him and knocked his teeth out. And humiliated him. But he was free," she said. "I got there without being caught."

Mrs. Delahanty spoke with a great surge of warmth and anger. "Humiliated him! When you were only trying to help him. Trying to rescue him. And you were black and blue for days yourself! What gratitude."

Cress said, "But he didn't want to be rescued, Mother. Not by me anyway. He said he liked being in the mush pot. He said . . . he got there on purpose . . . to observe. He gave me back the feathers I'd found for him. One was a road-runner feather. The only one he had."

"Well, you can start a feather collection of your own," said Mrs. Delahanty with energy. "I often see feathers when I'm walking through the orchard. After this I'll save them for you."

"I'm not interested in feathers," said Cress. Then she added, "I can get two bits an hour any time suckering trees for Mr. Hudson or cleaning blackboards at school. That would be two fifty a week at least. Plus the twelve seventy-five. How much do you suppose his teeth will be?"

"Cress," said her father, "you surely aren't going to let the Kibblers go on thinking you knocked their son down on purpose, are you? Do you want Edwin to think that?"

"Edwin doesn't really think that," Cress said. "He knows I was rescuing him. But now I've apologized—and if we pay for the new teeth and everything, maybe after a while he'll believe it."

She stood up and walked to the hall doorway. "I'm awfully tired," she said. "I guess I'll go to bed."

"But Cress," asked Mrs. Delahanty, "why do you want him to believe it? When it isn't true?"

Cress was already through the door, but she turned back to explain. "You don't knock people down you are sorry for," she said.

After Cress had gone upstairs Mrs. Delahanty said, "Well, John, you were right, of course."

"Right?" asked Mr. Delahanty, again forgetful.

"About Cress's being interested in the boys."

"Yes," said Mr. Delahanty. "Yes, I'm afraid I was."

Discussion

1. (a) In what state of mind do Mr. and Mrs. Delahanty wait for the arrival of the Kibblers? **(b)** What can you tell about their feelings for their daughter? **(c)** Which of the following words would you use to sum up these feelings—*worshipful, biased, overprotective, loyal?*

2. (a) What impression do you get of Mrs. Kibbler's personality? **(b)** How would you describe Mr. Kibbler?

3. (a) What do you learn about Cress's physical appearance? **(b)** What does her plan to pay Edwin's dental bill reveal about her personality? **(c)** What do you find out about her from what she says about Edwin?

4. On page 83, Edwin starts to speak but says only three words: "Nobody ever wants. . . ." **(a)** How do you think he intended to complete the sentence? **(b)** Why do you think Cress chooses this particular moment to interrupt Edwin?

5. Reread the exchange between Cress and her parents that begins " 'Cress,' said her father . . ." (85b, 3–85b, 7). **(a)** What does Cress want Edwin eventually to believe? Why do you think she wants him to believe this? **(b)** Explain Cress's final comment: "You don't knock people down you are sorry for."

6. (a) What are Mr. and Mrs. Delahanty's reactions to Cress's story about what happened on the school grounds? **(b)** Why do you think they now believe that Cress is interested in boys? **(c)** Do you agree with them? Why or why not?

Application
Characterization

"Oh, yes, I've heard of Edwin Kibbler. What's he like, anyway?"

If someone asked you this question, how would you respond? Using information the author supplies in "Cress to the Rescue," you should be able to describe quite a bit about Edwin.

1. Skim the story for details about Edwin's appearance and behavior, and for other characters' reactions and opinions. As you read each detail, ask yourself what it tells you about Edwin's personality.

2. What do Edwin's hunched posture, low voice, and downcast eyes suggest about his self-confidence?

3. The author does not include Edwin's own thoughts and feelings. Knowing what you do about Edwin, tell what you imagine he might be thinking during his meeting with the Delahantys.

Vocabulary
Context

Read the sentences of the story in which these words appear: *prominent* (81b, 7); *dogmatism* (80a, 10); *momentarily* (82a, 5); *diminished* (83a, 1); *boisterous* (83a, 11). Then read the following sentences, again paying careful attention to context. Finally, choose the appropriate definition for each word.

1. A *prominent* feature in Henry's face is his large, pointed chin. **(a)** hardly noticeable; **(b)** standing out; **(c)** new; **(d)** small.

2. Harry voiced his ideas so strongly and positively that there seemed little room for other viewpoints, and some students began to resent his *dogmatism.* **(a)** insisting on one's opinion; **(b)** negative attitude; **(c)** immature behavior; **(d)** uncertain manner.

3. Although Dudley was *momentarily* silent on hearing he had won, he soon began shouting the news to everyone within hearing. **(a)** unusually; **(b)** somewhat later; **(c)** for a little while; **(d)** surprisingly.

4. Rachel's three-layer birthday cake had *diminished* to the size of a cupcake before the party was over. **(a)** decreased; **(b)** increased; **(c)** ballooned; **(d)** darkened.

5. The child, with her usual *boisterous* behavior, ran around and around the room with the toy train shouting, ''All aboard!'' **(a)** quiet and shy; **(b)** ill-tempered; **(c)** cautious; **(d)** noisily cheerful.

Composition

Imagine that you have a problem you would like to talk over with someone. What kind of person do you think you could talk with most comfortably? What qualities would you like that person to have? Choose someone you know or a character from fiction who comes closest to the kind of person with whom you would like to discuss a problem.

Write one or two paragraphs describing this person's qualities. If you are writing about a real person, you might describe how he or she reacted when you have talked together. If you are writing about a fictional person, describe how you would *like* him or her to react. Be sure to explain why the qualities you are describing make this person someone you could feel close to.

(You may find the article ''Describing a Person or a Place'' in the Composition Guide helpful in writing this composition.)

Jessamyn West 1907–1984

Jessamyn West knew she was born to read and write even when she was three or four: she ''sat in a corner crying'' because she could not make out the words in a book she was holding.

A writer of novels and short stories, West often draws on her Quaker background (both of her grandmothers were Quaker preachers). Her most famous book, *The Friendly Persuasion,* is based on her childhood years in Indiana and was made into a popular film.

Surprisingly, West began her writing career unwillingly. She was a semi-invalid for many years and, unable to do much ''except perhaps crochet,'' decided to write stories. ''Talent,'' she remarks, ''is helpful in writing, but guts are absolutely necessary. Without the guts to try, the talent may never be discovered.''

Fable for When There's No Way Out

May Swenson

Grown too big for his skin,
and it grown hard,

without a sea and atmosphere—
he's drunk it all up—

5 his strength's inside him now,
but there's no room to stretch.

He pecks at the top
but his beak's too soft;

though instinct or ambition shoves,
10 he can't get through.

Barely old enough to bleed
and already bruised!

In a case this tough
what's the use

15 if you break your head
instead of the lid?

Despair tempts him
to just go limp:

Maybe the cell's
20 already a tomb,

and beginning end
in this round room.

Still, stupidly he pecks
and pecks, as if from under

25 his own skull—
yet makes no crack . . .

No crack until
he finally cracks,

and kicks and stomps.
30 What a thrill

and shock to feel
his little gaff[1] poke

through the floor!
A way he hadn't known or meant.

35 Rage works if reason won't.
When locked up, bear down.

---

1. **gaff** (gaf), here the bony, sharp spine on the back of the bird's leg.

Discussion

1. **(a)** At what point did you realize who "he" is in the poem? **(b)** What is the bird trying to do? What lines tell you so?

2. **(a)** Which lines suggest that the bird is tempted to give up? **(b)** What reason for giving up is suggested?

3. **(a)** In line 27, "crack" means "an opening." What is the meaning of "cracks" in line 28? **(b)** How does the bird finally succeed in his effort?

4. The poem is called a fable, which is a story that teaches a lesson. **(a)** What lesson do you think the bird has learned? **(b)** How might this poem influence *anyone* who is facing a situation where there seems to be no way out?

5. **(a)** In line 20 the shell is described figuratively as a "tomb." To what other things is the shell compared? **(b)** What phrase in the last stanza reinforces the comparison between the shell and a cell?

Composition

The bird in the poem finally breaks through its shell with "A way he hadn't known or meant." Sometimes a solution to a problem turns out to be one that you didn't consider at first—or one that comes as a complete surprise. You may have heard, for example, about the boy who helped a driver get a truck under a viaduct by suggesting that some air be let out of the truck's tires.

Write two paragraphs in which you tell about an unusual or surprising solution you found to some problem or predicament. Or, make up such a solution to some predicament. In one paragraph, describe the problem and the solutions that didn't work. In the second paragraph, describe the solution that finally worked and the way you arrived at it. Did you think for a long time, or did the solution come "out of the blue"?

Reread your paragraphs carefully. Will your readers be able to visualize the problem and solution you are describing? Revise your composition until you are confident it is clear. (You may find the article "Looking It Over" in the Composition Guide helpful in revising this composition.)

May Swenson 1919–

May Swenson is one of America's most noted modern poets. Born and raised in Logan, Utah, she now makes her home in New York. She has been a writer-in-residence at Purdue University and has given poetry readings and seminars at more than thirty other colleges and universities.

In much of her poetry Swenson plays with language—putting words together in unusual combinations and creating puns. Two of her most popular books are *Poems to Solve* and *More Poems to Solve,* collections of riddle-poems that can be enjoyed by both children and adults.

For Swenson, the enjoyment of poetry is "based in a craving to get through the curtains of things as they *appear,* to things as they *are,* and then into the larger, wilder space of things as they are *becoming.*"

My Delicate Heart Condition

Toni Cade Bambara

No wonder Aunt Hazel screamed so about my scary stories and Mary was always shushing me. We all had bad hearts.

My cousin Joanne has not been allowed to hang out with me for some time because she went and told Aunt Hazel that I scare her to death whenever she sleeps over at our house or I spend the weekend at hers. The truth is I sometimes like to tell stories about blood-thirsty vampires or ugly monsters that lurk in clothes closets or giant beetles that eat their way through the shower curtain, like I used to do at camp to entertain the kids in my bunk. But Joanne always cries and that makes the stories even weirder, like background music her crying. And too—I'm not going to lie about it—I get spookier on purpose until all the little crybabies are stuffing themselves under their pillows and throwing their sneakers at me and making such a racket that Mary the counselor has to come in and shine her flashlight around the bunkhouse. I play like I'm asleep. The rest of them are too busy blubbering and finding their way out from under the blankets to tell Mary that it's me. Besides, once they get a load of her standing against the moonlight in that long white robe of hers looking like a ghost, they just start up again and pretty soon the whole camp is awake. Anyway, that's what I do for fun. So Joanne hasn't been around. And this year I'll have to go to the circus by myself and to camp without her. My mother said on the phone to Aunt Hazel—"Good, keep Jo over there and maybe Harriet'll behave herself if she's got no one to show off to." For all the years my mother's known me, she still doesn't understand that my behaving has got nothing to do with who I hang out with. A private thing between me and me or maybe between me and the Fly family since they were the ones that first got me to sit through monster movies and withstand all the terror I could take.

For four summers now, me and the Fly family have had this thing going. A battle of nerves, you might say. Each year they raise the rope closer and closer to the very top of the tent—I hear they're going to perform outdoors this year and be even higher—and they stretch the rope further across the rings where the clowns and the pony riders perform. Each year they get bolder and more daring with their rope dancing and the swinging by the legs and flinging themselves into empty space making everyone throw up their hands and gasp for air until Mr. Fly at the very last possible second swings out on his bar to catch them up by the tips of their heels. Everyone just dies and clutches at their hearts. Everybody but me. I sit there calmly. I've trained myself. Joanne

used to die and duck her head under the benches and stay there till it was all over.

Last summer they really got bold. On the final performance just before the fair closed, and some revival type tent show[1] comes in and all the kids go off to camp, the Fly family performed without a net. I figured they'd be up to something so I made sure my stomach was like steel. I did ten push-ups before breakfast, twenty sit-ups before lunch, skipped dinner altogether. My brother Teddy kidded me all day—"Harriet's trying out for the Olympics." I passed up the icie man on the corner and the pizza and sausage stand by the schoolyard and the cotton candy and jelly apple lady and the pickle and penny candy boy, in fact I passed up all the stands that lead from the street down the little roadway to the fair grounds that used to be a swamp when we first moved from Baltimore to Jamaica, Long Island. It wasn't easy, I'm not going to lie, but I was taking no chances. Between the balloon man and the wheel of fortune was the usual clump of ladies from church who came night after night to try to win the giant punch bowl set on the top shelf above the wheel, but had to settle night after night for a jar of gumdrops or salt and pepper shakers or some other little thing from the bottom shelf. And from the wheel of fortune to the tent was at least a million stands selling B.B. bats and jawbreakers and gingerbread and sweet potato

---

1. *revival type tent show*, religious services performed by a traveling minister.

pie and frozen custard and—like I said it wasn't easy. A million ways to tempt you, to unsettle your stomach, and make you lose the battle to the Fly family.

I sat there almost enjoying the silly clowns who came tumbling out of a steamer trunk no bigger than the one we have in the basement where my mother keeps my old report cards and photographs and letters and things. And I almost enjoyed the fire eater and the knife thrower, but I was so close up I could see how there wasn't any real thrill. I almost enjoyed the fat-leg girls who rode the ponies two at a time and standing up, but their costumes weren't very pretty—just an ordinary polo shirt like you get if you run in the PAL[2] meets and short skirts you can wear on either side like the big girls wear at the roller rink. And I almost enjoyed the jugglers except that my Uncle Bubba can juggle the dinner plates better any day of the week so long as Aunt Hazel isn't there to stop him. I was impatient and started yawning. Finally all the clowns hitched up their baggy pants and tumbled over each other out of the ring and into the dark, the jugglers caught all the things that were up in the air and yawning just like me went off to the side. The pony girls brought their horses to a sudden stop that raised a lot of dust, then jumped down into the dirt and bowed. Then the ringmaster stepped into the circle of light and tipped his hat which was a little raggedy from where I was sitting and said—"And now, Ladieeez and Gentlemen, what you've alll been waiting forrr, the Main aTTRACtion, the FLY FAMILEEE." And everyone jumped up to shout like crazy as they came running out on their toes to stand in the light and then climb the ropes. I took a deep breath and folded my arms over my chest and a kid next to me went into hiding,

acting like she was going to tie her shoelaces.

There used to be four of them—the father, a big guy with a bald head and a bushy mustache and shoulders and arms like King Kong; a tall lanky mother whom you'd never guess could even climb into a high chair or catch anything heavier than a Ping-Pong ball to look at her; the oldest son who looked like his father except he had hair on his head but none on his face and a big face it was, so that no matter how high up he got you could always tell whether he was smiling or frowning or counting; the younger boy about thirteen, maybe, had a vacant stare like he was a million miles away feeding his turtles or something, anything but walking along a tightrope or flying through the air with his family. I had always liked to watch him because he was as cool as I was. But last summer the little girl got into the act. My grandmother says she's probably a midget 'cause no self-respecting mother would allow her child to be up there acting like a bird. "Just a baby," she'd say. "Can't be more than six years old. Should be home in bed. Must be a midget." My grandfather would give me a look when she started in and we'd smile at her together.

They almost got to me that last performance, dodging around with new routines and two at a time so that you didn't know which one Mr. Fly was going to save at the last minute. But he'd fly out and catch the little boy and swing over to the opposite stand where the big boy was flying out to catch them both by the wrists and the poor woman would be left kind of dangling there, suspended, then she'd do this double flip which would kill off everyone in the tent except me, of course, and swing out on the

2. *PAL,* Police Athletic League (New York).

very bar she was on in the first place. And then they'd mess around two or three flying at once just to confuse you until the big drum roll started and out steps the little girl in a party dress and a huge blindfold wrapped around her little head and a pink umbrella like they sell down in Chinatown. And I almost—I won't lie about it—I almost let my heart thump me off the bench. I almost thought I too had to tie my shoelaces. But I sat there. Stubborn. And the kid starts bouncing up and down on the rope like she was about to take off and tear through the canvas roof. Then out swings her little brother and before you know it, Fly Jr. like a great eagle with his arms flapping grabs up the kid, her eyeband in his teeth and swoops her off to the bar that's already got Mrs. Mr. and Big Bro on it and surely there's no room for him. And everyone's standing on their feet clutching at their faces. Everyone but me. Cause I know from the getgo[3] that Mr. and Mrs. are going to leave the bar to give Jr. room and fly over to the other side. Which is exactly what they do. The lady in front of me, Mrs. Perez, who does all the sewing in our neighborhood, gets up and starts shaking her hands like ladies do to get the fingernail polish dry and she says to me with her eyes jammed shut "I must go finish the wedding gowns. Tell me later who died." And she scoots through the aisle, falling all over everybody with her eyes still shut and never looks up. And Mrs. Caine taps me on the back and leans over and says, "Some people just can't take it." And I smile at her and at her twins who're sitting there with their mouths open. I fold my arms over my chest and just dare the Fly family to do their very worst.

The minute I got to camp, I ran up to the main house where all the counselors gather to say hello to the parents and talk with the directors. I had to tell Mary the latest doings with the Fly family. But she put a finger to her mouth like she sometimes does to shush me. "Let's not have any scary stuff this summer, Harriet," she said, looking over my shoulder at a new kid. This new kid, Willie, was from my old neighborhood in Baltimore so we got friendly right off. Then he told me that he had a romantic heart so I quite naturally took him under my wing and decided not to give him a heart attack with any ghost tales. Mary said he meant "rheumatic" heart, but I don't see any difference. So I told Mary to move him out of George's tent and give him a nicer counselor who'd respect his romantic heart. George used to be my play boyfriend when I first came to camp as a little kid and didn't know any better. But he's not a nice person. He makes up funny nicknames for people which aren't funny at all. Like calling Eddie Michaels the Watermelon Kid or David Farmer Charcoal Plenty which I really do not appreciate and especially from a counselor. And once he asked Joanne, who was the table monitor, to go fetch a pail of milk from the kitchen. And the minute she got up, he started hatching a plot, trying to get the kids to hide her peanut butter sandwich and put spiders in her soup. I had to remind everyone at the table that Joanne was my first cousin by blood, and I would be forced to waste the first bum that laid a hand on her plate. And ole George says, "Oh don't be a dumbhead, Harriet. Jo's so stupid she won't even notice." And I told him right then and there that I was not his play girlfriend anymore and would rather marry the

3. *getgo*, slang term meaning "beginning."

wolfman than grow up and be his wife. And just in case he didn't get the message, that night around campfire when we were all playing Little Sally Walker sittin' in a saucer and it was my turn to shake it to the east and to shake it to the west and to shake it to the very one that I loved the best—I shook straight for Mr. Nelson the lifeguard, who was not only the ugliest person in camp but the arch enemy of ole George.

And that very first day of camp last summer when Willie came running up to me to get in line for lunch, here comes George talking some simple stuff about "What a beautiful head you have, Willie. A long, smooth, streamlined head. A sure sign of superior gifts. Definitely genius proportions." And poor Willie went for it, grinning and carrying on and touching his head, which if you want to know the truth is a bullet head and that's all there is to it. And he's turning to me every which way, like he's modeling his head in a fashion show. And the minute his back is turned, ole George makes a face about Willie's head and all the kids in the line bust out laughing. So I had to beat up a few right then and there and finish off the rest later in the shower for being so stupid, laughing at a kid with a romantic heart.

One night in the last week of August when the big campfire party is held, it was very dark and the moon was all smoky, and I just couldn't help myself and started in with a story about the great caterpillar who was going to prowl through the tents and nibble off everybody's toes. And Willie started this whimpering in the back of his throat so I had to switch the story real quick to something cheerful. But before I could do that, ole George picked up my story and added a wicked witch who put spells on city kids who come to camp, and a hunchback dwarf that chopped up tents and bunk beds, and a one-eyed phantom giant who gobbled up the hearts of underprivileged kids. And every time he got to the part where the phantom ripped out a heart, poor Willie would get louder and louder until finally he started rolling around in the grass and screaming and all the kids went crazy and scattered behind the rocks almost kicking the fire completely out as they dashed off into the darkness yelling bloody murder. And the counselors could hardly round us all up—me, too, I'm not going to lie about it. Their little circles of flashlight bobbing in and out of the bushes along the patches of pine, bumping into each other as they scrambled for us kids. And poor Willie rolling around something awful, so they took him to the infirmary.

I was sneaking some ginger snaps in to him later that night when I hear Mary and another senior counselor fussing at ole George in the hallway.

"You've been picking on that kid ever since he got here, George. But tonight was the limit——"

"I wasn't picking on him, I was just trying to tell a story——"

"All that talk about hearts, gobblin' up hearts, and underpriv——"

"Yeh, you were directing it all at the little kid. You should be——"

"I wasn't talking about him. They're all underprivileged kids, after all. I mean all the kids are underprivileged."

I huddled back into the shadows and almost banged into Willie's iron bed. I was hoping he'd open his eyes and wink at me and tell me he was just fooling. That it wasn't so bad to have an underprivileged heart. But he just slept. "I'm an underprivileged kid too,'' I thought to myself. I knew it was a special camp, but I'd never realized. No wonder Aunt Hazel screamed so about my scary stories and my mother flicked off the TV when the monsters came on and Mary was always shushing me. We all had bad hearts. I crawled into the supply cabinet to wait for Willie to wake up so I could ask him about it all. I ate all the ginger snaps but I didn't feel any better. You have a romantic heart, I whispered to myself settling down among the bandages. You will have to be very careful.

It didn't make any difference to Aunt Hazel that I had changed, that I no longer told scary stories or dragged my schoolmates to the latest creature movie, or raced my friends to the edge of the roof, or held my breath, or ran under the train rail when the train was already in sight. As far as she was concerned, I was still the same ole spooky kid I'd always been. So Joanne was kept at home. My mother noticed the difference, but she said over the phone to my grandmother, ''She's acting very ladylike these days, growing up.'' I didn't tell her about my secret, that I knew about my

heart. And I was kind of glad Joanne wasn't around 'cause I would have blabbed it all to her and scared her to death. When school starts again, I decided, I'll ask my teacher how to outgrow my underprivileged heart. I'll train myself, just like I did with the Fly family.

''Well, I guess you'll want some change to go to the fair again, hunh?'' my mother said coming into my room dumping things in her pocketbook.

''No,'' I said. ''I'm too grown up for circuses.''

She put the money on the dresser anyway. I was lying, of course. I was thinking what a terrible strain it would be for Mrs. Perez and everybody else if while sitting there, with the Fly family zooming around in the open air a million miles above the ground, little Harriet Watkins should drop dead with a fatal heart attack behind them.

''I lost,'' I said out loud.

''Lost what?''

''The battle with the Fly family.''

She just stood there a long time looking at me, trying to figure me out, the way mothers are always doing but should know better. Then she kissed me goodbye and left for work.

Discussion

1. (a) What is the challenge that the Fly family represent to Harriet? (b) How does Harriet behave throughout the year to prepare herself for the Fly family's performance? (c) How does she prepare on the day of their performance?

2. Each summer, after the circus, Harriet goes to camp. (a) Why does Joanne no longer attend camp with Harriet? (b) What

is physically wrong with Willie? (c) How does the counselor George treat Willie? (d) How does Harriet treat Willie?

3. (a) What makes Harriet think she too has a ''romantic heart''? How does it change her behavior? (b) What is Harriet's mother's reaction to this change in behavior? (c) What does Harriet mean when she says she lost her battle with the Fly family?

4. At the beginning of the story, Harriet

explains her daring behavior as a "private thing between me and me or maybe between me and the Fly family . . . ." If Harriet's struggle to strengthen her nerve is the story's main conflict, would you say that her conflict is internal—"between me and me"—or external—"between me and the Fly family"? Why?

Toni Cade Bambara 1939–

Toni Cade Bambara's writing style is probably the result of her many interests and experiences. She has led an active and varied life: she has been a dancer, a teacher, and a director of educational projects. Beginning as a part-time writer in the early 1960s, Bambara became well-known ten years later when she edited and wrote the anthologies *The Black Woman* and *Tales and Stories for Black Folks.*

A number of Bambara's stories are about the everyday lives of young people and may reflect her early life in New York City. Her characters are spirited, sensitive, and independent.

Comment: Tell Me a Ghost Story

Have you ever watched a roller coaster and shuddered at how fast and dangerous it seems—even while you were waiting in line for your turn to ride on it? Do you like hearing ghost stories, walking through the "haunted house" at an amusement park, or watching monster movies? It is strange, perhaps, but true: people enjoy being frightened. In fact, many people purposely search out things that will give them a good scare.

All people, at certain times, feel afraid of something. As a child, one might be afraid of the dark; as an adult, one might be afraid of physical injury. Deliberately scaring themselves seems to be a way that people throughout history have devised of letting those fears out—perhaps even of laughing at them. Furthermore, by daring themselves to endure fearful situations, people can train themselves to deal calmly with other such situations. Certainly Harriet in "My Delicate Heart Condition" succeeds in building her courage this way.

Most of the time, however, frightening things are enjoyable only when one knows there is no real danger. Perhaps people, when they are physically safe, can enjoy imaginary fear because they feel pleasantly relieved upon "surviving" the scary situation. They can experience adventure along with the characters in a story who outsmart a terrifying monster. (Note that Harriet no longer finds fun in being afraid when she suspects she might have a heart attack.)

Of course some people go so far in their search for excitement as to seek out truly dangerous activities, like mountain climbing or car racing, that involve enough risk to satisfy their sense of accomplishment. The accomplishment, then, may be as much in overcoming fear as in actually performing the activity itself.

Boarding House

Ted Kooser

The blind man draws his curtains for the night
and goes to bed, leaving a burning light

above the bathroom mirror. Through the wall,
he hears the deaf man walking down the hall

5 in his squeaky shoes to see if there's a light
under the blind man's door, and all is right.

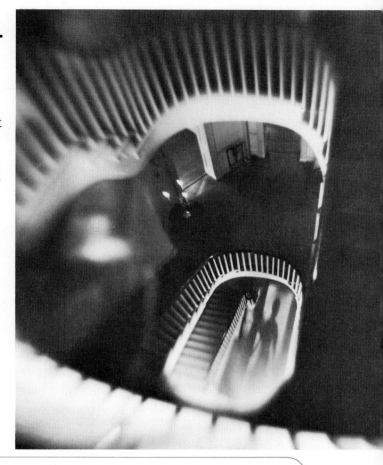

Discussion

1. What is the poem's setting?

2. (a) What is the effect of the light on the deaf man? **(b)** Do you think the blind man leaves his light on accidentally? Explain.

3. (a) What is noteworthy about the deaf man's shoes? **(b)** How is their effect on the blind man similar to the effect of the light on the deaf man?

4. On one level, this poem is about two disabled men who are dependent on each other for some things. On another level, the poem may be seen as a message for all people. What might this message be?

Ted Kooser 1939–

Born and raised in Iowa and currently living in Nebraska, Ted Kooser says of himself: "I am a poet, artist, and film-maker . . . . Most of my work reflects my interest in my surroundings here on the Great Plains."

In addition to teaching creative writing at the University of Nebraska, Kooser works as an underwriter for an insurance firm. He has published several books of poetry, including *Grass Country* and *Not Coming to Be Barked At.*

See **STEREOTYPE** Handbook of Literary Terms

The Ugly Duckling

A. A. Milne

In this most unlikely kingdom things are not quite what you expect them to be.

CHARACTERS

THE KING	DULCIBELLA
THE QUEEN	THE PRINCE SIMON
THE PRINCESS CAMILLA	CARLO
THE CHANCELLOR	

SCENE: *The Throne Room of the Palace; a room of many doors, or, if preferred, curtain-openings: simply furnished with three thrones for Their Majesties and Her Royal Highness the* PRINCESS CAMILLA—*in other words, with three handsome chairs. At each side is a long seat: reserved, as it might be, for His Majesty's Council (if any), but useful, as today, for other purposes. The* KING *is asleep on his throne with a handkerchief over his face. He is a king of any country from any story-book, in whatever costume you please. But he should be wearing his crown.*

A VOICE (*announcing*). His Excellency, the Chancellor! (*The* CHANCELLOR, *an elderly man in horn-rimmed spectacles, enters, bowing. The* KING *wakes up with a start and removes the handkerchief from his face.*)

KING (*with simple dignity*). I was thinking.

CHANCELLOR (*bowing*). Never, Your Majesty, was greater need for thought than now.

KING. That's what I was thinking. (*He struggles into a more dignified position.*) Well, what is it? More trouble?

CHANCELLOR. What we might call the old trouble, Your Majesty.

KING. It's what I was saying last night to the Queen. "Uneasy lies the head that wears a crown,"[1] was how I put it.

CHANCELLOR. A profound and original thought, which may well go down to posterity.

KING. You mean it may go down well with posterity. I hope so. Remind me to tell you some time of another little thing I

---

1. "*Uneasy . . . crown,*" a line from Shakespeare's play, *Henry IV, Part II.*

"The Ugly Duckling" by A. A. Milne.
Reprinted by permission of Curtis Brown Ltd.

said to Her Majesty: something about a fierce light beating on a throne.[2] Posterity would like that, too. Well, what is it?

CHANCELLOR. It is in the matter of Her Royal Highness's wedding.

KING. Oh . . . yes.

CHANCELLOR. As Your Majesty is aware, the young Prince Simon arrives today to seek Her Royal Highness's hand in marriage. He has been traveling in distant lands and, as I understand, has not—er—has not—

KING. You mean he hasn't heard anything.

CHANCELLOR. It is a little difficult to put this tactfully, Your Majesty.

KING. Do your best, and I will tell you afterwards how you got on.

CHANCELLOR. Let me put it this way. The Prince Simon will naturally assume that Her Royal Highness has the customary— so customary as to be in my own poor opinion, slightly monotonous—has what one might call the inevitable—so inevitable as to be, in my opinion again, almost mechanical—will assume that she has the, as *I* think of it, faultily faultless, icily regular, splendidly—

KING. What you are trying to say in the fewest words possible is that my daughter is not beautiful.

CHANCELLOR. Her beauty is certainly elusive, Your Majesty.

KING. It is. It has eluded you, it has eluded me, it has eluded everybody who has seen her. It even eluded the Court Painter. His last words were, "Well, I did my best." His successor is now painting the view across the water-meadows from the West Turret. He says his doctor has advised him to keep to landscape.

CHANCELLOR. It is unfortunate, Your Majesty, but there it is. One just cannot understand how it can have occurred.

KING. You don't think she takes after *me,* at all? You don't detect a likeness?

CHANCELLOR. Most certainly not, Your Majesty.

KING. Good. Your predecessor did.

CHANCELLOR. I have often wondered what happened to my predecessor.

KING. Well, now you know. (*There is a short silence.*)

CHANCELLOR. Looking at the bright side, although Her Royal Highness is not, strictly speaking, beautiful—

KING. Not, truthfully speaking, beautiful—

CHANCELLOR. Yet she has great beauty of character.

KING. My dear Chancellor, we are not considering Her Royal Highness's character, but her chances of getting married. You observe that there is a distinction.

CHANCELLOR. Yes, Your Majesty.

KING. Look at it from the suitor's point of view. If a girl is beautiful, it is easy to assume that she has, tucked away inside her, an equally beautiful character. But it is impossible to assume that an unattractive girl, however elevated in character, has, tucked away inside her, an equally beautiful face. That is, so to speak, not where you want it—tucked away.

CHANCELLOR. Quite so, Your Majesty.

KING. This doesn't, of course, alter the fact that the Princess Camilla is quite the nicest person in the Kingdom.

CHANCELLOR (*enthusiastically*). She is indeed, Your Majesty. (*Hurriedly*) With the exception, I need hardly say, of Your Majesty—and Her Majesty.

KING. Your exceptions are tolerated for their loyalty and condemned for their extreme fatuity.

CHANCELLOR. Thank you, Your Majesty.

---

2. *fierce . . . throne,* a reference to a line from a poem about King Arthur by Alfred, Lord Tennyson (1809-1892).

KING. As an adjective for your King, the word "nice" is ill-chosen. As an adjective for Her Majesty, it is—ill-chosen. (*At which moment* HER MAJESTY *comes in. The* KING *rises. The* CHANCELLOR *puts himself at right angles.*)

QUEEN (*briskly*). Ah. Talking about Camilla? (*She sits down.*)

KING (*returning to his throne*). As always, my dear, you are right.

QUEEN (*to the* CHANCELLOR). This fellow, Simon— What's he like?

CHANCELLOR. Nobody has seen him, Your Majesty.

QUEEN. How old is he?

CHANCELLOR. Five-and-twenty, I understand.

QUEEN. In twenty-five years he must have been seen by somebody.

KING (*to the* CHANCELLOR). Just a fleeting glimpse.

CHANCELLOR. I meant, Your Majesty, that no detailed report of him has reached this country, save that he has the usual personal advantages and qualities expected of a Prince, and has been traveling in distant and dangerous lands.

QUEEN. Ah! Nothing gone wrong with his eyes? Sunstroke or anything?

CHANCELLOR. Not that I am aware of, Your Majesty. At the same time, as I was venturing to say to His Majesty, Her Royal Highness's character and disposition are so outstandingly—

QUEEN. Stuff and nonsense. You remember what happened when we had the Tournament of Love last year.

CHANCELLOR. I was not myself present, Your Majesty. I had not then the honour of—I was abroad, and never heard the full story.

QUEEN. No; it was the other fool. They all rode up to Camilla to pay their homage—

it was the first time they had seen her. The heralds blew their trumpets, and announced that she would marry whichever Prince was left master of the field when all but one had been unhorsed. The trumpets were blown again, they charged enthusiastically into the fight, and— (*The* KING *looks nonchalantly at the ceiling and whistles a few bars.*)—don't do that.

KING. I'm sorry, my dear.

QUEEN (*to the* CHANCELLOR). And what happened? They all simultaneously fell off their horses and assumed a posture of defeat.

KING. One of them was not quite so quick as the others. I was very quick. I proclaimed him the victor.

QUEEN. At the Feast of Betrothal held that night—

KING. We were all very quick.

QUEEN. The Chancellor announced that by the laws of the country the successful suitor had to pass a further test. He had to give the correct answer to a riddle.

CHANCELLOR. Such undoubtedly is the fact, Your Majesty.

KING. There are times for announcing facts, and times for looking at things in a broad-minded way. Please remember that, Chancellor.

CHANCELLOR. Yes, Your Majesty.

QUEEN. I invented the riddle myself. Quite an easy one. What is it which has four legs and barks like a dog? The answer is, "A dog."

KING (*to the* CHANCELLOR). See that?

CHANCELLOR. Yes, Your Majesty.

KING. It isn't difficult.

QUEEN. He, however, seemed to find it so. He said an eagle. Then he said a serpent; a very high mountain with slippery sides; two peacocks; a moonlight night; the day after tomorrow—

KING. Nobody could accuse him of not trying.

QUEEN. *I* did.

KING. I *should* have said that nobody could fail to recognize in his attitude an appearance of doggedness.

QUEEN. Finally he said "Death." I nudged the King—

KING. Accepting the word "nudge" for the moment, I rubbed my ankle with one hand, clapped him on the shoulder with the other, and congratulated him on the correct answer. He disappeared under the table, and, personally, I never saw him again.

QUEEN. His body was found in the moat next morning.

CHANCELLOR. But what was he doing in the moat, Your Majesty?

KING. Bobbing about. Try not to ask needless questions.

CHANCELLOR. It all seems so strange.

QUEEN. What does?

CHANCELLOR. That Her Royal Highness, alone of all the Princesses one has ever heard of, should lack that invariable attribute of Royalty, supreme beauty.

QUEEN (*to the* KING). That was your Great-Aunt Malkin. She came to the christening. You know what she said.

KING. It was cryptic. Great-Aunt Malkin's besetting weakness. She came to *my* christening—she was one hundred and one then, and that was fifty-one years ago. (*To the* CHANCELLOR) How old would that make her?

CHANCELLOR. One hundred and fifty-two, Your Majesty.

KING (*after thought*). About that, yes. She promised me that when I grew up I should have all the happiness which my wife deserved. It struck me at the time— well, when I say "at the time," I was only a week old—but it did strike me as soon as anything could strike me—I mean of that nature—well, work it out for yourself, Chancellor. It opens up a most interesting field of speculation. Though naturally I have not liked to go into it at all deeply with Her Majesty.

QUEEN. I never heard anything less cryptic. She was wishing you extreme happiness.

KING. I don't think she was *wishing* me anything. However.

CHANCELLOR (*to the* QUEEN). But what, Your Majesty, did she wish Her Royal Highness?

QUEEN. Her other godmother—on my side— had promised her the dazzling beauty for which all the women in my family are famous—(*She pauses, and the* KING *snaps his fingers surreptitiously in the direction of the* CHANCELLOR.)

CHANCELLOR (*hurriedly*). Indeed, yes, Your Majesty. (*The* KING *relaxes.*)

QUEEN. And Great-Aunt Malkin said— (*To the* KING) —what were the words?

KING. 		*I give you with this kiss*
		A wedding day surprise.
		Where ignorance is bliss
		'Tis folly to be wise.[3]

I thought the last two lines rather neat. But what it *meant*—

QUEEN. We can all see what it meant. She was given beauty—and where is it? Great-Aunt Malkin took it away from her. The wedding day surprise is that there will never be a wedding day.

KING. Young men being what they are, my dear, it would be much more surprising if there *were* a wedding day. So how— (*The* PRINCESS *comes in. She is young, happy, healthy, but not beautiful. Or let*

---

3. *Where ignorance . . . be wise,* from "On a Distant Prospect of Eton College," by Thomas Gray (1716-1771).

us say that by some trick of make-up or arrangement of hair she seems plain to us: unlike the princess of the story-books.)

PRINCESS *(to the* KING*).* Hello, darling! *(Seeing the others)* Oh, I say! Affairs of state? Sorry.

KING *(holding out his hand).* Don't go, Camilla. *(She takes his hand.)*

CHANCELLOR. Shall I withdraw, Your Majesty?

QUEEN. You are aware, Camilla, that Prince Simon arrives today?

PRINCESS. He has arrived. They're just letting down the drawbridge.

KING *(jumping up).* Arrived! I must—

PRINCESS. Darling, you know what the drawbridge is like. It takes at *least* half an hour to let it down.

KING *(sitting down).* It wants oil. *(To the* CHANCELLOR*)* Have *you* been grudging it oil?

PRINCESS. It wants a new drawbridge, darling.

CHANCELLOR. Have I Your Majesty's permission—

KING. Yes, yes. *(The* CHANCELLOR *bows and goes out.)*

QUEEN. You've told him, of course? It's the only chance.

KING. Er—no. I was just going to, when—

QUEEN. Then I'd better. *(She goes to the door.)* You can explain to the girl; I'll have her sent to you. You've told Camilla?

KING. Er—no. I was just going to, when—

QUEEN. Then you'd better tell her now.

KING. My dear, are you sure—

QUEEN. It's the only chance left. *(Dramatically to heaven)* My daughter! *(She goes out. There is a little silence when she is gone.)*

KING. Camilla, I want to talk seriously to you about marriage.

PRINCESS. Yes, father.

KING. It is time that you learnt some of the facts of life.

PRINCESS. Yes, father.

KING. Now the great fact about marriage is that once you're married you live happy ever after. All our history books affirm this.

PRINCESS. And your own experience too, darling.

KING (with dignity). Let us confine ourselves to history for the moment.

PRINCESS. Yes, father.

KING. Of course, there *may* be an exception here and there, which, as it were, proves the rule; just as—oh, well, never mind.

PRINCESS (smiling). Go on, darling. You were going to say that an exception here and there proves the rule that all princesses are beautiful.

KING. Well—leave that for the moment. The point is that it doesn't matter *how* you marry, or *who* you marry, as long as you *get* married. Because you'll be happy ever after in any case. Do you follow me so far?

PRINCESS. Yes, father.

KING. Well, your mother and I have a little plan—

PRINCESS. Was that it, going out of the door just now?

KING. Er—yes. It concerns your waiting-maid.

PRINCESS. Darling, I have several.

KING. Only one that leaps to the eye, so to speak. The one with the—well, with everything.

PRINCESS. Dulcibella?

KING. That's the one. It is our little plan that at the first meeting she should pass herself off as the Princess—a harmless ruse, of which you will find frequent record in the history books—and allure Prince Si-mon to his—that is to say, bring him up to the—in other words, the wedding will take place immediately afterwards, and as quietly as possible—well, naturally in view of the fact that your Aunt Malkin is one hundred and fifty-two; and since you will be wearing the family bridal veil—which is no doubt how the custom arose—the surprise after the ceremony will be his. Are you following me at all? Your attention seems to be wandering.

PRINCESS. I was wondering why you needed to tell me.

KING. Just a precautionary measure, in case you happened to meet the Prince or his attendant before the ceremony; in which case, of course, you would pass yourself off as the maid—

PRINCESS. A harmless ruse, of which, also, you will find frequent record in the history books.

KING. Exactly. But the occasion need not arise.

A VOICE (announcing). The woman Dulcibella!

KING. Ah! (To the PRINCESS) Now, Camilla, if you just retire to your own apartments, I will come to you there when we are ready for the actual ceremony. (He leads her out as he is talking, and as he returns calls out:) Come in, my dear! (DULCIBELLA comes in. She is beautiful, but dumb.) Now don't be frightened, there is nothing to be frightened about. Has Her Majesty told you what you have to do?

DULCIBELLA. Y-yes, Your Majesty.

KING. Well now, let's see how well you can do it. You are sitting here, we will say. (He leads her to a seat.) Now imagine that I am Prince Simon. (He curls his moustache and puts his stomach in. She giggles.) You are the beautiful Princess Camilla whom he has never seen. (She *giggles again.)* This is a serious moment in your life, and you will find that a giggle will not be helpful. *(He goes to the door.)* I am announced: "His Royal Highness Prince Simon!" That's me being announced. Remember what I said about giggling. You should have a faraway look upon the face. *(She does her best.)* Farther away than that. *(She tries again.)* No, that's too far. You are sitting there, thinking beautiful thoughts—in maiden meditation, fancy-free,[4] as I remember saying to Her Majesty once . . . speaking of somebody else . . . fancy-free, but with the mouth definitely shut—that's better. I advance and fall upon one knee. *(He does so.)* You extend your hand graciously—*graciously;* you're not trying to push him in the face—that's better, and I raise it to my lips—so—and I kiss it— *(He kisses it warmly.)*—no, perhaps not so ardently as that, more like this *(He kisses it again.)* and I say, "Your Royal Highness, this is the most—er—Your Royal Highness, I shall ever be—no— Your Royal Highness, it is the proudest—" Well, the point is that *he* will say it, and it will be something complimentary, and then he will take your hand in both of his, and press it to his heart. *(He does so.)* And then—what do *you* say?

DULCIBELLA. Coo![5]

KING. No, *not* Coo.

DULCIBELLA. Never had anyone do *that* to me before.

KING. That also strikes the wrong note. What you want to say is, "Oh, Prince Simon!" . . . Say it.

DULCIBELLA *(loudly).* Oh, Prince Simon!

KING. No, no. You don't need to shout until he has said "What?" two or three times. Always consider the possibility that he *isn't* deaf. Softly, and giving the words a

dying fall, letting them play around his head like a flight of doves.

DULCIBELLA *(still a little over-loud).* O-o-o-h, Prinsimon!

KING. Keep the idea in your mind of a flight of *doves* rather than a flight of panic-stricken elephants, and you will be all right. Now I'm going to get up, and you must, as it were, *waft* me into a seat by your side. *(She starts wafting.)* Not rescuing a drowning man, that's another idea altogether, useful at times, but at the moment inappropriate. Wafting. Prince Simon will put the necessary muscles into play—all you require to do is to indicate by a gracious movement of the hand the seat you require him to take. Now! *(He gets up, a little stiffly, and sits next to her.)* That was better. Well, here we are. Now, I think you give me a look: something, let us say, halfway between the breathless adoration of a nun[6] and the voluptuous abandonment of a woman of the world; with an undertone of regal dignity, touched, as it were, with good comradeship. Now try that. *(She gives him a vacant look of bewilderment.)* Frankly, that didn't quite get it. There was just a little something missing. An absence, as it were, of all the qualities I asked for, and in their place an odd resemblance to an unsatisfied fish. Let us try to get it another way. Dulcibella, have you a young man of your own?

DULCIBELLA *(eagerly, seizing his hand).* Oo, yes, he's ever so smart, he's an archer, well not as you might say a real archer, he works in the armoury, but old Bottle-

---

4. *in . . . fancy-free,* a line from Shakespeare's play, *A Midsummer Night's Dream.*
5. *Coo,* a British slang expression of delight.
6. *breathless . . . nun,* a paraphrase of a line from "It Is a Beauteous Evening," a poem by William Wordsworth (1770-1850).

nose, *you* know who I mean, the Captain of the Guard, says the very next man they ever has to shoot, my Eg shall take his place, knowing Father and how it is with Eg and me, and me being maid to Her Royal Highness and can't marry me till he's a real soldier, but ever so loving, and funny like, the things he says. I said to him once, "Eg," I said—

KING (*getting up*). I rather fancy, Dulcibella, that if you think of Eg all the time, *say* as little as possible, and, when thinking of Eg, see that the mouth is not more than partially open, you will do very well. I will show you where you are to sit and wait for His Royal Highness. (*He leads her out. On the way he is saying:*) Now remember—*waft—waft—*not *hoick*.[7] (PRINCE SIMON *wanders in from the back unannounced. He is a very ordinary-looking young man in rather dusty clothes. He gives a deep sigh of relief as he sinks into the King's throne.* CAMILLA, *a new and strangely beautiful* CAMILLA, *comes in.*)

PRINCESS (*surprised*). Well!

PRINCE. Oh, hello!

PRINCESS. Ought you?

PRINCE (*getting up*). Do sit down, won't you?

PRINCESS. Who are you, and how did you get here?

PRINCE. Well, that's rather a long story. Couldn't we sit down? You could sit here if you liked, but it isn't very comfortable.

PRINCESS. That is the King's Throne.

PRINCE. Oh, is that what it is?

PRINCESS. Thrones are not meant to be comfortable.

PRINCE. Well, I don't know if they're meant to be, but they certainly aren't.

PRINCESS. Why were you sitting on the King's Throne, and who are you?

PRINCE. My name is Carlo.

PRINCESS. Mine is Dulcibella.

PRINCE. Good. And now couldn't we sit down?

PRINCESS (*sitting down on the long seat to the left of the throne, and, as it were, wafting him to a place next to her*). You may sit here, if you like. Why are you so tired? (*He sits down.*)

PRINCE. I've been taking very strenuous exercise.

PRINCESS. Is that part of the long story?

PRINCE. It is.

PRINCESS (*settling herself*). I love stories.

PRINCE. This isn't a story really. You see, I'm attendant on Prince Simon, who is visiting here.

PRINCESS. Oh? I'm attendant on Her Royal Highness.

PRINCE. Then you know what he's here for.

PRINCESS. Yes.

PRINCE. She's very beautiful, I hear.

PRINCESS. Did you hear that? Where have you been lately?

PRINCE. Traveling in distant lands—with Prince Simon.

PRINCESS. Ah! All the same, I don't understand. Is Prince Simon in the Palace now? The drawbridge *can't* be down yet!

PRINCE. I don't suppose it is. *And* what noise it makes coming down!

PRINCESS. Isn't it terrible?

PRINCE. I couldn't stand it any more. I just had to get away. That's why I'm here.

PRINCESS. But how?

PRINCE. Well, there's only one way, isn't there? That beech tree, and then a swing and a grab for the battlements, and don't ask me to remember it all— (*He shudders.*)

---

7. *hoick*, jerk or yank.

PRINCESS. You mean you came across the moat by that beech tree?

PRINCE. Yes. I got so tired of hanging about.

PRINCESS. But it's terribly dangerous!

PRINCE. That's why I'm so exhausted. Nervous shock. (*He lies back.*)

PRINCESS. Of course, it's different for *me*.

PRINCE (*sitting up*). Say that again. I must have got it wrong.

PRINCESS. It's different for me, because I'm used to it. Besides, I'm so much lighter.

PRINCE. You don't mean that *you*—

PRINCESS. Oh yes, often.

PRINCE. And I thought I was a brave man! At least, I didn't until five minutes ago, and now I don't again.

PRINCESS. Oh, but you are! And I think it's wonderful to do it straight off the first time.

PRINCE. Well, *you* did.

PRINCESS. Oh no, not the first time. When I was a child.

PRINCE. You mean that you crashed?

PRINCESS. Well, you only fall into the moat.

PRINCE. Only! Can you *swim?*

PRINCESS. Of course.

PRINCE. So you swam to the castle walls, and yelled for help, and they fished you out and walloped you. And next day you tried again. Well, if *that* isn't pluck—

PRINCESS. Of course I didn't. I swam back, and did it at once; I mean I tried again at once. It wasn't until the third time that I actually did it. You see, I was afraid I might lose my nerve.

PRINCE. Afraid she might lose her nerve!

PRINCESS. There's a way of getting over from this side, too; a tree grows out from the wall and you jump into another tree— I don't think it's quite so easy.

PRINCE. Not quite so easy. Good. You must show me.

PRINCESS. Oh, I will.

PRINCE. Perhaps it might be as well if you taught me how to swim first. I've often heard about swimming, but never—

PRINCESS. You can't swim?

PRINCE. No. Don't look so surprised. There are a lot of other things which I can't do. I'll tell you about them as soon as you have a couple of years to spare.

PRINCESS. You can't swim and yet you crossed by the beech tree! And you're *ever* so much heavier than I am! Now who's brave?

PRINCE (*getting up*). You keep talking about how light you are. I must see if there's anything in it. Stand up! (*She stands obediently and he picks her up.*) You're right, Dulcibella. I could hold you here forever. (*Looking at her*) You're very lovely. Do you know how lovely you are?

PRINCESS. Yes. (*She laughs suddenly and happily.*)

PRINCE. Why do you laugh?

PRINCESS. Aren't you tired of holding me?

PRINCE. Frankly, yes. I exaggerated when I said I could hold you forever. When you've been hanging by the arms for ten minutes over a very deep moat, wondering if it's too late to learn how to swim— (*He puts her down.*) —What I meant was that I should *like* to hold you forever. Why did you laugh?

PRINCESS. Oh, well, it was a little private joke of mine.

PRINCE. If it comes to that, I've got a private joke too. Let's exchange them.

PRINCESS. Mine's very private. One other woman in the whole world knows, and that's all.

PRINCE. Mine's just as private. One other man knows, and that's all.

PRINCESS. What fun. I love secrets . . . .

Well, here's mine. When I was born, one of my godmothers promised that I should be very beautiful.

PRINCE. How right she was.

PRINCESS. But the other one said this:

I give you with this kiss
A wedding day surprise.
Where ignorance is bliss
'Tis folly to be wise.

And nobody knew what it meant. And I grew up very plain. And then, when I was about ten, I met my godmother in the forest one day. It was my tenth birthday. Nobody knows this—except you.

PRINCE. Except us.

PRINCESS. Except us. And she told me what her gift meant. It meant that I *was* beautiful—but everybody else was to go on being ignorant, and thinking me plain, until my wedding day. Because, she said, she didn't want me to grow up spoilt and wilful and vain, as I should have done if everybody had always been saying how beautiful I was; and the best thing in the world, she said, was to be quite sure of yourself, but not to expect admiration from other people. So ever since then my mirror has told me I'm beautiful, and everybody else thinks me ugly, and I get a lot of fun out of it.

PRINCE. Well, seeing that Dulcibella is the result, I can only say that your godmother was very, very wise.

PRINCESS. And now tell me *your* secret.

PRINCE. It isn't such a pretty one. You see, Prince Simon was going to woo Princess Camilla, and he'd heard that she was beautiful and haughty and imperious—all *you* would have been if your godmother hadn't been so wise. And being a very ordinary-looking fellow himself, he was afraid she wouldn't think much of him, so

he suggested to one of his attendants, a man called Carlo, of extremely attractive appearance, that *he* should pretend to be the Prince, and win the Princess's hand; and then at the last moment they would change places—

PRINCESS. How would they do that?

PRINCE. The Prince was going to have been married in full armour—with his visor down.

PRINCESS *(laughing happily)*. Oh, what fun!

PRINCE. Neat, isn't it?

PRINCESS *(laughing)*. Oh, very . . . very . . . very.

PRINCE. Neat, but not so terribly *funny*. Why do you keep laughing?

PRINCESS. Well, that's another secret.

PRINCE. If it comes to that, *I've* got another one up my sleeve. Shall we exchange again?

PRINCESS. All right. You go first this time.

PRINCE. Very well. I am not Carlo. *(Standing up and speaking dramatically.)* I am Simon!—ow! *(He sits down and rubs his leg violently.)*

PRINCESS *(alarmed)*. What is it?

PRINCE. Cramp. *(In a mild voice, still rubbing)* I was saying that I was Prince Simon.

PRINCESS. Shall I rub it for you? *(She rubs.)*

PRINCE *(still hopefully)*. I am Simon.

PRINCESS. Is that better?

PRINCE *(despairingly)*. I am Simon.

PRINCESS. I know.

PRINCE. How did you know?

PRINCESS. Well, you told me.

PRINCE. But oughtn't you to swoon or something?

PRINCESS. Why? History records many similar ruses.

PRINCE *(amazed)*. Is that so? I've never read history. I thought I was being profoundly original.

PRINCESS. Oh, no! Now I'll tell you *my* secret. For reasons very much like your own the Princess Camilla, who is held to be extremely plain, feared to meet Prince Simon. Is the draw-bridge down yet?

PRINCE. Do your people give a faint, surprised cheer every time it gets down?

PRINCESS. Naturally.

PRINCE. Then it came down about three minutes ago.

PRINCESS. Ah! Then at this very moment your man Carlo is declaring his passionate love for my maid, Dulcibella. That, I think, is funny. *(So does the* PRINCE. *He laughs heartily.)* Dulcibella, by the way, is in love with a man she calls Eg, so I hope Carlo isn't getting carried away.

PRINCE. Carlo is married to a girl he calls "the little woman," so Eg has nothing to fear.

PRINCESS. By the way, I don't know if you heard, but I said, or as good as said, that I am the Princess Camilla.

PRINCE. I wasn't surprised. History, of which I read a great deal, records many similar ruses.

PRINCESS *(laughing)*. Simon!

PRINCE *(laughing)*. Camilla! *(He stands up.)* May I try holding you again? *(She nods. He takes her in his arms and kisses her.)* Sweetheart!

PRINCESS. You see, when you lifted me up before, you said, "You're very lovely," and my godmother said that the first person to whom I would seem lovely was the man I should marry; so I knew then that you were Simon and I should marry you.

PRINCE. I knew directly when I saw you that I should marry you, even if you were Dulcibella. By the way, which of you *am* I marrying?

PRINCESS. When she lifts her veil, it will be

Camilla. (*Voices are heard outside.*) Until then it will be Dulcibella.

PRINCE (*in a whisper*). Then goodbye, Camilla, until you lift your veil.

PRINCESS. Goodbye, Simon, until you raise your visor. (*The* KING *and* QUEEN *come in arm-in-arm, followed by* CARLO *and* DULCIBELLA, *also arm-in-arm. The* CHANCELLOR *precedes them, walking backwards, at a loyal angle.*)

PRINCE (*supporting the* CHANCELLOR *as an accident seems inevitable*). Careful! (*The* CHANCELLOR *turns indignantly round.*)

KING. Who and what is this? More accurately, who and what are all these?

CARLO. My attendant, Carlo, Your Majesty. He will, with Your Majesty's permission, prepare me for the ceremony. (*The* PRINCE *bows.*)

KING. Of course, of course!

QUEEN (*to* DULCIBELLA). Your maid, Dulcibella, is it not, my love? (DULCIBELLA *nods violently.*) I thought so. (*To* CARLO) *She* will prepare Her Royal Highness. (*The* PRINCESS *curtsies.*)

KING. Ah, yes. Yes. *Most* important.

PRINCESS (*curtsying*). I beg pardon, Your Majesty, if I've done wrong, but I found the gentleman wandering—

KING (*crossing to her*). Quite right, my dear, quite right. (*He pinches her cheek, and takes advantage of this kingly gesture to say in a loud whisper:*) We've pulled it off! (*They sit down; the* KING *and* QUEEN *on their thrones,* DULCIBELLA *on the princess's throne.* CARLO *stands behind* DULCIBELLA, *the* CHANCELLOR *on the right of the* QUEEN, *and the* PRINCE *and* PRINCESS *behind the long seat on the left.*)

CHANCELLOR (*consulting documents*). H'r'm! Have I Your Majesty's authority to put the final test to His Royal Highness?

QUEEN (*whispering to the* KING). Is this safe?

KING (*whispering*). Perfectly, my dear. I told him the answer a minute ago. (*Over his shoulder to* CARLO) Don't forget. *Dog.* (*Aloud*) Proceed, Your Excellency. It is my desire that the affairs of my country should ever be conducted in a strictly constitutional manner.

CHANCELLOR (*oratorically*). By the constitution of the country, a suitor to Her Royal Highness's hand cannot be deemed successful until he has given the correct answer to a riddle. (*Conversationally*) The last suitor answered incorrectly, and thus failed to win his bride.

KING. By a coincidence he fell into the moat.

CHANCELLOR (*to* CARLO). I have now to ask Your Royal Highness if you are prepared for the ordeal?

CARLO (*cheerfully*). Absolutely.

CHANCELLOR. I may mention, as a matter, possibly, of some slight historical interest to our visitor, that by the constitution of the country the same riddle is not allowed to be asked on two successive occasions.

KING (*startled*). What's that?

CHANCELLOR. This one, it is interesting to recall, was propounded exactly a century ago, and we must take it as a fortunate omen that it was well and truly solved.

KING (*to the* QUEEN). I may want my sword directly.

CHANCELLOR. The riddle is this. What is it which has four legs and mews like a cat?

CARLO (*promptly*). A dog.

KING (*still more promptly*). Bravo, bravo! (*He claps loudly and nudges the* QUEEN, *who claps too.*)

CHANCELLOR (*peering at his documents*). According to the records of the occasion to which I referred, the correct answer would seem to be—

PRINCESS (*to the* PRINCE). Say something, quick!

CHANCELLOR. —not dog, but—

PRINCE. Your Majesty, have I permission to speak? Naturally His Royal Highness could not think of justifying himself on such an occasion, but I think that with Your Majesty's gracious permission, I could—

KING. Certainly, certainly.

PRINCE. In our country, we have an animal to which we have given the name "dog," or, in the local dialect of the more mountainous districts, "doggie." It sits by the fireside and purrs.

CARLO. That's right. It purrs like anything.

PRINCE. When it needs milk, which is its staple food, it mews.

CARLO (*enthusiastically*). Mews like nobody's business.

PRINCE. It also has four legs.

CARLO. One at each corner.

PRINCE. In some countries, I understand, this animal is called a "cat." In one distant country to which His Royal Highness and I penetrated it was called by the very curious name of "hippopotamus."

CARLO. That's right. (*To the* PRINCE) Do you remember that ginger-coloured hippopotamus which used to climb onto my shoulder and lick my ear?

PRINCE. I shall never forget it, sir. (*To the* KING) So you see, Your Majesty—

KING. Thank you. I think that makes it perfectly clear. (*Firmly to the* CHANCELLOR) You are about to agree?

CHANCELLOR. Undoubtedly, Your Majesty. May I be the first to congratulate His Royal Highness on solving the riddle so accurately?

KING. You may be the first to see that all is in order for an immediate wedding.

CHANCELLOR. Thank you, Your Majesty.

(*He bows and withdraws. The* KING *rises, as do the* QUEEN *and* DULCIBELLA.)

KING (*to* CARLO). Doubtless, Prince Simon, you will wish to retire and prepare yourself for the ceremony.

CARLO. Thank you, sir.

PRINCE. Have I Your Majesty's permission to attend His Royal Highness? It is the custom of his country for Princes of the royal blood to be married in full armour, a matter which requires a certain adjustment—

KING. Of course, of course. (CARLO *bows to the* KING *and* QUEEN *and goes out. As the* PRINCE *is about to follow, the* KING *stops him.*) Young man, you have a quality of quickness which I admire. It is my pleasure to reward it in any way which commends itself to you.

PRINCE. Your Majesty is ever gracious. May I ask for my reward *after* the ceremony? (*He catches the eye of the* PRINCESS, *and they give each other a secret smile.*)

KING. Certainly. (*The* PRINCE *bows and goes out. To* DULCIBELLA.) Now, young woman, make yourself scarce. You've done your work excellently, and we will see that you and your—what was his name?

DULCIBELLA. Eg, Your Majesty.

KING. —that you and your Eg are not forgotten.

DULCIBELLA. Coo! (*She curtsies and goes out.*)

PRINCESS (*calling*). Wait for me, Dulcibella!

KING (*to the* QUEEN). Well, my dear, we may congratulate ourselves. As I remember saying to somebody once, "You have not lost a daughter, you have gained a son." How does he strike you?

QUEEN. Stupid.

KING. They made a very handsome pair, I thought, he and Dulcibella.

QUEEN. Both stupid.

KING. I said nothing about stupidity. What I *said* was that they were both extremely handsome. That is the important thing. *(Struck by a sudden idea)* Or isn't it?

QUEEN. What do *you* think of Prince Simon, Camilla?

PRINCESS. I adore him. We shall be so happy together.

KING. Well, of course you will. I told you so. Happy ever after.

QUEEN. Run along now and get ready.

PRINCESS. Yes, mother. *(She throws a kiss to them and goes out.)*

KING *(anxiously).* My dear, have we been wrong about Camilla all this time? It seemed to me that she wasn't looking *quite* so plain as usual just now. Did *you* notice anything?

QUEEN *(carelessly).* Just the excitement of the marriage.

KING *(relieved).* Ah, yes, that would account for it.

Curtain

Discussion

1. The title of this play comes from a fairy tale about an ugly duckling that grows up to be a beautiful swan. How does Princess Camilla's story parallel that of the ugly duckling?

2. (a) As the play opens, why are the King and the Chancellor concerned about Princess Camilla? (b) What had happened the previous year at the Tournament of Love? (c) How do the King, Queen, and Chancellor try to make certain this does not happen again?

3. (a) Why doesn't Princess Camilla tell anyone about her Great–Aunt Malkin's gift? (b) How does Great–Aunt Malkin's gift benefit Princess Camilla?

4. Explain how each of the following is different from what you would expect in a traditional fairy tale: (a) Prince Simon's appearance and behavior; (b) Princess Camilla's manner of speaking to her father; (c) the King's appearance in the opening scene; (d) the drawbridge; (e) the King and Queen's manner of speaking to each other in public.

5. Much of the dialogue in the play con-

tains humor. Find a line that you consider humorous; explain its meaning and, if necessary, its context.

Application
Stereotype

In the opening scene His Majesty is described as "a king of any country from any story-book." The King, wearing a crown and sitting on his throne, considers the fact that a prince is on his way "to seek Her Royal Highness's hand in marriage." You probably recognize these people and this situation as stereotypes because they have characteristics that are commonly found in many fairy tales.

1. How might Great-Aunt Malkin and her actions be considered stereotypes?

2. A stereotyped prince usually performs acts of great courage. What is Prince Simon's "courageous act"? Do you think A. A. Milne succeeds in making fun of this stereotype? Why or why not?

3. What other stereotypes—either characters or situations—do you find in this play?

Vocabulary
Affixes, Dictionary

Look closely at the structure of the itali-cized words in the following questions. Then answer the questions on a separate paper. You may find it necessary to check the meanings of the prefixes *in-, pre-,* and *un-* in the Glossary.

1. What is the root word of *precaution-ary?* Based on its structure, do you think *precautionary* means "having advance no-tice," "not being careful," or "taking care beforehand"?

2. If a person is known for her *invariable* cheerfulness, is she cheerful some of the time, most of the time, or all of the time? (To form the word *invariable,* the *y* in *vary* is changed to an *i.*)

3. An *orator* is a person known for skill and power in public speaking. In which of the following situations would you most likely expect to hear someone speaking *oratorically*—at a political convention, on a radio weather report, or on a TV game show?

4. The word *monotonous* is formed from *mono-* (from a Greek word meaning "one; single"), plus the root word *ton(e),* plus the suffix *-ous.* Do you think you would enjoy listening to someone who has a *mo-notonous* voice? Why or why not?

5. What is the root word of *undoubt-edly?* If a meal is *undoubtedly* the best you've ever eaten, is the good taste of the food to be doubted, not to be doubted, or to be doubted beforehand?

Composition

Although readers learn something about Great–Aunt Malkin by what other charac-ters say, she never appears on stage. What do you suppose she looks like? What might some of her personality traits be? Reread Princess Camilla's account of her meeting with Great–Aunt Malkin on her tenth birthday (107a, 2-4).

Write the dialogue you think took place between ten–year–old Camilla and Great–Aunt Malkin when they met in the forest. Use Princess Camilla's account as a basis for the content of your dialogue. Try to re-veal the characters' personalities by what they say and how they say it. You might include brief stage directions describing how they move and say their lines to help characterize Princess Camilla and Great–Aunt Malkin. Refer to "The Ugly Duck-ling" as a model for placement of charac-ters' names, stage directions, and punc-tuation.

A. A. Milne 1882–1956

A. A. Milne was born and educated in England. Although he earned a B. A. in mathematics, his occupations involved writing. He was a free-lance journalist and an editor of the British humor magazine *Punch,* as well as the celebrated creator of Winnie-the-Pooh. One of Pooh's friends, Christopher Robin, was modeled on Milne's own son.

In addition to stories, drama, and verse for young people, Milne produced many works for adults, including six novels and more than thirty plays.

Not Poor, Just Broke

Dick Gregory

The teacher thought he was a troublemaker, but he just wanted someone to know he was there.

I never learned hate at home, or shame. I had to go to school for that. I was about seven years old when I got my first big lesson. I was in love with a little girl named Helene Tucker, a light-complected little girl with pigtails and nice manners. She was always clean and she was smart in school. I think I went to school then mostly to look at her. I brushed my hair and even got me a little old handkerchief. It was a lady's handkerchief, but I didn't want Helene to see me wipe my nose on my hand. The pipes were frozen again, there was no water in the house, but I washed my socks and shirt every night. I'd get a pot, and go over to Mister Ben's grocery store, and stick my pot down into his soda machine. Scoop out some chopped ice. By evening the ice melted to water for washing. I got sick a'lot that winter because the fire would go out at night before the clothes were dry. In the morning I'd put them on, wet or dry, because they were the only clothes I had.

Everybody's got a Helene Tucker, a symbol of everything you want. I loved her for her goodness, her cleanness, her popularity. She'd walk down my street and my

brothers and sisters would yell, "Here comes Helene," and I'd rub my tennis sneakers on the back of my pants and wish my hair wasn't so nappy and the white folks' shirt fit me better. I'd run out on the street. If I knew my place and didn't come too close, she'd wink at me and say hello. That was a good feeling. Sometimes I'd follow her all the way home, and shovel the snow off her walk and try to make friends with her Momma and her aunts. I'd drop money on her stoop late at night on my way back from shining shoes in the taverns. And she had a Daddy, and he had a good job. He was a paper hanger.

I guess I would have gotten over Helene by summertime, but something happened in that classroom that made her face hang in front of me for the next twenty-two years. When I played the drums in high school it was for Helene and when I broke track records in college it was for Helene and when I started standing behind microphones and heard applause I wished Helene could hear it, too. It wasn't until I was twenty-nine years old and married and making money that I finally got her out of my system. Helene was sitting in that classroom when I learned to be ashamed of myself.

It was on a Thursday. I was sitting in the back of the room, in a seat with a chalk circle drawn around it. The idiot's seat, the troublemaker's seat.

The teacher thought I was stupid. Couldn't spell, couldn't read, couldn't do arithmetic. Just stupid. Teachers were never interested in finding out that you couldn't concentrate because you were so hungry, because you hadn't had any breakfast. All you could think about was noontime, would it ever come? Maybe you could sneak into the cloakroom and steal a bite of some kid's lunch out of a coat pocket. A bite of something. Paste. You can't really make a meal of paste, or put it on bread for a sandwich, but sometimes I'd scoop a few spoonfuls out of the paste jar in the back of the room. Pregnant people get strange tastes. I was pregnant with poverty. Pregnant with dirt and pregnant with smells that made people turn away, pregnant with cold and pregnant with shoes that were never bought for me, pregnant with five other people in my bed and no Daddy in the next room, and pregnant with hunger. Paste doesn't taste too bad when you're hungry.

The teacher thought I was a troublemaker. All she saw from the front of the room was a little black boy who squirmed in his idiot's seat and made noises and poked the kids around him. I guess she couldn't see a kid who made noises because he wanted someone to know he was there.

It was on a Thursday, the day before the Negro payday. The eagle always flew on Friday. The teacher was asking each student how much his father would give to the Community Chest.[1] On Friday night, each kid would get the money from his father, and on Monday he would bring it to the school. I decided I was going to buy me a Daddy right then. I had money in my pocket from shining shoes and selling papers, and whatever Helene Tucker pledged for her Daddy I was going to top it. And I'd hand the money right in. I wasn't going to wait until Monday to buy me a Daddy.

I was shaking, scared to death. The teacher opened her book and started calling out names alphabetically.

"Helene Tucker?"

"My Daddy said he'd give two dollars and fifty cents."

---

1. **Community Chest,** fund of money contributed voluntarily by people to support charity and welfare in their community.

"That's very nice, Helene. Very, very nice indeed."

That made me feel pretty good. It wouldn't take too much to top that. I had almost three dollars in dimes and quarters in my pocket. I stuck my hand in my pocket and held onto the money, waiting for her to call my name. But the teacher closed her book after she called everybody else in the class.

I stood up and raised my hand.

"What is it now?"

"You forgot me."

She turned toward the blackboard. "I don't have time to be playing with you, Richard."

"My Daddy said he'd . . ."

"Sit down, Richard, you're disturbing the class."

"My Daddy said he'd give . . . fifteen dollars."

She turned around and looked mad. "We are collecting this money for you and your kind, Richard Gregory. If your Daddy can give fifteen dollars you have no business being on relief."

"I got it right now, I got it right now, my Daddy gave it to me to turn in today, my Daddy said . . ."

"And furthermore," she said, looking right at me, her nostrils getting big and her lips getting thin and her eyes opening wide, "we know you don't have a Daddy."

Helene Tucker turned around, her eyes full of tears. She felt sorry for me. Then I couldn't see her too well because I was crying, too.

"Sit down, Richard."

And I always thought the teacher kind of liked me. She always picked me to wash the blackboard on Friday, after school.

That was a big thrill, it made me feel important. If I didn't wash it, come Monday the school might not function right.

"Where are you going, Richard?"

I walked out of school that day, and for a long time I didn't go back very often. There was shame there.

Now there was shame everywhere. It seemed like the whole world had been inside that classroom, everyone had heard what the teacher had said, everyone had turned around and felt sorry for me. There was shame in going to the Worthy Boys' Annual Christmas Dinner for you and your kind, because everybody knew what a worthy boy was. Why couldn't they just call it the Boys' Annual Dinner, why'd they have to give it a name? There was shame in wearing the brown and orange and white plaid mackinaw the welfare gave to three thousand boys. Why'd it have to be the same for everybody so when you walked down the street the people could see you were on relief? It was a nice warm mackinaw and it had a hood, and my Momma beat me and called me a little rat when she found out I stuffed it in the bottom of a pail full of garbage way over on Cottage Street. There was shame in running over to Mister Ben's at the end of the day and asking for his rotten peaches, there was shame in asking Mrs. Simmons for a spoonful of sugar, there was shame in running out to meet the relief truck. I hated that truck, full of food for you and your kind. I ran into the house and hid when it came. And then I started to sneak through alleys, to take the long way home so the people going into White's Eat Shop wouldn't see me. Yeah, the whole world heard the teacher that day, we all know you don't have a Daddy.

Discussion

1. (a) What reasons does Richard give for loving Helene Tucker? **(b)** What does Richard do in the hope of pleasing Helene?

2. (a) Describe Richard's behavior in school. **(b)** How does the teacher characterize Richard as a result of his behavior? **(c)** How does Richard explain his behavior to the reader?

3. It appears that Richard intended only to top Helene's father's pledge with his own earnings of nearly three dollars. What do you think causes Richard to come up with the clearly impossible pledge of fifteen dollars?

4. Richard says that after this incident at school, "there was shame everywhere." **(a)** What are three things that are shameful to Richard? **(b)** Which seems to have affected him most?

5. (a) Why do you think that Richard, in the years following this incident, considered his accomplishments to be "for Helene"? **(b)** When was Richard finally able to stop thinking about Helene? **(c)** In what ways must Richard's feelings about himself have changed?

Vocabulary
Word Origins

When you look up a word in a dictionary, you will often find, in addition to its definition, information about the word's origin—its *etymology* (et′ə mol′ə jē). Sometimes a word is based on a proper name. For example, *mackinaw,* the kind of woolen coat Richard throws away in the story, is named after Mackinaw City, a town in Michigan. During the 19th century, when Mackinaw City was a distribution center for supplies needed by trappers and Indians, the word *mackinaw* came to be applied to blankets and coats made of a certain kind of heavy wool.

Look up the etymologies of the following words in the Glossary. Explain from what proper name each word is derived:

1. leotard
2. sousaphone
3. frankfurter
4. malapropism
5. diesel

Dick Gregory 1932–

Though first known as a comedian, Dick Gregory has since won national attention as a writer, civil rights leader, and political activist. He frequently publicizes his concerns not only through his writing (he is author of more than a half-dozen books), but also by demonstrations and long-distance running. In his books and in performance, Gregory combines an urgent sense of social justice with a sharp sense of humor.

See **SYMBOL** Handbook of Literary Terms

Caged Bird

Maya Angelou

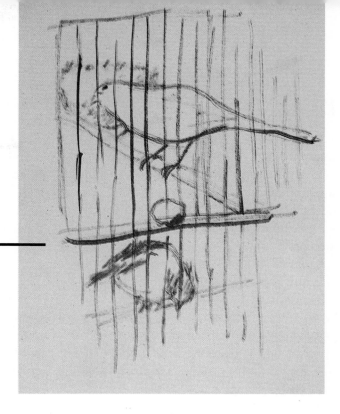

A free bird leaps
on the back of the wind
and floats downstream
till the current ends
5 and dips his wing
in the orange sun rays
and dares to claim the sky.

But a bird that stalks
down his narrow cage
10 can seldom see through
his bars of rage
his wings are clipped and
his feet are tied
so he opens his throat to sing.

15 The caged bird sings
with a fearful trill
of things unknown
but longed for still
and his tune is heard
20 on the distant hill
for the caged bird
sings of freedom.

The free bird thinks of another breeze
and the trade winds[1] soft through the sighing trees
25 and the fat worms waiting on a dawn-bright lawn
and he names the sky his own.

But a caged bird stands on the grave of dreams
his shadow shouts on a nightmare scream
his wings are clipped and his feet are tied
30 so he opens his throat to sing.

The caged bird sings
with a fearful trill
of things unknown
but longed for still
35 and his tune is heard
on the distant hill
for the caged bird
sings of freedom.

---

1. *trade winds,* winds that blow almost continually on a course toward the equator.

Discussion

1. What things are being contrasted in this poem?

2. **(a)** Describe the free bird's surroundings in stanzas 1 and 4. What is this bird doing? What is it thinking about? **(b)** Describe the caged bird's appearance in stanzas 2 and 5. What is this bird doing?

3. What is the speaker's explanation for why the caged bird sings?

4. In stanza 1, the free bird "leaps" and "dares." What other words suggesting human actions and emotions does the speaker use to describe both birds?

5. **(a)** Which two stanzas are the same? **(b)** What purpose is served by this repetition?

Application

Symbol

The birds in this poem look and act in many ways like typical birds: the free bird floats on the wind and dips a wing, and the caged bird has clipped wings and sings with a trill. There are suggestions, however, that the birds and their situations are symbolic of something beyond their obvious meaning—possibly of humans and their situations.

1. A bird with clipped wings could symbolize a person in what kind of situation?

2. A free bird daring "to claim the sky" might symbolize what kinds of human actions?

3. What circumstances could cause a person to feel "caged"? What do you think the cage symbolizes in this poem?

Maya Angelou 1928–

Maya Angelou was born in St. Louis and grew up in Arkansas and California. After studying music, dance, and drama, she became a professional actress and singer on stage and screen. Angelou is best known, however, for her writing of short stories, novels, plays, poetry, songs, and screenplays, including a ten-part series for television on African traditions in American life.

In the 1960s, Dr. Martin Luther King, Jr., asked Angelou to become the Northern Coordinator for the Southern Christian Leadership Conference. In 1975 she received the "Woman of the Year Award" in Communications from the *Ladies' Home Journal.*

Some of Angelou's best-known works are the autobiographical novels *I Know Why the Caged Bird Sings, Gather Together in My Name,* and *Heart of a Woman.*

from Homesick

Jean Fritz

She sang the song with her fingers crossed, but still she felt like a traitor. So one day she quit singing it.

In my father's study there was a large globe with all the countries of the world running around it. I could put my finger on the exact spot where I was and had been ever since I'd been born. And I was on the wrong side of the globe. I was in China in a city named Hankow,[1] a dot on a crooked line that seemed to break the country right in two. The line was really the Yangtse River,[2] but who would know by looking at a map what the Yangtse River really was?

Orange-brown, muddy mustard-colored. And wide, wide, wide. With a river smell that was old and came all the way up from the bottom. Sometimes old women knelt on the riverbank, begging the River God to return a son or grandson who may have drowned. They would wail and beat the earth to make the River God pay attention, but I knew how busy the River God must be. All those people on the Yangtse River!

---

1. *Hankow* (hän′kō′), a port in east China at the head of the ocean navigation on the Yangtse River.
2. *Yangtse* (yang′tsē) *River,* a river flowing from Tibet through China to the China Sea. It is the longest river in China. Also spelled *Yangtze.*

Men hauling water. Women washing clothes. Houseboats swarming with old people and young, chickens and pigs. Big crooked-sailed junks[3] with eyes painted on their prows so they could see where they were going. I loved the Yangtse River, but, of course, I belonged on the other side of the world. In America with my grandmother.

Twenty-five fluffy little yellow chicks hatched from our eggs today, my grandmother wrote.

I wrote my grandmother that I had watched a Chinese magician swallow three yards of fire.

The trouble with living on the wrong side of the world was that I didn't feel like a *real* American.

For instance. I could never be president of the United States. I didn't want to be president; I wanted to be a writer. Still, why should there be a *law* saying that only a person born in the United States could be president? It was as if I wouldn't be American enough.

Actually, I was American every minute of the day, especially during school hours. I went to a British school and every morning we sang "God Save the King." Of course the British children loved singing about their gracious king. Ian Forbes stuck out his chest and sang as if he were saving the king all by himself. Everyone sang. Even Gina Boss who was Italian. And Vera Sebastian who was so Russian she dressed the way Russian girls did long ago before the Revolution[4] when her family had to run away to keep from being killed.

But I wasn't Vera Sebastian. I asked my mother to write an excuse so I wouldn't have to sing, but she wouldn't do it. "When in Rome," she said, "do as the Romans do." What she meant was, "Don't make

trouble. Just sing." So for a long time I did. I sang with my fingers crossed but still I felt like a traitor.

Then one day I thought: If my mother and father were really and truly in Rome, they wouldn't do what the Romans did at all. They'd probably try to get the Romans to do what *they* did, just as they were trying to teach the Chinese to do what Americans did. (My mother even gave classes in American manners.)

So that day I quit singing. I kept my mouth locked tight against the king of England. Our teacher, Miss Williams, didn't notice at first. She stood in front of the room, using a ruler for a baton, striking each syllable so hard it was as if she were making up for the times she had nothing to strike.

"Make him vic-tor-i-ous," the class sang. It was on the strike of "vic" that Miss Williams noticed. Her eyes lighted on my mouth and when we sat down, she pointed her ruler at me.

"Is there something wrong with your voice today, Jean?" she asked.

"No, Miss Williams."

"You weren't singing."

"No, Miss Williams. It is not my national anthem."

"It is the national anthem we sing here," she snapped. "You have always sung. Even Vera sings it."

I looked at Vera with the big blue bow tied on the top of her head. Usually I felt sorry for her but not today. At recess I might even untie that bow, I thought. Just give it a yank. But if I'd been smart, I wouldn't have been looking at Vera. I

---

3. *junks* (jungks), Chinese sailing ships.
4. *Revolution,* the Russian Revolution, which overthrew the government of Nicholas II in 1917 and established what became the Communist government.

would have been looking at Ian Forbes and I would have known that, no matter what Miss Williams said, I wasn't through with the king of England.

Recess at the British School was nothing I looked forward to. Every day we played a game called prisoner's base, which was all running and shouting and shoving and catching. I hated the game, yet everyone played except Vera Sebastian. She sat on the sidelines under her blue bow like someone who had been dropped out of a history book. By recess I had forgotten my plans for that bow. While everyone was getting ready for the game, I was as usual trying to look as if I didn't care if I was the last one picked for a team or not. I was leaning against the high stone wall that ran around the schoolyard. I was looking up at a little white cloud skittering across the sky when all at once someone tramped down hard on my right foot. Ian Forbes. Snarling bulldog face. Heel grinding down on my toes. Head thrust forward the way an animal might before it strikes.

"You wouldn't sing it. So say it," he ordered. "Let me hear you say it."

I tried to pull my foot away but he only ground down harder.

"Say what?" I was telling my face please not to show what my foot felt.

"*God save the king.* Say it. Those four words. I want to hear you say it."

Although Ian Forbes was short, he was solid and tough and built for fighting. What was more, he always won. You had only to look at his bare knees between the top of his socks and his short pants to know that he would win. His knees were square. Bony and unbeatable. So of course it was crazy for me to argue with him.

"Why should I?" I asked. "Americans haven't said that since George the Third."[5]

He grabbed my right arm and twisted it behind my back.

"Say it," he hissed.

I felt the tears come to my eyes and I hated myself for the tears. I hated myself for not staying in Rome the way my mother had told me.

"I'll never say it," I whispered.

They were choosing sides now in the schoolyard and Ian's name was being called—among the first as always.

He gave my arm another twist. "You'll sing tomorrow," he snarled, "or you'll be sorry."

As he ran off, I slid to the ground, my head between my knees.

Oh, Grandma, I thought, why can't I be there with you? I'd feed the chickens for you. I'd pump water from the well, the way my father used to do.

It would be almost two years before we'd go to America. I was ten years old now; I'd be twelve then. But how could I think about *years*? I didn't even dare to think about the next day. After school I ran all the way home, fast so I couldn't think at all.

Our house stood behind a high stone wall which had chips of broken glass sticking up from the top to keep thieves away. I flung open the iron gate and threw myself through the front door.

"I'm home!" I yelled.

Then I remembered that it was Tuesday, the day my mother taught an English class at the Y.M.C.A. where my father was the director.

I stood in the hall, trying to catch my breath, and as always I began to feel small.

---

5. *George the Third,* king of England from 1760 to 1820. During his reign the American Revolution separated the U.S. from British rule.

It was a huge hall with ceilings so high it was as if they would have nothing to do with people. Certainly not with a mere child, not with me—the only child in the house. Once I asked my best friend, Andrea, if the hall made her feel little too. She said no. She was going to be a dancer and she loved space. She did a high kick to show how grand it was to have room.

Andrea Hull was a year older than I was and knew about everything sooner. She told me about commas, for instance, long before I took punctuation seriously. How could I write letters without commas? she asked. She made me so ashamed that for months I hung little wagging comma-tails all over the letters to my grandmother. She told me things that sounded so crazy I had to ask my mother if they were true.

I wished that Andrea were with me now, but she lived out in the country and I didn't see her often. Lin Nai-Nai, my amah,[6] was the only one around, and of course I knew she'd be there. It was her job to stay with me when my parents were out. As soon as she heard me come in, she'd called, "Tsai loushang,"[7] which meant that she was upstairs. She might be mending or ironing but most likely she'd be sitting by the window embroidering. And she was. She even had my embroidery laid out, for we had made a bargain. She would teach me to embroider if I would teach her English. I liked embroidering: the cloth stretched tight within my embroidery hoop while I filled in the stamped pattern with cross-stitches and lazy daisy flowers. The trouble was that lazy daisies needed French knots for their centers and I hated making French knots. Mine always fell apart, so I left them to the end. Today I had twenty lazy daisies waiting for their knots.

Lin Nai-Nai had already threaded my needle with embroidery floss.

"Black centers," she said, "for the yellow flowers."

I felt myself glowering. "American flowers don't have centers," I said and gave her back the needle.

Lin Nai-Nai looked at me, puzzled, but she did not argue. She was different from other amahs. She did not even come from the servant class, although this was a secret we had to keep from the other servants who would have made her life miserable, had they known. She had run away from her husband when he had taken a second wife. She would always have been Wife Number One and the Boss no matter how many wives he had, but she would rather be no wife than head of a string of wives. She was modern. She might look old-fashioned, for her feet had been bound up tight when she was a little girl so that they would stay small, and now, like many Chinese women, she walked around on little stumps stuffed into tiny cloth shoes. Lin Nai-Nai's were embroidered with butterflies. Still, she believed in true love and one wife for one husband. We were good friends, Lin Nai-Nai and I, so I didn't know why I felt so mean.

She shrugged. "English lesson?" she asked, smiling.

I tested my arm to see if it still hurt from the twisting. It did. My foot too. "What do you want to know?" I asked.

We had been through the polite phrases—Please, Thank you, I beg your pardon, Excuse me, You're welcome, Merry Christmas (which she had practiced but hadn't had a chance to use since this was only October).

---

6. *Lin Nai-Nai* (lin nī′nī′), *my amah* (ä′mə), maidservant.
7. *Tsai loushang* (tsī lō′shäng′).

"If I meet an American on the street," she asked, "how do I greet him?"

I looked her straight in the eye and nodded my head in a greeting. "Sewing machine," I said. "You say, 'Sew-ing machine.'"

She repeated after me, making the four syllables into four separate words. She got up and walked across the room, bowing and smiling. "Sew Ing Ma Shing." Part of me wanted to laugh at the thought of Lin Nai-Nai maybe meeting Dr. Carhart, our minister, whose face would surely puff up, the way it always did when he was flustered. But part of me didn't want to laugh at all. I didn't like it when my feelings got tangled, so I ran downstairs and played chopsticks on the piano. Loud and fast. When my sore arm hurt, I just beat on the keys harder.

Then I went out to the kitchen to see if Yang Sze-Fu,[8] the cook, would give me something to eat. I found him reading a Chinese newspaper, his eyes going up and down with the characters. (Chinese words don't march across flat surfaces the way ours do; they drop down cliffs, one cliff after another from right to left across a page.)

"Can I have a piece of cinnamon toast?" I asked. "And a cup of cocoa?"

Yang Sze-Fu grunted. He was smoking a cigarette, which he wasn't supposed to do in the kitchen, but Yang Sze-Fu mostly did what he wanted. He considered himself superior to common workers. You could tell because of the fingernails on his pinkies. They were at least two inches long, which was his way of showing that he didn't have to use his hands for rough or dirty work. He didn't seem to care that his fingernails were dirty, but maybe he couldn't keep such long nails clean.

He made my toast while his cigarette dangled out of the corner of his mouth, collecting a long ash that finally fell on the floor. He wouldn't have kept smoking if my mother had been there, although he didn't always pay attention to my mother. Never about butter pagodas, for instance. No matter how many times my mother told him before a dinner party, "No butter pagoda," it made no difference. As soon as everyone was seated, the serving boy, Wong Sze-Fu,[9] would bring in a pagoda and set it on the table. The guests would "oh" and "ah," for it was a masterpiece: a pagoda molded out of butter, curved roofs rising tier upon tier, but my mother could only think how unsanitary it was. For, of course, Yang Sze-Fu had molded the butter with his hands and carved the decorations with one of his long fingernails. Still, we always used the butter, for if my mother sent it back to the kitchen, Yang Sze-Fu would lose face[10] and quit.

When my toast and cocoa were ready, I took them upstairs to my room (the blue room) and while I ate, I began *Sara Crewe*[11] again. Now there was a girl, I thought, who was worth crying over. I wasn't going to think about myself. Or Ian Forbes. Or the next day. I wasn't. I wasn't.

And I didn't. Not all afternoon. Not all evening. Still, I must have decided what I was going to do because the next morning when I started for school and came to the corner where the man sold hot chestnuts, the corner where I always turned to go to school, I didn't turn. I walked straight ahead. I wasn't going to school that day.

I walked toward the Yangtse River. Past the store that sold paper pellets that opened

8. *Yang Sze-Fu* (yäng suʹfüʹ).
9. *Wong Sze-Fu* (wông suʹfüʹ).
10. *lose face,* lose dignity or self-respect.
11. *Sara Crewe,* published in 1888 by Frances Hodgson Burnett, a tale of neglected and misunderstood children who finally achieve happiness.

up into flowers when you dropped them in a glass of water. Then up the block where the beggars sat. I never saw anyone give money to a beggar. You couldn't, my father explained, or you'd be mobbed by beggars. They'd follow you everyplace; they'd never leave you alone. I had learned not to look at them when I passed and yet I saw. The running sores, the twisted legs, the mangled faces. What I couldn't get over was that, like me, each one of those beggars had only one life to live. It just happened that they had drawn rotten ones.

Oh, Grandma, I thought, we may be far apart but we're lucky, you and I. Do you even know how lucky? In America do you know?

This part of the city didn't actually belong to the Chinese, even though the beggars sat there, even though upper-class Chinese lived there. A long time ago other countries had just walked into China and divided up part of Hankow (and other cities) into sections, or concessions, which they called their own and used their own rules for governing. We lived in the French concession on Rue de Paris.[12] Then there was the British concession and the Japanese. The Russian and German concessions had been officially returned to China, but the people still called them concessions. The Americans didn't have one, although, like some of the other countries, they had gunboats on the river. In case, my father said. In case what? Just in case. That's all he'd say.

The concessions didn't look like the rest of China. The buildings were solemn and orderly with little plots of grass around them. Not like those in the Chinese part of the city: a jumble of rickety shops with people, vegetables, crates of quacking ducks, yard goods, bamboo baskets, and mangy dogs spilling onto a street so narrow it was hardly there.

The grandest street in Hankow was the Bund, which ran along beside the Yangtse River. When I came to it after passing the beggars, I looked to my left and saw the American flag flying over the American consulate building. I was proud of the flag and I thought maybe today it was proud of me. It flapped in the breeze as if it were saying ha-ha to the king of England.

Then I looked to the right at the Customs House, which stood at the other end of the Bund. The clock on top of the tower said nine-thirty. How would I spend the day?

I crossed the street to the promenade part of the Bund. When people walked here, they weren't usually going anyplace; they were just out for the air. My mother would wear her broad-brimmed beaver hat when we came and my father would swing his cane in that jaunty way that showed how glad he was to be a man. I thought I would just sit on a bench for the morning. I would watch the Customs House clock, and when it was time, I would eat the lunch I had brought along in my schoolbag.

I was the only one sitting on a bench. People did not generally "take the air" on a Wednesday morning and besides, not everyone was allowed here. The British had put a sign on the Bund, NO DOGS, NO CHINESE. This meant that I could never bring Lin Nai-Nai with me. My father couldn't even bring his best friend, Mr. T.K. Hu. Maybe the British wanted a place where they could pretend they weren't in China, I thought. Still, there were always Chinese workers around. In order to load and unload boats in the river, they had to

---

12. *Rue de Paris* (rʏ də pä rĕ′), Paris Street.

cross the Bund. All day they went back and forth, bent double under their loads, sweating and chanting in a tired, singsong way that seemed to get them from one step to the next.

To pass the time, I decided to recite poetry. The one good thing about Miss Williams was that she made us learn poems by heart and I liked that. There was one particular poem I didn't want to forget. I looked at the Yangtse River and pretended that all the busy people in the boats were my audience.

" 'Breathes there the man, with soul so dead,' " I cried, " 'Who never to himself hath said, This is my own, my native land!' "

I was so carried away by my performance that I didn't notice the policeman until he was right in front of me. Like all policemen in the British concession, he was a bushy-bearded Indian with a red turban wrapped around his head.

He pointed to my schoolbag. "Little miss," he said, "why aren't you in school?"

He was tall and mysterious-looking, more like a character in my Arabian Nights book[13] than a man you expected to talk to. I fumbled for an answer. "I'm going on an errand," I said finally. "I just sat down for a rest." I picked up my schoolbag and walked quickly away. When I looked around, he was back on his corner, directing traffic.

So now they were chasing children away too, I thought angrily. Well, I'd like to show them. Someday I'd like to walk a dog down the whole length of the Bund. A Great Dane. I'd have him on a leash—like this—(I put out my hand as if I were holding a leash right then) and he'd be so big and strong I'd have to strain to hold him back (I strained). I was so busy with my

Great Dane I was at the end of the Bund before I knew it. I let go of the leash, clapped my hands, and told my dog to go home. Then I left the Bund and the concessions and walked into the Chinese world.

My mother and father and I had walked here but not for many months. This part near the river was called the Mud Flats. Sometimes it was muddier than others, and when the river flooded, the flats disappeared under water. Sometimes even the fishermen's huts were washed away, knocked right off their long-legged stilts and swept down the river. But today the river was fairly low and the mud had dried so that it was cracked and cakey. Most of the men who lived here were out fishing, some not far from the shore, poling their sampans[14] through the shallow water. Only a few people were on the flats: a man cleaning fish on a flat rock at the water's edge, a woman spreading clothes on the dirt to dry, a few small children. But behind the huts was something I had never seen before. Even before I came close, I guessed what it was. Even then, I was excited by the strangeness of it.

It was the beginnings of a boat. The skeleton of a large junk, its ribs lying bare, its backbone running straight and true down the bottom. The outline of the prow was already in place, turning up wide and snubnosed, the way all junks did. I had never thought of boats starting from nothing, of taking on bones under their bodies. The eyes, I supposed, would be the last thing added. Then the junk would have life.

The builders were not there and I was

---

13. **Arabian Nights book,** a collection of ancient tales from Arabia, Persia, and India.
14. **sampans** (sam′panz), small boats used in China and throughout southeast Asia. A sampan is sculled by an oar at the stern and usually has a single sail and a cabin made of mats.

behind the huts where no one could see me as I walked around and around, marveling. Then I climbed inside and as I did, I knew that something wonderful was happening to me. I was a-tingle, the way a magician must feel when he swallows fire, because suddenly I knew that the boat was mine. No matter who really owned it, it was mine. Even if I never saw it again, it would be my junk sailing up and down the Yangtse River. My junk seeing the river sights with its two eyes, seeing them for me whether I was there or not. Often I had tried to put the Yangtse River into a poem so I could keep it. Sometimes I had tried to draw it, but nothing I did ever came close. But now, *now* I had my junk and somehow that gave me the river too.

I thought I should put my mark on the boat. Perhaps on the side of the spine. Very small. A secret between the boat and me. I opened my schoolbag and took out my folding penknife that I used for sharpening pencils. Very carefully I carved the Chinese character that was our name. Gau.[15] (In China my father was Mr. Gau, my mother was Mrs. Gau, and I was Little Miss Gau.) The builders would paint right over the character, I thought, and would never notice. But I would know. Always and forever I would know.

For a long time I dreamed about the boat, imagining it finished, its sails up, its eyes wide. Someday it might sail all the way down the Yangtse to Shanghai,[16] so I told the boat what it would see along the way because I had been there and the boat hadn't. After a while I got hungry and I ate my egg sandwich. I was in the midst of peeling an orange when all at once I had company.

A small boy, not more than four years old, wandered around to the back of the huts, saw me, and stopped still. He was wearing a ragged blue cotton jacket with a red cloth, pincushion-like charm around his neck which was supposed to keep him from getting smallpox. Sticking up straight from the middle of his head was a small pigtail which I knew was to fool the gods and make them think he was a girl. (Gods didn't bother much with girls; it was boys that were important in China.) He walked slowly up to the boat, stared at me, and then nodded as if he'd already guessed what I was. "Foreign devil," he announced gravely.

I shook my head. "No," I said in Chinese. "American friend." Through the ribs of the boat, I handed him a segment of orange. He ate it slowly, his eyes on the rest of the orange. Segment by segment, I gave it all to him. Then he wiped his hands down the front of his jacket.

"Foreign devil," he repeated.

"American friend," I corrected. Then I asked him about the boat. Who was building it? Where were the builders?

He pointed with his chin upriver. "Not here today. Back tomorrow."

I knew it would only be a question of time before the boy would run off to alert the people in the huts. "Foreign devil, foreign devil," he would cry. So I put my hand on the prow of the boat, wished it luck, and climbing out, I started back toward the Bund. To my surprise the boy walked beside me. When we came to the edge of the Bund, I squatted down so we would be on the same eye level.

"Good-bye," I said. "May the River God protect you."

For a moment the boy stared. When he

---

15. *Gau* (gou).
16. *Shanghai* (shang′hī′), a seaport in east China.

spoke, it was as if he were trying out a new sound. "American friend," he said slowly.

When I looked back, he was still there, looking soberly toward the foreign world to which I had gone.

The time, according to the Customs House clock, was five after two, which meant that I couldn't go home for two hours. School was dismissed at three-thirty and I was home by three-forty-five unless I had to stay in for talking in class. It took me about fifteen minutes to write "I will not talk in class" fifty times, and so I often came home at four o'clock. (I wrote up and down like the Chinese: fifty "I's," fifty "wills," and right through the sentence so I never had to think what I was writing. It wasn't as if I were making a promise.) To-day I planned to arrive home at four, my "staying-in" time, in the hope that I wouldn't meet classmates on the way.

Meanwhile I wandered up and down the streets, in and out of stores. I weighed my-self on the big scale in the Hankow Dispensary and found that I was as skinny as ever. I went to the Terminus Hotel and tried out the chairs in the lounge. At first I didn't mind wandering about like this. Half of my mind was still on the river with my junk, but as time went on, my junk began slipping away until I was alone with nothing but questions. Would my mother find out about today? How could I skip school tomorrow? And the next day and the next? Could I get sick? Was there a kind of long lie-abed sickness that didn't hurt?

I arrived home at four, just as I had planned, opened the door, and called out, "I'm home!" Cheery-like and normal. But I was scarely in the house before Lin Nai-Nai ran to me from one side of the hall and my mother from the other.

"Are you all right? Are you all right?"

Lin Nai-Nai felt my arms as if she expected them to be broken. My mother's face was white. "What happened?" she asked.

Then I looked through the open door into the living room and saw Miss Williams sitting there. She had beaten me home and asked about my absence, which of course had scared everyone. But now my mother could see that I was in one piece and for some reason this seemed to make her mad. She took me by the hand and led me into the living room. "Miss Williams said you weren't in school," she said. "Why was that?"

I hung my head, just the way cowards do in books.

My mother dropped my hand. "Jean will be in school tomorrow," she said firmly. She walked Miss Williams to the door. "Thank you for stopping by."

As soon as Miss Williams was gone and my mother was sitting down again, I burst into tears. Kneeling on the floor, I buried my head in her lap and poured out the whole miserable story. My mother could see that I really wasn't in one piece after all, so she listened quietly, stroking my hair as I talked, but gradually I could feel her stiffen. I knew she was remembering that she was a Mother.

"You better go up to your room," she said, "and think things over. We'll talk about it after supper."

I flung myself on my bed. What was there to think? Either I went to school and got beaten up. Or I quit.

After supper I explained to my mother and father how simple it was. I could stay at home and my mother could teach me, the way Andrea's mother taught her. Maybe I could even go to Andrea's house and study with her.

My mother shook her head. Yes, it was

simple, she agreed. I could go back to the British School, be sensible, and start singing about the king again.

I clutched the edge of the table. Couldn't she understand? I couldn't turn back now. It was too late.

So far my father had not said a word. He was leaning back, teetering on the two hind legs of his chair, the way he always did after a meal, the way that drove my mother crazy. But he was not the kind of person to keep all four legs of a chair on the floor just because someone wanted him to. He wasn't a turning-back person so I hoped maybe he would understand. As I watched him, I saw a twinkle start in his eyes and suddenly he brought his chair down slam-bang flat on the floor. He got up and motioned for us to follow him into the living room. He sat down at the piano and began to pick out the tune for "God Save the King."

A big help, I thought. Was he going to make me practice?

Then he began to sing:

"My country 'tis of thee,
Sweet land of liberty, . . ."

Of course! It was the same tune. Why hadn't I thought of that? Who would know what I was singing as long as I moved my lips? I joined in now, loud and strong.

"Of thee I sing."

My mother laughed in spite of herself. "If you sing that loud," she said, "you'll start a revolution."

"Tomorrow I'll sing softly," I promised. "No one will know." But for now I really let freedom ring.

Then all at once I wanted to see Lin Nai-Nai. I ran out back, through the courtyard that separated the house from the servants' quarters, and upstairs to her room.

"It's me," I called through the door and when she opened up, I threw my arms around her. "Oh, Lin Nai-Nai, I love you," I said. "You haven't said it yet, have you?"

"Said what?"

"Sewing machine. You haven't said it?"

"No," she said, "not yet. I'm still practicing."

"Don't say it, Lin Nai-Nai. Say 'Good day.' It's shorter and easier. Besides, it's more polite."

"Good day?" she repeated.

"Yes, that's right. Good day." I hugged her and ran back to the house.

The next day at school when we rose to sing the British national anthem, everyone stared at me, but as soon as I opened my mouth, the class lost interest. All but Ian Forbes. His eyes never left my face, but I sang softly, carefully, proudly. At recess he sauntered over to where I stood against the wall.

He spat on the ground. "You can be glad you sang today," he said. Then he strutted off as if he and those square knees of his had won again.

And, of course, I was glad.

Discussion

1. (a) What details about the setting help you imagine what the narrator sees and hears on the Yangtse River? (b) How does the narrator feel about the river?

2. (a) Why doesn't the narrator feel like "a *real* American"? (b) Why does she dislike singing "God Save the King" in school? (c) What does her mother advise her to do?

3. As the narrator is walking toward the

river (126a, 1), she thinks how lucky she and her grandmother are. What causes her to think this?

4. Describe the narrator's reactions to the following sights. Based on her reactions to these things, how would you characterize the narrator? **(a)** the American flag; **(b)** the sign, NO DOGS, NO CHINESE; **(c)** the traffic policeman; **(d)** the junk skeleton; **(e)** the small Chinese boy.

5. According to the narrator, what kind of person is her father?

6. (a) What does the narrator believe are her alternatives to attending the British school? **(b)** What other solution does her father come up with?

7. Why do you think the narrator decides to tell Lin Nai-Nai to say, "Good day"?

Vocabulary
Context, Dictionary

Often a dictionary entry has more than one definition for a word. When this happens, you must figure out which definition best fits the context of that word. Read the sentences of the story in which the following words appear. Then find each word in the Glossary and choose the definition that most clearly fits its context. Write that definition on your paper.

1. floss (124b, 1)
2. concession (126a, 2)
3. promenade (126b, 3)
4. flat (128b, 1)
5. character (129a, 1)

Composition

The narrator of "Homesick" mentions letters in which her grandmother describes farm life. What other things do you imagine that the narrator, having lived in China since she was born, would never have seen or experienced? Choose one thing that someone in another country would probably not have experienced, such as a Fourth of July parade, a Thanksgiving dinner, or a typical day at your school.

Write a letter describing one of these things to someone who has grown up in another country. Remember that the person to whom you are writing will have only your words to create a mental picture of what you describe. In addition to visual details, be sure to include appropriate sounds, smells, and/or tastes.

(You may find the article "Telling about an Event or an Experience" in the Composition Guide helpful in writing this composition.)

Jean Fritz 1915–

Jean Fritz is a distinguished author of books for young people, many of which deal with American history.

Fritz was born in Hankow, China; she based her book *Homesick: My Own Story,* from which this excerpt is taken, on childhood experiences in that country. The book was a Newbery Honor book and winner of the 1983 American Book Award for children's fiction.

Comment: Revolution in China

Jean Fritz lived in China from her birth in 1915 until she was twelve. These years for the United States were a time of enthusiasm, progress, and change. Women won the right to vote, Henry Ford produced the Model-T car, and Charles Lindbergh made the first solo flight across the Atlantic. Babe Ruth was hitting home runs, and Hollywood was coming out with "talkies"—films that had sound tracks. For China, these years were filled with changes of a different sort—changes involving the end of a form of government that had existed since ancient times.

For two thousand years, China was ruled by families, called dynasties, headed by an emperor or empress whose power was believed to have come from heaven. Most of the Chinese people were peasant farmers. Officials called mandarins controlled small areas by enforcing laws and collecting taxes. The Chinese called their country the "Central Kingdom" and considered all other countries uncivilized and inferior. A 1500-mile Great Wall discouraged northern invaders, while foreign trade ships, eager to obtain China's silks, teas, and porcelain, were allowed to dock at only one port.

In the 1800s Britain became increasingly impatient with China's trade restrictions, and war broke out. Britain's superior military easily won. With China's power weakened, other countries began demanding privileges. By the early 1900s thousands of British, French, Russians, Germans, and Americans were living and working in China. By the mid-1920s foreign countries controlled most Chinese industries.

In addition to growing resentful toward foreigners, many Chinese were becoming more and more dissatisfied with cruel and dishonest mandarins. In 1911 a revolution broke out in the Yangtse Valley, and the last dynasty was overthrown. The new republic was not strong. The appointed president was a military leader whose interests lay not in helping to form a democracy but in becoming emperor. When this man died in 1916, the country was in a state of confusion. Warlords—generals in charge of local districts—governed harshly while competing with each other for control of China. The few public services that had existed—roads, bridges, irrigation—collapsed. Many peasants fled to the cities where, in the concessions of foreign countries, they could find food and safety. This confusion continued for over a decade until a central government was established in 1927.

It was around this time that Jean and her family left China. Civil war was to continue until 1949, at which time the People's Republic of China was formed—the government that has remained until the present day.

Unit 2 Review: *Learning to Cope*

Content Review

1. **(a)** In what similar ways do the bird in "Fable for When There's No Way Out" and the "Caged Bird" cope with their frustration? **(b)** In what ways are their methods different? **(c)** How might the situations of both birds symbolize situations that humans sometimes experience?

2. Some people in this unit are characterized by their sensitivity to the situations of others. How do Cress Delahanty in "Cress to the Rescue" and Harriet Watkins in "My Delicate Heart Condition" illustrate this quality?

3. In "Homesick," the narrator solves her problem with the help of her father. What other characters in this unit deal with their problems through the help of others?

4. **(a)** Of all the characters in this unit, which do you think best learn to cope with a problem or predicament? Explain. **(b)** Which characters, if any, seem to be defeated by their problems?

Concept Review: Interpretation of New Material

Read carefully the short story below. Then use the questions that follow to review your understanding of the concepts and literary terms presented in this unit. If you wish, write your answers to the questions on a separate sheet of paper.

The Bracelet • *Yoshiko Uchida*

"Mama, is it time to go?"

I hadn't planned to cry, but the tears came suddenly, and I wiped them away with the back of my hand. I didn't want my older sister to see me crying.

"It's almost time, Ruri,"[1] my mother said gently. Her face was filled with a kind of sadness I had never seen before.

I looked around at my empty room. The clothes that Mama always told me to hang up in the closet, the junk piled on my dresser, the old rag doll I could never bear to part with; they were all gone. There was nothing left in my room, and there was noth-

ing left in the rest of the house. The rugs and furniture were gone, the pictures and drapes were down, and the closets and cupboards were empty. The house was like a gift box after the nice thing inside was gone; just a lot of nothingness.

It was almost time to leave our home, but we weren't moving to a nicer house or to a new town. It was April 21, 1942. The United

---

1. *Ruri* (rü rē).

"The Bracelet" by Yoshiko Uchida. Copyright © 1976 by Yoshiko Uchida. Reprinted by permission of the author.

Yoshiko Uchida (yōsh′kō ü chē dä).

States and Japan were at war, and every Japanese person on the West Coast was being evacuated by the government to a concentration camp. Mama, my sister Keiko,[2] and I were being sent from our home, and out of Berkeley, and eventually, out of California.

The doorbell rang, and I ran to answer it before my sister could. I thought maybe by some miracle, a messenger from the government might be standing there, tall and proper and buttoned into a uniform, come to tell us it was all a terrible mistake; that we wouldn't have to leave after all. Or maybe the messenger would have a telegram from Papa, who was interned in a prisoner-of-war camp in Montana because he had worked for a Japanese business firm.

The FBI had come to pick up Papa and hundreds of other Japanese community leaders on the very day that Japanese planes had bombed Pearl Harbor.[3] The government thought they were dangerous enemy aliens. If it weren't so sad, it would have been funny. Papa could no more be dangerous than the mayor of our city, and he was every bit as loyal to the United States. He had lived here since 1917.

When I opened the door, it wasn't a messenger from anywhere. It was my best friend, Laurie Madison, from next door. She was holding a package wrapped up like a birthday present, but she wasn't wearing her party dress, and her face drooped like a wilted tulip.

"Hi," she said. "I came to say goodbye."

She thrust the present at me and told me it was something to take to camp. "It's a bracelet," she said before I could open the package. "Put it on so you won't have to pack it." She knew I didn't have one inch of space left in my suitcase. We had been instructed to take only what we could carry into camp, and Mama had told us that we could each take only two suitcases.

"Then how are we ever going to pack the dishes and blankets and sheets they've told us to bring with us?" Keiko worried.

"I don't really know," Mama said, and she simply began packing those big impossible things into an enormous duffel bag— along with umbrellas, boots, a kettle, hot plate, and flashlight.

"Who's going to carry that huge sack?" I asked.

But Mama didn't worry about things like that. "Someone will help us," she said. "Don't worry." So I didn't.

Laurie wanted me to open her package and put on the bracelet before she left. It was a thin gold chain with a heart dangling on it. She helped me put it on, and I told her I'd never take it off, ever.

"Well, good-bye then," Laurie said awkwardly. "Come home soon."

"I will," I said, although I didn't know if I would ever get back to Berkeley again.

I watched Laurie go down the block, her long blond pigtails bouncing as she walked. I wondered who would be sitting in my desk at Lincoln Junior High now that I was gone. Laurie kept turning and waving, even walking backwards for a while, until she got to the corner. I didn't want to watch anymore, and I slammed the door shut.

The next time the doorbell rang, it was Mrs. Simpson, our other neighbor. She was going to drive us to the Congregational church, which was the Civil Control Station where all the Japanese of Berkeley were supposed to report.

It was time to go. "Come on, Ruri. Get your things," my sister called to me.

---

2. *Keiko* (kā kō).
3. *Pearl Harbor.* The Japanese attack on Pearl Harbor, a U.S. naval base in Hawaii, on December 7, 1941, was the immediate cause of American entry into World War II.

It was a warm day, but I put on a sweater and my coat so I wouldn't have to carry them, and I picked up my two suitcases. Each one had a tag with my name and our family number on it. Every Japanese family had to register and get a number. We were Family Number 13453.

Mama was taking one last look around our house. She was going from room to room, as though she were trying to take a mental picture of the house she had lived in for fifteen years, so she would never forget it.

I saw her take a long last look at the garden that Papa loved. The irises beside the fish pond were just beginning to bloom. If Papa had been home, he would have cut the first iris blossom and brought it inside to Mama. "This one is for you," he would have said. And Mama would have smiled and said, "Thank you, Papa San,"[4] and put it in her favorite cut-glass vase.

But the garden looked shabby and forsaken now that Papa was gone and Mama was too busy to take care of it. It looked the way I felt, sort of empty and lonely and abandoned.

When Mrs. Simpson took us to the Civil Control Station, I felt even worse. I was scared, and for a minute I thought I was going to lose my breakfast right in front of everybody. There must have been over a thousand Japanese people gathered at the church. Some were old and some were young. Some were talking and laughing, and some were crying. I guess everybody else was scared too. No one knew exactly what was going to happen to us. We just knew we were being taken to the Tanforan Racetracks, which the army had turned into a camp for the Japanese. There were fourteen other camps like ours along the West Coast.

What scared me the most were the soldiers standing at the doorway of the church hall. They were carrying guns with mounted bayonets. I wondered if they thought we would try to run away, and whether they'd shoot us or come after us with their bayonets if we did.

A long line of buses waited to take us to camp. There were trucks, too, for our baggage. And Mama was right; some men were there to help us load our duffel bag. When it was time to board the buses, I sat with Keiko and Mama sat behind us. The bus went down Grove Street and passed the small Japanese food store where Mama used to order her bean-curd cakes and pickled radish. The windows were all boarded up, but there was a sign still hanging on the door that read, "We are loyal Americans."

The crazy thing about the whole evacuation was that we were all loyal Americans. Most of us were citizens because we had been born here. But our parents, who had come from Japan, couldn't become citizens because there was a law that prevented any Asian from becoming a citizen. Now everybody with a Japanese face was being shipped off to concentration camps.

"It's stupid," Keiko muttered as we saw the racetrack looming up beside the highway. "If there were any Japanese spies around, they'd have gone back to Japan long ago."

"I'll say," I agreed. My sister was in high school and she ought to know, I thought.

When the bus turned into Tanforan, there were more armed guards at the gate, and I saw barbed wire strung around the entire grounds. I felt as though I were going into a prison, but I hadn't done anything wrong.

We streamed off the buses and poured

---

4. **Papa San** (pä pä sän). *San* is often added to the names of both men and women as a polite form of address.

into a huge room, where doctors looked down our throats and peeled back our eyelids to see if we had any diseases. Then we were given our housing assignments. The man in charge gave Mama a slip of paper. We were in Barrack 16, Apartment 40.

"Mama!" I said. "We're going to live in an apartment!" The only apartment I had ever seen was the one my piano teacher lived in. It was in an enormous building in San Francisco with an elevator and thick carpeted hallways. I thought how wonderful it would be to have our own elevator. A house was all right, but an apartment seemed elegant and special.

We walked down the racetrack looking for Barrack 16. Mr. Noma, a friend of Papa's,

helped us carry our bags. I was so busy looking around, I slipped and almost fell on the muddy track. Army barracks had been built everywhere, all around the racetrack and even in the center oval.

Mr. Noma pointed beyond the track toward the horse stables. "I think your barrack is out there."

He was right. We came to a long stable that had once housed the horses of Tanforan, and we climbed up the wide ramp. Each stall had a number painted on it, and when we got to 40, Mr. Noma pushed open the door.

"Well, here it is," he said, "Apartment 40."

The stall was narrow and empty and

dark. There were two small windows on each side of the door. Three folded army cots were on the dust-covered floor and one light bulb dangled from the ceiling. That was all. This was our apartment, and it still smelled of horses.

Mama looked at my sister and then at me. "It won't be so bad when we fix it up," she began. "I'll ask Mrs. Simpson to send me some material for curtains. I could make some cushions too, and . . . well . . . ." She stopped. She couldn't think of anything more to say.

Mr. Noma said he'd go get some mattresses for us. "I'd better hurry before they're all gone." He rushed off. I think he wanted to leave so that he wouldn't have to see Mama cry. But he needn't have run off, because Mama didn't cry. She just went out to borrow a broom and began sweeping out the dust and dirt. "Will you girls set up the cots?" she asked.

It was only after we'd put up the last cot that I noticed my bracelet was gone. "I've lost Laurie's bracelet!" I screamed. "My bracelet's gone!"

We looked all over the stall and even down the ramp. I wanted to run back down the track and go over every inch of ground we'd walked on, but it was getting dark and Mama wouldn't let me.

I thought of what I'd promised Laurie. I wasn't ever going to take the bracelet off, not even when I went to take a shower. And now I had lost it on my very first day in camp. I wanted to cry.

I kept looking for it all the time we were in Tanforan. I didn't stop looking until the day we were sent to another camp, called Topaz, in the middle of a desert in Utah. And then I gave up.

But Mama told me never mind. She said I didn't need a bracelet to remember Laurie, just as I didn't need anything to remember Papa or our home in Berkeley or all the people and things we loved and had left behind.

"Those are things we can carry in our hearts and take with us no matter where we are sent," she said.

And I guess she was right. I've never forgotten Laurie, even now.

---

1. The overall feeling in the first three paragraphs of the story is one of (a) fear; (b) anger; (c) sadness; (d) jealousy.

2. Ruri is moving because her family (a) has found a nicer home; (b) has lost touch with their father; (c) is being sent to a concentration camp; (d) wants to escape bombings by the Japanese.

3. Ruri's father is picked up by the FBI (a) on the day the Japanese bomb Pearl Harbor; (b) while he is working in the garden; (c) after World War II has ended; (d) on the same day his family leaves for the camp.

4. Leaders of the Japanese community on the West Coast are considered to be (a) dangerous enemy aliens; (b) loyal Americans; (c) possible candidates for political office; (d) good army recruits.

5. What type of charm is on the bracelet Laurie gives to Ruri?

6. Based on what she says and does, Laurie can be characterized as (a) bitter; (b) immature; (c) hopeful; (d) humorous.

7. To Ruri the bracelet symbolizes (a) her link to her grandparents in Japan; (b) her friendship with Laurie; (c) the bright future;

(d) a token of respect from her classmates.

8. Noticing how shabby her father's garden looks makes Ruri feel **(a)** angry and rebellious; **(b)** anxious that her father will blame her for not taking better care of it; **(c)** happy to be leaving it behind; **(d)** abandoned and lonely.

9. Does Ruri have a stereotyped idea of what apartments look like? Explain.

10. When Ruri loses the bracelet, her mother is **(a)** furious; **(b)** optimistic that they will find it; **(c)** reassuring that the bracelet is not necessary to remind her of her friend; **(d)** filled with despair.

Composition Review

Choose any one of the following assignments to write about. Unless you are told otherwise, assume you are writing for your classmates.

1. The characters of people are revealed by what they do, by what they say, and by what is said about them. Choose one of the characters in this unit or someone you know personally. On a separate paper, head three columns *actions, speech,* and *reactions of others.* Write details you know about your character under the headings that tell how you learned them.

Write three brief paragraphs in which you describe this person. From each column, choose those details that you think characterize the person most effectively. In each of your three paragraphs, include the details you have chosen from one column.

2. Both Richard in "Not Poor, Just Broke" and Ruri in "The Bracelet" have strong memories of someone they knew in their childhoods. How does Helene affect Richard both when he is a child and later on in his life? How do you think Laurie has affected Ruri so that Ruri has never forgotten her?

In one paragraph, compare and contrast the feelings Richard and Ruri have, as young people, for Helene and Laurie. In a second paragraph, compare and contrast the effects Helene and Laurie have on them as adults.

3. Most daily newspapers include articles about people whose lives seem interesting in some way. Look through a current issue of your newspaper to find one such article.

In no more than one page, tell why you think this particular person was chosen as the subject of a human–interest article. Tell whether or not you think this person deserves the special attention, and why.

unit 3

A poem can be many things, said many ways. It can touch softly, or it can beat like a fist against the ear. It can be about everything from running a race to helping someone on a bus, from sighting monsters to feeding pigeons. A poem can laugh, cry, sing, rage.

Poetry

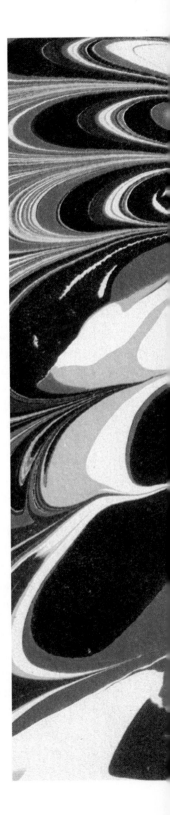

1

Stories

Poems can tell stories that are comic, mysterious, or just simply human.

The Story-Teller

Mark Van Doren

He talked, and as he talked
Wallpaper came alive;
Suddenly ghosts walked,
And four doors were five;

5 Calendars ran backward,
And maps had mouths;
Ships went tackward
In a great drowse;

Trains climbed trees,
10 And soon dripped down
Like honey of bees
On the cold brick town.

He had wakened a worm
In the world's brain,
15 And nothing stood firm
Until day again.

Discussion

1. (a) What happens when the story-teller talks? **(b)** What kinds of stories does he seem to be telling?

2. How does the speaker react to the story-teller? How can you tell?

3. To describe the effect the story-teller has on others, the speaker uses the figurative comparison of wakening "a worm in the world's brain." What is meant by this?

S*ea Monster*

W. S. Merwin

We were not even out of sight of land
That afternoon when we saw it. A good day
With the sea making[1] but still light. Not
One of us would have hesitated
5 As to where we were, or mistaken the brown
Cliffs or the town on top. Just after

(Continued)

---

1. *making,* beginning to become rough.

W. S. Merwin, "Sea Monster," in *The Drunk in the Furnace.*
Copyright © 1960 by W. S. Merwin. Reprinted with the
permission of David Higham Associates, Ltd. and Atheneum
Publishers from *The First Four Books of Poems.* Copyright ©
1975 by W. S. Merwin.

The noon watch, it was, that it slid
Into our sight: a darkness under
The surface, between us and the land, twisting
10 Like a snake swimming or a line of birds
In the air. Then breached, big as a church,
Right there beside us. None of us will
Agree what it was we saw then, but
None of us showed the least surprise, and truly
15 I felt none. I would say its eyes
Were like the sea when the thick snow falls
Onto it with a whisper and slides heaving
On the gray water. And looked at us
For a long time, as though it knew us, but
20 Did not harm us that time, sinking at last,
The waters closing like a rush of breath. Then
We were all ashamed at what we had seen,
Said it was only a sea-trick or
A dream we had all had together. As it
25 May have been, for since then we have forgotten
How it was that, on sea or land, once
We proved to ourselves that we were awake.

Discussion

1. (a) When and where do the people see the sea monster? (b) Does this setting—both time and place—seem important to the speaker? Why?

2. What similes are used to describe the following? Explain whether each seems appropriate: (a) the sea monster's way of swimming (lines 9–11); (b) its size (line 11); (c) its eyes (lines 15–18); (d) the way the waters close over it (line 21).

3. (a) How does the speaker interpret the look in the monster's eyes (lines 15–19)? (b) Why do you think the speaker describes the monster's eyes rather than some other feature?

4. (a) Why do you suppose that the people are "all ashamed" at what they see? (b) Why do they say it is "only a sea-trick or/A dream"? (c) Do you think they would have reacted differently if the visibility were poor? Explain.

*T*he Walrus and the Carpenter

Lewis Carroll

The sun was shining on the sea,
  Shining with all his might:
He did his very best to make
  The billows smooth and bright—
5 And this was odd, because it was
  The middle of the night.

The moon was shining sulkily,
  Because she thought the sun
Had got no business to be there
10   After the day was done—
"It's very rude of him," she said,
  "To come and spoil the fun!"

The sea was wet as wet could be,
  The sands were dry as dry.
15 You could not see a cloud, because
  No cloud was in the sky:
No birds were flying overhead—
  There were no birds to fly.

The Walrus and the Carpenter
20   Were walking close at hand;
They wept like anything to see
  Such quantities of sand:
"If this were only cleared away,"
  They said, "it would be grand!"

25 "If seven maids with seven mops
  Swept it for half a year,
Do you suppose," the Walrus said,
  "That they could get it clear?"
"I doubt it," said the Carpenter,
30   And shed a bitter tear.

"Oysters, come and walk with us!"
  The Walrus did beseech.
"A pleasant walk, a pleasant talk,
  Along the briny beach;
35 We cannot do with more than four,
  To give a hand to each."

The eldest Oyster looked at him,
  But never a word he said:
The eldest Oyster winked his eye,
40   And shook his heavy head—
Meaning to say he did not choose
  To leave the oyster-bed.[1]

(Continued)

---

1. *oyster-bed,* place such as a rock where many oysters attach themselves to live.

"The Walrus and the Carpenter" by Lewis Carroll from *Through the Looking-Glass* (Altemus, 1871).

But four young Oysters hurried up,
    All eager for the treat:
45 Their coats were brushed, their faces
      washed,
    Their shoes were clean and neat—
And this was odd, because, you know,
    They hadn't any feet.

Four other Oysters followed them,
50   And yet another four;
And thick and fast they came at last,
    And more, and more, and more—
All hopping through the frothy waves,
    And scrambling to the shore.

55 The Walrus and the Carpenter
    Walked on a mile or so,
And then they rested on a rock
    Conveniently low:
And all the little Oysters stood
60   And waited in a row.

"The time has come," the Walrus said,
    "To talk of many things;
Of shoes—and ships—and sealing-wax—[2]
    Of cabbages—and kings—
65 And why the sea is boiling hot—
    And whether pigs have wings."

"But wait a bit," the Oysters cried,
    "Before we have our chat;
For some of us are out of breath,
70   And all of us are fat!"
"No hurry!" said the Carpenter.
    They thanked him much for that.

"A loaf of bread," the Walrus said,
    "Is what we chiefly need:
75 Pepper and vinegar besides
    Are very good indeed—
Now if you're ready, Oysters dear,
    We can begin to feed."

"But not on us!" the Oysters cried,
80   Turning a little blue.[3]
"After such kindness, that would be
    A dismal thing to do!"
"The night is fine," the Walrus said,
    "Do you admire the view?

85 "It was so kind of you to come!
    And you are very nice!"
The Carpenter said nothing but
    "Cut us another slice:
I wish you were not quite so deaf—
90   I've had to ask you twice!"

"It seems a shame," the Walrus said,
    "To play them such a trick,
After we've brought them out so far,
    And made them trot so quick!"
95 The Carpenter said nothing but
    "The butter's spread too thick!"

"I weep for you," the Walrus said:
    "I deeply sympathize."
With sobs and tears he sorted out
100   Those of the largest size,
Holding his pocket-handkerchief
    Before his streaming eyes.

"O Oysters," said the Carpenter,
    "You've had a pleasant run!
105 Shall we be trotting home again?"
    But answer came there none—
And this was scarcely odd, because
    They'd eaten every one.

---

2. *sealing-wax,* a wax which is melted for use as a seal on letters, packages, etc. Often a design is made in the still-soft wax with a special stamp called a seal.
3. *blue,* a pun on *blue* meaning "sad" or—when referring to seafood—"spoiled."

Discussion

1. What hints are there in stanzas one and two that the poem is not to be taken seriously?

2. **(a)** How do the Walrus and Carpenter persuade the young Oysters to come with them? **(b)** What characteristics of the eldest Oyster make him seem like a wise old man? **(c)** What characteristics of the young Oysters make them seem like eager children?

3. "The time has come," the Walrus says in lines 61–62, "To talk of many things." What subjects does he then mention? Are these subjects likely to promote serious discussion? Explain.

4. Why do the Walrus and Carpenter call for bread and butter, pepper and vinegar?

5. **(a)** What situations in lines 1–6 and lines 46–48 does the speaker refer to as "odd"? **(b)** What occurs in lines 106–108 that is *not* ("scarcely") odd?

Application
Rhyme

Poets sometimes use rhyme to create effects in their poetry that can be anything from comic to serious.

1. Chart the rhyme scheme of the first stanza (lines 1–6). Is the same rhyme scheme used consistently throughout the other stanzas?

2. Where in the poem do internal rhymes occur? Are they used consistently throughout the poem?

3. Do the rhymes and the rhyme scheme in this poem have the effect of creating suspense, humor, sadness—or what?

Who has the harder job—a husband or a wife?
This old folk song from Missouri offers one answer.

Father Grumble

Anonymous

There was an old man lived under the hill,
As you may plainly see, see.
He said he could do more work in a day
Than his wife could do in three, three,
5 He said he could do more work in a day
Than his wife could do in three.

"Be it so, then," the old lady replied,
"But this you must allow,
That you go work in the house today
10 And I'll go follow the plow.

"But you must milk the Teeny cow,
For fear that she goes dry.
And you must feed the little pigs
That live in yonder sty.

15 "You must watch the speckled hen
For fear she lays away.
And you must wind the hank of yarn
Your wife spun yesterday.

"You must go to the dining-room
20 And scour up all the plates;
And don't forget the curly dog,
Or he'll eat all of the cakes.

"You must wash the dirty clothes
That hang upon the wall;
25 But don't forget the crooked stairs
Or you'll get an awful fall.

"Father Grumble" as printed in *Ballads and Songs Collected by the Missouri Folk-Lore Society*, edited by H. M. Belden (University of Missouri Studies, vol. 15), Columbia, 1940.

"You must churn the crock of cream
That stands upon the frame;
But don't forget the fat in the pot
30 Or 'twill all go up in a flame."

So the old woman she took the whip in her hand
To go and follow the plow,
And the old man he took the pail on his arm
To go and milk the cow.

35 But Teeny she hooked, and Teeny she crooked,
And Teeny turned up her nose;
And then she gave the old man such a kick
That the blood ran down to his toes.

He went to watch the speckled hen
40 For fear she'd lay away;
But he forgot to wind the yarn
His wife spun yesterday.   *(Continued)*

He then went to the dining-room
To scour up all the plates;
45 But he forgot the curly dog,
And he ate all of the cakes.

He went to wash the dirty clothes
That hung upon the wall;
But he forgot the crooked stairs,
50 And he got an awful fall.

He went to churn the crock of cream
That stood upon the frame;
But he forgot the fat in the pot,
And it all went up in a flame.

55 That night he swore by the light of the moon
And all the stars in heaven
His wife could do more work in a day
Than he could do in seven.

Discussion

1. What agreement do the old man and his wife make? Why do they make it?

2. (a) What things go wrong when the old man tries to do the housework? Why do these things happen? **(b)** What does the old man finally admit?

3. Is the song meant to entertain, to teach a moral, or both? Give reasons for your answer.

4. This story has been told and retold in many different versions for centuries. In your opinion, would the story have any special meaning if it were retold today in a modern setting? Explain. (The Comment on page 151 may help you answer this question.)

Composition

Were you ever in the position of having to "put up or shut up"? That is, did you ever have to try to prove an idle boast or exaggerated claim of some sort, as the old man who claims he can do three times as much work as his wife? Were your results comic or disastrous?

In no more than one page, describe the boast that you made and how you tried to fulfill it. Tell what things went wrong or what things went right. At the end, did you have to change your claim as the old man does—or could you stick to it?

(You may find the article "Telling about an Event or an Experience" in the Composition Guide helpful.)

Comment: Trading Places

Women have always done whatever jobs they had to do on the farm and in the community, and men have always done whatever jobs they had to do in the home. But there has existed for centuries a tradition that work can be divided into "women's work" and "men's work," and that people ought to stick to the work that suits them. From this tradition have come many stories and poems in which women and men "trade places." These works are usually comic, ending with the men in all kinds of trouble, as in "Father Grumble."

The Missouri folk song printed here is just one of many versions of this tale, going back to the Scottish ballad "John Grumlie," first published in 1825. The basic story is undoubtedly much older than that, however; another Scottish ballad on the same theme entitled "The Wife of Auchtermuchty"[1] dates from the sixteenth century or earlier.

Similar stories appear in the folk literature of many countries. In a Norwegian version, the husband who is keeping house remembers too late that he hasn't taken the cow out to pasture, and so to save time he decides to let the cow eat the grass that grows on the roof of their sod-thatched[2] farmhouse. He is able to get the cow onto the roof by bridging a plank across from a nearby hill, but then he worries that the cow might fall off. So he ties a rope around the cow's neck, runs the rope down the chimney and out the fireplace, and ties the other end to his own leg. When the cow does fall off the roof, the husband is dragged by the rope up the chimney, and when his wife finally comes home from working in the fields she finds her husband hanging upside down with his head in the cooking pot!

Today, with more women holding full-time jobs outside the home and more men doing some or all of the housework, one might wonder why any job was ever thought to "belong" to one group of people. But the stories based on this theme always deal with stereotypes instead of realistic characters, and the jobs are stereotyped, as well.

There may even be a moral of sorts concealed in the name of the character. For in all versions it is "Father Grumble" who grumbles first about his wife having an easier job. His grumbling is stopped only when he tries the job and fails at it. (For some reason, the women in these stories all seem to manage better at doing "men's work" than vice versa.) Perhaps, in the end, the message of this story is not so much that some people have easier jobs, but that all people should respect the jobs done by others.

---

1. *Auchtermuchty* (ôн′tər mùн′tē).
2. *sod-thatched,* having the roof thatched, or covered, with sod, a layer of grass and its roots.

How Tuesday Began

Kathleen Fraser

Don't let me lose you,
lady. We're jogging up
First Avenue in the sun,
nursing morning with
5 our habits.
I must have boarded before
you, where the bus stops
and the dusty nightgowns
beckon from Orchard St.
10 I must have pulled out
my book, peeled off my gloves,
and settled among the fumes
for a poem or two,
my habit.
15 I didn't see you,
black, filling the aisle
with your green housedress,
lowering each part of you
gently, in front of me,
20 maybe heaving a sigh, your
sorrow and habit.

Still, my eyes pulled
sideways. Someone old
moved without moving,
25 veins, vague eyes resisting
the aisle in front
of her, a journey
to be mastered upright,
seat by seat.
30 We rolled with the bus,
easy as rubber lifeboats
on troubled water.
But she hung to the same
space, sensing the movement
35 around her, sinking
in her own flesh.
Then you reached out, lady,
and pulled her in
beside you.
40 You were fading
and full of troubles, lady,
and you saw her drowning
and you reached out
and said, "I don't see
45 so good myself."

Discussion

1. What is the setting—both time and place—of this poem?

2. (a) What is the speaker's "habit" (line 14)? **(b)** How is the black woman described (lines 15–21)?

3. (a) Describe the progress of the old woman on the bus (lines 23–36). **(b)** What figurative language does the speaker use to describe the movements of the other passengers (lines 30–32)? **(c)** What does the black woman do?

4. (a) Has the action of the black woman affected the speaker in any particular way? How can you tell? **(b)** Do you think "How Tuesday Began" is an effective title for this poem? Why or why not?

Kathleen Fraser 1937–

Author of several books of poetry for both children and adults, Kathleen Fraser has also taught poetry and creative writing in New York, at the University of Iowa, and in San Francisco, where she now lives, married to another poet.

Dog at Night

Louis Untermeyer

At first he stirs uneasily in sleep
And, since the moon does not run off, unfolds
Protesting paws. Grumbling that he must keep
Both eyes awake, he whimpers; then he scolds
5 And, rising to his feet, demands to know
The stranger's business. You who break the dark
With insolent light, who are you? Where do you go?
But nothing answers his indignant bark.

The moon ignores him, walking on as though
10 Dogs never were. Stiffened to fury now,
His small hairs stand upright, his howls come fast,
And terrible to hear is the bow-wow
That tears the night. Stirred by this bugle-blast,
The farmer's hound grows active; without pause
15 Summons her mastiff and the cur that lies
Three fields away to rally to the cause.
And the next county wakes. And miles beyond
Throats ring themselves and brassy lungs respond
With threats, entreaties, bellowings and cries,
20 Chasing the white intruder down the skies.

Discussion

1. (a) What disturbs the dog? **(b)** Why doesn't he go back to sleep? **(c)** What makes the dog so furious?

2. (a) How is the moon described as if it were a person? **(b)** How is the dog described as if he were a person?

3. Find words that suggest the different noises made by the various dogs. How do these noises change from the beginning to the end of the poem?

4. Chart the rhyme scheme of "Dog at Night."

Vocabulary
Affixes, Dictionary

One way to find a root word is to remove what you think are prefixes or suf-

fixes and see what is left. This doesn't always work, however. For example, *in-* can sometimes be a prefix, as it is in *insane.* But if you remove *in-* from *insolent,* you do not get an English root. For words like these, you may need to use the dictionary.

Some of the following words are made up of an English root plus affixes. For these words, separate the parts with plus signs; then write a definition, like this: *in + sane,* "not sane; crazy." For any word that does not have an English root, copy it whole; then look it up in the Glossary and write the definition after it, like this: *insolent,* "boldly rude; insulting."

1. uneasily
2. indignant
3. active
4. entreaty
5. intruder

Events

Poems can stop time, so that exciting or special moments
can be examined more closely.

The Sprinters

Lillian Morrison

The gun explodes them.
Pummeling, pistoning they fly
In time's face.
A go at the limit,
5 A terrible try
To smash the ticking glass,
Outpace the beat
That runs, that streaks away
Tireless, and faster than they.

10 Beside ourselves
(It is for us they run!)

We shout and pound the stands
For one to win,
Loving him, whose hard
15 Grace-driven stride
Most mocks the clock
And almost breaks the bands
Which lock us in.

Discussion

1. **(a)** What is described in this poem? **(b)** Explain the meaning of the first line.

2. **(a)** What is the "ticking glass" (line 6)? **(b)** Who or what else are the sprinters competing against in lines 7–9?

3. **(a)** In what sense do the sprinters run "for us" (line 11)? **(b)** What are "the bands" mentioned in lines 17–18? **(c)** Does it seem possible that these bands will eventually be broken? Support your answer with words or lines from the poem. **(d)** What do you think would happen if a runner—or anyone else—succeeded in breaking those bands?

See **METAPHOR** Handbook of Literary Terms

Sky Diver

Adrien Stoutenburg

Grotesque, jumping out
like a clothed frog, helmet and glasses,
arms and legs wading the sky,
feet flapping before the cloth flower opens;
5 then suspended, poised,
an exclamation point upside-down,
and going down, swaying over corn and creeks
and highways scribbled
over the bones of fish and eagles.

10 There is the interim between air and earth,
time to study steeples
and the underwings of birds going over,
before the unseen chasm,
the sudden jaw open and hissing.

15 Lying here after the last jump
I see how fanatic roots are,
how moles breathe through darkness,
how deep the earth can be.

"Sky Diver" from *Short History of the Fur Trade* by Adrien
Stoutenburg. Copyright © 1968 by Adrien Stoutenburg.
Reprinted by permission of Houghton Mifflin Company and
Curtis Brown, Ltd.

Discussion

1. What is a sky diver? Describe the sport of sky diving.

2. **(a)** What is actually happening to the sky diver in lines 10–12? **(b)** Describe what emotions the sky diver seems to be experiencing in stanzas 1 and 2 (lines 1–14). Do these emotions change from line to line? Explain.

3. **(a)** Where is the sky diver in line 15? **(b)** In what ways are the details in lines 16–18 different from those in the rest of the poem? Why might this be so?

Application
Metaphor

Figurative language such as metaphors can help a reader imagine more vividly what is going on. When you think of the slow, deliberate motions of someone wading through deep water, for example, you can better visualize the metaphor of the sky diver "wading the sky."

1. What metaphors are used to describe the sky diver and equipment in lines 4 and 6?

2. What is suggested by the "sudden jaw open and hissing" in line 14?

3. Is the "clothed frog" in line 2 part of a metaphor? Explain.

Vocabulary
Pronunciation Key

For each numbered word, use your Glossary to figure out the pronunciation. Then choose, from the words that follow, the one that rhymes with the numbered word *or with its accented syllable* and write the letter of your choice on your paper.

1. grotesque: **(a)** low; **(b)** mess; **(c)** desk; **(d)** due.

2. poise: **(a)** is; **(b)** ice; **(c)** boys; **(d)** eyes.

3. interim: **(a)** win; **(b)** flint; **(c)** share; **(d)** him.

4. chasm: **(a)** daze; **(b)** has; **(c)** pass; **(d)** them.

5. fanatic: **(a)** ran; **(b)** rain; **(c)** fat; **(d)** sick.

Adrien Stoutenburg 1916–

Adrien Stoutenburg was born in Minnesota, has lived in Mexico and California, and now lives in New Mexico. A prolific author of both prose and poetry, she has also written under such pen names as Lace Kendall and Nelson Minier. Many of her books for juvenile readers, such as *Walk into the Wind,* are exciting adventure stories. Her poetry collection *Short History of the Fur Trade,* from which "Sky Diver" is taken, won the Commonwealth Club of California Silver Medal in 1969. Six record albums have been issued of stories from her books *American Tall Tale Animals* and *American Tall Tales.*

Jukebox Showdown

Victor Hernández Cruz

Two men got into a fight with a jukebox
The air was night and warm
Splattered all over the avenue
Was screws and bolts
5 Broken 45's all over the place
The police came and arrested all three
The police asked the jukebox questions
Then dropped quarters in

Originally entitled "Side 15" by Victor Hernández Cruz.
Copyright © 1976 by Victor Hernández Cruz. Reprinted by
permission.

Victor Hernández (er nän′des) **Cruz** (krüs).

Discussion

1. (a) Why do you think the two men got into a fight with the jukebox? **(b)** Have you ever felt like "fighting" with a machine? Explain.

2. In the last line, why do the police drop quarters in the jukebox?

3. (a) Which details in the poem seem realistic? **(b)** Which details seem unreal or fantastic?

Composition

What sort of questions do you ask an arrested jukebox? How does a jukebox answer?

Write an imaginary dialogue between a police officer and the jukebox. The questions of the officer should be serious and straightforward; the answers from the jukebox should consist of appropriate titles or lyrics from songs in the Top Forty. (This assignment might be written as a group project, with each member contributing one or more questions and answers which are then combined to form the dialogue.)

Victor Hernández Cruz 1949–

Born in Puerto Rico, Victor Hernández Cruz came to New York City when he was four years old. His poems have appeared in many publications, and he has published several collections of his work.

Breaking and Entering

Joyce Carol Oates

One of us touched the door and it swung open.

Slowly, we went inside,
Knowing better, we went inside.

The kitchen was darkened,
5 the light we'd left on in the hallway was out.
Downstairs, no sign of disorder.
Knowing better, we went upstairs.
If I had tried to caution you, you would have pulled away,
eager, anxious, needing to see——
10 and there in the bedroom
the acted-out drama, there
bureau drawers yanked out, overturned, thrown,
a skid mark on one wall——
our clothes tumbled together——
15 twisted, kicked, someone's fury run to earth.
On the doorframe there is a smear of blood.

Later, we will discover the smashed window in the basement;
the drops of a stranger's blood.
He must have been very small, the police said,
20 *to crawl through there.*
Later, slowly, as if shy of knowledge,
we discover things missing:
my wristwatch, a small typewriter,
a tarnished silver vase.

25 We are slowed-down, stupefied.
We want none of our possessions back,
we don't care what else has been stolen,
yet we talk about it constantly:
the mess! the surprise!

30 Later, we will transform it into an anecdote.
We will say, *One of us touched the door and it swung open.* . . .
knowing no way to explain the stupor, the despair,
the premonition of theft to come.

Discussion

1. What are some early signs that things are not as they should be in the house, even though there is no sign of disorder downstairs?

2. (a) How did the thief apparently enter the house? How did the thief apparently leave? **(b)** What do the police learn about the thief? **(c)** What seems to have been the thief's emotional state?

3. How would you characterize the people who live in the house? How have they been affected by the robbery?

4. Do you think you would react the way the speaker does if you discovered your home in a similar condition? Explain.

Joyce Carol Oates 1938–

At the age of twenty-five, Joyce Carol Oates published her first collection of short stories, though she had been writing poems and stories since childhood. "Before I could write," she says, "I drew pictures to tell my stories."

Oates teaches English at the University of Windsor, in Ontario, Canada. Her poems, stories, and novels have earned her several honors, including a National Book Award in 1970.

♂andelions

Deborah Austin

under cover of night and rain
the troops took over.
waking to total war in beleaguered houses
over breakfast we faced the batteries
5 marshalled by wall and stone, deployed
with a master strategy no one had suspected
and now all
firing

pow

10 all day, all yesterday
and all today
the barrage continued
deafening sight.
reeling now, eyes ringing from noise, from walking
15 gingerly over the mined lawns
exploded at every second
rocked back by the starshellfire
concussion of gold on green
bringing battle-fatigue
20 pow by lionface firefur pow by
goldburst shellshock pow by
whoosh   splat   splinteryellow   pow   by
pow   by   pow
tomorrow smoke drifts up
25 from the wrecked battalions,
all the ammunition, firegold fury, gone.
smoke
drifts
thistle-blown
30 over the war-zone, only

From *The Paradise of the World* by Deborah Austin. Published
by The Pennsylvania State University Press. Copyright © 1964
by The Pennsylvania State University. Reprinted by permission.

here and there, in the shade by the
peartree
pow   in the crack by the
curbstone   pow   and back of the
35 ashcan, lonely
guerrilla snipers, hoarding
their fire shrewdly
never

pow

40 surrender

Discussion

1. (a) Why does the speaker think that dandelions in the lawn are like exploding ammunition in a war zone? (b) How does the sudden appearance and eventual destruction of the blooms match what you know about the way dandelions grow? Try to match each step in their growth with phases of the battle.

2. Why do the people feel "beleaguered" (line 3) and suffer from "battle-fatigue" (line 19)?

3. (a) In line 13, the figurative expression "deafening sight" suggests an effect on the eyes similar to the effect of an explosion on the ears. Find other similar figurative expressions. (b) Is this poem a metaphor? Explain.

4. In your opinion, who will win this war? Explain your answer.

Vocabulary
Compound Words

A *compound word* is formed by combining two or more words. Some compounds mean just what you would expect when you combine the meanings of the words that form them. For example, *curbstone* = *curb + stone,* "the stone forming a curb along the edges of a street." Other compounds may have figurative meanings for which you must use your imagination. For example, what words form *splinteryellow?* How could a color come in pieces, or splinters? Does the context of the poem help answer this last question?

Write each of the following compounds on your paper, separating the parts with plus signs, as shown above. Then write a definition after each one. For some, you may need to use your imagination a bit.

1. battle-fatigue   6. peartree
2. firefur   7. shellshock
3. firegold   8. starshellfire
4. goldburst   9. thistle-blown
5. lionface   10. war-zone

See **RHYTHM** Handbook of Literary Terms

The Circus; Or One View of It

Theodore Spencer

Said the circus man, Oh what do you like
Best of all about my show—
The circular rings, three rings in a row,

"The Circus; Or One View of It" from *The Paradox in the Circle*
by Theodore Spencer. Copyright 1941 by New Directions
Publishing Corporation. Reprinted by permission of New
Directions.

With animals going around, around,
5 Tamed to go running round, around,
And around, round, around they go;
Or perhaps you like the merry-go-round,
Horses plunging sedately up,
Horses sedately plunging down,
10 Going around the merry-go-round;
Or perhaps you like the clown with a hoop,
Shouting, rolling the hoop around;
Or the elephants walking around in a ring
Each trunk looped to a tail's loop,
15 Loosely ambling around the ring;
How do you like this part of the show?   *(Continued)*

Everything's busy and on the go;
The peanut men cry out and sing,
The round fat clown rolls on the ground,
20   The trapeze ladies sway and swing,
The circus horses plunge around
The circular rings, three rings in a row;
Here they come, and here they go.
And here you sit, said the circus man,
25   Around in a circle to watch my show;
Which is show and which is you,
Now that we're here in this circus show,
Do I know? Do you know?
But hooray for the clowns and the merry-go-round,
30   The painted horses plunging round,
The live, proud horses stamping the ground,
And the clowns and the elephants swinging around;
Come to my show; hooray for the show,
Hooray for the circus all the way round!
35   Said the round exuberant circus man.
Hooray for the show! said the circus man.

Discussion

1. (a) To whom is the circus man talking? (b) What seems to be the purpose of his speech?

2. (a) How does he emphasize that "everything's busy and on the go"? Find words that give the feeling of constant movement. (b) What is the pattern of all this movement?

3. Reread lines 24-28. (a) Describe the seating arrangement of the audience. How is it similar to the pattern of the circus acts? (b) From whose viewpoint might the audience appear to be the show? (c) Is the question in line 26 playful or serious? Why do you think so?

4. Do you think the poem gives just "one view" of the circus, as the title suggests? Explain.

Application
Rhythm

Reread the poem aloud, emphasizing the important words and the naturally accented syllables. Pay attention to the punctuation.

1. Does the rhythm seem to be fairly regular throughout the poem?

2. Does the rhythm of the poem remind you of any rhythm or music that you have heard before? If so, describe it. Does the rhythm seem appropriate for the subject matter of the poem? Why or why not?

3 Portraits

Poems can sketch portraits of people or animals, of lives
that are simple or complex, happy or tragic.

See **HYPERBOLE** Handbook of Literary Terms

*t*akes talent

Don Marquis

there are two
kinds of human
beings in the world
so my observation
5 has told me
namely and to wit
as follows
firstly
those who
10 even though they
were to reveal
the secret of the universe
to you would fail
to impress you
15 with any sense
of the importance
of the news   *(Continued)*

"takes talent" from the book *the lives and times of archy and
mehitabel* by Don Marquis. Copyright 1926 by P. F. Collier &
Son, Co. Reprinted by permission of Doubleday & Company,
Inc. and Faber and Faber Limited.

Don Marquis (mär′kwis).

and secondly
those who could
20 communicate to you
that they had
just purchased
ten cents worth
of paper napkins
25 and make you
thrill and vibrate
with the intelligence
archy[1]

---

1. **archy.** Archy is a cockroach with the soul of a poet, a character created by New York *Sun* columnist Don Marquis. After most of the newspaper's employees had gone home at night, Archy would write letters on "the boss's" typewriter by hurling himself headfirst at the keys. Too light in weight to operate the shift key, he made no use of capitalization or punctuation in his writing.

Discussion

1. Describe and contrast the qualities involved in the "two/kinds of human/beings in the world."

2. (a) What does the title of this poem mean? (b) What comment on people is Archy making? (c) Does he see any hope for those who lack the "talent"?

3. (a) Is "takes talent" a humorous poem or a serious one? (b) Do you think Archy's comment should be taken seriously? Explain.

Application

Hyperbole

The exaggeration of hyperbole can heighten the effect of a statement.

1. What hyperbole is contained in lines 8–17? Why is it hyperbole?

2. What hyperbole is contained in lines 18–27? Why is it hyperbole?

3. What effect is created by these two hyperboles in combination?

Don Marquis 1878–1937

Within his lifetime Don Marquis was poet, playwright, short-story writer, and newspaper columnist. But today he is best remembered for his work in a field where talent is rare—humorous verse. Fame came to Marquis with the creation of Archy and Mehitabel, the cat who claimed to have once been Cleopatra. The quaint philosophies of the cat and the cockroach often filled Marquis's column in the New York *Sun,* and have been collected in a book entitled *the lives and times of archy and mehitabel.*

The cast of *The Me Nobody Knows* (1968).

Comment: Poetry on Stage

The earliest forms of poetry were always sung or recited aloud. Today, much of the effectiveness of poetry can be realized through performance. Many unusual and effective stage productions have been based on poetry.

The character of Archy, created by Don Marquis, wrote many poems like "takes talent" about life as seen by a cockroach. His special friend was an alley cat named Mehitabel, who considered herself a "lady." In a 1957 musical comedy called *Shinbone Alley,* Archy and Mehitabel were brought to life, singing and dancing along with other bugs, cats, and various alley dwellers.

The Me Nobody Knows, originally published in 1968, is a collection of writings by New York City students ranging in age from seven to eighteen. In poetry and prose, the young people wrote about their world and what was important to them—families, friends, growing up in the city. The stage version, speeches and songs set to rock music and performed by young people with no professional experience, won an award for the best off-Broadway musical. Some of the young authors saw the show and went backstage to meet the performers and comment on how well they had done.

A recent example of poetry on stage is *Cats,* in which the characters are an odd assortment of cats with even odder names like Rum Tum Tugger and Grizabella. The poems were originally written by T. S. Eliot, one of England's most influential poets, as letters to entertain his godchildren. In 1939 they were published in a collection entitled *Old Possum's Book of Practical Cats.* Then in 1981 Eliot's poems, set to music, opened in England to great success and later came to America. Thus, T. S. Eliot, winner of the 1948 Nobel Prize for Literature, also became the winner—years after his death—of the 1983 Tony (an award for excellence in the theater) for "best book of a musical."

Grandfather

James K. Cazalas

It puzzles me
That I cannot see
What grandfather can:
He is eighty with the eyes
5 Of a young Indian
Proving his manhood.

I stumbled in the deep yellow sand
And he walked over it easily.
I breathed hard and perspired
10 And he paced himself
Like an animal
With a long way to go.

A dollar-sized turtle
Struggling on its back
15 Was dying ten feet off the sand:
It was he who saw it
And turned it over.

When we returned home,
He took off his sneakers,
20 Took out his teeth,
And was an old, dying man.
But on the trail
He was Seneca[1]
And more a part of the earth
25 Than the sand we trod.

1. *Seneca*, member of the Seneca people, one of the five American Indian tribes which formed the powerful Iroquois nation.

"Grandfather" by James K. Cazalas from *Southwest Review*, Winter 1977, Vol. 62, No. 1. Reprinted by permission.

Discussion

1. (a) What actions of his grandfather does the speaker relate? (b) What description does the speaker give of his grandfather?

2. (a) What about his grandfather puzzles the speaker? (b) How does he become aware of these puzzling characteristics?

3. (a) What possible explanation is there for the fact that Grandfather "sees" better and moves along the trail with greater ease than someone much younger? (b) What change takes place in Grandfather when he returns home?

4. Do you know anyone like Grandfather—someone who sometimes seems much younger than his or her actual age? What about this person creates that impression?

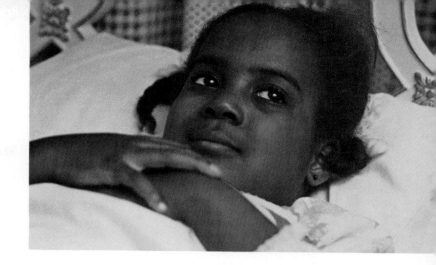

Nora

Gwendolyn Brooks

I was not sleeping when Brother said
"Good-bye!" and laughed and teased my head;
And went, like rockets, out of the door,
As he had done most days before.

5   But it was fun to curl between
The white warm sheets, and not be seen,

And stay, a minute more, alone,
Keeping myself for my very own.

"Nora" from *Bronzeville Boys and Girls* by Gwendolyn Brooks.
Copyright © 1956 by Gwendolyn Brooks Blakely. Reprinted by
permission of Harper & Row, Publishers, Inc.

Discussion

1. What happens in this poem?
2. (a) Contrast Nora's mood with the mood her brother seems to be in. **(b)** How do Nora and her brother seem to feel toward each other?
3. What do you think is meant by line 8?

Gwendolyn Brooks 1917–

At the age of thirteen, Gwendolyn Brooks published her first poem in a national children's magazine. She has been writing and receiving praise ever since. She won several awards with her first collection of poems, *A Street in Bronzeville. Annie Allen,* her second collection of poems, won a Pulitzer Prize in 1950.

Brooks lives in Chicago, where she continues to be involved with writing, teaching, and community work. One of her two children is named Nora.

Catalogue

Rosalie Moore

Cats sleep fat and walk thin.
Cats, when they sleep, slump;
When they wake, stretch and begin
Over, pulling their ribs in.
5 Cats walk thin.

Cats wait in a lump,
Jump in a streak.
Cats, when they jump, are sleek
As a grape slipping its skin—
10 They have technique.
Oh, cats don't creak.
They sneak.

Cats sleep fat.
They spread out comfort underneath them
15 Like a good mat,
As if they picked the place
And then sat;
You walk around one
As if he were the City Hall
20 After that.

If male,
A cat is apt to sing on a major scale;
This concert is for everybody, this
Is wholesale.
25 For a baton, he wields a tail.

(He is also found,
When happy, to resound
With an enclosed and private sound.)

A cat condenses.
30 He pulls in his tail to go under bridges,
And himself to go under fences.
Cats fit
In any size box or kit,
And if a large pumpkin grew under one,
35 He could arch over it.

When everyone else is just ready to go out,
The cat is just ready to come in.
He's not where he's been.
Cats sleep fat and walk thin.

Discussion

1. Which descriptive words and figurative expressions do you find most appropriate for a cat's movements? Which suggest a cat's personality traits?

2. (a) Do the many rhymes create an effect that is serious, lighthearted, irritated—or what? (b) In lines 26–28, how do the sounds of the words suggest the sounds that a cat sometimes makes?

3. (a) How does the speaker seem to feel about cats? (b) What lines especially suggest these feelings?

Composition

If you have a dog or other kind of pet, use "Catalogue" as a model to describe your own pet. First think of active verbs and descriptive words to tell how your pet sleeps, walks, jumps, etc. You might include words to tell how the animal sounds as well as how it looks.

Write a poem of no more than one page describing your pet. Use figurative expressions and, perhaps, hyperbole to create a vivid portrait. Title your poem "Dog-a-logue" or whatever seems appropriate. (If you wish, you may write this assignment in paragraph form.)

*J*amie

Elizabeth Brewster

When Jamie was sixteen,
Suddenly he was deaf. There were no songs,
No voices any more.
He walked about stunned by the terrible silence.
5 Kicking a stick, rapping his knuckles on doors,
He felt a spell of silence all about him,
So loud it made a whirring in his ears.
People moved mouths without a sound escaping:
He shuddered at the straining of their throats.
10 And suddenly he watched them with suspicion,
Wondering if they were talking of his faults,
Were pitying him or seeing him with scorn.
He dived into their eyes and dragged up sneers,
And sauntering the streets, imagined laughter behind him.
15 Working at odd jobs, ploughing, picking potatoes,
Chopping trees in the lumber woods in winter,
He became accustomed to an aimless and lonely labor.
He was solitary and unloquacious as a stone,
And silence grew over him like moss on an old stump.
20 But sometimes, going to town,
He was sore with the hunger for company among the people,
And, getting drunk, would shout at them for friendship,
Laughing aloud in the streets.
He returned to the woods,
25 And dreaming at night of a shining cowboy heaven
Where guns crashed through his deafness, woke morose,
And chopped the necks of pine trees in his anger.

"Jamie" by Elizabeth Brewster from *East Coast* published by Ryerson Press, 1951.
Reprinted by permission of the author.

Discussion

1. (a) In what ways are Jamie's relationships with people affected by his deafness? **(b)** What attempts does he make to gain the company of people? How successful are these attempts?

2. Jamie's reactions to his deafness change as time goes by. **(a)** How would you describe his reactions in lines 4–7? in lines 8–14? in lines 15–19? in lines 20–23? **(b)** What do the last four lines of the poem suggest about Jamie's future?

3. What do you feel toward Jamie—sympathy, pity, hope that he will be able to adjust to his disability—or something else? Explain.

Vocabulary
Combined Skills

Use your Glossary to answer the questions about the italicized words; write your answers on a separate paper.

1. Read the synonym study under the entry for *scorn.* From the three synonyms given, choose the best one to complete this sentence: Since he has become wealthy, he treats all his poor, unsuccessful relatives with ____.

2. When more than one pronunciation is given for a word, both are correct, but the one given first is considered more common. Write the two words from the pronunciation key that tell how the accented vowel sound in *saunter* can be pronounced.

3. Use the example sentences given for *accustomed* as models to write an example sentence of your own that demonstrates your understanding of the word.

4. Under what letter in the Glossary do you find *unloquacious—U* or *L*? Copy the sentence in lines 18–19 of the poem and substitute your definition for the word. Does your definition fit the context?

5. What was the original meaning of the Latin word from which *morose* comes? How does the current meaning of *morose* differ from that original meaning?

Elizabeth Brewster 1922–

Born and educated in New Brunswick, Canada, Elizabeth Brewster is considered by many to be among the most important Canadian poets. Much of her writing deals with the rich wilderness and harsh terrain of her homeland. She has published several collections of poetry and a novel, and her work frequently appears in magazines. She received the Canada Council's Senior Artists' awards in 1971–72, and again in 1976.

See **INVERSION** Handbook of Literary Terms

Still Life: Lady with Birds

Quandra Prettyman

She, in dowdy dress and dumpy,
clutching her black purse and brown paper bag,
comes bounty bearing and love bestows.

She, with birds for epaulets,[1]
5   thrusts such crusts as she has, such crumbs.
They cluster and grab and grabbing, sometimes, claw.

She, alone in this agony,
feeds them swiftly, firmly brushes them away,
speaking wild rantings to no one I see.

10 Sometimes one comes late,
finds no where to rest at her shoulders,
finds no crust to eat at her feet.

To that one, she
holds out her arm.
15 Him, she brings in.

---

1. **epaulets** (ep′ə lets), ornaments worn on the shoulders, usually of a uniform.

Discussion

1. **(a)** Describe the woman's appearance. **(b)** How do her actions contrast with her appearance?

2. In line 7, what might "this agony" refer to?

3. **(a)** Why does she brush some birds firmly away? **(b)** What bird does she treat differently? **(c)** Why might she treat that bird differently from the others?

4. In what ways is the behavior of the birds in this poem similar to some human behavior?

Application

Inversion

A sentence with inverted elements shouldn't be hard to read if you concentrate on the meaning instead of the form.

1. In this poem, who "comes bounty bearing and love bestows"? What elements are inverted here? Put them in their normal order.

2. In lines 13–14, the woman "holds out her arm." What does she hold it out to?

3. In line 15, what does she bring in?

4. What words are emphasized by the inversions in lines 13–15?

M*y Father Is a Simple Man*

Luis Omar Salinas

(for my father Alfredo)

I walk to town with my father
to buy a newspaper. He walks slower
than I do so I must slow up.
The street is filled with children.
5   We argue about the price
of pomegranates, I convince
him it is the fruit of scholars.
He has taken me on this journey
and it's been lifelong.
10 He's sure I'll be healthy
so long as I eat more oranges,
and tells me the orange
has seeds and so is perpetual;
and we too will come back
15 like the orange trees.
I ask him what he thinks   *(Continued)*

about death and he says
he will gladly face it when
it comes but won't jump
20 out in front of a car.
I'd gladly give my life
for this man with a sixth
grade education, whose kindness
and patience are true . . .
25 The truth of it is, he's the scholar,
and when the bitter-hard reality
comes at me like a punishing
evil stranger, I can always
remember that here was a man
30 who was a worker and provider,
who learned the simple facts
in life and lived by them,
who held no pretense.
And when he leaves without
35 benefit of fanfare or applause
I shall have learned what little
there is about greatness.

Discussion

1. What do the father and son talk about as they walk to town?

2. What is the "journey" that the speaker refers to in lines 8–9?

3. (a) What is the "bitter-hard reality" that will one day come (lines 26–28)? **(b)** Why might this reality seem like a "punishing / evil stranger" to the son?

4. What "simple facts" in life has the father learned? How do you suppose he has learned them?

5. When his father dies, the speaker says that he will have learned "what little / there is about greatness." Why do you think the speaker considers his father great?

Composition

The speaker says that he can always remember his father as "a man / who was a worker and provider, / who learned the simple facts / in life and lived by them, / who held no pretense." Think of someone you respect and admire—either a famous person or someone you know personally. List the qualities of that person which make him or her worthy of being honored.

Compose a tribute of no more than three sentences that could be engraved on a plaque or a trophy presented in honor of your subject. You will need to choose carefully among the qualities you have listed so that the tribute can be kept to just a few words. Title your composition with the name of your subject.

4

Reflections
Poems can express thoughts about life, wealth, beauty—
even about poetry.

Dreams

Langston Hughes

Hold fast to dreams
For if dreams die
Life is a broken-winged bird
That cannot fly.

5 Hold fast to dreams
For when dreams go
Life is a barren field
Frozen with snow.

Discussion

1. (a) What kind of dreams do you think
the speaker is talking about? **(b)** What two
metaphors are used to describe a life
without dreams? **(c)** In what ways are the
metaphors appropriate?

2. (a) How important do you think
dreams are? **(b)** Suggest some comparisons of your own that could be applied to
a life without dreams.

Langston Hughes 1902–1967

A man who lived to see many of his
dreams come true, Langston Hughes expressed himself in many types of writing—
novels, stories, plays, songs, movie
screenplays, travel articles, and children's
books. He is best known, however, as a
poet.

Born in Joplin, Missouri, he attended
high school in Cleveland, Ohio, where he
began writing poetry. Before graduating
from college he spent a year in Mexico,
worked as a seaman on trans-Atlantic voy-
ages, and held a job as a cook in Paris.

See **CONNOTATION/DENOTATION** Handbook of Literary Terms

*T*he Peaceable Tree

Fritz Eichenberg

A tree was dreaming—so the fable goes—
of pulling up its roots to see the world,
of which the owl had told him many stories.
He knew that birds can fly, that beasts can run,
5   and climb and jump from branch to branch.
The humans he had seen walked on two legs
or raced along on wheels—like lunatics.
''Yet,'' said the owl, an avid TV viewer

peeking through nightly windows,
10   "people are always talking about roots.
They search for them, write books about them,
travel long distances to dig them up,
are proud of them, like knights of their escutcheons."[1]
The tree was listening with rapt attention:
15   "I thank you, owl, as always, for your counsel;
you have convinced me that my dreams are wrong.
Woodpeckers knock me, squirrels annoy me
by hiding nuts in knotholes.
Old branches ache, drop off in heavy snow,
20   and storms sweep through my crown.
Yet spring will come, and little leaves
will sprout and rustle in the breeze.
Just as you say, the root's the thing!
I think I'll stay—
25   and sink them just a little deeper!"

---

1. **escutcheons.** An escutcheon (e skuch′ən) is a shield on which is displayed a coat of arms symbolizing one's family and associated with one's reputation and honor.

Discussion

1. Why does the tree want to pull up its roots?

2. **(a)** What reasons does the owl give for staying put? **(b)** How are people who are proud of their roots like knights who are proud of their escutcheons?

3. **(a)** What annoyances does the tree mention? **(b)** What makes up for those annoyances?

4. A fable is a story intended to teach a lesson, or moral. Put in your own words the lesson taught in this fable.

Application
Connotation/Denotation

1. What definition of *roots* would you ordinarily associate with a tree? Is that definition connotative or denotative?

2. What sort of *roots* are people always talking and writing about and traveling and searching for, according to the owl? Is that definition connotative or denotative?

3. What does the tree mean by "the root's the thing" in line 23?

Fritz Eichenberg 1901–

Fritz Eichenberg started as a newspaper artist in Germany, where he was born, and came to the United States in 1933. His work as a graphic artist and illustrator of classics and other books has been shown in several countries, in international exhibitions, and is housed in the collections of famous museums here and abroad. His favorite mediums are lithographs, wood engravings, and woodcuts.

*T*he clouds pass

Richard Garcia

The clouds pass in a blue sky
Too white to be true
Before winter sets in
The trees are spending all their money

5 I lie in gold
Above a green valley
Gold falls on my chest
I am a rich man.

Discussion

1. At what time of year is the poem set? How can you tell?

2. **(a)** What is meant by the metaphor in line 4? **(b)** Why might the speaker say that he is "rich"?

3. What emotions does the speaker seem to be feeling?

Composition

Many things besides money can make a person feel "rich"—family, good friends, contentment, small but definite successes, to name a few. Choose a time when you felt "rich" in one sense or another and consider just what it was that made that time so special to you.

Write a paragraph describing that time. Describe the setting, if it was important. If other people played a part, describe them and their actions. What did you actually do? Most important, what were your feelings about the whole situation? Try to describe your time in a way to make your reader share in your feeling of richness. (If you wish, you may write this assignment in the form of a poem.)

Snow Sculpture

Margaret Tsuda

There is nothing about
a snowplow
to suggest a
sculptor's mallet and chisel.
5 Nor does the
driver appear
unusually gifted.

Yet,
tutored by
10 rhythms of
sun-melt and
night-freeze,
blocks and mounds
heaped up by the
15 plow's dogged efforts
assume
shapes and forms
fantastic and beautiful,
abstract or figure-evoking,
20 turning both sides
of each street into
sculpture gardens.

Discussion

1. (a) What materials and tools does a sculptor use? **(b)** How is the snowplow like a sculptor's tool? **(c)** What do "sun-melt" and "night-freeze" accomplish?

2. (a) What other large, powerful machines have you seen that do beautiful work? **(b)** Suggest similes or other comparisons to describe their appearance or the work they do.

*B*ravado

Robert Frost

Have I not walked without an upward look
Of caution under stars that very well
Might not have missed me when they shot and fell?
It was a risk I had to take—and took.

"Bravado" from *The Poetry of Robert Frost* edited by Edward Connery Lathem. Copyright 1947, © 1969 by Holt, Rinehart and Winston. Copyright © 1975 by Lesley Frost Ballantine. Reprinted by permission of Holt, Rinehart and Winston, Publishers, the Estate of Robert Frost and Jonathan Cape Ltd.

Discussion

1. Put into statement form the question that is asked in lines 1-3.

2. (a) What is the "risk" the speaker takes? **(b)** Why is it necessary for the speaker to take it? **(c)** Does the speaker seem proud of taking that risk? Explain.

3. (a) In your opinion, how much risk is actually involved? **(b)** Might the speaker be referring to other risks, as well? Explain.

4. Why do you suppose the poem is entitled "Bravado" instead of "Bravery" or "Courage" or something else? (You may use the Glossary to help answer this question.)

How to Find Poems

Anita Skeen

They turn up everywhere, sometimes
in the most unexpected places.
Like Colby, Kansas.
(or even in Detroit, on a freeway,
5 in an Italian deli)
If you find footprints
in the snow on a January morning,
you know you've just missed one.
Be in the same spot earlier
10 tomorrow. Look in the cafeteria,
under lettuce. There will be fossils
of phrases passing themselves off
as red cabbage or beets.
Search in the gym
15 during basketball tournaments.
One may be spinning
precariously on the rim

like a ball. You will know it
by the rhythm when it
20 drops in. Peer between
feathers in eagle wings, inside
the velvet ears of beagles.
Follow the owner of beagles.
She knows the howl
25 of the lost line, the scent
of trapped words.
She prowls among blackberries,
under mushrooms, inside the eye
of the bat. Go there.
30 You will find poems.

Discussion

1. (a) Who do you think is the "you" the speaker is addressing? **(b)** What do you think that person will do with the poems he or she finds?

2. A number of specific places are listed (on a freeway, in the snow, etc.). If you have read poems about any of these places, tell about them.

3. In your own words, sum up what this poem says about where poems are to be found.

Anita Skeen 1946–

Born in Charleston, West Virginia, Anita Skeen has been artist-in-residence at YWCA camps and has participated in the Poet-in-the-Schools program and in the Squaw Valley, California, Community of Writers. Currently she teaches English and creative writing at Wichita State University in Kansas. In listing her "Wishes, Lies, and Dreams," Skeen says that she would like to write a novel, live in a cabin in the woods, have no telephone, take a cross-country bicycle trip, have her own printing press, work as a carpenter, and take a whole year to do nothing but write.

Unit 3 Review: *Poetry*

Content Review

1. Animals appear in several poems in this unit: "Sea Monster," "Dog at Night," "The Circus; Or One View of It," "Still Life: Lady with Birds," and "Catalogue." Compare the different feelings toward animals expressed in these poems.

2. People deal with problems in many ways. Identify the problem or conflict each of these characters has and explain how the character deals with it: **(a)** the people in "Sea Monster"; **(b)** the wife in "Father Grumble"; **(c)** the homeowners in "Breaking and Entering"; **(d)** Jamie; **(e)** the "Lady with Birds."

3. The following poems all contain rhyme. Some of them contain a regular rhythm; in others the rhythm is irregular. In your opinion, which poem makes the best use of rhyme and rhythm to express the meaning of the poem? **(a)** "The Story-Teller"; **(b)** "The Walrus and the Carpenter"; **(c)** "Father Grumble"; **(d)** "Dog at Night"; **(e)** "The Circus; Or One View of It"; **(f)** "Catalogue."

4. Identify the hyperbole in each of the following poems. What seems to be the purpose of the hyperbole in each? **(a)** "The Story-Teller"; **(b)** "The Walrus and the Carpenter"; **(c)** "Grandfather"; **(d)** "Catalogue."

5. Which is your favorite poem in this unit? Do you base your choice on the language, the emotion or feeling expressed, the subject matter or situation, or on something else? Explain.

Concept Review: Interpretation of New Material

Read the following poem carefully. Then use the questions that follow to review your understanding of the concepts and literary terms presented in this unit. If you wish, write your answers on a separate sheet of paper.

Sea Lullaby · *Elinor Wylie*

The old moon is tarnished
With smoke of the flood,
The dead leaves are varnished
With color like blood,

5 A treacherous smiler
With teeth white as milk,
A savage beguiler[1]
In sheathings of silk,

(Continued)

---

1. **beguiler,** a deceitful person.

Copyright 1921 by Alfred A. Knopf, Inc. and renewed 1949 by William Rose Benét. Reprinted from *Collected Poems of Elinor Wylie,* by permission of Alfred A. Knopf, Inc.

186 POETRY

The sea creeps to pillage,[2]
10 She leaps on her prey;
A child of the village
Was murdered today.

She came up to meet him
In a smooth golden cloak,
15 She choked him and beat him
To death, for a joke.

Her bright locks were tangled,
She shouted for joy,
With one hand she strangled
20 A strong little boy.

Now in silence she lingers
Beside him all night
To wash her long fingers
In silvery light.

---

2. *pillage*, to rob with violence; loot.

---

1. The title "Sea Lullaby" suggests that the poem will be about **(a)** a calm, restful sea; **(b)** a storm at sea; **(c)** children playing in the sea; **(d)** a sea animal.

2. In lines 1-2, the connotations of the words used suggest that what follows will be **(a)** ugly; **(b)** old-fashioned; **(c)** smoky; **(d)** beautiful.

3. List at least two words or phrases from the rest of the poem that further convey the feeling in the first two lines.

4. The metaphor "teeth white as milk" probably refers to the sea's **(a)** tides; **(b)** undercurrents; **(c)** breaking waves; **(d)** smooth surface.

5. In stanza four (lines 13-16) there is a strong contrast between **(a)** the sun and the sea; **(b)** the noise of the sea and the silence of the boy; **(c)** the beauty of the sea and the horror of what it does; **(d)** the beauty of the sea and the boy's fear of it.

6. The rhyme scheme is **(a)** abcb; **(b)** aabb; **(c)** abab; **(d)** abba.

7. Every line of the poem contains only two stresses. In nearly every line, the syllables stressed are **(a)** one and four; **(b)** two and five; **(c)** two and four; **(d)** three and five.

8. After the death of the boy, the sea **(a)** shouts for joy; **(b)** becomes quiet; **(c)** carries his body away; **(d)** becomes wild and stormy.

9. The poem leaves the reader with the impression that the sea is **(a)** always angry; **(b)** usually calm; **(c)** unchanging; **(d)** changeable.

10. What one word (not in the poem) would you use to tell what actually happens to the child?

Composition Review

1. Several poems in this unit focus not only on what people see and hear as they perform such activities as riding the bus, sky diving, feeding birds, and so on, but also on what they feel. Choose a sport or other activity and think about what you see and hear as you perform it. What emotions do you feel? Do your feelings change at different times?

Write one or two paragraphs describing your activity and your feelings in detail. Make your descriptions as vivid as possible by including figurative language. (If you wish, you may write this assignment in the form of a poem.)

2. Section three of this unit includes portraits of various characters. Choose a person that you know or "borrow" a character from literature or film. Decide on how you are going to picture the person.

(Describing a few specific actions will be better here than trying to tell a life story.)

Write a portrait of your character no more than a page in length. Use the various methods of characterization to make your portrait as real as possible. (If you wish, you may write this assignment in the form of a poem.)

3. A fable is a story made up to teach a moral, or useful lesson about life—as in "The Peaceable Tree." Decide on a lesson you want to express: choose a familiar saying such as "Look before you leap" or else write a lesson of your own. Think of a story that will teach that lesson.

Write a fable that is no more than a page in length. Include the lesson as a speech by a character or as a moral at the end. (If you wish, you may write this assignment in the form of a poem.)

All people born about the same time form a
generation. But generation also means producing,
causing something to be. Something said generates
an idea. Ideas and attitudes cause actions. And
sometimes, the way generations of people react to
each other can bring about a new way of looking
at the world.

Generations

Charles

Shirley Jackson

Charles was certainly a bad influence. But just who was he?

The day my son Laurie started kindergarten he renounced corduroy overalls with bibs and began wearing blue jeans with a belt. I watched him go off the first morning with the older girl next door, seeing clearly that an era of my life was ended, my sweet-voiced nursery-school tot replaced by a long-trousered, swaggering character who forgot to stop at the corner and wave good-bye to me.

He came home the same way, the front door slamming open, his hat on the floor, and the voice suddenly become raucous shouting, "Isn't anybody *here?*"

At lunch he spoke insolently to his father, spilled his baby sister's milk, and remarked that his teacher said we were not to take the name of the Lord in vain.

"How *was* school today?" I asked, elaborately casual.

"All right," he said.

"Did you learn anything?" his father asked.

Laurie regarded his father coldly. "I didn't learn nothing," he said.

"Anything," I said. "Didn't learn anything."

"The teacher spanked a boy, though," Laurie said, addressing his bread and butter. "For being fresh," he added, with his mouth full.

"What did he do?" I asked. "Who was it?"

Laurie thought. "It was Charles," he said. "He was fresh. The teacher spanked him and made him stand in a corner. He was awfully fresh."

"What did he do?" I asked again, but Laurie slid off his chair, took a cookie, and left, while his father was still saying, "See here, young man."

The next day Laurie remarked at lunch, as soon as he sat down, "Well, Charles was bad again today." He grinned enormously and said, "Today Charles hit the teacher."

"Good heavens," I said, mindful of the Lord's name. "I suppose he got spanked again?"

"He sure did," Laurie said. "Look up," he said to his father.

"What?" his father said, looking up.

"Look down," Laurie said. "Look at my thumb. Gee, you're dumb." He began to laugh insanely.

"Why did Charles hit the teacher?" I asked quickly.

"Because she tried to make him color

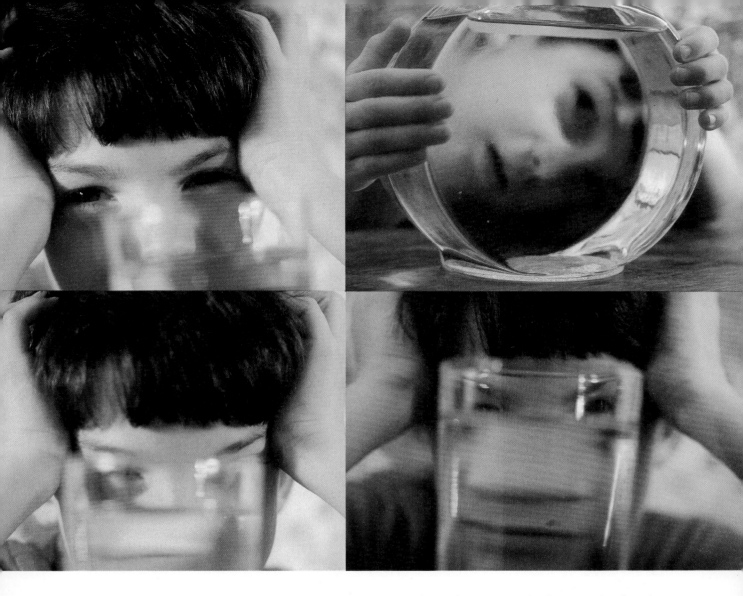

with red crayons,'' Laurie said. ''Charles wanted to color with green crayons so he hit the teacher and she spanked him and said nobody play with Charles but everybody did.''

The third day—it was Wednesday of the first week—Charles bounced a see-saw on the head of a little girl and made her bleed, and the teacher made him stay inside all during recess. Thursday Charles had to stand in a corner during story-time because he kept pounding his feet on the floor. Friday Charles was deprived of blackboard privileges because he threw chalk.

On Saturday I remarked to my husband, ''Do you think kindergarten is too unsettling for Laurie? All this toughness and bad grammar, and this Charles boy sounds like such a bad influence.''

''It'll be all right,'' my husband said reassuringly. ''Bound to be people like Charles in the world. Might as well meet them now as later.''

On Monday Laurie came home late, full of news. ''Charles,'' he shouted as he came up the hill; I was waiting anxiously on the front steps. ''Charles,'' Laurie yelled all the way up the hill. ''Charles was bad again.''

"Come right in," I said, as soon as he came close enough. "Lunch is waiting."

"You know what Charles did?" he demanded, following me through the door. "Charles yelled so in school they sent a boy in from first grade to tell the teacher she had to make Charles keep quiet, and so Charles had to stay after school. And so all the children stayed to watch him."

"What did he do?" I asked.

"He just sat there," Laurie said, climbing into his chair at the table. "Hi, Pop, y'old dust mop."

"Charles had to stay after school today," I told my husband. "Everyone stayed with him."

"What does this Charles look like?" my husband asked Laurie. "What's his other name?"

"He's bigger than me," Laurie said. "And he doesn't have any rubbers and he doesn't ever wear a jacket."

Monday night was the first Parent-Teachers meeting, and only the fact that the baby had a cold kept me from going; I wanted passionately to meet Charles's mother. On Tuesday Laurie remarked suddenly, "Our teacher had a friend come to see her in school today."

"Charles's mother?" my husband and I asked simultaneously.

"Naaah," Laurie said scornfully. "It was a man who came and made us do exercises, we had to touch our toes. Look." He climbed down from his chair and squatted down and touched his toes. "Like this," he said. He got solemnly back into his chair and said, picking up his fork, "Charles didn't even *do* exercises."

"That's fine," I said heartily. "Didn't Charles want to do the exercises?"

"Naaah," Laurie said. "Charles was so fresh to the teacher's friend he wasn't *let* do exercises."

"Fresh again," I said.

"He kicked the teacher's friend," Laurie said. "The teacher's friend told Charles to touch his toes like I just did and Charles kicked him."

"What are they going to do about Charles, do you suppose?" Laurie's father asked him.

Laurie shrugged elaborately. "Throw him out of school, I guess," he said.

Wednesday and Thursday were routine; Charles yelled during story hour and hit a boy in the stomach and made him cry. On Friday Charles stayed after school again and so did all the other children.

With the third week of kindergarten Charles was an institution in our family; the baby was being a Charles when he filled his wagon full of mud and pulled it through the kitchen; even my husband, when he caught his elbow in the telephone cord and pulled telephone, ashtray, and a bowl of flowers off the table, said, after the first minute, "Looks like Charles."

During the third and fourth weeks it looked like a reformation in Charles; Laurie reported grimly at lunch on Thursday of the third week, "Charles was so good today the teacher gave him an apple."

"What?" I said, and my husband added warily, "You mean Charles?"

"Charles," Laurie said. "He gave the crayons around and he picked up the books afterward and the teacher said he was her helper."

"What happened?" I asked incredulously.

"He was her helper, that's all," Laurie said, and shrugged.

"Can this be true, about Charles?" I

asked my husband that night. "Can something like this happen?"

"Wait and see," my husband said cynically. "When you've got a Charles to deal with, this may mean he's only plotting."

He seemed to be wrong. For over a week Charles was the teacher's helper; each day he handed things out and he picked things up; no one had to stay after school.

"The PTA meeting's next week again," I told my husband one evening. "I'm going to find Charles's mother there."

"Ask her what happened to Charles," my husband said. "I'd like to know."

"I'd like to know myself," I said.

On Friday of that week things were back to normal. "You know what Charles did today?" Laurie demanded at the lunch table, in a voice slightly awed. "He told a little girl to say a word and she said it and the teacher washed her mouth out with soap and Charles laughed."

"What word?" his father asked unwisely, and Laurie said, "I'll have to whisper it to you, it's so bad." He got down off his chair and went around to his father. His father bent his head down and Laurie whispered joyfully. His father's eyes widened.

"Did Charles tell the little girl to say *that?*" he asked respectfully.

"She said it *twice,*" Laurie said. "Charles told her to say it *twice.*"

"What happened to Charles?" my husband asked.

"Nothing," Laurie said. "He was passing out the crayons."

Monday morning Charles abandoned the little girl and said the evil word himself three or four times, getting his mouth washed out with soap each time. He also threw chalk.

My husband came to the door with me that evening as I set out for the PTA meeting. "Invite her over for a cup of tea after the meeting," he said. "I want to get a look at her."

"If only she's there," I said prayerfully.

"She'll be there," my husband said. "I don't see how they could hold a PTA meeting without Charles's mother."

At the meeting I sat restlessly, scanning each comfortable matronly face, trying to determine which one hid the secret of Charles. None of them looked to me haggard enough. No one stood up in the meeting and apologized for the way her son had been acting. No one mentioned Charles.

After the meeting I identified and sought out Laurie's kindergarten teacher. She had a plate with a cup of tea and a piece of chocolate cake; I had a plate with a cup of tea and a piece of marshmallow cake. We maneuvered up to one another cautiously, and smiled.

"I've been so anxious to meet you," I said. "I'm Laurie's mother."

"We're all so interested in Laurie," she said.

"Well, he certainly likes kindergarten," I said. "He talks about it all the time."

"We had a little trouble adjusting, the first week or so," she said primly, "but now he's a fine little helper. With occasional lapses, of course."

"Laurie usually adjusts very quickly," I said. "I suppose this time it's Charles's influence."

"Charles?"

"Yes," I said, laughing, "you must have your hands full in that kindergarten, with Charles."

"Charles?" she said. "We don't have any Charles in the kindergarten."

Discussion

1. In the first paragraph, why does the narrator feel that "an era of my life was ended"?

2. (a) How does Laurie behave at home after his first morning at school? **(b)** What does Laurie tell about Charles's behavior at school?

3. (a) Describe the ways Laurie's teacher tries to change Charles's behavior. **(b)** Which of these methods seems to work best?

Application
Inference

Understanding the story "Charles" depends on making inferences. Correct inferences can be made by paying close attention to the characters' speeches and actions—particularly Laurie's.

1. On learning there is no Charles in the kindergarten, who do you infer is the troublemaker in Laurie's class?

2. How does Laurie's behavior at home help you make this inference?

3. Laurie describes Charles in these words: "He's bigger than me. And he doesn't have any rubbers, and he doesn't ever wear a jacket." Once you discover who Charles is, what inferences about Laurie can you make from this description?

Vocabulary
Context

Use context clues to figure out the meanings of the italicized words in these sentences. Write the letters of the best answers on your paper.

1. He talks back to his teacher, ignores his father, and makes fun of his mother— have you ever seen such an *insolent* child? **(a)** clever; **(b)** loud; **(c)** friendly; **(d)** rude.

2. The crows' cawing sounded loud and *raucous,* especially in contrast to the doves' gentle cooing. **(a)** sweet; **(b)** harsh; **(c)** distant; **(d)** pleasant.

3. Even though he had loved and cared for the stray dog, Greg *renounced* his claim to the animal when its former owners appeared. **(a)** gave up; **(b)** announced; **(c)** demanded; **(d)** renewed.

4. Because she was unsure whether or not the thief had a gun, the policewoman approached him *warily.* **(a)** kindly; **(b)** cautiously; **(c)** angrily; **(d)** clumsily.

5. Because the two shots were fired *simultaneously,* they sounded like one very loud shot. **(a)** carelessly; **(b)** into the ground; **(c)** hesitantly; **(d)** at the same time.

Shirley Jackson 1919–1965

Laurie, the child in "Charles," is modeled on a real person—Shirley Jackson's first child. The story appears, among other places, in Jackson's *Life Among the Savages,* which she once called "a disrespectful memoir of my children."

Born in San Francisco, Jackson spent most of her married life in Bennington, Vermont. In addition to writing humorous stories of domestic life, she was equally at home writing spine-chilling Gothic thrillers.

*f*or sapphires[1]

Carolyn M. Rodgers

(for mama and daddy)

my daddy don't know
the same lady
i do. i know mama
he knows "suga."
5   and when daddy looks at mama
i wonder does he see
the wrinkles around
the tight mouth, stiff
factory used fingers
10   uh yellow skin,
begun to fade. . . .

and when mama talks
how does he hear? i hear
anger, pride, strength and love
15 crouched low in the throat,
any, ready to spring.
      but daddy calls mama "suga"
      and uh beacon is behind his eyes,
      he buys Chanel and coats
20   with fur collars. . . .

i wonder what lady does daddy know?

---

1. **sapphires** (saf′īrz), a slang expression for unpopular or unattractive girls or women, from the transparent, rich blue stone used as a gem.

"for sapphires," copyright © 1971 by Carolyn M. Rodgers from *How I Got Ovah* by Carolyn M. Rodgers. Reprinted by permission of Doubleday & Company, Inc.

Discussion

1. **(a)** What does the speaker see when she looks at her mother? **(b)** What does she hear when her mother talks?

2. **(a)** What does the speaker's father call this same woman? What does he buy her? **(b)** What does the metaphor in line 18 suggest about the father's feelings? **(c)** Describe the lady you think "daddy" knows.

3. Of the two pictures of "mama" presented in the poem, which do you think is the "true" picture? Explain.

Carolyn M. Rodgers 1942–

Formerly a counselor and language arts instructor, Carolyn Rodgers began a full-time writing career after being encouraged by Gwendolyn Brooks, the Pulitzer-Prize-winning poet.

Rodgers's first work appeared in *Black World;* since then she has published several volumes of poetry and has served as writer-in-residence at Malcolm X College in Chicago.

Mr. Mendelsohn

Nicholasa Mohr

"Man, I don't get you. You got a whole apartment next door all to yourself—six rooms! And you gotta come here to eat in this crowded kitchen. Why?"

Psst . . . psst, Mr. Mendelsohn, wake up. Come on now!" Mrs. Suárez[1] said in a low quiet voice. Mr. Mendelsohn had fallen asleep again, on the large armchair in the living room. He grasped the brown shiny wooden cane and leaned forward, his chin on his chest. The small black skullcap that was usually placed neatly on the back of his head had tilted to one side, covering his right ear. "Come on now. It's late, and time to go home." She tapped him on the shoulder and waited for him to wake up. Slowly, he lifted his head, opened his eyes, and blinked.

"What time is it?" he asked.

"It's almost midnight. Caramba![2] I didn't even know you was still here. When I came to shut off the lights, I saw you was sleeping."

"Oh . . . I'm sorry. O.K., I'm leaving." With short, slow steps he followed Mrs. Suárez over to the front door.

"Go on now," she said, opening the door. "We'll see you tomorrow."

He walked out into the hallway, stepped about three feet to the left, and stood before the door of his apartment. Mrs. Suárez waited, holding her door ajar, while he carefully searched for the right key to each lock. He had to open seven locks in all.

A small fluffy dog standing next to Mrs. Suárez began to whine and bark.

"Shh—sh, Sporty! Stop it!" she said. "You had your walk. Shh."

"O.K.," said Mr. Mendelsohn, finally opening his door. "Good night." Mrs. Suárez smiled and nodded.

"Good night," she whispered, as they both shut their doors simultaneously.

Mr. Mendelsohn knocked on the door and waited; then tried the doorknob. Turning and pushing, he realized the door was locked, and knocked again, this time more forcefully. He heard Sporty barking and footsteps coming toward the door.

"Who's there?" a child's voice asked.

"It's me—Mr. Mendelsohn! Open up, Yvonne." The door opened, and a young girl, age nine, smiled at him.

---

1. **Mrs. Suárez** (swä´res).
2. **caramba!** (kä räm´bä), goodness!

"Mr. Mendelsohn" from *El Bronx Remembered* by Nicholasa Mohr. Copyright © 1975 by Nicholasa Mohr. Reprinted by permission of Harper & Row, Publishers, Inc.

Nicholasa Mohr (nē kô lä´sä môr).

"Mami! It's el Señor[3] Mr. Mendelsohn again."

"Tell him to come on in, muchacha!"[4] Mrs. Suárez answered.

"My mother says come on in."

He followed Yvonne and the dog, who leaped up, barking and wagging his tail. Mr. Mendelsohn stood at the kitchen entrance and greeted everyone.

"Good morning to you all!" He had just shaved and trimmed his large black mustache. As he smiled broadly, one could see that most of his teeth were missing. His large bald head was partially covered by his small black skullcap. Thick dark grey hair grew in abundance at the lower back of his head, coming around the front above his ears into short sideburns. He wore a clean white shirt, frayed at the cuffs. His worn-out pinstripe trousers were held up by a pair of dark suspenders. Mr. Mendelsohn leaned on his brown shiny cane and carried a small brown paper bag.

"Mr. Mendelsohn, come into the kitchen," said Mrs. Suárez, "and have some coffee with us." She stood by the stove. A boy of eleven, a young man of about seventeen, and a young pregnant woman were seated at the table.

"Sit here," said the boy, vacating a chair. "I'm finished eating." He stood by the entrance with his sister Yvonne, and they both looked at Mr. Mendelsohn and his paper bag with interest.

"Thank you, Georgie," Mr. Mendelsohn said. He sat down and placed the bag on his lap.

The smell of freshly perked coffee and boiled milk permeated the kitchen.

Winking at everyone, the young man asked, "Hey, what you got in that bag you holding onto, huh, Mr. Mendelsohn?" They all looked at each other and at the old man, amused. "Something special, I bet!"

"Well," the old man replied. "I thought your mama would be so kind as to permit me to make myself a little breakfast here today . . . so." He opened the bag, and began to take out its contents. "I got two slices of rye bread, two tea bags. I brought one extra, just in case anybody would care to join me for tea. And a jar of herrring in sour cream."

"Sounds delicious!" said the young man, sticking out his tongue and making a face. Yvonne and Georgie burst out laughing.

"Shh . . . sh." Mrs. Suárez shook her head and looked at her children disapprovingly. "Never mind, Julio!" she said to the young man. Turning to Mr. Mendelsohn, she said, "You got the same like you brought last Saturday, eh? You can eat with us anytime. How about some fresh coffee? I just made it. Yes?" Mr. Mendelsohn looked at her, shrugging his shoulders. "Come on, have some," she coaxed.

"O.K.," he replied. "If it's not too much bother."

"No bother," she said, setting out a place for the old man. "You gonna have some nice fresh bread with a little butter— it will go good with your herring." Mrs. Suárez cut a generous slice of freshly baked bread with a golden crust and buttered it. "Go on, eat. There's a plate and everything for your food. Go on, eat . . . ."

"Would anyone care for some?" Mr. Mendelsohn asked. "Perhaps a tea bag for a cup of tea?"

"No . . . no thank you, Mr. Mendelsohn," Mrs. Suárez answered. "Everybody

---

3. *Mami* (mä′mē). . .*el Señor* (el sä nyôr′).
4. *muchacha* (mü chä′chä), girl.

here already ate. You go ahead and eat. You look too skinny; you better eat. Go on, eat your bread."

The old man began to eat vigorously.

"Can I ask you a question?" Julio asked the old man. "Man, I don't get you. You got a whole apartment next door all to yourself—six rooms! And you gotta come here to eat in this crowded kitchen. Why?"

"First of all, today is Saturday, and I thought I could bring in my food and your mama could turn on the stove for me. You know, in my religion you can't light a fire on Saturday."[5]

"You come here anytime; I turn on the stove for you, don't worry," Mrs. Suárez said.

"Man, what about other days? We been living here for about six months, right?" Julio persisted. "And you do more cooking here than in your own place."

"It doesn't pay to turn on the gas for such a little bit of cooking. So I told the gas company to turn it off . . . for good! I got no more gas now, only an electric hot plate," the old man said.

Julio shook his head and sighed. "I don't know——"

"Julio, chico!" snapped Mrs. Suárez, interrupting him, "Basta[6]—it doesn't bother nobody." She looked severely at her son and shook her head. "You gotta go with your sister to the clinic today, so you better get ready now. You too, Marta."

"O.K., Mama," she answered, "but I wanted to see if I got mail from Ralphy today."

"You don't got time. I'll save you the mail; you read it when you get back. You and Julio better get ready; go on." Reluctantly, Marta stood up and yawned, stretching and arching her back.

"Marta," Mr. Mendelsohn said, "you taking care? . . . You know, this is a very delicate time for you."

"I am, Mr. Mendelsohn. Thank you."

"I raised six sisters," the old man said. "I ought to know. Six . . . and married them off to fine husbands. Believe me, I've done my share in life." Yvonne and Georgie giggled and poked each other.

"He's gonna make one of his speeches," they whispered.

". . . I never had children. No time to get married. My father died when I was eleven. I went to work supporting my mother and six younger sisters. I took care of them, and today they are all married, with families. They always call and want me to visit them. I'm too busy and I have no time . . . ."

"Too busy eating in our kitchen," whispered Julio. Marta, Georgie, and Yvonne tried not to laugh out loud. Mrs. Suárez reached over and with a wooden ladle managed a light but firm blow on Julio's head.

". . . Only on the holidays, I make some time to see them. But otherwise, I cannot be bothered with all that visiting." Mr. Mendelsohn stopped speaking and began to eat again.

"Go on, Marta and Julio, you will be late for the clinic," Mrs. Suárez said. "And you two? What are you doing there smiling like two monkeys? Go find something to do!"

Quickly, Georgie and Yvonne ran down the hallway, and Julio and Marta left the kitchen.

Mrs. Suárez sat down beside the old man.

"Another piece of bread?" she asked.

"No, thank you very much . . . . I'm full. But it was delicious."

---

5. *in my religion. . .on Saturday.* Saturday is the Jewish Sabbath, a day of rest and worship. For many Jews, the restrictions against work on the Sabbath apply to such tasks as the lighting of stoves.
6. *chico* (chē′kô). . .*basta* (bäs′tä), boy. . .stop; enough.

"You too skinny—you don't eat right, I bet." Mrs. Suárez shook her head. "Come tomorrow and have Sunday supper with us."

"I really couldn't."

"Sure, you could. I always make a big supper and there is plenty. All right? Mr. Suárez and I will be happy to have you."

"Are you sure it will be no bother?"

"What are you talking for the bother all the time? One more person is no bother. You come tomorrow. Yes?"

The old man smiled broadly and nodded. This was the first time he had been invited to Sunday supper with the family.

Mrs. Suárez stood and began clearing away the dishes. "O.K., you go inside; listen to the radio or talk to the kids or something. I got work to do."

Mr. Mendelsohn closed his jar of herring and put it back into the bag. "Can I leave this here till I go?"

"Leave it; I put it in the refrigerator for you."

Leaning on his cane, Mr. Mendelsohn stood up and walked out of the kitchen and down the long hallway into the living room. It was empty. He went over to a large armchair by the window. The sun shone through the window, covering the entire armchair and Mr. Mendelsohn. A canary cage was also by the window, and two tiny yellow birds chirped and hopped back and forth energetically. Mr. Mendelsohn felt drowsy; he shut his eyes. So many aches and pains, he thought. It was hard to sleep at night, but here, well . . . the birds began to chirp in unison and the old man opened one eye, glancing at them, and smiled. Then he shut his eyes once more and fell fast asleep.

When Mr. Mendelsohn opened his eyes, Georgie and Yvonne were in the living room. Yvonne held a deck of playing cards and Georgie read a comic book. She looked at the old man and, holding up the deck of cards, asked "Do you wanna play a game of War? Huh, Mr. Mendelsohn?"

"I don't know how to play that," he answered.

"It's real easy. I'll show you. Come on . . . please!"

"Well," he shrugged, "sure, why not? Maybe I'll learn something."

Yvonne took a small maple end table and a wooden chair, and set them next to Mr. Mendelsohn. "Now . . ." she began, "I'll shuffle the cards and you cut, and then I throw down a card and you throw down a card and the one with the highest card wins. O.K.? And then, the one with the most cards of all wins the game. O.K.?"

"That's all?" he asked.

"That's all. Ready?" she asked, and sat down. They began to play cards.

"You know, my sister Jennie used to be a great card player," said Mr. Mendelsohn.

"Does she still play?" asked Yvonne.

"Oh . . ." Mr. Mendelsohn laughed. "I don't know any more. She's already married and has kids. She was the youngest in my family—like you."

"Did she go to P.S. 39? On Longwood Avenue?"

"I'm sure she did. All my sisters went to school around here."

"Wow! You must be living here a long time, Mr. Mendelsohn."

"Forty-five years!" said the old man.

"Wowee!" Yvonne whistled. "Georgie, did you hear? Mr. Mendelsohn been living here for forty-five whole years!"

Georgie put down his comic book and looked up.

"Really?" he asked, impressed.

"Yes, forty-five years this summer we

moved here. But in those days things were different, not like today. No sir! The Bronx has changed. Then, it was the country. That's right! Why, look out the window. You see the elevated trains on Westchester Avenue? Well, there were no trains then. That was once a dirt road. They used to bring cows through there.''

"Oh, man!" Georgie and Yvonne both gasped.

"Sure. These buildings were among the first apartment houses to go up. Four stories high, and that used to be a big accomplishment in them days. All that was here was mostly little houses, like you still see here and there. Small farms, woodlands . . . like that.''

"Did you see any Indians?" asked Georgie.

"What do you mean, Indians?" laughed the old man. "I'm not that old, and this here was not the Wild West." Mr. Mendelsohn saw that the children were disappointed. He added quickly, "But we did have carriages with horses. No cars and lots of horses.''

"That's what Mami says they have in Puerto Rico—not like here in El Bronx," said Yvonne.

"Yeah," Georgie agreed. "Papi[7] says he rode a horse when he was a little kid in Puerto Rico. They had goats and pigs and all them things. Man, was he lucky.''

"Lucky?" Mr. Mendelsohn shook his head. "You—you are the lucky one today! You got school and a good home and clothes. You don't have to go out to work and support a family like your papa and I had to do, and miss an education. You can learn and be somebody someday.''

"Someday," said Yvonne, "we are gonna get a house with a yard and all. Mami says that when Ralphy gets discharged from the Army, he'll get a loan from the govern-ment and we can pay to buy a house. You know, instead of rent.''

Mrs. Suárez walked into the living room with her coat on, carrying a shopping bag.

"Yvonne, take the dog out for a walk, and Georgie come on! We have to go shopping. Get your jacket.''

Mr. Mendelsohn started to rise. "No," she said, "stay . . . sit down. It's O.K. You can stay and rest if you want.''

"All right, Mrs. Suárez," Mr. Mendelsohn said.

"Now don't forget tomorrow for Sunday supper, and take a nap if you like.''

Mr. Mendelsohn heard the front door slam shut, and the apartment was silent. The warmth of the bright sun made him drowsy once more. It was so nice here, he thought, a house full of people and kids— like it used to be. He recalled his sisters and his parents . . . the holidays . . . the arguments . . . the laughing. It was so empty next door. He would have to look for a smaller apartment, near Jennie, someday. But not now. Now, it was just nice to sleep and rest right here. He heard the tiny birds chirping and quietly drifted into a deep sleep.

Mr. Mendelsohn rang the bell, then opened the door. He could smell the familiar cooking odors of Sunday supper. For two years he had spent every Sunday at his neighbors'. Sporty greeted him, jumping affectionately and barking.

"Shh—sh . . . down. Good boy," he said, and walked along the hallway toward the kitchen. The room was crowded with people and the stove was loaded with large pots of food, steaming and puffing. Mrs. Suárez was busy basting a large roast. Looking up, she saw Mr. Mendelsohn.

---

7. **Papi** (pä′pē).

"Come in," she said, "and sit down." Motioning to Julio, who was seated, she continued, "Julio, you are finished, get up and give Mr. Mendelsohn a seat." Julio stood up.

"Here's the sponge cake," Mr. Mendelsohn said, and handed the cake box he carried to Julio, who put it in the refrigerator.

"That's nice . . . . Thank you," said Mrs. Suárez, and placed a cup of freshly made coffee before the old man.

"Would anyone like some coffee?" Mr. Mendelsohn asked. Yvonne and Georgie giggled, looked at one another, and shook their heads.

"You always say that!" said Yvonne.

"One of these days," said Ralphy, "I'm gonna say, 'Yes, give me your coffee,' and you won't have none to drink." The children laughed loudly.

"Don't tease him," Mrs. Suárez said, half smiling. "Let him have his coffee."

"He is just being polite, children," Mr. Suárez said, and shifting his chair closer to Mr. Mendelsohn, he asked, "So . . . Mr. Mendelsohn, how you been? What's new? You O.K.?"

"So-so, Mr. Suárez. You know, aches and pains when you get old. But there's nothing you can do, so you gotta make the best of it."

Mr. Suárez nodded sympathetically, and they continued to talk. Mr. Mendelsohn saw the family every day, except for Mr. Suárez and Ralphy, who both worked a night shift.

Marta appeared in the entrance, holding a small child by the hand.

"There he is, Tato,"[8] she said to the child, and pointed to Mr. Mendelsohn.

"Oh, my big boy! He knows, he knows he's my best friend," Mr. Mendelsohn said, and held the brown shiny cane out toward Tato. The small boy grabbed the cane and, shrieking with delight, walked toward Mr. Mendelsohn.

"Look at that, will you?" said Ralphy. "He knows Mr. Mendelsohn better than me, his own father."

"That's because they are always together," smiled Marta. "Tato is learning to walk with his cane!"

Everyone laughed as they watched Tato climbing the old man's knee. Bending over, Mr. Mendelsohn pulled Tato onto his lap.

"Oh . . . he's getting heavy," said Mrs. Suárez. "Be careful."

"Never mind," Mr. Mendelsohn responded, hugging Tato. "That's my best boy. And look how swell he walks, and he's not even nineteen months."

"What a team," Julio said. "Tato already walks like Mr. Mendelsohn and pretty soon he's gonna complain like him, too . . . ." Julio continued to tease the old man, who responded good-naturedly, as everyone laughed.

After coffee, Mr. Mendelsohn sat on the large armchair in the living room, waiting for supper to be ready. He watched with delight as Tato walked back and forth with the cane. Mr. Mendelsohn held Tato's blanket, stuffed bear, and picture book.

"Tato," he called out, "come here. Let me read you a book—come on. I'm going to read you a nice story."

Tato climbed onto the chair and into Mr. Mendelsohn's lap. He sucked his thumb and waited. Mr. Mendelsohn opened the picture book.

"O.K. Now . . . ." He pointed to the picture. "A is for Alligators. See that? Look at that big mouth and all them teeth . . . ." Tato yawned, nestled back, and closed his

---

8. *Tato* (tä′tō).

eyes. The old man read a few more pages and shut the book.

The soft breathing and sucking sound that Tato made assured Mr. Mendelsohn that the child was asleep. Such a smart kid. What a great boy, he said to himself. Mr. Mendelsohn was vaguely aware of a radio program, voices, and the small dog barking now and then, just before he too fell into a deep sleep.

This Sunday was very much like all the others; coffee first, then he and Tato would play a bit before napping in the large armchair. It had become a way of life for the old man. Only the High Holy Days and an occasional invitation to a family event, such as a marriage or funeral and so on, would prevent the old man from spending Sunday next door.

It had all been so effortless. No one ever asked him to leave, except late at night when he napped too long. On Saturdays, he tried to observe the Sabbath and brought in his meal. They lit the stove for him.

Mrs. Suárez was always feeding him, just like Mama. She also worried about me not eating, the old man had said to himself, pleased. At first, he had been cautious and had wondered about the food and the people that he was becoming so involved with. That first Sunday, the old man had looked suspiciously at the food they served him.

"What is it?" he had asked. Yvonne and Georgie had started giggling, and had looked at one another. Mrs. Suárez had responded quickly and with anger, cautioning her children; speaking to them in Spanish.

"Eat your food, Mr. Mendelsohn. You too skinny," she had told him.

"What kind of meat is it?" Mr. Mendelsohn insisted.

"It's good for you, that's what it is," Mrs. Suárez answered.

"But I——" Mr. Mendelsohn started.

"Never mind—it's good for you. I prepare everything fresh. Go ahead and eat it," Mrs. Suárez had interrupted. There was a silence as Mr. Mendelsohn sat still, not eating.

"You know, I'm not allowed to eat certain things. In my religion we have dietary laws. This is not—pork or something like it, is it?"

"It's just . . . chicken. Chicken! That's what it is. It's delicious . . . and good for you," she had said with conviction.

"It doesn't look like chicken to me."

"That's because you never ate no chicken like this before. This here is—is called Puerto Rican chicken. I prepare it special. So you gonna eat it. You too skinny."

Mr. Mendelsohn had tried to protest, but Mrs. Suárez insisted. "Never mind. Now I prepare everything clean and nice. You eat the chicken; you gonna like it. Go on!"

And that was all.

Mr. Mendelsohn ate his Sunday supper from then on without doubt or hesitation, accepting the affection and concern that Mrs. Suárez provided with each plateful.

That night in his own apartment, Mr. Mendelsohn felt uneasy. He remembered that during supper, Ralphy had mentioned that his G.I. loan had come through. They would be looking for a house soon, everyone agreed. Not in the Bronx; farther out, near Yonkers: It was more like the country there.

The old man tossed and turned in his bed. That's still a long way off. First, they have to find the house and everything. You don't move just like that! he said to himself.

It's gonna take a while, he reasoned, putting such thoughts out of his mind.

Mr. Mendelsohn looked at his quarters.

"I told you, didn't I? See how nice this is?" his sister Jennie said. She put down the large sack of groceries on the small table.

It was a fair-sized room with a single bed, a bureau, a wooden wardrobe closet, a table, and two chairs. A hot plate was set on a small white refrigerator, and a white metal kitchen cabinet was placed alongside.

"We'll bring you whatever else you need, Louis," Jennie went on. "You'll love it here, I'm sure. There are people your own age, interested in the same things. Here—let's get started. We'll put your things away and you can get nicely settled."

Mr. Mendelsohn walked over to the window and looked out. He saw a wide avenue with cars, taxis, and buses speeding by. "It's gonna take me two buses, at least, to get back to the old neighborhood," he said.

"Why do you have to go back there?" Jennie asked quickly. "There is nobody there any more, Louis. Everybody moved!"

"There's shul . . . ."[9]

"There's shul right here. Next door you have a large temple. Twice you were robbed over there. It's a miracle you weren't hurt! Louis, there is no reason for you to go back. There is nothing over there, nothing," Jennie said.

"The trouble all started with that rooming house next door. Those people took in all kinds . . . ." He shook his head. "When the Suárez family lived there we had no problems. But nobody would talk to the landlord about those new people—only me. Nobody cared."

"That's all finished," Jennie said, looking at her watch. "Now look how nice it is here. Come on, let's get started." She began to put the groceries away in the refrigerator and cabinet.

"Leave it, Jennie," he interrupted. "Go on . . . . I'll take care of it. You go on home. You are in a hurry."

"I'm only trying to help," Jennie responded.

"I know, I know. But I lived in one place for almost fifty years. So don't hurry me." He looked around the room. "And I ain't going nowhere now . . . ."

Shaking her head, Jennie said, "Look—this weekend we have a wedding, but next weekend Sara and I will come to see you. I'll call the hotel on the phone first, and they'll let you know. All right?"

"Sure." He nodded.

"That'll be good, Louis. This way you will get a chance to get settled and get acquainted with some of the other residents." Jennie kissed Mr. Mendelsohn affectionately. The old man nodded and turned away. In a moment, he heard the door open and shut.

Slowly, he walked to the sack of groceries and finished putting them away. Then, with much effort, he lifted a large suitcase onto the bed. He took out several photographs. Then he set the photographs upright, arranging them carefully on the bureau. He had pictures of his parents' wedding and of his sisters and their families. There was a photograph of his mother taken just before she died, and another one of Tato.

That picture was taken when he was about two years old, the old man said to

---

9. **shul** (shül), synagogue; a Jewish place of worship and religious study.

himself. Yes, that's right, on his birthday . . . . There was a party. And Tato was already talking. Such a smart kid, he thought, smiling. Last? Last when? he wondered. Time was going fast for him. He shrugged. He could hardly remember what year it was lately. Just before they moved! He remembered. That's right, they gave him the photograph of Tato. They had a nice house around Gunhill Road someplace, and they had taken him there once. He recalled how exhausted he had been after the long trip. No one had a car, and they had had to take a train and buses. Anyway, he was glad he remembered. Now he could let them know he had moved, and tell them all about what happened to the old neighborhood. That's right, they had a telephone now. Yes, he said to himself, let me finish here, then I'll go call them. He continued to put the rest of his belongings away.

Mr. Mendelsohn sat in the lobby holding onto his cane and a cake box. He had told the nurse at the desk that his friends were coming to pick him up this Sunday. He looked eagerly toward the revolving doors. After a short while, he saw Ralphy, Julio, and Georgie walk through into the lobby.

"Deliveries are made in the rear of the building," he heard the nurse at the desk say as they walked toward him.

"These are my friends, Mrs. Read," Mr. Mendelsohn said, standing. "They are here to take me out."

"Oh, well," said the nurse. "All right; I didn't realize. Here he is then. He's been talking about nothing else but this visit." Mrs. Read smiled.

Ralphy nodded, then spoke to Georgie. "Get Mr. Mendelsohn's overcoat."

Quickly, Mr. Mendelsohn put on his coat, and all four left the lobby.

"Take good care of him now . . ." they heard Mrs. Read calling. "You be a good boy now, Mr. Mendelsohn."

Outside, Mr. Mendelsohn looked at the young men and smiled.

"How's everyone?" he asked.

"Good," Julio said. "Look, that's my pickup truck from work. They let me use it sometimes when I'm off."

"That's a beautiful truck. How's everyone? Tato? How is my best friend? And Yvonne? Does she like school? And your Mama and Papa? . . . Marta? . . ."

"Fine, fine. Everybody is doing great. Wait till you see them. We'll be there in a little while," said Julio. "With this truck, we'll get there in no time."

Mr. Mendelsohn sat in the kitchen and watched as Mrs. Suárez packed food into a shopping bag. Today had been a good day for the old man; he had napped in the old armchair and spent time with the children. Yvonne was so grown up, he almost had not recognized her. When Tato remembered him, Mr. Mendelsohn had been especially pleased. Shyly, he had shaken hands with the old man. Then he had taken him into his room to show Mr. Mendelsohn all his toys.

"Now I packed a whole lotta stuff in this shopping bag for you. You gotta eat it. Eat some of my Puerto Rican chicken—it's good for you. You too skinny. You got enough for tomorrow and for another day. You put it in the refrigerator. Also I put some rice and other things."

He smiled as she spoke, enjoying the attention he received.

"Julio is gonna drive you back before it gets too late," she said. "And we gonna pick you up again and bring you back to eat with us. I bet you don't eat right." She shook her head. "O.K.?"

"You shouldn't go through so much bother," he protested mildly.

"Again with the bother? You stop that! We gonna see you soon. You take care of yourself and eat. Eat! You must nourish yourself, especially in such cold weather."

Mr. Mendelsohn and Mrs. Suárez walked out into the living room. The family exchanged good-byes with the old man. Tato, feeling less shy, kissed Mr. Mendelsohn on the cheek.

Just before leaving, Mr. Mendelsohn embraced Mrs. Suárez for a long time, as everybody watched silently.

"Thank you," he whispered.

"Thank you? For what?" Mrs. Suárez said. "You come back soon and have Sunday supper with us. Yes?" Mr. Mendelsohn nodded and smiled.

It was dark and cold out. He walked with effort. Julio carried the shopping bag. Slowly, he got into the pickup truck. The ride back was bumpy and uncomfortable for Mr. Mendelsohn. The cold wind cut right through into the truck, and the old man was aware of the long winter ahead.

His eyelids were so heavy he could hardly open them. Nurses scurried about busily. Mr. Mendelsohn heard voices.

"Let's give him another injection. It will help his breathing. Nurse! Nurse! The patient needs . . . ."

The voices faded. He remembered he had gone to sleep after supper last—last when? How many days have I been here . . . here in the hospital? Yes, he thought, now I know where I am. A heart attack, the doctor had said, and then he had felt even worse. Didn't matter; I'm too tired. He heard voices once more, and again he

barely opened his eyes. A tall thin man dressed in white spoke to him.

"Mr. Mendelsohn, can you hear me? How do you feel now? More comfortable? We called your family. I spoke to your sister, Mrs. Wiletsky. They should be here very soon. You feeling sleepy? Good . . . . Take a little nap—go on. We'll wake you when they get here, don't worry. Go on now . . . ."

He closed his eyes, thinking of Jennie. She'll be here soon with Esther and Rosalie and Sara. All of them. He smiled. He was so tired. His bed was by the window and a bright warm sash of sunshine covered him almost completely. Nice and warm, he thought, and felt comfortable. The pain had lessened, practically disappeared. Mr. Mendelsohn heard the birds chirping and Sporty barking. That's all right, Mrs. Suárez would let him sleep. She wouldn't wake him up, he knew that. It looked like a good warm day; he planned to take Tato for a walk later. That's some smart kid, he thought. Right now he was going to rest.

"This will be the last of it, Sara."

"Just a few more things, Jennie, and we'll be out of here."

The two women spoke as they packed away all the items in the room. They opened drawers and cabinets, putting things away in boxes and suitcases.

"What about these pictures on the bureau?" asked Sara.

Jennie walked over and they both looked at the photographs.

"There's Mama and Papa's wedding picture. Look, there's you, Sara, when Jonathan was born. And Esther and . . . look, he's got all the pictures of the entire family." Jennie burst into tears.

"Come on, Jennie; it's all over, honey.

He was sick and very old.'' The older woman comforted the younger one.

Wiping her eyes, Jennie said, ''Well, we did the best we could for him, anyway.''

''Who is this?'' asked Sara, holding up Tato's photo.

''Let me see,'' said Jennie. ''Hummm . . . that must be one of the people in that family that lived next door in the old apartment on Prospect Avenue. You know—remember that Spanish family? He used to visit with them. Their name was . . . Díaz or something like that, I think. I can't remember.''

''Oh yes,'' said Sara. ''Louis mentioned them once in a while, yes. They were nice to him. What shall we do with it? Return it?''

''Oh,'' said Jennie, ''that might be rude. What do you think?''

''Well, I don't want it, do you?''

''No,'' Jennie hesitated. ''. . . But let's just put it away. Maybe we ought to tell them what happened. About Louis.'' Sara shrugged her shoulders. ''Maybe I'll write to them,'' Jennie went on, ''if I can find out where they live. They moved. What do you say?''

''I don't care, really,'' Sara sighed. ''I have a lot to do yet. I have to meet Esther at the lawyer's to settle things. And I still have to make supper. So let's get going.''

Both women continued to pack, working efficiently and with swiftness. After a while, everything was cleared and put away in boxes and suitcases.

''All done!'' said Sara.

''What about this?'' asked Jennie, holding up Tato's photograph.

''Do what you want,'' said Sara. ''I'm tired. Let's go.''

Looking at the photograph, Jennie slipped it into one of the boxes. ''I might just write and let them know.''

The two women left the room, closing the door behind them.

Discussion

1. About how many years are covered in the story? How can you tell?

2. Considering his actions and the things he thinks and talks about, how would you characterize Mr. Mendelsohn?

3. **(a)** How does Mrs. Suárez seem to feel about Mr. Mendelsohn? How does she show this? **(b)** What is the attitude of the older children toward Mr. Mendelsohn? Does their relationship with him change? **(c)** How is Tato's relationship with Mr. Mendelsohn different from the others'? Why might this be so?

4. Julio asks Mr. Mendelsohn why he eats in their kitchen when he has his own apartment. **(a)** What answers does Mr. Mendelsohn give him? **(b)** In your opinion, are these the only or even the most important reasons?

5. **(a)** Why does Mr. Mendelsohn move from his apartment? **(b)** What does Jennie consider to be the advantages of the new location? **(c)** Although Jennie insists that ''there is nothing'' in the old neighborhood, what things might still be there for Mr. Mendelsohn?

6. After their brother has died, Jennie says to Sara, ''We did the best we could for him.'' **(a)** What do you infer is the relationship between Mr. Mendelsohn and his sisters? **(b)** In your opinion, did the sisters do the best they could for him?

Application
Point of View

The amount of information a reader gets about each character in a story depends on the point of view from which the narrator tells the story. After answering the following questions, decide from which of the four major points of view "Mr. Mendelsohn" is told.

1. Is the narrator a character in the story or an outsider?

2. Do you know what Mr. Mendelsohn does? what he thinks?

3. Do you know what the other characters do? what they think?

Vocabulary
Dictionary

Replace the italicized phrase in each of the following sentences with the word from the list that has the same meaning. (You will not use one of the listed words.) Refer to your Glossary if you need help.

ajar	permeated
conviction	unison
injection	vacated

1. At the end of the concert the whole chorus sang in *harmonious combination.*

2. It is his *firm belief* that all it takes to be successful is strong willpower.

3. The police stated that the hotel room had been *abandoned and left empty* just thirty minutes before they arrived.

4. By leaving the back door *slightly open,* they hoped to encourage their wandering cat to return home.

5. The poisonous gas fumes soon *spread throughout* the windowless room.

Composition

Mr. Mendelsohn tells the Suárez family that he raised six sisters after their father died and that he now visits them and their families on holidays. During the story he also forms a strong attachment to the Suárezes. In your opinion, which "family"—his sisters or the Suárezes—does Mr. Mendelsohn feel closer to? Why? Complete this statement: "Mr. Mendelsohn probably considers his family to be _____." Now recall from the story events, comments by characters, etc., that could help prove the statement you have completed, and make a list of them.

Write a composition of about one page in which you explain and support your statement. (You may use the statement as a topic sentence if you wish, or you may rewrite it as you need.) Use items from your list to help support your point.

(You may find the article "Supporting a Point" in the Composition Guide helpful in writing this composition.)

Nicholasa Mohr 1935–

Nicholasa Mohr turned to writing only after she had already earned a reputation as a painter and printmaker. Her first book, *Nilda,* which she illustrated herself, received many awards. *El Bronx Remembered, In Nueva York,* and *Felita,* also award-winning books, established Mohr's reputation as an accomplished author and as a spokeswoman for the Puerto Rican people.

*T*hank You, Ma'am

Langston Hughes

He did not trust the woman *not* to trust him. And he did not want to be mistrusted now.

She was a large woman with a large purse that had everything in it but a hammer and nails. It had a long strap, and she carried it slung across her shoulder. It was about eleven o'clock at night, and she was walking alone, when a boy ran up behind her and tried to snatch her purse. The strap broke with the tug the boy gave it from behind. But the boy's weight and the weight of the purse caused him to lose his balance. Instead of taking off full blast, the boy fell on his back on the sidewalk, and his legs flew up. The large woman simply turned around and kicked him right square in his blue-jeaned sitter. She shook him until his teeth rattled. Then she reached down and picked the boy up by his shirt.

After that the woman said, "Pick up my pocketbook, boy, and give it here."

She still held him tightly. But she bent down enough to let him pick up her purse. Then she said, "Now ain't you ashamed of yourself?"

Firmly gripped by his shirt front, the boy said, "Yes'm."

The woman said, "What did you want to do it for?"

The boy said, "I didn't aim to."

She said, "You lie!"

By that time two or three people passed, turned to look, and some stood watching.

"If I turn you loose, will you run?" asked the woman.

"Yes'm," said the boy.

"Then I won't turn you loose," said the woman. She did not release him.

"Lady, I'm sorry," whispered the boy.

"Um-hum! Your face is dirty. I got a great mind to wash your face for you. Ain't you got nobody home to tell you to wash your face?"

"No'm," said the boy.

"Then it will get washed this evening," said the large woman, starting up the street, dragging the frightened boy behind her.

He looked as if he were fourteen or fifteen, thin and wild, in tennis shoes and blue jeans.

The woman said, "You ought to be my son. I would teach you right from wrong. Least I can do right now is to wash your face. Are you hungry?"

"No'm," said the boy. "I just want you to turn me loose."

"Was I bothering you when I turned that corner?" asked the woman.

"No'm."

"But you put yourself in contact with *me,*" said the woman. "If you think that contact is not going to last a while, you got another thought coming. When I get through with you, sir, you are going to remember Mrs. Luella Bates Washington Jones."

"Thank You, Ma'am" from *The Langston Hughes Reader* by Langston Hughes. Published by George Braziller, Inc. Copyright © 1958 by Langston Hughes. Reprinted by permission of Harold Ober Associates Incorporated.

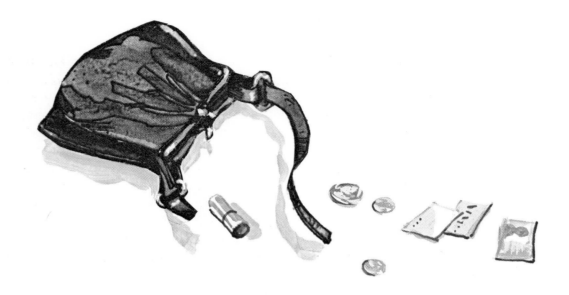

Sweat popped out on the boy's face, and he began to struggle. Mrs. Jones stopped, jerked him around in front of her, put a half nelson about his neck, and continued to drag him up the street. When she got to her door, she dragged the boy inside, down a hall, and into a large room at the rear of the house. She switched on the light and left the door open. The boy could hear other roomers laughing and talking. Some of their doors were open, too; so he knew he and the woman were not alone. The woman still had him by the neck in the middle of her room.

She said, "What is your name?"

"Roger," answered the boy.

"Then, Roger, you go to that sink and wash your face," said the woman. She turned him loose—at last. Roger looked at the door—and went to the sink.

"Let the water run until it gets warm," she said. "Here's a clean towel."

"You gonna take me to jail?" asked the boy, bending over the sink.

"Not with that face. I would not take you nowhere," said the woman. "Here I am trying to get home to cook me a bite to eat, and you snatch my pocketbook! Maybe you ain't been to your supper, either, late as it be. Have you?"

"There's nobody home at my house," said the boy.

"Then we'll eat," said the woman. "I believe you're hungry—or been hungry—to try to snatch my pocketbook!"

"I want a pair of suede shoes," said the boy.

"Well, you didn't have to snatch *my* pocketbook to get some suede shoes," said Mrs. Luella Bates Washington Jones. "You could of asked me."

"Ma'am?"

The water dripping from his face, the boy looked at her. There was a long pause. A very long pause. After drying his face and not knowing what else to do, the boy dried it again. Then he turned around. The door was open. He would make a dash for it down the hall. He would run, run, run, *run!*

The woman was sitting on the day bed. After a while she said, "I were young once and I wanted things I could not get."

There was another long pause. The boy's mouth opened. Then he frowned, not knowing he frowned.

The woman said, "Um-hum! You thought I was going to say, *but I didn't snatch people's pocketbooks*. Well, I wasn't going to say that." Pause. Silence. "I have done things, too, which I would not tell you, son—neither tell God, if He didn't already know. Everybody's got something in common. Sit you down while I fix us something to eat. You might run that comb through your hair so you will look presentable."

In another corner of the room behind a screen was a gas plate and an icebox. Mrs. Jones got up and went behind the screen. The woman did not watch the boy to see if he was going to run now. She didn't watch her purse, which she left behind her on the day bed. But the boy took care to sit on the far side of the room, away from the purse. He thought she could easily see him out of the corner of her eye if she wanted to. He did not trust the woman *not* to trust him. And he did not want to be mistrusted now.

"Do you need somebody to go to the store," asked the boy, "to get some milk or something?"

"Don't believe I do," said the woman, "unless you want sweet milk yourself. I was going to make cocoa out of this canned milk I got here."

"That will be fine," said the boy.

She heated some lima beans and ham, made the cocoa, and set the table. The woman did not ask the boy anything about where he lived, or his folks, or anything else that would embarrass him. Instead, as they ate, she told him about her job in a hotel beauty shop, what the work was like, and how all kinds of women came in and out. Then she cut him half of her ten-cent cake.

"Eat some more, son," she said.

When they finished eating, she got up and said, "Now here, take this ten dollars and buy yourself some suede shoes. And, next time, do not make the mistake of latching onto my pocketbook nor nobody else's—because shoes got by devilish ways will burn your feet. I got to get my rest now. But from here on in, son, I hope you will behave yourself."

She led him down the hall to the front door and opened it. "Good night! Behave yourself, boy!" she said as he went down the steps.

The boy wanted to say something more than "Thank you, ma'am," to Mrs. Luella Bates Washington Jones. Although his lips moved, he couldn't even say that as he turned at the foot of the stairs and looked up at the large woman in the door. Then she shut the door.

Discussion

1. What happens to Roger as he grabs Mrs. Jones's purse, and how does Mrs. Jones react?

2. How does Mrs. Jones treat Roger once they get to her home?

3. Mrs. Jones says, "I have done things, too, which I would not tell you, son . . . . Everybody's got something in common."
(a) Why do you infer she tells Roger this?
(b) What effect does her comment seem to have on Roger?

4. (a) Why can't Roger say, "Thank you, ma'am" to Mrs. Jones? (b) Do you think Roger's encounter with Mrs. Jones will have a lasting effect on him? Why or why not?

*F*ather and the "1812"

Todd Rolf Zeiss

As the music began to build to the grand climax, Father stood and raised his shotgun . . . .

My father, Jahnos Kovach,[1] was a brick-layer. He lived in Milwaukee, and in the days before trade unions he was also a carpenter, a plasterer, a plumber, an electrician and a cabinetmaker. He knew how to mend harnesses, set saws, tune pianos, and repair bicycles. He could build a house from foundation to roof, tear apart an automobile and put it together again, and sharpen knives so they would hold an edge.

But most of all he wanted to become a musician.

Grandfather, a locksmith, watchmaker and master gunsmith, disapproved. Music was all right—in its place. There was nothing wrong with listening to the opera over WTMJ on Sunday afternoons or going to the band concerts in Washington Park on holidays. But a man should have a trade—something he did with his hands. And he should have something to show for his efforts when he was done. What had a musician to show when the concert was over?

There were arguments. At first merely disagreements, with a remark here, a comment there, an emphatic gesture or two. The remarks became epithets and the comments grew into tirades. Hands waved in the air. There were shouts, accusations. And one day father left.

But it was already too late. His fingers, bruised and calloused by brick and stone, had no touch for keys, no agility for frets or stops, no feeling for strings. His lips, cracked a thousand times by the winter cold and blistered a thousand more by the summer wind, were no good for mouthpieces or reeds. His voice had limited itself to a narrow range between "D" above middle "C" and "A" an octave below, making tenor too high and baritone too low.

His ear was good—excellent, in fact. To him the most complicated scores of Bach, Beethoven and Wagner[2] were child's play. He knew every entrance, release, crescendo and decrescendo[3] by heart.

He could conduct. We watched him many times, my brother and I, in later years when he thought he was alone. Standing before the radio or the Victrola,[4] he would wave his arms in the air, cueing the horns, quieting the strings, bringing in the entire ensemble and, flapping and soaring like an eagle, he would raise the orchestra to a deafening crescendo of cymbals and tympani and chimes. We lay on the floor and peered beneath the curtain which separated the parlor from the hall. We could never keep still for very long and our giggling always gave us away. When he heard us, fa-

---

1. *Jahnos Kovach* (yä′nōsh kō′väch).
2. *Bach. . .Wagner.* Bach (bäk) 1685-1750, Beethoven (bā′ tō vən) 1770-1827, and Wagner (väg′ nər) 1813-1883 were all German composers.
3. *crescendo* (krə shen′dō) *and decrescendo* (dē′krə shen′dō), increase and decrease in force or loudness. [*Italian*]
4. *Victrola* (vik trō′lə), a trade name for an early kind of phonograph.

Todd Rolf Zeiss (zīs).

ther would turn round, and we could never be certain what was going to happen next. Sometimes he would scowl ferociously and charge forward, roaring like a bear, his huge calloused hand describing an arc through the air which ended abruptly with a whack on our posteriors as we scrambled in retreat. Other times, however, that same large hand would beckon to us, and father would say, "Come, Jahni.[5] Come, Karl. Come and listen." We would go in. "Hear the horns," he would say, lifting us to his lap. "Listen to the cello play counterpoint.[6] Now it starts to build." A wave of his hand would fill the room with sound, and as his hand rose, the music would rise—up and up it would go, whirling and swirling, higher and higher, carrying us with it. His hand would drop and the music would fall—soft, so soft we could hear his heart beating.

But there were too many conductors already, and nobody was the least bit interested in one who could not play a single instrument, so father did the next best thing. He bought a three-storied brownstone on Juneau Avenue just a few blocks from the Forstkeller[7] where the symphony orchestra rehearsed, married a woman who was an excellent cook and opened a boarding house with special rates for musicians. Because of the low rates, the musicians came. Because of the wonderful meals, and because mother always had something to eat waiting for them when they returned from a late rehearsal or an evening concert, they stayed.

There were other inducements, too. The price of concert tickets, which the musicians could often get for nothing, was deducted from the rent, and if one of them happened to be out of a job for a week or two, which was often the case, music lessons were considered adequate compensa-

tion. As a consequence my brother Karl learned to pay the piano, the oboe, and the clarinet, and I the violin, the viola, the cello, and the bass violin.

As his patronage increased, father grew happier and happier. He would come home tired after a hard day's bricklaying or plastering, and the talk with the musicians at the dinner table seemed to revive him. After the meal they would adjourn to the parlor for wine and cigars and the discussion would continue, often until midnight. Sometimes they put a record on the Victrola and discussed orchestration. Other times one of the musicians would get out his violin or sit at our piano (a marvelous old Steinway upright whose tone was the equal of any grand), or a group of them would form an ensemble and play into the small hours of the morning. Karl and I often sneaked downstairs in our pajamas to listen to those impromptu concerts, but mother usually caught us and sent us back to bed where we lay awake for hours, listening to the muted strains as they seeped through the plaster and reverberated along the heavy timbers until, I like to think, the entire house was filled with the spirit of some dead composer.

But in the midst of father's happiness lay a strong sense of frustration. Taking his family to the concert every Sunday was not the same as playing in the orchestra. Hearing his sons play music, although it brought him great satisfaction, was not as satisfying as playing it himself would have been. Being among musicians was not the same as being one of them.

Once he came very close to being one of them. A famous pianist of German extrac-

5. *Jahni* (yä′ni).
6. *play counterpoint,* add one melody to another as an accompaniment.
7. *Forstkeller* (fôrsht′kel′ər).

tion whose concert tours always included several performances in Milwaukee and who invariably stayed at our house because he liked the food, planned on one occasion to play several piano variations written by Dr. Prager, the conductor of the Milwaukee Symphony. Because this was to be a surprise (the programs, Dr. Prager was told, were "inexcusably delayed" at the printers, and newspapers carrying announcements of the event listed only "some variations"), and because the variations were still in manuscript and had to be secretly purloined, Herr Schmidt[8] (so I shall call him) had had little time to practice them and required a page-turner. He had intended to use for this purpose his secretary and valet, a slender, dyspeptic Frenchman, but before the concert was to begin, the man became violently ill. He said it was something he had eaten.

Herr Schmidt stalked up and down the parlor in his white tie and tails. "Fifteen minutes before the concert!" he stormed. "If he was going to get sick, why couldn't he at least have given us time to find a replacement? I'll have to cancel the variations; that's all there is to it. My poor friend Prager: what a disappointment! But where can we possibly find a page-turner at this hour?"

Father volunteered.

"You are a musician, too?" the pianist asked, somewhat surprised, since father had come home late that evening and was still dressed in his overalls.

"No," father replied. "I am a bricklayer. But I read music quite well and I am certain I can turn pages as efficiently and as quietly as that idiot secretary of yours, who can't recognize good food even when it stares him in the face. Besides," he continued, throwing his great arm around Herr

Schmidt's shoulders and turning on his warmest smile which, we used to say, could win a lamb from a wolf, "we were planning a little smorgasbord after the concert in honor of you and Dr. Prager."

Herr Schmidt threw up his hands. Father dashed upstairs and returned a few minutes later, wearing the skinny Frenchman's tuxedo, its sleeves and shoulders bulging, trouser cuffs turned under, and a large safety-pin hidden behind the white tie, fastening the collar.

We hurriedly drove downtown to the Pabst Theatre. The orchestra was already tuning up, and mother, Karl and I just had time to get ourselves seated before Dr. Prager and Herr Schmidt walked onto the stage. They were greeted by warm and sustained applause.

The first half of the concert went well with Dr. Prager, the orchestra and Herr Schmidt performing beautifully the "Concerto in E-flat" by Liszt.[9]

The Prager variations opened the second half of the concert. As father and Herr Schmidt walked onto the stage, Karl and I applauded wildly. All went well, with father proving himself an able assistant. But in the middle of the second variation, the accent pedal on the piano began to squeak. The audience stirred. Herr Schmidt, with true professional fortitude, continued as if nothing unusual were happening. But every time he pressed the pedal, it squeaked. Herr Schmidt grew visibly annoyed.

At the end of the variation, father stood up, whispered something to Herr Schmidt and hurried off stage. A moment later he returned, carrying the toolbox which he always kept in the car. Before anyone could think of pulling the curtain, he was down on

---

8. **Herr Schmidt** (her shmit), Mr. Schmidt. [*German*]
9. **Liszt** (list), a Hungarian composer 1811-1886.

his knees beneath the piano, toolbox open, working on the pedal with screwdriver, wrench and oil-can.

Herr Schmidt tested the pedal: it no longer squeaked.

Father closed his toolbox, got up, carried it off stage and returned, brushing dust and sweeping wax from the Frenchman's tuxedo. They continued with the next variation. When it was over, the audience, forgetting for the moment its concert manners, burst into applause.[10] Herr Schmidt rose, bowed, bowed again, then sat down to begin the next variation. The audience continued to applaud. Herr Schmidt stood, bowed once more, and sat again. The applause continued.

"Kovach!" we shouted. "Kovach!"

Herr Schmidt heard us. He smiled, rose again and extended his hand to father. Father stood up, bowed stiffly, gave Herr Schmidt's hand a rough shake, and sat down quickly. The applause died and they finished the variations.

For father, it was not the same as being a musician. It was true that much of the applause Herr Schmidt had received that evening was meant for father, and that father had saved the concert; but being able to repair a piano, however important it might have been at the moment, was not the same as being able to play it.

In the late 'twenties and early 'thirties Milwaukee became quite well known for its music. Every week-end during the summer there were concerts in the Blatz Open Air Theatre in Washington Park, and as the weather grew colder, the orchestra moved indoors to the Pabst Theatre downtown. Because we had a short concert season and it was easy for our musicians to find work during the off-season at downtown theatres like the Palace and the Majestic, and at jazz spots and burlesque houses, we were able to hold within the city itself the solid core of musicians so necessary to a good orchestra. Although we often had guest conductors and guest performers, the orchestra itself had very few itinerant members.

But music was not consigned only to our musicians. It was everywhere. One could walk down any street in the residential districts and hear a cacophony of instruments practicing scales, exercises and recital numbers. People walking to and from work hummed arias from Puccini's "Madame Butterfly," Mozart's "Magic Flute" or "The Marriage of Figaro." One could hear them whistling the theme from Haydn's[11] "Surprise Symphony" or from Beethoven's "Eroica." In the winter it was there too, but hushed and muted. Blending with the silent snowfall of a winter night, it lay encased behind closed doors and tightly sealed windows, waiting for spring to set it free again.

For father it was like an eternal winter. His desire to play music, to contribute to the sound of an orchestra, lay dormant like a hibernating animal, restless, stirring with the first pre-dawn of spring.

Musicians came to Milwaukee from all over the world, and soon our orchestra was playing two concerts a week, Saturday evening and Sunday afternoon. Generally one of these concerts, usually the one on Sunday, was directed by a guest conductor.

On one of these occasions the guest conductor was a famous Italian, a very particular and exacting man who had never before been in our city. He had just completed a world-wide tour and the stop at

---

10. **forgetting. . .applause.** During a performance of a musical composition in several parts, the audience generally holds its applause until the end.
11. **Puccini's . . . Haydn's.** Puccini (pü chē′nē) 1858-1924 was an Italian composer; Mozart (mōt′särt) 1756-1791 and Haydn (hīd′n) 1732-1809 were Austrian composers.

Milwaukee was to be its triumphant close. Instead of the usual two, he was scheduled to direct three weekend concerts, and his concluding selection for the Sunday evening performance was to be Tchaikovsky's "1812 Overture."[12]

The musicians at our house were buzzing with excitement. Some of them were nervous; they had heard of the Italian's incendiary temperament and they feverishly hoped nothing would go wrong. The great maestro arrived on the Thursday morning and immediately plunged the orchestra into a whirlwind of rehearsals. They rehearsed and rehearsed until each number was measure perfect. All went well until Friday evening when they rehearsed the "1812 Overture."

Near the end of the overture, which was written to celebrate the Russian victory over Napoleon and which was to be the grand climax of the maestro's triumphant tour, there is a notation for cannon. "Ordnance is to be fired nineteen times." Our orchestra had no cannon. The young man who headed the percussion section, a tympanist named Otto who lived at our boarding house, planned merely to substitute bass drum and tympani, which was often done. When the first stroke of ordnance fell, Otto pounded the tympani and another fellow beat the bass drum.

The maestro stopped the orchestra. "Where is the cannon?" he asked.

"We have none, sir," Otto replied.

"No cannon?" the maestro asked with cold incredulity. "None, sir," said Otto. "We will substitute bass drum and tympani."

"But the score calls for cannon," insisted the maestro, his voice rising. "Tchaikovsky asks for cannon. And I demand cannon!"

"But, sir—we have none," Otto cried.

"Then get one," the maestro screamed, ending the discussion.

The following morning Otto borrowed father's car and chased all over Milwaukee looking for some sort of cannon. But there was none to be had. At noon he remarked plaintively, "If only I could find something, a shotgun, anything . . . ."

"I have a shotgun," father replied.

It was a marvelous gun. Father had inherited it from grandfather. It was an eight-gauge double-barrel, a journeyman's piece made by grandfather to display his craftsmanship for entry into the gunsmiths' guild. It had external dragon-shaped hammers, a fancy brass triggerguard, engraved Damascus barrels[13] with two tiny ivory beads for sights and an ivory butt plate. Its stock and fore-end were of burled walnut, polished smooth as glass. Inlaid on either side of the stock was an ivory dragon and there was a small pewter shield at the wrist, stamped with grandfather's initials, "J.K." Father used it for shooting ducks along the Milwaukee River. But if Otto wished, he would remove the shot from a box of shells and it could be used for the concert.

There was one stipulation; father would have to shoot it himself. It was a family treasure, he explained, and if anything should happen to it . . . .

Otto agreed, and that afternoon he brought father and the shotgun to rehearsal. Out of curiosity, Karl and I tagged along and hid in the wings.

"We could find no cannon," Otto ex-

---

12. **Tchaikovsky's "1812 Overture."** Tchaikovsky (chī kôf′skē) 1840-1893 was a Russian composer whose "1812 Overture" has become a popular favorite for its stirring conclusion written for actual cannon and church bells.

13. **Damascus** (də mas′kəs) **barrels,** barrels of Damascus steel, a kind of ornamented steel with fine wavy lines.

plained to the maestro, "but my friend, Jahnos Kovach, has kindly consented to lend us his shotgun." The maestro smiled. "There is one condition," Otto continued. "The shotgun is a family treasure and Herr Kovach insists that he shoot it himself."

Again the Italian smiled. "Certainly," he replied. "Herr Kovach is a musician, of course?"

"I am a bricklayer," father said with quiet dignity.

"A bricklayer! First there is no cannon; and now, I suppose, I am to have a *bricklayer* playing in my orchestra!"

"I read music quite well," said father, "and I assure you I can play the shotgun."

The maestro was furious. They argued violently. The conductor, jumping up and down and waving his hands in the air, yapped and squeaked like a puppy-dog. Father, standing solidly with his massive arms folded across his barrel of a chest, growled and rumbled in response. As the argument grew more and more heated, Karl and I became more and more concerned. How long could father hold his temper? How long would it be before one of his immense fists descended upon this noisy little creature and . . .

But a temperamental Italian is no match for a determined Hungarian. In the end, father won. They rehearsed the "1812 Overture."

Bang . . . bang. Father had fired only two shots of the initial volley of ordnance when the maestro stopped the orchestra.

"Do you call that a cannon?" the Italian asked acidly. "It's not even a pop-gun." The men in the orchestra laughed. Father's leathered cheeks grew red. "It must be louder," the conductor cried, savoring his immediate victory, "much, much louder."

"I can make it louder," father said.

"Then do it," the maestro replied. "And don't fire another shot until you do."

Making the shots louder was no problem. Father merely pulled out the wads in the shells and filled them with a triple load of powder. What bothered him was that he had had no chance to rehearse with the orchestra. The first five shots were to follow with a single measure of one another at a tempo of *allegro vivace.*[14] He would have to load both barrels, fire both, reload, fire both again, reload again and fire one—all within five seconds.

For the rest of the afternoon father retreated to the parlor. We could hear the metronome ticking and father counting, "One and two and a three and four and a one." And each time we could hear the hammers of the shotgun click, the shotgun break and snap shut. But the timing was off. The metronome always came out one beat ahead.

That evening father did not go with us to the maestro's first concert, and when we returned we heard him working on something in the basement. Late that night I remember waking to the faint ticking of the metronome and the snap and click of the shotgun. But I was too drowsy to take serious note of it and rolled over and quickly fell asleep again.

The following morning father said nothing. He accompanied the rest of us to church, which was unusual as he generally let mother take care of the family's religion. But I noted that he was especially devout during the silent prayer.

That afternoon we all went to the maestro's second concert, and although we particularly enjoyed a selection by Dvořák,[15]

---

14. allegro vivace (ə leg′rō vē vä′chä), fast and very lively. [*Italian*]
15. Dvořák (dvôr′zhäk), a Czech composer 1841-1904.

the concert was generally a disappointment. When we returned home and the musicians were munching on a light between-concerts-snack mother had prepared, we listened to them grumbling their dissatisfaction with the maestro. He was too severe, they said, too tied to the notations. He gave the music no chance to sing.

That evening father put on the tuxedo he had rented especially for the occasion, slipped his shotgun into its case, and we all headed back to the Pabst Theatre. Our seats were to the right in the front row of the balcony where we could see the entire stage. On the backs of our programs, listed at the bottom of the percussion section we found father's name, Jahnos Kovach, in neat hand lettering. Otto had got hold of the programs, and he and other musicians staying at our house had spent the entire morning printing it on every one.

The musicians filed onto the stage. The oboe sounded his concert "A"[16] and the orchestra began tuning up. The maestro entered and walked to the podium. There was a smattering of applause. I felt a moment of panic, not seeing father on the stage and thinking, perhaps, the maestro had refused him his part. But then I realized there would be nothing for him to do during the first half of the concert and he had chosen to remain backstage. I could imagine him poking into every aspect of theatre apparatus and asking the lighting technicians an interminable stream of questions.

The first half of the concert went well. The audience was appreciative but not over enthusiastic. When the musicians returned after the intermission, father assumed his place with the percussionists at the rear of the stage. He removed his shotgun from its case, carefully examined both barrels to make certain they were not fouled, took out

an oil-rag and began polishing the barrels and the stock. He then pulled from his pocket a curious device which looked like a beat strap-hinge with a spring attached and taped it to the breech of the gun.

Otto came over and they shook hands. The maestro entered and walked to the podium amid light applause.

As the "1812 Overture" began, father sat quietly, his shotgun across his knees, his arms folded, his sunburned face glowing like a red lantern among the pale faces of the musicians. The overture moved slowly for several minutes and then began to build, gathering momentum for the grand climax. As it did so, father got out his triple-load shells and placed them in a neat row on his music stand, clipping several of them to the device he had taped to the gun. At the entrance of the French horns, father stood up and lifted his shotgun. Mother nibbled on her handkerchief. I crossed my fingers and sat on them. But brother Karl, who was still young enough to have supreme faith in his father, sat on the edge of his seat in excited but confident expectation.

With a dramatic gesture, the maestro pointed at father.

Ka-whoom! ka-whoom! ka-whoom! ka-whoom! ka-whoom! The initial volley thundered from the rear of the stage. A great cloud of white smoke engulfed the orchestra and rolled out into the auditorium. For a moment everything stopped.

The conductor waved his arms furiously and one by one the awestruck musicians gathered their wits and began to play again. As the music approached the next cannon shot, the musicians tightened up, the music became pinched and sharp. The maestro tried frantically to wave father off. But fa-

---

16. **concert "A,"** a certain note for all the musicians to tune their instruments to.

ther's consummate musicianship, like rare wine bottled for years and at last uncorked, could not be contained.

Ka-whoom! went the shotgun. Everyone jumped. *Ka-whoom! ka-whoom!*

Suddenly the orchestra caught hold. It began to play as it had never played before in a mad attempt to equal and incorporate the shotgun blasts. *Ka-whoom!* The maestro could barely be seen behind the thick curtain of smoke. *Ka-whoom!* The orchestra played without him. *Ka-whoom!* The strings raced wildly up and down. *Ka-whoom!* The horns and trumpets came in.

Ka-whoom! The tympani and chimes. The orchestra hurled itself through the closing measures of the overture, hammered out the final series of concluding chords, built them up and up to the firm and final statement of the last resolving note.

The audience jumped to its feet with great applause.

When it was all over and we and the musicians had gathered round the table for a late celebration dinner, father stood up, and lifting a glass of his best Hungarian wine in one hand and his concert program in the other, said, ''Gentlemen, to music.''

Discussion

1. (a) What does Father do for a living? **(b)** What circumstances prevented him from becoming a musician?

2. (a) How does the boarding house help satisfy Father's desire for music? **(b)** How does Father's desire affect the narrator and his brother?

3. (a) How does Father contribute to Herr Schmidt's piano concert? **(b)** Why is Father not entirely satisfied?

4. How does Father's rehearsal and performance with the shotgun illustrate his skills as a craftsman and a musician?

5. The story is told from the point of view of one of Father's children. How might the story be different if Father himself were the narrator?

Vocabulary
Combined Skills

When a word contains one or more affixes, locating the root may help you figure out the meaning of the whole word.

Many English words have roots that come from a foreign language, but they can still give you clues to the meaning of the words. For example, knowing that the Latin root *port* means ''to carry,'' you can guess that the English word *portable* means ''able to be carried.''

Study the five Vocabulary words below and the Greek or Latin roots from which they are derived. Then complete each sentence on a separate paper with the appropriate Vocabulary word. (You may look up the meanings of certain affixes in the Glossary if you need to.)

fortitude	fortis—strong
cacophony	phonē—sound
incredulity	crēdere—believe
technician	technē—skill; craft
interminable	terminus—end

1. Hana simply couldn't believe she had won the race, and there was a look of ____ on her face when she claimed the trophy.

2. Marcy showed such _____ while her broken arm was being set that the doctor admired her courage and strength.

3. For Don, who hadn't seen his friend for several months, the wait for Jeremy's train seemed _____, never ending.

4. In order that the stained-glass window be repaired properly, Larry called someone skilled in working with glass, and the _____ who fixed it did a fine job.

5. Scott could hear a _____ of cackling chickens in the barnyard, and nothing he did could muffle the sounds.

Comment: The "Pieces" of Literature

Todd Rolf Zeiss writes that Father, in "Father and the '1812,' " is based largely upon his grandfather.

"While I was growing up in Appleton, Wisconsin, Grandfather Zeiss, an amazing man full of surprises, came to live with us. An immigrant carpenter, he had arrived sometime during the 1870s in Chicago, where he became a successful builder. Grandfather Zeiss was a lover of fine literature and music, and he would seat me in his lap in his old cane-seated rocker and sing me German folk songs. He also used to read me long passages from German poetry and from the Bible.

"My father is also a grand storyteller and used to regale us with many wonderful tales of hunting, fishing, and being a country doctor on the plains of North Dakota during the 'thirties."

From his father and grandfather, Zeiss learned a great deal about storytelling.

"My father, too, was a great lover of music, especially opera, and would often take my brother and me to concerts where we heard so many singers and instrumentalists I can't remember them all. Yet, while we enjoyed their performances, we never held these people in great awe, and I remember my father saying after a performance of a certain string quartet, 'Phew! That was a lot of sawing!'

"Both my father and grandfather were very handy fellows, and my brother and I learned a great deal from them about tools, making furniture, and building houses while working with them in our basement workshop."

This general background furnishes many pieces for "Father and the '1812.' "

While Zeiss was in high school, one of his music teachers used to tell him tales of music and musicians. One of the teacher's stories was about a man who roomed with him and several other musicians from the Milwaukee Symphony in the same boardinghouse. "This fellow was totally unmusical, yet he wanted very much to play with the others in the symphony. Finally they arranged for him to shoot the shotgun in the *1812 Overture*. After the first resounding shot, however—which did indeed startle the musicians—they hustled the poor fellow from the stage, and he never got to finish the number.

"I had often thought there was a short story tucked away in the anecdote, but the anecdote itself was spare. It was not until years later, when I was attending a concert during which the piano pedal began to squeak, prompting me to think, 'If my grandfather were here, he'd have that fixed in a minute,' that all the pieces for the story fell into place."

Paw-Paw

Laurence Yep

In this excerpt from *Child of the Owl,* Casey Young is twelve years old. Her mother is dead; her father is in the hospital after an accident. She has spent an uncomfortable time with the family of her Uncle Phil and is now being taken to live with her grandmother in San Francisco's Chinatown.

It was like we'd gone through an invisible wall into another world. There was a different kind of air in Chinatown, lighter and brighter. I mean, on the north side there were the American bars and joints; on the west, the mansions and hotels of Nob Hill; and on the other two sides were the tall skyscrapers where insurance men or lawyers spent the day. And they were pushing all the sunshine and all the buildings of Chinatown together—like someone had taken several square miles of buildings and squeezed it until people and homes were compressed into a tiny little half of a square mile. I didn't know what to make of the buildings either. They were mostly three- or four-story stone buildings but some had fancy balconies, and others had decorations on them like curved tile roofs—one building had bright yellow balconies decorated with shiny, glazed purple dolphins—and there was a jumble of neon signs, dark now in the daytime, jammed all together. Most of the buildings, though, had some color to them—bright reds and rich golds with some green thrown in.

But it was the people there that got me. I don't think I'd ever seen so many Chinese in my life before this. Some were a rich, dark tan while others were as pale as Caucasians. Some were short with round faces and wide, full-lipped mouths and noses squashed flat, and others were tall with thin faces and high cheekbones that made their eyes look like the slits in a mask. Some were dressed in regular American style while others wore padded silk jackets. All of them crowding into one tiny little patch of San Francisco.

Funny, but I felt embarrassed. Up until then I had never thought about skin colors because in the different places where we had lived, there were just poor people in all different colors. But now all of a sudden I saw all these funny brown people running around, a lot of them gabbling away at one another. I started to roll up the car window to try to shut out the sound and I noticed that my hand on the window handle was colored a honey kind of tan like some of the people outside. I took my hand off the handle and stared at it.

"What's the matter now?" Uncle Phil asked. We'd gotten caught in a momentary traffic snarl. I turned to see that Phil's face

was brown as my hand. Phil adjusted his tie uneasily and growled, "What're you looking at?"

I looked ahead, keeping my eyes on the glove compartment. My father and I had never talked much about stuff like this. I knew more about race horses than I knew about myself—I mean myself as a Chinese. I looked at my hands again, thinking they couldn't be my hands, and then I closed my eyes and felt their outline, noticing the tiny fold of flesh at the corners. Maybe it was because I thought of myself as an American and all Americans were supposed to be white like on TV or in books or in movies, but now I felt like some mad scientist had switched bodies on me like in all those monster movies, so that I had woken up in the wrong one.

Suddenly I felt like I was lost. Like I was going on this trip to this place I had always heard about and I was on the only road to that place but the signs kept telling me I was going to some other place. When I looked in the glove compartment to check my maps, I found I'd brought the wrong set of maps. And the road was too narrow to turn around in and there was too much traffic anyway so I just had to keep on going . . . and getting more and more lost. It gave me the creeps so I kept real quiet.

Phil headed up Sacramento Street—a steep, slanting street that just zoomed on and on up to the top of Nob Hill, where the rich people lived and where they had the swanky hotels. Phil turned suddenly into a little dead-end alley wide enough for only one car. On one side was a one-story Chinese school of brick so old or so dirty that the bricks were practically a purple color. On the other side as we drove by was a small parking lot with only six spaces for cars. Phil stopped the car in the middle of

the alley and I could see the rest of it was filled with apartment houses. Somewhere someone had a window open and the radio was blaring out. I couldn't find the place where it was coming from but I did see someone's diapers and shirts hung in the windows and on the fire escape of one apartment.

"Why do they hang their laundry in the windows?" I asked Phil.

"That's what people from Hong Kong use for curtains," Phil grumbled.

The sidewalk in front of the house was cracked like someone had taken a sledgehammer to it, and there were iron grates over the lower windows. The steps up to the doorway were old, worn concrete painted red. To the left were the mailboxes, which had Chinese words for the names or had no labels at all. To the right were the doorbells to all the nine apartments. Phil picked out the last and rang. He jabbed his thumb down rhythmically. Three short. Three long. Three short.

"Why are you doing that?" I asked.

"Signaling your grandmother," he grumbled. "She never answers just one buzz like any normal person, or even just three bursts. It's got to be nine buzzes in that way or she doesn't open the door. She says her friends know what she means."

So did I. It was Morse code for SOS.[1] The buzzer on the door sounded like an angry bee. Phil opened the door, putting his back against it and fighting against the heavy spring that tried to swing it shut. "Go on. Up three flights. Number nine. Remember now. You call her Paw-Paw."

"What's Paw-Paw?"

"Maternal grandmother. Chinese have a

---

1. **SOS.** These three letters, in telegraphic code, are the international signal for help.

different word for every relation. Like I'm your *kauh-fu*—your maternal uncle. Actually your grandmother's name is *Ah Paw* but when you're close to someone, you repeat the word, so it's Paw-Paw."

"I don't know any Chinese," I said.

Phil grunted. "You don't have to worry about talking to her. She learned pretty good English when she was a maid to some rich Americans."

"When did she do that?"

"Just after your grandfather died. I was only a baby then. But she quit once Jeanie finished high school. She got tired of leaving Chinatown."

I walked into an old, dim hallway and climbed up the wooden steps. As I turned an angle on the stairs, I saw light burning fierce and bright from a window. When I came to it, I looked out at the roof of the Chinese school next door. Someone had thrown some old 45's and a pair of sneakers down there. If I were some kind of kid that felt sorry for herself, I would almost have said that was the way I felt: like some piece of old ugly junk that was being kicked around on the discard pile.

I didn't stay by the window long, though, because Phil was coming up the stairs and I didn't want to act like his kids' stories about Paw-Paw had scared me. Anybody could be better than Uncle Phil and his family . . . I hoped. I stopped by the number-nine room, afraid to knock. It could not be the right place because I could hear rock music coming through the doorway. I scratched my head and checked the numbers on the other doors on the landing. Phil was still a flight down, huffing and puffing up the steps with my duffel bag—it wasn't that heavy; Phil was just that much out of shape. "Go on. Go on. Knock, you little idiot," he called up the stairwell.

I shrugged. It wasn't any of my business. I knocked at the door. I heard about six bolts and locks being turned. Finally the door swung open and I saw a tiny, pleasant, round-faced woman smiling at me. Her cheeks were a bright red. Her gray hair was all curly and frizzy around her head and a pair of rimless, thick eyeglasses perched on her nose. She was round and plump, wearing a sweater even on a hot day like this, a pair of cotton black slacks, and a pair of open heeled, flat slippers.

"Paw-Paw?" I asked.

"Hello. Hello." She opened up her arms and gave me a big hug, almost crushing me. It was funny, but I suddenly found myself holding on to her. Underneath all the soft layers of clothing I could feel how hard and tough she was. She patted me on the back three times and then left me for a moment to turn down her radio. It really was her old, white, beat-up radio playing rock music.

"Hey, how about a hand?" Phil puffed as he finally got to the landing.

Paw-Paw shuffled out to the landing in her slippered feet and made shooing motions. "You can go home now. We can do all right by ourselves."

Phil heaved his shoulders up and down in a great sigh and set the bag down. "Now, Momma——"

"Go on home," she said firmly. "We need time by ourselves."

I saw that Phil must have had some fine speech all prepared, probably warning Paw-Paw about me and warning me about ingratitude. He was not about to give up such an opportunity to make a speech.

"Now, Momma——"

"Go on. You're still not too old for a swat across the backside."

Phil ran his hand back and forth along

the railing. "Really, Momma. You oughtn't——"

"Go on," Paw-Paw raised her hand.

Phil gulped. The thought of having a former district president of the lawyers spanked by his own mother must have been too much for him. He turned around and started down the steps. He still had to get in the last word though.

"You mind your Paw-Paw, young lady. You hear me?" he shouted over his shoulder.

I waited till I heard the door slam. "Do you know what those buzzes stand for?"

"Do you?" Her eyes crinkled up.

"It stands for SOS. But where did you learn it?"

"When I worked for the American lady, her boy had a toy . . . what do you call it?" She made a tapping motion with her finger.

"Telegraph?"

"Yes. It's a good joke on such a learned man, no?" Her round red face split into a wide grin and then she began to giggle and when she put her hand over her mouth, the giggle turned into a laugh.

I don't think that I had laughed in all that time since my father's accident a month ago. It was like all the laughter I hadn't been able to use came bubbling up out of some hidden well—burst out of the locks and just came up. Both of us found ourselves slumping on the landing, leaning our heads against the banister, and laughing.

Finally Paw-Paw tilted up her glasses and wiped her eyes. "Philip always did have too much dignity for one person. Ah." She leaned back against the railing on the landing before the stairwell, twisting her head to look at me. "You'll go far," she nodded. "Yes, you will. Your eyebrows are beautifully curved, like silkworms. That means you'll be clever. And your ears are small and close to your head and shaped a certain way. That means you're adventurous and win much honor."

"Really?"

She nodded solemnly. "Didn't you know? The face is the map of the soul." Then she leaned forward and raised her glasses and pointed to the corners of her eyes where there were two small hollows, just shadows, really. "You see those marks under my eyes?"

"Yes." I added after a moment, "Paw-Paw."

"Those marks, they mean I have a temper."

"Oh." I wondered what was to happen next.

She set her glasses back on her nose. "But I will make a deal with you. I can keep my temper under control if you can do the same with your love of adventure and intelligence. You see, people, including me, don't always understand a love of adventure and intelligence. Sometimes we mistake them for troublemaking."

"I'll try." I grinned.

I went and got my bag then and brought it inside Paw-Paw's place and looked around, trying to figure out where I'd put it. Her place wasn't more than ten by fifteen feet and it was crowded with her stuff. Her bed was pushed lengthwise against the wall next to the doorway leading out to the landing. To the right of the door was another doorway, leading to the small little cubicle of a kitchen, and next to that door was her bureau. The wall opposite the bed had her one window leading out to the fire escape and giving a view of the alley, which was so narrow that it looked like we could have shaken hands with the people in the apartment house across from us. Beneath the window was a stack of newspapers for wrapping up the garbage. Next to the window was a table with a bright red-and-orange-flower tablecloth. Paw-Paw pulled aside her chair and her three-legged stool and told me to put my bag under the table. A metal cabinet and stacks of boxes covered the rest of the wall and the next one had hooks from which coats and other stuff in plastic bags hung.

In the right corner of the old bureau were some statues and an old teacup with some dirt in it and a half-burnt incense stick stuck into it. The rest of the top, though, was covered with old photos in little cardboard covers. They filled the bureau top and the mirror too, being stuck into corners of the mirror or actually taped onto the surface.

Next to the photos were the statues. One was about eight inches high in white porcelain of a pretty lady holding a flower and with the most patient, peaceful expression on her face. To her left was a statue of a man with a giant-sized, bald head. And then there were eight little statues, each only about two inches high. "Who are they?" I asked.

"Statues of some holy people," Paw-Paw said reluctantly.

There was something familiar about the last statue on Paw-Paw's bureau. It was of a fat, balding god with large ears, who had little children crawling over his lap and climbing up his shoulders. "Hey," I said. "Is that the happy god?"

Paw-Paw looked puzzled. "He's not the god of happiness."

"But they call him the happy god. See?" I pulled my father's little plastic charm out of my pocket and pointed to the letters on the back. *Happy God—Souvenir of Chinatown.*

Paw-Paw didn't even try to read the lettering. Maybe my father had already shown it to her long ago. "He's not the god of happiness. He just looks happy. He's the Buddha—the Buddha who will come in the future. He's smiling because everyone will be saved by that time and he can take a vacation. The children are holy people who become like children again."

"What about the others, Paw-Paw?"

"I don't have the words to explain," Paw-Paw said curtly, like the whole thing was embarrassing her.

I sat down by the table on the stool, which was painted white with red flowers. "Sure you do. I think your English is better than mine."

"You don't want to know any of that stuff." With her index finger Paw-Paw rubbed hard against some spot on the tablecloth. "That stuff's only for old people. If I tell you any more, you'll laugh at it like all other young people do." There was bitter hurt and anger in her voice.

I should have left her alone, I guess; but we had been getting close to one another and suddenly I'd found this door between us—a door that wouldn't open. I wasn't so much curious now as I was desperate: I didn't want Paw-Paw shutting me out like that. "I won't laugh, Paw-Paw. Honest."

"That stuff's only for old people who are too stupid to learn American ways," she insisted stubbornly.

"Well, maybe I'm stupid too."

"No." Paw-Paw pressed her lips together tightly; and I saw that no matter how much I pestered her, I wasn't going to get her to tell me any more about the statues on her bureau. We'd been getting along so great before that I was sorry I'd ever started asking questions.

We both sat, each in our own thoughts,

until almost apologetically Paw-Paw picked up a deck of cards from the table. "Do you play cards?"

"Some," I said. "Draw poker. Five-card stud. Things like that."

Paw-Paw shuffled the cards expertly. "Poker is for old men who like to sit and think too much. Now I know a game that's for the young and quick."

"What's that?"

"Slapjack." She explained that each of us took half of a deck and stacked it in front without looking at it. Then we would take turns taking the top card off and putting it down in the middle. Whenever a jack appeared, the first one to put her hand over the pile of cards got it. She then mixed the new cards with all the cards she still had in front of her. The first one to get all the cards won the game. It would sound like the advantage was with the person who was putting out the card at the time, but she was supposed to turn up the card away from her so she couldn't see it before the other player.

Paw-Paw had played a lot of card games, since she lived by herself, so she seemed to know when the jacks were going to come up. For a while all you could hear was the *slap-slap-slap*ping of cards and sometimes our hands smacking one another trying to get the pile. And sometimes I'd have more cards and sometimes Paw-Paw would. Eventually, though, she beat me. She shuffled the deck again. "You're a pretty good player," she grudged.

"Not as good as you, though."

Paw-Paw shuffled the cards, tapping them against the table so the cards in the pack were all even. "We used to play all the time. Your mother, Phil, everyone. We'd hold big contests and make plenty of noise. Only when Phil got older, he only wanted to play the games fancy Americans played

like—what's that word for a road that goes over water?"

"A bridge? Phil wanted to play bridge."

"Yes." Paw-Paw put the deck on the table. I wandered over to the bed.

The radio was in a little cabinet built into the headboard of the bed. I lay down on the bed and looked at the radio dial. "Do you like rock music, Paw-Paw?"

"It's fun to listen to," Paw-Paw said, "and besides, *Chinese Hour* is on that station every night."

"*Chinese Hour?*"

"An hour of news and songs all in Chinese." Paw-Paw slipped the cards back carefully into their box. "They used to have some better shows on that station like mystery shows."

"I bet I could find some." I started to reach for the dial.

"Don't lose that station." Paw-Paw seemed afraid suddenly.

"Don't worry, Paw-Paw, I'll be able to get your station back for you." It was playing "Monster Mash" right then. I twisted the dial to the right and the voices and snatches of song slid past and then I turned the dial back to her station, where "Monster Mash" was still playing. "See?"

"As long as you could get it back," Paw-Paw said reluctantly.

I fiddled with the dial some more until I got hold of *Gunsmoke*. It'd gone off the air years ago but some station was playing reruns. Paw-Paw liked that, especially the deep voice of the marshal. It was good to sit there in the darkening little room, listening to Marshal Dillon inside your head and picturing him as big and tall and striding down the dusty streets of Dodge City. And I got us some other programs too, shows that Paw-Paw had never been able to listen to before.

Don't get the idea that Paw-Paw was stupid. She just didn't understand American machines that well. She lived with them in a kind of truce where she never asked much of them if they wouldn't ask much of her.

"It's getting near eight," Paw-Paw said anxiously. It was only when I got the station back for her that she began to relax. "I was always so worried that I would not be able to get back the station, I never tried to listen to others. Look what I missed."

"But you have me now, Paw-Paw," I said.

"Yes," Paw-Paw smiled briefly, straightening in her chair. "I guess I do."

Discussion

1. Although Casey is of Chinese ancestry, she admits she knows little about her cultural heritage. **(a)** What makes Casey conscious of her Chinese origin? **(b)** How does she feel when she becomes aware of the physical characteristics that identify her as Chinese? **(c)** What shows that she knows little about the customs, culture, or beliefs of Chinese people?

2. **(a)** Why is Casey staying with Paw-Paw? **(b)** What do you infer about her past actions and reputation? How might these be connected to her stay?

3. How is Paw-Paw able to make Casey feel comfortable and accepted?

4. **(a)** How does Paw-Paw characterize her son Phil? **(b)** Do his speech and actions justify her characterization? Explain. **(c)** How does Paw-Paw characterize her granddaughter Casey? **(d)** How does Paw-Paw characterize herself? Do her speech and actions justify her characterization? Explain.

Composition

Although her grandmother is a part of the Chinatown world that seems so strange, Casey soon finds that she and the old woman are in some ways alike.

Compare and contrast Casey with her grandmother. In what ways are they alike? How are they different? Some things you might consider are background, language, religion, sense of humor, and personality.

Write a composition of about one page in which you discuss the likenesses and differences between Casey and her grandmother. You will have to decide whether it will be more effective to discuss their likenesses in one paragraph and their differences in another or to discuss first a likeness, then a difference, and so on.

(You may find the article "Finding Likenesses and Differences" in the Composition Guide helpful in writing this composition.)

Laurence Yep 1948–

Laurence Yep was born in San Francisco and attended grammar school in Chinatown. Having been influenced by a variety of cultures, Yep says, "I have no one culture to call my own . . . . However, in my writing I can create my own." This variety of cultures shows in much of his writing, as it does in *Child of the Owl*, the novel from which "Paw-Paw" is excerpted. He has written several novels for young people and a number of short stories.

Comment: Chinatown

There are Chinatowns in many cities, but San Francisco's Chinatown has the largest Chinese population of any city outside Asia. Today it is one of the major tourist attractions in the San Francisco area. Shops, restaurants, and even school buildings have been constructed especially to imitate a picturesque Oriental-style architecture—upward-curving tiled roofs which are supposed to throw back to the skies any bad luck or misfortune that may rain down from heaven. Oriental clothing, art, furniture, porcelain, and toys fill the shops, and food of all descriptions is available for tourists as well as residents.

Although there are historical records to show that people from China settled in the Americas more than 2500 years ago, the first large group of Chinese immigrants came to California as a result of the discovery of gold in the 1840s. These adventurous pioneers came to mine gold, along with the other "forty-niners" who flocked to the state from all over the world hoping to make their fortunes.

Goldminers in California.

Later, when the first transcontinental railroad was being constructed, the railroad companies recruited and imported men from China as laborers. Soon the Chinese made up a large percentage of the work crews; they often did the most hazardous work and were an important reason why the railroad was completed in record time. But they were always isolated because of their differences in language and culture, and there was no effective communication between the Chinese and white workers.

After the railroad was completed in 1869, thousands of Chinese men were left without a way to earn a living. Since there was a financial depression in California at the time, many unemployed Americans were quick to blame the Chinese workers for allegedly accepting a lower pay scale and for taking jobs away from them. Such anti-Chinese feeling produced many discriminatory state laws and local ordinances. These laws not only prevented other Chinese from entering the United States but also prevented the men who were here from bringing over their families, from owning land, from attending public schools, and from applying for U.S. citizenship. Mob violence occasionally occurred during this time; some Chinese were abused physically and even killed, and others were ruined financially when crowds invaded Chinatowns and destroyed their shops and burned their homes. In 1943, 1952, and 1965 the discriminatory laws against the Chinese were repealed. Equality of rights and opportunities became law in the United States.

omen

Alice Walker

They were women then
My mama's generation
Husky of voice—Stout of
Step
5 With fists as well as
Hands
How they battered down
Doors
And ironed
10 Starched white
Shirts
How they led
Armies
Headragged Generals
15 Across mined
Fields
Booby-trapped
Ditches

To discover books
20 Desks
A place for us
How they knew what we
Must know
Without knowing a page
25 Of it
Themselves.

I shall write of the old men I knew
And the young men
I loved
30 And of the gold toothed women
Mighty of arm
Who dragged us all
To church.

Copyright © 1970 by Alice Walker. Reprinted from her volume *Revolutionary Petunias and Other Poems* by permission of Harcourt Brace Jovanovich, Inc. and Julian Bach Literary Agency, Inc.

Discussion

1. (a) What physical characteristics do the women have? **(b)** What does the speaker mean by saying the women had "fists as well as/Hands"? **(c)** Who are the "Headragged Generals"?

2. (a) For what reason have the women "battered down/Doors" and "led/Armies . . . Across mined/Fields"? **(b)** If these phrases are metaphors for difficulties that faced the women, what might some of these difficulties have been?

3. What did the women know "Without knowing a page/Of it/Themselves"?

4. Is the speaker's attitude toward these women admiring or critical, grateful or resentful? Explain.

Alice Walker 1944—

Alice Walker is known for her powerful portrayal of the experience of black people, especially families, in America. Her writing has been called "candid," "truthful," and "convincing." She is the author of a number of poetry and short story collections and novels. In 1983 her novel *The Color Purple* received an American Book Award and a Pulitzer Prize.

A Celebration of Grandfathers Rudolfo A. Anaya

I am glad I knew my grandfather.

Buenos días le de Dios, abuelo.''[1] God give you a good day, grandfather. This is how I was taught as a child to greet my grandfather, or any grown person. It was a greeting of respect, a cultural value to be passed on from generation to generation, this respect for the old ones.

The old people I remember from my childhood were strong in their beliefs, and as we lived daily with them we learned a wise path of life to follow. They had something important to share with the young, and when they spoke the young listened. These old *abuelos* and *abuelitas*[2] had worked the earth all their lives, and so they knew the value of nurturing, they knew the sensitivity of the earth. They knew the rhythms and cycles of time, from the preparation of the earth in the spring to the digging of the *acequias*[3] that brought the water to the dance of harvest in the fall. They shared good times and hard times. They helped each other through the epidemics and the personal tragedies, and they shared what little they had when the hot winds burned the land and no rain came. They learned that to survive one had to share in the process of life.

My grandfather was a plain man, a farmer from the valley called Puerto de Luna on the Pecos River.[4] He was probably a descendant of those people who spilled over the mountain from Taos, following the Pecos River in search of farmland. There in that river valley he settled and raised a large family.

Bearded and walrus-mustached, he stood five feet tall, but to me as a child he was a giant. I remember him most for his silence. In the summers my parents sent me to live with him on his farm, for I was to learn the ways of a farmer. My uncles also lived in that valley, there where only the flow of the river and the whispering of the wind marked time. For me it was a magical place.

I remember once, while out hoeing the fields, I came upon an anthill, and before I knew it I was badly bitten. After he had covered my welts with the cool mud from the irrigation ditch, my grandfather calmly said: "Know where you stand." That is the way he spoke, in short phrases, to the point.

One very dry summer, the river dried to a trickle, there was no water for the fields. The young plants withered and died. In my sadness and with the impulse of youth I said, "I wish it would rain!" My grandfather touched me, looked up into the sky and whispered, "Pray for rain." In his language there was a difference. He felt connected to the cycles that brought the rain or kept it from us. His prayer was a meaningful ac-

---

1. *Buenos días le de Dios, abuelo* (bwe′nôs dē′äs le de dē′ôs ä bwe′lô). [*Spanish*]
2. *abuelos* (ä bwe′lôs) *and abuelitas* (ä bwe lē′täs), grandfathers and grandmothers.
3. *acequias* (ä se kwē′äs), irrigation ditches.
4. *Puerto de Luna* (pwer′tô de lü′nä) . . . *Pecos* (pe′kôs) *River*.

Rudolfo A. Anaya (ä nä′yä).

tion, because he was a participant with the forces that filled our world, he was not a bystander.

A young man died at the village one summer. A very tragic death. He was dragged by his horse. When he was found I cried, for the boy was my friend. I did not understand why death had come to one so young. My grandfather took me aside and said: "Think of the death of the trees and the fields in the fall. The leaves fall, and everything rests, as if dead. But they bloom again in the spring. Death is only this small transformation in life."

These are the things I remember, these fleeting images, few words.

I remember him driving his horse-drawn wagon into Santa Rosa in the fall when he brought his harvest produce to sell in the town. What a tower of strength seemed to come in that small man huddled on the seat of the giant wagon. One click of his tongue and the horses obeyed, stopped or turned as he wished. He never raised his whip. How unlike today when so much teaching is done with loud words and threatening hands.

I would run to greet the wagon, and the wagon would stop. *"Buenos días le de Dios, abuelo,"* I would say. *"Buenos días te de Dios, mi hijo,"*[5] he would answer and smile, and then I could jump up on the wagon and sit at his side. Then I, too, became a king as I rode next to the old man who smelled of earth and sweat and the other deep aromas from the orchards and fields of Puerto de Luna.

We were all sons and daughters to him. But today the sons and daughters are breaking with the past, putting aside *los abuelitos*.[6] The old values are threatened, and threatened most where it comes to these relationships with the old people. If we don't take the time to watch and feel the years of their final transformation, a part of our humanity will be lessened.

I grew up speaking Spanish, and oh! how difficult it was to learn English. Sometimes I would give up and cry out that I couldn't learn. Then he would say, *"Ten paciencia."*[7] Have patience. *Paciencia,* a word with the strength of centuries, a word that said that someday we would overcome. "You have to learn the language of the Americanos," he said. "Me, I will live my last days in my valley. You will live in a new time."

A new time did come, a new time is here. How will we form it so it is fruitful? We need to know where we stand. We need to speak softly and respect others, and to share what we have. We need to pray not for material gain, but for rain for the fields, for the sun to nurture growth, for nights in which we can sleep in peace, and for a harvest in which everyone can share. Simple lessons from a simple man. These lessons he learned from his past which was as deep and strong as the currents of the river of life.

He was a man; he died. Not in his valley, but nevertheless cared for by his sons and daughters and flocks of grandchildren. At the end, I would enter his room which carried the smell of medications and Vicks. Gone were the aroma of the fields, the strength of his young manhood. Gone also was his patience in the face of crippling old age. Small things bothered him; he shouted or turned sour when his expectations were not met. It was because he could not care for himself, because he was returning to that state of childhood, and all those wishes and desires were now wrapped in a crumbling old body.

"Ten paciencia," I once said to him, and he smiled. "I didn't know I would grow this old," he said.

I would sit and look at him and remember what was said of him when he was a young man. He could mount a wild horse and break it, and he could ride as far as any man. He could dance all night at a dance, then work the *acequia* the following day. He helped the neighbors, they helped him. He married, raised children. Small legends, the kind that make up everyman's life.

---

5. *mi hijo* (mē ē′hō), my son.
6. *los abuelitos* (lôs ä bwe lē′tọs), grandparents.
7. *Ten paciencia* (ten pä sē en′sē ä).

He was ninety-four when he died. Family, neighbors, and friends gathered; they all agreed he had led a rich life. I remembered the last years, the years he spent in bed. And as I remember now, I am reminded that it is too easy to romanticize old age. Sometimes we forget the pain of the transformation into old age, we forget the natural breaking down of the body. My grandfather pointed to the leaves falling from the tree. So time brings with its transformation the often painful, wearing-down process. Vision blurs, health wanes; even the act of walking carries with it the painful reminder of the autumn of life. But this process is something to be faced, not something to be hidden away by false images. Yes, the old can be young at heart, but in their own way, with their own dignity. They do not have to copy the always-young image of the Hollywood star.

I returned to Puerto de Luna last summer, to join the community in a celebration of the founding of the church. I drove by my grandfather's home, my uncles' ranches, the neglected adobe washing down into the earth from whence it came. And I wondered, how might the values of my grandfather's generation live in our own? What can we retain to see us through these hard times? I was to become a farmer, and I became a writer. As I plow and plant my words, do I nurture as my grandfather did in his fields and orchards? The answers are not simple.

"They don't make men like that anymore," is a phrase we hear when one does honor to a man. I am glad I knew my grandfather. I am glad there are still times when I can see him in my dreams, hear him in my reverie. Sometimes I think I catch a whiff of that earthy aroma that was his smell. Then I smile. How strong these people were to leave such a lasting impression.

So, as I would greet my *abuelo* long ago, it would help us all to greet the old ones we know with this kind and respectful greeting: "*Buenos días le de Dios.*"

Discussion

1. (a) Describe the grandfather's physical appearance and manner of speaking. (b) Why is the narrator sent to stay with his grandfather during the summers?

2. The narrator says that the old people "had something important to share with the young." (a) What knowledge of farming do they pass on to young people? (b) What lessons about life does the narrator as a boy learn from his grandfather? (c) How does the narrator think these lessons can be applied in his everyday life?

3. What advice from his grandfather is the narrator later able to return to the old man?

Rudolfo A. Anaya 1937–

Rudolfo Anaya was born into a Spanish-speaking family in Pastura, New Mexico, where, he says, "everyone tells stories . . . . I learned from the old storytellers how to recreate the narrative and pass it on."

Anaya currently teaches English and American literature at the University of New Mexico. In addition to teaching and writing, he has participated in workshops dealing with such topics as cultural awareness, Mexican culture, and Chicano literature.

A Christmas Memory

Truman Capote

He was only seven; she was sixty-something. They were distant cousins who had only each other. Now grown, Buddy recalls Christmas and his unusual friend.

Imagine a morning in late November. A coming of winter morning more than twenty years ago. Consider the kitchen of a spreading old house in a country town. A great black stove is its main feature; but there is also a big round table and a fireplace with two rocking chairs placed in front of it. Just today the fireplace commenced its seasonal roar.

A woman with shorn white hair is standing at the kitchen window. She is wearing tennis shoes and a shapeless gray sweater over a summery calico dress. She is small and sprightly, like a bantam hen; but, due to a long youthful illness, her shoulders are pitifully hunched. Her face is remarkable—not unlike Lincoln's, craggy like that, and tinted by sun and wind; but it is delicate too, finely boned, and her eyes are sherry-colored and timid. "Oh my," she exclaims, her breath smoking the windowpane, "it's fruitcake weather!"

The person to whom she is speaking is myself. I am seven; she is sixty-something. We are cousins, very distant ones, and we have lived together—well, as long as I can remember. Other people inhabit the house, relatives; and though they have power over us, and frequently make us cry, we are not, on the whole, too much aware of them. We are each other's best friend. She calls me Buddy, in memory of a boy who was formerly her best friend. The other Buddy died in the 1880's, when she was still a child. She is still a child.

"I knew it before I got out of bed," she says, turning away from the window with a purposeful excitement in her eyes. "The courthouse bell sounded so cold and clear. And there were no birds singing; they've gone to warmer country, yes indeed. Oh, Buddy, stop stuffing biscuit and fetch our buggy. Help me find my hat. We've thirty cakes to bake."

It's always the same: a morning arrives in November, and my friend, as though officially inaugurating the Christmas time of year that exhilarates her imagination and fuels the blaze of her heart, announces: "It's fruitcake weather! Fetch our buggy. Help me find my hat."

The hat is found, a straw cartwheel corsaged with velvet roses out-of-doors has faded: it once belonged to a more fashionable relative. Together, we guide our buggy,

a dilapidated baby carriage, out to the garden and into a grove of pecan trees. The buggy is mine; that is, it was bought for me when I was born. It is made of wicker, rather unraveled, and the wheels wobble like a drunkard's legs. But it is a faithful object; springtimes, we take it to the woods and fill it with flowers, herbs, wild fern for our porch pots; in the summer, we pile it with picnic paraphernalia and sugar-cane fishing poles and roll it down to the edge of a creek; it has its winter uses, too: as a truck for hauling firewood from the yard to the kitchen, as a warm bed for Queenie, our tough little orange and white rat terrier who has survived distemper and two rattlesnake bites. Queenie is trotting beside it now.

Three hours later we are back in the kitchen hulling a heaping buggyload of windfall pecans. Our backs hurt from gathering them: how hard they were to find (the main crop having been shaken off the trees and sold by the orchard's owners, who are not us) among the concealing leaves, the frosted, deceiving grass. Caaarackle! A cheery crunch, scraps of miniature thunder sound as the shells collapse and the golden mound of sweet oily ivory meat mounts in the milk-glass bowl. Queenie begs to taste, and now and again my friend sneaks her a mite, though insisting we deprive ourselves. "We mustn't, Buddy. If we start, we won't stop. And there's scarcely enough as there is. For thirty cakes." The kitchen is growing dark. Dusk turns the window into a mirror: our reflections mingle with the rising moon as we work by the fireside in the firelight. At last, when the moon is quite high, we toss the final hull into the fire and, with joined sighs, watch it catch flame. The buggy is empty, the bowl is brimful.

We eat our supper (cold biscuits, bacon, blackberry jam) and discuss tomorrow. Tomorrow the kind of work I like best begins: buying. Cherries and citron, ginger and vanilla and canned Hawaiian pineapple, rinds and raisins and walnuts and whiskey and oh, so much flour, butter, so many eggs, spices, flavorings: why, we'll need a pony to pull the buggy home.

But before these purchases can be made, there is the question of money. Neither of us has any. Except for skinflint sums persons in the house occasionally provide (a dime is considered very big money); or what we earn ourselves from various activities: holding rummage sales, selling buckets of handpicked blackberries, jars of homemade jam and apple jelly and peach preserves, rounding up flowers for funerals and weddings. Once we won seventy-ninth prize, five dollars, in a national football contest. Not that we know a fool thing about football. It's just that we enter any contest we hear about: at the moment our hopes are centered on the fifty-thousand-dollar Grand Prize being offered to name a new brand of coffee (we suggested "A.M."; and after some hesitation, for my friend thought it perhaps sacrilegious, the slogan "A.M.! Amen!"). To tell the truth, our only *really* profitable enterprise was the Fun and Freak Museum we conducted in a backyard woodshed two summers ago. The Fun was a stereopticon with slide views of Washington and New York lent us by a relative who had been to those places (she was furious when she discovered why we'd borrowed it); the Freak was a three-legged biddy chicken hatched by one of our own hens. Everybody hereabouts wanted to see that biddy: we charged grownups a nickel, kids two cents. And took in a good twenty dollars before the museum shut down due to the decease of the main attraction.

But one way and another we do each

year accumulate Christmas savings, a Fruit-cake Fund. These moneys we keep hidden in an ancient bead purse under a loose board under the floor under a chamber pot under my friend's bed. The purse is seldom removed from this safe location except to make a deposit, or, as happens every Saturday, a withdrawal; for on Saturdays I am allowed ten cents to go to the picture show. My friend has never been to a picture show, nor does she intend to: "I'd rather hear you tell the story, Buddy. That way I can imagine it more. Besides, a person my age shouldn't squander their eyes. When the Lord comes, let me see him clear." In addition to never having seen a movie, she has never: eaten in a restaurant, traveled more than five miles from home, received or sent a telegram, read anything except funny papers and the Bible, worn cosmetics, cursed, wished someone harm, told a lie on purpose, let a hungry dog go hungry. Here are a few things she has done, does do: killed with a hoe the biggest rattlesnake ever seen in this county (sixteen rattles), dip snuff (secretly), tame hummingbirds (just try it) till they balance on her finger, tell ghost stories (we both believe in ghosts) so tingling they chill you in July, talk to herself, take walks in the rain, grow the prettiest japonicas in town, know the recipe for every sort of old-time Indian cure, including a magical wart-remover.

Now, with supper finished, we retire to the room in a faraway part of the house where my friend sleeps in a scrap-quilt-covered iron bed painted rose pink, her favorite color. Silently, wallowing in the pleasures of conspiracy, we take the bead purse from its secret place and spill its contents on the scrap quilt. Dollar bills, tightly rolled and green as May buds. Somber fifty-cent pieces, heavy enough to weight a dead man's eyes. Lovely dimes, the liveliest coin, the one that really jingles. Nickels and quarters, worn smooth as creek pebbles. But mostly a hateful heap of bitter-odored pennies. Last summer others in the house contracted to pay us a penny for every twenty-five flies we killed. Oh, the carnage of August: the flies that flew to heaven! Yet it was not work in which we took pride. And, as we sit counting pennies, it is as though we were back tabulating dead flies. Neither of us has a head for figures; we count slowly, lose track, start again. According to her calculations, we have $12.73. According to mine, exactly $13. "I do hope you're wrong, Buddy. We can't mess around with thirteen. The cakes will fall. Or put somebody in the cemetery. Why, I wouldn't dream of getting out of bed on the thirteenth." This is true: she always spends thirteenths in bed. So, to be on the safe side, we subtract a penny and toss it out the window.

Of the ingredients that go into our fruit-cakes, whiskey is the most expensive, as well as the hardest to obtain: state laws forbid its sale. But everybody knows you can buy a bottle from Mr. Haha Jones. And the next day, having completed our more prosaic shopping, we set out for Mr. Haha's business address, a "sinful" (to quote public opinion) fish-fry and dancing café down by the river. We've been there before, and on the same errand; but in previous years our dealings have been with Haha's wife, an iodine-dark Indian woman with brassy peroxided hair and a dead-tired disposition. Actually, we've never laid eyes on her husband, though we've heard that he's an Indian too. A giant with razor scars across his cheeks. They call him Haha because he's so gloomy, a man who never laughs. As we approach his café (a large log cabin festooned inside and out with chains of garish-gay naked lightbulbs and standing by the river's muddy edge under the shade of river trees where moss drifts through the branches like gray mist) our steps slow down. Even Queenie stops prancing and sticks close by. People have been murdered in Haha's café. Cut to pieces. Hit on the head. There's a case coming up in court next month. Naturally these goings-on happen at night when the colored lights cast crazy patterns and the Victrola wails. In the daytime Haha's is shabby and deserted. I knock at the door, Queenie barks, my friend calls: "Mrs. Haha, ma'am? Anyone to home?"

Footsteps. The door opens. Our hearts overturn. It's Mr. Haha Jones himself! And he *is* a giant; he *does* have scars; he *doesn't* smile. No, he glowers at us through Satan-tilted eyes and demands to know: "What you want with Haha?"

For a moment we are too paralyzed to tell. Presently my friend half-finds her voice, a whispery voice at best: "If you please, Mr. Haha, we'd like a quart of your finest whiskey."

His eyes tilt more. Would you believe it? Haha is smiling! Laughing, too. "Which one of you is a drinkin' man?"

"It's for making fruitcakes, Mr. Haha. Cooking."

This sobers him. He frowns. "That's no way to waste good whiskey." Nevertheless, he retreats into the shadowed café and seconds later appears carrying a bottle of daisy yellow unlabeled liquor. He demonstrates its sparkle in the sunlight and says: "Two dollars."

We pay him with nickels and dimes and pennies. Suddenly, jangling the coins in his hand like a fistful of dice, his face softens. "Tell you what," he proposes, pouring the money back into our bead purse, "just send me one of them fruitcakes instead."

"Well," my friend remarks on our way home, "there's a lovely man. We'll put an extra cup of raisins in *his* cake."

The black stove, stoked with coal and firewood, glows like a lighted pumpkin. Eggbeaters whirl, spoons spin round in bowls of butter and sugar, vanilla sweetens the air, ginger spices it; melting, nose-tingling odors saturate the kitchen, suffuse the house, drift out to the world on puffs of chimney smoke. In four days our work is done. Thirty-one cakes, dampened with whiskey, bask on window sills and shelves.

Who are they for?

Friends. Not necessarily neighbor friends: indeed, the larger share are intended for persons we've met maybe once, perhaps not at all. People who've struck our fancy. Like President Roosevelt. Like the Reverend and Mrs. J. C. Lucey, Baptist missionaries to Borneo who lectured here last winter. Or the little knife grinder who comes through town twice a year. Or Abner Packer, the driver of the six o'clock bus from Mobile, who exchanges waves with us every day as he passes in a dust-cloud whoosh. Or the young Wistons, a California couple whose car one afternoon broke down outside the house and who spent a pleasant hour chatting with us on the porch (young Mr. Wiston snapped our picture, the only one we've ever had taken). Is it because my friend is shy with everyone *except* strangers that these strangers, and merest acquaintances, seem to us our truest friends? I think yes. Also, the scrapbooks we keep of thank-you's on White House stationery, time-to-time communications from California and Borneo, the knife grinder's penny post cards, make us feel connected to eventful worlds beyond the kitchen with its view of a sky that stops.

Now a nude December fig branch grates against the window. The kitchen is empty, the cakes are gone; yesterday we carted the last of them to the post office, where the cost of stamps turned our purse inside out. We're broke. That rather depresses me, but my friend insists on celebrating—with two inches of whiskey left in Haha's bottle. Queenie has a spoonful in a bowl of coffee (she likes her coffee chicory-flavored and strong). The rest we divide between a pair of jelly glasses. We're both quite awed at the prospect of drinking straight whiskey; the taste of it brings screwed-up expressions and sour shudders. But by and by we begin to sing, the two of us singing different songs simultaneously. I don't know the words to mine, just: *Come on along, come on along, to the dark-town strutters' ball.* But I can dance: that's what I mean to be, a tap dancer in the movies. My dancing shadow rollicks on the walls; our voices rock the chinaware; we giggle: as if unseen hands were tickling us. Queenie rolls on her back, her paws plow the air, something like a grin stretches her black lips. Inside myself, I feel warm and sparky as those crumbling logs, carefree as the wind in the chimney. My friend waltzes round the stove, the hem of her poor calico skirt pinched between her fingers as though it were a party dress: *Show me the way to go home,* she sings, her tennis shoes squeaking on the floor. *Show me the way to go home.*

Enter: two relatives. Very angry. Potent with eyes that scold, tongues that scald. Listen to what they have to say, the words tumbling together into a wrathful tune: "A child of seven! whiskey on his breath! are you out of your mind? feeding a child of seven! must be loony! road to ruination! re-member Cousin Kate? Uncle Charlie? Uncle Charlie's brother-in-law? shame! scandal! humiliation! kneel, pray, beg the Lord!"

Queenie sneaks under the stove. My friend gazes at her shoes, her chin quivers, she lifts her skirt and blows her nose and runs to her room. Long after the town has gone to sleep and the house is silent except for the chimings of clocks and the sputter of fading fires, she is weeping into a pillow already as wet as a widow's handkerchief.

"Don't cry," I say, sitting at the bottom of her bed and shivering despite my flannel nightgown that smells of last winter's cough syrup, "don't cry," I beg, teasing her toes, tickling her feet, "you're too old for that."

"It's because," she hiccups, "I *am* too old. Old and funny."

"Not funny. Fun. More fun than anybody. Listen. If you don't stop crying you'll be so tired tomorrow we can't go cut a tree."

She straightens up. Queenie jumps on the bed (where Queenie is not allowed) to lick her cheeks. "I know where we'll find pretty trees, Buddy. And holly, too. With berries big as your eyes. It's way off in the woods. Farther than we've ever been. Papa used to bring us Christmas trees from there: carry them on his shoulder. That's fifty years ago. Well, now: I can't wait for morning."

Morning. Frozen rime lusters the grass; the sun, round as an orange and orange as hot-weather moons, balances on the horizon, burnishes the silvered winter woods. A wild turkey calls. A renegade hog grunts in the undergrowth. Soon, by the edge of knee-deep, rapid-running water, we have to abandon the buggy. Queenie wades the stream first, paddles across barking complaints at the swiftness of the current, the pneumonia-making coldness of it. We follow, holding our shoes and equipment (a hatchet, a burlap sack) above our heads. A mile more: of chastising thorns, burs and briers that catch at our clothes; of rusty pine needles brilliant with gaudy fungus and molted feathers. Here, there, a flash, a flutter, an ecstasy of shrillings reminds us that not all the birds have flown south. Always, the path unwinds through lemony sun pools and pitch vine tunnels. Another creek to cross: a disturbed armada of speckled trout froths the water round us, and frogs the size of plates practice belly flops; beaver workmen are building a dam. On the farther shore, Queenie shakes herself and trembles. My friend shivers, too: not with cold but enthusiasm. One of her hat's ragged roses sheds a petal as she lifts her head and inhales the pine-heavy air. "We're almost there; can you smell it, Buddy?" she says, as though we were approaching an ocean.

And, indeed, it is a kind of ocean. Scented acres of holiday trees, prickly-leafed holly. Red berries shiny as Chinese bells: black crows swoop upon them screaming. Having stuffed our burlap sacks with enough greenery and crimson to garland a dozen windows, we set about choosing a tree. "It should be," muses my friend, "twice as tall as a boy. So a boy can't steal the star." The one we pick is twice as tall as me. A brave handsome brute that survives thirty hatchet strokes before it keels with a creaking, rending cry. Lugging it like a kill, we commence the long trek out. Every few yards we abandon the struggle, sit down and pant. But we have the strength of triumphant huntsmen; that and the tree's virile, icy perfume revive us, goad us on. Many compliments accompany our sunset return along the red clay road to town; but my friend is sly and noncommittal when pas-

sers-by praise the treasure perched on our buggy: what a fine tree and where did it come from? "Yonderways," she murmurs vaguely. Once a car stops and the rich mill owner's lazy wife leans out and whines: "Give ya two-bits cash for that ol' tree." Ordinarily my friend is afraid of saying no; but on this occasion she promptly shakes her head: "We wouldn't take a dollar." The mill owner's wife persists. "A dollar, my foot! Fifty cents. That's my last offer. Goodness, woman, you can get another one." In answer, my friend gently reflects: "I doubt it. There's never two of anything."

Home: Queenie slumps by the fire and sleeps till tomorrow, snoring loud as a human.

A trunk in the attic contains: a shoebox of ermine tails (off the opera cape of a curious lady who once rented a room in the house), coils of frazzled tinsel gone gold with age, one silver star, a brief rope of dilapidated, undoubtedly dangerous candylike light bulbs. Excellent decorations, as far as they go, which isn't far enough: my friend wants our tree to blaze "like a Baptist window," droop with weighty snows of ornament. But we can't afford the made-in-Japan splendors at the five-and-dime. So we do what we've always done: sit for days at the kitchen table with scissors and crayons and stacks of colored paper. I make sketches and my friend cuts them out: lots of cats, fish too (because they're easy to draw), some apples, some watermelons, a few winged angels devised from saved-up sheets of Hershey-bar tin foil. We use safety pins to attach these creations to the tree; as a final touch, we sprinkle the branches with shredded cotton (picked in August for this purpose). My friend, surveying the effect, clasps her hands together. "Now honest, Buddy. Doesn't it look good

enough to eat?'' Queenie tries to eat an angel.

After weaving and ribboning holly wreaths for all the front windows, our next project is the fashioning of family gifts. Tie-dye scarves for the ladies, for the men a home-brewed lemon and licorice and aspirin syrup to be taken ''at the first Symptoms of a Cold and after Hunting.'' But when it comes time for making each other's gifts, my friend and I separate to work secretly. I would like to buy her a pearl-handled knife, a radio, a whole pound of chocolate-covered cherries (we tasted some once, and she always swears: ''I could live on them, Buddy, Lord yes I could—and that's not taking His name in vain''). Instead, I am building her a kite. She would like to give me a bicycle (she's said so on several million occasions: ''If only I could, Buddy. It's bad enough in life to do without something *you* want; but confound it, what gets my goat is not being able to give somebody something you want *them* to have. Only one of these days I will, Buddy. Locate you a bike. Don't ask how. Steal it, maybe''). Instead, I'm fairly certain that she is building me a kite—the same as last year, and the year before: the year before that we exchanged slingshots. All of which is fine by me. For we are champion kite-fliers who study the wind like sailors; my friend, more accomplished than I, can get a kite aloft when there isn't enough breeze to carry clouds.

Christmas Eve afternoon we scrape together a nickel and go to the butcher's to buy Queenie's traditional gift, a good gnawable beef bone. The bone, wrapped in funny paper, is placed high in the tree near the silver star. Queenie knows it's there. She squats at the foot of the tree staring up in a trance of greed: when bedtime arrives she refuses to budge. Her excitement is equaled by my own. I kick the covers and turn my pillow as though it were a scorching summer's night. Somewhere a rooster crows: falsely, for the sun is still on the other side of the world.

''Buddy, are you awake?'' It is my friend, calling from her room, which is next to mine; and an instant later she is sitting on my bed holding a candle. ''Well, I can't sleep a hoot,'' she declares. ''My mind's jumping like a jack rabbit. Buddy, do you think Mrs. Roosevelt will serve our cake at dinner?'' We huddle in the bed, and she squeezes my hand I-love-you. ''Seems like your hand used to be so much smaller. I guess I hate to see you grow up. When you're grown up, will we still be friends?'' I say always. ''But I feel so bad, Buddy. I wanted so bad to give you a bike. I tried to sell my cameo Papa gave me. Buddy''—she hesitates, as though embarrassed—''I made you another kite.'' Then I confess that I made her one, too; and we laugh. The candle burns too short to hold. Out it goes, exposing the starlight, the stars spinning at the window like a visible caroling that slowly, slowly daybreak silences. Possibly we doze; but the beginnings of dawn splash us like cold water: we're up, wide-eyed and wandering while we wait for others to waken. Quite deliberately my friend drops a kettle on the kitchen floor. I tap-dance in front of closed doors. One by one the household emerges, looking as though they'd like to kill us both; but it's Christmas, so they can't. First, a gorgeous breakfast: just everything you can imagine—from flapjacks and fried squirrel to hominy grits and honey-in-the-comb. Which puts everyone in a good humor except my friend and I. Frankly, we're so impatient to get at the presents we can't eat a mouthful.

Well, I'm disappointed. Who wouldn't be? With socks, a Sunday school shirt, some handkerchiefs, a hand-me-down sweater and a year's subscription to a religious magazine for children. *The Little Shepherd*. It makes me boil. It really does.

My friend has a better haul. A sack of Satsumas,[1] that's her best present. She is proudest, however, of a white wool shawl knitted by her married sister. But she *says* her favorite gift is the kite I built her. And it *is* very beautiful; though not as beautiful as the one she made me, which is blue and scattered with gold and green Good Conduct stars; moreover, my name is painted on it, "Buddy."

"Buddy, the wind is blowing."

The wind is blowing, and nothing will do till we've run to a pasture below the house where Queenie has scooted to bury her bone (and where, a winter hence, Queenie will be buried, too). There, plunging through the healthy waist-high grass, we unreel our kites, feel them twitching at the string like sky fish as they swim into the wind. Satisfied, sunwarmed, we sprawl in the grass and peel Satsumas and watch our kites cavort. Soon I forget the socks and hand-me-down sweater. I'm as happy as if we'd already won the fifty-thousand-dollar Grand Prize in that coffee-naming contest.

"My, how foolish I am!" my friend cries, suddenly alert, like a woman remembering too late she has biscuits in the oven. "You know what I've always thought?" she asks in a tone of discovery, and not smiling at me but a point beyond. "I've always thought a body would have to be sick and dying before they saw the Lord. And I imagined that when He came it would be like looking at the Baptist window: pretty as colored glass with the sun pouring through, such a shine you don't know it's getting dark. And it's been a comfort: to think of that shine taking away all the spooky feeling. But I'll wager it never happens. I'll wager at the very end a body realizes the Lord has already shown Himself. That things as they are"—her hand circles in a gesture that gathers clouds and kites and grass and Queenie pawing earth over her bone—"just what they've always seen, was seeing Him. As for me, I could leave the world with today in my eyes."

This is our last Christmas together.

Life separates us. Those who Know Best decide that I belong in a military school. And so follows a miserable succession of bugle-blowing prisons, grim reveille-ridden summer camps. I have a new home too. But it doesn't count. Home is where my friend is, and there I never go.

And there she remains, puttering around the kitchen. Alone with Queenie. Then alone. ("Buddy dear," she writes in her wild hard-to-read script, "yesterday Jim Macy's horse kicked Queenie bad. Be thankful she didn't feel much. I wrapped her in a Fine Linen sheet and rode her in the buggy down to Simpson's pasture where she can be with all her Bones . . . .") For a few Novembers she continues to bake her fruitcakes single-handed; not as many, but some: and, of course, she always sends me "the best of the batch." Also, in every letter she encloses a dime wadded in toilet paper: "See a picture show and write me the story." But gradually in her letters she tends to confuse me with her other friend, the Buddy who died in the 1880's; more and more thirteenths are not the only days she stays in bed: a morning arrives in November, a leafless birdless coming of winter morning, when she cannot rouse herself to exclaim: "Oh my, it's fruitcake weather!"

---

1. *Satsumas*, a type of orange.

And when that happens, I know it. A message saying so merely confirms a piece of news some secret vein had already received, severing from me an irreplaceable part of myself, letting it loose like a kite on a broken string. That is why, walking across a school campus on this particular December morning, I keep searching the sky. As if I expected to see, rather like hearts, a lost pair of kites hurrying toward heaven.

Discussion

1. **(a)** What is the setting of the story? **(b)** From whose point of view is it told?
2. **(a)** How do Buddy and the old woman feel toward one another? **(b)** How are they different from the rest of the household? **(c)** Point out the passages you think are most effective in showing their friendship.
3. Reread the passage in which Buddy lists the things his friend has and has not done (241a, lines 15 to 33). **(a)** Based on this passage, how would you characterize Buddy's friend? **(b)** How do you feel toward her?
4. This story deals with a series of rather ordinary events. Why do they make such a lasting impression on the boy?

Application
Imagery

The first sentence of "A Christmas Memory" asks you to "imagine a morning in late November," and throughout the selection Truman Capote uses vivid sensory imagery. Choose one scene in which the images are particularly successful in helping you mentally experience what Buddy and his friend are experiencing.

1. Point out the images and the senses to which they appeal.
2. Explain how the imagery helps you become involved in the scene.

Composition

The experiences Buddy describes—baking cakes, buying groceries, decorating a Christmas tree, flying kites—are not unusual. It is Buddy's special friend who makes them remain vivid in his memory. Recall something that you might long have forgotten, except that someone or something has made it special in your memory. What details stand out most in your mind?

Write a page or two in which you describe this experience. Use sensory images where they are appropriate and helpful. Remember that you must make your readers understand why this experience was *not* ordinary to you.

(You may find the article "Describing a Person or Place" in the Composition Guide helpful in writing this composition.)

Truman Capote 1924–

Truman Capote began writing when still a child; in fact, in school nothing *but* writing interested him. After publishing many stories in local newspapers, he wrote his first major prize-winning story at the age of nineteen. Since then he has written numerous stories and novels ranging in scope from nightmarish tragedy to light comedy. Much of his writing reflects his Southern background.

Unit 4 Review: *Generations*

Content Review

1. How do the stories and poems in this unit show the influence of people on each other, especially the influence of one *generation* upon another? Give examples from selections to support your answer.

2. (a) Do the selections in this unit show young people and adults in conflict or in relative harmony? **(b)** Which selection do you think best displays the relationship that ought to exist between young people and adults?

3. Choose one selection from the unit and explain how you think the events and ideas might change if a different point of view were used. For example, do you think the picture of "mama's generation"

in "Women" would change if the women themselves told about their actions? How might the story be affected if we saw things exclusively from the point of view of the teacher in "Charles"?

4. To generate something is to cause or produce something. In "Charles," Laurie generates a new "pretend" personality. In "Thank You, Ma'am," Mrs. Jones generates new respect in Roger. Mr. Mendelsohn and Paw-Paw generate new understandings of different ages and cultures. Which selection in this unit do you think does the best job of generating a new or different way of looking at people, actions, or attitudes? Explain.

Concept Review: Interpretation of New Material

This selection is taken from the autobiography of Margaret Mead, well known for her work in anthropology—the study of the origin and development of the human race. Read the selection carefully; then answer the questions that follow it.

On Being a Granddaughter • *Margaret Mead*

My paternal grandmother, who lived with us from the time my parents married until she died in 1927, while I was studying anthropological collections in German museums, was the most decisive influence in my life. She sat at the center of our household. Her room—and my mother always saw to it that she had the best room, spacious and sunny, with a fireplace if possible—was the place to which we immediately went when we came in from playing or home from school. There my father went when he ar-

rived in the house. There we did our lessons on the cherrywood table with which she had begun housekeeping and which, later, was my dining room table for twenty-five years. There, sitting by the fire, erect and intense, she listened to us and to all of Mother's friends and to our friends. In my early childhood she was also very active—cooking, preserving, growing flowers in the garden, and attentive to all the activities of the country and the farm . . . .

My mother was trustworthy in all matters that concerned our care. Grandma was trustworthy in a quite different way. She meant exactly what she said, always. If you borrowed her scissors, you returned them. In like case, Mother would wail ineffectually, "Why does everyone borrow my scissors and never return them?" and Father would often utter idle threats. But Grandma never threatened. She never raised her voice. She simply commanded respect and obedience by her complete expectation that she would be obeyed. And she never gave silly orders . . . . Grandma never said, "Do this because Grandma says so," or "because Grandma wants you to do it." She simply said, "Do it," and I knew from her tone of voice that it was necessary.

My grandmother grew up in the little town of Winchester, in Adams County, Ohio, which two of my great-great-grandfathers had founded. She was one of nine children who reached adulthood . . . .

My grandmother began school teaching quite young, at a time when it was still somewhat unusual for a girl to teach school. When my grandfather, who was also a teacher, came home from the Civil War, he married my grandmother and they went to college together. They also graduated together. She gave a graduation address in the morning and my grandfather, who gave one in the afternoon, was introduced as the husband of Mrs. Mead who spoke this morning.

My grandfather was a school superintendent . . . . He died when my father was six. Two days later the principal took his place and my grandmother took the principal's place. From then on she taught, sometimes in high school, sometimes small children, until she came to live with us when my parents married. It was the small children in whom she was most interested, and I have the notes she took on the schools she observed during a visit to Philadelphia before my parents' marriage.

She understood many things that are barely recognized in the wider educational world even today . . . . She thought that memorizing mere facts was not very important and that drill was stultifying. The result was that I was not well drilled in geography or spelling. But I learned to observe the world around me and to note what I saw—to observe flowers and children and baby chicks. She taught me to read for the sense of what I read and to enjoy learning.

With the exception of the two years I went to kindergarten . . . and the year I was eight, . . . she taught me until I went to high school and even then helped me with my lessons when my teachers were woefully inadequate, as they often were. I never expected any teacher to know as much as my parents or my grandmother did . . . .

Grandma was a wonderful storyteller, and she had a set of priceless, individually tailored anecdotes with which American grandparents of her day brought up children. There was the story of the little boys who had been taught absolute, quick obedience. One day when they were out on the prairie, their father shouted, "Fall down on your faces!" They did, and the terrible prairie fire swept over them *and they weren't hurt*. There was also the story of three boys at school, each of whom received a cake sent from home. One hoarded his, and the mice ate it; one ate all of his, and he got sick; and who do you think had the best time?—why, of course, the one who shared his cake with his friends. Then there was the little boy who ran away from home and stayed away all day. When he came home after supper, he found

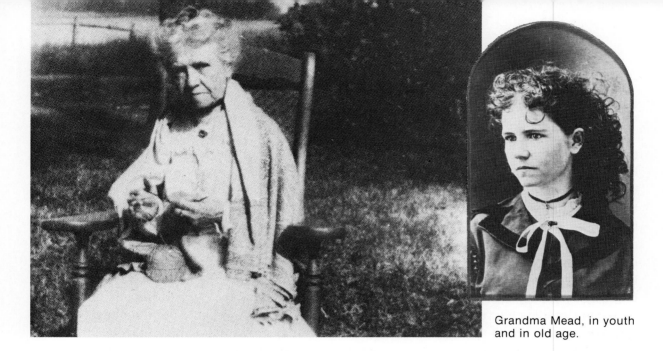

Grandma Mead, in youth and in old age.

the family sitting around the fire and nobody said a word. Not a word. Finally, he couldn't stand it anymore and said, "Well, I see you have the same old cat!" And there was one about a man who was so lazy he would rather starve than work. Finally, his neighbors decided to bury him alive. On the way to the cemetery they met a man with a wagonload of unshelled corn. He asked where they were going. When they told him that they were going to bury that no-good man alive, the owner of the corn took pity on him and said, "I tell you what. I will give you this load of corn. All you will have to do is shell it." But the lazy man said, "Drive on, boys!"

Because Grandma did so many things with her hands, a little girl could always tag after her, talking and asking questions and listening. Side by side with Grandma, I learned to peel apples, to take the skin off tomatoes by plunging them into scalding water, to do simple embroidery stitches, and to knit. Later, during World War I, when I had to cook for the whole household, she taught me a lot about cooking, for example, just when to add a lump of butter, something that always had to be concealed from

Mother, who thought that cooking with butter was extravagant.

While I followed her about as she carried out the endless little household tasks that she took on, supplementing the work of the maids or doing more in between maids—and we were often in between—she told me endless tales about Winchester. She told me about her school days and about the poor children who used to beg the cores of apples from the rich children who had whole apples for lunch. She told me about Em Eiler, who pushed Aunt Lou off a rail fence into a flooded pasture lot; about Great-aunt Louisian, who could read people's minds and tell them everything they had said about her and who had been a triplet and was so small when she was born that she would fit into a quart cup; about Grace, who died from riding a trotting horse too hard, which wasn't good for girls; and about the time Lida cut off Anna Louise's curls and said, "Now they won't say 'pretty little girl' anymore." My great-grandfather used to say such a long grace, she told me, that one of her most vivid memories was of standing, holding a log she had started to put on the fire, for what seemed to be hours for fear of interrupting him. All this was as real to me as if I had lived it myself . . . .

Mother never ceased to resent the fact that Grandma lived with us, but she gave her her due. Grandma never "interfered"—never tried to teach the children anything religious that had not previously been introduced by my mother, and in disagreements between my mother and father she always took my mother's side. When my father threatened to leave my mother, Grandma told him firmly that she would stay with her and the children.

When Grandma was angry, she sat and held her tongue. I used to believe that this involved some very mysterious . . . trick. She was so still, so angry, and so determined not to speak, not to lose her temper. And she never did. But not losing her temper came out of her eyes like fire. Years later, when I was given a picture of her as a young woman, I felt that I had looked very like her at the same age. But when I actually compared pictures of me with the one of her, I looked milky mild. Not until the birth of her great-great-granddaughter, my daughter's daughter Sevanne Margaret, did that flashing glance reappear in the family . . . .

I think it was my grandmother who gave me my ease in being a woman. She was unquestionably feminine—small and dainty and pretty . . . . She had gone to college when this was a very unusual thing for a girl to do, she had a firm grasp of anything she paid attention to, she had married and had a child, and she had a career of her own. All this was true of my mother, as well. But my mother was filled with passionate resentment about the condition of women, as perhaps my grandmother might have been had my grandfather lived and had she borne five children and had little opportunity to use her special gifts and training. As it was, the two women I knew best were mothers and had professional training. So I had no reason to doubt that brains were suitable for a woman. And as I had my father's kind of mind—which was also his mother's—I learned that the mind is not sex-typed.

The content of my conscience came from my mother's concern for other people and the state of the world, and from my father's insistence that the only thing worth doing is to add to the store of exactly known facts. But the strength of my conscience came from Grandma, who meant what she said . . . .

---

1. Is Grandma the mother of Mr. or Mrs. Mead?

2. Readers learn about Grandma from the point of view of **(a)** her son; **(b)** Grandma herself; **(c)** her husband; **(d)** her granddaughter.

3. In the Mead household, Grandma **(a)** usually stays in her room by herself; **(b)** takes little responsibility for raising the children; **(c)** is at the center of the family's life; **(d)** has everyone else wait on her.

4. What job was Grandma trained for?

5. Margaret Mead thinks her grandmother is trustworthy because Grandma **(a)** never tells on the children; **(b)** takes Margaret's part in many family arguments; **(c)** secretly lends Margaret money; **(d)** always means what she says.

6. Grandma's view of education is that children **(a)** need strict discipline; **(b)** need complete freedom; **(c)** can learn a lot by observing; **(d)** should learn by memorizing.

7. One can infer that the message behind Grandma's story about the little boys and the prairie fire (250b, 3) is **(a)** children should not go into the wilderness without their parents; **(b)** children should always obey their elders; **(c)** there are steps people can take to protect themselves in a fire; **(d)** people shouldn't build fires in dry areas.

8. What part of Grandma's face always gives away the fact that she is angry?

9. Margaret Mead thinks the reason that her mother feels "passionate resentment about the condition of women" (252b, 1) is that she **(a)** has little chance to use her own education; **(b)** is a widow with five children to support; **(c)** knows that Margaret cannot get a good job because she is a woman; **(d)** grew up at a time when women's rights were becoming an important issue.

10. Which of the following statements best describes the Mead family as they are seen in this selection? **(a)** They have many beautiful family traditions; **(b)** they spend much of their time arguing; **(c)** They are poorly educated; **(d)** they stress mutual respect and learning.

Composition Review

Choose one of the following assignments to write about. Assume you are writing for your classmates.

1. It is sometimes said that the older people get, the more set in their ways they become. Choose Paw-Paw, Mr. Mendelsohn, or Buddy's friend in "A Christmas Memory." List beliefs, habits, or attitudes from earlier years that the character continues to cling to as he or she grows older. Then list the things your character says or does that indicate a willingness to adjust to new ideas. Choose the appropriate ending to your topic sentence: _____ is (a) set in his/her ways; (b) open to new ideas; (c) attached to the past but is willing to adjust to new ideas.

Write a composition of one or two pages in which you discuss your subject's personality in light of one of the three topics. Include items from your lists that best support your point.

2. Who is the most admirable character you have encountered in this unit? In your judgment, what makes the character most admirable? Does the admiration you feel have anything to do with the age or generation of the character?

Write a character sketch of the person chosen. Use specific examples from the selection or from your own experiences to explain why you admire this character.

3. Some characters in this unit can be credited with generating, or causing, certain attitudes in others. For example, Jahnos Kovach in "Father and the '1812'" generates in his children the appreciation of both music and skillful craftsmanship. The mothers in "Women" generate in the speaker a respect for their determination to obtain advantages for their children. Choose any character in the unit and jot down ways he or she is able to generate certain attitudes in others. Does the character affect others by speech? by actions? by an unusual personality trait?

Write a composition in which you explain how the character you have chosen generates the attitudes described. You might conclude with your opinion about whether or not these new attitudes could be helpful in one's life, and why.

unit 5

Around a campfire, in a banquet hall, or from a stage; accompanied by music or speaking into hushed silence, storytellers since the beginning of time have told their tales.

The Well-Told Tale

The Tell-Tale Heart

Edgar Allan Poe

What is it about the old man's eye that makes the narrator's blood run cold?

True!—nervous—very, very dreadfully nervous I had been and am; but why *will* you say that I am mad? The disease had sharpened my senses—not destroyed—not dulled them. Above all was the sense of hearing acute. I heard all things in the heavens and in the earth. I heard many things in hell. How, then, am I mad? Hearken! and observe how healthily—how calmly I can tell you the whole story.

It is impossible to say how first the idea entered my brain; but once conceived, it haunted me day and night. Object there was none. Passion there was none. I loved the old man. He had never wronged me. He had never given me insult. For his gold I had no desire. I think it was his eye! Yes, it was this! One of his eyes resembled that of a vulture—a pale blue eye, with a film over it. Whenever it fell upon me, my blood ran cold; and so by degrees—very gradually—I made up my mind to take the life of the old man, and thus rid myself of the eye forever.

Now this is the point. You fancy me mad. Madmen know nothing. But you should have seen *me*. You should have seen how wisely I proceeded—with what caution—with what foresight—with what dissimulation I went to work! I was never kinder to the old man than during the whole week before I killed him. And every night,

about midnight, I turned the latch of his door and opened it—oh, so gently! And then, when I had made an opening sufficient for my head, I put in a dark lantern,[1] all closed, closed, so that no light shone out, and then I thrust in my head. Oh, you would have laughed to see how cunningly I thrust it in! I moved it slowly—very, very slowly, so that I might not disturb the old man's sleep. It took me an hour to place my whole head within the opening so far that I could see him as he lay upon his bed. Ha!—would a madman have been so wise as this? And then, when my head was well in the room, I undid the lantern cautiously—oh, so cautiously—cautiously (for the hinges creaked)—I undid it just so much that a single thin ray fell upon the vulture eye. And this I did for seven long nights—every night just at midnight—but I found the eye always closed; and so it was impossible to do the work; for it was not the old man who vexed me, but his Evil Eye. And every morning, when the day broke, I went boldly into the chamber, and spoke courageously to him, calling him by name in a hearty tone, and inquiring how he had passed the

---

1. **dark lantern,** a lantern whose light can be hidden by a cover over the opening.

The Complete Works of Edgar Allan Poe, edited by James A. Harrison (17 vols.). New York: AMS Press, 1902.

night. So you see he would have been a very profound old man, indeed, to suspect that every night, just at twelve, I looked in upon him while he slept.

Upon the eighth night I was more than usually cautious in opening the door. A watch's minute hand moves more quickly than did mine. Never before that night had I *felt* the extent of my own powers—of my sagacity. I could scarcely contain my feelings of triumph. To think that there I was, opening the door, little by little, and he not even to dream of my secret deeds or thoughts. I fairly chuckled at the idea; and perhaps he heard me; for he moved on the bed suddenly, as if startled. Now you may think that I drew back—but no. His room was as black as pitch with the thick darkness (for the shutters were close fastened, through fear of robbers), and so I knew that he could not see the opening of the door, and I kept pushing it on steadily, steadily.

I had my head in, and was about to open the lantern, when my thumb slipped upon the tin fastening, and the old man sprang up in the bed, crying out—"Who's there?"

I kept quite still and said nothing. For a whole hour I did not move a muscle, and in the meantime I did not hear him lie down. He was still sitting up in the bed listening—just as I have done, night after night, hearkening to the death watches[2] in the wall.

Presently I heard a slight groan, and I knew it was the groan of mortal terror. It was not a groan of pain or of grief—oh, no!—it was the low stifled sound that arises from the bottom of the soul when overcharged with awe. I knew the sound well. Many a night, just at midnight, when all the world slept, it has welled up from my own bosom, deepening, with its dreadful echo, the terrors that distracted me. I say I knew it well. I knew what the old man felt, and pitied him, although I chuckled at heart. I knew that he had been lying awake ever since the first slight noise, when he had turned in the bed. His fears had been ever since growing upon him. He had been trying to fancy them causeless, but could not. He had been saying to himself: "It is nothing but the wind in the chimney—it is only a mouse crossing the floor," or "It is merely a cricket which has made a single chirp." Yes, he had been trying to comfort himself with these suppositions; but he had found all in vain. *All in vain;* because Death, in approaching him, had stalked with his black shadow before him, and enveloped the victim. And it was the mournful influence of the unperceived shadow that caused him to feel—although he neither saw nor heard—to *feel* the presence of my head within the room.

When I had waited a long time, very patiently, without hearing him lie down, I resolved to open a little—a very, very little crevice in the lantern. So I opened it—you cannot imagine how stealthily, stealthily—until, at length, a single dim ray, like the thread of the spider, shot from out the crevice and full upon the vulture eye.

It was open—wide, wide open—and I grew furious as I gazed upon it. I saw it with perfect distinctness—all a dull blue, with a hideous veil over it that chilled the very marrow in my bones; but I could see nothing else of the old man's face or person, for I had directed the ray as if by instinct, precisely upon the spot.

And now have I not told you that what you mistake for madness is but overacuteness of the senses?—now, I say, there came to my ears a low, dull, quick sound, such as a watch makes when enveloped in

2. *death watches,* small beetles that live in wood and make a ticking sound.

cotton. I knew *that* sound well too. It was the beating of the old man's heart. It increased my fury, as the beating of a drum stimulates the soldier into courage.

But even yet I refrained and kept still. I scarcely breathed. I held the lantern motionless. I tried how steadily I could maintain the ray upon the eye. Meantime the hellish tattoo of the heart increased. It grew quicker and quicker, and louder and louder every instant. The old man's terror *must* have been extreme! It grew louder, I say, louder every moment!—do you mark me well? I have told you that I am nervous: so I am. And now at the dead hour of the night, amid the dreadful silence of that old house, so strange a noise as this excited me to uncontrollable terror. Yet, for some minutes longer I refrained and stood still. But the beating grew louder, louder! I thought the heart must burst. And now a new anxiety seized me—the sound would be heard by a neighbor! The old man's hour had come! With a loud yell, I threw open the lantern and leaped into the room. He shrieked once—once only. In an instant I dragged him to the floor, and pulled the heavy bed over him. I then smiled gaily, to find the deed so far done. But, for many minutes, the heart beat on with a muffled sound. This, however, did not vex me; it would not be heard through the wall. At length it ceased. The old man was dead. I removed the bed and examined the corpse. Yes, he was stone, stone dead. I placed my hand upon the heart and held it there many minutes. There was no pulsation. He was stone dead. His eye would trouble me no more.

If still you think me mad, you will think so no longer when I describe the wise precautions I took for the concealment of the body. The night waned, and I worked hastily, but in silence. First of all I dismembered the corpse. I cut off the head and the arms and the legs.

I then took up three planks from the flooring of the chamber, and deposited all between the scantlings. I then replaced the boards so cleverly, so cunningly, that no human eye—not even *his*—could have detected anything wrong. There was nothing to wash out—no stain of any kind—no bloodspot whatever. I had been too wary for that. A tub had caught all—ha! ha!

When I had made an end of these labors, it was four o'clock—still dark as midnight. As the bell sounded the hour, there came a knocking at the street door. I went down to open it with a light heart—for what had I *now* to fear? There entered three men, who introduced themselves, with perfect suavity, as officers of the police. A shriek had been heard by a neighbor during the night; suspicion of foul play had been aroused; information had been lodged at the police office, and they (the officers) had been deputed to search the premises.

I smiled—for *what* had I to fear? I bade the gentlemen welcome. The shriek, I said, was my own in a dream. The old man, I mentioned, was absent in the country. I took my visitors all over the house. I bade them search—search *well*. I led them, at length, to *his* chamber. I showed them his treasures, secure, undisturbed. In the enthusiasm of my confidence, I brought chairs into the room, and desired them *here* to rest from their fatigues, while I myself, in the wild audacity of my perfect triumph, placed my own seat upon the very spot beneath which reposed the corpse of the victim.

The officers were satisfied. My *manner* had convinced them. I was singularly at ease. They sat, and while I answered cheerily, they chatted of familiar things. But, ere long, I felt myself getting pale and wished them gone. My head ached, and I fancied a ringing in my ears: but still they sat and still chatted. The ringing became more distinct; it continued and became more distinct; I talked more freely to get rid of the feeling; but it continued and gained definiteness—until, at length, I found that the noise was *not* within my ears.

No doubt I now grew *very* pale—but I talked more fluently, and with a heightened voice. Yet the sound increased—and what could I do? It was *a low, dull, quick sound—much such a sound as a watch makes when enveloped in cotton.* I gasped for breath—and yet the officers heard it not. I talked more quickly—more vehemently; but the noise steadily increased. I arose and argued about trifles, in a high key and with violent gesticulations, but the noise steadily increased. Why *would* they not be gone? I paced the floor to and fro with heavy strides, as if excited to fury by the observation of the men—but the noise steadily increased. Oh, what *could* I do? I foamed—I raved—I swore! I swung the chair upon which I had been sitting, and grated it upon the boards, but the noise arose over all and continually increased. It grew louder—louder—*louder!* And still the men chatted pleasantly, and smiled. Was it possible they heard not? No, no! They heard!—they suspected!—they *knew!*—they were making a mockery of my horror!—this I thought, and this I think. But anything was better than this agony! Anything was more tolerable than this derision! I could bear those hypocritical smiles no longer! I felt that I must scream or die!—and now—again!—hark! louder! louder! louder! *louder!*——

"Villains!" I shrieked, "dissemble no more! I admit the deed!—tear up the planks!—here, here!—it is the beating of his hideous heart!"

Discussion

1. From what point of view is the story told?

2. (a) Why does the narrator want to kill the old man? (b) How does he go about carrying out his plans? (c) Why do his plans go wrong?

3. Throughout the story the narrator insists that he is not mad. (a) What proofs does he offer of his sanity? (b) What do you infer about the narrator's sanity by the end of the story? Cite passages from the selection to support your inference.

4. This story was written over one hundred years ago. Why do you think it is still widely read?

Application
Mood

The choice of setting, details, images, and words all contribute to the total feeling that is the mood of "The Tell-Tale Heart."

1. What is the setting of this story? What does this setting suggest about the mood?

2. How do the events of the story contribute to the mood?

3. Edgar Allan Poe believed that a short story should create a "single emotional effect." What emotional effect, or mood, do you think Poe was trying to achieve in this story? Pick out phrases and sentences that help create this mood.

Vocabulary
Word Origins

Use your Glossary to answer the following questions. Write your answers on a separate piece of paper.

1. From which language does *tattoo* originally come?

2. What is the meaning of the Old English word from which *stalk* comes?

3. Based on the word's origin, ''Don't react so *vehemently*'' means which of the following? ''Don't ask any questions''; ''Don't get so carried away''; ''Don't complain so much.''

4. *Fancy* is a contraction of what word?

5. How has *trifle* changed from its original form and meaning in Old French?

Composition

Assume that you are one of the police officers who come to inquire about the shriek heard in the night. How would you describe the behavior of the narrator—from your point of view? First reread the ending of the story, beginning with 259b, 2. Jot down a few notes that will help you keep in mind the actual events you will write about.

In a page or two, narrate the events of that night beginning with your arrival. Use the pronoun ''I.'' Describe the appearance of the house during your search. Describe the man's appearance and behavior. Do you notice anything strange about him? What are your thoughts during the chat ''about familiar things'' that leads to the man's confession? What happens afterwards?

(You may find the article ''Being Someone Else'' in the Composition Guide helpful in writing this composition.)

Edgar Allan Poe 1809–1849

The life of Edgar Allan Poe was, for the most part, a tragic one. Orphaned at an early age, Poe was taken in by the wealthy Allan family of Virginia. Following his attendance at English schools and instruction by private tutors, Poe attended the University of Virginia for a year. He also attended the military academy at West Point for a short time but was expelled. Increasing friction between Poe and his foster father led to a final break between the two when Poe was twenty-three.

Forced to make his own living, Poe turned to writing and editing. He achieved success as a poet and literary critic but especially as a short-story writer. Poe believed that a short story should be written so as to produce a single emotional effect within the reader: all events, characters, ideas, and words should be chosen and manipulated solely for the purpose of achieving this effect. Few writers have used this formula more effectively than did Poe himself. Among his most famous short stories are ''The Pit and the Pendulum,'' ''The Cask of Amontillado,'' ''The Fall of the House of Usher,'' and his detective stories ''The Gold Bug'' and ''The Purloined Letter.''

*L*ord Randal

Old Ballad

"O where ha you been, Lord Randal, my son?
And where ha you been, my handsome young man?"
"I ha been at the greenwood; Mother, mak my bed soon,
For I'm wearied wi huntin, and fain wad lie down."[1]

5 "An wha met ye there, Lord Randal, my son?
An wha met you there, my handsome young man?"
"O I met wi my true-love; Mother, mak my bed soon,
For I'm wearied wi huntin, and fain wad lie down."

"And what did she give you, Lord Randal, my son?
10 And what did she give you, my handsome young man?"
"Eels fried in a pan;[2] Mother, mak my bed soon,
For I'm wearied wi huntin, and fain wad lie down."

"And wha gat your leavins,[3] Lord Randal, my son?
And wha gat your leavins, my handsome young man?"
15 "My hawks and my hounds; Mother, mak my bed soon,
For I'm wearied wi huntin, and fain wad lie down."

"And what becam of them, Lord Randal, my son?
And what becam of them, my handsome young man?"
"They stretched their legs out an died; Mother, mak my
     bed soon,
20 For I'm wearied wi huntin, and fain wad lie down."

"O I fear you are poisoned, Lord Randal, my son!
I fear you are poisoned, my handsome young man!"
"O yes, I am poisoned; Mother, mak my bed soon,
For I'm sick at the heart, and I fain wad lie down."

(Continued)

---

1. *I . . . fain wad lie down,* I need to lie down. *Down* is pronounced in the
Scottish manner (dün) to rhyme with *soon.*
2. *Eels fried in a pan,* a method of poisoning that appears in many old ballads.
3. *wha gat your leavins,* who ate the food you didn't eat?

English and Scottish Popular Ballads. Helen Child Sargent and George Lymann
Kittredge, eds. Boston: Houghton Mifflin Company, 1904, 1932.

25 "What d'ye leave to your mother, Lord Randal, my son?
What d'ye leave to your mother, my handsome young
     man?"
"Four and twenty milk kye;[4] Mother, mak my bed soon,
For I'm sick at the heart, and I fain wad lie down."

"What d'ye leave to your sister, Lord Randal, my son?
30 What d'ye leave to your sister, my handsome young
     man?"
"My gold and my silver; Mother, mak my bed soon,
For I'm sick at the heart, and I fain wad lie down."

"What d'ye leave to your brother, Lord Randal, my son?
What d'ye leave to your brother, my handsome young
     man?"
35 "My houses and my lands; Mother, mak my bed soon,
For I'm sick at the heart, and I fain wad lie down."

"What d'ye leave to your true-love, Lord Randal, my
     son?
What d'ye leave to your true-love, my handsome young
     man?"
"I leave her hell and fire; Mother, mak my bed soon,
40 For I'm sick at the heart, and I fain wad lie down."

---

4. *kye,* cows.

Discussion

1. (a) Who is asking the question in the first two lines of the poem? (b) Who answers in lines 3–4? (c) How is the story told throughout?

2. (a) What is the situation at the opening of "Lord Randal"? Describe the scene. (b) Why do you think the mother asks Lord Randal what he has eaten (line 9)?

3. In many ballads, phrases or whole

lines are repeated much as they appeared before, with new details added slowly, one by one. **(a)** At what point does Lord Randal give a new reason for wanting to lie down? What is his real reason? **(b)** Why do you think he does not tell this to his mother earlier?

4. (a) How do you learn who is responsible for Lord Randal's condition? **(b)** What do you think are the mother's purposes for asking what Lord Randal will leave her, his sister and brother, and his true-love?

5. Discuss how a mood of suspense is created by the way in which the story is told.

Comment: Old Ballads

During the Middle Ages, wandering minstrels traveled throughout the countryside of England and the rest of Europe singing songs in exchange for food and lodging. These songs the minstrels sang are called *ballads.* No one is certain how old the first ballads are, who their authors were, or how they came to be written. But whatever their origins, ballads were sung for hundreds of years. Different versions arose as people, moving from one place to another, forgot some of the older lines, substituted new ones of their own, or made changes to suit the time and place. Centuries went by before these ballads were written down in any permanent form. Today we have a number of versions of some of the same ballads.

Although ballads sprang from many sources and often underwent drastic revisions in the telling, there are certain distinctive features common to most ballads. First of all, the ballad is a highly dramatic story told in verse, with an emphasis on action. Ballads deal with basic subjects like treachery, cunning, death, love, jealousy. Few of the old ballads are humorous. Most of them are tragic, dealing with sensational events—but they do so objectively, with little or no emotion or moralizing.

Ballads often contain dialogue, and their stories deal with a limited number of characters and incidents. There is little description; only those facts are included which are necessary for narrating the action. To do this, the minstrels often used a kind of shorthand, using stereotyped characters and actions which are sometimes almost symbolic. For example, the crowing of a rooster means "morning" to us now as it did in the Middle Ages, and the giving of a ring still symbolizes engagement or marriage. The making of a bed usually meant preparing a deathbed or coffin, and feeding someone eels meant poisoning, although these actions no longer carry the same significance to us as they did to earlier audiences.

Another feature is the characteristic verse form used in most of the old ballads. The stanzas are composed of four lines, and the second and fourth lines of each stanza rhyme. Phrases or whole lines are very often repeated, and rhythm usually follows a quite definite pattern.

Shooting the Moon

A Yao[1] folktale

retold by Catherine Edwards Sadler

Imagine a sharp-cornered moon so fiery hot that people on earth are scorched by its heat.

Long ago, in ancient times, there was no moon nor any stars. The sun alone dominated the sky and when it set for the night, the world was wrapped in utter darkness.

Then, suddenly, a fiery moon appeared in the sky. It had sharp edges and corners and was hotter than any sun. So fierce were its rays that it scorched the crops and burned the people below.

And there was little anyone could do. Long into the night the suffering folk mopped their brows and tossed miserably in their beds.

There lived at that time a young married couple. The man was called Ya La[2] and he was a fine archer. Each day he climbed to the top of the mountain to hunt. His wife was called Ni Wo[3] and she spent her day embroidering fine cloth.

Now Ni Wo was a good woman and she cared greatly for her people. So one day she told her husband, "This moon is too hot for mankind. We cannot stand by and let it cause such suffering. You are the best archer in the region, surely you can shoot down this wretched moon."

So Ya La took up his bow and arrow and climbed back up to the top of the mountain. There he took a deep, determined breath, pulled back his bowstring as far as it would bear and shot an arrow at

---

1. **Yao** (you), a people living chiefly in the mountainous regions of southwest China, northern Thailand, and Laos.
2. **Ya La** (yä′lä′).
3. **Ni Wo** (nē′wō′).

Catherine Edwards Sadler, "Shooting the Moon," A Yao Folktale, in *Treasure Mountain: Folktales from Southern China.* Copyright © 1982 by Catherine Edwards Sadler. Reprinted with the permission of Atheneum Publishers and Toni Mendez, Inc.

that fiery moon. The arrow sailed high up into the sky directly toward the moon, but it did not reach its mark. Halfway it turned and began to fall back to earth. Ya La shot arrow after arrow at the fiery moon, but try as he might his arrows always fell short. Ya La remained at the mountaintop until his last arrow was shot. Then he looked sorrowfully at the moon above that was causing his people so much pain. He knew his hollow-cheeked people could not survive its poisonous rays for long. But the archer Ya La did not know what to do.

At that very moment there came a cracking sound from behind him. Turning round, he found himself face to face with a weathered, worn-looking old man. The man bowed to Ya La and began to speak:

"Deep in the southern mountain there lives the strong tiger. You must eat its flesh if you wish your arrows to reach the moon. You must make its tail your bow and his tendon your bowstring. In the northern mountain there lives a tall deer; you must use the tip of his antler for your arrow. Then shoot the fiery moon till it spins."

The archer bowed to the old man in return and went home. He told his wife of his strange meeting and the words the old man had said. Then they spoke of how they could capture the strong tiger and the tall deer.

"You are a fine archer, Ya La," Ni Wo said. "Can you not shoot them with your bow and arrow?"

"I have often tried," Ya La replied. "But the tiger's hide is thick and the deer is quick. No, I must use a net to catch the strong tiger and the tall deer."

So Ni Wo cut her own hair for her husband's net. And as her hair fell to the ground, new hair grew back in its place. Then the good wife wove her hair into an enormous net. She worked for thirty days and thirty nights, until at last she was satisfied that it was strong enough to capture the tiger and the deer. Then husband and wife went to the southern mountain.

The journey was long and hard-going and the couple often had to climb high cliffs and wade through ravines, but they encouraged each other until at last they reached the tiger's den. There they placed Ni Wo's net. It was not very long before the huge beast stepped out of his den in search of food. In an instant he was caught up in the net and struggling for his freedom. His cries could be heard over the mountains and through the valleys, but Ni Wo's net was strong. Then the archer and his wife killed the tiger and dragged him home. But they did not remain for long. They gathered up their net and started for the northern mountain. They had to travel over dried lakes and through dense forests, but they plodded on until at last they reached their destination. There they set their net and waited for the tall deer. In time they caught the deer and tightened their net about him. He butted it with his strong, sharp horns, but Ni Wo's net was well made and it did not rip. And so the brave couple killed the tall deer and dragged it home as well.

Then Ni Wo prepared a meal of the tiger's flesh and Ya La ate. Soon his strength increased so that he could twist metal with his bare hands. He made a bow with the tiger's tail and a bowstring with the tiger's tendon. He shaped an arrow from the tall deer's horn and climbed once again to the mountaintop.

Ya La looked up at the blazing fiery moon. Then he pulled back the tendon bowstring. The deer-horn arrow sailed up— higher and higher—until it reached the moon. Suddenly there was a great noise. Sparks lit up the sky. The arrow bounded back to earth where Ya La placed it again in his bow. Over and over he shot the arrow and each time it hit the moon, an edge or a corner broke off and the pieces scattered across the sky. A hundred times Ya La shot the single arrow. And when he was done the moon was round and smooth and spinning like a top. And throughout the sky were shining stars, each formed from a fragment of the fiery moon. But still the moon was hot—still it scorched the fields and burned the people. So Ya La went home with his head hung low.

"Ni Wo," he said sadly to his wife. "I no longer know what to do. The moon is as hot as ever. If only we could somehow cover up its poisonous rays."

Now at that moment Ni Wo was working on a lovely embroidery. It was a picture of an ideal garden with a tall Cassia tree,[4] under which sat the image of Ni Wo. A little hut, much like her own, stood to the side. And in the meadow in the distance cows and sheep lazily grazed. She was just about to embroider the image of her husband herding the flock when he came home.

"Take this embroidery and tie it to your arrowhead," she said at once. "Then shoot it up at the moon. Perhaps it will cover the moon and curtain its fiery heat."

So Ya La took his wife's embroidery and went once more to the mountaintop. And there he strung his bow and shot his deer-horn arrow. Higher and higher it rose until it reached the fiery moon. Ni Wo's embroidery unwrapped and spread smoothly across the moon. The air suddenly became cool and pleasant. And Ya La could hear the sound of his people's laughter and merriment as they danced at the base of the mountain.

He remained for some time at the mountaintop admiring the new cool moon. There were shapes and forms across its surface, but at first he paid them little attention. Then, suddenly, they seemed to move. He strained his eyes to make out the forms . . . surely, that was his own wife's image upon the moon! And it seemed to be beckoning to him!

Meanwhile, Ni Wo was standing in front of her door admiring her husband's work when she too saw the image on the moon. No sooner had she seen it than she began to rise up—higher and higher—until at last she reached the moon and merged with her own image.

Ya La watched in despair as his dear wife sailed up through the sky to the new moon. He shouted wildly:

"Ni Wo, Ni Wo, my beloved wife. Do not leave me! Why did you not embroider me into your cloth? Oh, Ni Wo, I cannot live without you. Please, please come back!"

But Ni Wo could not come back. She cried out and pulled at her hair in torment. As she did her hair became longer and longer. She braided it and when the moon spun around and faced the mountaintop she dipped it down toward her Ya La. He desperately stretched out his hands and just caught hold of the end of his wife's braid. Then he scaled up it—higher and higher—until at last he was in the arms of his dear wife, Ni Wo.

And if you look up at the cool moon you will see them there, the archer and his wife. Sometimes she is sitting under the Cassia tree while Ya La herds their flock. But other times they are standing arm in arm, gazing out at the thousands of glittering stars that once—long, long ago—belonged to a fiery moon.

---

4. *Cassia* (kash′ə) *tree,* a variety of laurel tree found in southern China.

Discussion

1. **(a)** What extraordinary powers do Ya La and Ni Wo have? **(b)** What other magical elements are present?

2. **(a)** Why does Ya La attempt to shoot the moon in the first place? **(b)** What advice does he get from the old man? **(c)** What must Ya La and Ni Wo do in order to follow this advice?

3. **(a)** When Ya La finally manages to shoot the moon, what does he accomplish? **(b)** What problem still remains? **(c)** How do Ya La and Ni Wo solve this further problem?

4. How do Ya La and Ni Wo become separated and then reunited at the end of the story?

5. Folktales are often about typical people and situations that people commonly experience. **(a)** What human emotions are expressed in this folktale? **(b)** What customs are described that seem to reflect life in the country where the folktale originated?

6. This story, like many myths, explains the origins of certain things in nature. What natural things are explained in this folktale?

Composition

Science tells us that the moon was probably never hot, and common sense tells us that no one could shoot the moon even with a magical bow and arrow. In your opinion, do such elements of fantasy and magic make "Shooting the Moon" more or less enjoyable? Choose one of the following topics to write about: (1) Scientific knowledge makes it impossible to enjoy fantasy; (2) Enjoyment of fantasy is not spoiled by knowing a story is not scientifically accurate. Think of examples and specific details from "Shooting the Moon" or from other myths or folktales you have read to support your argument.

Write no more than one page in which you explain and defend your point of view. You may use the topic sentences as given above or change them to suit your needs. Choose your points carefully to convince a reader of your position.

(You may find the article "Supporting a Point" in the Composition Guide helpful in writing this composition.)

Catherine Edwards Sadler

Although Catherine Edwards Sadler was born in California, she lived and grew up in England and Switzerland. For a number of years she worked as an editor of children's books, and when she and her husband, Alan, visited China a few years ago, she wrote *Two Chinese Families,* which includes photographs by Alan Sadler. Her interest in China encouraged her to collect and retell folktales from southern China in a collection called *Treasure Mountain.* "Shooting the Moon" is from that collection. The Sadlers now live in New York City with their son.

The Ghost That Jim Saw

Bret Harte

Why, as to that, said the engineer,
Ghosts ain't things we are apt to fear;
Spirits don't fool with levers much,
And throttle-valves don't take to such;
5   And as for Jim,
      What happened to him
Was one half fact, and t'other half whim!

Running one night on the line, he saw
A house—as plain as the moral law—
10 Just by the moonlit bank, and thence
Came a drunken man with no more sense
    Than to drop on the rail
    Flat as a flail,
As Jim drove by with the midnight mail.

15 Down went the patents—steam reversed.
Too late! for there came a "thud." Jim cursed
As the fireman, there in the cab with him,
Kinder stared in the face of Jim,
    And says, "What now?"
20   Says Jim, "What now!
I've just run over a man,—that's how!"

The fireman stared at Jim. They ran
Back, but they never found house nor man,—
Nary a shadow within a mile.
25 Jim turned pale, but he tried to smile,
    Then on he tore
    Ten mile or more,
In quicker time than he'd made afore.

(Continued)

Would you believe it! the very next night
30 Up rose that house in the moonlight white,
Out comes the chap and drops as before,
Down goes the brake and the rest encore;
    And so, in fact,
    Each night that act
35 Occurred, till folks swore Jim was cracked.

Humph! let me see; it's a year now, 'most,
That I met Jim, East, and says, "How's your ghost?"
"Gone," says Jim; "and more, it's plain
That ghost don't trouble me again.
40   I thought I shook
    That ghost when I took
A place on an Eastern line,—but look!

"What should I meet, the first trip out,
But the very house we talked about,
45 And the selfsame man! 'Well,' says I, 'I guess
It's time to stop this 'yer foolishness.'
    So I crammed on steam,
    When there came a scream
From my fireman, that jest broke my dream:

50 " 'You've killed somebody!' Says I, 'Not much!
I've been thar often, and thar ain't no such,
And now I'll prove it!' Back we ran,
And—darn my skin!—but thar *was* a man
    On the rail, dead,
55   Smashed in the head!—
Now I call that meanness!'" That's all Jim said.

Discussion

1. (a) Who is the speaker in this poem?
(b) How does the speaker seem to feel about ghosts?

2. What happens to Jim night after night until people claim he is "cracked"?

3. (a) Why does Jim move East?
(b) What happens his first trip out in his new job? **(c)** How is Jim's reaction different from the way he had reacted before?

4. What do you think Jim means when he calls the discovery of the dead body "meanness"?

5. In line 7 the narrator says that what happens to Jim is "one half fact, and t'other half whim." **(a)** What seems to be fact in this poem? **(b)** A *whim* is defined as "a sudden fancy or notion; a freakish idea." What would you describe as whim in this poem?

6. How would you explain what happens to Jim?

Bret Harte 1836–1902

Bret Harte is most famous for his stories and poems about the Gold Rush days in the old West. To add realism to his work, Harte included much *local color*—the distinctive customs, peculiarities, and other details associated with a certain place and time. His collection *The Luck of Roaring Camp, and Other Stories* is filled with such local color details, humor, and portraits of odd but lovable characters. Harte and other authors of his time felt that they should record directly the slang and "fractured grammar" of their characters in order to make their work as accurate and realistic as possible.

*T*he Ransom of Red Chief
O. Henry

Bill was to be scalped at daybreak and Sam was to be broiled at the stake. At first neither took the idea seriously.

It looked like a good thing: but wait till I tell you. We were down South, in Alabama—Bill Driscoll and myself—when this kidnaping idea struck us. It was, as Bill afterward expressed it, "during a moment of temporary mental apparition";[1] but we didn't find that out till later.

There was a town down there, as flat as a flannel-cake, and called Summit, of course. It contained inhabitants of as undeleterious[2] and self-satisfied a class of peasantry as ever clustered around a Maypole.

Bill and me had a joint capital of about six hundred dollars, and we needed just two thousand dollars more to pull off a fraudulent town-lot scheme in western Illinois with. We talked it over on the front steps of the Hotel. Philoprogenitiveness,[3] says we, is strong in semi-rural communities; therefore, and for other reasons, a kidnaping project ought to do better there than in the radius of newspapers that send reporters out in plain clothes to stir up talk about such things. We knew that Summit couldn't get after us with anything stronger than constables and, maybe, some lackadaisical bloodhounds and a diatribe or two in the *Weekly Farmers' Budget*. So, it looked good.

We selected for our victim the only child of a prominent citizen named Ebenezer Dorset. The father was respectable and tight, a mortgage fancier and a stern, upright collection-plate passer and forecloser. The kid was a boy of ten, with bas-relief freckles, and hair the color of the cover of the magazine you buy at the newsstand when you want to catch a train. Bill and me figured that Ebenezer would melt down for a ransom of two thousand dollars to a cent. But wait till I tell you.

About two miles from Summit was a little mountain, covered with a dense cedar brake. On the rear elevation of this mountain was a cave. There we stored provisions.

One evening after sundown, we drove in a buggy past old Dorset's house. The kid was in the street, throwing rocks at a kitten on the opposite fence.

"Hey, little boy!" says Bill, "would you like to have a bag of candy and a nice ride?"

---

1. *apparition,* Bill means *aberration,* a temporary disorder of the mind.
2. *undeleterious,* harmless.
3. *Philoprogenitiveness,* love of offspring.

The boy catches Bill neatly in the eye with a piece of brick.

"That will cost the old man an extra five hundred dollars," says Bill, climbing over the wheel.

That boy put up a fight like a welterweight cinnamon bear; but, at last, we got him down in the bottom of the buggy and drove away. We took him up to the cave, and I hitched the horse in the cedar brake.

After dark I drove the buggy to the little village, three miles away, where we had hired it, and walked back to the mountain.

Bill was pasting court-plaster over the scratches and bruises on his features. There was a fire burning behind the big rock at the entrance of the cave, and the boy was watching a pot of boiling coffee, with two buzzard tail-feathers stuck in his red hair. He points a stick at me when I come up, and says:

"Ha! cursed paleface, do you dare to enter the camp of Red Chief, the terror of the plains?"

"He's all right now," says Bill, rolling up his trousers and examining some bruises on his shins. "We're playing Indian. We're making Buffalo Bill's show look like magic-lantern views of Palestine in the town hall. I'm Old Hank, the Trapper, Red Chief's captive, and I'm to be scalped at daybreak. By Geronimo! that kid can kick hard."

Yes, sir, that boy seemed to be having the time of his life. The fun of camping out in a cave had made him forget that he was a captive himself. He immediately christened me Snake-eye, the Spy, and announced that, when his braves returned from the warpath, I was to be broiled at the stake at the rising of the sun.

Then we had supper; and he filled his mouth full of bacon and bread and gravy, and began to talk. He made a during-dinner speech something like this:

"I like this fine. I never camped out before; but I had a pet 'possum once, and I was nine last birthday. I hate to go to school. Rats ate up sixteen of Jimmy Talbot's aunt's speckled hen's eggs. Are there any real Indians in these woods? I want some more gravy. Does the trees moving make the wind blow? We had five puppies. What makes your nose so red, Hank? My

father has lots of money. Are the stars hot? I whipped Ed Walker twice, Saturday. I don't like girls. You dassent catch toads unless with a string. Do oxen make any noise? Why are oranges round? Have you got beds to sleep on in this cave? Amos Murray has got six toes. A parrot can talk, but a monkey or a fish can't. How many does it take to make twelve?"

Every few minutes he would remember that he was a pesky redskin, and pick up his stick rifle and tiptoe to the mouth of the cave to rubber for the scouts of the hated paleface. Now and then he would let out a war-whoop that made Old Hank the Trapper shiver. That boy had Bill terrorized from the start.

"Red Chief," says I to the kid, "would you like to go home?"

"Aw, what for?" says he. "I don't have any fun at home. I hate to go to school. I like to camp out. You won't take me back home again, Snake-eye, will you?"

"Not right away," says I. "We'll stay here in the cave awhile."

"All right!" says he. "That'll be fine. I never had such fun in all my life."

We went to bed about eleven o'clock. We spread down some wide blankets and quilts and put Red Chief between us. We weren't afraid he'd run away. He kept us awake for three hours, jumping up and reaching for his rifle and screeching: "Hist! pard," in mine and Bill's ears, as the fancied crackle of a twig or the rustle of a leaf revealed to his young imagination the stealthy approach of the outlaw band. At last, I fell into a troubled sleep, and dreamed that I had been kidnaped and chained to a tree by a ferocious pirate with red hair.

Just at daybreak, I was awakened by a series of awful screams from Bill. They weren't yells, or howls, or shouts, or whoops, or yawps, such as you'd expect from a manly set of vocal organs—they were simply indecent, terrifying, humiliating screams, such as women emit when they see ghosts or caterpillars. It's an awful thing to hear a strong, desperate, fat man scream incontinently in a cave at daybreak.

I jumped up to see what the matter was. Red Chief was sitting on Bill's chest, with one hand twined in Bill's hair. In the other he had the sharp case-knife we used for slicing bacon; and he was industriously and realistically trying to take Bill's scalp, according to the sentence that had been pronounced upon him the evening before.

I got the knife away from the kid and made him lie down again. But, from that moment, Bill's spirit was broken. He laid down on his side of the bed, but he never closed an eye again in sleep as long as that boy was with us. I dozed off for a while, but along toward sun-up I remembered that Red Chief had said I was to be burned at the stake at the rising of the sun. I wasn't nervous or afraid; but I sat up and lit my pipe and leaned against a rock.

"What you getting up so soon for, Sam?" asked Bill.

"Me?" says I. "Oh, I got a kind of pain in my shoulder. I thought sitting up would rest it."

"You're a liar!" says Bill. "You're afraid. You was to be burned at sunrise, and you was afraid he'd do it. And he would, too, if he could find a match. Ain't it awful, Sam? Do you think anybody will pay out money to get a little imp like that back home?"

"Sure," said I. "A rowdy kid like that is just the kind that parents dote on. Now, you and the Chief get up and cook breakfast, while I go up on the top of this mountain and reconnoiter."

I went up on the peak of the little mountain and ran my eye over the contiguous vicinity. Over towards Summit I expected to see the sturdy yeomanry of the village armed with scythes and pitchforks beating the countryside for the dastardly kidnapers. But what I saw was a peaceful landscape dotted with one man ploughing with a dun mule. Nobody was dragging the creek; no couriers dashed hither and yon, bringing tidings of no news to the distracted parents. There was a sylvan attitude of somnolent sleepiness pervading that section of the external outward surface of Alabama that lay exposed to my view. "Perhaps," says I to myself, "it has not yet been discovered that the wolves have borne away the tender lambkin from the fold. Heaven help the wolves!" says I, and I went down the mountain to breakfast.

When I got to the cave I found Bill backed up against the side of it, breathing hard, and the boy threatening to smash him with a rock half as big as a cocoanut.

"He put a red-hot boiled potato down my back," explained Bill, "and then mashed it with his foot; and I boxed his ears. Have you got a gun about you, Sam?"

I took the rock away from the boy and kind of patched up the argument. "I'll fix you," says the kid to Bill. "No man ever yet struck the Red Chief but he got paid for it. You better beware!"

After breakfast the kid takes a piece of leather with strings wrapped around it out of his pocket and goes outside the cave unwinding it.

"What's he up to now?" says Bill, anxiously. "You don't think he'll run away, do you, Sam?"

"No fear of it," says I. "He don't seem to be much of a home body. But we've got to fix up some plan about the ransom.

There don't seem to be much excitement around Summit on account of his disappearance; but maybe they haven't realized yet that he's gone. His folks may think he's spending the night with Aunt Jane or one of the neighbors. Anyhow, he'll be missed today. Tonight we must get a message to his father demanding the two thousand dollars for his return."

Just then we heard a kind of war whoop, such as David might have emitted when he knocked out the champion Goliath.[4] It was a sling that Red Chief had pulled out of his pocket, and he was whirling it around his head.

I dodged, and heard a heavy thud and a kind of a sigh from Bill, like a horse gives out when you take his saddle off. A rock the size of an egg had caught Bill just behind his left ear. He loosened himself all over and fell in the fire across the frying pan of hot water for washing the dishes. I dragged him out and poured cold water on his head for half an hour.

By and by, Bill sits up and feels behind his ear and says: "Sam, do you know who my favorite biblical character is?"

"Take it easy," says I. "You'll come to your senses presently."

"King Herod,"[5] says he. "You won't go away and leave me here alone, will you, Sam?"

I went out and caught that boy and shook him until his freckles rattled.

"If you don't behave," says I, "I'll take you straight home. Now, are you going to be good, or not?"

"I was only funning," says he, sullenly. "I didn't mean to hurt Old Hank. But what did he hit me for? I'll behave, Snake-eye, if you won't send me home, and if you'll let me play the Black Scout today."

"I don't know the game," says I.

"That's for you and Mr. Bill to decide. He's your playmate for the day. I'm going away for a while, on business. Now, you come in and make friends with him and say you are sorry for hurting him, or home you go, at once."

I made him and Bill shake hands, and then I took Bill aside and told him I was going to Poplar Grove, a little village three miles from the cave, and find out what I could about how the kidnaping had been regarded in Summit. Also, I thought it best to send a peremptory letter to old man Dorset that day, demanding the ransom and dictating how it should be paid.

"You know, Sam," says Bill, "I've stood by you without batting an eye in earthquakes, fire and flood—in poker games, dynamite outrages, police raids, train robberies, and cyclones. I never lost my nerve yet till we kidnaped that two-legged skyrocket of a kid. He's got me going. You won't leave me long with him, will you, Sam?"

"I'll be back some time this afternoon," says I. "You must keep the boy amused and quiet till I return. And now we'll write the letter to old Dorset."

Bill and I got paper and pencil and worked on the letter while Red Chief, with a blanket wrapped around him, strutted up and down, guarding the mouth of the cave. Bill begged me tearfully to make the ransom fifteen hundred dollars instead of two thousand. "I ain't attempting," says he, "to decry the celebrated moral aspect of parental affection, but we're dealing with humans, and it ain't human for anybody to give up two thousand dollars for that forty-pound

---

4. **Goliath,** in the Bible, a Philistine giant whom David killed with a stone from a sling.
5. **King Herod,** King of Judea, a tyrant who at the time of Jesus Christ's birth ordered all the male infants of Bethlehem killed.

chunk of freckled wildcat. I'm willing to take a chance at fifteen hundred dollars. You can charge the difference up to me."

So, to relieve Bill, I acceded, and we collaborated a letter that ran this way:

Ebenezer Dorset, Esq.:

We have your boy concealed in a place far from Summit. It is useless for you or the most skillful detectives to attempt to find him. Absolutely, the only terms on which you can have him restored to you are these: We demand fifteen hundred dollars in large bills for his return; the money to be left at midnight tonight at the same spot and in the same box as your reply—as hereinafter described. If you agree to these terms, send your answer in writing by a solitary messenger tonight at half-past eight o'clock. After crossing Owl Creek on the road to Poplar Grove, there are three large trees about a hundred yards apart, close to the fence of the wheat field on the right-hand side. At the bottom of the fence post, opposite the third tree, will be found a small pasteboard box.

The messenger will place the answer in this box and return immediately to Summit.

If you attempt any treachery or fail to comply with our demand as stated, you will never see your boy again.

If you pay the money as demanded, he will be returned to you safe and well within three hours. These terms are final, and if you do not accede to them no further communication will be attempted.

TWO DESPERATE MEN

I addressed this letter to Dorset, and put it in my pocket. As I was about to start, the kid comes up to me and says:

"Aw, Snake-eye, you said I could play the Black Scout while you was gone."

"Play it, of course," says I. "Mr. Bill will play with you. What kind of a game is it?"

"I'm the Black Scout," says Red Chief, "and I have to ride to the stockade to warn the settlers that the Indians are coming. I'm tired of playing Indian myself. I want to be the Black Scout."

"All right," says I. "It sounds harmless to me. I guess Mr. Bill will help you foil the pesky savages."

"What am I to do?" asks Bill, looking at the kid suspiciously.

"You are the hoss," says Black Scout. "Get down on your hands and knees. How can I ride to the stockade without a hoss?"

"You'd better keep him interested," said I, "till we get the scheme going. Loosen up."

Bill gets down on his all fours, and a look comes in his eye like a rabbit's when you catch it in a trap.

"How far is it to the stockade, kid?" he asks, in a husky manner of voice.

"Ninety miles," says the Black Scout. "And you have to hump yourself to get there on time. Whoa, now!"

The Black Scout jumps on Bill's back and digs his heels in his side.

"For Heaven's sake," says Bill, "hurry back, Sam, as soon as you can. I wish we hadn't made the ransom more than a thousand. Say, you quit kicking me or I'll get up and warm you good."

I walked over to Poplar Grove and sat around the postoffice and store, talking with the chaw-bacons that came in to trade. One whiskerando says that he hears Summit is all upset on account of Elder Ebenezer Dorset's boy having been lost or stolen. That was all I wanted to know. I bought some smoking tobacco, referred casually to the price of black-eyed peas, posted my letter surreptitiously, and came away. The post-master said the mail-carrier would come by in an hour to take the mail to Summit.

When I got back to the cave Bill and the boy were not to be found. I explored the vicinity of the cave, and risked a yodel or two, but there was no response.

So I lighted my pipe and sat down on a mossy bank to await developments.

In about half an hour I heard the bushes rustle, and Bill wabbled out into the little glade in front of the cave. Behind him was the kid, stepping softly like a scout, with a broad grin on his face. Bill stopped, took off his hat, and wiped his face with a red handkerchief. The kid stopped about eight feet behind him.

"Sam," says Bill, "I suppose you'll think I'm a renegade, but I couldn't help it. I'm a grown person with masculine proclivities and habits of self-defense, but there is a time when all systems of egotism and predominance fail. The boy is gone. I sent him home. All is off. There was martyrs in old times," goes on Bill, "that suffered death rather than give up the particular graft they enjoyed. None of 'em ever was subjugated to such supernatural tortures as I have been. I tried to be faithful to our articles of depredation;[6] but there came a limit."

"What's the trouble, Bill?" I asks him.

"I was rode," says Bill, "the ninety miles to the stockade, not barring an inch. Then, when the settlers was rescued, I was given oats. Sand ain't a palatable substitute. And then, for an hour I had to try to explain to him why there was nothin' in holes, how a road can run both ways, and what makes the grass green. I tell you, Sam, a human can only stand so much. I takes him by the neck of his clothes and drags him down the mountain. On the way he kicks my legs black and blue from the knees down; and I've got to have two or three bites on my thumb and hand cauterized.

"But he's gone"—continues Bill—"gone home. I showed him the road to Summit and kicked him about eight feet nearer there at one kick. I'm sorry we lose the ransom; but it was either that or Bill Driscoll to the madhouse."

Bill is puffing and blowing, but there is a look of ineffable peace and growing content on his rose-pink features.

"Bill," says I, "there isn't any heart disease in your family, is there?"

"No," says Bill, "nothing chronic except malaria and accidents. Why?"

"Then you might turn around," says I, "and have a look behind you."

Bill turns and sees the boy, and loses his complexion and sits down plump on the ground and begins to pluck aimlessly at grass and little sticks. For an hour I was afraid of his mind. And then I told him that my scheme was to put the whole job through immediately and that we would get the ransom and be off with it by midnight if old Dorset fell in with our proposition. So Bill braced up enough to give the kid a weak sort of a smile and a promise to play the Russian in a Japanese war with him as soon as he felt a little better.

I had a scheme for collecting that ransom without danger of being caught by counterplots that ought to commend itself to professional kidnapers. The tree under which the answer was to be left—and the money later on—was close to the road fence with big, bare fields on all sides. If a

---

6. *articles of depradation.* Bill means *articles of confederation,* a contract or agreement. The constitution adopted by the thirteen original states was called the Articles of Confederation.

gang of constables should be watching for anyone to come for the note, they could see him a long way off crossing the fields or in the road. But no, sirree! At half-past eight I was up in that tree as well hidden as a tree toad, waiting for the messenger to arrive.

Exactly on time, a half-grown boy rides up the road on a bicycle, locates the pasteboard box at the foot of the fencepost, slips a folded piece of paper into it, and pedals away again back toward Summit.

I waited an hour and then concluded the thing was square. I slid down the tree, got the note, slipped along the fence till I struck the woods, and was back at the cave in another half an hour. I opened the note, got near the lantern, and read it to Bill. It was written with a pen in a crabbed hand, and the sum and substance of it was this:

Two Desperate Men.

Gentlemen: I received your letter today by post, in regard to the ransom you ask for the return of my son. I think you are a little high in your demands, and I hereby make you a counter-proposition, which I am inclined to believe you will accept. You bring Johnny home and pay me two hundred and fifty dollars in cash, and I agree to take him off your hands. You had better come at night, for the neighbors believe he is lost, and I couldn't be responsible for what they would do to anybody they saw bringing him back. Very respectfully,

EBENEZER DORSET.

"Great Pirates of Penzance," says I; "of all the impudent——"

But I glanced at Bill, and hesitated. He had the most appealing look in his eyes I ever saw on the face of a dumb or a talking brute.

"Sam," says he, "what's two hundred and fifty dollars, after all? We've got the money. One more night of this kid will send me to a bed in Bedlam.[7] Besides being a thorough gentleman, I think Mr. Dorset is a spendthrift for making us such a liberal offer. You ain't going to let the chance go, are you?"

"Tell you the truth, Bill," says I, "this little he ewe lamb has somewhat got on my nerves too. We'll take him home, pay the ransom, and make our getaway."

We took him home that night. We got him to go by telling him that his father had bought a silver-mounted rifle and a pair of moccasins for him, and we were to hunt bears the next day.

It was just twelve o'clock when we knocked at Ebenezer's front door. Just at the moment when I should have been abstracting the fifteen hundred dollars from the box under the tree, according to the original proposition, Bill was counting out two hundred and fifty dollars into Dorset's hand.

When the kid found out we were going to leave him at home he started up a howl like a calliope and fastened himself as tight as a leech to Bill's leg. His father peeled him away gradually, like a porous plaster.

"How long can you hold him?" asks Bill.

"I'm not as strong as I used to be," says old Dorset, "but I think I can promise you ten minutes."

"Enough," says Bill. "In ten minutes I shall cross the Central, Southern, and Middle Western States, and be legging it trippingly for the Canadian border."

And, as dark as it was, and as fat as Bill was, and as good a runner as I am, he was a good mile and a half out of Summit before I could catch up with him.

---

7. **Bedlam,** popular name for the hospital of St. Mary of Bethlehem, an insane asylum in London, England.

Discussion

1. **(a)** What circumstances make the kidnaping of the Dorset boy seem attractive at first to Bill and the narrator, Sam? **(b)** Is there any indication in the first few pages of the story that the kidnaping may not succeed? If so, where?

2. **(a)** How would you characterize Bill and Sam? **(b)** What kind of boy does Johnny, or "Red Chief," prove himself to be? **(c)** In your opinion, are any of these characters stereotypes? Explain.

3. **(a)** Near the middle of the story, who seems to be in control? **(b)** Is this situation unusual in any way? Explain.

4. What is unexpected about the outcome of the story?

5. **(a)** Find at least two examples of hyperbole in statements by Bill or Sam. **(b)** What effect does this hyperbole create?

Application
Tone

Practically any given subject can be made to seem serious or silly, depending on how it is handled. An author's choice of words and details reveals his or her attitude toward that subject and establishes the tone of the work.

1. Do Bill and Sam take their kidnaping plot seriously, or not?

2. Does the author seem to take Bill and Sam's plot seriously? How does the author's attitude influence the way you, the reader, regard Bill and Sam and their activities?

3. How would you describe the tone of this story? Is this the tone you would expect in a story about a criminal plot? Why or why not?

Vocabulary
Context, Pronunciation Key

Use your Glossary to answer the following questions, and write the answers on your paper. Be sure you know the meaning of each Vocabulary word.

1. Does the accent in *fraudulent* fall on the first, second, or third syllable?

2. Does the first syllable of *bas-relief* rhyme with *ha, lace,* or *glass?*

3. Does the first syllable of *stealthy* rhyme with *reel, tell,* or *mail?*

4. Does the syllable in *reconnoiter* that has a primary accent rhyme with *deck, boy,* or *her?*

5. Does the accented syllable in *contiguous* rhyme with *don, dig,* or *flu?*

6. Does the *sc* in *scythe* sound like the *sc* in *scare,* in *scent,* or in *conscience?*

7. Does the *mn* in *somnolent* sound like the *mn* in *autumn* or in *gymnasium?*

8. Does the syllable in *collaborate* that has a primary accent rhyme with *babe, tab, bat,* or *mate?*

9. Does the accent in *proclivity* fall on the second, third, or fourth syllable?

10. In the context of the story (282b, 1), should *abstract* be pronounced (ab'strakt) or (ab strakt')?

O. Henry 1862–1910

O. Henry's real name was William Sydney Porter. He was born in Greensboro, North Carolina, but after a brief schooling he drifted off to Texas, where he became a bank teller, began writing pieces for newspapers, and founded his own humor magazine called *The Rolling Stone* (1894–1895). Charged with embezzling bank funds, he fled to Central America but returned to Texas to turn himself in. Although his loss of a small sum was a technical mismanagement rather than crime, he was tried, convicted, and sentenced to prison. During his three-year imprisonment he took the pen name O. Henry and continued writing. After his release he went to New York, where he remained the rest of his life.

O. Henry's fine gift of skill as a writer of humorous stories with ingenious plots and surprise endings gained him enormous popularity. He wrote so many short stories that nine collections were published during his life and eight more after his death. In 1918 the O. Henry Memorial Awards were established to be awarded each year to the authors of the best short stories.

The Highwayman

Alfred Noyes

Part One:
The wind was a torrent of darkness among the gusty trees;
The moon was a ghostly galleon tossed upon cloudy seas;
The road was a ribbon of moonlight over the purple moor;
And the highwayman came riding—
5   Riding—riding—
The highwayman came riding, up to the old inn door.

He'd a French cocked hat on his forehead, a bunch of lace at his chin,
A coat of the claret velvet, and breeches of brown doeskin;
They fitted with never a wrinkle; his boots were up to the thigh!
10 And he rode with a jeweled twinkle,
His pistol butts a-twinkle,
His rapier hilt a-twinkle, under the jeweled sky.

Over the cobbles he clattered and clashed in the dark inn yard;
And he tapped with his whip on the shutters, but all was locked and barred;
15 He whistled a tune to the window, and who should be waiting there
But the landlord's black-eyed daughter,
Bess, the landlord's daughter,
Plaiting a dark red love knot into her long black hair.

And dark in the dark old inn yard a stable-wicket creaked
20 Where Tim the ostler listened; his face was white and peaked;
His eyes were hollows of madness, his hair like moldy hay,
But he loved the landlord's daughter,
The landlord's red-lipped daughter;
Dumb as a dog he listened, and he heard the robber say—

25 "One kiss, my bonny sweetheart; I'm after a prize tonight;
But I shall be back with the yellow gold before the morning light;
Yet, if they press me sharply, and harry me through the day,
Then look for me by moonlight,
Watch for me by moonlight,
30 I'll come to thee by moonlight, though hell should bar the way."

"The Highwayman" from *Collected Poems* in One Volume, by Alfred Noyes. Copyright 1906, renewed 1934 by Alfred Noyes. Reprinted by permission of J. B. Lippincott Company and Hugh Noyes.

He rose upright in the stirrups; he scarce could reach her hand,
But she loosened her hair i' the casement! His face burned like a brand
As the black cascade of perfume came tumbling over his breast;
And he kissed its waves in the moonlight
35   (Oh, sweet black waves in the moonlight!);
Then he tugged at his rein in the moonlight, and galloped away to the West.

(Continued)

Part Two:
He did not come in the dawning; he did not come at noon;
And out o' the tawny sunset, before the rise o' the moon,
When the road was a gypsy's ribbon, looping the purple moor,
40 A redcoat troop came marching—
    Marching—marching—
King George's men came marching, up to the old inn door.

They said no word to the landlord; they drank his ale instead;
But they gagged his daughter and bound her to the foot of her narrow bed;
45 Two of them knelt at her casement, with muskets at their side!
There was death at every window,
    And hell at one dark window,
For Bess could see, through her casement, the road that *he* would ride.

They had tied her up to attention, with many a sniggering jest;
50 They had bound a musket beside her, with the barrel beneath her breast!
"Now keep good watch!" and they kissed her.
She heard the dead man say:
Look for me by moonlight,
    Watch for me by moonlight,
55 *I'll come to thee by moonlight, though hell should bar the way!*

She twisted her hands behind her, but all the knots held good!
She writhed her hands till her fingers were wet with sweat or blood!
They stretched and strained in the darkness, and the hours crawled by like years,
Till, now, on the stroke of midnight,
60   Cold on the stroke of midnight,
The tip of one finger touched it! The trigger at least was hers!

The tip of one finger touched it; she strove no more for the rest!
Up she stood, to attention, with the barrel beneath her breast.
She would not risk their hearing; she would not strive again;
65 For the road lay bare in the moonlight,
    Blank and bare in the moonlight,
And the blood of her veins in the moonlight throbbed to her love's refrain.

Tlot-tlot; tlot-tlot! Had they heard it? The horse-hoofs ringing clear;
Tlot-tlot, tlot-tlot, in the distance! Were they deaf that they did not hear?
70 Down the ribbon of moonlight, over the brow of the hill,
The highwayman came riding—
    Riding—riding—
The redcoats looked to their priming! She stood up, straight and still!

Tlot-tlot, in the frosty silence! *Tlot-tlot,* in the echoing night!
75 Nearer he came and nearer! Her face was like a light!
Her eyes grew wide for a moment; she drew one last deep breath;
Then her finger moved in the moonlight,
    Her musket shattered the moonlight,
Shattered her breast in the moonlight and warned him—with her death.

80 He turned; he spurred to the westward; he did not know who stood
Bowed, with her head o'er the musket, drenched with her own red blood!
Not till the dawn he heard it; and slowly blanched to hear
How Bess, the landlord's daughter,
    The landlord's black-eyed daughter,
85 Had watched for her love in the moonlight, and died in the darkness there.

Back he spurred like a madman, shrieking a curse to the sky,
With the white road smoking behind him, and his rapier brandished high!
Blood-red were his spurs i' the golden noon; wine-red was his velvet coat,
When they shot him down on the highway,
90   Down like a dog on the highway,
And he lay in his blood on the highway, with the bunch of lace at his throat.

And still of a winter's night, they say, when the wind is in the trees,
When the moon is a ghostly galleon tossed upon cloudy seas,
When the road is a ribbon of moonlight over the purple moor,
95 *A highwayman comes riding—*
    Riding—riding—
A highwayman comes riding, up to the old inn door.

Over the cobbles he clatters and clangs in the dark inn yard;
And he taps with his whip on the shutters, but all is locked and barred;
100 *He whistles a tune to the window, and who should be waiting there*
But the landlord's black-eyed daughter,
    Bess, the landlord's daughter,
Plaiting a dark red love knot into her long black hair.

Discussion

1. (a) Tell the major events in the plot of "The Highwayman." **(b)** How do you infer the king's soldiers know where to set their trap to capture the highwayman?

2. How would you describe the mood of this poem? What details help create this mood?

3. Read aloud the first stanza to get a

sense of the rhythm of the whole poem. **(a)** What sounds are suggested by the rhythm of lines 4–6? **(b)** Does the rhythm seem appropriate to the poem? Explain.

4. **(a)** List at least three metaphors in the poem. **(b)** In the fourth stanza, what similes are used to describe Tim the ostler? Why do you think he is portrayed in this way? **(c)** What other similes are in the poem?

5. Alfred Noyes once commented, "The point of the poem is not that the highwayman was a highwayman, but that the heroine was a heroine." What do you think the author meant?

Comment: Highwaymen, Footpads, and Rufflers

If you were a wealthy person in eighteenth-century England, a journey of any kind could be an extremely dangerous venture. The streets and roads about London were infested with highwaymen, footpads (highwaymen without horses), and rufflers (today we would call them "muggers"). Highway robbery was an almost daily occurrence. The outlaws grew so bold, according to one source, that they once posted notices on the doors of the rich, warning everyone who ventured out of town to carry at least ten gold coins and a watch—or risk a penalty of death.

During this "golden age of crime" a Prime Minister, the Prince of Wales, and the Lord Mayor of London all had expensive encounters with robbers. Queen Anne once narrowly missed an ambush when her coach was delayed: a waiting band of highwaymen attacked another coach by mistake. A later monarch, George II, was not so fortunate. While walking in Kensington Gardens, he was confronted by a lone highwayman and was forced to give up his money, his watch, and the buckles of his shoes.

In a time when organized police forces were unheard of, the principal means of fighting crime was to offer large rewards for the capture of criminals. An unfortunate side effect of this system was that it made possible the extraordinary double career of Jonathan Wild. On one hand, Wild was a master criminal, plotting thefts, receiving stolen goods. On the other hand, Wild was the most successful "thief-taker" of all, and made an additional profit by returning stolen goods to their owners—for a fee. If a thief objected to Wild's leadership, he was quickly betrayed to the authorities, and Wild pocketed another reward. Like many of the highwaymen he dealt with, Wild eventually finished his career at the end of a rope, betrayed in his own turn.

There are many obvious parallels between the highwaymen of eighteenth-century England and the outlaws of the American West. A further parallel exists in the mysterious process by which brutal and greedy men of both eras have become figures of folklore and legend.

The Lady, or the Tiger?

Frank R. Stockton

She loved the young man, but she could not have him. The choice she had to make cost her days and nights of anguish.

In the very olden time, there lived a semi-barbaric king, whose ideas, though somewhat polished and sharpened by the progressiveness of distant Latin neighbors,[1] were still large, florid, and untrammeled, as became the half of him which was barbaric. He was a man of exuberant fancy, and, withal, of an authority so irresistible that, at his will, he turned his varied fancies into facts. He was greatly given to self-communing; and, when he and himself agreed upon anything, the thing was done. When every member of his domestic and political systems moved smoothly in its appointed course, his nature was bland and genial; but whenever there was a little hitch, and some of his orbs got out of their orbits, he was blander and more genial still, for nothing pleased him so much as to make the crooked straight, and crush down uneven places.

Among the borrowed notions by which his barbarism had become semifixed was that of the public arena, in which, by exhibitions of manly and beastly valor, the minds of his subjects were refined and cultured.

But even here the exuberant and barbaric fancy asserted itself. The arena of the king was built, not to give the people an opportunity of hearing the rhapsodies of dying gladiators, nor to enable them to view the inevitable conclusion of a conflict between religious opinions and hungry jaws, but for purposes far better adapted to widen and develop the mental energies of the people. This vast amphitheater, with its encircling galleries, its mysterious vaults, and its unseen passages, was an agent of poetic justice, in which crime was punished, or virtue rewarded, by the decrees of an impartial and incorruptible chance.

When a subject was accused of a crime of sufficient importance to interest the king, public notice was given that on an appointed day the fate of the accused person would be decided in the king's arena, a structure which well deserved its name; for, although its form and plan were borrowed from afar, its purpose emanated solely from the brain of this man, who, every barley-corn a king,[2] knew no tradition to which he owed more allegiance than pleased his fancy, and who ingrafted on every adopted form of human thought and action the rich growth of his barbaric idealism.

When all the people had assembled in the galleries, and the king, surrounded by his court, sat high up on his throne of royal state on one side of the arena, he gave a signal, a door beneath him opened, and the

---

1. *Latin neighbors,* peoples of the ancient Roman empire.
2. *every barleycorn a king.* A barleycorn is a measurement used in former times equal to one-third of an inch. *Barleycorn* is here substituted in the usual phrase "every inch a king" to create a humorous effect of antiquity.

From *The Lady, or the Tiger and Other Stories* by Frank R. Stockton (Charles Scribner's Sons, 1884).

accused subject stepped out into the amphitheater. Directly opposite him, on the other side of the enclosed space, were two doors, exactly alike and side by side. It was the duty and the privilege of the person on trial to walk directly to these doors and open one of them. He could open either door he pleased; he was subject to no guidance or influence but that of the aforementioned impartial and incorruptible chance. If he opened the one, there came out of it a hungry tiger, the fiercest and most cruel that could be procured, which immediately sprang upon him and tore him to pieces, as a punishment for his guilt. The moment that the case of the criminal was thus decided, doleful iron bells were clanged, great wails went up from the hired mourners posted on the outer rim of the arena, and the vast audience, with bowed heads and downcast hearts, wended slowly their homeward way, mourning greatly that one so young and fair, or so old and respected, should have merited so dire a fate.

But if the accused person opened the other door, there came forth from it a lady, the most suitable to his years and station that his majesty could select among his fair subjects; and to this lady he was immediately married, as a reward for his innocence. It mattered not that he might already possess a wife and family or that his affections might be engaged upon an object of his own selection; the king allowed no such subordinate arrangements to interfere with his great scheme of retribution and reward. The exercises, as in the other instance, took place immediately, and in the arena. Another door opened beneath the king, and a priest, followed by a band of choristers and dancing maidens blowing joyous airs on golden horns and treading an epithalamic measure, advanced to where the pair stood,

side by side, and the wedding was promptly and cheerily solemnized. Then the gay brass bells rang forth their merry peals, the people shouted glad hurrahs, and the innocent man, preceded by children strewing flowers on his path, led his bride to his home.

This was the king's semibarbaric method of administering justice. Its perfect fairness is obvious. The criminal could not know out of which door would come the lady; he opened either he pleased, without having the slightest idea whether, in the next instant, he was to be devoured or married. On some occasions the tiger came out of one door, and on some out of the other. The decisions of this tribunal were not only fair, they were positively determinate; the accused person was instantly punished if he found himself guilty, and, if innocent, he was rewarded on the spot, whether he liked it or not. There was no escape from the judgments of the king's arena.

The institution was a very popular one. When the people gathered together on one of the great trial days, they never knew whether they were to witness a bloody slaughter or a hilarious wedding. This element of uncertainty lent an interest to the occasion which it could not otherwise have attained. Thus, the masses were entertained and pleased, and the thinking part of the community could bring no charge of unfairness against this plan; for did not the accused person have the whole matter in his own hands?

This semibarbaric king had a daughter as blooming as his most florid fancies and with a soul as fervent and imperious as his own. As is usual in such cases, she was the apple of his eye and was loved by him above all humanity. Among his courtiers was a young man of that fineness of blood

and lowness of station common to the conventional heroes of romance who love royal maidens. This royal maiden was well satisfied with her lover, for he was handsome and brave to a degree unsurpassed in all this kingdom, and she loved him with an ardor that had enough of barbarism in it to make it exceedingly warm and strong. This love affair moved on happily for many months, until one day the king happened to discover its existence. He did not hesitate nor waver in regard to his duty in the premises. The youth was immediately cast into prison, and a day was appointed for his trial in the king's arena. This, of course, was an especially important occasion, and his majesty, as well as all the people, was greatly interested in the workings and development of this trial. Never before had such a case occurred; never before had a subject dared to love the daughter of the king. In after-

years such things became commonplace enough, but then they were, in no slight degree, novel and startling.

The tiger cages of the kingdom were searched for the most savage and relentless beasts, from which the fiercest monster might be selected for the arena, and the ranks of maiden youth and beauty throughout the land were carefully surveyed by competent judges, in order that the young man might have a fitting bride in case fate did not determine for him a different destiny. Of course, everybody knew that the deed with which the accused was charged had been done. He had loved the princess, and neither he, she, nor anyone else thought of denying the fact, but the king would not think of allowing any fact of this kind to interfere with the workings of the tribunal, in which he took such great delight and satisfaction. No matter how the affair turned out, the youth would be disposed of, and the king would take an aesthetic pleasure in watching the course of events, which would determine whether or not the young man had done wrong in allowing himself to love the princess.

The appointed day arrived. From far and near the people gathered and thronged the great galleries of the arena, and crowds, unable to gain admittance, massed themselves against its outside walls. The king and his court were in their places opposite the twin doors—those fateful portals so terrible in their similarity.

All was ready. The signal was given. A door beneath the royal party opened, and the lover of the princess walked into the arena. Tall, beautiful, fair, his appearance was greeted with a low hum of admiration and anxiety. Half the audience had not known so grand a youth had lived among them. No wonder the princess loved him! What a terrible thing for him to be there!

As the youth advanced into the arena, he turned, as the custom was, to bow to the king, but he did not think at all of that royal personage; his eyes were fixed upon the princess who sat to the right of her father. Had it not been for the moiety of barbarism in her nature, it is probable that lady would not have been there, but her intense and fervid soul would not allow her to be absent on an occasion in which she was so terribly interested.

From the moment that the decree had gone forth, that her lover should decide his fate in the king's arena, she had thought of nothing, night or day, but this great event and the various subjects connected with it. Possessed of more power, influence, and force of character than anyone who had ever before been interested in such a case, she had done what no other person had done—she had possessed herself of the secret of the doors. She knew in which of the two rooms that lay behind those doors stood the cage of the tiger, with its open front, and in which waited the lady. Through these thick doors, heavily curtained with skins on the inside, it was impossible that any noise or suggestion should come from within to the person who should approach to raise the latch of one of them, but gold and the power of a woman's will had brought the secret to the princess.

And not only did she know in which room stood the lady ready to emerge, all blushing and radiant, should her door be opened, but she knew who the lady was. It was one of the fairest and loveliest of the damsels of the court who had been selected as the reward of the accused youth should he be proved innocent of the crime of aspiring to one so far above him, and the princess hated her. Often had she seen, or imagined that she had seen, this fair creature throwing glances of admiration upon the person of her lover, and sometimes she thought these glances were perceived and even returned. Now and then she had seen them talking together; it was but for a moment or two, but much can be said in a brief space; it may have been on most unimportant topics, but how could she know that? The girl was lovely, but she had dared to raise her eyes to the loved one of the princess, and, with all the intensity of the savage blood transmitted to her through long lines of wholly barbaric ancestors, she hated the woman who blushed and trembled behind that silent door.

When her lover turned and looked at her, and his eye met hers as she sat there paler and whiter than anyone in the vast ocean of anxious faces about her, he saw, by that power of quick perception which is given to those whose souls are one, that she knew behind which door crouched the tiger and behind which stood the lady. He had expected her to know it. He understood her nature, and his soul was assured that she would never rest until she had made plain to herself this thing, hidden to all other lookers-on, even to the king. The only hope for the youth in which there was any element of certainty was based upon the success of the princess in discovering this mystery, and the moment he looked upon her, he saw she had succeeded, as in his soul he knew she would succeed.

Then it was that his quick and anxious glance asked the question: "Which?" It was as plain to her as if he shouted it from where he stood. There was not an instant to be lost. The question was asked in a flash; it must be answered in another.

Her right arm lay on the cushioned parapet before her. She raised her hand, and made a slight, quick movement toward the right. No one but her lover saw her. Every eye but his was fixed on the man in the arena.

He turned, and with a firm and rapid step he walked across the empty space. Every heart stopped beating, every breath was held, every eye was fixed immovably upon that man. Without the slightest hesitation, he went to the door on the right and opened it.

Now, the point of the story is this: Did the tiger come out of that door, or did the lady?

The more we reflect upon this question, the harder it is to answer. It involves a study of the human heart which leads us through devious mazes of passion, out of which it is difficult to find our way. Think of it, fair reader, not as if the decision of the question depended upon yourself, but upon that hot-blooded, semibarbaric princess, her soul at a white heat beneath the combined fires of despair and jealousy. She had lost him, but who should have him?

How often, in her waking hours and in her dreams, had she started in wild horror and covered her face with her hands as she thought of her lover opening the door on the other side of which waited the cruel fangs of the tiger!

But how much oftener had she seen him at the other door! How in her grievous reveries had she gnashed her teeth and torn her hair, when she saw his start of rapturous delight as he opened the door of the lady! How her soul had burned in agony when she had seen him rush to meet that woman, with her flushing cheek and sparkling eye of triumph; when she had seen him lead her forth, his whole frame kindled with the joy of recovered life; when she had heard the glad shouts from the multitude, and the wild ringing of the happy bells; when she had seen the priest, with his joyous followers, advance to the couple and make them man and wife before her very eyes; and when she had seen them walk away together upon their path of flowers, followed by the tremendous shouts of the hilarious multitude, in which her one despairing shriek was lost and drowned!

Would it not be better for him to die at once, and go to wait for her in the blessed regions of semibarbaric futurity?

And yet, that awful tiger, those shrieks, that blood!

Her decision had been indicated in an instant, but it had been made after days and nights of anguished deliberation. She had known she would be asked, she had decided what she would answer, and without the slightest hesitation, she had moved her hand to the right.

The question of her decision is one not to be lightly considered, and it is not for me to presume to set myself up as the one person able to answer it. And so I leave it with all of you: Which came out of the opened door—the lady, or the tiger?

Discussion

1. **(a)** Describe the king's method for achieving justice. **(b)** The narrator says of this method, "Its perfect fairness is obvious." In what ways might the method be considered "fair"? **(c)** In what ways might the method be unfair?

2. When does this story take place? What effect does this setting have upon what happens?

3. **(a)** Describe the character of the princess. **(b)** What is her attitude toward the young lady selected to be the young man's bride? **(c)** How does this attitude complicate her position?

4. Some readers of this story have felt cheated because the author does not say for certain what is behind the door that the princess chooses for the young man. **(a)** Why do you suppose the author might have chosen to end the story in this way? **(b)** Do you think that an author has an obligation to eliminate all uncertainty for readers? Explain.

5. What choice do you think the princess makes? Give reasons for your view.

Vocabulary
Antonyms, Dictionary

Look up each of the following words in the Glossary. Then match each word in Column A with its *antonym* (the word most opposite it in meaning) in Column B. Write the pairs of antonyms on your paper. Be sure you spell all the words correctly.

Column A	*Column B*
novel	fervid
subordinate	doleful
rapturous	commonplace
bland	genial
savage	imperious

Composition

The expression "on the horns of a dilemma" is often used to refer to a situation in which one has to choose between two equally unpleasant alternatives. Have you ever found yourself in such a situation? What did you do?

In one paragraph describe a dilemma of your own in which you were caught between two equally unpleasant—or equally tempting—choices. Describe the choices and explain why your decision was a difficult one. In a second paragraph explain which one you finally chose, and why. Did you ever regret the choice you made? Why or why not?

See **FORESHADOWING** Handbook of Literary Terms

To Build a Fire

Jack London

He was alone, and it was seventy-five degrees below zero. Could he make it to camp before the cold conquered him?

Day had broken cold and gray, exceedingly cold and gray, when the man turned aside from the main Yukon trail[1] and climbed the high earth bank, where a dim and little-traveled trail led eastward through the fat spruce timberland. It was a steep bank, and he paused for breath at the top, excusing the act to himself by looking at his watch. It was nine o'clock. There was no sun or hint of sun, though there was not a cloud in the sky. It was a clear day, and yet there seemed an intangible pall over the face of things, a subtle gloom that made the day dark and that was due to the absence of sun. This fact did not worry the man. He was used to the lack of sun. It had been days since he had seen the sun, and he knew that a few more days must pass before that cheerful orb, due south, would just peep above the skyline and dip immediately from view.

The man flung a look back along the way he had come. The Yukon lay a mile wide and hidden under three feet of ice. On top of this ice were as many feet of snow. It was all pure white, rolling in gentle undulations where the ice jams of the freeze-up had formed. North and south, as far as his eye could see, it was unbroken white, save for a dark hairline that curved and twisted from around the spruce-covered island to the south and that curved and twisted away into the north, where it disappeared behind another spruce-covered island. This dark hairline was the trail—the main trail—that led south five hundred miles to the Chilcoot Pass, Dyea,[2] and salt water, and that led north seventy miles to Dawson, and still on to the north a thousand miles to Nulato, and finally to St. Michael on the Bering Sea,[3] a thousand miles and half a thousand more.

But all this—the mysterious, far-reaching hairline trail, the absence of sun from the sky, the tremendous cold, and the strangeness and weirdness of it all—made no impression on the man. It was not because he was long used to it. He was a newcomer in the land, a *chechaquo*,[4] and this was his first winter. The trouble with him

---

1. **Yukon** (yü′kon) **trail,** a trail which runs through the Yukon, a territory in northwestern Canada.
2. **Chilcoot** (chil′küt) **Pass, Dyea** (dī′ā). Chilcoot Pass is a mountain pass in British Columbia, the territory just south of the Yukon. At the time of the story, Dyea was a town in western British Columbia, south of Chilcoot Pass.
3. **Dawson . . . Bering Sea.** Dawson is a city in the western part of the Yukon. Nulato (nü lä′tō) is a city in western Alaska. St. Michael is a port city on the western coast of Alaska.
4. *chechaquo* (chē chä′kō), a newcomer; greenhorn; tenderfoot. [*Spanish*]

Slightly abridged from *Lost Faces* by Jack London. Published by The Macmillan Company (1909). Reprinted by permission of the estate of the author.

was that he was without imagination. He was quick and alert in the things of life, but only in the things, not in the significances. Fifty degrees below zero meant eighty-odd degrees of frost. Such a fact impressed him as being cold and uncomfortable, and that was all. It did not lead him to meditate upon his frailty as a creature of temperature, and upon man's frailty in general, able only to live within certain narrow limits of heat and cold; and, from there on, it did not lead him to the conjectural field of immortality and man's place in the universe. Fifty degrees below zero stood for a bite of frost that hurt and that must be guarded against by the use of mittens, ear flaps, warm moccasins, and thick socks. Fifty degrees below zero was to him just precisely fifty degrees below zero. That there should be anything more to it than that was a thought that never entered his head.

As he turned to go on, he spat speculatively. There was a sharp, explosive crackle that startled him. He spat again. And again, in the air, before it could fall to the snow, the spittle crackled. He knew that at fifty below spittle cracked on the snow, but this spittle had cracked in the air. Undoubtedly it was colder than fifty below—how much colder he did not know. But the temperature did not matter. He was bound for the old claim on the left fork of Henderson Creek where the boys were already. They had come over across the divide from the Indian Creek country, while he had come the roundabout way to take a look at the possibilities of getting out logs in the spring from the islands in the Yukon. He would be in to camp by six o'clock; a bit after dark, it was true, but the boys would be there, a fire would be going, and a hot supper would be ready. As for lunch, he pressed his hand against the protruding bundle under his jacket. It was also under his shirt, wrapped up in a handkerchief and lying against the naked skin. It was the only way to keep the biscuits from freezing. He smiled agreeably to himself as he thought of those biscuits, each cut open and sopped in bacon grease, and each enclosing a generous slice of fried bacon.

He plunged in among the big spruce trees. The trail was faint. A foot of snow had fallen since the last sled had passed over, and he was glad he was without a sled, traveling light. In fact, he carried nothing but the lunch wrapped in the handkerchief. He was surprised, however, at the cold. It certainly was cold, he concluded, as he rubbed his numb nose and cheekbones with his mittened hand. He was a warm-whiskered man, but the hair on his face did not protect the high cheekbones and the eager nose that thrust itself aggressively into the frosty air.

At the man's heels trotted a dog, a big native husky, the proper wolf dog, gray-coated and without any visible or temperamental difference from its brother, the wild wolf. The animal was depressed by the tremendous cold. It knew that it was no time for traveling. Its instinct told it a truer tale than was told to the man by the man's judgment. In reality, it was not merely colder than fifty below zero; it was colder than sixty below, than seventy below. It was seventy-five below zero. Since the freezing point is thirty-two above zero, it meant that one hundred and seven degrees of frost obtained. The dog did not know anything about thermometers. Possibly in its brain there was no sharp consciousness of a condition of very cold such as was in the man's brain. But the brute had its instinct. It experienced a vague but menacing apprehension that subdued it and made it slink along at the man's heels, and that made it ques-

tion eagerly every unwonted movement of the man as if expecting him to go into camp or to seek shelter somewhere and build a fire. The dog had learned fire, and it wanted fire, or else to burrow under the snow and cuddle its warmth away from the air.

The frozen moisture of its breathing had settled on its fur in a fine powder of frost, and especially were its jowls, muzzle, and eyelashes whitened by its crystalled breath. The man's red beard and mustache were likewise frosted, but more solidly, the deposit taking the form of ice and increasing with every warm, moist breath he exhaled. Also, the man was chewing tobacco, and the muzzle of ice held his lips so rigidly that he was unable to clear his chin when he expelled the juice. The result was that a crystal beard of the color and solidity of amber was increasing its length on his chin. If he fell down it would shatter itself, like glass, into brittle fragments. But he did not mind the appendage. It was the penalty all tobacco chewers paid in that country, and he had been out before in two cold snaps. They had not been so cold as this, he knew, but by the spirit thermometer at Sixty Mile[5] he knew they had been registered at fifty below and at fifty-five.

He held on through the level stretch of woods for several miles, crossed a wide flat, and dropped down a bank to the frozen bed of a small stream. This was Henderson Creek, and he knew he was ten miles from the forks. He looked at his watch. It was ten o'clock. He was making four miles an hour, and he calculated that he would arrive at the forks at half-past twelve. He decided to celebrate that event by eating his lunch there.

The dog dropped in again at his heels, with a tail drooping discouragement, as the man swung along the creek bed. The furrow of the old sled trail was plainly visible, but a dozen inches of snow covered the marks of the last runners. In a month no man had come up or down that silent creek. The man held steadily on. He was not much given to thinking, and just then, particularly, he had nothing to think about save that he would eat lunch at the forks and that at six o'clock he would be in camp with the boys. There was nobody to talk to, and, had there been, speech would have been impossible because of the ice muzzle on his mouth. So he continued monotonously to chew tobacco and to increase the length of his amber beard.

Once in a while the thought reiterated itself that it was very cold and that he had never experienced such cold. As he walked along he rubbed his cheekbones and nose with the back of his mittened hand. He did this automatically, now and again changing hands. But, rub as he would, the instant he stopped his cheekbones went numb and the following instant the end of his nose went numb. He was sure to frost his cheeks; he knew that, and experienced a pang of regret that he had not devised a nose strap of the sort Bud wore in cold snaps. Such a strap passed across the cheeks as well and saved them. But it didn't matter much, after all. What were frosted cheeks? A bit painful, that was all; they were never serious.

Empty as the man's mind was of thoughts, he was keenly observant, and he noticed the changes in the creek, the curves and bends and timber jams, and always he sharply noted where he placed his feet. Once, coming around a bend, he shied abruptly, like a startled horse, curved away from the place where he had been walking, and retreated several paces back along the

5. *Sixty Mile*, a village in the western part of the Yukon near the Alaskan border.

trail. The creek he knew was frozen clear to the bottom—no creek could contain water in that arctic winter—but he knew also that there were springs that bubbled out from the hillsides and ran along under the snow and on top of the ice of the creek. He knew that the coldest snaps never froze these springs, and he knew likewise their danger. They were traps. They hid pools of water under the snow that might be three inches deep, or three feet. Sometimes a skin of ice half an inch thick covered them, and in turn was covered by the snow. Sometimes there were alternate layers of water and ice skin, so that when one broke through, he kept on breaking through for a while, sometimes wetting himself to the waist.

That was why he had shied in such panic. He had felt the give under his feet and heard the crackle of a snow-hidden ice skin. And to get his feet wet in such a temperature meant trouble and danger. At the very least it meant delay, for he would be forced to stop and build a fire, and, under its protection, to bare his feet while he dried his socks and moccasins. He stood and studied the creek bed and its banks and decided that the flow of water came from the right. He reflected awhile, rubbing his nose and cheeks, then skirted to the left, stepping gingerly and testing the footing for each step. Once clear of the danger, he took a fresh chew of tobacco and swung along at his four-mile gait.

In the course of the next two hours he came upon several similar traps. Usually the snow above the hidden pools had a sunken, candied appearance that advertised the danger. Once again, however, he had a close call, and once, suspecting danger, he compelled the dog to go on in front. The dog did not want to go. It hung back until the man shoved it forward, and then it went quickly across the white, unbroken surface. Suddenly it broke through, floundered to one side, and got away to firmer footing. It had wet its forefeet and legs, and almost immediately the water that clung to it turned to ice. It made quick efforts to lick the ice off its legs, then dropped down in the snow and began to bite out the ice that had formed between the toes. This was a matter of instinct. To permit the ice to remain would mean sore feet. It did not know this. It merely obeyed the mysterious prompting that arose from the deep crypts of its being. But the man knew, having achieved a judgment on the subject, and he removed the mitten from his right hand and helped tear out the ice particles. He did not expose his fingers more than a minute, and was astonished at the swift numbness that smote them. It certainly was cold. He pulled on the mitten hastily, and beat the hand savagely across his chest.

At twelve o'clock the day was at its brightest. Yet the sun was too far south on its winter journey to clear the horizon. The bulge of the earth intervened between it and Henderson Creek, where the man walked under a clear sky at noon and cast no shadow. At half-past twelve, to the minute, he arrived at the forks of the creek. He was pleased at the speed he had made. If he kept it up, he would certainly be with the boys by six. He unbuttoned his jacket and shirt and drew forth his lunch. The action consumed no more than a quarter of a minute, yet in that brief moment the numbness laid hold of the exposed fingers. He did not put the mitten on, but, instead, struck the fingers a dozen sharp smashes against his leg. Then he sat down on a snow-covered log to eat. The sting that followed upon the striking of his fingers against his leg ceased so quickly that he was startled. He had no chance to take a bite of biscuit. He struck the fingers repeatedly and returned them to the mitten, baring the other hand for the purpose of eating. He tried to take a mouthful but the ice muzzle prevented. He had forgotten to build a fire and thaw out. He chuckled at his foolishness, and as he chuckled he noted the numbness creeping into the exposed fingers. Also, he noted that the stinging which had first come to his toes when he sat down was already passing away. He wondered whether the toes were warm or numb. He moved them inside the moccasins and decided that they were numb.

He pulled the mitten on hurriedly and stood up. He was a bit frightened. He stamped up and down until the stinging returned into the feet. It certainly was cold, was his thought. That man from Sulphur Creek had spoken the truth when telling how cold it sometimes got in the country. And he had laughed at him at the time! That showed one must not be too sure of things. There was no mistake about it, it *was* cold. He strode up and down, stamping his feet and threshing his arms, until reassured by the returning warmth. Then he got out matches and proceeded to make a fire. From the undergrowth, where high water of the previous spring had lodged a supply of seasoned twigs, he got his firewood. Working carefully from a small beginning, he soon had a roaring fire, over which he thawed the ice from his face and in the protection of which he ate his biscuits. For the moment the cold of space was outwitted. The dog took satisfaction in the fire, stretching out close enough for warmth and far enough away to escape being singed.

When the man had finished, he filled his pipe and took his comfortable time over a smoke. Then he pulled on his mittens, settled the ear flaps of his cap firmly about his ears, and took the creek trail up the left fork. The dog was disappointed and yearned back toward the fire. This man did not know cold. Possibly all the generations of his ancestry had been ignorant of cold, of real cold, of cold one hundred and seven degrees below freezing point. But the dog knew; all its ancestry knew, and it had inherited the knowledge. And it knew that it was not good to walk abroad in such fearful cold. It was the time to lie snug in a hole in the snow and wait for a curtain of cloud to be drawn across the face of outer space whence this cold came. On the other hand, there was no keen intimacy between the dog and the man. The one was the toil slave of the other, and the only caresses it had ever received were the caresses of the whip lash and of harsh and menacing throat sounds that threatened the whip lash. So the dog made no effort to communicate its apprehension to the man. It was not concerned in the welfare of the man; it was for its own sake that it yearned back toward the fire. But the man whistled and spoke to it with the sound of whip lashes, and the dog swung in at the man's heels and followed after.

The man took a chew of tobacco and proceeded to start a new amber beard. Also, his moist breath quickly powdered with white his mustache, eyebrows, and lashes. There did not seem to be so many springs on the left fork of the Henderson, and for half an hour the man saw no signs of any. And then it happened. At a place where there were no signs, where the soft, unbroken snow seemed to advertise solidity beneath, the man broke through. It was not deep. He wet himself halfway to the knees before he floundered out to the firm crust.

He was angry and cursed his luck aloud. He had hoped to get into camp with the boys at six o'clock, and this would delay him an hour, for he would have to build a fire and dry out his footgear. This was imperative at that low temperature—he knew that much; and he turned aside to the bank which he climbed. On top, tangled in the underbrush about the trunks of several small spruce trees, was a high-water deposit of dry firewood—sticks and twigs, principally, but also larger portions of seasoned branches and fine, dry, last year's grasses. He threw down several large pieces on top of the snow. This served for a foundation and prevented the young flame from drowning itself in the snow it otherwise would melt. The flame he got by touching a match to a small shred of birch bark that he took from his pocket. This burned even more readily than paper. Placing it on the foundation, he fed the young flame with wisps of dry grass and with the tiniest dry twigs.

He worked slowly and carefully, keenly aware of his danger. Gradually, as the flame grew stronger, he increased the size of the twigs with which he fed it. He squatted in the snow, pulling the twigs out from their entanglement in the brush and feeding directly to the flame. He knew there must be no failure. When it is seventy-five below zero, a man must not fail in his first attempt to build a fire—that is, if his feet are wet. If his feet are dry, and he fails, he can run along the trail for half a mile and restore his circulation. But the circulation of wet and freezing feet cannot be restored by running when it is seventy-five below. No matter how fast he runs, the wet feet will freeze the harder.

All this the man knew. The old-timer on Sulphur Creek had told him about it the previous fall, and now he was appreciating the advice. Already all sensation had gone out of his feet. To build a fire he had been forced to remove his mittens, and the fingers had quickly gone numb. His pace of four miles an hour had kept his heart pumping blood to the surface of his body and to all the extremities. But the instant he stopped, the action of the pump eased down. The cold of space smote the unprotected tip of the planet, and he, being of that unprotected tip, received the full force of the blow. The blood of his body recoiled before it. The blood was alive, like the dog, and like the dog it wanted to hide away and cover itself up from the fearful cold. So long as he walked four miles an hour, he pumped that blood, willy-nilly, to the surface, but now it ebbed away and sank down into the recesses of his body. The extremities were the first to feel its absence. His wet feet froze the faster, and his exposed fingers numbed the faster, though they had not yet begun to freeze. Nose and cheeks were already freezing, while the skin of all his body chilled as it lost its blood.

But he was safe. Toes and nose and cheeks would be only touched by the frost, for the fire was beginning to burn with strength. He was feeding it with twigs the size of his finger. In another minute he would be able to feed it with branches the size of his wrist, and then he could remove his wet footgear, and, while it dried, he could keep his naked feet warm by the fire, rubbing them at first, of course, with snow. The fire was a success. He was safe. He remembered the advice of the old-timer on Sulphur Creek and smiled. The old-timer had been very serious in laying down the law that no man must travel alone in the Klondike[6] after fifty below. Well, here he

6. *Klondike* (klon′dīk), a region in the western part of the Yukon territory.

was; he had had the accident; he was alone; and he had saved himself. Those old-timers were rather womanish, some of them, he thought. All a man had to do was to keep his head, and he was all right. Any man who was a man could travel alone. But it was surprising, the rapidity with which his cheeks and nose were freezing. And he had not thought his fingers could go lifeless in so short a time. Lifeless they were, for he could scarcely make them move together to grip a twig, and they seemed remote from his body and from him. When he touched a twig, he had to look and see whether or not he had hold of it. The wires were pretty well down between him and his finger ends.

All of which counted for little. There was the fire, snapping and crackling and promising life with every dancing flame. He started to untie his moccasins. They were coated with ice; the thick German socks were like sheaths of iron halfway to the knees; and the moccasin strings were like rods of steel all twisted and knotted as by some conflagration. For a moment he tugged with his numb fingers; then, realizing the folly of it, he drew his sheath knife.

But before he could cut the strings, it happened. It was his own fault or, rather, his mistake. He should not have built the fire under the spruce tree. He should have built it in the open. But it had been easier to pull the twigs from the brush and drop them directly on the fire. Now the tree under which he had done this carried a weight of snow on its boughs. No wind had blown for weeks, and each bough was fully freighted. Each time he had pulled a twig he had communicated a slight agitation to the tree—an imperceptible agitation, so far as he was concerned, but an agitation sufficient to bring about the disaster. High up in the tree one bough capsized its load of snow. This fell on the boughs beneath, capsizing them. This process continued, spreading out and involving the whole tree. It grew like an avalanche, and it descended without warning upon the man and the fire, and the fire was blotted out! Where it had burned was a mantle of fresh and disordered snow.

The man was shocked. It was as though he had just heard his own sentence of death. For a moment he sat and stared at the spot where the fire had been. Then he grew very calm. Perhaps the old-timer on Sulphur Creek was right. If he had only had a trail mate he would have been in no danger now. The trail mate could have built the fire. Well, it was up to him to build the fire over again, and this second time there must be no failure. Even if he succeeded, he would most likely lose some toes. His feet must be badly frozen by now, and there would be some time before the second fire was ready.

Such were his thoughts, but he did not sit and think them. He was busy all the time they were passing through his mind. He made a new foundation for a fire, this time in the open, where no treacherous tree could blot it out. Next he gathered dry grasses and tiny twigs from the high-water flotsam. He could not bring his fingers together to pull them out, but he was able to gather them by the handful. In this way he got many rotten twigs and bits of green moss that were undesirable, but it was the best he could do. He worked methodically, even collecting an armful of the larger branches to be used later when the fire gathered strength. And all the while the dog sat and watched him, a certain yearning wistfulness in its eyes, for it looked upon him as the fire provider, and the fire was slow in coming.

When all was ready, the man reached in his pocket for a second piece of birch bark. He knew the bark was there, and, though he could not feel it with his fingers, he could hear its crisp rustling as he fumbled for it. Try as he would, he could not clutch hold of it. And all the time, in his consciousness, was the knowledge that each instant his feet were freezing. This thought tended to put him in a panic, but he fought against it and kept calm. He pulled on his mittens with his teeth, and threshed his arms back and forth, beating his hands with all his might against his sides. He did this sitting down, and he stood up to do it; and all the while the dog sat in the snow, its wolf brush of a tail curled around warmly over its forefeet, its sharp wolf ears pricked forward intently as it watched the man. And the man, as he beat and threshed with his arms and hands, felt a great surge of envy as he regarded the creature that was warm and secure in its natural covering.

After a time he was aware of the first faraway signals of sensation in his beaten fingers. The faint tingling grew stronger till it evolved into a stinging ache that was excruciating but which the man hailed with satisfaction. He stripped the mitten from his right hand and fetched forth the birch bark. The exposed fingers were quickly going numb again. Next he brought out his bunch of sulphur matches. But the tremendous cold had already driven the life out of his fingers. In his effort to separate one match from the others, the whole bunch fell in the snow. He tried to pick it out of the snow, but failed. The dead fingers could neither touch nor clutch. He was very careful. He drove the thought of his freezing feet, and nose, and cheeks, out of his mind, devoting his whole soul to the matches. He watched, using the sense of vision in place of that of touch, and when he saw his fingers on each side of the bunch, he closed them—that is, he willed to close them, for the wires were down, and the fingers did not obey. He pulled the mitten on the right hand, and beat it fiercely against his knee. Then, with both mittened hands, he scooped the bunch of matches, along with much snow, into his lap. Yet he was no better off.

After some manipulation he managed to get the bunch between the heels of his mittened hands. In this fashion he carried it to his mouth. The ice crackled and snapped when, by a violent effort, he opened his mouth. He drew the lower jaw in, curled the upper lip out of the way, and scraped the bunch with his upper teeth in order to separate a match. He succeeded in getting one, which he dropped on his lap. He was no better off. He could not pick it up. Then he devised a way. He picked it up in his teeth and scratched it on his leg. Twenty times he scratched before he succeeded in lighting it. As it flamed he held it with his teeth to the birch bark. But the burning brimstone went up his nostrils and into his lungs, causing him to cough spasmodically. The match fell into the snow and went out.

The old-timer on Sulphur Creek was right, he thought in the moment of controlled despair that ensued: after fifty below, a man should travel with a partner. He beat his hands but failed in exciting any sensation. Suddenly he bared both hands, removing the mittens with his teeth. He caught the whole bunch between the heels of his hands. His arm muscles not being frozen enabled him to press the hand heels tightly against the matches. Then he scratched the bunch along his leg. It flared into flame, seventy sulphur matches at once! There was no wind to blow them out. He kept his head to one side to escape the fumes, and held the blazing bunch to the birch bark. As he so held it, he became aware of sensation in his hand. His flesh was burning. He could smell it. Deep down below the surface he could feel it. The sensation developed into pain that grew acute. And still he endured it, holding the flame of the matches clumsily to the bark that would not light readily because his own burning hands were in the way, absorbing most of the flame.

At last, when he could endure no more, he jerked his hands apart. The blazing matches fell sizzling into the snow, but the birch bark was alight. He began laying dry grasses and the tiniest twigs on the flame. He could not pick and choose, for he had to lift the fuel between the heels of his hands. Small pieces of rotten wood and green moss clung to the twigs, and he bit them off as well as he could with his teeth. He cherished the flame carefully and awkwardly. It meant life, and it must not perish. The withdrawal of blood from the surface of his body now made him begin to shiver, and he grew more awkward. A large piece of green moss fell squarely on the little fire. He tried to poke it out with his fingers, but his shivering frame made him poke too far, and he disrupted the nucleus of the little fire, the burning grasses and tiny twigs separating and scattering. He tried to poke them together again, but in spite of the tenseness of the effort, his shivering got away with him, and the twigs were hopelessly scattered. Each twig gushed a puff of smoke and went out. The fire provider had failed. As he looked apathetically about him, his eyes chanced on the dog, sitting across the ruins of the fire from him, in the snow, making restless, hunching movements, slightly lifting one forefoot and then the other, shifting its weight back and forth on them with wistful eagerness.

The sight of the dog put a wild idea into his head. He remembered the tale of the man, caught in a blizzard, who killed a steer and crawled inside the carcass and so was saved. He would kill the dog and bury his hands in the warm body until the numbness went out of them. Then he could build another fire. He spoke to the dog, calling it to him, but in his voice was a strange note of fear that frightened the animal, who had never known the man to speak in such a way before. Something was the matter, and its suspicious nature sensed danger—it knew not what danger, but somewhere, somehow, in its brain arose an apprehension of the man. It flattened its ears down at the sound of the man's voice, and its restless, hunching movements and the liftings and shiftings of its forefeet became more pronounced; but it would not come to the man. He got on his hands and knees and crawled toward the dog. This unusual posture again excited suspicion, and the animal sidled mincingly away.

The man sat up in the snow for a moment and struggled for calmness. Then he pulled on his mittens, by means of his teeth, and got up on his feet. He glanced down at first in order to assure himself that he was really standing up, for the absence of sensation in his feet left him unrelated to the earth. His erect position in itself started to drive the webs of suspicion from the dog's mind, and when he spoke peremptorily, with the sound of whip lashes in his voice, the dog rendered its customary allegiance and came to him. As it came within reaching distance, the man lost his control. His arms flashed out to the dog, and he experienced genuine surprise when he discovered that his hands could not clutch, that there

was neither bend nor feeling in the fingers. He had forgotten for the moment that they were frozen and that they were freezing more and more. All this happened quickly, and before the animal could get away, he encircled its body with his arms. He sat down in the snow and in this fashion held the dog, while it snarled and whined and struggled.

But it was all he could do, hold its body encircled in his arms and sit there. He realized that he could not kill the dog. There was no way to do it. With his helpless hands he could neither draw nor hold his sheath knife nor throttle the animal. He released it, and it plunged wildly away, with tail between its legs and still snarling. It halted forty feet away and surveyed him curiously, with ears sharply pricked forward.

The man looked down at his hands in order to locate them, and found them hanging on the ends of his arms. It struck him as curious that one should have to use his eyes in order to find out where his hands were. He began threshing his arms back and forth, beating the mittened hands against his sides. He did this for five minutes, violently, and his heart pumped enough blood up to the surface to put a stop to his shivering. But no sensation was aroused in the hands. He had an impression that they hung like weights on the ends of his arms, but when he tried to run the impression down, he could not find it.

A certain fear of death, dull and oppressive, came to him. This fear quickly became poignant as he realized that it was no longer a mere matter of freezing his fingers and toes, or of losing his hands and feet, but that it was a matter of life and death with the chances against him. This threw him into a panic, and he turned and ran up the creek bed along the old, dim trail. The dog joined in behind and kept up with him. He ran blindly, without intention, in fear such as he had never known in his life. Slowly, as he plowed and floundered through the snow, he began to see things again—the banks of the creek, the old timber jams, the leafless aspens, and the sky. The running made him feel better. He did not shiver. Maybe, if he ran on, his feet would thaw out, and, anyway, if he ran far enough, he would reach camp and the boys. Without doubt he would lose some fingers and toes and some of his face, but the boys would take care of him, and save the rest of him when he got there. And at the same time there was another thought in his mind that said he would never get to the camp and the boys, that it was too many miles away, that the freezing had too great a start on him, and that he would soon be stiff and dead. This thought he kept in the background and refused to consider. Sometimes it pushed itself forward and demanded to be heard, but he thrust it back and strove to think of other things.

It struck him as curious that he could run at all on feet so frozen that he could not feel them when they struck the earth and took the weight of his body. He seemed to himself to skim along above the surface and to have no connection with the earth. Somewhere he had once seen a winged Mercury,[7] and he wondered if Mercury felt as he felt when skimming over the earth.

His theory of running until he reached camp and the boys had one flaw in it: he lacked the endurance. Several times he stumbled, and finally he tottered, crumpled up, and fell. When he tried to rise, he failed. He must sit and rest, he decided, and next time he would merely walk and keep on going. As he sat and regained his breath, he noted that he was feeling quite warm and comfortable. He was not shivering, and it even seemed that a warm glow had come to his chest and trunk. And yet, when he touched his nose or cheeks, there was no sensation. Running would not thaw them out. Nor would it thaw out his hands and feet. Then the thought came to him that the frozen portions of his body must be extending. He tried to keep this thought down, to forget it, to think of something else; he was aware of the panicky feeling that it caused, and he was afraid of the panic. But the thought asserted itself and persisted, until it produced a vision of his body totally frozen. This was too much, and he made another wild run along the trail. Once he slowed down to a walk, but the thought of the freezing extending itself made him run again.

And all the time the dog ran with him, at his heels. When he fell down a second time, it curled its tail over its forefeet and sat in front of him, facing him, curiously eager and intent. The warmth and security of the animal angered him, and he cursed it till it flattened down its ears appeasingly. This time the shivering came more quickly upon the man. He was losing in his battle with the frost. It was creeping into his body from all sides. The thought of it drove him on, but he ran no more than a hundred feet when he staggered and pitched headlong. It was his last panic. When he had recovered his breath and control, he sat up and entertained in his mind the conception of meeting death with dignity. However, the conception did not come to him in such

7. **Mercury,** in Roman mythology, the messenger of the gods. He is usually depicted as having wings on his sandals.

terms. His idea of it was that he had been making a fool of himself, running around like a chicken with its head cut off—such was the simile that occurred to him. Well, he was bound to freeze anyway, and he might as well take it decently. With this new-found peace of mind came the first glimmerings of drowsiness. A good idea, he thought, to sleep off to death. It was like taking an anesthetic. Freezing was not so bad as people thought. There were lots worse ways to die.

He pictured the boys finding his body next day. Suddenly he found himself with them, coming along the trail and looking for himself. And, still with them, he came around a turn in the trail and found himself lying in the snow. He did not belong with himself any more, for even then he was out of himself, standing with the boys and looking at himself in the snow. It certainly was cold, was his thought. When he got back to the States he could tell the folks what real cold was. He drifted on from this to a vision of the old-timer on Sulphur Creek. He could see him quite clearly, warm and comfortable, and smoking a pipe.

"You were right, old hoss; you were right," the man mumbled to the old-timer of Sulphur Creek.

Then the man drowsed off into what seemed to him the most comfortable and satisfying sleep he had ever known. The dog sat facing him and waiting. The brief day drew to a close in a long, slow twilight. There were no signs of a fire to be made, and, besides, never in the dog's experience had it known a man to sit like that in the snow and make no fire. As the twilight drew on, its eager yearning for the fire mastered it, and with a great lifting and shifting of forefeet, it whined softly, then flattened its ears down in anticipation of being chidden by the man. But the man remained silent. Later the dog whined loudly. And still later it crept close to the man and caught the scent of death. This made the animal bristle and back away. A little longer it delayed, howling under the stars that leaped and danced and shone brightly in the cold sky. Then it turned and trotted up the trail in the direction of the camp it knew, where were the other food providers and fire providers.

Discussion

1. **(a)** What is the setting of this story? **(b)** Why is the setting important? **(c)** What details in the early part of the story make you aware of the intense cold?

2. **(a)** What advice was given by the old-timer at Sulphur Creek? **(b)** What was the man's reaction to this advice before he started on his journey?

3. **(a)** How do the dog's reactions to the cold differ from those of the man?

(b) Why do you suppose the dog's reactions are included in the story?

4. According to medical research, prolonged exposure to cold can have a deadly effect on the mind, as well as on the body: one can lose awareness, memory, and the ability to think clearly.
(a) Find passages in which the man experiences these symptoms. **(b)** What physical symptoms does the man experience before his death?

5. The narrator states that the trouble

with the man is that he is without imagination (295b,1). **(a)** What examples of the man's thoughts or behavior support this statement? **(b)** Do you agree that this is the man's basic problem? Explain.

Application
Foreshadowing

Foreshadowing can add plausibility and/or suspense to a narrative by partially preparing a reader for what is to come and making the reader want to find out what actually happens.

1. At what point in the story are you aware that the narrator is foreshadowing a tragic ending?

2. Cite passages that foreshadow the ending.

3. Do you think the ending is appropriate? Why or why not?

Vocabulary
Dictionary, Inflected Forms

Past tenses of regular verbs are formed by adding *d* or *ed*. Sometimes it is necessary to make a spelling change, such as doubling a final consonant as in *expel-expelled,* or changing a final *y* to *i* as in *shy-shied.*

Past tenses of irregular verbs, however, are not formed in the same way. For example, the past tense of *bind* is *bound,* and the past tense of *spit* is *spat.* For such words you may need to use a dictionary.

Look up each of the following italicized words in the Glossary to see what the present tense of the word is. If you do not know the meaning of the present tense,

look that up as well. On your paper, rewrite the sentence, substituting a definition in your own words for the italicized word.

1. The man *flung* a look back along the way he had come.

2. Numbness *smote* his fingers in less than a minute.

3. He *strode* through the snow, trying to warm his feet by exercise.

4. The man *strove* not to think about freezing to death.

5. The dog crouched in fear of being *chidden* by his master.

Jack London 1876–1916

The financial problems of his family forced Jack London to leave school and go to work at the age of fourteen. After several years of wandering around the country, he returned home to San Francisco and completed high school. Later London enrolled at the University of California but attended for only a short time.

In 1896, after the gold rush to the Klondike had begun, he went to Alaska. He found no gold, but the experiences of the prospectors and trappers of the region gave him the materials for the stories he was to write. Back in San Francisco, he supported himself and his family by working at odd jobs, writing and studying in his spare time. By 1913 he was one of the best-known writers in the country.

Jack London's stories about Alaska during the gold rush are still widely read. Among his best-known books are his novels *Call of the Wild* and *White Fang,* and a collection of shorter pieces, *Sun Dog Trial and Other Stories.*

Unit 5 Review: *The Well-Told Tale*

Content Review

1. Which of the stories in this unit are basically realistic? What elements or techniques used in these stories make them seem true to life?

2. Which of the stories have elements of fantasy? For each one, describe what you consider to be fantastic.

3. Some of the main characters in this unit face unusual stress. Identify the stress that each of the following characters faces and explain how each character reacts to it: **(a)** the murderer in "The Tell-Tale Heart"; **(b)** Jim in "The Ghost That Jim Saw"; **(c)** Bill in "The Ransom of Red Chief"; **(d)** Bess in "The Highwayman"; **(e)** the princess in "The Lady, or the Tiger?"; **(f)** the man in "To Build a Fire."

4. **(a)** Some of the selections in this unit have endings that have a surprise twist. Which endings seemed unexpected to you? Why? **(b)** In which selections in this unit are the endings foreshadowed?

Concept Review: Interpretation of New Material

Read the following story carefully. Then on a separate sheet of paper, write your answers to the questions that follow it; do not write in your book.

Lazy Peter and His Three-Cornered Hat • *Ricardo E. Alegría*

This is the story of Lazy Peter, a shameless rascal of a fellow who went from village to village making mischief.

One day Lazy Peter learned that a fair was being held in a certain village. He knew that a large crowd of country people would be there selling horses, cows, and other farm animals and that a large amount of money would change hands. Peter, as usual, needed money, but it was not his custom to work for it. So he set out for the village, wearing a red three-cornered hat.

The first thing he did was to stop at a stand and leave a big bag of money with the owner, asking him to keep it safely until he returned for it. Peter told the man that when he returned for the bag of money, one corner of his hat would be turned down, and that was how the owner of the stand would know him. The man promised to do this, and Peter thanked him. Then he went to the drugstore in the village and gave the drug-

---

Ricardo Alegría (ä lä grē′ä).

gist another bag of money, asking him to keep it until he returned with one corner of his hat turned up. The druggist agreed, and Peter left. He went to the church and asked the priest to keep another bag of money and to return it to him only when he came back with one corner of his hat twisted to the side. The priest said fine, that he would do this.

Having disposed of three bags of money, Peter went to the edge of the village where the farmers were buying and selling horses and cattle. He stood and watched for a while until he decided that one of the farmers must be very rich indeed, for he had sold all of his horses and cows. Moreover, the man seemed to be a miser who was never satisfied but wanted always more and more money. This was Peter's man! He stopped beside him. It was raining; and instead of keeping his hat on to protect his head, he took it off and wrapped it carefully in his cape, as though it were very valuable. It puzzled the farmer to see Peter stand there with the rain falling on his head and his hat wrapped in his cape.

After a while he asked, "Why do you take better care of your hat than of your head?"

Peter saw that the farmer had swallowed the bait, and smiling to himself, he said that the hat was the most valuable thing in all the world and that was why he took care to protect it from the rain. The farmer's curiosity increased at this reply, and he asked Peter what was so valuable about a red three-cornered hat. Peter told him that the hat worked for him; thanks to it, he never had to work for a living because, whenever he put the hat on with one of the corners turned over, people just handed him any money he asked for.

The farmer was amazed and very interested in what Peter said. As money-getting was his greatest ambition, he told Peter that he couldn't believe a word of it until he saw the hat work with his own eyes. Peter assured him that he could do this, for he, Peter, was hungry, and the hat was about to start working since he had no money with which to buy food.

With this, Peter took out his three-cornered hat, turned one corner down, put it on his head, and told the farmer to come along and watch the hat work. Peter took the farmer to the stand. The minute the owner looked up, he handed over the bag of money Peter had left with him. The farmer stood with his mouth open in astonishment. He didn't know what to make of it. But of one thing he was sure—he had to have that hat!

Peter smiled and asked if he was satisfied, and the farmer said yes, he was. Then he asked Peter if he would sell the hat. This was just what Lazy Peter wanted, but he said no, that he was not interested in selling the hat because, with it, he never had to work and he always had money. The farmer said he thought that was unsound reasoning because thieves could easily steal a hat, and wouldn't it be safer to invest in a farm with cattle? So they talked, and Peter pretended to be impressed with the farmer's arguments. Finally he said yes, that he saw the point, and if the farmer would make him a good offer, he would sell the hat. The farmer, who had made up his mind to have the hat at any price, offered a thousand pesos.[1] Peter laughed aloud and said he could make as much as that by just putting his hat on two or three times.

As they continued haggling over the price, the farmer grew more and more determined to have that hat until, finally, he offered all he had realized from the sale of his horses and cows—ten thousand pesos in gold. Peter still pretended not to be interested, but he chuckled to himself, thinking of the trick he was about to play on the farmer. All right, he said, it was a deal. Then the farmer grew cautious and told Peter that, before he handed over the ten thousand pesos, he would like to see the hat work again. Peter said that was fair enough. He put on the hat with one of the corners turned up and went with the farmer to the drugstore.

The moment the druggist saw the turned-up corner, he handed over the money Peter had left with him. At this the farmer was convinced and very eager to set the hat to work for himself. He took out a bag containing ten thousand pesos in gold and was about to hand it to Peter when he had a change of heart and thought better of it. He asked Peter please to excuse him, but he had to see the hat work just once more before he could part with his gold. Peter said that that was fair enough, but now he would have to ask the farmer to give him the fine horse he was riding as well as the ten thousand pesos in gold. The farmer's interest in the hat revived, and he said it was a bargain!

Lazy Peter put on his hat again, doubled over one of the corners, and told the farmer that, since he still seemed to have doubts, this time he could watch the hat work in the church. The farmer was delighted with this, his doubts were stilled, and he fairly beamed thinking of all the money he was going to make once that hat was his.

They entered the church. The priest was hearing confession, but when he saw Peter with his hat, he said, "Wait here, my son," and he went to the sacristy and returned with the bag of money Peter had left with him. Peter thanked the priest, then knelt and asked for a blessing before he left. The farmer had seen everything and was fully convinced of the hat's magic powers. As soon as they left the church, he gave Peter the ten thousand pesos in gold and told him to take the horse, also. Peter tied the bag of pesos to the saddle, gave the hat to the farmer, begging him to take good care of it, spurred his horse, and galloped out of town.

As soon as he was alone, the farmer burst out laughing at the thought of the trick

---

1. **pesos.** A peso (pä′sō) is the monetary unit of several Central American and South American countries.

he had played on Lazy Peter. A hat such as this was priceless! He couldn't wait to try it. He put it on with one corner turned up and entered the butcher shop. The butcher looked at the hat, which was very handsome indeed, but said nothing. The farmer turned around, then walked up and down until the butcher asked him what he wanted. The farmer said he was waiting for the bag of money. The butcher laughed aloud and asked if he was crazy. The farmer thought that there must be something wrong with the way he had folded the hat. He took it off and doubled another corner down. But this had no effect on the butcher. So he decided to try it out some other place. He went to the Mayor of the town.

The Mayor, to be sure, looked at the hat but did nothing. The farmer grew desperate and decided to go to the druggist who had given Peter a bag of money. He entered and stood with the hat on. The druggist looked at him but did nothing.

The farmer became very nervous. He began to suspect that there was something very wrong. He shouted at the druggist, "Stop looking at me and hand over the bag of money!"

The druggist said he owed him nothing, and what bag of money was he talking about, anyway? As the farmer continued to shout about a bag of money and a magic hat, the druggist called the police. When they arrived, he told them that the farmer had gone out of his mind and kept demanding a bag of money. The police questioned the farmer, and he told them about the magic hat he had bought from Lazy Peter. When he heard the story, the druggist explained that Peter had left a bag of money, asking that it be returned when he appeared with a corner of his hat turned up. The owner of the stand and the priest told the same story. And I am telling you the farmer was so angry that he tore the hat to shreds and walked home.

---

1. The *fair* in this story refers to the kind of gathering where people (a) compete for prizes; (b) go on rides and play games; (c) buy and sell goods and livestock; (d) dance around a pole.

2. The first two paragraphs of the story contain examples of (a) symbolism; (b) foreshadowing; (c) simile and metaphor; (d) mood and tone.

3. How many people does Peter give bags of money to?

4. The people that Peter gives money to are supposed to recognize him by (a) his appearance; (b) the color of his hat; (c) what he does to a corner of his hat; (d) a secret word.

5. The reason Peter gives money to these people is that (a) he needs a safe place to keep his money; (b) he wants their money in return; (c) the money is counterfeit; (d) he hopes to trick someone into thinking his hat is magic.

6. Peter chooses the farmer because the man (a) has agreed to sell him a horse; (b) had tricked Peter out of money in the past; (c) seems to be a fine, deserving person; (d) seems to be a greedy, rich miser.

7. According to the story Peter tells the

farmer, what do people do when he puts on his hat in a certain way?

8. Peter finally agrees to accept in trade for the hat **(a)** all of the farmer's cattle; **(b)** the farmer's horse and ten thousand pesos; **(c)** three bags of gold; **(d)** half the farmer's land.

9. Which of the following statements best describes this story? **(a)** The plot is realistic, and the characters are believable individuals; **(b)** The plot is not very realistic, and the characters are stereotypes; **(c)** The plot is not very realistic, but the characters are believable individuals; **(d)** The plot is realistic, but the characters are stereotypes.

10. Many folktales have a moral, either directly stated or implied. The moral of this story is **(a)** Misers should learn to spend money more freely; **(b)** Greed can make fools of people who should know better; **(c)** You should be neither a borrower nor a lender; **(d)** People who live in glass houses shouldn't throw stones.

Composition Review

1. Assume that you are Johnny "Red Chief" Dorset. Soon after you return to school, you are asked to write an account of your kidnaping for the school newspaper. In planning your article, you might want to consider the following points: how you were captured by Sam and Bill, what you did while you were with them, what you thought of the two men, how you felt when they took you back home.

Write your account in the form of a narrative, using the pronoun "I." Limit your story to two pages. Write a headline and use the byline "Johnny Dorset."

2. Assume that you are the princess in "The Lady, or the Tiger?" It is the night before your lover is to go into the arena, and you have just made your decision about which door you will indicate to him.

Write a one-to-two-page entry for your diary, explaining the dilemma you faced, how you felt about it, what your final decision is, and your reasons for making it. The diary is for no one else to see, so you need only explain your own feelings, not convince anyone else of how right you are.

3. People with clever ideas or plans often make the mistake of thinking that no one can outsmart them. The following characters are all criminals who fail in their crimes: the murderer in "The Tell-Tale Heart"; "The Highwayman"; Sam and Bill in "The Ransom of Red Chief." Choose one of these stories and consider what the plan is and why it fails.

In a few paragraphs, explain the character's plan and why he thinks no one can outsmart him. What people and circumstances finally cause him to be outsmarted? Is his downfall his own fault, or is he "doomed from the start"?

unit **6**

Things are not quite as they usually are: A roller coaster disappears into the clouds. A man who couldn't read becomes a genius. A reassembled skeleton gets up and runs away. A man finds himself one hundred years back in time. Things are somehow out of control.

Out of Control

*F*light of the Roller-Coaster

Raymond Souster

Once more around should do it, the man confided . . .

And sure enough, when the roller-coaster reached the peak
Of the giant curve above me—screech of its wheels
Almost drowned by the shriller cries of the riders—

5 Instead of the dip and plunge with its landslide of screams
It rose in the air like a movieland magic carpet, some wonderful bird,

---

"Flight of the Roller-Coaster" is reprinted from *Collected Poems of Raymond Souster* by permission of Oberon Press.

Raymond Souster (sos′tər).

And without fuss or fanfare swooped slowly across the amusement park,
Over Spook's Castle, ice-cream booths, shooting-gallery; and losing no height

Made the last yards above the beach, where the cucumber-cool
10 Brakeman in the last seat saluted
A lady about to change from her bathing-suit.

Then, as many witnesses duly reported, headed leisurely over the water,
Disappearing mysteriously all too soon behind a low-lying flight of clouds.

Discussion

1. (a) What happens in lines 2-6? **(b)** Describe the images of sound and sight in these lines.

2. (a) What happens to the roller coaster? **(b)** Does the brakeman seem alarmed by what happens? **(c)** What might you infer from his reaction?

3. (a) What words are used to describe the pace of the roller coaster's flight? **(b)** What does the phrase "all too soon" (line 13) imply?

4. Which word or words would you use to describe the mood of the poem—*terrifying, amusing, spooky, calm, strange, tense, fanciful*?

Vocabulary
Word Origins

Which word do you think came first in our language, *greed* or *greedy*? Although *greed* probably looks like the original word, to which the suffix *-y* was added, this is not the case. The original word was the adjective *greedy,* from which the noun *greed* developed. A word formed in this way is called a *back-formation.* The Vocabulary word *fanfare,* meaning "a short tune or call played on horns," was a back-formation in French before it was borrowed into English.

In each of the following sentences the italicized word is a back-formation. The word needed to fill the blank in the sentence is the word from which the italicized word developed. Write that word on your paper. (You may need to look up the italicized word in the Glossary for its origin and, if necessary, its meaning.)

1. The person who chose to *burgle* our house was skillful: much was stolen, and no clues to the identity of the _____ were found.

2. Jack found a large *splat* of paint on the floor even though he had tried not to _____ any.

3. Since she could not speak French well, Jill's attempts to be *couth* by ordering in French from the menu only made her appear _____.

4. Because the boiling liquid would not *jell,* we finally gave up trying to make our own _____ and bought some at the store.

5. Dale tried to *enthuse* me about going to the soil exhibit, but I couldn't build up much _____ about seeing different kinds of soil.

*T*he Greatest Gift

Philip Van Doren Stern

When George said, "Give me just one good reason why I should be alive," he got his reason—and more.

The little town straggling up the hill was bright with colored Christmas lights. But George Pratt did not see them. He was leaning over the railing of the iron bridge, staring down moodily at the black water. The current eddied and swirled like liquid glass, and occasionally a bit of ice, detached from the shore, would go gliding downstream to be swallowed up in the shadows under the bridge.

The water looked paralyzingly cold. George wondered how long a man could stay alive in it. The glassy blackness had a strange, hypnotic effect on him. He leaned still farther over the railing . . .

"I wouldn't do that if I were you," a quiet voice beside him said.

George turned resentfully to a little man he had never seen before. He was stout, well past middle age, and his round cheeks were pink in the winter air as though they had just been shaved.

"Wouldn't do what?" George asked sullenly.

"What you were thinking of doing."

"How do you know what I was thinking?"

"Oh, we make it our business to know a lot of things," the stranger said easily.

George wondered what the man's business was. He was a most unremarkable little person, the sort you would pass in a crowd and never notice. Unless you saw his bright blue eyes, that is. You couldn't forget them, for they were the kindest, sharpest eyes you ever saw. Nothing else about him was noteworthy. He wore a moth-eaten old fur cap and a shabby overcoat that was stretched tightly across his paunchy belly. He was carrying a small black satchel. It wasn't a doctor's bag—it was too large for that and not the right shape. It was a salesman's sample kit, George decided distastefully. The fellow was probably some sort of peddler, the kind who would go around poking his sharp little nose into other people's affairs.

"Looks like snow, doesn't it?" the stranger said, glancing up appraisingly at the overcast sky. "It'll be nice to have a white Christmas. They're getting scarce these days—but so are a lot of things." He turned to face George squarely. "You all right now?"

"Of course I'm all right. What made you think I wasn't? I——"

George fell silent before the stranger's quiet gaze.

The little man shook his head. "You

Slightly abridged from "The Greatest Gift" copyright 1943, 1944 by Philip Van Doren Stern.

know you shouldn't think of such things—and on Christmas Eve of all times! You've got to consider Mary—and your mother too.''

George opened his mouth to ask how this stranger could know his wife's name, but the fellow anticipated him. ''Don't ask me how I know such things. It's my business to know 'em. That's why I came along this way tonight. Lucky I did too.'' He glanced down at the dark water and shuddered.

''Well, if you know so much about me,'' George said, ''give me just one good reason why I should be alive.''

The little man made a queer chuckling sound. ''Come, come, it can't be that bad. You've got your job at the bank. And Mary and the kids. You're healthy, young, and—''

''And sick of everything!'' George cried. ''I'm stuck here in this mudhole for life, doing the same dull work day after day. Other men are leading exciting lives, but I—well, I'm just a small-town bank clerk that even the Army didn't want. I never did anything really useful or interesting, and it looks as if I never will. I might just as well be dead. I might better be dead. Sometimes I wish I were. In fact, I wish I'd never been born!''

The little man stood looking at him in the growing darkness. ''What was that you said?'' he asked softly.

''I said I wish I'd never been born,'' George repeated firmly. ''And I mean it too.''

The stranger's pink cheeks glowed with excitement. ''Why that's wonderful! You've solved everything. I was afraid you were going to give me some trouble. But now you've got the solution yourself. You wish you'd never been born. All right! Okay! You haven't!''

''What do you mean?'' George growled.

''You haven't been born. Just that. You haven't been born. No one here knows you. You have no responsibilities—no job—no wife—no children. Why, you haven't even a mother. You couldn't have, of course. All your troubles are over. Your wish, I am happy to say, has been granted—officially.''

''Nuts!'' George snorted and turned away.

The stranger ran after him and caught him by the arm.

''You'd better take this with you,'' he said, holding out his satchel. ''It'll open a lot of doors that might otherwise be slammed in your face.''

''What doors in whose face?'' George scoffed. ''I know everybody in this town. And besides, I'd like to see anybody slam a door in my face.''

''Yes, I know,'' the little man said patiently. ''But take this anyway. It can't do any harm and it may help.'' He opened the satchel and displayed a number of brushes. ''You'd be surprised how useful these can be as introduction—especially the free ones. These, I mean.'' He hauled out a plain little handbrush. ''I'll show you how to use it.'' He thrust the satchel into George's reluctant hands and began: ''When the lady of the house comes to the door you give her this and then talk fast. You say: 'Good evening, Madam. I'm from the World Cleaning Company, and I want to present you with this handsome and useful brush absolutely free—no obligation to purchase anything at all.' After that, of course, it's a cinch. Now

you try it.'' He forced the brush into George's hand.

George promptly dropped the brush into the satchel and fumbled with the catch, finally closing it with an angry snap. ''Here,'' he said, and then stopped abruptly, for there was no one in sight.

The little stranger must have slipped away into the bushes growing along the river bank, George thought. He certainly wasn't going to play hide-and-seek with him. It was nearly dark and getting colder every minute. He shivered and turned up his coat collar.

The street lights had been turned on, and Christmas candles in the windows glowed softly. The little town looked remarkably cheerful. After all, the place you grew up in was the one spot on earth where you could really feel at home. George felt a sudden burst of affection even for crotchety old Hank Biddle whose house he was passing. He remembered the quarrel he had had when his car had scraped a piece of bark out of Hank's big maple tree. George looked up at the vast spread of leafless branches towering over him in the darkness. The tree must have been growing there since Indian times. He felt a sudden twinge of guilt for the damage he had done. He had never stopped to inspect the wound, for he was ordinarily afraid to have Hank catch him even looking at the tree. Now he stepped out boldly into the roadway to examine the huge trunk.

Hank must have repaired the scar or painted it over, for there was no sign of it. George struck a match and bent down to look more closely. He straightened up with an odd, sinking feeling in his stomach. There wasn't any scar. The bark was smooth and undamaged.

He remembered what the little man at

the bridge had said. It was all nonsense, of course, but the non-existent scar bothered him.

When he reached the bank, he saw that something was wrong. The building was dark, and he knew he had turned the vault light on. He noticed, too, that someone had left the window shades up. He ran around to the front. There was a battered old sign fastened on the door. George could just make out the words:

FOR RENT OR SALE

Apply JAMES SILVA, *Real Estate*

Perhaps it was some boys' trick, he thought wildly. Then he saw a pile of ancient leaves and tattered newspapers in the bank's ordinarily immaculate doorway. And the windows looked as though they hadn't been washed in years. A light was still burning across the street in Jim Silva's office. George dashed over and tore the door open.

Jim looked up from his ledgerbook in surprise. "What can I do for you, young man?" he said in the polite voice he reserved for potential customers.

"The bank," George said breathlessly. "What's the matter with it?"

"The old bank building?" Jim Silva turned around and looked out of the window. "Nothing that I can see. Wouldn't like to rent or buy it, would you?"

"You mean—it's out of business?"

"For a good ten years. Went bust. Stranger 'round these parts, ain't you?"

George sagged against the wall. "I was here some time ago," he said weakly. "The bank was all right then. I even knew some of the people who worked there."

"Didn't know a feller named Marty Jenkins, did you?"

"Marty Jenkins! Why, he——" George was about to say that Marty had never

worked at the bank—couldn't have, in fact, for when they had both left school they had applied for a job there and George had gotten it. But now, of course, things were different. He would have to be careful. "No, I didn't know him," he said slowly. "Not really, that is. I'd heard of him."

"Then maybe you heard how he skipped out with fifty thousand dollars. That's why the bank went broke. Pretty near ruined everybody around here." Silva was looking at him sharply. "I was hoping for a minute maybe you'd know where he is. I lost plenty in that crash myself. We'd like to get our hands on Marty Jenkins."

"Didn't he have a brother? Seems to me he had a brother named Arthur."

"Art? Oh, sure. But he's all right. He don't know where his brother went. It's had a terrible effect on him, too. It's too bad—and hard on his wife. He married a nice girl."

George felt the sinking feeling in his stomach again. "Who did he marry?" he demanded hoarsely. Both he and Art had courted Mary.

"Girl named Mary Thatcher," Silva said cheerfully. "She lives up on the hill just this side of the church—Hey! Where are you going?"

But George had bolted out of the office. He ran past the empty bank building and turned up the hill. For a moment he thought of going straight to Mary. The house next to the church had been given them by her father as a wedding present. Naturally Art Jenkins would have gotten it if he had married Mary. George wondered whether they had any children. Then he knew he couldn't face Mary—not yet anyway. He decided to visit his parents and find out more about her.

There were candles burning in the windows of the little weatherbeaten house on the side street, and a Christmas wreath was hanging on the glass panel of the front door. George raised the gate latch with a loud click. A dark shape on the porch jumped up and began to growl. Then it hurled itself down the steps, barking ferociously.

"Brownie!" George shouted. "Brownie, you old fool, stop that! Don't you know me?" But the dog advanced menacingly and drove him back behind the gate. The porch light snapped on, and George's father stepped outside to call the dog off. The barking subsided to a low, angry growl.

His father held the dog by the collar while George cautiously walked past. He could see that his father did not know him. "Is the lady of the house in?" he asked.

His father waved toward the door. "Go on in," he said cordially. "I'll chain this dog up. She can be mean with strangers."

His mother, who was waiting in the hallway, obviously did not recognize him. George opened his sample kit and grabbed the first brush that came to hand. "Good evening, ma'am," he said politely. "I'm from the World Cleaning Company. We're giving out a free sample brush. I thought you might like to have one. No obligation. No obligation at all . . ." His voice faltered.

His mother smiled at his awkwardness. "I suppose you'll want to sell me something. I'm not really sure I need any brushes."

"No'm. I'm not selling anything," he assured her. "The regular salesman will be around in a few days. This is just—well, just a Christmas present from the company."

"How nice," she said. "You people never gave away such good brushes before."

"This is a special offer," he said. His father entered the hall and closed the door.

"Won't you come in for a while and sit down?" his mother said. "You must be tired walking so much."

"Thank you, ma'am. I don't mind if I do." He entered the little parlor and put his bag down on the floor. The room looked different somehow, although he could not figure out why.

"I used to know this town pretty well," he said to make conversation. "Knew some of the townspeople. I remember a girl named Mary Thatcher. She married Art Jenkins, I heard. You must know them."

"Of course," his mother said. "We know Mary well."

"Any children?" he asked casually.

"Two—a boy and a girl."

George sighed audibly.

"My, you must be tired," his mother said. "Perhaps I can get you a cup of tea."

"No'm, don't bother," he said. "I'll be having supper soon." He looked around the little parlor, trying to find out why it looked different. Over the mantlepiece hung a framed photograph which had been taken on his kid brother Harry's sixteenth birthday. He remembered how they had gone to Potter's studio to be photographed together. There was something queer about the picture. It showed only one figure—Harry's.

"That your son?" he asked.

His mother's face clouded. She nodded but said nothing.

"I think I met him, too," George said hesitantly. "His name's Harry, isn't it?"

His mother turned away, making a strange choking noise in her throat. Her husband put his arm clumsily around her shoulder. His voice, which was always mild and gentle, suddenly became harsh. "You couldn't have met him," he said. "He's been dead a long while. He was drowned the day that picture was taken."

George's mind flew back to the long-ago August afternoon when he and Harry had visited Potter's studio. On their way home they had gone swimming. Harry had been seized with a cramp, he remembered. He had pulled him out of the water and had thought nothing of it. But suppose he hadn't been there!

"I'm sorry," he said miserably. "I guess I'd better go. I hope you like the brush. And I wish you both a very Merry Christmas." There, he had put his foot in it again, wishing them a Merry Christmas when they were thinking about their dead son.

Brownie tugged fiercely at her chain as George went down the porch steps and accompanied his departure with a hostile, rolling growl.

He wanted desperately now to see Mary. He wasn't sure he could stand not being recognized by her, but he had to see her.

The lights were on in the church, and the choir was making last-minute preparations for Christmas vespers.[1] The organ had been practicing "Holy Night" evening after evening until George had become thoroughly sick of it. But now the music almost tore his heart out.

He stumbled blindly up the path to his own house. The lawn was untidy, and the flower bushes he had kept carefully trimmed were neglected and badly sprouted. Art Jenkins could hardly be expected to care for such things.

When he knocked at the door there was a long silence, followed by the shout of a child. Then Mary came to the door.

At the sight of her, George's voice almost failed him. "Merry Christmas,

ma'am," he managed to say at last. His hand shook as he tried to open the satchel.

When George entered the living room, unhappy as he was, he could not help noticing with a secret grin that the too-high-priced blue sofa they often had quarreled over was there. Evidently Mary had gone through the same thing with Art Jenkins and had won the argument with him too.

George got his satchel open. One of the brushes had a bright blue handle and vari-colored bristles. It was obviously a brush not intended to be given away, but George didn't care. He handed it to Mary. "This would be fine for your sofa," he said.

"My, that's a pretty brush," she exclaimed. "You're giving it away free?"

He nodded solemnly. "Special introductory offer. It's one way for the company to keep excess profits down—share them with its friends."

She stroked the sofa gently with the brush, smoothing out the velvety nap. "It is a nice brush. Thank you. I——" There was a sudden scream from the kitchen, and two small children rushed in. A little, homely-faced girl flung herself into her mother's arms, sobbing loudly as a boy of seven came running after her, snapping a toy pistol at her head. "Mommy, she won't die," he yelled. "I shot her a hunert times, but she won't die."

He looks just like Art Jenkins, George thought. Acts like him too.

The boy suddenly turned his attention to him. "Who're you?" he demanded belligerantly. He pointed his pistol at George and pulled the trigger. "You're dead!" he cried. "You're dead. Why don't you fall down and die?"

There was a heavy step on the porch.

---

1. **vespers,** late afternoon or evening worship.

The boy looked frightened and backed away. George saw Mary glance apprehensively at the door.

Art Jenkins came in. He stood for a moment in the doorway. His face was very red. "Who's this?" he demanded.

"He's a brush salesman," Mary tried to explain. "He gave me this brush."

"Brush salesman!" Art sneered. "Well, tell him to get outa here. We don't want no brushes." Art lurched across the room to the sofa where he sat down suddenly. "An' we don't want no brush salesmen neither."

George looked despairingly at Mary. Her eyes were begging him to go. Art had lifted his feet up on the sofa and was sprawling out on it, muttering unkind things about brush salesmen. George went to the door, followed by Art's son who kept snapping his pistol at him and saying: "You're dead—dead—dead!"

Perhaps the boy was right, George thought when he reached the porch. Maybe he was dead, or maybe this was all a bad dream from which he might eventually awake. He wanted to find the little man on the bridge again and try to persuade him to cancel the whole deal.

He hurried down the hill and broke into a run when he neared the river. George was relieved to see the little stranger standing on the bridge. "I've had enough," he gasped. "Get me out of this—you got me into it."

The stranger raised his eyebrows. "I got you into it! I like that! You were granted your wish. You got everything you asked for. You're the freest man on earth now. You have no ties. You can go anywhere—do anything. What more can you possibly want?"

"Change me back," George pleaded. "Change me back—please. Not just for my

sake but for others too. You don't know what a mess this town is in. You don't understand. I've got to get back. They need me here."

"I understand right enough," the stranger said slowly. "I just wanted to make sure you did. You had the greatest gift of all conferred upon you—the gift of life, of being a part of this world and taking a part in it. Yet you denied that gift." As the stranger spoke, the church bell high up on the hill sounded, calling the townspeople to Christmas vespers. Then the downtown church bell started ringing.

"I've got to get back," George said desperately. "You can't cut me off like this. Why, it's murder!"

"Suicide rather, wouldn't you say?" the stranger murmured. "You brought it on yourself. However, since it's Christmas Eve—well, anyway, close your eyes and keep listening to the bells." His voice sank lower. "Keep listening to the bells . . ."

George did as he was told. He felt a cold, wet snowdrop touch his cheek—and then another and another. When he opened his eyes, the snow was falling fast, so fast that it obscured everything around him. The little stranger could not be seen, but then neither could anything else. The snow was so thick that George had to grope for the bridge railing.

As he started toward the village, he thought he heard someone saying: "Merry Christmas," but the bells were drowning out all rival sounds, so he could not be sure.

When he reached Hank Biddle's house he stopped and walked out into the roadway, peering down anxiously at the base of the big maple tree. The scar was there, thank Heaven! He touched the tree affectionately. He'd have to do something about the wound—get a tree surgeon or something. Anyway, he'd evidently been changed back. He was himself again. Maybe it was all a dream, or perhaps he had been hypnotized by the smooth-flowing black water. He had heard of such things.

At the corner of Main and Bridge Streets he almost collided with a hurrying figure. It was Jim Silva, the real estate agent. "Hello, George," Jim said cheerfully. "Late tonight, ain't you? I should think you'd want to be home early on Christmas Eve."

George drew a long breath. "I just wanted to see if the bank is all right. I've got to make sure the vault light is on."

"Sure it's on. I saw it as I went past."

"Let's look, huh?" George said, pulling at Silva's sleeve. He wanted the assurance of a witness. He dragged the surprised real estate dealer around to the front of the bank where the light was gleaming through the falling snow. "I told you it was on," Silva said with some irritation.

"I had to make sure," George mumbled. "Thanks—and Merry Christmas!" Then he was off like a streak, running up the hill.

He was in a hurry to get home, but not in such a hurry that he couldn't stop for a moment at his parents' house, where he wrestled with Brownie until the friendly old bulldog waggled all over with delight. He grasped his startled brother's hand and wrung it frantically, wishing him an almost hysterical Merry Christmas. Then he dashed across the parlor to examine a certain photograph. He kissed his mother, joked with his father, and was out of the house a few seconds later, stumbling and slipping on the newly fallen snow as he ran on up the hill.

The church was bright with light, and the choir and the organ were going full tilt. George flung the door to his home open and called out at the top of his voice: "Mary! Where are you? Mary! Kids!"

His wife came toward him, dressed for going to church, and making gestures to silence him. "I've just put the children to bed," she protested. "Now they'll——" But not another word could she get out of her mouth, for he smothered it with kisses, and then he dragged her up to the children's room, where he violated every tenet of parental behavior by madly embracing his son and his daughter and waking them up thoroughly.

It was not until Mary got him downstairs that he began to be coherent. "I thought I'd lost you. Oh, Mary, I thought I'd lost you!"

"What's the matter, darling?" she asked in bewilderment.

He pulled her down on the sofa and kissed her again. And then, just as he was about to tell her about his queer dream, his fingers came in contact with something lying on the seat of the sofa. His voice froze.

He did not even have to pick the thing up, for he knew what it was. And he knew that it would have a blue handle and vari-colored bristles.

Discussion

1. (a) At the beginning of the story, what does it appear George intends to do? **(b)** What are his complaints about his life?

2. (a) Describe the stranger's appearance. What is unusual about his eyes? **(b)** What surprising things does the stranger know about George?

3. (a) What differences appear in the town as a result of George's never having been born? **(b)** What causes George to change his attitude toward life?

4. (a) According to the stranger, what is the greatest gift? **(b)** Who—or what—do you infer the stranger is?

Application
Theme

In figuring out the theme—the main idea—of a work of literature, consider its topic, the events of the plot, and the attitudes of the characters. Ask yourself: What opinion, if any, is being expressed about the topic?

1. Consider the differences in the town as a result of George's never having been born. What do these differences make George realize about himself and his life?

2. In your own words, what is the theme of the story? Is the theme stated or implied?

Vocabulary
Affixes

Suffixes often change the way a word can be used in a sentence. For example, the adjective *abrupt* might be used in this way: Sandy stopped with an *abrupt* movement. The suffix -*ly* changes the word to an adverb that might be used in this way: Sandy stopped *abruptly*. At the same time, the meaning is changed from "unexpected" to "in an unexpected manner."

Listed below are five words that have suffixes. In each sentence pair that follows, note how the root word is used. Write out the sentences on your paper, using the appropriate Vocabulary word to fill the blank. Remember that the spellings of some words change when certain suffixes are added.

coherent
solemnly
assurance
audibly
parental

1. Ronald took care to *assure* Arlene that he would be on time. Ronald's _____, however, was not always reliable.

2. Her teacher's advice about driving carefully was similar to a warning from a *parent*. Anne appreciated her teacher's _____ concern.

3. Sharon was so confused that her thoughts did not seem to *cohere.* She tried in vain to give a _____ report of the accident.

4. The graduation ceremony was a *solemn* affair. The graduates helped set the tone by marching _____ down the aisle.

5. Carolyn's voice was not *audible* to those in the back rows. We asked her to speak more _____.

Composition

At the end of the story, George is about to tell Mary about his "dream" of never having been born when he discovers on the sofa a brush that he knew "would have a blue handle and vari-colored bristles." If the story were to continue, what do you think would happen next? Would George ask Mary about the brush? If so, how do you think Mary would account for it? Do you think a brush salesman really did come to the door that night? If so, what did he look and act like?

Write a composition of about one page in which you continue the story beyond its present conclusion. You may describe what happens from the point of view of the third-person narrator or in the form of a dialogue between George and Mary, or you might use a combination of both narration and dialogue.

Philip Van Doren Stern 1900–1984

Philip Van Doren Stern began his career in advertising and also became a designer for two publishing firms while writing mystery stories under the name of "Peter Storme." In addition to publishing a number of short stories, he has written extensively about the Civil War; his 1958 history *An End to Valor* received the F. Pratt Award as the best nonfiction Civil War book of the year. He has also written about photography, cars, travel, and prehistoric art. Educated at Rutgers, Stern later received an honorary degree from that university and in 1960 received a Guggenheim fellowship.

Comment: Short Story into Film

Many television and movie screenplays have been based on short stories and novels. A reader must use the words in a story to make mental images of characters and events. In a film, however, the images that the audience sees on the screen are decided upon by the screenwriter and director. Adaptations, or changes, are often made so that the characters and events are as vivid on the screen as they are in the original written work.

Some adaptations are made in order to suit a story to the special qualities of film. Films rely on sights and sounds, movement and conversation. For example, the 1946 film *It's a Wonderful Life,* adapted from Philip Van Doren Stern's story "The Greatest Gift," opens with a conversation among angels, seen as glowing stars in the sky. The angel Clarence is being given a chance to earn his wings. Clarence appears on the bridge and jumps into the freezing water himself, forcing George to abandon his suicide and rescue Clarence. The meeting in the film of George and the angel is thereby filled with action.

Sometimes characters and events are added so that a film audience can better understand personalities and conflicts. In flashbacks of George's life, the audience sees George save his brother from drowning, save another life by preventing an accidental poisoning, take over the family business, and marry Mary Thatcher. Although he dreams of college and travel, his plans are always frustrated. A constant threat is Mr. Potter, a power-hungry banker added to the plot.

Through these scenes, viewers can sympathize with George's despair and, at the same time, with Clarence's hopes of restoring George's will to live. When George chooses not to have been born, the changes are visually shocking: He reels down a Main Street that has become a noisy tangle of neon lights and unattractive businesses. In the conclusion, the townspeople demonstrate George's importance to them by donating money to save his business from ruin. Finally, instead of a brush to "prove" that the events have taken place, a bell rings. A bell rings, Clarence has told George, when an angel gets his wings.

A further adaptation of "The Greatest Gift" was made for television in 1977. The role of George Bailey, played by James Stewart in the 1946 version, becomes Mary Bailey, played by Marlo Thomas. The angel is also a female, named Clara.

See **ALLITERATION** Handbook of Literary Terms

*T*he Mewlips

J. R. R. Tolkien

The shadows where the Mewlips dwell
    Are dark and wet as ink,
And slow and softly rings their bell,
    As in the slime you sink.

5 You sink into the slime, who dare
    To knock upon their door,
While down the grinning gargoyles stare
    And noisome waters pour.

Beside the rotting river-stand
10   The drooping willows weep,
And gloomily the gorcrows stand
    Croaking in their sleep.

Over the Merlock Mountains a long and weary way,
In a mouldy valley where the trees are grey,
15 By a dark pool's borders without wind or tide,
Moonless and sunless, the Mewlips hide.

The cellars where the Mewlips sit
    Are deep and dank and cold
With single sickly candle lit;
20   And there they count their gold.

(Continued)

Their walls are wet, their ceilings drip;
    Their feet upon the floor
Go softly with a squish-flap-flip,
    As they sidle to the door.

25 They peep out slyly; through a crack
    Their feeling fingers creep
And when they've finished, in a sack
    Your bones they take to keep.

Beyond the Merlock Mountains, a long and lonely road,
30   Through the spider-shadows and the marsh of Tode,
And through the wood of hanging trees and the gallowsweed,
    You go to find the Mewlips—and the Mewlips feed.

Discussion

1. The speaker says the Mewlips live "Beyond the Merlock Mountains." **(a)** What images are used to describe the kinds of places the Mewlips can be found? **(b)** What do all these places have in common?

2. (a) In stanzas 1 and 2, what first happens to those who visit the Mewlips? **(b)** What happens by stanzas 7 and 8?

3. What is the mood of the poem?

Application
Alliteration

The use of alliteration in a piece of writing helps create certain effects through sounds. In addition, it often emphasizes the meaning of the lines in which it occurs or emphasizes the mood of the entire work.

1. What repeated sound occurs in lines 3 and 4? Do you think this alliteration helps get across the meaning of the lines? Explain.

2. In what other lines does alliteration occur?

3. How does alliteration help create the mood of the poem?

J. R. R. Tolkien 1892–1973

J. R. R. Tolkien is best known for *The Hobbit* and his three-book fantasy *The Lord of the Rings,* which take place in a land inhabited by men, hobbits, elves, and other creatures. As a boy in rural England, Tolkien "desired dragons with a profound desire." Later, as an Oxford University professor, he began writing fairy tales for his children. Still, Tolkien believed that fantasy is not just for children, but provides for any age not only an escape from the real world but also the ability to return to the real world with a fresh outlook.

Rain, Rain, Go Away

Isaac Asimov

The new neighbors seemed to be sweet, but they were also a little strange.

There she is again,'' said Lillian Wright as she adjusted the venetian blinds carefully. ''There she is, George.''

''There who is?'' asked her husband, trying to get satisfactory contrast on the TV so that he might settle down to the ball game.

''Mrs. Sakkaro,'' she said, and then, to forestall her husband's inevitable ''Who's that?'' added hastily, ''The new neighbors, for goodness sake.''

''Oh.''

''Sunbathing. Always sunbathing. I wonder where her boy is. He's usually out on a nice day like this, standing in that tremendous yard of theirs and throwing the ball against the house. Did you ever see him, George?''

''I've heard him. It's a version of the Chinese water torture.[1] Bang on the wall, biff on the ground, smack in the hand. Bang, biff, smack, bang, biff——''

''He's a *nice* boy, quiet and well-behaved. I wish Tommie would make friends with him. He's the right age, too, just about ten, I should say.''

''I didn't know Tommie was backward about making friends.''

''Well, it's hard with the Sakkaros. They keep so to themselves. I don't even know what Mr. Sakkaro does.''

''Why should you? It's not really anyone's business what he does.''

''It's odd that I never see him go to work.''

''No one ever sees me go to work.''

''You stay home and write. What does *he* do?''

''I dare say Mrs. Sakkaro knows what Mr. Sakkaro does and is all upset because she doesn't know what *I* do.''

''Oh, George.'' Lillian retreated from the window and glanced with distaste at the television. (Schoendienst was at bat.) ''I think we should make an effort; the neighborhood should.''

''What kind of an effort?'' George was comfortable on the couch now, with a king-size Coke in his hand, freshly opened and frosted with moisture.

''To get to know them.''

''Well, didn't you, when she first moved in? You said you called.''

''I said hello but, well, she'd just moved in and the house was still upset, so that's all it could be, just hello. It's been two months now and it's still nothing more than hello, sometimes. —She's so odd.''

''Is she?''

''She's always looking at the sky; I've seen her do it a hundred times and she's never been out when it's the least bit cloudy. Once, when the boy was out playing, she called to him to come in, shouting

---

1. **Chinese water torture,** a form of torture in which the victim is driven mad by the constant, measured drip of water on his or her head.

that it was going to rain. I happened to hear her and I thought, wouldn't you know and me with a wash on the line, so I hurried out and, you know, it was broad sunlight. Oh, there were some clouds, but nothing, really."

"Did it rain, eventually?"

"Of course not. I just had to run out in the yard for nothing."

George was lost amid a couple of base hits and a most embarrassing bobble that meant a run. When the excitement was over and the pitcher was trying to regain his composure, George called out after Lillian, who was vanishing into the kitchen, "Well, since they're from Arizona, I dare say they don't know rainclouds from any other kind."

Lillian came back into the living room with a patter of high heels. "From where?"

"From Arizona, according to Tommie."

"How did Tommie know?"

"He talked to their boy, in between ball chucks, I guess, and he told Tommie they came from Arizona and then the boy was called in. At least, Tommie says it might have been Arizona, or maybe Alabama or some place like that. You know Tommie and his nontotal recall. But if they're that nervous about the weather, I guess it's Arizona and they don't know what to make of a good rainy climate like ours."

"But why didn't you ever tell me?"

"Because Tommie only told me this morning and because I thought he must have told you already and, to tell the absolute truth, because I thought you could just manage to drag out a normal existence even if you never found out. Wow——"

The ball went sailing into the right field stands and that was that for the pitcher.

Lillian went back to the venetian blinds and said, "I'll simply just have to make her

acquaintance. She looks *very* nice. —Oh, look at that, George."

George was looking at nothing but the TV.

Lillian said, "I know she's staring at that cloud. And now she'll be going in. Honestly."

George was out two days later on a reference search in the library and came home with a load of books. Lillian greeted him jubilantly.

She said, "Now, you're not doing anything tomorrow."

"That sounds like a statement, not a question."

"It *is* a statement. We're going out with the Sakkaros to Murphy's Park."

"With——"

"With the next-door neighbors, George. *How* can you never remember the name?"

"I'm gifted. How did it happen?"

"I just went up to their house this morning and rang the bell."

"That easy?"

"It wasn't easy. It was hard. I stood there, jittering, with my finger on the doorbell, till I thought that ringing the bell would be easier than having the door open and being caught standing there like a fool."

"And she didn't kick you out?"

"No. She was sweet as she could be. Invited me in, knew who I was, said she was so glad I had come to visit. *You* know."

"And you suggested we go to Murphy's Park."

"Yes. I thought if I suggested something that would let the children have fun, it would be easier for her to go along with it. She wouldn't want to spoil a chance for her boy."

"A mother's psychology."

"But you should see her home."

"Ah. You had a reason for all this. It comes out. You wanted the Cook's tour.[2] But, please, spare me the color-scheme details. I'm not interested in the bedspreads, and the size of the closets is a topic with which I can dispense."

It was the secret of their happy marriage that Lillian paid no attention to George. She went into the color-scheme details, was most meticulous about the bedspreads, and gave him an inch-by-inch description of closet-size.

"And *clean*? I have never seen any place so spotless."

"If you get to know her, then, she'll be setting you impossible standards and you'll have to drop her in self-defense."

"Her kitchen," said Lillian, ignoring him, "was so spanking clean you just couldn't believe she ever used it. I asked for a drink of water and she held the glass underneath the tap and poured slowly so that not one drop fell in the sink itself. It wasn't affectation. She did it so casually that I just knew she always did it that way. And when she gave me the glass she held it with a clean napkin. Just hospital-sanitary."

"She must be a lot of trouble to herself. Did she agree to come with us right off?"

"Well—not right off. She called to her husband about what the weather forecast was, and he said that the newspapers all said it would be fair tomorrow but that he was waiting for the latest report on the radio."

"*All* the newspapers said so, eh?"

"Of course, they all just print the official weather forecast, so they would all agree. But I think they do subscribe to all the newspapers. At least I've watched the bundle the newsboy leaves——"

"There isn't much you miss, is there?"

"Anyway," said Lillian severely, "she called up the weather bureau and had them tell her the latest and she called it out to her husband and they said they'd go, except they said they'd phone us if there were any unexpected changes in the weather."

"All right. Then we'll go."

The Sakkaros were young and pleasant, dark and handsome. In fact, as they came down the long walk from their home to where the Wright automobile was parked, George leaned toward his wife and breathed into her ear, "So *he's* the reason."

"I wish he were," said Lillian. "Is that a handbag he's carrying?"

"Pocket-radio. To listen to weather forecasts, I bet."

The Sakkaro boy came running after them, waving something which turned out to be an aneroid barometer,[3] and all three got into the back seat. Conversation was turned on and lasted, with neat give-and-take on impersonal subjects, to Murphy's Park.

The Sakkaro boy was so polite and reasonable that even Tommie Wright, wedged between his parents in the front seat, was subdued by example into a semblance of civilization. Lillian couldn't recall when she had spent so serenely pleasant a drive.

She was not the least disturbed by the fact that, barely to be heard under the flow of the conversation, Mr. Sakkaro's small radio was on, and she never actually saw him put it occasionally to his ear.

It was a beautiful day at Murphy's Park;

---

2. **Cook's tour,** a quick, well-organized tour in which attractions are viewed only briefly, so-called after a British travel agent.
3. **aneroid** (an′ə roid′) **barometer,** an instrument in which changes in air pressure are registered on a dial, used in predicting probable changes in the weather. The "falling" barometer, mentioned later, means that the air pressure is increasing and that rain is likely.

hot and dry without being too hot; and with a cheerfully bright sun in a blue, blue sky. Even Mr. Sakkaro, though he inspected every quarter of the heavens with a careful eye and then stared piercingly at the barometer, seemed to have no fault to find.

Lillian ushered the two boys to the amusement section and bought enough tickets to allow one ride for each on every variety of centrifugal thrill that the park offered.

"Please," she had said to a protesting Mrs. Sakkaro, "let this be my treat. I'll let you have your turn next time."

When she returned, George was alone. "Where——" she began.

"Just down there at the refreshment stand. I told them I'd wait here for you and we would join them." He sounded gloomy.

"Anything wrong?"

"No, not really, except that I think he must be independently wealthy."

"What?"

"I don't know what he does for a living. I hinted——"

"Now who's curious?"

"I was doing it for you. He said he's just a student of human nature."

"How philosophical. That would explain all those newspapers."

"Yes, but with a handsome, wealthy man next door, it looks as though I'll have impossible standards set for me, too."

"Don't be silly."

"And he doesn't come from Arizona."

"He doesn't?"

"I said I heard he was from Arizona. He looked so surprised, it was obvious he didn't. Then he laughed and asked if he had an Arizona accent."

Lillian said thoughtfully, "He has some kind of accent, you know. There are lots of Spanish-ancestry people in the Southwest, so he could still be from Arizona. Sakkaro could be a Spanish name."

"Sounds Japanese to me. —Come on, they're waving. Oh, look what they've bought."

The Sakkaros were each holding three sticks of cotton candy, huge swirls of pink foam consisting of threads of sugar dried out of frothy syrup that had been whipped about in a warm vessel. It melted sweetly in the mouth and left one feeling sticky.

The Sakkaros held one out to each Wright, and out of politeness the Wrights accepted.

They went down the midway, tried their hand at darts, at the kind of poker game where balls were rolled into holes, at knocking wooden cylinders off pedestals. They took pictures of themselves and recorded their voices and tested the strength of their handgrips.

Eventually they collected the youngsters, who had been reduced to a satisfactorily breathless state of roiled-up insides, and the Sakkaros ushered theirs off instantly to the refreshment stand. Tommie hinted the extent of his pleasure at the possible purchase of a hot-dog and George tossed him a quarter. He ran off, too.

"Frankly," said George, "I prefer to stay here. If I see them biting away at another cotton candy stick I'll turn green and sicken on the spot. If they haven't had a dozen apiece, I'll eat a dozen myself."

"I know, and they're buying a handful for the child now."

"I offered to stand Sakkaro a hamburger and he just looked grim and shook his head. Not that a hamburger's much, but after enough cotton candy, it ought to be a feast."

"I know. I offered her an orange drink and the way she jumped when she said no, you'd think I'd thrown it in her face. —Still, I suppose they've never been to a place like this before and they'll need time to adjust to the novelty. They'll fill up on cotton candy and then never eat it again for ten years.''

"Well, maybe.'' They strolled toward the Sakkaros. "You know, Lil, it's clouding up.''

Mr. Sakkaro had the radio to his ear and was looking anxiously toward the west.

"Uh-oh," said George, "he's seen it. One gets you fifty, he'll want to go home."

All three Sakkaros were upon him, polite but insistent. They were sorry, they had had a wonderful time, a marvelous time, the Wrights would have to be their guests as soon as it could be managed, but now, really, they had to go home. It looked stormy. Mrs. Sakkaro wailed that all the forecasts had been for fair weather.

George tried to console them. "It's hard to predict a local thunderstorm, but even if it were to come, and it mightn't, it wouldn't last more than half an hour on the outside."

At which comment, the Sakkaro youngster seemed on the verge of tears, and Mrs. Sakkaro's hand, holding a handkerchief, trembled visibly.

"Let's go home," said George in resignation.

The drive back seemed to stretch interminably. There was no conversation to speak of. Mr. Sakkaro's radio was quite loud now as he switched from station to station, catching a weather report every time. They were mentioning "local thundershowers" now.

The Sakkaro youngster piped up that the barometer was falling, and Mrs. Sakkaro, chin in the palm of her hand, stared dolefully at the sky and asked if George could not drive faster, please.

"It does look rather threatening, doesn't it?" said Lillian in a polite attempt to share their guests' attitude. But then George heard her mutter, "Honestly!" under her breath.

A wind had sprung up, driving the dust of the weeks-dry road before it, when they entered the street on which they lived, and the leaves rustled ominously. Lightning flickered.

George said, "You'll be indoors in two minutes, friends. We'll make it."

He pulled up at the gate that opened onto the Sakkaros' spacious front yard and got out of the car to open the back door. He thought he felt a drop. They were *just* in time.

The Sakkaros tumbled out, faces drawn with tension, muttering thanks, and started off toward their long front walk at a dead run.

"Honestly," began Lillian, "you would think they were——"

The heavens opened and the rain came down in giant drops as though some celestial dam had suddenly burst. The top of their car was pounded with a hundred drum sticks, and halfway to their front door the Sakkaros stopped and looked despairingly upward.

Their faces blurred as the rain hit; blurred and shrank and ran together. All three shriveled, collapsing within their clothes, which sank down into three sticky-wet heaps.

And while the Wrights sat there, transfixed with horror, Lillian found herself unable to stop the completion of her remark: "——made of sugar and afraid they would melt.''

Discussion

1. (a) What things does Lillian Wright tell her husband that she has noticed about their new neighbors, the Sakkaros? **(b)** How does George Wright respond at first to his wife's curiosity?

2. (a) What seems to be the Sakkaros' main concern? **(b)** How is their behavior in keeping with this concern?

3. (a) What happens to the Sakkaros at the end of the story? **(b)** What clues throughout the story foreshadow the conclusion?

4. Where do you infer the Sakkaros come from?

5. Has the tone of the story prepared you to accept the fate of the Sakkaros as tragic, comic, or something else? Explain.

Vocabulary
Context, Dictionary

Look up the following words in the Glossary to determine their meaning. Then decide which would best complete each of the sentences below. Write that word on your paper.

> affectation
> attitude
> composure
> resignation
> semblance

1. Daniel had spent only two weeks in London, so his friends in Florida knew his English accent was a temporary _____.

2. When the children begged her to ride with them on the roller coaster, Janet sighed in _____ and went with them.

3. The diving champion was known for her ability to keep her _____ in tensely competitive situations.

4. By shoving clothes, books, and toys under the bed, Randy was able to create a _____ of order in his room.

5. Todd's casual _____ toward dress was shown especially when he arrived at the formal dinner in tennis shoes.

Composition

If water is deadly to the Sakkaros because they are made of sugar, what must the place they come from be like? What kind of climate has it? What do the people and animals live on? Is there any plant life? If so, what does it look like, and how does it survive? What might people do for a living? for entertainment?

Write a composition of about one page in which you describe the place—another planet, perhaps—the Sakkaros come from. In choosing the details to include in your description, consider the questions in the preceding paragraph as well as any others you think of.

(You may find the article "Describing a Person or a Place" in the Composition Guide helpful in writing this composition.)

Isaac Asimov 1920–

Hooked on science fiction by age nine, Isaac Asimov has become a leading writer of science fiction and of science texts for the general reader. His best-known science fiction includes the *Foundation* series and a collection of stories called *I, Robot*.

Skeleton Fixer

Leslie Marmon Silko

What happened here?
she asked
Some kind of accident?
Words like bones
5 scattered all over the place . . . .

Old Man Badger traveled
from place to place
searching for skeleton bones.
There was something
10 only he could do with them.

On the smooth sand
Old Man Badger started laying
   out the bones.
It was a great puzzle for him.
He started with the toes
15 He loved their curve
like a new moon,
like a white whisker hair.

Without thinking
he knew their direction,
20 laying each toe bone
to walk east.
"I know,
it must have been this way.
Yes,"
25 he talked to himself as he worked.

He strung the spine bones
as beautiful as any shell necklace.

The leg bones were running
so fast
30 dust from the ankle joints
surrounded the wind.

"Oh poor dear one who left your bones here
I wonder who you are?"
Old Skeleton Fixer spoke to the bones
35 Because things don't die
they fall to pieces maybe,
get scattered or separate,
but Old Badger Man can tell
how they once fit together.

40 Though he didn't recognize the bones
he could not stop;
he loved them anyway.

He took great care with the ribs
marveling at the structure
45 which had contained the lungs and heart.
Skeleton Fixer had never heard of
such things as souls.
He was certain
only of bones.

50 But where a heart once beat
there was only sand.
"Oh I will find you one—
somewhere around here!"
And a yellow butterfly
55 flew up from the grass at his feet.

"Ah! I know how your breath left you—
Like butterflies over an edge,
not falling but fluttering
their wings rainbow colors—
60 Wherever they are
your heart will be."   *(Continued)*

He worked all day
He was so careful with this one—
it felt like the most special of all.
65 Old Man Badger didn't stop
until the last spine bone
was arranged at the base of the tail.

"A'moo'ooh,[1] my dear one
these words are bones,"
70 he repeated this
four times
    Pa Pa Pa Pa!
    Pa Pa Pa Pa!
    Pa Pa Pa Pa!
75 Pa Pa Pa Pa!

Old Coyote Woman jumped up
and took off running.
She never even said "thanks."

Skeleton Fixer
80 shook his head slowly.

"It is surprising sometimes," he said
"how these things turn out."
But he never has stopped fixing
the poor scattered bones he finds.

---

1. **A'moo'ooh** (ä mü′ō), a Laguna Pueblo expression of endearment for a young child.

Discussion

1. (a) What is the Skeleton Fixer's name? **(b)** What does he search for? Why?

2. (a) How does the Skeleton Fixer feel about his task? **(b)** What lines tell you this?

3. (a) What does the Skeleton Fixer find to use for the skeleton's heart? **(b)** Why is this appropriate to use?

4. (a) Who does the skeleton turn out to be? **(b)** What does the skeleton do once it is put back together?

5. (a) How does the Skeleton Fixer react to the skeleton's actions? **(b)** What does his reaction suggest about his personality?

Leslie Marmon Silko 1948–

Leslie Marmon Silko grew up at Laguna Pueblo, a Pueblo Indian reservation in New Mexico. There, she listened to tales of the Pueblo Indians. Such tales, she believes, have the power to bring people together.

Silko's books include *The Man to Send Rain Clouds,* a collection of stories; *Ceremony,* a novel; and *Storyteller,* a collection of prose and poetry in which she uses her own experiences, especially those with her family, to re-create stories that resemble ancient tales. In 1981 Silko won a MacArthur Prize Fellowship. The select group of winners, talented people in a variety of fields, are given a five-year income so that they can continue their creative work without financial worries. "I write," says Silko, "because I love the stories, the feelings, the words."

See **IRONY** Handbook of Literary Terms

*B*ack There

Rod Serling

If you could return to the past, what would you change? What *could* you change?

CHARACTERS

PETER CORRIGAN, a young man
JACKSON, member of the Washington Club
MILLARD, member of the Washington Club
WHITAKER, member of the Washington Club
WILLIAM, attendant at the Washington Club
ATTENDANT ONE, at the Washington Club
ATTENDANT TWO, at the Washington Club
MRS. LANDERS, landlady of a rooming house

LIEUTENANT
LIEUTENANT'S WIFE
POLICE CAPTAIN
POLICEMAN
POLICE OFFICER
JONATHAN WELLINGTON
LANDLADY
NARRATOR

Act One

Scene One

Exterior of club at night. Near a large front entrance of double doors is a name plaque in brass which reads "The Washington Club, Founded 1858." In the main hall of the building is a large paneled foyer with rooms leading off on either side. An attendant, WILLIAM, *carrying a tray of drinks, crosses the hall and enters one of the rooms. There are four men sitting around in the aftermath of a card game.* PETER COR-RIGAN *is the youngest, then two middle-aged men named* WHITAKER *and* MILLARD, *and* JACKSON, *the oldest, a white-haired man in his sixties, who motions the tray from the attendant over to the table.*

JACKSON. Just put it over here, William, would you?

WILLIAM. Yes, sir. (*He lays the tray down and walks away from the table.*)

CORRIGAN. Now what's your point? That if it were possible for a person to go back in time there'd be nothing in the world to prevent him from altering the course of history—is that it?

MILLARD. Let's say, Corrigan, that you go back in time. It's October, 1929. The day before the stock market crashed.[1] You know on the following morning that the securities are going to tumble into an abyss. Now using that prior knowledge,

---

1. *stock market crashed.* In October, 1929, stocks suddenly became greatly devalued, leading to a nationwide financial disaster and the ruin of many people.

there's a hundred things you can do to protect yourself.

CORRIGAN. But I'm an anachronism back there. I don't really belong back there.

MILLARD. You could sell out the day before the crash.

CORRIGAN. But what if I did and that started the crash earlier? Now history tells us that on October 24th, 1929, the bottom dropped out of the stock market. That's a fixed date. October 24th, 1929. It exists as an event in the history of our times. It *can't* be altered.

MILLARD. And I say it can. What's to prevent it? What's to prevent me, say, from going to a broker[2] on the morning of October 23rd?

CORRIGAN. Gentlemen, I'm afraid I'll have to leave this time travel to H. G. Wells.[3] I'm much too tired to get into any more metaphysics[4] this evening. And since nobody has ever gone back in time, the whole blamed thing is much too theoretical. I'll probably see you over the weekend.

WHITAKER. Don't get lost back in time now, Corrigan.

CORRIGAN. I certainly shall not. Good night, everybody.

VOICES. Good night, Pete. Good night, Corrigan. See you tomorrow.

(CORRIGAN *walks out into the hall and heads toward the front door.*)

WILLIAM (*going by*). Good night, Mr. Corrigan.

CORRIGAN. Good night, William. (*Then he looks at the elderly man a little more closely.*) Everything all right with you, William? Looks like you've lost some weight.

WILLIAM (*with a deference built of a forty-year habit pattern*). Just the usual worries, sir. The stars and my salary are fixed. It's the cost of living that goes up. (CORRIGAN *smiles, reaches in his pocket, starts to hand him a bill.*)

WILLIAM. Oh no, sir, I couldn't.

CORRIGAN (*forcing it into his hand*). Yes, you can, William. Bless you and say hello to your wife for me.

WILLIAM. Thank you so much, sir. (*A pause*) Did you have a coat with you?

CORRIGAN. No. I'm rushing the season a little tonight, William. I felt spring in the air. Came out like this.

WILLIAM (*opening the door*). Well, April *is* spring, sir.

CORRIGAN. It's getting there. What is the date, William?

WILLIAM. April 14th, sir.

CORRIGAN. April 14th. (*Then he turns and grins at the attendant.*) 1965—right?

WILLIAM. I beg your pardon, sir? Oh, yes, sir. 1965.

CORRIGAN (*going out*). Good night, William. Take care of yourself. (*He goes out into the night.*)

Scene Two

Exterior of the club. The door closes behind CORRIGAN. *He stands there near the front entrance. The light from the street light illuminates the steps. There's the sound of chimes from the distant steeple clock.* CORRIGAN *looks at his wristwatch, holding it out toward the light so it can be seen more clearly. Suddenly his face takes on a strange look. He shuts his eyes and rubs his temple. Then he looks down at his wrist again. This time the light has*

---

2. broker, a person who buys and sells stocks and bonds for a client.
3. H. G. Wells, 1866-1946, an English writer known particularly for his prophetic science fiction. One of his best-known novels is *The Time Machine*, about traveling in time.
4. metaphysics (met′ə fiz′iks), the philosophical study of such concepts as time, space, and reality.

changed. *It's a wavery, moving light, different from what it had been.* CORRIGAN *looks across toward the light again. It's a gaslight[5] now. He reacts in amazement. The chimes begin to chime again, this time eight times. He once again looks at the watch, but instead of a wristwatch there is just a fringe of lace protruding from a coat. There is no wristwatch at all. He grabs his wrist, pulling at the lace and coat. He's dressed now in a nineteenth-century costume. He looks down at himself, looks again toward the gaslight that flickers, and then slowly backs down from the steps staring at the building from which he's just come. The plaque reads "Washington Club." He jumps the steps two at a time, slams against the front door, pounding on it. After a long moment the door opens. An* ATTENDANT, *half undressed, stands there peering out into the darkness.*

ATTENDANT ONE. Who is it? What do you want?

CORRIGAN. I left something in there.

(He starts to push his way in and the ATTENDANT *partially closes the door on him.)*

ATTENDANT ONE. Now here you! The Club is closed this evening.

CORRIGAN. The devil it is. I just left here a minute ago.

ATTENDANT ONE *(peers at him).* You did what? You drunk, young man? That it? You're drunk, huh?

CORRIGAN. I am not drunk. I want to see Mr. Jackson or Mr. Whitaker, or William. Let me talk to William. Where is he now?

ATTENDANT ONE. Who?

CORRIGAN. William. What's the matter with you? Where did *you* come from? *(Then he looks down at his clothes.)* What's the idea of this? *(He looks up. The door has been shut. He pounds on it again, shouting.)* Hey! Open up!

VOICE *(from inside).* You best get away from here or I'll call the police. Go on. Get out of here.

(CORRIGAN backs away from the door, goes down to the sidewalk, stands there, looks up at the gaslight, then up and down the street, starts at the sound of noises. It's the clip-clop of horses' hooves and the rolling, squeaky sound of carriage wheels. He takes a few halting, running steps out into the street. He bites his lip, looks around.)

CORRIGAN *(under his breath).* I'll go home. That's it. Go home. I'll go home. *(He turns and starts to walk and then run down the street, disappearing into the night.)*

Scene Three

Hallway of rooming house. There is the sound of a doorbell ringing. MRS. LANDERS, *the landlady, comes out from the dining room and goes toward the door.*

MRS. LANDERS. All right. All right. Have a bit of patience. I'm coming. *(Opening door)* Yes?

CORRIGAN. Is this 19 West 12th Street?

MRS. LANDERS. That's right. Whom did you wish to see?

CORRIGAN. I'm just wondering if . . .

(He stands there trying to look over her shoulder. MRS. LANDERS *turns to look behind her and then suspiciously back toward* CORRIGAN.)

MRS. LANDERS. Whom did you wish to see, young man?

CORRIGAN. I . . . I used to live here. It's the oldest building in this section of town.

---

5. gaslight. Gas was used for lighting on streets and in buildings chiefly during the nineteenth century.

MRS. LANDERS (stares at him). How's that?

CORRIGAN (wets his lips). What I mean is . . . as I remember it . . . it was the oldest——

MRS. LANDERS. Well now really, young man. I can't spend the whole evening standing here talking about silly things like which is the oldest building in the section. Now if there's nothing else——

CORRIGAN (blurting it out). Do you have a room?

MRS. LANDERS (opens the door just a little bit wider so that she can get a better look at him; looks him up and down and appears satisfied). I have a room for acceptable boarders. Do you come from around here?

CORRIGAN. Yes. Yes, I do.

MRS. LANDERS. Army veteran?

CORRIGAN. Yes. Yes, as a matter of fact I am.

MRS. LANDERS (looks at him again up and down). Well, come in. I'll show you what I have.

(She opens the door wider and CORRIGAN enters. She closes it behind him. She looks expectantly up toward his hat and CORRIGAN rather hurriedly and abruptly removes it. He grins, embarrassed.)

CORRIGAN. I'm not used to it.

MRS. LANDERS. Used to what?

CORRIGAN (points to the hat in his hand). The hat. I don't wear a hat very often.

MRS. LANDERS (again gives him her inventory look, very unsure of him now). May I inquire as to what your business is?

CORRIGAN. I'm an engineer.

MRS. LANDERS. Really. A professional man. Hmmm. Well, come upstairs and I'll show you.

(She points to the stairs that lead off the hall and CORRIGAN starts up as an army officer and his wife come down them.)

MRS. LANDERS (smiling). Off to the play?

LIEUTENANT. That's right, Mrs. Landers. Dinner at The Willard and then off to the play.

MRS. LANDERS. Well, enjoy yourself. And applaud the President for me!

LIEUTENANT. We'll certainly do that.

LIEUTENANT'S WIFE. Good night, Mrs. Landers.

MRS. LANDERS. Good night, my dear. Have a good time. This way, Mr. Corrigan.

(The LIEUTENANT and CORRIGAN exchange a nod as they pass on the stairs. As they go up the steps, CORRIGAN suddenly stops and MRS. LANDERS almost bangs into him.)

MRS. LANDERS. Now what's the trouble?

CORRIGAN (whirling around). What did you say?

MRS. LANDERS. What did I say to whom? When?

CORRIGAN. To the lieutenant. To the officer. What did you just say to him?

(The LIEUTENANT has turned. His wife tries to lead him out, but he holds out his hand to stop her so that he can listen to the conversation from the steps.)

CORRIGAN. You just said something to him about the President.

LIEUTENANT (walking toward the foot of the steps). She told me to applaud him. Where might your sympathies lie?

MRS. LANDERS (suspiciously). Yes, young man. Which army were you in?

CORRIGAN (wets his lips nervously). The Army of the Republic,[6] of course.

LIEUTENANT (nods, satisfied). Then why make such a thing of applauding President Lincoln? That's his due, we figure.

MRS. LANDERS. That and everything else, may the good Lord bless him.

---

6. **Army of the Republic,** the northern army, or Federal Army, in the United States Civil War.

CORRIGAN (*takes a step down the stairs, staring at the* LIEUTENANT). You're going to a play tonight?

(*The* LIEUTENANT *nods.*)

LIEUTENANT'S WIFE (*at the door*). We may or we may not, depending on when my husband makes up his mind to get a carriage in time to have dinner and get to the theater.

CORRIGAN. What theater? *What* play?

LIEUTENANT. Ford's Theater, of course.

CORRIGAN (*looking off, his voice intense*). Ford's Theater. Ford's Theater.

LIEUTENANT. Are you all right? I mean do you feel all right?

CORRIGAN (*whirls around to stare at him*). What's the name of the play?

LIEUTENANT (*exchanges a look with his wife*). I beg your pardon?

CORRIGAN. The play. The one you're going to tonight at Ford's Theater. What's the name of it?

LIEUTENANT'S WIFE. It's called "Our American Cousin."

CORRIGAN (*again looks off thoughtfully*). "Our American Cousin" and Lincoln's going to be there. (*He looks from one to the other, first toward the landlady on the steps, then down toward the soldier and his wife.*) And it's April 14th, 1865, isn't it? Isn't it April 14th, 1865? (*He starts down the steps without waiting for an answer. The* LIEUTENANT *stands in front of him.*)

LIEUTENANT. Really, sir, I'd call your actions most strange.

(CORRIGAN *stares at him briefly as he goes by, then goes out the door, looking purposeful and intent.*)

Scene Four

*Alley at night. On one side is the stage door with a sign over it reading "Ford's Thea-*ter." CORRIGAN *turns the corridor into the alley at a dead run. He stops directly under the light, looks left and right, then vaults over the railing and pounds on the stage door.*

CORRIGAN (*shouting*). Hey! Hey, let me in! President Lincoln is going to be shot tonight!

(*He continues to pound on the door and shout.*)

Act Two

Scene One

Police station at night. It's a bare receiving room with a POLICE CAPTAIN *at a desk. A long bench on one side of the room is occupied by sad miscreants awaiting disposition. There is a line of three or four men standing in front of the desk with several policemen in evidence. One holds onto* CORRIGAN *who has a bruise over his eye and his coat is quite disheveled. The* POLICE CAPTAIN *looks up to him from a list.*

CAPTAIN. Now what's this one done? (*He peers up over his glasses and eyes* CORRIGAN *up and down.*) Fancy Dan with too much money in his pockets, huh?

CORRIGAN. While you idiots are sitting here, you're going to lose a President!

(*The* CAPTAIN *looks inquiringly toward the* POLICEMAN.)

POLICEMAN. That's what he's been yellin' all the way over to the station. And that's what the doorman at the Ford Theater popped him on the head for. (*He nods toward* CORRIGAN.) Tried to pound his way right through the stage door. Yellin' some kind of crazy things about President Lincoln goin' to get shot.

CORRIGAN. President Lincoln *will* be shot! Tonight. In the theater. A man named Booth.

CAPTAIN. And how would you be knowin' this? I suppose you're clairvoyant or something. Some kind of seer or wizard or something.

CORRIGAN. I only know what I know. If I told you *how* I knew, you wouldn't believe me. Look, keep me here if you like. Lock me up.

CAPTAIN (*motions toward a* TURNKEY,[7] *points to cell block door*). Let him sleep it off.

(*The* TURNKEY *grabs* CORRIGAN'S *arm and starts to lead him out of the room.*)

CORRIGAN (*shouting as he's led away*). Well you better hear me out. Somebody better get to the President's box at the Ford Theater. Either keep him out of there or put a cordon of men around him. A man named John Wilkes Booth is going to assassinate him tonight!

(*He's pushed through the door leading to the cell block. A tall man in cape and black moustache stands near the open door at the other side. He closes it behind him, takes a step into the room, then with a kind of very precise authority, he walks directly over to the* CAPTAIN'S *table, shoving a couple of people aside as he does so with a firm gentleness. When he reaches the* CAPTAIN'S *table he removes a card from his inside pocket, puts it on the table in front of the* CAPTAIN.)

WELLINGTON. Wellington, Captain. Jonathan Wellington.

(*The* CAPTAIN *looks at the card, peers at it over his glasses, then looks up toward the tall man in front of him. Obviously the man's manner and dress impresses him. His tone is respectful and quiet.*)

CAPTAIN. What can I do for you, Mr. Wellington?

WELLINGTON. That man you just had incarcerated. Mr. Corrigan I believe he said his name was.

CAPTAIN. Drunk, sir. That's probably what he is.

WELLINGTON. Drunk or . . . (*He taps his head meaningfully.*) Or perhaps, ill. I wonder if he could be remanded in my custody. He might well be a war veteran and I'd hate to see him placed in jail.

CAPTAIN. Well, that's real decent of you, Mr. Wellington. You say you want him remanded in *your* custody?

WELLINGTON. Precisely. I'll be fully responsible for him. I think perhaps I might be able to help him.

CAPTAIN. All right, sir. If that's what you'd like. But I'd be careful of this one if I was you! There's a mighty bunch of crackpots running the streets these days and many of them his like, and many of them dangerous too, sir. (*He turns toward* TURNKEY.) Have Corrigan brought back out here. This gentleman's going to look after him. (*Then he turns to* WELLINGTON.) It's real decent of you, sir. Real decent indeed.

WELLINGTON. I'll be outside. Have him brought out to me if you would.

CAPTAIN. I will indeed, sir.

(WELLINGTON *turns. He passes the various people who look at him and make room for him. His walk, his manner, his positiveness suggest a commanding figure and everyone reacts accordingly. The* CAPTAIN *once again busies himself with his list and is about to check in the next prisoner, when a young* POLICE OFFICER *alongside says:*)

POLICE OFFICER. Begging your pardon, Captain.

CAPTAIN. What is it?

POLICE OFFICER. About that Corrigan, sir.

CAPTAIN. What about him?

---

7. *turnkey,* jailer.

POLICE OFFICER. Wouldn't it be wise, sir, if——

CAPTAIN (*impatiently*). If what?

POLICE OFFICER. He seemed so positive, sir. So sure. About the President, I mean.

CAPTAIN (*slams on the desk with vast impatience*). What would you have us do? Send all available police to the Ford Theater? And on what authority? On the word of some demented fool who probably left his mind someplace in Gettysburg.[8] If I was you, mister, I'd be considerably more thoughtful at sizing up situations or you'll not advance one-half grade the next twenty years. Now be good enough to stand aside and let me get on with my work.

POLICE OFFICER (*very much deterred by all this, but pushed on by a gnawing sense of disquiet*). Captain, it wouldn't hurt.

CAPTAIN (*interrupting with a roar*). It wouldn't hurt if what?

POLICE OFFICER. I was going to suggest, sir, that if perhaps we place extra guards in the box with the President——

CAPTAIN. The President has all the guards he needs. He's got the whole Federal Army at his disposal and if they're satisfied with his security arrangements, then I am too and so should you. Next case!

(*The young* POLICE OFFICER *bites his lip and looks away, then stares across the room thoughtfully. The door opens and the* TURNKEY *leads* CORRIGAN *across the room and over to the door. He opens it and points out.* CORRIGAN *nods and walks outside. The door closes behind him. The young* POLICE OFFICER *looks briefly at the* CAPTAIN, *then puts his cap on and starts out toward the door.*)

Scene Two

Lodging-house, WELLINGTON'S *room.* WELLINGTON *is pouring wine into two glasses.* CORRIGAN *sits in a chair, his face in his hands. He looks up at the proffered drink and takes it.*

WELLINGTON. Take this. It'll make you feel better. (CORRIGAN *nods his thanks, takes a healthy swig of the wine, puts it down, then looks up at the other man.*) Better?

CORRIGAN (*studying the man*). Who are you anyway?

WELLINGTON (*with a thin smile*). At the moment I'm your benefactor and apparently your only friend. I'm in the Government service, but as a young man in college I dabbled in medicine of a sort.

CORRIGAN. Medicine?

WELLINGTON. Medicine of the mind.

CORRIGAN (*smiles grimly*). Psychiatrist.

WELLINGTON (*turning to him*). I don't know the term.

CORRIGAN. What about the symptoms?

WELLINGTON. They *do* interest me. This story you were telling about the President being assassinated.

CORRIGAN (*quickly*). What time *is* it?

WELLINGTON. There's time. (*Checks a pocket watch*) A quarter to eight. The play won't start for another half hour. What gave you the idea that the President would be assassinated?

CORRIGAN. I happen to know, that's all.

WELLINGTON (*again the thin smile*). You have a premonition?

CORRIGAN. I've got a devil of a lot more than a premonition. Lincoln *will* be assassinated. (*Then quickly*) Unless somebody tries to prevent it.

WELLINGTON. *I* shall try to prevent it. If you can convince me that you're neither drunk nor insane.

---

8. *Gettysburg* (get'iz berg'), a town in Pennsylvania, the site of one of the major battles of the Civil War in July, 1863.

CORRIGAN (on his feet). If I told you what I was, you'd be convinced I *was* insane. So all I'm *going* to tell you is that I happen to know for a fact that a man named John Wilkes Booth will assassinate President Lincoln in his box at the Ford Theater. I don't know what time it's going to happen . . . that's something I forgot—but——

WELLINGTON (softly). Something you forgot?

CORRIGAN (takes a step toward him). Listen, please—— (He stops suddenly, and begins to waver. He reaches up to touch the bruise over his head.)

WELLINGTON (takes out a handkerchief and hands it to CORRIGAN). Here. That hasn't been treated properly. You'd best cover it.

CORRIGAN (very, very shaky, almost faint, takes the handkerchief, puts it to his head and sits back down weakly). That's . . .

that's odd. *(He looks up, still holding the handkerchief.)*

WELLINGTON. What is?

CORRIGAN. I'm so . . . I'm so faint all of a sudden. So weak. It's almost as if I were——

WELLINGTON. As if you were what?

CORRIGAN *(with a weak smile)*. As if I'd suddenly gotten drunk or some—*(He looks up, desperately trying to focus now as his vision starts to become clouded.)* I've never . . . I've never felt like this before. I've never—*(His eyes turn to the wine glass on the table. As his eyes open wide, he struggles to his feet.)* You . . . you devil! You drugged me, didn't you! *(He reaches out to grab* WELLINGTON, *half struggling in the process.)* You drugged me, didn't you!

WELLINGTON. I was forced to, my young friend. You're a very sick man and a sick man doesn't belong in jail. He belongs in a comfortable accommodation where he can sleep and rest and regain his . . . *(He smiles a little apologetically.)* his composure, his rationale. Rest, Mr. Corrigan. I'll be back soon.

(He turns and starts toward the door. CORRIGAN *starts to follow him, stumbles to his knees, supports himself on one hand, looks up as* WELLINGTON *opens the door.)*

CORRIGAN. Please . . . please, you've got to believe me. Lincoln's going to be shot tonight.

WELLINGTON *(smiling again)*. And *that's* odd! Because . . . perhaps I'm *beginning* to believe you! Good night, Mr. Corrigan. Rest well. *(He turns and goes out of the room, closing the door behind him. We hear the sound of the key being inserted, the door locked.)*

*(*CORRIGAN *tries desperately to rise and*

then weakly falls over on his side. He crawls toward the door. He scrabbles at it with a weak hand.)*

CORRIGAN *(almost in a whisper)*. Please . . . please . . . somebody . . . let me out. I wasn't kidding . . . I know . . . *the President's going to be assassinated!* (His arm, supporting him, gives out and he falls to his face, then in a last effort, he turns himself over so that he's lying on his back.)*

(There is a sound of a heavy knocking on the door. Then a LANDLADY'S *voice from outside.)*

LANDLADY. There's no need to break it open, Officer. I've got an extra key. Now if you don't mind, stand aside.

(There's the sound of the key inserted in the lock and the door opens. The young POLICE OFFICER *from earlier is standing there with an angry-faced* LANDLADY *behind him. The* POLICE OFFICER *gets down on his knees, props up* CORRIGAN'S *head.)*

POLICE OFFICER. Are you all right? What happened?

CORRIGAN. What time is it? *(He grabs the* OFFICER, *almost pulling him over.)* You've got to tell me what time it is.

POLICE OFFICER. It's ten-thirty-five. Come on, Corrigan. You've got to tell me what you know about this. You may be a madman or a drunk or I don't know what— but you've got me convinced and I've been everywhere from the Mayor's office to the Police Commissioner's home trying to get a special guard for the President.

CORRIGAN. Then go yourself. Find out where he's sitting and get right up alongside of him. He'll be shot from behind. That's the way it happened. Shot from behind. And then the assassin jumps from the box to the stage and he runs out of the wings.

POLICE OFFICER (*incredulous*). You're telling me this as if, as if it has already happened.

CORRIGAN. It *has* happened. It happened a hundred years ago and I've come back to see that it *doesn't* happen. (*Looking beyond the* POLICE OFFICER) Where's the man who brought me in here? Where's Wellington?

LANDLADY (*peering into the room*). Wellington? There's no one here by that name.

CORRIGAN (*waves a clenched fist at her, still holding the handkerchief*). Don't tell me there's no one here by that name. He brought me in here. He lives in this room.

LANDLADY. There's no one here by that name.

CORRIGAN (*holds the handkerchief close to his face, again waving his fist*). I tell you the man who brought me here was named——

(*He stops abruptly, suddenly caught by something he sees on the handkerchief. His eyes slowly turn to stare at it in his hand. On the border are the initials J.W.B.*)

CORRIGAN. J.W.B.?

LANDLADY. Of course! Mr. John Wilkes Booth who lives in this room and that's who brought you here.

CORRIGAN. He said his name was Wellington! And *that's* why he drugged me. (*He grabs the* POLICE OFFICER *again.*) He gave me wine and he drugged me. He didn't want me to stop him. He's the one who's going to do it. Listen, you've got to get to that theater. You've got to stop him. John Wilkes Booth! He's going to kill Lincoln. Look, get out of here now! Will you stop him? Will you——

(*He stops abruptly, his eyes look up. All three people turn to look toward the window. There's the sound of crowd noises building, suggestive of excitement, and then almost a collective wail, a mournful, universal chant that comes from the streets, and as the sound builds we suddenly hear intelligible words that are part of the mob noise.*)

VOICES. The President's been shot. President Lincoln's been assassinated. Lincoln is dying.

(*The* LANDLADY *suddenly bursts into tears. The* POLICE OFFICER *rises to his feet, his face white.*)

POLICE OFFICER. Oh my dear God! You were right. You *did* know. Oh . . . my . . . dear . . . God!

(*He turns almost trance-like and walks out of the room. The* LANDLADY *follows him.* CORRIGAN *rises weakly and goes to the window, staring out at the night and listening to the sounds of a nation beginning its mourning. He closes his eyes and puts his head against the window pane and with fruitless, weakened smashes, hits the side of the window frame as he talks.*)

CORRIGAN. I tried to tell you. I tried to warn you. Why didn't anybody listen? Why? Why didn't anyone listen to me?

(*His fist beats a steady staccato on the window frame.*)

Scene Three

The Washington Club at night. CORRIGAN *is pounding on the front door of the Washington Club.* CORRIGAN *is standing there in modern dress once again. The door opens. An* ATTENDANT *we've not seen before appears.*

ATTENDANT TWO. Good evening, Mr. Corrigan. Did you forget something, sir?

(CORRIGAN *walks past the* ATTENDANT, *through the big double doors that lead to the card room as in Act One. His three friends are in the middle of a discussion. The fourth man at the table, sitting in his seat, has his back to the camera.)*

MILLARD *(looking up).* Hello, Pete. Come on over and join tonight's bull session. It has to do with the best ways of amassing a fortune. What are your tried-and-true methods?

CORRIGAN *(his voice intense and shaky).* We were talking about time travel, about going back in time.

JACKSON *(dismissing it).* Oh that's old stuff. We're on a new tack now. Money and the best ways to acquire it.

CORRIGAN. Listen . . . listen, I want to tell you something. This is true. If you go back into the past you can't change anything. *(He takes another step toward the table.)* Understand? You can't change anything.

(The men look at one another, disarmed by the intensity of CORRIGAN'S tone.)

JACKSON *(rises, softly).* All right, old man, if you say so. *(Studying him intensely)* Are you all right?

CORRIGAN *(closing his eyes for a moment).* Yes . . . yes, I'm all right.

JACKSON. Then come on over and listen to a lot of palaver from self-made swindlers. William here has the best method.

CORRIGAN. William?

(He sees the attendant from Act One but now meticulously dressed, a middle-aged millionaire obviously, with a totally different manner, who puts a cigarette in a holder with manicured hands in the manner of a man totally accustomed to wealth. WILLIAM looks up and smiles.)

WILLIAM. Oh yes. My method for achieving security is by far the best. You simply inherit it. It comes to you in a beribboned box. I was telling the boys here, Corrigan. My great-grandfather was on the po-

lice force here in Washington on the night of Lincoln's assassination. He went all over town trying to warn people that something might happen. *(He holds up his hands in a gesture.)* How he figured it out, nobody seems to know. It's certainly not recorded any place. But because there was so much publicity, people never forgot him. He became a police chief, then a councilman, did some wheeling and dealing in land and became a millionaire. What do you say we get back to our bridge, gentlemen?

(JACKSON takes the cards and starts to shuffle. WILLIAM turns in his seat once again.)

WILLIAM. How about it, Corrigan? Take a hand?

CORRIGAN. Thank you, William, no. I think I'll . . . I think I'll just go home.

(He turns very slowly and starts toward the exit. Over his walk we hear the whispered, hushed murmurings of the men at the table.)

VOICES. Looks peaked, doesn't he? Acting so strangely. I wonder what's the matter with him.

(CORRIGAN walks into the hall and toward the front door.)

NARRATOR'S VOICE. Mr. Peter Corrigan, lately returned from a place "Back There"; a journey into time with highly questionable results. Proving, on one hand, that the threads of history are woven tightly and the skein of events cannot be undone; but, on the other hand, there are small fragments of tapestry that *can* be altered. Tonight's thesis, to be taken as you will, in *The Twilight Zone!*[9]

---

9. The Twilight Zone, the name of the television program on which "Back There" was originally produced.

Discussion

1. At the beginning of the play, what is Corrigan's opinion about the possibility of changing history?

2. (a) On leaving the Washington Club, what unusual things does Corrigan notice? **(b)** How does he react?

3. A number of clues help the reader, along with Corrigan, infer what event in history is about to happen. **(a)** What is the date? **(b)** What war has just ended? **(c)** What play is taking place and where? **(d)** What famous person will be at the play?

4. Corrigan tries to convince several people of what is about to happen. How do the following people respond: **(a)** the doorman at the Ford Theater; **(b)** the police captain; **(c)** the police officer; **(d)** Wellington?

5. In the end, does Corrigan learn whether or not history can be changed? Explain.

Application

Irony

1. At the beginning of the play, Corrigan insists that history "*can't* be altered." In light of his opinion, what is ironic about Corrigan's situation throughout most of the play?

2. Why is it ironic that Jonathan Wellington helps release Corrigan from prison and calls himself Corrigan's benefactor and friend?

3. Throughout the play, Corrigan tries to convince people that Lincoln is about to be assassinated. How are these encounters examples of dramatic irony?

4. When Corrigan tells the police captain that a man named Booth will shoot Lincoln, the captain replies, "I suppose you're clairvoyant or something. Some kind of seer or wizard or something." What kind of irony is this? Explain.

Composition

If you could improve the course of history by changing the fate of one historically significant person, who would that person be? Would you prevent the assassination of Dr. Martin Luther King, Jr. or John F. Kennedy? Would you cause Hitler or Napoleon to lose, early in their careers, the support of their followers? What effects would your change of history have on the world?

In a composition of one or two pages, discuss the change you would make in one person's fate. Explain how you would go about changing events if you could travel back in time with the knowledge you have now. Support your choice by explaining the positive effects the change would have.

(You may find the article "Supporting a Point" in the Composition Guide helpful in writing this composition.)

Rod Serling 1924–1975

After two years at a Cincinnati radio station and six years writing for a television station, Rod Serling began his noted career as a free-lance television screenwriter. He is best known for his work in writing, producing, and narrating the series *The Twilight Zone* and *Rod Serling's Night Gallery.*

Serling considered it a writer's job to make audiences aware of problems in society, and many of his scripts attack various forms of prejudice. Among Serling's numerous awards are six Emmys for television scripts and a Golden Globe Award for Best Director.

Comment: Traveling in Time

"Where does time go?" This question, so commonly asked by small children, is something most of us have wondered about at one time or another. It seems that people have always been interested in the passage of time and the possibility of traveling through time. Many writers have used this theme. Washington Irving's story "Rip Van Winkle," published in 1819, is about a man who falls asleep in New York's Catskill Mountains and awakens twenty years later. Not only has his beard grown a foot, but the Revolutionary War has been fought. The reactions of the townspeople to Rip's return and Rip's own reactions to the changes he sees provide many amusing scenes. In *A Connecticut Yankee in King Arthur's Court,* a novel by Mark Twain published in 1889, a nineteenth-century American mechanic is knocked unconscious. He awakens under a tree near legendary Camelot in the England of a much earlier century and proceeds to outdo Merlin the magician and King Arthur's best knights.

In 1894 appeared *The Time Machine,* H. G. Wells's celebrated novel about a man who travels in a machine into the distant future. This novel was among the first to link events of fantasy or fiction with believable—if not actual—scientific background, and it was enormously popular.

In 1895, Wells and a friend applied for a patent on a machine that would create the same effects that Wells had written about in his novel. The machine was designed to have moving floors and walls. Films and slides would portray different time eras on screens as the machine's operator "traveled" into the past or the future. Unfortunately, Wells could not afford to build the machine.

In 1960, a film of *The Time Machine* was made, and Wells's time machine idea was used again in the 1979 film *Time After Time.* Although the plot of *Time After Time* is fictitious, the main character is the author H. G. Wells. In the film, Wells invents a real time machine and uses it to chase a criminal from London in the past to modern-day San Francisco.

The possibilities of time travel continue to fascinate scientists as well as writers and film makers. Although several scientific theories seem to rule out the chance of entering past or future time, for writers, the topic of time travel holds an unlimited number of plots and possibilities.

*M*anhunt

George H. Gurley, Jr.

My hound and I are tracking an escape
    artist.
His trail is always fresh.
He taunts us with clues,
Leaves fingerprints on everything I touch.
Whenever we arrive he's just checked out,
His cigarettes still burning in my rooms.

He leads us further from home
And I have to use the things he leaves
    behind,
Dressing in his wrinkled suits
Eating his leftovers
Drying off with his soggy towel.

He cuts the corner ahead of us,
His car disappears in a van.
He slips through drapes,

15 Edges along parapets,
Jumps from boxcar roofs.
My hound tugs at his leash.

It's been going on so long
I'm beginning to talk like him.
20 Fugitives relay my dreams,
He passes the baton to me.
Lying awake in his pajamas
I hear his breathing
On the other side of the wall.

25 Sometimes I think I've almost got my
    man.
After dinner, alone in my room,
When I reach for the paper or a match,
My old hound sniffs at me and growls.

"Manhunt" by George H. Gurley, Jr. from Wichita
(Kansas) Public Schools *Literary Calendar* 1983.
Reprinted by permission of the author.

Discussion

1. (a) What clues does the "escape artist" leave in stanza 1? (b) In stanza 2, what things belonging to the "escape artist" does the speaker end up using?

2. (a) What is the hound's reaction to the speaker in the last stanza? (b) How do you account for this?

3. (a) Do you think the speaker is really looking for another person? Why or why not? (b) If not, whom might the speaker be looking for?

George H. Gurley, Jr.

George H. Gurley, Jr. lives in Lawrence, Kansas and works in the real estate business. He also teaches composition part time at the University of Missouri at Kansas City and Washburn University. Gurley has published two collections of poetry, *Home Movies* and *Fugues in the Plumbing,* and has contributed poems to numerous magazines. A playwright as well as a poet, Gurley's play, *Cures,* won first prize in a contest sponsored by the Missouri Arts Council.

Flowers for Algernon

Daniel Keyes

Before, they laughed at Charlie Gordon for his ignorance and dullness; now, they hate him for his knowledge and understanding. What do they want of him?

Progris riport 1—march 5

Dr. Strauss says I shud rite down what I think and every thing that happins to me from now on. I dont know why but he says its importint so they will see if they will use me. I hope they use me. Miss Kinnian says maybe they can make me smart. I want to be smart. My name is Charlie Gordon. I am 37 years old. I have nuthing more to rite now so I will close for today.

progris riport 2—march 6

I had a test today. I think I faled it. And I think maybe now they wont use me. What happind is a nice young man was in the room and he had some white cards and ink spillled all over them. He sed Charlie what do yo see on this card. I was very skared even tho I had my rabits foot in my pockit because when I was a kid I always faled tests in school and I spillled ink to.

I told him I saw a inkblot. He said yes and it made me feel good. I thot that was all but when I got up to go he said Charlie we are not thru yet. Then I dont remember so good but he wantid me to say what was in the ink. I dint see nuthing in the ink but he said there was picturs there other pepul saw some picturs. I couldnt see any picturs. I reely tryed. I held the card close up and then far away. Then I said if I had my glases I coud see better I usally only ware my glases in the movies or TV but I said

they are in the closit in the hall. I got them. Then I said let me see that card agen I bet Ill find it now.

I tryed hard but I only saw the ink. I told him maybe I need new glases. He rote something down on a paper and I got skared of faling the test. I told him it was a very nice inkblot with littel points all around the edges. He looked very sad so that wasnt it. I said please let me try agen. Ill get it in a few minits becaus Im not so fast somtimes. Im a slow reeder too in Miss Kinnians class for slow adults but I'm trying very hard.

He gave me a chance with another card that had 2 kinds of ink spilled on it red and blue.

He was very nice and talked slow like Miss Kinnian does and he explained it to me that it was a *raw shok*.[1] He said pepul see things in the ink. I said show me where. He said think. I told him I think a inkblot but that wasn't rite eather. He said what does it remind you—pretend something. I closed my eyes for a long time to pretend. I told him I pretend a fowntan pen with ink leeking all over a table cloth.

I dont think I passed the *raw shok* test.

---

1. *raw shok,* Rorschach (rôr′shäk) test, a psychological test used to measure personality traits and general intelligence.

Slightly abridged from "Flowers for Algernon" by Daniel Keyes. Copyright 1959 by Mercury Press, Inc.; originally appeared in the *Magazine of Fantasy and Science Fiction;* reprinted by permission of the author and his agent, Robert P. Mills.

progris riport 3—martch 7

Dr Strauss and Dr Nemur say it dont matter about the inkblots. They said that maybe they will still use me. I said Miss Kinnian never gave me tests like that one only spelling and reading. They said Miss Kinnian told that I was her bestist pupil in the adult nite school because I tryed the hardist and I reely wantid to lern. They said how come you went to the adult nite scool all by yourself Charlie. How did you find it. I said I asked pepul and sumbody told me where I shud go to lern to read and spell good. They said why did you want to. I told them becaus all my life I wantid to be smart and not dumb. But its very hard to be smart. They said you know it will probly be tempirery. I said yes. Miss Kinnian told me. I dont care if it herts.

Later I had more crazy tests today. The nice lady who gave it to me told me the name and I asked her how do you spellit so I can rite it my progris riport. THEMATIC APPERCEPTION TEST.[2] I dont know the frist 2 words but I know what *test* means. You got to pass it or you get bad marks. This test lookd easy becaus I coud see the pictures. Only this time she dint want me to tell her the picturs. That mixd me up. She said make up storys about the pepul in the picturs.

I told her how can you tell storys about pepul you never met. I said why shud I make up lies. I never tell lies any more becaus I always get caut.

She told me this test and the other one the raw-shok was for getting personality. I laffed so hard. I said how can you get that thing from inkblots and fotos. She got sore and put her picturs away. I don't care. It was sily. I gess I faled that test too.

Later some men in white coats took me to a difernt part of the hospitil and gave me

a game to play. It was like a race with a white mouse. They called the mouse Algernon. Algernon was in a box with a lot of twists and turns like all kinds of walls and they gave me a pencil and paper with lines and lots of boxes. On one side it said START and on the other end it said FINISH. They said it was *amazed*[3] and that Algernon and me had the same *amazed* to do. I dint see how we could have the same *amazed* if Algernon had a box and I had a paper but I dint say nothing. Anyway there wasnt time because the race started.

One of the men had a watch he was trying to hide so I wouldnt see it so I tryed not to look and that made me nervus.

Anyway that test made me feel worser than all the others because they did it over 10 times with different *amazeds* and Algernon won everytime. I dint know that mice were so smart. Maybe thats because Algernon is a white mouse. Maybe white mice are smarter than other mice.

progris riport 4—Mar 8

Their going to use me! Im so exited I can hardly write. Dr Nemur and Dr Strauss had a argament about it first. Dr Nemur was in the office when Dr Strauss brot me in. Dr Nemur was worryed about using me but Dr Strauss told him Miss Kinnian rekemmended me the best from all the people who she was teaching. I like Miss Kinnian becaus shes a very smart teacher. And she said Charlie your going to have a second chance. If you volenteer for this experament you mite get smart. They dont know if it will be perminint but theirs a chance. Thats why I said ok even when I was scared because she said it was an opera-

---

2. *Thematic Apperception Test,* another psychological test.
3. *amazed,* a maze, a network of paths through which one must find one's way.

shun. She said dont be scared Charlie you done so much with so little I think you deserv it most of all.

So I got scaird when Dr. Nemur and Dr. Strauss argud about it. Dr. Strauss said I had something that was very good. He said I had a good *motorvation*. I never even knew I had that. I felt proud when he said that not every body with an eye-q of 68[4] had that thing. I dont know what it is or where I got it but he said Algernon had it too. Algernons *motorvation* is the cheese they put in his box. But it cant be that because I didn't eat any cheese this week.

Then he told Dr Nemur something I dint understand so while they were talking I wrote down some of the words.

He said Dr. Nemur I know Charlie is not what you had in mind as the first of your new brede of intelek** (coudnt get the word) superman. But most people of his low ment** are host** and uncoop** they are usually dull apath** and hard to reach. He has a good natcher hes intristed and eager to please.

Dr Nemur said remember he will be the first human beeng ever to have his intellijence tripled by surgicle meens.

Dr. Strauss said exakly. Look at how well hes lerned to read and write for his low mentel age its as grate an acheve** as you and I lerning einstines therey of **vity without help. That shows the inteness motorvation. Its comparat** a tremen** achev** I say we use Charlie.

I dint get all the words but it sounded like Dr Strauss was on my side and like the other one wasnt.

Then Dr Nemur nodded he said all right maybe your right. We will use Charlie. When he said that I got so exited I jumped up and shook his hand for being so good to me. I told him thank you doc you wont be sorry for giving me a second chance. And I mean it like I told him. After the operashun Im gonna try to be smart. Im gonna try awful hard.

progris riport 5—Mar 10

Im skared. Lots of the nurses and the people who gave me the tests came to bring me candy and wish me luck. I hope I have luck. I got my rabits foot and my lucky penny. Only a black cat crossed me when I was comming to the hospitil. Dr Strauss says dont be supersitis Charlie this is science. Anyway Im keeping my rabits foot with me.

I asked Dr Strauss if Ill beat Algernon in the race after the operashun and he said maybe. If the operashun works Ill show that mouse I can be as smart as he is. Maybe smarter. Then Ill be abel to read better and spell the words good and know lots of things and be like other people. I want to be smart like other people. If it works perminint they will make everybody smart all over the wurld.

They dint give me anything to eat this morning. I dont know what that eating has to do with getting smart. Im very hungry and Dr. Nemur took away my box of candy. That Dr Nemur is a grouch. Dr Strauss says I can have it back after the operashun. You cant eat befor a operashun. . . .

progress report 6—Mar 15

The operashun dint hurt. He did it while I was sleeping. They took off the bandijis from my head today so I can make a PROGRESS REPORT. Dr. Nemur who looked at some of my other ones says I spell PROGRESS wrong and told me how

---

4. *eye-q of 68.* An average I.Q. is 100.

to spell it and REPORT too. I got to try and remember that.

I have a very bad memary for spelling. Dr. Strauss says its ok to tell about all the things that happin to me but he says I should tell more about what I feel and what I think. When I told him I dont know how to think he said try. All the time when the bandijis were on my eyes I tryed to think. Nothing happened. I dont know what to think about. Maybe if I ask him he will tell me how I can think now that Im suppose to get smart. What do smart people think about. Fancy things I suppose. I wish I knew some fancy things alredy.

progress report 7—Mar 19

Nothing is happining. I had lots of tests and different kinds of races with Algernon. I hate that mouse. He always beats me. Dr. Strauss said I got to play those games. And he said some time I got to take those tests over again. Those inkblots are stupid. And those pictures are stupid too. I like to draw a picture of a man and a woman but I wont make up lies about people.

I got a headache from trying to think so much. I thot Dr Strauss was my frend but he dont help me. He dont tell me what to think or when Ill get smart. Miss Kinnian dint come to see me. I think writing these progress reports are stupid too.

progress report 8—Mar 23

Im going back to work at the factory. They said it was better I shud go back to work but I cant tell anyone what the oper-ashun was for and I have to come to the hospitil for an hour evry night after work. They are gonna pay me mony every month for learning to be smart.

Im glad Im going back to work because I miss my job and all my frends and all the fun we have there.

Dr Strauss says I shud keep writing things down but I dont have to do it every day just when I think of something or something speshul happins. He says dont get discoridged because it takes time and it happins slow. He says it took a long time with Algernon before he got 3 times smarter than he was before. Thats why Algernon beats me all the time because he had that operashun too. That makes me feel better. I coud probly do that *amazed* faster than a reglar mouse. Maybe some day Ill beat him. That would be something. So far Algernon looks smart perminent.

Mar 25 (I dont have to write PROG-RESS REPORT on top any more just when I hand it in once a week for Dr Nemur. I just have to put the date on. That saves time)

We had a lot of fun at the factery today. Joe Carp said hey look where Charlie had his operashun what did they do Charlie put some brains in. I was going to tell him but I remembered Dr Strauss said no. Then Frank Reilly said what did you do Charlie forget your key and open your door the hard way. That made me laff. Their really my friends and they like me.

Sometimes somebody will say hey look at Joe or Frank or George he really pulled a Charlie Gordon. I dont know why they say that but they always laff. This morning Amos Borg who is the 4 man at Donnegans used my name when he shouted at Ernie the office boy. Ernie lost a packige. He said Ernie what are you trying to be a Charlie Gordon. I dont understand why he said that.

Mar 28. Dr. Strauss came to my room tonight to see why I dint come in like I was suppose to. I told him I dont like to race with Algernon any more. He said I dont have to for a while but I shud come in. He had a present for me. I thot it was a little television but it wasnt. He said I got to turn it on when I go to sleep. I said your kidding why shud I turn it on when Im going to sleep. Who ever herd of a thing like that. But he said if I want to get smart I got to do what he says. I told him I dint think I was going to get smart and he puts his hand on my sholder and said Charlie you dont know it yet but your getting smarter all the time. You wont notice for a while. I think he was just being nice to make me feel good because I dont look any smarter.

Oh yes I almost forgot. I asked him when I can go back to the class at Miss Kinnians school. He said I wont go their. He said that soon Miss Kinnian will come to the hospitil to start and teach me speshul.

Mar 29 That crazy TV kept up all night. How can I sleep with something yelling crazy things all night in my ears. And the nutty pictures. Wow. I don't know what it says when Im up so how am I going to know when Im sleeping.

Dr Strauss says its ok. He says my brains are lerning when I sleep and that will help me when Miss Kinnian starts my lessons in the hospitl (only I found out it isn't a hospitil its a labatory.) I think its all crazy. If you can get smart when your sleeping why do people go to school. That thing I don't think will work. I use to watch the late show and the late late show on TV all the time and it never made me smart. Maybe you have to sleep while you watch it.

progress report 9—April 3

Dr Strauss showed me how to keep the TV turned low so now I can sleep. I don't hear a thing. And I still dont understand what it says. A few times I play it over in the morning to find out what I lerned when I was sleeping and I don't think so. Miss Kinnian says Maybe its another langwidge. But most times it sounds american. It talks faster than even Miss Gold who was my teacher in 6 grade.

I told Dr. Strauss what good is it to get smart in my sleep. I want to be smart when Im awake. He says its the same thing and I have two minds. Theres the *subconscious* and the *conscious* (thats how you spell it). And one dont tell the other one what its doing. They dont even talk to each other. Thats why I dream. And boy have I been having crazy dreams. Wow. Ever since that night TV. The late late late show. I forgot to ask him if it was only me or if everybody had those two minds.

(I just looked up the word in the dictionary Dr. Strauss gave me. The word is *subconscious. adj. Of the nature of mental operations not yet present in consciousness; as, subconscious conflict of desires.*) There's more but I still dont know what it means. This isnt a very good dictionary for dumb people like me.

Anyway the headache is from the party. My friends from the factery Joe Carp and Frank Reilly invited me to go to Muggsys Saloon for some drinks. I don't like to drink but they said we will have lots of fun. I had a good time.

Joe Carp said I shoud show the girls how I mop out the toilet in the factory and he got me a mop. I showed them and everyone laffed when I told that Mr. Donnegan said I was the best janiter he ever had because I like my job and do it good and never miss a day except for my operashun.

I said Miss Kinnian always said Charlie be proud of your job because you do it good.

Everybody laffed and we had a good time and they gave me lots of drinks and Joe said Charlie is a card when hes potted. I dont know what that means but everybody likes me and we have fun. I cant wait to be smart like my best friends Joe Carp and Frank Reilly.

I dont remember how the party was over but I think I went out to buy a newspaper and coffe for Joe and Frank and when I came back there was no one their. I looked for them all over till late. Then I dont remember so good but I think I got sleepy or sick. A nice cop brot me back home Thats what my landlady Mrs Flynn says.

But I got a headache and a big lump on my head. I think maybe I fell but Joe Carp says it was the cop they beat up drunks some times. I don't think so. Miss Kinnian says cops are to help people. Anyway I got a bad headache and Im sick and hurt all over. I dont think Ill drink anymore.

April 6 I beat Algernon! I dint even know I beat him until Burt the tester told me. Then the second time I lost because I got so exited I fell off the chair before I finished. But after that I beat him 8 more times. I must be getting smart to beat a smart mouse like Algernon. But I don't *feel* smarter.

I wanted to race Algernon some more but Burt said thats enough for one day. They let me hold him for a minit. Hes not so bad. Hes soft like a ball of cotton. He blinks and when he opens his eyes their black and pink on the eges.

I said can I feed him because I felt bad to beat him and I wanted to be nice and make friends. Burt said no Algernon is a very specshul mouse with an operashun like mine, and he was the first of all the animals to stay smart so long. He told me Algernon is so smart that every day he has to solve a test to get his food. Its a thing like a lock on a door that changes every time Algernon goes in to eat so he has to lern something new to get his food. That made me sad because if he couldn't lern he would be hungry.

I don't think its right to make you pass a test to eat. How would Dr Nemur like it to have to pass a test every time he wants to eat. I think Ill be friends with Algernon.

April 9 Tonight after work Miss Kinnian was at the laboratory. She looked like she was glad to see me but scared. I told her dont worry Miss Kinnian Im not smart yet and she laffed. She said I have confidence in you Charlie the way you struggled so hard to read and right better than all the others. At werst you will have it for a littel wile and your doing somthing for science.

We are reading a very hard book. Its called *Robinson Crusoe* about a man who gets merooned on a dessert Iland. Hes smart and figers out all kinds of things so he can have a house and food and hes a good swimmer. Only I feel sorry because hes all alone and has no frends. But I think their must be somebody else on the iland because theres a picture with his funny umbrella looking at footprints. I hope he gets a frend and not be lonly.

April 10 Miss Kinnian teaches me to spell better. She says look at a word and close your eyes and say it over and over until you remember. I have lots of truble with *through* that you say *threw* and *enough* and *tough* that you dont say *enew* and *tew*. You got to say *enuff* and *tuff*. Thats how I use to write it before I started to get smart. Im confused but Miss Kinnian says theres no reason in spelling.

Apr 14 Finished *Robinson Crusoe*. I want to find out more about what happens to him but Miss Kinnian says thats all there is. *Why.*

Apr 15 Miss Kinnian says Im lerning fast. She read some of the Progress Reports and she looked at me kind of funny. She says Im a fine person and Ill show them all. I asked her why. She said never mind but I shouldnt feel bad if I find out everybody isnt nice like I think. She said for a person who god gave so little to you done more then a lot of people with brains they never even used. I said all my friends are smart people but there good. They like me and they never did anything that wasnt nice. Then she got something in her eye and she had to run out to the ladys room.

Apr 16 Today, I lerned, the *comma,* this is a comma (,) a period, with a tail, Miss Kinnian, says its important, because, it makes writing, better, she said, somebody, coud lose, a lot of money, if a comma, isnt, in the, right place, I dont have, any money, and I dont see, how a comma, keeps you, from losing it,

Apr 17 I used the comma wrong. Its punctuation. Miss Kinnian told me to look up long words in the dictionary to lern to spell them. I said whats the difference if you can read it anyway. She said its part of your education so now on Ill look up all the words Im not sure how to spell. It takes a long time to write that way but I only have to look up once and after that I get it right.

You got to mix them up, she showed? me'' how. to mix! them (and now; I can! mix up all kinds'' of punctuation, in! my writing? There, are lots! of rules? to lern; but Im gettin'g them in my head.

One thing I like about, Dear Miss Kinnian: (thats the way it goes in a business letter if I ever go into business) is she, always gives me' a reason'' when—I ask. She's a gen'ius! I wish I cou'd be smart'' like, her;

(Puncuation, is; fun!)

April 18 What a dope I am! I didn't even understand what she was talking about. I read the grammar book last night and it explanes the whole thing. Then I saw it was the same way as Miss Kinnian was trying to tell me, but I didn't get it.

Miss Kinnian said that the TV working in my sleep helped out. She and I reached a plateau. Thats a flat hill.

After I figured out how punctuation worked, I read over all my old Progress Reports from the beginning. Boy, did I have crazy spelling and punctuation! I told Miss Kinnian I ought to go over the pages and fix all the mistakes but she said, "No, Charlie, Dr. Nemur wants them just as they are. That's why he let you keep them after they were photostated, to see your own progress. You're coming along fast, Charlie."

That made me feel good. After the lesson I went down and played with Algernon. We don't race any more.

April 20 I feel sick inside. Not sick like for a doctor, but inside my chest it feels empty like getting punched and a heartburn at the same time. I wasn't going to write about it, but I guess I got to, because its important. Today was the first time I ever stayed home from work.

Last night Joe Carp and Frank Reilly invited me to a party. There were lots of girls and some men from the factory. I remembered how sick I got last time I drank too much, so I told Joe I didn't want anything to drink. He gave me a plain coke instead.

We had a lot of fun for a while. Joe said I should dance with Ellen and she would teach me the steps. I fell a few times and I couldn't understand why because no one else was dancing besides Ellen and me. And all the time I was tripping because somebody's foot was always sticking out.

Then when I got up I saw the look on Joe's face and it gave me a funny feeling in my stomach. "He's a scream," one of the girls said. Everybody was laughing.

"Look at him. He's blushing. Charlie is blushing."

"Hey, Ellen, what'd you do to Charlie? I never saw him act like that before."

I didn't know what to do or where to turn. Everyone was looking at me and laughing and I felt naked. I wanted to hide. I ran outside and I threw up. Then I walked home. It's a funny thing I never knew that Joe and Frank and the others liked to have me around all the time to make fun of me.

Now I know what it means when they say "to pull a Charlie Gordon."

I'm ashamed.

progress report 11

April 21 Still didn't go into the factory. I told Mrs. Flynn my landlady to call and tell Mr. Donnegan I was sick. Mrs. Flynn looks at me very funny lately like she's scared.

I think it's a good thing about finding out how everybody laughs at me. I thought about it a lot. It's because I'm so dumb and I don't even know when I'm doing something dumb. People think it's funny when a dumb person can't do things the same way they can.

Anyway, now I know I'm getting smarter every day. I know punctuation and I can spell good. I like to look up all the hard words in the dictionary and I remember them. I'm reading a lot now, and Miss Kinnian says I read very fast. Sometimes I even understand what I'm reading about, and it stays in my mind. There are times when I can close my eyes and think of a page and it all comes back like a picture.

Besides history, geography, and arithmetic, Miss Kinnian said I should start to learn foreign languages. Dr. Strauss gave me some more tapes to play while I sleep. I still don't understand how that conscious and unconscious mind works, but Dr. Strauss says not to worry yet. He asked me to promise that when I start learning college subjects next week I wouldn't read any books on psychology—that is, until he gives me permission.

I feel a lot better today, but I guess I'm still a little angry that all the time people were laughing and making fun of me because I wasn't so smart. When I become intelligent like Dr. Strauss says, with three times my I.Q. of 68, then maybe I'll be like everyone else and people will like me.

I'm not sure what an I.Q. is. Dr. Nemur said it was something that measured how intelligent you were—like a scale in the drugstore weighs pounds. But Dr. Strauss had a big argument with him and said an I.Q. didn't weigh intelligence at all. He said an I.Q. showed how much intelligence you could get, like the numbers on the outside of a measuring cup. You still had to fill the cup up with stuff.

Then when I asked Burt, who gives me my intelligence tests and works with Algernon, he said that both of them were wrong (only I had to promise not to tell them he said so). Burt says that the I.Q. measures a lot of different things including some of the things you learned already, and it really isn't any good at all.

So I still don't know what I.Q. is except that mine is going to be over 200 soon. I didn't want to say anything, but I don't see how if they don't know *what* it is, or *where* it is—I don't see how they know *how much* of it you've got.

Dr. Nemur says I have to take a *Rorschach Test* tomorrow. I wonder what *that* is.

April 22 I found out what a Rorschach is. It's the test I took before the operation—the one with the inkblots on the pieces of cardboard.

I was scared to death of those inkblots. I knew the man was going to ask me to find the pictures and I knew I couldn't. I was thinking to myself, if only there was some way of knowing what kind of pictures were hidden there. Maybe there weren't any pictures at all. Maybe it was just a trick to see if I was dumb enough to look for something that wasn't there. Just thinking about that made me sore at him.

"All right, Charlie," he said, "you've seen these cards before, remember?"

"Of course I remember."

The way I said it, he knew I was angry, and he looked surprised. "Yes, of course. Now I want you to look at this. What might this be? What do you see on this card? People see all sorts of things in these inkblots. Tell me what it might be for you—what it makes you think of."

I was shocked. That wasn't what I had expected him to say. "You mean there are no pictures hidden in those inkblots?"

He frowned and took off his glasses. "What?"

"Pictures. Hidden in the inkblots. Last time you told me everyone could see them and you wanted me to find them too."

He explained to me that the last time he had used almost the exact same words he was using now. I didn't believe it, and I still have the suspicion that he misled me at the time just for the fun of it. Unless—I don't know any more—could I have been *that* feeble-minded?

We went through the cards slowly. One looked like a pair of bats tugging at something. Another one looked like two men fencing with swords. I imagined all sorts of things. I guess I got carried away. But I didn't trust him any more, and I kept turning them around, even looking on the back to see if there was anything there I was supposed to catch. While he was making his notes, I peeked out of the corner of my eye to read it. But it was all in code that looked like this:

$$WF + A \quad DdF - Ad \text{ orig.} \quad WF - A$$
$$SF + obj$$

The test still doesn't make sense to me. It seems to me that anyone could make up lies about things that they didn't really imagine? Maybe I'll understand it when Dr. Strauss lets me read up on psychology.

April 25 I figured out a new way to line up the machines in the factory, and Mr. Donnegan says it will save him ten thousand dollars a year in labor and increased production. He gave me a $25 bonus.

I wanted to take Joe Carp and Frank Reilly out to lunch to celebrate, but Joe said he had to buy some things for his wife, and Frank said he was meeting his cousin for lunch. I guess it'll take a little time for them to get used to the changes in me. Everybody seems to be frightened of me. When I went over to Amos Borg and tapped him, he jumped up in the air.

People don't talk to me much any more

or kid around the way they used to. It makes the job kind of lonely.

April 27 I got up the nerve today to ask Miss Kinnian to have dinner with me tomorrow night to celebrate my bonus.

At first she wasn't sure it was right, but I asked Dr. Strauss and he said it was okay. Dr. Strauss and Dr. Nemur don't seem to be getting along so well. They're arguing all the time. This evening I heard them shouting. Dr. Nemur was saying that it was *his* experiment and *his* research, and Dr. Strauss shouted back that he contributed just as much, because he found me through Miss Kinnian and he performed the operation. Dr. Strauss said that someday thousands of neurosurgeons might be using his technique all over the world.

Dr. Nemur wanted to publish the results of the experiment at the end of this month. Dr. Strauss wanted to wait a while to be sure. Dr. Strauss said Dr. Nemur was more interested in the Chair of Psychology at Princeton[5] than he was in the experiment. Dr. Nemur said Dr. Strauss was nothing but an opportunist trying to ride to glory on *his* coattails.

When I left afterwards, I found myself trembling. I don't know why for sure, but it was as if I'd seen both men clearly for the first time. I remember hearing Burt say Dr. Nemur had a shrew of a wife who was pushing him all the time to get things published so he could become famous. Burt said that the dream of her life was to have a big-shot husband.

April 28 I don't understand why I never noticed how beautiful Miss Kinnian really is. She has brown eyes and feathery brown hair that comes to the top of her neck. She's only thirty-four! I think from the be-

ginning I had the feeling that she was an unreachable genius—and very, very old. Now, every time I see her she grows younger and more lovely.

We had dinner and a long talk. When she said I was coming along so fast I'd be leaving her behind, I laughed.

"It's true, Charlie. You're already a better reader than I am. You can read a whole page at a glance while I can take in only a few lines at a time. And you remember every single thing you read. I'm lucky if I can recall the main thoughts and the general meaning."

"I don't feel intelligent. There are so many things I don't understand."

She took out a cigarette and I lit it for her. "You've got to be a *little* patient. You're accomplishing in days and weeks what it takes normal people to do in a lifetime. That's what makes it so amazing. You're like a giant sponge now, soaking things in. Facts, figures, general knowledge. And soon you'll begin to connect them, too. You'll see how different branches of learning are related. There are many levels, Charlie, like steps on a giant ladder that take you up higher and higher to see more and more of the world around you.

"I can see only a little bit of that, Charlie, and I won't go much higher than I am now, but you'll keep climbing up and up, and see more and more, and each step will open new worlds that you never even knew existed." She frowned. "I hope . . . I just hope——"

"What?"

"Never mind, Charles. I just hope I wasn't wrong to advise you to go into this in the first place."

---

5. *Chair of Psychology at Princeton,* an appointment as professor of psychology at Princeton University.

I laughed. "How could that be? It worked, didn't it? Even Algernon is still smart."

We sat there silently for a while and I knew what she was thinking about as she watched me toying with the chain of my rabbit's foot and my keys. I didn't want to think of that possibility any more than elderly people want to think of death. I *knew* that this was only the beginning. I knew what she meant about levels because I'd seen some of them already. The thought of leaving her behind made me sad.

I'm in love with Miss Kinnian.

progress report 12

April 30 I've quit my job with Donnegan's Plastic Box Company. Mr. Donnegan insisted it would be better for all concerned if I left. What did I do to make them hate me so?

The first I knew of it was when Mr. Donnegan showed me the petition. Eight hundred names, everyone in the factory, except Fanny Girden. Scanning the list quickly, I saw at once that hers was the only missing name. All the rest demanded that I be fired.

Joe Carp and Frank Reilly wouldn't talk to me about it. No one else would either, except Fanny. She was one of the few people I'd known who set her mind to something and believed it no matter what the rest of the world proved, said or did—and Fanny did not believe that I should have been fired. She had been against the petition on principle and despite the pressure and threats she'd held out.

"Which don't mean to say," she remarked, "that I don't think there's something mighty strange about you, Charlie. Them changes. I don't know. You used to be a good, dependable, ordinary man—not too bright maybe, but honest. Who knows what you done to yourself to get so smart all of a sudden. Like everybody around here's been saying, Charlie, it's not right."

"But how can you say that, Fanny? What's wrong with a man becoming intelligent and wanting to acquire knowledge and understanding of the world around him?"

She stared down at her work and I turned to leave. Without looking at me, she said: "It was evil when Eve listened to the snake and ate from the tree of knowledge. It was evil when she saw that she was naked. If not for that none of us would ever have to grow old and sick, and die."[6]

Once again, now, I have the feeling of shame burning inside me. This intelligence has driven a wedge between me and all the people I once knew and loved. Before, they laughed at me and despised me for my ignorance and dullness; now, they hate me for my knowledge and understanding. What do they want of me?

They've driven me out of the factory. Now I'm more alone than ever before. . . .

May 15 Dr. Strauss is very angry at me for not having written any progress reports in two weeks. He's justified because the lab is now paying me a regular salary. I told him I was too busy thinking and reading. When I pointed out that writing was such a slow process that it made me impatient with my poor handwriting, he suggested I learn to type. It's much easier to write now because I can type seventy-five words a minute. Dr. Strauss continually reminds me of the need to speak and write simply so people will be able to understand me.

---

6. *"It was evil . . . die."* Fanny is referring to the biblical story of the fall of Adam and Eve and their expulsion by God from the Garden of Eden. [Genesis 2]

I'll try to review all the things that happened to me during the last two weeks. Algernon and I were presented to the *American Psychological Association* sitting in convention with the *World Psychological Association*. We created quite a sensation. Dr. Nemur and Dr. Strauss were proud of us.

I suspect that Dr. Nemur, who is sixty—ten years older than Dr. Strauss—finds it necessary to see tangible results of his work. Undoubtedly the result of pressure by Mrs. Nemur.

Contrary to my earlier impressions of him, I realize that Dr. Nemur is not at all a genius. He has a very good mind, but it struggles under the spectre of self-doubt. He wants people to take him for a genius. Therefore it is important for him to feel that his work is accepted by the world. I believe that Dr. Nemur was afraid of further delay because he worried that someone else might make a discovery along these lines and take the credit from him.

Dr. Strauss on the other hand might be called a genius, although I feel his areas of knowledge are too limited. He was educated in the tradition of narrow specialization; the broader aspects of background were neglected far more than necessary—even for a neurosurgeon.

I was shocked to learn the only ancient languages he could read were Latin, Greek, and Hebrew, and that he knows almost nothing of mathematics beyond the elementary levels of the calculus of variations. When he admitted this to me, I found myself almost annoyed. It was as if he'd hidden this part of himself in order to deceive me, pretending—as do many people I've discovered—to be what he is not. No one I've ever known is what he appears to be on the surface.

Dr. Nemur appears to be uncomfortable around me. Sometimes when I try to talk to him, he just looks at me strangely and turns away. I was angry at first when Dr. Strauss told me I was giving Dr. Nemur an inferiority complex. I thought he was mocking me and I'm oversensitive at being made fun of.

How was I to know that a highly respected psycho-experimentalist like Nemur was unacquainted with Hindustani and Chinese? It's absurd when you consider the work that is being done in India and China today in the very field of his study.

I asked Dr. Strauss how Nemur could refute Rahajamati's attacks on his method if Nemur couldn't even read them in the first place. That strange look on Strauss's face can mean only one of two things. Either he doesn't want to tell Nemur what they're saying in India, or else—and this worries me—Dr. Strauss doesn't know either. I must be careful to speak and write clearly and simply so people won't laugh.

May 18 I am very disturbed. I saw Miss Kinnian last night for the first time in over a week. I tried to avoid all discussions of intellectual concepts and to keep the conversation on a simple, everyday level, but she just stared at me blankly and asked me what I meant about the mathematical variance equivalent in Dorbermann's *Fifth Concerto*.

When I tried to explain she stopped me and laughed. I guess I got angry, but I suspect I'm approaching her on the wrong level. No matter what I try to discuss with her, I am unable to communicate. I must review Vrostadt's equations on *Levels of Semantic Progression*. I find I don't communicate with people much any more. Thank God for books and music and things

I can think about. I am alone at Mrs. Flynn's boarding house most of the time and seldom speak to anyone.

May 20 I would not have noticed the new dishwasher, a boy of about sixteen, at the corner diner where I take my evening meals if not for the incident of the broken dishes.

They crashed to the floor, sending bits of white china under the tables. The boy stood there, dazed and frightened, holding the empty tray in his hand. The catcalls from the customers (the cries of "hey, there go the profits!" . . . "*Mazeltov!*"[7] . . . and "well, *he* didn't work here very long . . ." which invariably seem to follow the breaking of glass or dishware in a public restaurant) all seemed to confuse him.

When the owner came to see what the excitement was about, the boy cowered as if he expected to be struck. "All right! All right, you dope," shouted the owner, "don't just stand there! Get the broom and sweep that mess up. A broom . . . a broom, you idiot! It's in the kitchen!"

The boy saw he was not going to be punished. His frightened expression disappeared and he smiled as he came back with the broom to sweep the floor. A few of the rowdier customers kept up the remarks, amusing themselves at his expense.

"Here, sonny, over here there's a nice piece behind you . . ."

"He's not so dumb. It's easier to break 'em than wash 'em!"

As his vacant eyes moved across the crowd of onlookers, he slowly mirrored their smiles and finally broke into an uncertain grin at the joke he obviously did not understand.

I felt sick inside as I looked at his dull, vacuous smile, the wide, bright eyes of a child, uncertain but eager to please. They were laughing at him because he was mentally retarded.

And I had been laughing at him too.

Suddenly I was furious at myself and all those who were smirking at him. I jumped up and shouted, "Shut up! Leave him alone! It's not his fault he can't understand! He can't help what he is! But he's still a human being!"

The room grew silent. I cursed myself for losing control. I tried not to look at the boy as I walked out without touching my food. I felt ashamed for both of us.

How strange that people of honest feelings and sensibility, who would not take advantage of a man born without arms or eyes—how such people think nothing of abusing a man born with low intelligence. It infuriated me to think that not too long ago I had foolishly played the clown.

And I had almost forgotten.

I'd hidden the picture of the old Charlie Gordon from myself because now that I was intelligent it was something that had to be pushed out of my mind. But today in looking at that boy, for the first time I saw what I had been. *I was just like him!*

Only a short time ago, I learned that people laughed at me. Now I can see that unknowingly I joined with them in laughing at myself. That hurts most of all.

I have often reread my progress reports and seen the illiteracy, the childish naïveté, the mind of low intelligence peering from a dark room through the keyhole at the dazzling light outside. I see that even in my dullness I knew I was inferior, and that other people had something I lacked—something denied me. In my mental blindness, I thought it was somehow connected

---

7. *Mazeltov!*, a Yiddish expression meaning, in this case, "May you have better luck in the future."

with the ability to read and write, and I was sure that if I could get those skills I would automatically have intelligence too.

Even a feeble-minded man wants to be like other men.

A child may not know how to feed itself, or what to eat, yet it knows of hunger.

This then is what I was like. I never knew. Even with my gift of intellectual awareness, I never really knew.

This day was good for me. Seeing the past more clearly, I've decided to use my knowledge and skills to work in the field of increasing human intelligence levels. Who is better equipped for this work? Who else has lived in both worlds? These are my people. Let me use my gift to do something for them.

Tomorrow, I will discuss with Dr. Strauss how I can work in this area. I may be able to help him work out the problems of widespread use of the technique which was used on me. I have several good ideas of my own.

There is so much that might be done with this technique. If I could be made into a genius, what about thousands of others like myself? What fantastic levels might be achieved by using this technique on normal people? On *geniuses?*

There are so many doors to open. I am impatient to begin.

progress report 13

May 23 It happened today. Algernon bit me. I visited the lab to see him as I do occasionally, and when I took him out of his cage, he snapped at my hand. I put him back and watched him for a while. He was unusually disturbed and vicious.

May 24 Burt, who is in charge of the experimental animals, tells me that Algernon

is changing. He is less cooperative; he refuses to run the maze any more; general motivation has decreased. And he hasn't been eating. Everyone is upset about what this may mean.

May 25 They've been feeding Algernon, who now refuses to work the shifting-lock problem. Everyone identifies me with Algernon. In a way we're both the first of our kind. They're all pretending that Algernon's behavior is not necessarily significant for me. But it's hard to hide the fact that some of the other animals who were used in this experiment are showing strange behavior.

Dr. Strauss and Dr. Nemur have asked me not to come to the lab any more. I know what they're thinking but I can't accept it. I am going ahead with my plans to carry their research forward. With all due respect to both these fine scientists, I am well aware of their limitations. If there is an answer, I'll have to find it out for myself. Suddenly, time has become very important to me.

May 29 I have been given a lab of my own and permission to go ahead with the research. I'm on to something. Working day and night. I've had a cot moved into the lab. Most of my writing time is spent on the notes which I keep in a separate folder, but from time to time I feel it necessary to put down my moods and thoughts from sheer habit.

I find the *calculus of intelligence* to be a fascinating study. Here is the place for the application of all the knowledge I have acquired.

May 31 Dr. Strauss thinks I'm working too hard. Dr. Nemur says I'm trying to cram a lifetime of research and thought into a few weeks. I know I should rest, but I'm driven on by something inside that won't let me stop. I've got to find the reason for the sharp regression in Algernon. I've got to know *if* and *when* it will happen to me.

June 4

LETTER TO DR. STRAUSS *(copy)*

Dear Dr. Strauss:

Under separate cover I am sending you a copy of my report entitled, "The Algernon-Gordon Effect: A Study of Structure and Function of Increased Intelligence," which I would like to have published.

As you see, my experiments are completed. I have included in my report all of my formulae, as well as mathematical analysis in the appendix. Of course, these should be verified.

Because of its importance to both you and Dr. Nemur (and need I say to myself, too?) I have checked and rechecked my results a dozen times in the hope of finding an error. I am sorry to say the results must stand. Yet for the sake of science, I am grateful for the little bit that I here add to the knowledge of the function of the human mind and of the laws governing the artificial increase of human intelligence.

I recall your once saying to me that an experimental *failure* or the *disproving* of a theory was as important to the advancement of learning as a success would be. I know now that this is true. I am sorry, however, that my own contribution to the field must rest upon the ashes of the work of two men I regard so highly.

Yours truly,
Charles Gordon

June 5 I must not become emotional. The facts and the results of my experiments are clear, and the more sensational aspects of my own rapid climb cannot obscure the fact that the tripling of intelligence by the surgical technique developed by Drs. Strauss and Nemur must be viewed as having little or no practical applicability (at the present time) to the increase of human intelligence.

As I review the records and data on Algernon, I see that although he is still in his physical infancy, he has regressed mentally. Motor activity is impaired; there is a general reduction of glandular activity; there is an accelerated loss of coordination.

There are also strong indications of progressive amnesia.

As will be seen by my report, these and other physical and mental deterioration syndromes can be predicted with significant results by the application of my formula.

The surgical stimulus to which we were both subjected has resulted in an intensification and acceleration of all mental processes. The unforeseen development, which I have taken the liberty of calling the *Algernon-Gordon Effect,* is the logical extension of the entire intelligence speed-up. The hypothesis here proven may be described simply in the following terms: Artificially increased intelligence deteriorates at a rate of time directly proportional to the quantity of the increase.

I feel that this, in itself, is an important discovery.

As long as I am able to write, I will continue to record my thoughts in these progress reports. It is one of my few pleasures. However, by all indications, my own mental deterioration will be very rapid.

I have already begun to notice signs of emotional instability and forgetfulness, the first symptoms of the burnout.

June 10 Deterioration progressing. I have

become absent-minded. Algernon died two days ago. Dissection shows my predictions were right. His brain had decreased in weight and there was a general smoothing out of cerebral convolutions, as well as a deepening and broadening of brain fissures.[8]

I guess the same thing is or will soon be happening to me. Now that it's definite, I don't want it to happen.

I put Algernon's body in a cheese box and buried him in the back yard. I cried.

June 15 Dr. Strauss came to see me again. I wouldn't open the door and I told him to go away. I want to be left to myself. I am touchy and irritable. I feel the darkness closing in. It's hard to throw off thoughts of suicide. I keep telling myself how important this journal will be.

It's a strange sensation to pick up a book you enjoyed just a few months ago and discover you don't remember it. I remembered how great I thought John Milton was, but when I picked up *Paradise Lost* I couldn't understand it at all. I got so angry I threw the book across the room.

I've got to try to hold on to some of it. Some of the things I've learned. Oh, God, please don't take it all away.

June 19 Sometimes, at night, I go out for a walk. Last night, I couldn't remember where I lived. A policeman took me home. I have the strange feeling that this has all happened to me before—a long time ago. I keep telling myself I'm the only person in the world who can describe what's happening to me.

June 21 Why can't I remember? I've got to fight. I lie in bed for days and I don't know who or where I am. Then it all comes back to me in a flash. Fugues of amnesia.

Symptoms of senility—second childhood. I can watch them coming on. It's so cruelly logical. I learned so much and so fast. Now my mind is deteriorating rapidly. I won't let it happen. I'll fight it. I can't help thinking of the boy in the restaurant, the blank expression, the silly smile, the people laughing at him. No—please—not that again. . . .

June 22 I'm forgetting things that I learned recently. It seems to be following the classic pattern—the last things learned are the first things forgotten. Or is that the pattern? I'd better look it up again. . . .

I reread my paper on the *Algernon-Gordon Effect* and I get the strange feeling that it was written by someone else. There are parts I don't even understand.

Motor activity impaired. I keep tripping over things, and it becomes increasingly difficult to type.

June 23 I've given up using the typewriter. My coordination is bad. I feel I'm moving slower and slower. Had a terrible shock today. I picked up a copy of an article I used in my research, Krueger's *Uber psychische Ganzheit,* to see if it would help me understand what I had done. First I thought there was something wrong with my eyes. Then I realized I could no longer read German. I tested myself in other languages. All gone.

June 30 A week since I dared to write again. It's slipping away like sand through my fingers. Most of the books I have are too hard for me now. I get angry with them

---

8. *His brain . . . fissures.* There seems to be a direct relationship between intelligence and brain size, and between intelligence and the number of cerebral convolutions (folds or ridges on the surface of the brain).

because I know that I read and understood them just a few weeks ago.

I keep telling myself I must keep writing these reports so that somebody will know what is happening to me. But it gets harder to form the words and remember spellings. I have to look up even simple words in the dictionary now and it makes me impatient with myself.

Dr. Strauss comes around almost every day, but I told him I wouldn't see or speak to anybody. He feels guilty. They all do. But I don't blame anyone. I knew what might happen. But how it hurts.

July 7 I don't know where the week went. Todays Sunday I know because I can see through my window people going to church. I think I stayed in bed all week but I remember Mrs. Flynn bringing food to me a few times. I keep saying over and over I've got to do something but then I forget or maybe its just easier not to do what I say I'm going to do.

I think of my mother and father a lot these days. I found a picture of them with me taken at a beach. My father has a big ball under his arm and my mother is holding me by the hand. I dont remember them the way they are in the picture. All I remember is my father drunk most of the time and arguing with mom about money.

He never shaved much and he used to scratch my face when he hugged me. My Mother said he died but Cousin Miltie said he heard his dad say that my father ran away with another woman. When I asked my mother she slapped me and said my father was dead. I dont think I ever found out the truth but I dont care much. (He said he was going to take me to see cows on a farm once but he never did. He never kept his promises. . . .)

July 10 My landlady Mrs. Flynn is very worried about me. She says the way I lay around all day and dont do anything I remind her of her son before she threw him out of the house. She said she doesn't like loafers. If Im sick its one thing, but if Im a loafer thats another thing and she won't have it. I told her I think Im sick.

I try to read a little bit every day, mostly stories, but sometimes I have to read the same thing over and over again because I don't know what it means. And its hard to write. I know I should look up all the words in the dictionary but its so hard and Im so tired all the time.

Then I got the idea that I would only use the easy words instead of the long hard ones. That saves time. I put flowers on Algernons grave about once a week. Mrs. Flynn thinks Im crazy to put flowers on a mouses grave but I told her that Algernon was special.

July 14 Its sunday again. I dont have anything to do to keep me busy now because my television set is broke and I dont have any money to get it fixed. (I think I lost this months check from the lab. I don't remember)

I get awful headaches and asperin doesnt help me much. Mrs. Flynn knows Im really sick and she feels very sorry for me. Shes a wonderful woman whenever someone is sick.

July 22 Mrs. Flynn called a strange doctor to see me. She was afraid I was going to die. I told the doctor I wasnt too sick and I only forget sometimes. He asked me did I have any friends or relatives and I said no I dont have any. I told him I had a friend called Algernon once but he was a mouse and we used to run races together. He looked at me kind of funny like he thought I was crazy. He smiled when I told him I used to be a genius. He talked to me like I was a baby and he winked at Mrs. Flynn. I got mad and chased him out because he was making fun of me the way they all used to.

July 24 I have no more money and Mrs. Flynn says I got to go to work somewhere and pay the rent because I havent paid for two months. I dont know any work but the job I used to have at Donnegans Box Company. I dont want to go back because they all knew me when I was smart and maybe they'll laugh at me. But I dont know what else to do to get money.

July 25 I was looking at some of my old progress reports and its very funny but I cant read what I wrote. I can make out some of the words but they dont make sense.

Miss Kinnian came to the door but I said go away I don't want to see you. She cried and I cried too but I wouldnt let her in because I didn't want her to laugh at me. I told her I didnt like her any more. I told her I didnt want to be smart any more. That's not true. I still love her and I still want to be smart but I had to say that so shed go away. She gave Mrs. Flynn money to pay the rent. I dont want that. I got to get a job.

Please . . . please let me not forget how to read and write. . . .

July 27 Mr. Donnegan was very nice when I came back and asked him for my old job of janitor. First he was very suspicious but I told him what happened to me and he looked very sad and put his hand on my shoulder and said Charlie Gordon you got guts.

Everybody looked at me when I came downstairs and started working in the toilet sweeping it out like I used to. I told myself Charlie if they make fun of you dont get sore because you remember their not so smart as you once thot they were. And besides they were once your friends and if they laughted at you that doesnt meant anything because they liked you too.

One of the new men who came to work there after I went away made a nasty crack he said hey Charlie I hear your a very smart fella a real quiz kid. Say something intelligent. I felt bad but Joe Carp came over and grabbed him by the shirt and said leave him alone you lousy cracker or I'll break your neck. I didnt expect Joe to take my part so I guess hes really my friend.

Later Frank Reilly came over and said Charlie if anybody bothers you or trys to take advantage you call me or Joe and we will set em straight. I said thanks Frank and I got choked up so I had to turn around and go into the supply room so he wouldnt see me cry. Its good to have friends.

July 28 I did a dumb thing today I forgot I wasn't in Miss Kinnians class at the adult center any more like I use to be. I went in and sat down in my old seat in the back of the room and she looked at me funny and she said Charles. I dint remember she ever called me that before only Charlie so I said hello Miss Kinnian Im redy for my lesin today only I lost my reader that we was using. She startid to cry and run out of the room and everybody looked at me and I saw they wasnt the same pepul who use to be in my class.

Then all of a suddin I remembered some things about the operashun and me getting smart and I said holy smoke I reely pulled a Charlie Gordon that time. I went away before she come back to the room.

Thats why Im going away from New York for good. I dont want to do nothing like that agen. I dont want Miss Kinnian to feel sorry for me. Evry body feels sorry at the factery and I dont want that eather so Im going someplace where nobody knows that Charlie Gordon was once a genus and now he cant even reed a book or rite good.

Im taking a cuple of books along and even if I cant reed them Ill practise hard and maybe I wont forget every thing I lerned. If I try reel hard maybe Ill be a littel bit smarter then I was before the operashun. I got my rabits foot and my luky penny and maybe they will help me.

If you ever reed this Miss Kinnian dont be sorry for me Im glad I got a second chanse to be smart becaus I lerned a lot of things that I never even new were in this world and Im grateful that I saw it all for a littel bit. I dont know why Im dumb agen or what I did wrong maybe its because I dint try hard enuff. But if I try and practis very hard maybe Ill get a littl smarter and know what all the words are. I remember a littel bit how nice I had a feeling with the blue book that has the torn cover when I red it. Thats why Im gonna keep trying to get smart so I can have that feeling agen. Its a good feeling to know things and be smart. I wish I had it rite now if I did I would sit down and reed all the time. Anyway I bet Im the first dumb person in the world who ever found out somthing important for science. I remember I did somthing but I dont remember what. So I gess its like I did it for all the dumb pepul like me.

Goodbye Miss Kinnian and Dr. Strauss and evreybody. And P.S. please tell Dr Nemur not to be such a grouch when pepul laff at him and he would have more frends. Its easy to make frends if you let pepul laff at you. Im going to have lots of frends where I go.

P.P.S. Please if you get a chanse put some flowrs on Algernons grave in the bak yard. . . .

Discussion

1. (a) How does Charlie come to be considered for the operation? (b) What qualities, apart from low intelligence, are reasons for his being chosen?

2. (a) What is Charlie's attitude toward Algernon at the start of their association? (b) How and why does this attitude change?

3. Miss Kinnian, Charlie's landlady, and the factory workers all have different attitudes toward Charlie at different times in the story. Explain how each feels about Charlie (a) before his operation; (b) as his intelligence increases; and (c) as his intelligence slips away.

4. As a result of his increased understanding, Charlie sees people in a new light. Explain the changes in Charlie's view of (a) Joe Carp and Frank Reilly; (b) Dr. Nemur and Dr. Strauss; and (c) Miss Kinnian.

5. (a) What is ironic about Charlie's laughter during the incident involving the dishwasher at the restaurant? (b) What does Charlie realize for the first time? (c) What goal does this realization give Charlie?

6. (a) What is the first indication of Algernon's deterioration? (b) In what ways does Algernon change mentally and physically? (c) How is Charlie's deterioration similar to Algernon's?

7. This story is written in the form of a journal kept by Charlie. What method or methods of characterization are emphasized by this technique of telling a story?

8. (a) To what event in the story does the title refer? (b) In light of Charlie's relation to Algernon, how might the title be symbolic?

9. What do you think is the theme of this story?

Vocabulary
Combining Forms

A *combining form* is a word part that combines with words or with other combining forms to make new words. The combining form *psycho-* comes from the Greek word *psychē,* meaning "mind." The Vocabulary word *psycho-experimentalist,* then, means "one who does experiments on the mind or about the mind." Another common combining form is *-logy,* meaning "science of," as in *volcanology,* "the science or study of volcanoes."

On a separate paper, write the words from Column A. After each word, write the correct definition from Column B.

Column A	Column B
psychoanalysis	mental therapy
psychology	analysis of the mind
psychohistory	science of the mind
psychotherapy	measurement of mental function
psychometrics	tal function
	history written from a psychological point of view

Composition

Imagine an event or experience that does not appear in this story that you, as Charlie Gordon, are going to write about in your journal. You are writing after the operation has taken place—either while you are gaining your new intelligence or while you are losing it. Some events you might write about as Charlie are: a conversation with a newspaper reporter who is interviewing you; the purchase of a book in a bookstore; an unexpected meeting with a former sixth-grade classmate; the purchase of a pet mouse to keep at home.

Write a one-page progress report as if you were Charlie Gordon at some point after your operation. After you have written your progress report, you might have classmates read it to see if they can discover at what point after the operation you are presenting Charlie's ideas and feelings.

(You may find the article "Being Someone Else" in the Composition Guide helpful in writing this composition.)

Daniel Keyes 1927–

Of "Flowers for Algernon" Daniel Keyes writes, "I recall clearly the brief note in my 'idea folder' something like: 'What would happen if a person's intelligence could be increased by surgery or something like that?' But that's all it was—an idea—until more than five years later a retarded boy said to me: 'Mr. Keyes, if I try hard and become smart will they put me into a regular class and let me be like everyone else?' The impact of those words stayed with me for a long time afterwards, until one day idea fused with character and I began to write 'Flowers for Algernon.'"

Since its first publication the short story has appeared in numerous books and magazines, has been translated into several languages, and has been adapted for television under the title "The Two Worlds of Charlie Gordon." The story won the Science Fiction Writers of America Hugo Award in 1959. In 1966 Keyes published a novel-length version of the story which won the Nebula Award, and in 1968 the movie version, *Charly,* was produced. In 1980, the musical play *Charlie and Algernon* was produced in New York City. Keyes currently teaches English at Ohio University, Athens.

Unit 6 Review: *O**ut of Control***

Content Review

1. Very often, stories of fantasy, science fiction, and the like are believable because they involve situations and characters that we encounter in real life. Of the selections in this unit, which is the most believable? the least believable? Give reasons for your answers.

2. **(a)** In your opinion, which stories in this unit do not have a theme? **(b)** For the stories you think do have a theme, state the theme briefly.

3. In which selections in this unit do you find irony? Is it verbal, situational, or dramatic irony in each case? Explain.

4. Consider the following statement: ''Good literature deals with real people and events. Literature that involves fantasy or the supernatural is just not worth reading.'' Do you agree? Why or why not? Which selection in this unit best proves your point? Explain.

Concept Review: Interpretation of New Material

Read carefully the poem below. Then use the questions that follow to review your understanding of the concepts and literary terms presented in this unit. Write your answers to the questions on a separate sheet of paper.

Metropolitan Nightmare • *Stephen Vincent Benét*

It rained quite a lot that spring. You woke in the morning
And saw the sky still clouded, the streets still wet,
But nobody noticed so much, except the taxis
And the people who parade. You don't, in a city.
5　The parks got very green. All the trees were green
Far into July and August, heavy with leaf,
Heavy with leaf and the long roots boring and spreading,
But nobody noticed that but the city gardeners
And they don't talk.

''Metropolitan Nightmare'' by Stephen Vincent Benét from *The Selected Works of Stephen Vincent Benét* (Holt, Rinehart and Winston, Inc.). Copyright 1933 by Stephen Vincent Benét. Copyright renewed © 1961 by Rosemary Carr Benét. Reprinted by permission of Brandt & Brandt Literary Agents, Inc.

Oh, on Sundays, perhaps you'd notice:
     Walking through certain blocks, by the shut, proud houses
     With the windows boarded, the people gone away,
     You'd suddenly see the queerest small shoots of green
     Poking through cracks and crevices in the stone
15   And a bird-sown flower, red on a balcony,
     And then you made jokes about grass growing in the streets
     And politics and grass-roots[1]—and there were songs
     And gags and a musical show called "Hot and Wet."
     It all made a good box[2] for the papers. When the flamingo
20   Flew into a meeting of the Board of Estimate,
     The new mayor acted at once and called the photographers.
     When the first green creeper crawled upon Brooklyn Bridge,
     They thought it was ornamental. They let it stay.

     That was the year the termites came to New York
25   And they don't do well in cold climates—but listen, Joe,
     They're only ants, and ants are nothing but insects.
     It was funny and yet rather wistful, in a way
     (As Heywood Broun pointed out in the *World-Telegram*)[3]
     To think of them looking for wood in a steel city.
30   It made you feel about life. It was too divine.
     There were funny pictures by all the smart, funny artists
     And Macy's[4] ran a terribly clever ad:
     "The Widow's Termite"[5] or something.
                                          There was no
35   Disturbance. Even the Communists didn't protest
     And say they were Morgan hirelings.[6] It was too hot,
     Too hot to protest, too hot to get excited,
     An even African heat, lush, fertile and steamy,
     That soaked into bone and mind and never once broke.
40   The warm rain fell in fierce showers and ceased and fell.
     Pretty soon you got used to it always being that way.

                                    (Continued)

---

1. *grass-roots,* a term used in politics to refer to all the ordinary citizens of a political district, here used as a pun.
2. *box,* feature story set off by lines in a newspaper.
3. *Heywood Broun . . . World Telegram,* a popular columnist who wrote for the New York *World-Telegram.*
4. *Macy's,* large New York department store.
5. *"Widow's Termite,"* a word play on "widow's mite," a term from the Bible referring to any small contribution willingly given by a poor person. [Mark 12:42]
6. *Even the Communists . . . Morgan hirelings.* Even the Communists didn't accuse the termites of working for J. Pierpont Morgan, the wealthy New York capitalist.

You got used to the changed rhythm, the altered beat,
To people walking slower, to the whole bright
Fierce pulse of the city slowing, to men in shorts,
45 To the new sun-helmets from Best's[7] and the cops'
        white uniforms,
And the long noon-rest in the offices, everywhere.
It wasn't a plan or anything. It just happened.
The fingers tapped slower, the office-boys
Dozed on their benches, the bookkeeper yawned at
        his desk.
50 The A.T.&T.[8] was the first to change the shifts
And establish an official siesta-room;
But they were always efficient. Mostly it just
Happened like sleep itself, like a tropic sleep,
Till even the Thirties[9] were deserted at noon
55 Except for a few tourists and one damp cop.
They ran boats to see the big lilies on the North River
But it was only the tourists who really noticed
The flocks of rose-and-green parrots and parakeets
Nesting in the stone crannies of the Cathedral.
60 The rest of us had forgotten when they first came.

There wasn't any real change, it was just a heat spell,
A rain spell, a funny summer, a weather-man's joke,
In spite of the geraniums three feet high
In the tin-can gardens of Hester and Desbrosses.[10]
65 New York was New York. It couldn't turn inside out.
When they got the news from Woods Hole about the
        Gulf Stream,[11]
The *Times* ran an adequate story.

(Continued)

---

7. Best's, New York department store.
8. A.T.&T., the huge American Telephone and Telegraph
Corporation.
9. Thirties, the garment district in New York from 30th to 39th
Streets. Its principal thoroughfare is 34th Street, where both the
Empire State Building and Macy's stand.
10. Hester and Desbrosses, slum districts.
11. Woods Hole . . . Gulf Stream. The Marine Biological
Laboratory is at Woods Hole, a town on the eastern tip of Cape
Cod in Massachusetts; the Gulf Stream, the Atlantic Ocean
current originating in the Gulf of Mexico, affects weather in the
United States and western Europe. The laboratory has noted a
definite alteration in the Gulf current, indicating a permanent
change in climate.

But nobody reads those stories but science-cranks.
Until, one day, a somnolent city-editor
70 Gave a new cub the termite yarn to break his teeth on.
The cub was just down from Vermont, so he took his time.
He was serious about it. He went around.
He read all about termites in the Public Library
And it made him sore when they fired him.
75   So, one evening,
Talking with an old watchman, beside the first
Raw girders of the new Planetopolis Building
(Ten thousand brine-cooled offices, each with shower)
He saw a dark line creeping across the rubble
80 And turned a flashlight on it.
                                        "Say, buddy," he said,
"You better look out for those ants. They eat wood, you know,
They'll have your shack down in no time."
                                        The watchman spat.
85 "Oh, they've quit eating wood," he said in a casual voice,
"I thought everybody knew that."
                                        —And, reaching down,
He pried from the insect jaws the bright crumb of steel.

---

1. The events in the poem take place in
(a) Chicago; (b) Miami; (c) New York City;
(d) Honolulu.

2. The first unusual occurrence in the
city is a large amount of (a) snow; (b) rain;
(c) hail; (d) wind.

3. When the creeper of a plant first
grows onto a bridge, people (a) like its
looks; (b) tear it down; (c) get tangled in it;
(d) swing on it.

4. Among the people who notice the
changes are (a) tourists; (b) city gardeners;
(c) taxi drivers; (d) all of the above.

5. The change in climate is eventually
linked to (a) creatures from another planet;
(b) the Gulf Stream; (c) an eclipse of the
moon; (d) the sun.

6. Of the following adjectives, all are
used to describe the city except (a) lush;
(b) fertile; (c) chilly; (d) steamy.

7. A cub reporter, one of the people to
take the termites seriously, is fired. This is
an example of (a) tone; (b) foreshadowing;
(c) inference; (d) irony.

8. Is the attitude of most of the people
similar to the cub reporter's attitude or the
watchman's attitude?

9. In lines 85-88, what does the watchman imply the termites are now eating?

10. Which of the following best states the
theme of the poem? (a) A city's climate
changes, and termites cause trouble.
(b) People are often so self-absorbed that
they fail to notice important changes in their
lives; (c) Tourists are observant people;
(d) Cities should not be built with steel.

Composition Review

1. In "The Greatest Gift," the stranger tells George that life is the greatest gift. What—besides life—might another character in this unit consider the greatest gift to be? The greatest gift for Charlie Gordon in "Flowers for Algernon," for example, might be intelligence. For Corrigan in "Back There," it might be the ability to travel through time. For the speaker in "Flight of the Roller Coaster," it may be the ability to fly. Choose one of these characters to write about or any other character from the unit. Consider what reasons your chosen character might have for his or her opinion.

Write a composition of about one page in which you tell what one person in this unit might consider the greatest gift to be. Use details from the selection—events, conversations, etc.—to help explain why this person might feel this way.

2. If you could become for one hour a character in one of this unit's selections, who would you become? Would you like to be a passenger on a flying roller coaster? someone who travels in time? one of the Mewlips? a "Skeleton Fixer"? Why would you choose this character? Do you like his or her personality? the opportunities he or she has? the surroundings?

Write a one-page composition in which you explain why you would choose to be a certain character. What would you do in the hour you are this character? You may use events from the selection or make up new situations you think appropriate.

3. In each of the selections in this unit, someone or something is out of control. That is, the normal state of affairs is somehow disturbed. Imagine that you are doing something usual—buttering your toast, perhaps, or walking to a class—when suddenly the situation takes on unexpected and unusual qualities. What happens, and how do you react? What is the outcome?

In a composition of one or two pages, describe an imaginary experience in which some everyday occurrence goes out of control. Write as yourself and use the first person.

unit 7

The ancient Greeks believed that their gods were immortal. In a way they were right, for the gods live on in our language, in our literature, and most of all in those timeless stories—the myths themselves.

Greek Myths

Introduction

A series of feathery clouds moves in formation across the sky. After a heavy downpour, a rainbow appears near the horizon. Lightning flashes, and a tree—or a person—is destroyed. The seasons change regularly in a never-ending cycle. Night follows day, the tide is high for six hours, then low for six. Today we see these phenomena and explain them through science. Ancient peoples saw them too, and wondered. Their wonder led to the composition of myths—stories that offer explanations for the marvels of nature and that often involve gods and goddesses in those explanations.

By the time the civilization of Greece had become established, these myths, thousands of years older, had become more detailed. The sky, the earth, the sea, the underworld—each had its own gods who had responsibilities that were more or less clearly defined.

Myths were passed by word of mouth from person to person and region to region, often carried by professional storytellers. With the passage of time, as different storytellers retold the myths, the details sometimes blurred or came into conflict, so that there are often several different versions of the same basic story.

In addition, some of the myths became more sophisticated as the storytellers included elements of symbolism and philosophy. For example, one myth tells us that Zeus,[1] who ruled the gods, developed a dreadful headache. To give him relief, another god split open his head, and out

sprang Athene, adult and fully clad in armor. We can marvel, or we can laugh. But Athene was the Greek goddess of wisdom—and where should wisdom have its source, if not in the mind of the ruler of the gods?

It may surprise us that some Greek myths show the gods in a comic, irreverent, even unfavorable light. The ancient Greeks saw their gods as complete beings, possessing both good and bad traits, and they did not limit their myths to the good traits.

The major gods, called the Olympians, were twelve in number, headed by Zeus. Most of them dwelt with Zeus in a huge palace, enveloped by clouds, on the top of Mount Olympus, the highest mountain in Greece. Lesser deities lived on earth, in the sea, and in the underworld. Sometimes the gods fell in love with humans. Their children could then be either human or immortal. The word *demigod* is usually used to describe one of those half-human, half-divine beings who had attained immortal status. On the other hand, the familiar word *hero* was originally used to identify those half-human, half-divine beings who retained their mortal status but were unusually strong and brave.

Greek mythology also provided creatures that were part human, part animal. Almost always these were dangerous or man-eating monsters like the Minotaur, part man and

---

1. See Glossary of Proper Names on pages 446–447 for pronunciation and identification of characters and places mentioned in the Introduction and in all the selections in this unit.

part bull, who devoured sacrificial victims. On rare occasions these monsters could be relatively harmless, like the mischievous Pan, half human and half goat.

Whatever the origin or meaning of individual myths, they do show us that the ancient Greeks had inquiring minds and excellent imaginations.

We no longer believe that the sun is a golden chariot, that lightning is a spear, that the constellations were once living beings. And yet the heritage of myth that has come down to us across the centuries remains fascinating.

The ancient Greeks believed their gods to be immortal. In a way that they might not have expected, they were right, for the gods live on in our language, in our literature, and most of all in those timeless stories, the myths themselves.

Zeus

as told by **Bernard Evslin**

Huge, twisted creatures taller than trees attacked the young gods furiously.

Cronos, father of the gods, who gave his name to time, married his sister Rhea, goddess of earth. Now, Cronos had become king of the gods by killing his father, Oranos, the First One. The dying Oranos had prophesied, saying, "You murder me now and steal my throne—but one of your own sons will dethrone you, for crime begets crime."

So Cronos was very careful. One by one, he swallowed his children as they were born. First three daughters—Hestia, Demeter, and Hera; then two sons—Hades and Poseidon. One by one, he swallowed them all.

Rhea was furious. She was determined that he should not eat her next child who she felt sure would be a son. When her time came, she crept down the slope of Olympus to a dark place to have her baby. It was a son, and she named him Zeus. She hung a golden cradle from the branches of an olive tree and put him to sleep there. Then she went back to the top of the mountain. She took a rock and wrapped it in swaddling clothes and held it to her breast, humming a lullaby. Cronos came snorting and bellowing out of his great bed, snatched the bundle from her and swallowed it, clothes and all.

Reprinted by permission of Scholastic Magazines, Inc. from *Heroes, Gods, and Monsters of the Greek Myths* by Bernard Evslin. Copyright © 1966, 1967 by Scholastic Magazines, Inc.

Rhea stole down the mountainside to the swinging golden cradle and took her son down into the fields. She gave him to a shepherd family to raise, promising that their sheep would never be eaten by wolves.

Here Zeus grew to be a beautiful young boy, and Cronos, his father, knew nothing about him. Finally, however, Rhea became lonely for him and brought him back to the court of the gods, introducing him to Cronos as the new cupbearer. Cronos was pleased because the boy was beautiful.

One night Rhea and Zeus prepared a special drink. They mixed mustard and salt with the nectar. Next morning, after a mighty swallow, Cronos vomited up first a stone, and then Hestia, Demeter, Hera, Hades, and Poseidon—who, being gods, were still undigested, still alive. They thanked Zeus and immediately chose him to be their leader.

Then a mighty battle raged. Cronos was joined by the Titans, his half-brothers, huge, twisted, dark creatures taller than trees, whom he kept pent up in the mountains until there was fighting to be done. They attacked the young gods furiously. But Zeus had allies too. He had gone to darker caverns—caves under caves under caves, deep in the mountainside—formed by the first bubbles of the cooling earth.

Here Cronos thousands of centuries before (a short time in the life of a god) had pent up other monsters, the one-eyed Cyclopes and the Hundred-handed Ones. Zeus unshackled these ugly cousins and led them against the Titans.

There was a great rushing and tumult in the skies. The people on earth heard mighty thunder and saw mountains shatter. The earth quaked and tidal waves rolled as the gods fought. The Titans were tall as trees, and old Cronos was a crafty leader. He attacked fiercely, driving the young gods before him. But Zeus had laid a trap. Halfway up the slope of Olympus, he whistled for his cousins, the Hundred-handed Ones, who had been lying in ambush. They took up huge boulders, a hundred each, and hurled them downhill at the Titans. The Titans thought the mountain itself was falling on them. They broke ranks and fled.

The young goat-god Pan was shouting with joy. Later he said that it was his shout that made the Titans flee. That is where we get the word "panic."

Now the young gods climbed to Olympus, took over the castle, and Zeus became their king. No one knows what happened to Cronos and his Titans. But sometimes mountains still explode in fire and the earth still quakes, and no one knows exactly why.

Discussion

1. **(a)** Why does Cronos swallow his children? **(b)** How is the infant Zeus spared this fate?

2. In what way is the prophecy of Oranos fulfilled?

3. How is the earth affected by the battle of the gods?

4. Does strength or cleverness determine who wins the battle between the young gods and the old? Explain.

Poseidon

as told by **Bernard Evslin**

Poseidon's character is unpredictable—like the wild sea that he chose for his kingdom.

After Cronos was deposed, the three sons threw dice for his empire. Zeus, the youngest, won and chose the sky. Poseidon smiled to himself because the sky was empty, and he knew that the impulsive Zeus had chosen it because it looked so high. And now, he, Poseidon, could choose as he would have done if he had won. He chose the sea. He had always wanted it; it

Reprinted by permission of Scholastic Magazines, Inc. from *Heroes, Gods, and Monsters of the Greek Myths* by Bernard Evslin. Copyright © 1966, 1967 by Scholastic Magazines, Inc.

is the best place for adventures and secrets and makes claim on land and sky. Hades, who was always unlucky, had to take the underworld. The earth was held as a commonwealth and left to the goddesses to manage.

Poseidon left Olympus and came to his kingdom. He immediately set about building a huge underwater palace with a great pearl and coral throne. He needed a queen and chose Thetis, a beautiful Nereid, or water nymph. But it was prophesied that any son born to Thetis would be greater than his father, so Poseidon decided to try elsewhere. The prophecy came true. The son of Thetis was Achilles.

Poseidon chose another Nereid named Amphitrite. But like his brother Zeus, he was a great traveler and had hundreds of children in different places. He was a very difficult god, changeful and quarrelsome. He did bear grudges; but he could be pleased, and then his smile was radiant. He liked jokes and thought up very curious forms for his creatures. He liked to startle nymphs with monsters, and concocted the octopus, the squid, the sea-polyp or jellyfish, the swordfish, blowfish, sea cow, and many others. Once, trying to appease Amphitrite's jealous rage, he thought up the dolphin and gave it to her as a gift.

He was greedy and aggressive, always trying to add to his kingdom. Once he claimed Attica as his own and stabbed his trident into the hillside where the Acropolis still stands, and a spring of salt water spouted. Now, the people of Athens did not want to belong to the kingdom of the sea. They were afraid of Poseidon, who had a habit of seizing all the youth of a town when he was in the mood. So they prayed to be put under the protection of another god. Athene heard their prayers. She came down and planted an olive tree by the side of the spring. Poseidon was enraged. His face darkened, and he roared with fury, raising a storm. A fishing fleet was blown off the sea and never came to port. He challenged Athene to single combat and threatened to stir up a tidal wave to break over the city if she refused. She accepted. But Zeus heard the sound of this quarreling and came down and decreed a truce. Then all the gods sat in council to hear the rival claims. After hearing both Athene and Poseidon, they voted to award the city to Athene because her olive tree was the better gift. After that, Athenians had to be very careful when they went to sea, and were often unfortunate in their naval battles.

Poseidon was very fond of Demeter and pursued her persistently.

Finally Demeter said, "Give me a gift. You have made creatures for the sea; now make me a land animal. But a beautiful one, the most beautiful ever seen."

She thought she was safe, because she believed he could make only monsters. She was amazed when he made her a horse, and gasped with delight when she saw it. And Poseidon was so struck by his handiwork that he swiftly made a herd of horses that began to gallop about the meadow, tossing their heads, flirting their tails, kicking up their back legs, and neighing joyously. And he was so fascinated by the horses that he forgot all about Demeter and leaped on one and rode off. Later he made another herd of green ones for his undersea stables. But Demeter kept the first herd; from that all the horses in the world have descended.

Another story says it took Poseidon a

full week to make the horse. During that time he made and cast aside many other creatures that didn't come out right. But he simply threw them away without killing them, and they made their way into the world. From them have come the camel, the hippopotamus, the giraffe, the donkey, and the zebra.

Discussion

1. (a) Describe the division of Cronos's empire after he is deposed. **(b)** What are Poseidon's feelings about the division?

2. (a) Why does Poseidon not marry Thetis? **(b)** Who does become his queen? **(c)** What special creature does he later think up and give his queen?

3. (a) How does Athene come to be the protector of Athens? **(b)** How does Poseidon seem to react to this?

4. This myth explains the origin of some natural phenomena, or things that occur in nature. Which are explained and what are some of the explanations?

Vocabulary
Combined Skills

The *trident* that Poseidon carries is a particular kind of spear. Look up *trident* in the Glossary. What are the meanings of *tri-* and *dent,* the prefix and root from which *trident* is formed?

Use your Glossary to answer the following questions about the italicized words, all of which contain either *tri-* or *dent.*

1. How many languages does a *trilingual* person speak?

2. Name at least three things that one can *indent.*

3. According to its etymology, what is *dentifrice* used for?

4. A *dandelion* is so-named because of the resemblance of its leaves to what?

5. Which italicized words in this exercise are *trisyllabic?*

Persephone

retold by **Anne Terry White**

When the goddess of the harvest mourned for her lost daughter, the earth withered.

Deep under Mt. Aetna, the gods had buried alive a number of fearful, fire-breathing giants. The monsters heaved and struggled to get free. And so mightily did they shake the earth that Hades, the king of the underworld, was alarmed.

"They may tear the rocks asunder and leave the realm of the dead open to the light of day," he thought. And mounting his golden chariot, he went up to see what damage had been done.

Now the goddess of love and beauty, fair Aphrodite, was sitting on a mountainside playing with her son, Eros. She saw Hades as he drove around with his coalblack horses and she said:

"My son, there is one who defies your power and mine. Quick! Take up your darts! Send an arrow into the breast of that dark monarch. Let him, too, feel the pangs of love. Why should he alone escape them?"

At his mother's words, Eros leaped lightly to his feet. He chose from his quiver his sharpest and truest arrow, fitted it to his bow, drew the string, and shot straight into Hades' heart.

The grim King had seen fair maids enough in the gloomy underworld over which he ruled. But never had his heart been touched. Now an unaccustomed warmth stole through his veins. His stern eyes softened. Before him was a blossoming valley, and along its edge a charming girl was gathering flowers. She was Persephone, daughter of Demeter, goddess of the harvest. She had strayed from her companions, and now that her basket overflowed with blossoms, she was filling her apron with lilies and violets. The god looked at Persephone and loved her at once. With one sweep of his arm he caught her up and drove swiftly away.

"Mother!" she screamed, while the flowers fell from her apron and strewed the ground. "Mother!"

And she called on her companions by name. But already they were out of sight, so fast did Hades urge the horses on. In a few moments they were at the River Cyane. Persephone struggled, her loosened girdle fell to the ground, but the god held her tight. He struck the bank with his trident. The earth opened, and darkness swallowed them all—horses, chariot, Hades, and weeping Persephone.

From end to end of the earth Demeter sought her daughter. But none could tell her where Persephone was. At last, worn out and despairing, the goddess returned to Sicily. She stood by the River Cyane, where Hades had cleft the earth and gone down into his own dominions.

Now a river nymph had seen him carry off his prize. She wanted to tell Demeter where her daughter was, but fear of Hades

---

kept her dumb. Yet she had picked up the girdle Persephone had dropped, and this the nymph wafted on the waves to the feet of Demeter.

The goddess knew then that her daughter was gone indeed, but she did not suspect Hades of carrying her off. She laid the blame on the innocent land.

"Ungrateful soil!" she said. "I made you fertile. I clothed you in grass and nourishing grain, and this is how you reward me. No more shall you enjoy my favors!"

That year was the most cruel mankind had ever known. Nothing prospered, nothing grew. The cattle died, the seed would not come up, men and oxen toiled in vain. There was too much sun. There was too much rain. Thistles and weeds were the only things that grew. It seemed that all mankind would die of hunger.

"This cannot go on," said mighty Zeus. "I see that I must intervene." And one by one he sent the gods and goddesses to plead with Demeter.

But she had the same answer for all: "Not till I see my daughter shall the earth bear fruit again."

Zeus, of course, knew well where Persephone was. He did not like to take from his brother the one joyful thing in his life, but he saw that he must if the race of man was to be preserved. So he called Hermes to him and said:

"Descend to the underworld, my son. Bid Hades release his bride. Provided she has not tasted food in the realm of the dead, she may return to her mother forever."

Down sped Hermes on his winged feet, and there in the dim palace of the king, he found Persephone by Hades' side. She was pale and joyless. Not all the glittering treasures of the underworld could bring a smile to her lips.

"You have no flowers here," she would say to her husband when he pressed gems upon her. "Jewels have no fragrance. I do not want them."

When she saw Hermes and heard his message, her heart leaped within her. Her cheeks grew rosy and her eyes sparkled, for she knew that Hades would not dare to disobey his brother's command. She sprang up, ready to go at once. Only one thing troubled her—that she could not leave the underworld forever. For she had accepted a pomegranate from Hades and sucked the sweet pulp from four of the seeds.[1]

With a heavy heart Hades made ready

---

1. *four of the seeds.* Technically, Persephone would have to remain in the underworld permanently because she had eaten those seeds. But Zeus arranged a compromise allowing her to leave, on condition that she spend a portion of each year with Hades.

his golden car. He helped Persephone in while Hermes took up the reins.

"Dear wife," said the King, and his voice trembled as he spoke, "think kindly of me, I pray you. For indeed I love you truly. It will be lonely here these eight months you are away. And if you think mine is a gloomy palace to return to, at least remember that your husband is great among the immortals. So fare you well—and get your fill of flowers!"

Straight to the temple of Demeter at Eleusis, Hermes drove the black horses.

The goddess heard the chariot wheels and, as a deer bounds over the hills, she ran out swiftly to meet her daughter. Persephone flew to her mother's arms. And the sad tale of each turned into joy in the telling.

So it is to this day. One third of the year Persephone spends in the gloomy abode of Hades—one month for each seed that she tasted. Then Nature dies, the leaves fall, the earth stops bringing forth. In spring Persephone returns, and with her come the flowers, followed by summer's fruitfulness and the rich harvest of fall.

Discussion

1. (a) Why does Hades kidnap Persephone? (b) Whom does Demeter wrongfully blame for Persephone's disappearance? What revenge does she take? (c) Why and how does Zeus intervene with Demeter? What is her answer? (d) What decision does Zeus finally make?

2. Describe the physical changes that take place in Persephone while in the underworld. How do you account for these?

3. (a) Under what conditions may Persephone be released from the underworld? (b) Since Persephone has eaten four seeds, what is to be her fate?

4. This myth is somewhat different from most in that the gods are shown displaying "human" emotions such as love, despair, and sympathy. Cite several instances of their display of such emotions.

5. (a) How does this myth explain the changing of the seasons? (b) In this version of the myth, Persephone eats four seeds. Other retellings give different numbers—five, six, or seven seeds. How would you account for this variation?

Composition

Myths that contain an explanation of some natural phenomenon or element of nature are called nature myths, or science myths. Choose one of the following phenomena and think of an explanation for it: rainbows, the color of the sky, eclipses of the sun, the difference between raindrops and snowflakes, why crickets chirp, why elephants have trunks. The character you choose as the one responsible for the phenomenon can be either mortal or immortal, but be sure to include at least one Greek god or goddess somewhere in your explanation.

Write your own "nature myth" one or two pages long. Describe, first of all, what the earth was like before the events you relate. Then tell the story of how your chosen phenomenon was created. (The Glossary of Proper Names on pages 446-447 may help you by providing a complete list of gods and goddesses mentioned in this unit, as well as typical Greek names for mortals.)

Arachne

as told by **Olivia Coolidge**

Arachne believed that her skill was greater than that of anyone— even a goddess.

Arachne was a maiden who became famous throughout Greece, though she was neither wellborn nor beautiful and came from no great city. She lived in an obscure little village, and her father was a humble dyer of wool. In this he was very skillful, producing many varied shades, while above all he was famous for the clear, bright scarlet which is made from shellfish, and which was the most glorious of all the colors used in ancient Greece. Even more skillful than her father was Arachne. It was her task to spin the fleecy wool into a fine, soft thread and to weave it into cloth on the high-standing loom within the cottage. Arachne was small and pale from much working. Her eyes were light and her hair was a dusty brown, yet she was quick and graceful, and her fingers, roughened as they were, went so fast that it was hard to follow their flickering movements. So soft and even was her thread, so fine her cloth, so gorgeous her embroidery, that soon her products were known all over Greece. No one had ever seen the like of them before.

At last Arachne's fame became so great that people used to come from far and wide to watch her working. Even the graceful nymphs would steal in from stream or forest and peep shyly through the dark doorway, watching in wonder the white arms of Arachne as she stood at the loom and threw the shuttle from hand to hand between the hanging threads, or drew out the long wool, fine as a hair, from the distaff[1] as she sat spinning. "Surely Athene herself must have taught her," people would murmur to one another. "Who else could know the secret of such marvelous skill?"

Arachne was used to being wondered at, and she was immensely proud of the skill that had brought so many to look on her. Praise was all she lived for, and it displeased her greatly that people should think anyone, even a goddess, could teach her anything. Therefore when she heard them murmur, she would stop her work and turn around indignantly to say, "With my own ten fingers I gained this skill, and by hard practice from early morning till night. I never had time to stand looking as you people do while another maiden worked. Nor if

---

1. **distaff,** a stick, slit at one end, to hold wool or flax for spinning into thread by hand.

I had, would I give Athene credit because the girl was more skillful than I. As for Athene's weaving, how could there be finer cloth or more beautiful embroidery than mine? If Athene herself were to come down and compete with me, she could do no better than I.''

One day when Arachne turned round with such words, an old woman answered her, a grey old woman, bent and very poor, who stood leaning on a staff and peering at Arachne amid the crowd of onlookers. "Reckless girl," she said, "how dare you claim to be equal to the immortal gods themselves? I am an old woman and have seen much. Take my advice and ask pardon of Athene for your words. Rest content with your fame of being the best spinner and weaver that mortal eyes have ever beheld.''

"Stupid old woman," said Arachne indignantly, "who gave you a right to speak in this way to me? It is easy to see that you were never good for anything in your day, or you would not come here in poverty and rags to gaze at my skill. If Athene resents my words, let her answer them herself. I have challenged her to a contest, but she, of course, will not come. It is easy for the gods to avoid matching their skill with that of men.''

At these words the old woman threw down her staff and stood erect. The wondering onlookers saw her grow tall and fair and stand clad in long robes of dazzling white. They were terribly afraid as they realized that they stood in the presence of Athene. Arachne herself flushed red for a moment, for she had never really believed that the goddess would hear her. Before the group that was gathered there she would not give in; so pressing her pale lips together in obstinacy and pride, she led the

goddess to one of the great looms and set herself before the other. Without a word both began to thread the long woolen strands that hang from the rollers, and between which the shuttle moves back and forth. Many skeins lay heaped beside them to use, bleached white, and gold, and scarlet, and other shades, varied as the rainbow. Arachne had never thought of giving credit for her success to her father's skill in dyeing, though in actual truth the colors were as remarkable as the cloth itself.

Soon there was no sound in the room but the breathing of the onlookers, the whirring of the shuttles, and the creaking of the wooden frames as each pressed the thread up into place or tightened the pegs by which the whole was held straight. The excited crowd in the doorway began to see that the skill of both in truth was very nearly equal, but that, however the cloth might turn out, the goddess was the quicker of the two. A pattern of many pictures was growing on her loom. There was a border of twined branches of the olive, Athene's favorite tree, while in the middle, figures began to appear. As they looked at the

glowing colors, the spectators realized that Athene was weaving into her pattern a last warning to Arachne. The central figure was the goddess herself competing with Poseidon for possession of the city of Athens; but in the four corners were mortals who had tried to strive with gods and pictures of the awful fate that had overtaken them. The goddess ended a little before Arachne and stood back from her marvelous work to see what the maiden was doing.

Never before had Arachne been matched against anyone whose skill was equal, or even nearly equal to her own. As she stole glances from time to time at Athene and saw the goddess working swiftly, calmly, and always a little faster than herself, she became angry instead of frightened, and an evil thought came into her head. Thus as Athene stepped back a pace to watch Arachne finishing her work, she saw that the maiden had taken for her design a pattern of scenes which showed evil or unworthy actions of the gods, how they had deceived fair maidens, resorted to trickery, and appeared on earth from time to time in the form of poor and humble peo-

ple. When the goddess saw this insult glowing in bright colors on Arachne's loom, she did not wait while the cloth was judged, but stepped forward, her grey eyes blazing with anger, and tore Arachne's work across. Then she struck Arachne across the face. Arachne stood there a moment, struggling with anger, fear, and pride. "I will not live under this insult," she cried, and seizing a rope from the wall, she made a noose and would have hanged herself.

The goddess touched the rope and touched the maiden. "Live on, wicked girl," she said. "Live on and spin, both you and your descendants. When men look at you they may remember that it is not wise to strive with Athene." At that the body of Arachne shrivelled up; and her legs grew tiny, spindly, and distorted. There before the eyes of the spectators hung a little dusty brown spider on a slender thread.

All spiders descend from Arachne, and as the Greeks watched them spinning their thread wonderfully fine, they remembered the contest with Athene and thought that it was not right for even the best of men to claim equality with the gods.

Discussion

1. (a) Why has Arachne become famous throughout Greece? **(b)** What part does her father have in her fame? **(c)** Does she acknowledge her father's role?

2. (a) Why do you suppose Athene disguises herself as an old woman? **(b)** While in disguise, what advice does Athene give Arachne? **(c)** How does Arachne react to this advice?

3. (a) Describe the pattern that Athene weaves. **(b)** Why might she have selected this pattern? **(c)** Describe the pattern that Arachne weaves. **(d)** Why might she have chosen this pattern? **(e)** How does the weaving contest end?

4. To the ancient Greeks one of the greatest sins was *hubris* (hyü′bris), excessive pride that leads to rudeness and disrespect, especially to the gods. Is Arachne guilty of this sin? Explain.

5. Do you think Arachne deserves her fate? Why or why not?

Composition

How do you think Arachne feels as Athene changes her into a spider? Do you think Arachne still has human thoughts and emotions as a spider? What must they be? Consider the story of Arachne from her point of view, beginning with the moment that the "grey old woman" calls her "reckless girl" and continuing through Arachne's transformation into a spider.

Write an account of these events in the first person (use the pronoun "I"). Remember that Arachne undergoes many emotional changes during and after the weaving contest before her physical change. Try to make Arachne appear to your readers as a real, believable person.

(You may find the article "Being Someone Else" in the Composition Guide helpful in writing this composition.)

Comment: Transformations in Myth

Arachne was transformed, and thus spiders were created. Throughout Greek mythology runs a strong theme of such magical changes of shape. Transformation myths account for the origins of certain animals, flowers, trees, mountains—even stars.

Narcissus (när sis'əs) was such a beautiful young man that all the women who saw him longed to be his. Not interested in them or their broken hearts, however, Narcissus went on his cruel way, scorning love. Those he had wounded prayed to the gods that Narcissus be punished, and the prayer was answered. One day as he knelt by a pool for a drink, he saw in the clear water a beautiful face and form and immediately fell in love with it. He could not reach the object of his love, but he could not bear to leave it. So there he remained, leaning over the pool, gazing at his own reflection until at length he turned into the flower that is still called narcissus.

One of those who loved Narcissus was Echo, a nymph condemned never to use her voice except to repeat what was said to her. Unable to express her love or to say anything but others' words, she hid herself in a lonely cave and wasted away from longing until only her voice remained. To this day, Echo's voice lingers in caves and on mountainsides, echoing whatever is said to her.

Zeus once fell in love with a young woman named Callisto (kə lis'tō), who bore him a son. Hera, in a fit of jealousy, turned Callisto into a bear. Later when the son was grown, he encountered the bear one day when he was hunting. Not knowing who she was, he was about to shoot his mother when Zeus carried her up to the sky and placed her among the stars, where she is known as the Great Bear (Ursa Major, also called the Big Dipper). Her son was placed near her and called the Lesser Bear. Hera, still jealous, forbade the Bears ever to descend into the ocean; of all the constellations, they alone never set below the horizon.

A fisherman named Glaucus (glô'kəs) one day spread his catch out on a grassy meadow near the shore. As they touched the grass, the fish began to jump about and dive back into the sea. Amazed, Glaucus tasted the grass and immediately felt possessed to jump into the water. The gods of the sea saved him by turning him into a merman with green flowing hair and beard and a body tapering to a fish-like tail. His new form did not prevent him from falling in love with the nymph Scylla (sil'ə), but she was frightened and fled from him. Glaucus then asked Circe (sėr'sē), the enchantress, for a potion to cause Scylla to love him. Circe fell in love with Glaucus herself, however, and instead of a love potion mixed a powerful poison, which she poured into the bay where Scylla swam. When Scylla entered the water her body became covered with horrible growths of barking heads. In that spot the monster Scylla remained, destroying in her rage the sailors on ships that passed. At last she was transformed into a rock; in this new form she is still dangerous to sailors and their ships.

The Gorgon's Head

as told by **Nathaniel Hawthorne**

It was a dangerous adventure Perseus had undertaken. How was he going to avoid being turned to stone?

Perseus was the son of Danaë, who was the daughter of a king. When Perseus was a very little boy, some wicked people put his mother and himself into a chest and set them afloat upon the sea. The wind drove the chest away from the shore while Danaë clasped her child closely and dreaded that some big wave would dash over them both. The chest sailed on, however, until it floated so near an island that it got entangled in a fisherman's net and was drawn out upon the sand. The island was called Seriphus, and it was reigned over by King Polydectes, who happened to be the fisherman's brother.

This fisherman was an exceedingly humane and upright man. He showed great kindness to Danaë and her little boy and continued to befriend them until Perseus had grown to be a handsome youth, very strong and active, and skillful in the use of arms.

Long before this time, King Polydectes had seen the two strangers—the mother and her child—who had come to his dominions in a floating chest. As he was not good and kind, like his brother the fisherman, but extremely wicked, he resolved to send Perseus on a dangerous enterprise in which he would probably be killed and then to do some great mischief to Danaë herself. So this bad-hearted king spent a long while in considering what was the most dangerous thing that a young man could possibly undertake to perform. At last he sent for the youthful Perseus.

The young man came to the palace and found the king sitting upon his throne.

"Perseus," said King Polydectes, smiling craftily upon him, "you are grown up a fine young man. You and your good mother have received a great deal of kindness from myself as well as from my worthy brother the fisherman, and I suppose you would not be sorry to repay some of it."

"Please your Majesty," answered Perseus, "I would willingly risk my life to do so."

"Well then," continued the king, still with a cunning smile, "I have a little adventure to propose to you; and as you are a brave and enterprising youth, you will doubtless look upon it as an opportunity of distinguishing yourself. You must know, my good Perseus, I think of getting married to the beautiful Princess Hippodamia, and it is customary on these occasions to make the bride a present of some farfetched and elegant curiosity. I have been a little perplexed where to obtain anything likely to please a princess of her exquisite taste. But this morning I have thought of precisely the article."

An abridgement of "The Gorgon's Head" by Nathaniel Hawthorne from *A Wonder-Book and Tanglewood Tales* (Houghton Mifflin, 1923, 1951), pages 21-48.

"And can I assist your Majesty in obtaining it?" cried Perseus eagerly.

"You can if you are as brave a youth as I believe you to be," replied King Polydectes. "The bridal gift which I have set my heart on presenting to the beautiful Hippodamia is the head of the Gorgon Medusa with the snaky locks; and I depend on you to bring it to me. And in cutting off the Gorgon's head, be careful to make a clean stroke so as not to injure its appearance. You must bring it home in the very best condition."

Perseus left the palace but was scarcely out of hearing before Polydectes burst into a laugh, being greatly amused, wicked king that he was, to find how readily the young man fell into the snare. The news quickly spread abroad. Everybody rejoiced, for most of the inhabitants of the island were as wicked as the king himself and would have liked nothing better than to see some enormous mischief happen to Danaë and her son.

Now there were three Gorgons alive at that period, and they were the most strange and terrible monsters that had ever been since the world was made. Instead of locks of hair they had each of them a hundred enormous snakes growing on their heads, all alive, twisting, wriggling, curling, and thrusting out their venomous tongues. The teeth of the Gorgons were terribly long tusks; their hands were made of brass; and their bodies were all over scales, hard and impenetrable as iron. They had wings, too; every feather in them was pure, bright, glittering, burnished gold, and they looked very dazzling when the Gorgons were flying about in the sunshine.

But the worst thing about these abominable Gorgons was that if once a poor mortal fixed his eyes full upon one of their faces, he was certain, that very instant, to be changed from warm flesh and blood into cold and lifeless stone!

Thus it was a very dangerous adventure that the wicked King Polydectes had contrived. Perseus himself could not help seeing that he had very little chance of coming safely through it and that he was far more likely to become a stone image than to bring back the head of Medusa. Not only must he fight with and slay this golden-winged, iron-scaled, long-tusked, brazen-clawed, snaky-haired monster, but he must do it with his eyes shut or, at least, without so much as a glance at the enemy with whom he was contending.

So disconsolate did these thoughts make him that Perseus could not bear to tell his mother what he had undertaken to do. He therefore took his shield, girded on his sword, and crossed over from the island to the mainland, where he sat down in a solitary place and hardly refrained from shedding tears.

But while he was in this sorrowful mood, he heard a voice close beside him.

"Perseus," said the voice, "why are you sad?"

He lifted his head from his hands and behold! there was a stranger in the solitary place. It was an intelligent and remarkably shrewd-looking young man, with a cloak over his shoulders, an odd sort of cap on his head, a strangely twisted staff in his hand, and a short and very crooked sword hanging by his side. The stranger had such a cheerful, knowing, and helpful aspect that Perseus could not help feeling his spirits grow livelier as he gazed at him. So Perseus wiped his eyes and answered the stranger. "I am not so very sad," said he, "only thoughtful about an adventure that I have undertaken."

"Oho!" answered the stranger. "Well, tell me all about it, and possibly I may be of service to you. Perhaps you may have heard of me. I have more names than one, but the name of Quicksilver[1] suits me as well as any other. Tell me what the trouble is, and we will talk the matter over and see what can be done."

The stranger's words and manner put Perseus into quite a different mood from his former one. So he let the stranger know, in few words, precisely what the case was—how King Polydectes wanted the head of Medusa with the snaky locks as a bridal gift for the beautiful Princess Hippodamia and how he had undertaken to get it for him but was afraid of being turned into stone.

"And that would be a great pity," said Quicksilver with his mischievous smile. "You would make a very handsome marble statue, it is true, and it would be a considerable number of centuries before you crumbled away; but, on the whole, one would rather be a young man for a few years than a stone image for a great many."

"Oh, far rather!" exclaimed Perseus. "And besides, what would my dear mother do if her beloved son were turned into a stone?"

"Well, well, let us hope that the affair will not turn out so very badly," replied Quicksilver in an encouraging tone. "I am the very person to help you, if anybody can. My sister[2] and myself will do our utmost to bring you safe through the adventure, ugly as it now looks."

"Your sister?" repeated Perseus.

"Yes, my sister," said the stranger. "She is very wise, I promise you; and as for myself, I generally have all my wits about me. If you follow our advice, you need not fear being a stone image yet awhile. But, first of all, you must polish your shield till you can see your face in it as distinctly as in a mirror."

This seemed to Perseus rather an odd beginning of the adventure. However, he immediately set to work and scrubbed the shield with so much diligence that it very quickly shone like the moon at harvest-time. Quicksilver looked at it with a smile and nodded his approbation. Then taking off his own short and crooked sword, he girded it about Perseus instead of the one which he had before worn.

"No sword but mine will answer your purpose," observed he. "The blade has a most excellent temper and will cut through iron and brass as easily as through the slenderest twig. And now we will set out. The next thing is to find the Three Gray Women, who will tell us where to find the Nymphs."

"The Three Gray Women!" cried Perseus. "Pray who may the Three Gray Women be? I never heard of them before."

"They are three very strange old ladies," said Quicksilver, laughing. "They have but one eye among them and only one tooth. Moreover, you must find them out by starlight or in the dusk of the evening for they never show themselves by the light either of the sun or moon."

"But," said Perseus, "why should I waste my time with these Three Gray Women? Would it not be better to set out at once in search of the terrible Gorgons?"

"No, no," answered his friend. "There are other things to be done before you can find your way to the Gorgons. Come, let us be stirring!"

They accordingly set out and walked at a pretty brisk pace, so brisk indeed that

---

1. *Quicksilver,* the god Hermes.
2. *my sister,* the goddess Athene, although she is not named in the story.

Perseus found it rather difficult to keep up with his nimble friend. To say the truth, he had a singular idea that Quicksilver was furnished with a pair of winged shoes. And when Perseus looked sideways at him, he seemed to see wings on the side of his head. But, at all events, the twisted staff[3] evidently enabled him to proceed so fast that Perseus began to be out of breath.

"Here!" cried Quicksilver at last, "take you the staff, for you need it a great deal more than I. Are there no better walkers than yourself in the island of Seriphus?"

"I could walk pretty well," said Perseus, glancing slyly at his companion's feet, "if I had only a pair of winged shoes."

"We must see about getting you a pair," answered Quicksilver.

But the staff helped Perseus along so bravely that he no longer felt the slightest weariness. He and Quicksilver now walked onward at their ease, and Quicksilver told stories about his former adventures and how well his wits had served him on various occasions. Perseus listened eagerly in the hope of brightening his own wits by what he heard.

At last he happened to recollect that Quicksilver had spoken of a sister who was to lend her assistance. "Where is she?" he inquired. "Shall we not meet her soon?"

"All at the proper time," said his companion. "But this sister of mine, you must understand, is quite a different sort of character from myself. She seldom smiles, never laughs, and makes it a rule not to utter a word unless she has something particularly profound to say. In short, she is so immoderately wise that many people call her wisdom personified."

---

3. **winged shoes. . . . twisted staff.** Hermes (Quicksilver) is often represented in art as wearing a winged cap and winged sandals and carrying a staff with two snakes wound around it.

By this time it had grown quite dusk. They were now come to a very wild and desert place, overgrown with shaggy bushes. All was waste and desolate in the gray twilight, which grew every moment more obscure. Perseus looked about him rather disconsolately and asked Quicksilver whether they had a great deal farther to go.

"Hist!" whispered his companion. "Make no noise! This is just the time and place to meet the Three Gray Women. Be careful that they do not see you before you see them, for though they have but a single eye among the three, it is as sharp-sighted as half a dozen common eyes."

"But what must I do," asked Perseus, "when we meet them?"

Quicksilver explained to Perseus how the Three Gray Women managed with their one eye, changing it from one to another as if it had been a pair of spectacles. When one of the three had kept the eye a certain time, she took it out of the socket and passed it to one of her sisters, who immediately clapped it into her own head and enjoyed a peep at the visible world. Thus, at the instant when the eye was passing from hand to hand, neither of the poor old ladies was able to see a wink.

Perseus was so astonished that he almost fancied his companion was joking with him.

"You will soon find whether I tell the truth or no," observed Quicksilver. "Hush! There they come, now!"

Perseus looked earnestly through the dusk of the evening, and there, sure enough, he descried the Three Gray Women. As they came nearer, he saw that two of them had but the empty socket of an eye in the middle of their foreheads. But in the middle of the third sister's forehead there was a very large, bright, and piercing eye, which sparkled like a great diamond in a ring. She who chanced to have the eye in her forehead led the other two by the hands, peeping sharply about her all the while—so much that Perseus dreaded lest she should see right through the thick clump of bushes behind which he and Quicksilver had hidden themselves.

But before they reached the clump of bushes, one of the Three Gray Women spoke. "Sister! Sister Scarecrow!" cried she, "you have had the eye long enough. It is my turn now!"

"Let me keep it a moment longer, Sister Nightmare," answered Scarecrow. "I thought I had a glimpse of something behind that thick bush."

"Well, and what of that?" retorted Nightmare peevishly. "Can't I see into a thick bush as easily as yourself? The eye is mine as well as yours, and I know the use of it as well as you."

But here the third sister, whose name was Shakejoint, began to complain and said that it was her turn to have the eye. To end the dispute, old Dame Scarecrow took the eye out of her forehead and held it forth in her hand.

"Take it, one of you," cried she, "and quit this foolish quarreling."

Both Nightmare and Shakejoint put out their hands, groping eagerly to snatch the eye. But being both alike blind, they could not easily find where Scarecrow's hand was, and Scarecrow, being now just as much in the dark as Shakejoint and Nightmare, could not at once meet either of their hands in order to put the eye into it. Thus were all three in utter darkness from too impatient a desire to see.

Quicksilver could scarcely help laughing aloud. "Now is your time!" he whispered to

Perseus. "Quick, quick! before they can clap the eye into either of their heads!"

In an instant Perseus leaped from behind the clump of bushes and made himself master of the prize. The marvelous eye, as he held it in his hand, shone very brightly and seemed to look up into his face with a knowing air. But the Gray Women knew nothing of what had happened, and each supposing that one of her sisters was in possession of the eye, they began their quarrel anew. At last Perseus thought it right to explain the matter.

"My good ladies," said he, "pray do not be angry with one another. If anybody is in fault, it is myself, for I have the honor to hold your very brilliant and excellent eye in my own hand!"

"You! you have our eye! And who are you?" screamed the Three Gray Women all in a breath, for they were terribly frightened at hearing a strange voice. "Oh, what shall we do, sisters? We are all in the dark! Give us our eye! Give us our one, precious, solitary eye!"

"Tell them," whispered Quicksilver to Perseus, "that they shall have back the eye as soon as they direct you where to find the Nymphs who have the flying slippers, the magic wallet, and the helmet of darkness."

"My dear ladies," said Perseus, "there is no occasion for putting yourselves into such a fright. You shall have back your eye safe and sound and as bright as ever, the moment you tell me where to find the Nymphs."

"The Nymphs! Sisters, what Nymphs does he mean?" screamed Scarecrow. "There are a great many Nymphs—some that go ahunting in the woods and some that live inside of trees and some that have a comfortable home in fountains of water. We know nothing at all about them."

All this while the Three Gray Women were groping with their outstretched hands and trying their utmost to get hold of Perseus. But he took good care to keep out of their reach.

"I hold your eye fast in my hand," said he, "and shall keep it until you please to tell me where to find these Nymphs. The Nymphs, I mean, who keep the enchanted wallet, the flying slippers, and the what is it?—the helmet of invisibility."

"Mercy on us, sisters! what is the young man talking about?" exclaimed Scarecrow, Nightmare, and Shakejoint. "A pair of flying slippers, quoth he! His heels would quickly fly higher than his head if he were silly enough to put them on. And a helmet of invisibility! How could a helmet make him invisible unless it were big enough for him to hide under it? And an enchanted wallet! What sort of a contrivance may that be, I wonder? No, no, good stranger! we can tell you nothing of these marvelous things."

Perseus was just on the point of restoring their eye and asking pardon for his rudeness, but Quicksilver caught his hand.

"Don't let them make a fool of you!" said he. "Keep fast hold of the eye and all will go well."

The Gray Women, finding that there was no other way of recovering it, at last told Perseus what he wanted to know. No sooner had they done so, than he immediately clapped the eye into the vacant socket in one of their foreheads, thanked them for their kindness, and bade them farewell. Before the young man was out of hearing, however, they had got into a new dispute because he happened to have given the eye to Scarecrow, who had already taken her turn of it.

Quicksilver and Perseus, in the meantime, were making the best of their way in quest of the Nymphs. They proved to be very different persons from Nightmare, Shakejoint, and Scarecrow, for they were young and beautiful; and instead of one eye amongst the sisterhood, each Nymph had two exceedingly bright eyes of her own with which she looked very kindly at Perseus. They seemed to be acquainted with Quicksilver, and they made no difficulty about giving him the valuable articles that were in their custody. In the first place, they brought out what appeared to be a small purse made of deer skin and curiously embroidered, and they bade him be sure and keep it safe. This was the magic wallet. The Nymphs next produced a pair of slippers with a nice little pair of wings at the heel of each.

"Put them on, Perseus," said Quicksilver. "You will find yourself as light-heeled as you can desire for the remainder of our journey."

When Perseus had got on these wonderful slippers, he was altogether too buoyant to tread on earth. Making a step or two, upward he popped into the air and found it very difficult to clamber down again. Quicksilver laughed at his companion's involuntary activity and told him that he must not be in so desperate a hurry but must wait for the invisible helmet.

The good-natured Nymphs had the helmet, with its dark tuft of waving plumes, all in readiness to put upon his head. And the instant the helmet was put on, there was no longer any Perseus to be seen. Nothing but empty air!

"Where are you, Perseus?" asked Quicksilver.

"Why, here, to be sure!" answered Perseus out of the transparent atmosphere. "Don't you see me?"

"No indeed!" answered his friend. "But if I cannot see you, neither can the Gorgons. Follow me, therefore, and we will try your dexterity in using the winged slippers."

With these words, Quicksilver's whole figure rose lightly into the air, and Perseus followed.

It was now deep night. Perseus looked upward and saw the round, bright, silvery moon and thought that he should desire nothing better than to soar up thither and spend his life there. Then he looked downward again and saw the earth with its seas and lakes and the silver courses of its rivers, and its snowy mountain-peaks and the breadth of its fields and the dark cluster of its woods, and its cities of white marble. With the moonshine sleeping over the whole scene, it was as beautiful as the moon or any star could be. The bravest sights were the meteors that gleamed suddenly out, as if a bonfire had been kindled in the sky, and made the moonshine pale for as much as a hundred miles around them.

As the two companions flew onward, Perseus fancied that he could hear the rustle of a garment close by his side; yet only Quicksilver was visible.

"Whose garment is this," inquired Perseus, "that keeps rustling close beside me in the breeze?"

"Oh, it is my sister's!" answered Quicksilver. "She is coming along with us, as I told you she would."

By this time they had come within sight of the great ocean and were soon flying over it. Far beneath them the waves tossed themselves tumultuously in mid-sea or foamed against the rocky cliffs. Just then a voice spoke in the air close by him, a woman's voice, melodious, though grave and mild.

"Perseus," said the voice, "there are the Gorgons."

"Where?" exclaimed Perseus. "I cannot see them."

"On the shore of that island beneath you," replied the voice. "A pebble dropped from your hand would strike in the midst of them."

Straight downward, two or three thousand feet below him, Perseus perceived a small island with the sea breaking into white foam all around its rocky shore except on one side, where there was a beach of snowy sand. He descended towards it, and, looking earnestly at a cluster or heap of brightness at the foot of a precipice of black rocks, there were the terrible Gorgons! They lay fast asleep, soothed by the thunder of the sea. The moonlight glistened on their steely scales and on their golden wings, which drooped idly over the sand. Their brazen claws, horrible to look at, were thrust out and clutched the wave-beaten fragments of rock, while the sleeping Gorgons dreamed of tearing some poor mortal all to pieces. The snakes that served them instead of hair seemed likewise to be asleep, although now and then one would writhe and lift its head and thrust out its forked tongue, emitting a drowsy hiss.

Luckily for Perseus, their faces were completely hidden from him. Had he but looked one instant at them, he would have fallen heavily out of the air, an image of senseless stone.

"Now," whispered Quicksilver as he hovered by the side of Perseus. "Now is your time to do the deed! Be quick, for if one of the Gorgons should awake, you are too late!"

"Which shall I strike at?" asked Perseus, drawing his sword and descending a little lower. "Which of the three is Medusa?"

"Be cautious," said the calm voice which had before spoken to him. "One of the Gorgons is stirring in her sleep and is just about to turn over. That is Medusa. Do not look at her! Look at the reflection of her face and figure in the bright mirror of your shield and take care that you do not miss your first stroke."

Perseus now understood Quicksilver's motive for so earnestly exhorting him to polish his shield. In its surface he could safely look at the reflection of the Gorgon's face. And there it was, that terrible countenance mirrored in the brightness of the shield with the moonlight falling over it and displaying all its horror. The snakes kept twisting themselves over the forehead. It was the fiercest and most horrible face that ever was seen or imagined, and yet with a strange, fearful, and savage kind of beauty in it. The eyes were closed, and the Gorgon was still in a deep slumber, but there was an unquiet expression disturbing her features, as if the monster was troubled with an ugly dream. She gnashed her white tusks and dug into the sand with her brazen claws.

The snakes, too, seemed to feel Medusa's dream and to be made more restless by it. They twined themselves into tumultuous knots, writhed fiercely, and uplifted a hundred hissing heads without opening their eyes.

Perseus flew cautiously downward, still keeping his eyes on Medusa's face as reflected in his shield. The nearer he came, the more terrible did the snaky visage and metallic body of the monster grow. At last, when he found himself hovering over her within arm's length, Perseus uplifted his sword while, at the same instant, each separate snake upon the Gorgon's head stretched threateningly upward, and Me-

Artists through the centuries have depicted
Medusa with her snaky locks. Above, a
stone carving from an ancient Greek temple
in Sicily; below, an oil painting by
Michelangelo Caravaggio (Italian, 1565–
1609); below left, a painting from a Greek
water jar (about 490 B.C.); above left, a
modern interpretation.

dusa unclosed her eyes. But she awoke too late. The sword was sharp, the stroke fell like a lightning-flash, and the head of the wicked Medusa tumbled from her body!

"Admirably done!" cried Quicksilver. "Make haste and clap the head into your magic wallet."

To the astonishment of Perseus, the small, embroidered wallet which he had hung about his neck and which had hitherto been no bigger than a purse grew all at once large enough to contain Medusa's head. As quick as thought, he snatched it up with the snakes still writhing upon it and thrust it in.

"Your task is done," said the calm voice. "Now fly, for the other Gorgons will do their utmost to take vengeance for Medusa's death."

It was indeed necessary to take flight, for the other two monsters awoke with yells and screeches and hurtled upward into the air, brandishing their brass talons, gnashing their horrible tusks, and flapping their huge wings so wildly that some of the golden feathers were shaken out and floated down upon the shore. The snakes sent forth a hundred-fold hiss, and Medusa's snakes answered them out of the magic wallet. But as Perseus wore the helmet of invisibility, the Gorgons knew not in what direction to follow him, nor did he fail to make the best use of the winged slippers by soaring upward a perpendicular mile or so. At that height, when the screams of those abominable creatures sounded faintly beneath him, he made a straight course for the island of Seriphus in order to carry Medusa's head to King Polydectes.

Perseus went straight to the palace and was immediately ushered into the presence of the king. Polydectes by no means rejoiced to see him, for he had felt almost certain in his own evil mind that the Gorgons would have torn the poor young man to pieces and have eaten him up, out of the way. However, seeing him safely returned, he put the best face he could upon the matter.

"Have you performed your promise?" inquired he. "Have you brought me the head of Medusa with the snaky locks? If not, young man, it will cost you dear."

"Yes, please your Majesty," answered Perseus. "I have brought you the Gorgon's head, snaky locks and all!"

"Indeed! Pray let me see it," quoth King Polydectes. "It must be a very curious spectacle, if all that travelers tell about it be true!"

"Your Majesty is right," replied Perseus. "It is really an object that will be pretty certain to fix the regards of all who look at it. And if your Majesty think fit, I would suggest that a holiday be proclaimed and that all your Majesty's subjects be summoned to behold this wonderful curiosity. Few of them, I imagine, have seen a Gorgon's head before and perhaps never may again!"

The king well knew that his subjects were an idle set of reprobates, and very fond of sightseeing. So he sent out heralds and messengers in all directions to blow the trumpet at the street-corners and in the market-places and wherever two roads met and summon everybody to court. Thither, accordingly, came a great multitude of good-for-nothing vagabonds, all of whom out of pure love of mischief would have been glad if Perseus had met with some ill-hap in his encounter with the Gorgons. They ran as fast as they could to the palace and shoved and pushed and elbowed one another in their eagerness to get near a balcony on which Perseus showed himself, holding the embroidered wallet in his hand.

On a platform within full view of the balcony sat the mighty King Polydectes amid his evil counselors, and with his flattering courtiers in a semicircle round about him. Monarch, counselors, courtiers, and subjects all gazed eagerly towards Perseus.

"Show us the head! Show us the head!" shouted the people, and there was a fierceness in their cry as if they would tear Perseus to pieces unless he should satisfy them with what he had to show. "Show us the head of Medusa with the snaky locks!"

A feeling of sorrow and pity came over the youthful Perseus.

"O King Polydectes," cried he, "and ye many people. I am very loath to show you the Gorgon's head!"

"Ah, the villain and coward!" yelled the people, more fiercely than before. "He is making game of us! He has no Gorgon's head!"

The evil counselors whispered bad advice in the king's ear, the courtiers murmured that Perseus had shown disrespect to their royal lord and master, and the great King Polydectes himself waved his hand and ordered him, on his peril, to produce the head.

"Show me the Gorgon's head, or I will cut off your own!"

And Perseus sighed.

"This instant," repeated Polydectes, "or you die!"

"Behold it, then!" cried Perseus in a voice like the blast of a trumpet.

And suddenly holding up the head, not an eyelid had time to wink before the wicked King Polydectes, his evil counselors, and all his fierce subjects were all fixed forever in the look and attitude of that moment! At the first glimpse of the terrible head of Medusa they whitened into marble! And Perseus thrust the head back into his wallet and went to tell his dear mother that she need no longer be afraid of the wicked King Polydectes.

Discussion

1. (a) How does Perseus react at first to the idea of going on an "adventure" for King Polydectes? (b) How does he react after hearing what the king wants him to do? (c) What is King Polydectes' real reason for giving Perseus this task?

2. (a) How does Quicksilver treat Perseus from the start? (b) How does Perseus react to Quicksilver's offer of help? (c) What actual practical assistance does Quicksilver give?

3. What sensory imagery is used to describe the following: (a) the flight of Perseus and Quicksilver (408b, 3); (b) the Gorgons (403a, 4 and 409a, 4)?

4. Explain how each of the following objects helps Perseus in carrying out his task: (a) Quicksilver's staff; (b) the winged slippers; (c) the helmet of invisibility; (d) the polished shield; (e) the magic wallet.

5. Perseus tells King Polydectes that the Gorgon's head is "pretty certain to fix the regards of all who look at it." One interpretation of his statement is that the head will catch their attention. What other interpretation is possible?

6. What is ironic about the ending in which the king and most of his subjects

are turned to stone?

7. What seems to be the author's attitude toward the story and its characters? Would you describe the tone of the story as sad and sympathetic, lighthearted and amused, bitter and angry, or neutral and objective? Explain.

Vocabulary

Usage

Certain words and word forms may puzzle you because they are not common or else are used in uncommon ways. For example, what does *brave* mean in the following sentence? "But the staff helped Perseus along so *bravely* that he no longer felt the slightest weariness." The usual meaning "without fear" doesn't make sense here, but if you look up *brave* in the Glossary, you will find a further definition: "ARCHAIC. fine; excellent." The staff, then, helped Perseus *excellently.*

The label ARCHAIC means that a word or its meaning generally appears only in old books or in books written in the style of an earlier time. Other similar labels are INFORMAL, SLANG, DIALECT, and OBSOLETE. Dictionaries have additional ways of explaining the usage of words. One is to include a usage note after an entry, designated by ➤ or some similar device.

Look up the following italicized words in your Glossary (all have either labels or usage notes designated by ➤) and answer the questions. Be sure you know the meanings of all the words.

1. What label does *quoth* have?

2. In what sort of writing is *bade* chiefly used?

3. Rewrite this sentence, substituting a definition for the italicized word: "King Polydectes expected Perseus to meet with some *ill-hap* in his encounter with the Gorgons." (Hint: Look up the root *hap.*)

4. Why don't you hear *ye* used more often today?

5. When should you use *loath* instead of *loathe?*

Composition

The winged slippers, helmet of invisibility, and magic wallet that the Nymphs give Perseus certainly come in handy when he goes after Medusa. If you were going after a monster, what sort of magical equipment would you wish to have? First decide what monster you are going to capture or defeat. Then imagine a single piece of magical equipment that you would need to get past the monster's defenses and defeat it. (The article "Strange Combinations" on page 437 describes several monsters from Greek mythology; you may choose one of these monsters or make one up yourself.)

In your composition of a page or two, describe first the monster you are after. Be sure to explain the monster's powers and why it is almost impossible to defeat. Then describe your magical equipment and how you will use it. (You may wish also to explain how you obtain this equipment.) Perseus carried the head of Medusa back to King Polydectes and turned him to stone with it. What will you do with your monster once you have defeated it?

Daedalus

retold by **Anne Terry White**

"Not even the eagle soars as high as this!" the boy thought.

In the days when King Minos ruled Crete and his mighty navy ranged the seas, there lived in Athens a man by the name of Daedalus. And his name was known as far and wide as that of Minos. For Daedalus was the greatest architect and sculptor of his time. There was nothing his ingenious mind could not design or his skillful hands execute. And his statues were so real that people said they lived. It seemed that at any moment they might move a hand or take a step or open their lips and speak.

His young nephew, Talus, also had clever hands and a creative mind. So his mother placed him with her brother that the boy might learn his marvelous skills. But Talus had a genius of his own and even more imagination. Walking on the shore one day, he picked up the backbone of a fish. Idly he drew the strong, sharp spines forward and back across a piece of driftwood. They cut deep into the wood. He went home and notched a metal blade all along one edge—and he had a saw. Another time he fixed two iron rods together at the tip. He held one firmly upright against the earth and moved the other slowly around. It made a perfect circle—he had invented the compass.

Talus was a pupil to make any teacher excited and proud. But not Daedalus. Instead of being pleased, he was frightened and sorely jealous.

"Talus will soon surpass me!" he thought.

He could not bear the idea of a rival, and came to hate the boy. And one day, when they stood together on a height, Daedalus pushed Talus off to his death.

He had not planned the deed. It had been a sudden, crazy impulse. The next instant, horrified at what he had done, he rushed down to the boy. But it was too late. Talus was dead, and not all the wonderful skills of Daedalus could call him back. Clearly, if Daedalus wished to save his own life, he must flee. So he left Athens and wandered miserably from place to place, until at last he left Greece altogether and crossed the sea to Crete.

King Minos was delighted to have the Athenian in his realm. The King had something in mind that called for the genius of Daedalus. Minos possessed a fearful monster, with the head and shoulders of a bull and the legs and trunk of a man. The creature was called the Minotaur—that is, the Bull of Minos. The King wanted a suitable place to keep the Minotaur. The building must be such that neither the monster himself nor any victim sent in to be devoured by him could possibly escape from it.

So, at the King's command, Daedalus designed the labyrinth. The building was a bewildering maze of passages. They turned back upon themselves, crisscrossed, and went round and round without leading anywhere. Once inside the labyrinth, it was all but impossible to find the way out again. Even Daedalus himself was once nearly lost.

King Minos was delighted with Daedalus's work and held him in highest favor. Yet Daedalus was less than pleased, for he felt himself to be no better than a prisoner in Crete. The King was so afraid Daedalus would reveal the secret of the labyrinth that he would not let him leave the island. And for that very reason Daedalus yearned to go. With what envy he watched the birds winging their way through the sky!

One day, as his eyes followed the graceful sea birds cleaving the ocean of air, an idea came to him.

"King Minos may shut my way out by land and by sea," he thought, "but he does not control the air."

And he began to study the flight of birds and to observe how their wings are fashioned. He watched the little song birds fold and unfold their wings, watched how they rose from the ground, flew down from the trees, and went to and fro. He also watched the herons slowly flapping their great wings. He watched the eagles soar and swoop. He saw, too, how their feathers overlapped one another—where they were large and where they were small.

When he thought he understood the secrets of flight, Daedalus went to a nesting place he knew of and gathered feathers of various sizes. And in a chamber close to the roof he began to build wings. First he laid down a row of the tiniest feathers, then a row of larger ones overlapping them, and yet larger ones beyond these. He fastened the feathers together in the middle with thread and at the bottom with wax. And when he had built on enough rows, he bent them around into a gentle curve to look like real birds' wings.

His young son Icarus stood by and watched his father work. Laughing, the boy caught the feathers when they blew away in the wind. He pressed his thumb into the yellow wax to soften it for his father, hindering more than he helped.

When Daedalus had finished the pair of wings, he put them on. He raised himself in the air and hovered there. He moved the wings just as he had seen birds do, and lo! he could fly. Icarus clapped his hands together in delight.

"Make me a pair of wings, too, father!" he cried.

Then Daedalus made a second pair of wings and prepared his son to fly.

"Now I warn you, Icarus," Daedalus said, "not to be reckless. Be wise, not bold. Take a course midway between heaven and earth. For if you fly too high, the sun will scorch your feathers. And if you fly too low, the sea will wet them. Take me for your guide. Follow me and you will be safe."

All the time he was speaking, Daedalus was fastening the wings to his son's shoulders. His hands trembled as he thought of the great adventure before them. At the same time, he was worried about the boy. He did not know whether he could quite trust Icarus to obey. As he adjusted his own wings and kissed the excited child, tears ran down Daedalus's face.

"Remember," he repeated for the last time. "Heed my words and stay close to me!"

Then he rose on his wings and flew from the housetop. Icarus followed.

Daedalus kept a watchful eye on the boy, even as a mother bird does when she has brought a fledgling out of its nest in the treetops and launched it in the air. It was early morning. Few people were about. But

here and there a plowman in the field or a
fisherman tending his nets caught sight of
them.

"They must be gods!" the simple toilers
cried, and they bent their bodies in reverent
worship.

Father and son flew far out over the sea.
Daedalus was no longer worried about Icarus, who managed his wings as easily as a
bird. Already the islands of Delos and Paros
were behind them. Calymne, rich in honey,
was on their right hand. But now Icarus began to yield to the full delight of his new-
found powers. He wanted to soar and
swoop. How thrilling it was to rise to a
height, close his wings, and speed down,
down, like a thunderbolt, then turn and rise
again!

Time after time Icarus tried it, each time daring greater heights. Then, forgetting his father's warning, he soared higher still, far up into the cloudless sky.

"Not even the eagle soars as high as this!" the boy thought. "I am like the gods that keep the wide heaven."

As the words crossed his mind, he felt a warm stream flow over his shoulders. He had come too close to the blazing sun, and the sweet-smelling wax that bound the feathers was melting. With a shock of terror he felt himself hurtling downward. His wings, broken in a thousand parts, were hurtling downward, too. In vain Icarus moved his arms up and down—he could get no hold on the air.

"Father!" he shrieked. "Father! Help! I am falling."

Even as he cried, the deep blue water of the sea—that ever since has been called Icarian—closed over him.

"Icarus! Icarus! Where are you?" Daedalus cried, turning in every direction and searching the air behind, above, and all around. Then his eyes fell on the sea. Tufts of feathers were floating on the crest of the waves.

Too well he understood their meaning. Folding his great wings, he came to earth on the nearest island and fixed his streaming eyes upon the sea. He beat his breast. Wildly he clutched his hair.

"O Icarus, my son!" he wailed. "Even so fell Talus whom my envy slew! The gods have avenged him." He ripped off his glorious wings and stamped upon them. "Cursed be the skill that wrought my son's destruction!" he cried.

Days afterwards, the body of Icarus washed to the shore. There, on the lonely island which bears the boy's name, Daedalus buried his only son.

Discussion

1. (a) Why must Daedalus flee from Athens? (b) Why does King Minos welcome him? (c) How does Daedalus plan to escape from Crete with his son Icarus?

2. Like many fathers before him, Daedalus tells his son, "Take me for your guide. Follow me and you will be safe." (a) What happens when Icarus disobeys? (b) How might Daedalus's warning to Icarus be updated to apply to advice given by a modern parent to his or her child?

3. This myth touches on two concepts important to the Greeks. The first of these is *hubris* (hyü′bris), excessive pride that leads to disrespect to the gods. (a) Is Daedalus guilty of hubris? (b) Is Icarus guilty of it? Explain.

4. A second concept important to the Greeks is *nemesis* (nem′ə sis), by which an evil deed is appropriately punished. (Nemesis was the goddess of vengeance or divine punishment.) In what sense might the story of Daedalus serve as an illustration of nemesis?

5. The phrase "the price of progress" suggests that an invention or development can have bad as well as good results.
(a) What "price" does Talus pay for his ingenuity? (b) What "price" does Daedalus pay for building the labyrinth? for achieving flight?

The gods and mortals of myth live on in our
language and in our literature—as in this
poem about a modern-day Icarus.

I, *Icarus*

Alden Nowlan

There was a time when I could fly. I swear it.
Perhaps, if I think hard for a moment, I can even tell you the year.
My room was on the ground floor at the rear of the house.
My bed faced a window.
5 Night after night I lay on my bed and willed myself to fly.
It was hard work, I can tell you.
Sometimes I lay perfectly still for an hour before I felt my body rising from the bed.
I rose slowly, slowly, until I floated three or four feet above the floor.
Then, with a kind of swimming motion, I propelled myself toward the window.

10 Outside, I rose higher and higher, above the pasture fence, above the clothesline, above
    the dark, haunted trees beyond the pasture.
And, all the time, I heard the music of the flutes.
It seemed the wind made this music.
And sometimes there were voices singing.
All of this was a long time ago and I cannot remember the words the voices sang,
15 But I know I flew when I heard them.

Discussion

1. **(a)** How would you describe the speaker in this poem? **(b)** What details suggest that the setting is *not* ancient Greece?

2. In your own words describe the experience the speaker relates.

3. **(a)** What similarities are there between the experience related here and that of Icarus in the myth "Daedalus"? What differences are there? **(b)** Why do you think the poem is entitled "I, Icarus"? **(c)** What details besides the title suggest the influence of Greek myths on the speaker?

Theseus

as told by **Bernard Evslin**

Theseus cried to the wind, "I will be a king . . . or I will not be at all."

Young Theseus had a secret. He lived with his mother in a little hut on a wild sea-battered part of the coast called Troezen. For all his poor house and worn-out clothes, he was very proud, for he had a secret: he knew that he was the son of a king. His mother had told him the story one night when their day's catch of fish had been very bad and they were hungry.

"A king, truly," she said. "And one day you will know his name."

"But mother, then why are you not a queen and I a prince? Why don't we live in a palace instead of a hovel?"

"Politics, my son," she said sadly. "All politics . . . . You're too young to understand, but your father has a cousin, a very powerful lord with fifty sons. They are waiting for your father to die so they can divide the kingdom. If they knew he had a son of his own to inherit it, they would kill the son immediately."

"When can I go to him? When can I go there and help my father?"

"When you're grown. When you know how to fight your enemies."

This was Theseus's secret . . . and he needed a secret to keep him warm in those long, cold, hard years. One of his worst troubles was his size. His being small for his age bothered him terribly, for how could he become a great fighter and help his father against terrible enemies if he couldn't even hold his own against the village boys? He exercised constantly by running up and down the cliffs, swimming in the roughest seas, lifting logs and rocks, bending young trees; and indeed he grew much stronger, but he was still very dissatisfied with himself.

A Voice from the Sea

One day, when he had been beaten in a fight with a larger boy, he felt so gloomy that he went down to the beach and lay on the sand watching the waves, hoping that a big one would come along and cover him.

"I will not live this way!" he cried to the wind. "I will not be small and weak and poor. I will be a king, a warrior . . . or I will not be at all."

And then it seemed that the sound of the waves turned to a deep-voiced lullaby, and Theseus fell asleep—not quite asleep, perhaps, because he was watching a great white gull smashing clams open by dropping them on the rocks below. Then the bird swooped down and stood near Theseus's head looking at him, and spoke, "I can crack clams open because they are heavy. Can I do this with shrimps or scallops? No . . . they are too light. Do you know the answer to my riddle?"

"Is it a riddle?"

"A very important one. The answer is this: do not fear your enemy's size, but use it against him. Then his strength will be-

Reprinted by permission of Scholastic Magazines, Inc. from *Heroes, Gods, and Monsters of the Greek Myths* by Bernard Evslin. Copyright © 1966, 1967 by Scholastic Magazines, Inc.

come yours. When you have used this secret, come back, and I will tell you a better one.''

Theseus sat up, rubbing his eyes. Was it a dream? Had the gull been there, speaking to him? Could it be? What did it all mean? Theseus thought and thought; then he leaped to his feet and raced down the beach, up the cliff to the village where he found the boy who had just beaten him and slapped him across the face. When the boy, who was almost as big as a man, lunged toward him swinging his big fist, Theseus caught the fist and pulled in the same direction. The boy, swung off balance by his own power, went spinning off his feet and landed headfirst.

"Get up," said Theseus. "I want to try that again."

The big fellow lumbered to his feet and rushed at Theseus, who stooped suddenly. The boy went hurtling over him and landed in the road again. This time he lay still.

"Well," said Theseus, "that was a smart gull."

One by one, Theseus challenged the largest boys of the village; and, by being swift and sure and using their own strength against them, he defeated them all.

Then, he returned to the beach and lay on the sand, watching the waves, and listening as the crashing became a lullaby. Once again, his eyes closed, then opened. The great white seagull was pacing the sand near him.

"Thank you," said Theseus.

"Don't thank me," said the gull. "Thank your father. I am but his messenger."

"My father, the king?"

"King, indeed. But not the king your mother thinks."

"What do you mean?"

"Listen now . . . . Your father rules no paltry stretch of earth. His domain is as vast as all the seas, and all that is beneath them, and all that the seas claim. He is the Earthshaker, Poseidon.''

"Poseidon . . . my father?"

"You are his son."

"Then why does my mother not know? How can this be?"

"You must understand, boy, that the gods sometimes fall in love with beautiful maidens of the earth, but they cannot appear to the maidens in their own forms. The gods are too large, too bright, too terrifying, so they must disguise themselves. Now, when Poseidon fell in love with your mother, she had just been secretly married to Aegeus, king of Athens. Poseidon disguised himself as her new husband, and you, you are his son. One of many, very many; but he seems to have taken a special fancy to you and plans great and terrible things for you . . . if you have the courage.''

"I have the courage," said Theseus. "Let me know his will."

"Tomorrow," said the seagull, "you will receive an unexpected gift. Then you must bid farewell to your mother and go to Athens to visit Aegeus. Do not go by sea. Take the dangerous overland route, and your adventures will begin.''

The waves made great crashing music. The wind crooned. A blackness crossed the boy's mind. When he opened his eyes the gull was gone, and the sun was dipping into the sea.

"Undoubtedly a dream," he said to himself. "But the last dream worked. Perhaps this one will too."

The next morning there was a great excitement in the village. A huge stone had appeared in the middle of the road. In this stone was stuck a sword halfway up to its hilt; and a messenger had come from the oracle at Delphi[1] saying that whoever pulled the sword from the stone was a king's son and must go to his father.

When Theseus heard this, he embraced his mother and said, "Farewell."

"Where are you going, my son?"

"To Athens. This is the time we have been waiting for. I shall take the sword from the stone and be on my way."

"But, son, it is sunk so deeply. Do you think you can? Look . . . look . . . the strongest men cannot budge it. There is the smith trying . . . and there the Captain of the Guard . . . and look . . . look at that giant herdsman trying. See how he pulls and grunts. Oh, son, I fear the time is not yet."

"Pardon me," said Theseus, moving through the crowd. "Let me through, please. I should like a turn."

When the villagers heard this, heard the short fragile-looking youth say these words, they exploded in laughter.

"Delighted to amuse you," said Theseus. "Now, watch this."

Theseus grasped the sword by the hilt and drew it from the stone as easily as though he were drawing it from a scabbard; he bowed to the crowd and stuck the sword in his belt. The villagers were too stunned to say anything. They moved apart as he approached, making room for him to pass. He smiled, embraced his mother again, and set out on the long road to Athens.

The Road

The overland road from Troezen to Athens was the most dangerous in the world. It was infested not only by bandits but also giants, ogres, and sorcerers who lay in wait for travelers and killed them for their money, or their weapons, or just for sport.

Those who had to make the trip usually went by boat, preferring the risk of shipwreck and pirates to the terrible mountain brigands. If the trip overland had to be made, travelers banded together, went heavily armed, and kept watch as though on a military march.

Theseus knew all this, but he did not give it a second thought. He was too happy to be on his way . . . leaving his poky little village and his ordinary life. He was off to the great world and adventure. He welcomed the dangers that lay in wait. "The more, the better," he thought. "Where there's danger, there's glory. Why, I shall be disappointed if I am *not* attacked."

He was not to be disappointed. He had not gone far when he met a huge man in a bearskin carrying an enormous brass club. This was Corynetes, the cudgeler, terror of travelers. He reached out a hairy hand, seized Theseus by the throat and lifted his club, which glittered in the hot sunlight.

"Pardon me," said Theseus. "What are you planning to do?"

"Bash in your head."

"Why?"

"That's what I do."

"A beautiful club you have there, sir," said Theseus. "So bright and shiny. You know, it's a positive honor to have my head bashed in with a weapon like this."

"Pure brass," growled the bandit.

"Mmm . . . but is it really brass? It might be gilded wood, you know. A brass club would be too heavy to lift."

"Not too heavy for me," said the bandit, "and it's pure brass. Look . . . ."

He held out his club, which Theseus ac-

---

1. **oracle at Delphi.** An oracle (ôr′ə kəl) is a shrine or place where it was thought that a god provided answers to questions. The shrine of Apollo in the town of Delphi (del′ fī) was one of the most famous oracles.

cepted, smiling. Swinging it in a mighty arc he cracked the bandit's head as if it were an egg.

"Nice balance to this," said Theseus. "I think I'll keep it." He shouldered the club and walked off.

The road ran along the edge of the cliff above the burning blue sea. He turned a bend in the road and saw a man sitting on a rock. The man held a great battle-ax in his hand; he was so large that the ax seemed more like a hatchet.

"Stop!" said the man.

"Good day," said Theseus.

"Now listen, stranger, everyone who passes this way washes my feet. That's the toll. Any questions?"

"One. Suppose I don't?"

"Then I'll simply cut off your head," said the man, "unless you think that little twig you're carrying will stop this ax."

"I was just asking," said Theseus. "I'll be glad to wash your feet, sir. Personal hygiene is very important, especially on the road."

"What?"

"I said I'll do it."

Theseus knelt at the man's feet and undid his sandals, thinking hard. He knew who this man was; he had heard tales of him. This was Sciron who was notorious for keeping a pet turtle that was as large for a turtle as Sciron was for a man and was trained to eat human flesh. This giant turtle swam about at the foot of the cliff waiting for Sciron to kick his victims over. Theseus glanced swiftly down the cliffside. Sure enough, he saw the great blunt head of the turtle lifted out of the water, waiting.

Theseus took Sciron's huge foot in his hand, holding it by the ankle. As he did so, the giant launched a mighty kick. Theseus was ready. When the giant kicked, Theseus

pulled, dodging swiftly out of the way as the enormous body hurtled over him, over and down, splashing the water cliff-high as it hit. Theseus saw the turtle swim toward the splash. He arose, dusted off his knees, and proceeded on his journey.

The road dipped now, running past a grove of pines.

"Stop!"

He stopped. There was another huge brute of a man facing him. First Theseus thought that Sciron had climbed back up the cliff somehow; but then he realized that this must be Sciron's brother, of whom he had also heard. This fellow was called Pityocamptes, which means "pine-bender." He was big enough and strong enough to press pine trees to the ground. It was his habit to bend a tree just as a passerby approached and ask the newcomer to hold it for a moment. The traveler, afraid not to oblige, would grasp the top of the tree. Then Pityocamptes with a great jeering laugh would release his hold. The pine tree would spring mightily to its full height, flinging the victim high in the air, so high that the life was dashed out of him when he hit the ground. Then the bandit would search his pockets, chuckling all the while, as he was a great joker. Now he said to Theseus, "Wait, friend. I want you to do me a favor."

He reached for a pine tree and bent it slowly to earth like an enormous bow. "Just hold this for a moment like a good fellow, will you?"

"Certainly," said Theseus.

Theseus grasped the tree, set his feet, clenched his teeth, let his mind go dark and all his strength flow downward, through his legs, into the earth, anchoring him to the earth like a rock. Pityocamptes let go, expecting to see Theseus fly into the air.

Nothing happened. The pine stayed bent. The lad was holding it, legs rigid, arms trembling. The giant could not believe his eyes. He thought he must have broken the pine while bending it. He leaned his head closer to see. Then Theseus let go. The tree snapped up, catching the giant under the chin, knocking him unconscious. Theseus bent the tree again, swiftly bound the giant's wrists to it. He pulled down another pine and tied Pityocamptes' legs to that . . . and then let both pines go. They sprang apart. Half of Pityocamptes hung from one tree, half from the other. Vultures screamed with joy and fed on both parts impartially. Theseus wiped the pine tar from his hands and continued on his way.

By now it was nightfall, and he was very weary. He came to an inn where light was coming from the window, smoke from the chimney. But it was not a cozy sight as the front yard was littered with skulls and other bones.

"They don't do much to attract guests," thought Theseus. "Well . . . I'm tired. It has been a gruesome day. I'd just as soon go to bed now without any more fighting. On the other hand, if an adventure comes my way, I must not avoid it. Let's see what this bone-collector looks like."

He strode to the door and pounded on it, crying, "Landlord! Landlord, ho!"

The door flew open. In it was framed a greasy-looking giant, resembling Sciron and the pine-bender, but older, filthier, with long, tangled gray hair and a blood-stained gray beard. He had great meaty hands like grappling hooks.

"Do you have a bed for the night?" said Theseus.

"A bed? That I have. Come with me."

He led Theseus to a room where a bed stood—an enormous ugly piece of furniture, hung with leather straps, and chains, and shackles.

"What are all those bolts and bindings for?" said Theseus.

"To keep you in bed until you've had your proper rest."

"Why should I wish to leave the bed?"

"Everyone else seems to. You see, this is a special bed, exactly six feet long from head to foot. And I am a very neat, orderly person. I like things to fit. Now, if the guest is too short for the bed, we attach those chains to his ankles and stretch him. Simple."

"And if he's too long?" said Theseus.

"Oh, well then we just lop off his legs to the proper length."

"I see."

"But don't worry about that part of it. You look like a stretch job to me. Go ahead, lie down."

"And if I do, then you will attach chains to my ankles and stretch me—if I understand you correctly."

"You understand me fine. Lie down."

"But all this stretching sounds uncomfortable."

"You came here. Nobody invited you. Now you've got to take the bad with the good."

"Yes, of course," said Theseus. "I suppose if I decided not to take advantage of your hospitality . . . I suppose you'd *make* me lie down, wouldn't you?"

"Oh, sure. No problem."

"How? Show me."

The inn-keeper, whose name was Procrustes, reached out a great hand, put it on Theseus's chest, and pushed him toward the bed. Theseus took his wrist, and, as the big man pushed, he pulled . . . in the swift shoulder-turning downward snap he had taught himself. Procrustes flew over his shoulder and landed on the bed. Theseus bolted him fast, took up an ax, and chopped off his legs as they dangled over the footboards. Then, because he did not wish the fellow to suffer, chopped off his head too.

"As you have done by travelers, so are you done by," said Theseus. "You have made your bed, old man. Now lie on it."

He put down the ax, picked up his club, and resumed his journey, deciding to sleep in the open because he found the inn unpleasant.

Athens

Athens was not yet a great city in those days, but it was far more splendid than any Theseus had seen. He found it quite beautiful with arbors and terraces and marble temples. After the adventures of the road, however, he found it strangely dull. He suffered too from humiliation for, although he was the king's son, his father was in a very weak position so he could not be a real prince. It was his father's powerful cousin, the tall black-browed Pallas with his fifty fierce sons, who actually ran things. Their estate was much larger and finer than the castle, their private army stronger than the Royal Guard, and Theseus could not bear it.

"Why was I given the sign?" he stormed. "Why did I pull the sword from the stone and come here to Athens? To skulk in the castle like a runaway slave? What difference does it make, Father, how *many* there are? After we fight them, there will be many less. Let's fight! Right now!"

"No," said Aegeus, "we cannot. Not yet. It would not be a battle, it would be suicide. They must not know you are here. I am sorry now I had you come all the way to Athens. It is too dangerous. I should have kept you in some little village some-

where, outside of town, where we could have seen each other every day, but where you would not be in such danger."

"Well, if I am no use here, let me go to Crete!" cried Theseus. "If I can't fight our enemies at home, let me try my hand abroad."

"Crete! . . . Oh, my dear boy, no, no . . ." and the old man fell to lamenting, for it was in these days that Athens, defeated in a war with Crete, was forced by King Minos to pay a terrible tribute. He demanded that each year the Athenians send him seven of their most beautiful maidens, seven of their strongest men. These were

taken to the labyrinth and offered to the monster who lived there—the dread Minotaur, half man and half bull. Year after year they were taken from their parents, these seven maidens and seven youths, and were never heard of again. Now the day of tribute was approaching again.

Theseus offered to go himself as one of the seven young men and take his chances with the monster. He kept hammering at his father, kept producing so many arguments, was so electric with impatience and rage, that finally his father consented, and the name Theseus was entered among those who were to be selected for tribute. The

night before he left, he embraced Aegeus and said, "Be of good heart, dear sire. I traveled a road that was supposed to be fatal before and came out alive. I met quite a few unpleasant characters on my journey and had a few anxious moments, but I learned from them that the best weapon you can give an enemy is your own fear. So . . . who can tell? I may emerge victorious from the labyrinth and lead my companions home safely. Then I will be known to the people of Athens and will be able to rouse them against your tyrant cousins and make you a real king."

"May the gods protect you, son," said

Aegeus. "I shall sacrifice to Zeus and to Ares, and to our own Athene, every day, and pray for your safety."

"Don't forget Poseidon," said Theseus.

"Oh, yes, Poseidon too," said Aegeus. "Now do this for me, son. Each day I shall climb the Hill of the Temple, and from there watch over the sea . . . watching for your ship to return. It will depart wearing black sails, as all the sad ships of tribute do; but if you should overcome the Minotaur, please, I pray you, raise a white sail. This will tell me that you are alive and save a day's vigil."

"That I will do," said Theseus. "Watch for the white sail . . . ."

Crete

All Athens was at the pier to see the black-sailed ship depart. The parents of the victims were weeping and tearing their clothing. The maidens and the young men, chosen for their beauty and courage, stood on the deck trying to look proud; but the sound of lamentation reached them, and they wept to see their parents weep. Then Theseus felt the cords of his throat tighten with rage. He stamped his foot on the deck and shouted, "Up anchor, and away!" as though he were the captain of the vessel. The startled crew obeyed, and the ship moved out of the harbor.

Theseus immediately called the others to him. "Listen to me," he said. "You are not to look upon yourselves as victims, or victims you will surely be. The time of tribute has ended. You are to regard this voyage not as a submission but as a military expedition. Everything will change, but first you must change your own way of looking at things. Place your faith in my hands, place yourselves under my command. Will you?"

"We will!" they shouted.

"Good. Now I want every man to instruct every girl in the use of the sword and the battle-ax. We may have to cut our way to freedom. I shall also train you to respond to my signals—whistles, hand-movements—for if we work as a team, we may be able to defeat the Minotaur and confound our enemies."

They agreed eagerly. They were too young to live without hope, and Theseus's words filled them with courage. Every day he drilled them, man and maiden alike, as though they were a company of soldiers. He taught them to wrestle in the way he had invented. And this wild young activity, this sparring and fencing, so excited the crew, that they were eager to place themselves under the young man's command.

"Yes," he said, "I will take your pledges. You are Athenians. Right now that means you are poor, defeated, living in fear. But one day 'Athenian' will be the proudest name in the world, a word to make warriors quake in their armor, kings shiver upon their thrones!"

Now Minos of Crete was the most powerful king in all the world. His capital, Knossos, was the gayest, richest, proudest city in the world; and the day, each year, when the victims of the Minotaur arrived from Athens, was always a huge feast-day. People mobbed the streets—warriors with shaven heads and gorgeous feathered cloaks, women in jewels, children, farmers, great swaggering bullherders, lithe bullfighters, dwarfs, peacocks, elephants, and slaves, slaves, slaves from every country known to man. The streets were so jammed no one could walk freely, but the King's Guard kept a lane open from quayside to palace. And here, each year, the fourteen victims were marched so that the whole city could see them—marched past the crowds to the palace to be presented to the king to have their beauty approved before giving them to the Minotaur.

On this day of arrival, the excited harbormaster came puffing to the castle, fell on his knees before the throne, and gasped, "Pity, great king, pity . . . ."

And then in a voice strangled with fright the harbormaster told the king that one of the intended victims, a young man named Theseus, demanded a private audience with Minos before he would allow the Athenians to disembark.

"My warships!" thundered Minos. "The harbor is full of triremes.[2] Let the ship be seized, and this Theseus and his friends dragged here through the streets."

"It cannot be, your majesty. Their vessel stands over the narrow neck of the harbor. And he swears to scuttle it right there, blocking the harbor, if any of our ships approach."

"Awkward . . . very awkward," murmured Minos. "Quite resourceful for an Athenian, this young man. Worth taking a look at. Let him be brought to me."

Thereupon Theseus was informed that the king agreed to see him privately. He was led to the palace, looking about eagerly as he was ushered down the lane past the enormous crowd. He had never seen a city like this. It made Athens look like a little fishing village. He was excited and he walked proudly, head high, eyes flashing. When he came to the palace, he was introduced to the king's daughters, two lovely young princesses, Ariadne and Phaedra.

"I regret that my queen is not here to greet you," said Minos. "But she has become attached to her summer house in the labyrinth and spends most of her time there."

The princesses were silent, but they never took their eyes off Theseus. He could not decide which one he preferred. Ariadne, he supposed—the other was really still a little girl. But she had a curious cat-faced look about her that intrigued him. However, he could not give much thought to this; his business was with the king.

Finally, Minos signaled the girls to leave the room, and motioned Theseus toward his throne. "You wanted to see me alone," he said. "Here I am. Speak."

"I have a request, your majesty. As the son of my father, Aegeus, King of Athens, and his representative in this court, I ask you formally to stop demanding your yearly tribute."

"Oh, heavens," said Minos. "I thought you would have something original to say. And you come with this threadbare old petition. I have heard it a thousand times and refused it a thousand times."

"I know nothing of what has been done before," said Theseus. "But only of what I must do. You laid this tribute upon Athens to punish the city, to show the world that you were the master. But it serves only to degrade you and show the world that you are a fool."

"Feeding you to the Minotaur is much too pleasant a finale for such an insolent rascal," said Minos. "I shall think of a much more interesting way for you to die—perhaps several ways."

"Let me explain what I mean," said Theseus. "Strange as it seems, I do not hate you. I admire you. You're the most powerful king in the world and I admire power. In fact, I intend to imitate your career. So what I say, I say in all friendliness, and it is this: when you take our young men and

---

2. triremes. A trireme (trī′rēm′) was a Greek warship having three rows of oars on each side.

women and shut them in the labyrinth to be devoured by the Minotaur, you are making the whole world forget Minos, the great general Minos, the wise king. What you are forcing upon their attention is Minos, the betrayed husband, the man whose wife disliked him so much she ran away. And this image of you is what people remember. Drop the tribute, I say, and you will once again live in man's mind as warrior, lawgiver, and king.''

"You are an agile debater," said Minos, "as well as a very reckless young man, saying these things to me. But there is a flaw in your argument. If I were to drop the tribute, my subjects would construe this as an act of weakness. They would be encouraged to launch conspiracies against me. Other countries under my sway would be encouraged to rebel. It cannot be done.''

"I can show you a graceful way to let the tribute lapse. One that will not be seen as a sign of weakness. Just tell me how to kill the monster."

"Kill the monster, eh? And return to Athens a hero? And wipe out your enemies there? And then subdue the other cities of Greece until you become leader of a great alliance? And then come visit me again with a huge fleet and an enormous army, and topple old Minos from his throne . . . ? Do I describe your ambitions correctly?''

"The future does not concern me," said Theseus. "I take one thing at a time. And the thing that interests me now is killing the Minotaur.''

"Oh, forget the Minotaur," said Minos. "How do you know there is one? How do you know it's not some maniac there who ties sticks to his head? Whatever it is, let him rot there in the labyrinth with his mad mother. I have a better plan for you. My sons are dead. My daughter Ariadne, I no-tice, looks upon you with favor. Marry her, and become my heir. One day you will rule Crete and Athens both . . . and all the cities of the sea.''

"Thank you, sir. I appreciate your offer. But I came here to fight a monster."

"You are mad."

"Perhaps. But this is the only way I know how to be. When I am your age, when the years have thinned my blood, when rage has cooled into judgment, then I will go in for treaties, compromises. Now, I must fight.''

"Why is the young fool so confident?" thought Minos to himself. "He acts like a man who knows he is protected by the gods. Can it be true what they say? Is he really the son of Poseidon? Do I have that kind of enemy on my hands? If so, I will make doubly sure to get rid of him.''

Then he said aloud, "You are wrong to refuse my offer. I suppose you are made so wildly rash by some old gossip in your little village that you are the son of this god or that. Those mountain villages of yours, they're ridiculous. Every time a child does something out of the way, all the crones and hags get together and whisper, 'He's the son of a god, really the son of a god.' Is that the way of it? Tell the truth now.''

"My truth," said Theseus, "is that I am the son of Poseidon.''

"Poseidon, eh? No less. Well, how would you like to prove it?''

"Why should I care to prove it? *I* know. That's enough for me. The whole world has heard that you are the son of Zeus, who courted your mother, Europa, in the guise of a white bull. Everyone has heard this tale; few disbelieve it. But can you prove it?''

"Come with me," said Minos.

He led him out of the palace, beyond the

wall, to a cliff overlooking the sea. He stood tall, raised his arms, and said, "Father Zeus, make me a sign."

Lightning flashed so furiously that the night became brighter than day, and the sky spoke in thunder. Then Minos dropped his arms; the light stopped pulsing in the sky, and the thunder was still.

"Well," said Minos. "Have I proved my parentage?"

"It's an impressive display. I suppose it proves something."

"Then show me you are the son of Poseidon."

Minos took the crown from his head and threw it over the cliff into the sea. They heard the tiny splash far below.

"If you are his son, the sea holds no terror for you. Get me my crown," said Minos.

Without a moment's hesitation, Theseus stepped to the edge of the cliff and leaped off. As he fell, he murmured, "Father, help me now."

Down he plunged, struck the black water and went under, shearing his way through until he felt his lungs bursting. But he did not kick toward the surface. He let out the air in his chest in a long tortured gasp, and then, breathed in. No strangling rush of water, but a great lungful of sweet cool air . . . and he felt himself breathing as naturally as a fish. He swam down, down, and as he swam his eyes became accustomed to the color of the night sea; he moved in a deep green light. And the first thing he saw was the crown gleaming on the bottom. He swam down and picked it up.

Theseus stood on the ocean bottom holding the crown in his hand and said, "All thanks, Father Poseidon."

He waited there for the god to answer him, but all he saw were dark gliding shapes, creatures of the sea passing like shadows. He swam slowly to the surface, climbed the cliff, and walked to where Minos was waiting.

"Your crown, sir."

"Thank you."

"Are you convinced now that Poseidon is my father?"

"I am convinced that the water is more shallow here than I thought. Convinced that you are lucky."

"Luck? Is that not another word for divine favor?"

"Perhaps. At any rate, I am also convinced that you are a dangerous young man. So dangerous that I am forced to strip you of certain advantages allowed those who face the Minotaur. You will carry neither sword nor ax, but only your bare hands . . . and your luck, of course. I think we will not meet again. So farewell." He whistled sharply. His Royal Guard appeared, surrounded Theseus, and marched him off to a stone tower at the edge of the labyrinth. There they locked him up for the night.

An hour before dawn Ariadne appeared in his cell and said, "I love you, Theseus. I will save you from death if you promise to take me back to Athens with you."

"And how do you propose to save me, lovely princess?"

"Do you know what the labyrinth is? It is a hedge of a thousand lanes, all leading in, and only one leading out. And this one is so concealed, has so many twists and turns and secret windings that no one can possibly find his way out. Only I can travel the labyrinth freely. I will lead you in and hide you. I will also lead you around the central chamber where the Minotaur is and lead you out again. You will not even see the monster. Since no one has ever found his way out of the maze, Minos will assume that you have killed the Minotaur, and you will have a chance to get to your ship and escape before the trick is discovered. But you must take me with you.''

"It cannot be,'' said Theseus.

"Don't you believe me? It's all true. Look . . . .''

She took from her tunic a ball of yellow silk thread and dropped it on the floor. The ball swiftly rolled across the room, unwinding itself as it went. It rolled around the bench, wrapped itself around one of Theseus's ankles, rolled up the wall, across the ceiling and down again. Then Ariadne tugged sharply on her end of the thread, and the ball reversed itself, rolling back the way it had come, reeling in its thread as it rolled. Back to Ariadne it rolled and leaped into her hand.

"This was made for me by old Daedalus,'' said Ariadne. "It was he who built the labyrinth, you know. And my father shut him up in it too. I used to go visit him there. He made me this magic ball of thread so that I would always be able to find my way to him, and find my way back. He was very fond of me.''

"I'm getting very fond of you too,'' said Theseus.

"Do you agree?'' cried Ariadne. "Will you let me guide you in the labyrinth and teach you how to avoid the monster, and fool my father? Say you will. Please . . . .''

"I'll let you guide me through the maze,'' said Theseus. "Right to where the monster dwells. You can stay there and watch the fight. And when it's over, you can lead me back.''

"No, no, I won't be able to. You'll be dead! It's impossible for you to fight the Minotaur.''

"It is impossible for me not to.''

"You won't even be armed.''

"I have always traveled light, sweet princess, and taken my weapons from the enemy. I see no reason to change my habits now. Are you the kind of girl who seeks to change a man's habits? If you are, I don't think I will take you back to Athens.''

"Oh, please, do not deny me your love,'' she said. "I will do as you say.''

The next morning when the Royal Guard led Theseus out of the tower and forced him into the outer lane of the labyrinth, Ariadne was around the first bend, waiting. She tied one end of the thread to a branch of the hedge, then dropped the ball to the ground. It rolled slowly, unwinding; they followed, hand in hand. It was pleasant, walking in the labyrinth. The hedge grew tall above their heads and was heavy with little white sweet-smelling flowers. The lane turned and twisted and turned again, but the ball of thread ran ahead, and they followed it. Theseus heard a howling.

"Sounds like the wind,'' he said.

"No, it is not the wind. It is my mad mother, howling.''

They walked farther. They heard a rumbling, crashing sound.

"What's that?''

"That is my brother. He's hungry.''

They continued to follow the ball of thread. Now the hedges grew so tall the branches met above their heads, and it was dark. Ariadne looked up at him, sadly. He bent his head and brushed her lips in a kiss.

"Please don't go to him,'' she said. "Let me lead you out now. He will kill you. He has the strength of a bull and the cunning of a man.''

"Who knows?'' said Theseus. "Perhaps he has the weakness of a man and the stupidity of a bull.'' He put his hand over her mouth. "Anyway, let me think so because I

Paintings on two vases from
ancient Greece show Theseus
fighting the Minotaur. On the
vase at the right, Ariadne stands
facing Theseus.

must fight him, you see, and I'd rather not frighten myself beforehand.''

The horrid roaring grew louder and louder. The ball of thread ran ahead, ran out of the lane, into an open space. And here, in a kind of meadow surrounded by the tall hedges of the labyrinth, stood the Minotaur.

Theseus could not believe his eyes. The thing was more fearsome than in his worst dreams. What he had expected was a bull's head on a man's body. What he saw was something about ten feet tall shaped like a man, like an incredibly huge and brutally muscular man, but covered with a short dense brown fur. It had a man's face, but a squashed, bestialized one, with poisonous red eyes, great blunt teeth, and thin leathery lips. Sprouting out of its head were two long, heavy, polished horns. Its feet were hooves, razor sharp; its hands were shaped like a man's hands, but much larger and hard as horn. When it clenched them they were great fists of bone.

It stood pawing the grass with a hoof, peering at Theseus with its little red eyes. There was a bloody slaver on its lips.

Now, for the first time in all his battles, Theseus became unsure of himself. He was confused by the appearance of the monster. It filled him with a kind of horror that was beyond fear, as if he were wrestling a giant spider. So when the monster lowered its head and charged, thrusting those great bone lances at him, Theseus could not move out of the way.

There was only one thing to do. Drawing himself up on tiptoe, making himself as narrow as possible, he leaped into the air and seized the monster's horns. Swinging himself between the horns, he somersaulted onto the Minotaur's head, where he crouched, gripping the horns with desperate strength. The monster bellowed with rage and shook its head violently. But Theseus held on. He thought his teeth would shake out of his head; he felt his eyeballs rattling in their sockets. But he held on.

Now, if it can be done without one's being gored, somersaulting between the horns is an excellent tactic when fighting a real bull; but the Minotaur was not a real bull; it had hands. So when Theseus refused to be shaken off but stood on the head between the horns trying to dig his heels into the beast's eyes, the Minotaur stopped shaking his head, closed his great horny fist, big as a cabbage and hard as a rock, and struck a vicious backward blow, smashing his fist down on his head, trying to squash Theseus as you squash a beetle.

This is what Theseus was waiting for. As soon as the fist swung toward him, he jumped off the Minotaur's head, and the fist smashed between the horns, full on the skull. The Minotaur's knees bent, he staggered and fell over; he had stunned himself. Theseus knew he had only a few seconds before the beast would recover his strength. He rushed to the monster, took a horn in both hands, put his foot against the ugly face, and putting all his strength in a sudden tug, broke the horn off at the base. He leaped away. Now he, too, was armed, and with a weapon taken from the enemy.

The pain of the breaking horn goaded the Minotaur out of his momentary swoon. He scrambled to his feet, uttered a great choked bellow, and charged toward Theseus, trying to hook him with his single horn. Bone cracked against bone as Theseus parried with his horn. It was like a duel now, the beast thrusting with his horn, Theseus parrying, thrusting in return. Since the Minotaur was much stronger, it forced Theseus back—back until it had Theseus pinned against the hedge. As soon as he felt the first touch of the hedge, Theseus disengaged, ducked past the Minotaur, and raced to the center of the meadow, where he stood, poised, arm drawn back. For the long pointed horn made as good a javelin as it did a sword, and so could be used at a safer distance.

The Minotaur whirled and charged again. Theseus waited until he was ten paces away, and then whipped his arm forward, hurling the javelin with all his strength. It entered the bull's neck and came out the other side. But so powerful was the Minotaur's rush, so stubborn his bestial strength, that he trampled on with the sharp horn through his neck and ran right over Theseus, knocking him violently to the ground. Then it whirled to try to stab Theseus with its horn; but the blood was spouting fast now, and the monster staggered and fell on the ground beside Theseus.

Ariadne ran to the fallen youth. She turned him over, raised him in her arms; he was breathing. She kissed him. He opened his eyes, looked around, and saw the dead Minotaur; then he looked back at her and smiled. He climbed to his feet, leaning heavily on Ariadne.

"Tell your thread to wind itself up again, princess. We're off for Athens."

When Theseus came out of the labyrinth there was an enormous crowd of Cretans gathered. They had heard the sound of fighting, and, as the custom was, had gathered to learn of the death of the hostages. When they saw the young man covered with dirt and blood, carrying a broken horn, with Ariadne clinging to his arm, they raised a great shout.

Minos was there, standing with his arms folded. Phaedra was at his side. Theseus bowed to him and said, "Your majesty, I have the honor to report that I have rid your kingdom of a foul monster."

"Prince Theseus," said Minos. "According to the terms of the agreement, I must release you and your fellow hostages."

"Your daughter helped me, king. I have promised to take her with me. Have you any objection?"

"I fancy it is too late for objections. The women of our family haven't had much luck in these matters. Try not to be too beastly to her."

"Father," said Phaedra, "she will be lonesome there in far-off Athens. May I not go with her and keep her company?"

"You too?" said Minos. He turned to Theseus. "Truly, young man, whether or not Poseidon has been working for you, Aphrodite surely has."

"I will take good care of your daughters, king," said Theseus. "Farewell."

And so, attended by the Royal Guard, Theseus, his thirteen happy companions, and the two Cretan princesses, walked through the mobbed streets from the palace to the harbor. There they boarded their ship.

It was a joyous ship that sailed northward from Crete to Athens. There was feasting and dancing night and day. And every young man aboard felt himself a hero too, and every maiden a princess. And Theseus was lord of them all, drunk with strength and joy. He was so happy he forgot his promise to his father—forgot to tell the crew to take down the black sail and raise a white one.

King Aegeus, keeping a lonely watch on the Hill of the Temple, saw first a tiny speck on the horizon. He watched it for a long time and saw it grow big and then bigger. He could not tell whether the sail was white or black; but as it came nearer, his heart grew heavy. The sail seemed to be dark. The ship came nearer, and he saw that it wore a black sail. He knew that his son was dead.

"I have killed him," he cried. "In my weakness, I sent him off to be killed. I am unfit to be king, unfit to live. I must go to Tartarus immediately and beg his pardon there."

And the old king leaped from the hill, dived through the steep air into the sea far below, and was drowned. He gave that lovely blue, fatal stretch of water its name for all time—the Aegean Sea.

Theseus, upon his return to Athens, was hailed as king. The people worshipped him. He swiftly raised an army, wiped out his powerful cousins, and then led the Athenians forth into many battles, binding all the cities of Greece together in an alliance. Then, one day he returned to Crete to reclaim the crown of Minos which once he had recovered from the sea.

Discussion

1. (a) Theseus's early years are difficult. What secret helps him get through this period? (b) What is the point of the riddle that the gull tells Theseus, and how does Theseus test it? (c) What does the gull later tell Theseus about his father? (d) What feat does Theseus perform in the presence of the villagers before he leaves, and what does it signify?

2. The term "poetic justice" is often applied to situations in which people are defeated or punished by the same treatments they customarily use on others. Cite at least three examples of poetic justice from Theseus's experiences on the road to Athens.

3. (a) Why is Theseus eager to journey to Crete after only a short stay in Athens? (b) Why is Aegeus so reluctant to allow Theseus to make the journey? (c) What signal is Theseus supposed to make to Aegeus if he is successful?

4. (a) In which episodes is Theseus mainly dependent on cleverness? (b) In which episodes is he dependent on his strength? (c) In which does he rely on assistance from others, human or divine?

5. Explain the irony in the following statements: (a) "Delighted to amuse you" (422a, 7); (b) "It's a positive honor to have my head bashed in with a weapon like this" (422b, 7); (c) "Personal hygiene is very important, especially on the road" (424a, 8).

6. Repeated throughout this myth is a pattern of the larger and stronger being defeated by the smaller and weaker. (a) List as many examples of this pattern as you can. (b) What is the effect of this repetition, and what does it suggest to you about the theme of this myth?

Vocabulary
Context, Roots

The italicized words in each of the statements on the next page explain or define the root of one of the listed words. Read each statement; then write on your paper the word from the list that best completes it. (You will not use one of the listed words.)

alliance   disembark
bestialized parentage
disengage   submission

1. Alice does not know who her *mother and father* are; in other words, she is not sure of her _____.

2. He thinks that Fred's crimes have ____ him and turned him into an *animal.*

3. If you *give in* to what she wants with no argument now, she will only expect more acts of _____ from you in the future.

4. If you don't want to *take part* in conversations that waste your time, try to ____ yourself gracefully and walk away.

5. Often throughout history various *nations joined together* have called themselves an _____.

Comment: Strange Combinations

The strange creatures called the Gorgons and the Minotaur belong to a large and bizarre collection of monsters that appear in Greek myths. Other well-known oddities include:

A dreaded, fire-breathing monster, the Chimera (kə mir′ə) was a zoo on four legs. She was a lion in front, a goat in the middle, and a snake (or dragon) behind—complete with the heads of each creature. (The word *chimera* today is used to refer to an absurd, impossible idea or fancy.) The Chimera was eventually killed by the hero Bellerophon (bə ler′ə fon) mounted on the flying horse Pegasus (peg′ə səs). According to one version, Bellerophon defeated the monster by poking a lump of lead into her fiery mouth: the lead melted and the Chimera was choked to death.

The Hydra (hī′drə) was a monstrous serpent with nine poisonous heads. As part of his Twelve Labors, the great hero Heracles (her′ə klēz′) was ordered to kill the Hydra. At first Heracles had a terrible time: when he cut off one head, two more sprouted in its place. Heracles solved the problem by using fire to sear the necks. The Hydra's last head was immortal, so Heracles buried it under a large rock.

Centaurs (sen′tôrz) had four legs like horses, but their heads, arms, and chests were human. Most centaurs were brutal, ill-tempered creatures who lived on raw flesh, but one, Chiron (kī′ron), was wise and gentle. He trained many of the Greek heroes in music, hunting, and medicine.

The Sirens were sisters with the faces of maidens and the feathered bodies of birds. The Sirens could sing beautifully—but it was fatal to hear them do so. Sailors were lured to shipwreck, drowning, or starvation by Siren songs; human bones cluttered the island on which the Sirens lived (in some accounts, the Sirens devoured their spellbound listeners). One man who heard the Sirens and survived to tell about it was Ulysses (yü lis′ēz), who plugged the ears of his crew and had himself tied securely to the ship's mast. The Sirens were so enraged by this clever escape that they flung themselves into the sea and drowned.

Minotaur

Robert Fisher

in the middle of the sea lies an island
in the middle of the island stands a palace
in the middle of the palace is a maze
of darkened rooms and alleyways
5 endless walls and hidden doors
miles and miles of corridors
here shadows fall and footsteps sound
echoing along the ground
here is my home
10 I am minotaur
half-man half-bull
shaggy-headed golden horns
hear me bellow hear my roar
see the slavering of my jaw
15 round the corner here I wait
flaring nostrils sniff the air
for here or somewhere a door may open
and I will enter

your dream
20 of the sea
and in the middle of the sea lies an island
in the middle of the island stands a palace
in the middle of the palace is a maze
of darkened rooms and alleyways
25 endless walls and hidden doors
miles and miles of corridors
here shadows fall and footsteps sound
echoing along the ground
here is my home
30 I am . . . waiting

Discussion

1. (a) From what point of view is this poem related? Who is the speaker? (b) Whom does the speaker seem to be addressing?

2. (a) Which details about the Minotaur and the labyrinth are the same in this poem as in "Theseus"? (b) Which details are different? How would you account for this difference? (Reviewing the Introduction on pages 388-389 may help you answer this question.)

3. In what ways is the structure of the poem itself like a maze or labyrinth?

4. In lines 18-19 the speaker says, "I will enter/your dream. . . ." In your opinion, is this poem meant to represent a dream experience or a real one? Explain.

Phaëthon

retold by **Edith Hamilton**

For a few thrilling moments, Phaëthon felt like the Lord of the Sky. But suddenly the chariot was swinging to and fro—he had lost control!

The palace of the Sun was a radiant place. It shone with gold and gleamed with ivory and sparkled with jewels. Everything without and within flashed and glowed and glittered. It was always high noon there. Shadowy twilight never dimmed the brightness. Darkness and night were unknown. Few among mortals could have long endured that unchanging brilliancy of light, but few had ever found their way thither.

Nevertheless, one day a youth, mortal on his mother's side, dared to approach. Often he had to pause and clear his dazzled eyes, but the errand which had brought him was so urgent that his purpose held fast and he pressed on, up to the palace, through the burnished doors, and into the throneroom where surrounded by a blinding, blazing splendor the Sun-god sat. There the lad was forced to halt. He could bear no more.

Nothing escapes the eyes of the Sun. He saw the boy instantly and he looked at him very kindly. "What brought you here?" he asked. "I have come," the other answered boldly, "to find out if you are my father or not. My mother said you were, but the boys at school laugh when I tell them I am your son. They will not believe me. I told my mother and she said I had better go and ask you." Smiling, the Sun took off his crown of burning light so that the lad could look at him without distress. "Come here, Phaëthon," he said. "You are my son. Clymene told you the truth. I expect you will not

doubt my word too? But I will give you a proof. Ask anything you want of me and you shall have it. I call the Styx to be witness to my promise, the river of the oath of the Gods."

No doubt Phaëthon had often watched the Sun riding through the heavens and had told himself with a feeling, half awe, half excitement, "It is my father up there." And then he would wonder what it would be like to be in that chariot, guiding the steeds along that dizzy course, giving light to the world. Now at his father's words this wild dream had become possible. Instantly he cried, "I choose to take your place, Father. That is the only thing I want. Just for a day, a single day, let me have your car to drive."

The Sun realized his own folly. Why had he taken that fatal oath and bound himself to give in to anything that happened to enter a boy's rash young head? "Dear lad," he said, "this is the only thing I would have refused you. I know I cannot refuse. I have sworn by the Styx. I must yield if you persist. But I do not believe you will. Listen while I tell you what this is you want. You are Clymene's son as well as mine. You are mortal and no mortal could drive my chariot. Indeed, no god except myself can do

that. The ruler of the gods cannot. Consider the road. It rises up from the sea so steeply that the horses can hardly climb it, fresh though they are in the early morning. In mid-heaven it is so high that even I do not like to look down. Worst of all is the descent, so precipitous that the Sea-gods waiting to receive me wonder how I can avoid falling headlong. To guide the horses, too, is a perpetual struggle. Their fiery spirits grow hotter as they climb and they scarcely suffer my control. What would they do with you?

"Are you fancying that there are all sorts of wonders up there, cities of the gods full of beautiful things? Nothing of the kind. You will have to pass beasts, fierce beasts of prey, and they are all that you will see. The Bull, the Lion, the Scorpion, the great Crab,[1] each will try to harm you. Be persuaded. Look around you. See all the goods the rich world holds. Choose from them your heart's desire and it shall be yours. If what you want is to be proved my son, my fears for you are proof enough that I am your father."

But none of all this wise talk meant anything to the boy. A glorious prospect opened before him. He saw himself proudly standing in that wondrous car, his hands triumphantly guiding those steeds which Jove himself could not master. He did not give a thought to the dangers his father detailed. He felt not a quiver of fear, not a doubt of his own powers. At last the Sun gave up trying to dissuade him. It was hopeless, as he saw. Besides, there was not time. The moment for starting was at hand. Already the gates of the east glowed purple, and Dawn had opened her courts full of rosy light. The stars were leaving the sky; even the lingering morning star was dim.

There was need for haste, but all was ready. The seasons, the gatekeepers of Olympus, stood waiting to fling the doors wide. The horses had been bridled and yoked to the car. Proudly and joyously Phaëthon mounted it and they were off. He had made his choice. Whatever came of it he could not change now. Not that he wanted to in that first exhilarating rush through the air, so swift that the East Wind was outstripped and left far behind. The horses' flying feet went through the low-banked clouds near the ocean as through a thin sea mist and then up and up in the clear air, climbing the height of heaven. For a few ecstatic moments Phaëthon felt himself the Lord of the Sky. But suddenly there was a change. The chariot was swinging wildly to and fro; the pace was faster; he had lost control. Not he, but the horses were directing the course. That light weight in the car, those feeble hands clutching the reins, had told them their own driver was not there. They were the masters then. No one else could command them. They left the road and rushed where they chose, up, down, to the right, to the left. They nearly wrecked the chariot against the Scorpion; they brought up short and almost ran into the Crab. By this time the poor charioteer was half fainting with terror, and he let the reins fall.

That was the signal for still more mad and reckless running. The horses soared up to the very top of the sky and then, plunging headlong down, they set the world on fire. The highest mountains were the first to burn, Ida and Helicon, where the Muses dwell, Parnassus, and heaven-piercing Olympus. Down their slopes the flame ran

---

1. **the Bull . . .the great Crab,** the constellations of Taurus, Leo, Scorpio, and Cancer, respectively.

to the low-lying valleys and the dark forest lands, until all things everywhere were ablaze. The springs turned into steam; the rivers shrank. It is said that it was then the Nile fled and hid his head, which still is hidden.

In the car Phaëthon, hardly keeping his place there, was wrapped in thick smoke and heat as if from a fiery furnace. He wanted nothing except to have this torment and terror ended. He would have welcomed death. Mother Earth, too, could bear no more. She uttered a great cry which reached up to the gods. Looking down from Olympus they saw that they must act quickly if the world was to be saved. Jove seized his thunderbolt and hurled it at the rash, repentant driver. It struck him dead, shattered the chariot, and made the maddened horses rush down into the sea.

Phaëthon all on fire fell from the car through the air to the earth. The mysterious river Eridanus, which no mortal eyes have ever seen, received him and put out the flames and cooled the body. The naiads, in pity for him, so bold and so young to die, buried him and carved upon the tomb:—

Here Phaëthon lies
    who drove the Sun-god's car.
Greatly he failed,
    but he had greatly dared.

His sisters, the Heliades, the daughters of Helios, the Sun, came to his grave to mourn for him. There they were turned into poplar trees, on the bank of the Eridanus,

Where sorrowing they weep into the
    stream forever.
And each tear as it falls shines in
    the water
A glistening drop of amber.

Discussion

1. What natural phenomenon is this myth based on? How did the ancient Greeks explain this phenomenon?

2. **(a)** Why does Phaëthon go to the palace of the Sun? **(b)** What request does he make of the Sun? **(c)** Against what dangers does the Sun warn Phaëthon? **(d)** Why does the Sun finally agree to Phaëthon's request?

3. What are the "beasts" that Phaëthon encounters in the sky?

4. What actually happens to Phaëthon?

5. Which of the following statements best expresses the theme of this myth? **(a)** Don't try to be a show-off in things you really know nothing about; **(b)** A young man ignores his father's warning and insists on a special privilege which leads to his death; **(c)** Human beings are not meant to ride through the air or to control things of nature; **(d)** A rash choice, made in ignorance and stubbornly followed through, can lead to disaster.

See **SATIRE** Handbook of Literary Terms

**Here the same legend is retold—
with a modern twist.**

Phaëthon

Morris Bishop

Apollo through the heavens rode
   In glinting gold attire;
His car was bright with chrysolite,
   His horses snorted fire.
5 He held them to their frantic course
   Across the blazing sky.
His darling son was Phaëthon,
   Who begged to have a try.

"The chargers are ambrosia-fed,[1]
10   They barely brook control;
On high beware the Crab, the Bear,
   The Serpent round the Pole;
Against the Archer[2] and the Bull
   Thy form is all unsteeled!"
15 But Phaëthon could lay it on;
   Apollo had to yield.

Out of the purple doors of dawn
   Phaëthon drove the horses;
They felt his hand could not command,
20   They left their wonted courses.
And from the chariot Phaëthon
   Plunged like a falling star—
And so, my boy, no, no, my boy,
   You cannot take the car.

---

1. ambrosia-fed. In myths, ambrosia (am brō′zhə) was the food of the gods; here, the horses are fed it as well.
2. the Bear . . . the Archer, constellations. The Bear is Ursa Major (which includes the Big Dipper); the Serpent round the Pole probably refers to Draco; the Archer is Sagittarius.

Discussion

1. (a) Who is the speaker in this poem? **(b)** Whom is the speaker addressing?

2. How are the speaker and the person being addressed similar to Apollo and Phaëthon? How are they different?

3. Does the speaker make any significant changes in the story of the myth? If so, what are they?

Application
Satire

A satire can deal with major social and political problems or with minor human absurdities, but in all cases satire uses humor of some sort to make its point.

1. At a certain point the speaker stops retelling the story of Phaëthon and makes a modern application of the myth. Which lines contain this modern application?

2. (a) Does the story of the myth seem appropriate for the modern application being made? Explain. **(b)** In your opinion, is the language of the poem appropriate for the point being made? Why or why not?

3. Is this poem in any sense a parody? Explain.

4. Which of the following best describes what this poem is satirizing? **(a)** ancient Greek myths; **(b)** certain kinds of poetry; **(c)** modern parent-child relationships; **(d)** the supposed power of the ancient gods.

Composition

In the myth, Phaëthon's father, the Sun, tries to talk him out of driving the sun chariot but finally gives in—with disastrous consequences to Phaëthon. In the poem, the father absolutely refuses to let his son take the car. Do you think that parents should let young people make their own mistakes (and pay for those mistakes themselves) or do you think that parents should be firm in what they will and will not allow their children to do? Complete this statement as you choose: Parents *(should/should not)* allow their children freedom to make mistakes. Plan carefully an argument to support your statement and think of examples that are relevant to your argument.

Write a composition of one or two pages, using the statement you have completed as a topic sentence. Support your argument in a way that will convince your readers of your point of view. If you wish, use "Phaëthon" or other myths as examples, but base your argument mostly on current situations you are familiar with.

(You may find the article "Supporting a Point" in the Composition Guide helpful in writing this composition.)

Glossary of Proper Names

Achilles (ə kil′ēz), son of Thetis who became a famous warrior and hero.

Acropolis (ə krop′ə lis), high, fortified section of Athens. Some of its ruins are still standing.

Aegean (i jē′ən) **Sea,** sea between Greece and Turkey, named for Aegeus who drowned himself in it.

Aegeus (ē′jüs, ē jē′əs), king of Athens.

Aetna (et′nə), **Mount,** volcano located in northeast Sicily. It is still active.

Amphitrite (am′fə trī′tē), wife of Poseidon.

Aphrodite (af′rə dī′tē), goddess of love and beauty. Roman name: Venus.

Apollo (ə pol′ō), god of the sun, poetry, music, prophecy, and healing. Also called Helios. Roman name: Phoebus (fē′ bəs) Apollo.

Arachne (ə rak′nē), woman who lost a weaving contest to Athene and was changed into a spider.

Ares (er′ēz, ar′ēz), god of war. Roman name: Mars.

Ariadne (ar′ē ad′nē), princess of Crete who helped Theseus.

Athene (ə thē′nē), goddess of wisdom, of weaving and other household arts, and of warfare. Roman name: Minerva (mə nèr′və).

Athenian (ə thē′nē ən, ə thē′nyən), native of Athens.

Athens (ath′ənz), capital city of ancient Greece.

Attica (at′ə kə), southern region of Greece.

Baucis (bô′sis), old peasant woman who entertained Zeus and Hermes.

Calymne (kə lim′nē), island in the Aegean Sea.

Clymene (klim′ə nē), mother of Phaëthon.

Corynetes (kôr′ə nē′tēz), giant bandit who murdered travelers by bashing their heads with a brass club.

Cretan (krēt′n), native of Crete.

Crete (krēt), Greek island in the Mediterranean, southeast of Greece.

Cronos (krō′nəs), father of the gods of Olympus.

Cyane (sī′ə nē), river in Sicily.

Cyclops (sī′klops), *pl.* **Cyclopes** (sī klō′pēz), one of a race of giants, children of Oranos, each having only one eye in the center of the forehead.

Daedalus (ded′l əs), skilled workman who constructed the labyrinth in Crete; with his son Icarus he escaped from imprisonment by using wings he built of feathers fastened by wax.

Danaë (dan′ā ē), mother of Perseus.

Delos (dē′los), island in the Aegean Sea.

Demeter (di mē′tər), goddess of agriculture and the harvest. Roman name: Ceres (sir′ēz).

Eleusis (i lü′sis), city in ancient Greece, near Athens.

Eridanus (ē rid′ə nəs), river in Italy.

Eros (ir′os, er′os), son of Aphrodite. Roman name: Cupid.

Europa (yu̇ rō′pə), mother of King Minos of Crete.

Gorgon (gôr′gən), any of three sister monsters having snakes for hair and faces so horrible that anyone who looked at them turned to stone.

Hades (hā′dēz), god of the underworld, which is often called by his name. Roman name: Pluto.

Heliades (hē lī′ ə dēz), daughters of Helios.

Helicon (hel′ə kon, hel′ə kən), **Mount,** mountain in southern Greece.

Helios (hē′lē os), god of the sun, pictured driving a chariot drawn by four horses through the heavens. Also called Apollo.

Hera (hir′ə), wife of Zeus and queen of the gods; goddess of women and marriage. Roman name: Juno (jü′nō).

Hermes (hər′mēz), messenger of the gods and guide who brings the souls of the dead to the underworld; god of travel, business, invention, and cunning. Roman name: Mercury (''Quicksilver'').

Hestia (hes′tē ə), goddess of hearth and home. Roman name: Vesta (ves′tə).

Hippodamia (hip′ō də mī′ə), princess betrothed to King Polydectes.

Icarian (i ker′ē ən, ī ker′ē ən) **Sea,** named after Icarus, who drowned in it.

Icarus (ik′ər əs), son of Daedalus. While escaping from Crete on wings that Daedalus had made, Icarus flew so high that the sun melted the wax with

a hat	i it	oi oil	ch child	(a in about
ā age	ī ice	ou out	ng long	e in taken
ä far	o hot	u cup	sh she	ə = { i in pencil
e let	ō open	u̇ put	th thin	o in lemon
ē equal	ô order	ü rule	ᵀH then	(u in circus
ėr term			zh measure	< = derived from

which his wings were made, and he drowned in the sea.

Ida (ī'də), **Mount,** mountain in northwest Asia Minor overlooking the Aegean Sea.

Jove (jōv). See Zeus.

Knossos (nos'əs), captial city of ancient Crete.

Medusa (mə dü'sə, mə dyü'sə), one of the three Gorgons, or horrible monsters with snakes for hair. She was slain by Perseus.

Minos (mī'nəs, mī'nos), king of Crete.

Minotaur (min'ə tôr), monster with a bull's head and a man's body, killed by Theseus.

Muse (myüz), one of the nine goddesses of the fine arts and sciences.

Naiad (nā'ad, nī'ad), nymph guarding a river, stream, or spring.

Nereid (nir'ē id), any one of fifty daughters of Nereus (nir'ē əs), a sea god.

Nile (nīl), river in East Africa, the longest in the world.

Nymph (nimf), any one of lesser goddesses of nature who lived in seas, rivers, fountains, springs, hills, woods, or trees.

Olympus (ō lim'pəs), **Mount,** mountain in northeastern Greece, considered the home of the major Greek gods.

Oranus (ôr ān'əs), the "First One," the ancestor of all gods.

Pallas (pal'əs), cousin of King Aegeus and a challenger to Aegeus' position as ruler of Athens.

Pan (pan), god of flocks, forests, and shepherds. His body was half human, but with the legs, horns, and ears of a goat.

Parnassus (pär nas'əs), **Mount,** mountain in central Greece, sacred to Apollo and the Muses.

Paros (per'os, par'os), island in the Aegean Sea.

Persephone (pər sef'ə nē), daughter of Demeter. Hades fell in love with her and carried her off to rule the underworld with him. Roman name: Proserpina (prō sėr'pə nə).

Perseus (pėr'sē əs, pėr'syüs), son of Zeus and Danaë who slew Medusa.

Phaedra (fē'drə), princess of Crete.

Phaëthon (fā'ə thon), son of Helios who tried unsuccessfully to drive the sun chariot.

Philemon (fi lē'mon), old peasant man who entertained Zeus and Hermes.

Pityocamptes (pit'ē ō kamp'tēz), giant bandit who murdered travelers by slinging them in the air with a bent pine tree.

Polydectes (pol'ē dek'tēz), wicked king of the Island of Seriphus.

Poseidon (pə sīd'n), god of the sea. Roman name: Neptune.

Procrustes (prō krus'tēz), giant innkeeper who murdered travelers by stretching them or cutting them to fit his bed.

Quicksilver. See Hermes.

Rhea (rē'ə), goddess of the earth.

Sciron (sī'ron), giant bandit who kicked travelers into the sea to be eaten by a giant turtle.

Seriphis (sə rī'fəs), island ruled by King Polydectes.

Sicily (sis'ə lē), largest island in the Mediterranean, near the southwest tip of the Italian peninsula.

Styx (stiks), river in the underworld that the souls of the dead must cross to reach Hades.

Talus (tā'ləs), nephew of Daedalus. Daedalus killed Talus because he was jealous of the boy's skill.

Tartarus (tär'tər əs), region of punishment located below Hades. Sometimes the term refers to the whole underworld.

Theseus (thē'süs, thē'sē əs), son of Poseidon who killed the Minotaur in the labyrinth.

Thetis (thē'tis), nymph whom Poseidon considered as a wife. She became the mother of Achilles.

Titan (tīt'n), any one of the gigantic offspring of Oranos; called the "first race."

Troezen (trē'zən), ancient seacoast town in Greece.

Zeus (züs), chief god of Olympus, ruler of gods and humans. Roman names: Jupiter, Jove.

Unit 7 Review: *Greek Myths*

Content Review

1. Many of the myths in this unit explain natural phenomena. Where and how are the following explained: **(a)** volcanoes and earthquakes; **(b)** sunrise and sunset; **(c)** seasonal changes; **(d)** creation of various animals?

2. Reread the myths dealing with Zeus, Poseidon, and Hades (the "Persephone" myth) and think of other myths in which these gods are mentioned or appear briefly. Characterize each as best you can, keeping in mind—and making reference to—the part of the world each one rules.

3. The following characters all have direct encounters with deities. For each, explain how the character came to encounter a god or goddess and what resulted from the encounter: **(a)** Arachne; **(b)** Perseus; **(c)** Phaëthon.

4. Many mortals in this unit have a particular skill or are unusually clever. **(a)** In which myths does skill or cleverness lead to success? **(b)** In which does skill or cleverness lead to disaster?

5. The introduction to this unit explains that the word *hero* was orginally applied to a mortal who had a god as one parent and a human as the other and who was unusually brave and strong. Compare Theseus and Perseus ("The Gorgon's Head") as heroes, including the ways in which they fulfill these qualifications. Which do you think is the greater hero? Explain.

6. The ancient Greeks believed in "the golden mean"—in being moderate and sensible in all things and in avoiding extremes and excesses. Which of the myths is this unit seem to demonstrate this principle by showing that moderation is good or that excess is bad?

Concept Review:
Interpretation of New Material

Read the myth below; then on a separate sheet of paper, write your answers to the questions that follow it.

Baucis and Philemon • retold by *Olivia Coolidge*

One time Zeus and Hermes came down to earth in human form and traveled through a certain district, asking for food and shelter as they went. For a long time they found nothing but refusals from both rich and poor until at last they came to a little, one-room cottage rudely thatched with reeds from the nearby marsh, where dwelled a poor old couple, Baucis and Philemon.

"Baucis and Philemon" from *Greek Myths* by Olivia E. Coolidge. Copyright 1949 and © renewed 1977 by Olivia E. Coolidge. Reprinted by permission of Houghton Mifflin Company.

The two had little to offer, since they lived entirely from the produce of their plot of land and a few goats, fowl, and pigs. Nevertheless they were prompt to ask the strangers in and to set their best before them. The couch that they pulled forward for their guests was roughly put together from willow boughs, and the cushions on it were stuffed with straw. One table leg had to be propped up with a piece of broken pot, but Baucis scrubbed the top with fragrant mint and set some water on the fire. Meanwhile Philemon ran out into the garden to fetch a cabbage and then lifted down a piece of home-cured bacon from the blackened beam where it hung. While these were cooking, Baucis set out her best delicacies on the table. There were ripe olives, sour cherries pickled in wine, fresh onions and radishes, cream cheese, and eggs baked in the ashes of the fire. There was a big earthenware bowl in the midst of the table to mix their crude, homemade wine with water.

The second course had to be fruit, but there were nuts, figs, dried dates, plums, grapes, and apples, for this was their best season of the year. Philemon had even had it in mind to kill their only goose for dinner, and there was a great squawking and cackling that went on for a long time. Poor old Philemon wore himself out trying to catch that goose, but somehow the animal always got away from him until the guests bade him let it be, for they were well served as it was. It was a good meal, and the old couple kept pressing their guests to eat and drink, caring nothing that they were now consuming in one day what would ordinarily last them a week.

At last the wine sank low in the mixing bowl, and Philemon rose to fetch some more. But to his astonishment as he lifted the wineskin to pour, he found the bowl was full again as though it had not been touched at all. Then he knew the two strangers must be gods, and he and Baucis were awed and afraid. But the gods smiled kindly at them, and the younger, who seemed to do most of the talking, said, "Philemon, you have welcomed us beneath your roof this day when richer men refused us shelter. Be sure those shall be punished who would not help the wandering stranger, but you shall have whatever reward you choose. Tell us what you will have."

The old man thought for a little with his eyes bent on the ground, and then he said: "We have lived together here for many years, happy even though the times have been hard. But never yet did we see fit to turn a stranger from our gate or to seek a reward for entertaining him. To have spoken with the immortals face to face is a thing few men can boast of. In this small cottage, humble though it is, the gods have sat at meat. It is as unworthy of the honor as we are. If, therefore, you will do something for us, turn this cottage into a temple where the gods may always be served and where we may live out the remainder of our days in worship of them."

"You have spoken well," said Hermes, "and you shall have your wish. Yet is there not anything that you would desire for yourselves?"

Philemon thought again at this, stroking his straggly beard, and he glanced over at old Baucis with her thin, grey hair and her rough hands as she served at the table, her feet bare on the floor of trodden earth. "We have lived together for many years," he said again, "and in all that time there has never been a word of anger between us. Now, at last, we are growing old and our long companionship is coming to an end. It is the only thing that has helped us in the bad times and the source of our joy in the good. Grant us this one request, that when we come to die, we may perish in the same hour and neither of us be left without the other."

He looked at Baucis and she nodded in approval, so the old couple turned their eyes on the gods.

"It shall be as you desire," said Hermes. "Few men would have made such a good and moderate request."

Thereafter the house became a temple, and the neighbors, amazed at the change, came often to worship and left offerings for the support of the aged priest and priestess there. For many years Baucis and Philemon lived in peace, passing from old to extreme old age. At last, they were so old and bowed that it seemed they could only walk at all if they clutched one another. But still every evening they would shuffle a little way down the path that they might turn and look together at the beautiful little temple and praise the gods for the honor bestowed on them. One evening it took them longer than ever to reach the usual spot, and there they turned arm in arm to look back, thinking perhaps that it was the last time their limbs would support them so far. There as they stood, each one felt the other stiffen and change and only had time to turn and say once, "Farewell," before they disappeared. In their place stood two tall trees growing closely side by side with branches interlaced. They seemed to nod and whisper to each other in the passing breeze.

---

1. The two gods involved in this selection are **(a)** Hermes and Athene; **(b)** Poseidon and Apollo; **(c)** Zeus and Hermes; **(d)** Demeter and Zeus.

2. In what form do the two gods travel the earth?

3. Baucis and Philemon support themselves by **(a)** poultry and livestock they have raised for sale; **(b)** their garden and a few animals; **(c)** gifts from their neighbors; **(d)** Philemon's work as a carpenter.

4. At first the old couple think that their guests are **(a)** gods; **(b)** officials from the village; **(c)** long-forgotten friends; **(d)** passing strangers.

5. Baucis and Philemon offer their guests **(a)** lodging for the night; **(b)** a donkey to carry their belongings for them; **(c)** fine pottery that Baucis has made; **(d)** a large meal.

6. What do Baucis and Philemon realize when the wine bowl suddenly becomes full again?

7. Told they can have whatever gift they want, Baucis and Philemon first ask that **(a)** the gods visit them again; **(b)** their cottage be turned into a temple; **(c)** they might never have to go hungry; **(d)** they might live forever.

8. Name at least two virtues, or good qualities, that Baucis and Philemon possess.

9. Baucis and Philemon do not die but are transformed into **(a)** statues; **(b)** farm animals; **(c)** trees; **(d)** mountains.

10. From this myth one can infer that the ancient Greeks greatly admired the quality of **(a)** showing generous hospitality; **(b)** always telling the truth; **(c)** working hard all one's life; **(d)** having no fear of death.

Composition Review

1. The gods and goddesses that appear in selections in this unit possess many of the same qualities or characteristics—both good and bad—that humans have. Briefly review "Zeus," "Poseidon," and "Persephone" and list some of the "human" characteristics displayed by the gods in those selections.

Write a composition of one or two pages in which you describe some of these human characteristics. Choose carefully the characteristics that you can support with specific examples. Try especially to include those that are displayed by more than one god. Where do you suppose the writers and tellers of these myths got their ideas about how the gods and goddesses behave?

2. Theseus and Perseus ("The Gorgon's Head") are both representatives of the Greek concept of a hero. Consider these two characters in terms of the following: (a) cleverness; (b) strength and courage; (c) help received from human and nonhuman sources; (d) an "impossible" task; (e) a successful conclusion.

In a few paragraphs describe what you think of as a "typical" Greek hero. Use at least one specific example from the story of either Theseus or Perseus to illustrate each of the five points given above. If you wish, you may also compare this typical Greek hero to a typical modern hero.

3. Theseus's punishments for the giants along the road are examples of poetic justice because they are punishments that are particularly appropriate to the situations. Of the situations that follow, choose two that you think best demonstrate poetic justice: (a) Arachne being changed into a spider; (b) King Polydectes being turned to stone; (c) Icarus falling to his death; (d) Phaëthon being destroyed by a thunderbolt.

Explain in a few paragraphs your understanding of poetic justice as it applies to the two situations you have chosen. Describe as much of your chosen situations as you need to in order to use them as examples.

"I see the eight of us . . . as if we were a little piece of blue heaven, surrounded by heavy black rain clouds. The round, clearly defined spot where we stand is still safe, but the clouds gather more closely about us and the circle which separates us from the approaching danger closes more and more tightly."

The Diary of Anne Frank

Introduction

When Anne Frank was thirteen years old, her family had to leave their home in Amsterdam, the Netherlands. The Franks were Jews, and, during World War II, no Jew was safe in lands controlled by the Nazis (nä′tsēs)—the German National Socialist Party that sought to conquer Europe.

Earlier Otto Frank, his wife Edith, and their two daughters Margot and Anne had fled Frankfort, Germany. In Amsterdam Mr. Frank became an importer for Travis, Inc. In May, 1940, the Nazi army captured the Netherlands, and in July, 1942, the Franks went into hiding in a secret apartment to escape persecution.

On her thirteenth birthday, Anne received a diary from her father. Into the diary Anne recorded the hopes, fears, joys, and frustrations of living for twenty-five months in cramped quarters under constant tension. That diary, on which this drama is based, remains a living tribute to the dignity, courage, and perseverance of the human spirit.

The Diary of Anne Frank

Dramatized by Frances Goodrich and Albert Hackett
(based upon the book, *Anne Frank: The Diary of a Young Girl*)

CHARACTERS

MR. OTTO FRANK (frängk)

MIEP (mēp) GIES (Hēs)

MR. VAN DAAN (fän dän′)

MRS. PETRONELLA (pet′rə nel′ə) VAN DAAN

PETER VAN DAAN

MRS. EDITH FRANK

MARGOT (mär′gət) FRANK

ANNE FRANK

MR. KRALER (krä′lər)

MR. DUSSEL (düs′əl)

The Time: During the years of World War II and immediately thereafter.
The Place: Amsterdam.
There are two acts.

Act One

Scene One

The scene remains the same throughout the play. It is the top floor of a warehouse and office building in Amsterdam, Holland. The sharply peaked roof of the building is outlined against a sea of other rooftops, stretching away into the distance. Nearby is the belfry of a church tower, the Westertoren, whose carillon rings out the hours. Occasionally faint sounds float up from below: the voices of children playing in the street, the tramp of marching feet, a boat whistle from the canal.

The three rooms of the top floor and a small attic space above are exposed to our view. The largest of the rooms is in the center, with two small rooms, slightly raised, on either side. On the right is a bathroom, out of sight. A narrow steep flight of stairs at the back leads up to the attic. The rooms are sparsely furnished with a few chairs, cots, a table or two. The windows are painted over, or covered with makeshift blackout curtains. In the main room there is a sink, a gas ring for cooking, and a woodburning stove for warmth.

The room on the left is hardly more than a closet. There is a skylight in the sloping ceiling. Directly under this room is a small steep stairwell, with steps leading down to a door. This is the only entrance from the building below. When the door is opened we see that it has been concealed on the outer side by a bookcase attached to it.

The curtain rises on an empty stage. It is late afternoon, November, 1945.

The rooms are dusty, the curtains in rags. Chairs and tables are overturned.

The door at the foot of the small stairwell swings open. MR. FRANK *comes up the steps into view. He is a gentle, cultured Euro-pean in his middle years. There is still a trace of a German accent in his speech.*

He stands looking slowly around, making a supreme effort at self-control. He is weak, ill. His clothes are threadbare.

After a second he drops his rucksack on the couch and moves slowly about. He opens the door to one of the smaller rooms, and then abruptly closes it again, turning away. He goes to the window at the back, looking off at the Westertoren as its carillon strikes the hour of six; then he moves restlessly on.

From the street below we hear the sound of a barrel organ and children's voices at play. There is a many-colored scarf hanging from a nail. MR. FRANK *takes it, putting it around his neck. As he starts back for his rucksack, his eye is caught by something lying on the floor. It is a woman's white glove. He holds it in his hand and suddenly all of his self-control is gone. He breaks down, crying.*

We hear footsteps on the stairs. MIEP GIES *comes up, looking for* MR. FRANK. MIEP *is a Dutch girl of about twenty-two. She wears a coat and hat, ready to go home. She is pregnant. Her attitude toward* MR. FRANK *is protective, compassionate.*

MIEP. Are you all right, Mr. Frank?

MR. FRANK (*quickly controlling himself*). Yes, Miep, yes.

MIEP. Everyone in the office has gone home . . . It's after six. (*Then pleading*) Don't stay up here, Mr. Frank. What's the use of torturing yourself like this?

MR. FRANK. I've come to say good-by . . . I'm leaving here, Miep.

MIEP. What do you mean? Where are you going? Where?

MR. FRANK. I don't know yet. I haven't decided.

MIEP. Mr. Frank, you can't leave here! This

is your home! Amsterdam is your home. Your business is here, waiting for you . . . You're needed here . . . Now that the war is over, there are things that . . .

MR. FRANK. I can't stay in Amsterdam, Miep. It has too many memories for me. Everywhere there's something . . . the house we lived in . . . the school . . . that street organ playing out there . . . I'm not the person you used to know, Miep. I'm a bitter old man. *(Breaking off)* Forgive me. I shouldn't speak to you like this . . . after all that you did for us . . . the suffering . . .

MIEP. No. No. It wasn't suffering. You can't say we suffered. *(As she speaks, she straightens a chair which is overturned.)*

MR. FRANK. I know what you went through, you and Mr. Kraler. I'll remember it as long as I live. *(He gives one last look around.)* Come, Miep. *(He starts for the steps, then remembers his rucksack, going back to get it.)*

MIEP *(hurrying up to a cupboard)*. Mr. Frank, did you see? There are some of your papers here. *(She brings a bundle of papers to him.)* We found them in a heap of rubbish on the floor . . . after you left.

MR. FRANK. Burn them. *(He opens his rucksack to put the glove in it.)*

MIEP. But, Mr. Frank, there are letters, notes . . .

MR. FRANK. Burn them. All of them.

MIEP. Burn *this?* *(She hands him a paperbound notebook.)*

MR. FRANK *(quietly)*. Anne's diary. *(He opens the diary and begins to read.)* "Monday, the sixth of July, nineteen forty-two." *(To MIEP)* Nineteen forty-two. Is it possible, Miep? . . . Only three years ago. *(As he continues his reading, he sits down on the couch.)* "Dear Diary, since you and I are going to be great

friends, I will start by telling you about myself. My name is Anne Frank. I am thirteen years old. I was born in Germany the twelfth of June, nineteen twenty-nine. As my family is Jewish, we emigrated to Holland when Hitler[1] came to power."

(As MR. FRANK reads on, another voice joins his, as if coming from the air. It is ANNE'S VOICE.)

MR. FRANK *and* ANNE. "My father started a business, importing spice and herbs. Things went well for us until nineteen forty. Then the war came, and the Dutch capitulation, followed by the arrival of the Germans. Then things got very bad for the Jews."

(MR. FRANK'S VOICE dies out. ANNE'S VOICE continues alone. The lights dim slowly to darkness. The curtain falls on the scene.)

ANNE'S VOICE. You could not do this and you could not do that. They forced Father out of his business. We had to wear yellow stars. I had to turn in my bike. I couldn't go to a Dutch school any more. I couldn't go to the movies, or ride in an automobile, or even on a streetcar, and a million other things. But somehow we children still managed to have fun. Yesterday Father told me we were going into hiding. Where, he wouldn't say. At five o'clock this morning Mother woke me and told me to hurry and get dressed. I was to put on as many clothes as I could. It would look too suspicious if we walked along carrying suitcases. It wasn't until we were on our way that I learned where we were going. Our hiding place was to be upstairs in the building where Father used to have his business. Three other

---

1. *Hitler,* Adolf Hitler (ā′dôlf hit′lər), 1889–1945, German National Socialist leader, dictator of Germany from 1933 to 1945.

people were coming in with us . . . the Van Daans and their son Peter . . . Father knew the Van Daans but we had never met them . . .

(During the last lines the curtain rises on the scene. The lights dim on. ANNE'S VOICE *fades out.)*

Discussion

1. (a) What is the time setting for this scene? **(b)** What is the general appearance of the rooms?

2. (a) What do you learn about Otto Frank in this scene? **(b)** What reason does Mr. Frank give Miep for his decision to leave Amsterdam?

3. (a) What information do you get about Anne from the first entry in her diary? **(b)** What information does the diary give about the war and its effect on the Jews?

Scene Two

It is early morning, July, 1942. The rooms are bare, as before, but they are now clean and orderly.

MR. VAN DAAN, *a tall, portly man in his late forties, is in the main room, pacing up and down, nervously smoking a cigarette. His clothes and overcoat are expensive and well cut.*

MRS. VAN DAAN *sits on the couch, clutching her possessions, a hatbox, bags, etc. She is a pretty woman in her early forties. She wears a fur coat over her other clothes.*

PETER VAN DAAN *is standing at the window of the room on the right, looking down at the street below. He is a shy, awkward boy of sixteen. He wears a cap, a raincoat, and long Dutch trousers, like "plus fours."[1] At his feet is a black case, a carrier for his cat.*

The yellow Star of David[2] is conspicuous on all of their clothes.

MRS. VAN DAAN *(rising, nervous, excited).* Something's happened to them! I know it!

MR. VAN DAAN. Now, Kerli![3]

MRS. VAN DAAN. Mr. Frank said they'd be here at seven o'clock. He said . . .

MR. VAN DAAN. They have two miles to walk. You can't expect . . .

MRS. VAN DAAN. They've been picked up. That's what's happened. They've been taken . . .

(MR. VAN DAAN indicates that he hears someone coming.)

MR. VAN DAAN. You see?

(PETER takes up his carrier and his schoolbag, etc. and goes into the main room as MR. FRANK comes up the stairwell from below. MR. FRANK looks much younger now. His movements are brisk, his manner confident. He wears an overcoat and carries his hat and a small cardboard box. He crosses to the VAN DAANS, shaking hands with each of them.)

MR. FRANK. Mrs. Van Daan, Mr. Van Daan, Peter. *(Then, in explanation of their lateness)* There were too many of the Green Police[4] on the streets . . . We had to take the long way around.

---

1. *plus fours,* loose knickers that come down below the knee.
2. *Star of David,* a six-pointed star, a religious symbol of the Jewish people. In Nazi-occupied countries all Jews were required to wear a Star of David prominently displayed on their clothing.
3. *Kerli* (ker′lē).
4. *Green Police,* a branch of the Nazi police who wore green uniforms.

(Up the steps come MARGOT FRANK, MRS.
FRANK, MIEP—*not pregnant now—and* MR.
KRALER. *All of them carry bags, pack-*
ages, and so forth. The Star of David is
conspicuous on all of the FRANKS' *cloth-*
ing. MARGOT *is eighteen, beautiful, quiet,*
shy. MRS. FRANK *is a young mother,*
gently bred, reserved. She, like MR.
FRANK, *has a slight German accent.* MR.
KRALER *is a Dutchman, dependable,*
kindly.

As MR. KRALER *and* MIEP *go upstage[5] to*
put down their parcels, MRS. FRANK *turns*
back to call ANNE.*)*

MRS. FRANK. Anne?

*(*ANNE *comes running up the stairs. She*
is thirteen, quick in her movements, inter-
ested in everything, mercurial in her emo-
tions. She wears a cape, long wool socks
and carries a schoolbag.)

MR. FRANK *(introducing them).* My wife,
Edith. Mr. and Mrs. Van Daan *(*MRS.
FRANK *hurries over, shaking hands with*
them.) . . . their son, Peter . . . my
daughters, Margot and Anne.

*(*ANNE *gives a polite little curtsy as she*
shakes MR. VAN DAAN'S *hand. Then she*
immediately starts off on a tour of inves-
tigation of her new home, going upstairs
to the attic room.

MIEP *and* MR. KRALER *are putting the*
various things they have brought on the
shelves.)

MR. KRALER. I'm sorry there is still so much
confusion.

MR. FRANK. Please. Don't think of it. After
all, we'll have plenty of leisure to arrange
everything ourselves.

MIEP *(to* MRS. FRANK*).* We put the stores of
food you sent in here. Your drugs are
here . . . soap, linen here.

MR. FRANK. Thank you, Miep.

MIEP. I made up the beds . . . the way Mr.

Frank and Mr. Kraler said. *(She starts*
out.) I have to hurry. I've got to go to the
other side of town to get some ration
books[6] for you.

MRS. VAN DAAN. Ration books? If they see
our names on ration books, they'll know
we're here.

MR. KRALER. There isn't anything . . .

MIEP. Don't worry. Your
names won't be on them.
(As she hurries out) I'll be
up later.

(Together)

MR. FRANK. Thank you, Miep.

MRS. FRANK *(to* MR. KRALER*).* It's illegal,
then, the ration books? We've never
done anything illegal.

MR. FRANK. We won't be living here exactly
according to regulations.

(As MR. KRALER *reassures* MRS. FRANK, *he*
takes various small things, such as
matches, soap, etc., from his pockets,
handing them to her.)

MR. KRALER. This isn't the black market,
Mrs. Frank. This is what we call the
white market[7] . . . helping all of the
hundreds and hundreds who are hiding
out in Amsterdam.

(The carillon is heard playing the quarter-
hour before eight. MR. KRALER *looks at*
his watch. ANNE *stops at the window as*
she comes down the stairs.)

ANNE. It's the Westertoren!

MR. KRALER. I must go. I must be out of here
and downstairs in the office before the
workmen get here. *(He starts for the*
stairs leading out.) Miep or I, or both of

---

5. **upstage,** toward the back of the stage. *Down,* or *downstage,*
means toward the front of the stage.
6. **ration books,** books of coupons which allowed the bearer to
buy a fixed amount of provisions or food.
7. **black market . . . white market.** Black market goods are sold
illegally, usually at a very high price. The goods the Franks were
receiving (white market) were donated by people wishing to
help the Jews.

us, will be up each day to bring you food and news and find out what your needs are. Tomorrow I'll get you a better bolt for the door at the foot of the stairs. It needs a bolt that you can throw yourself and open only at our signal. (*To* MR. FRANK) Oh . . . You'll tell them about the noise?

MR. FRANK. I'll tell them.

MR. KRALER. Good-by then for the moment. I'll come up again, after the workmen leave.

MR. FRANK. Good-by, Mr. Kraler.

MRS. FRANK (*shaking his hand*). How can we thank you?

(*The others murmur their good-bys.*)

MR. KRALER. I never thought I'd live to see the day when a man like Mr. Frank would have to go into hiding. When you think—

(*He breaks off, going out.* MR. FRANK *follows him down the steps, bolting the door after him. In the interval before he returns,* PETER *goes over to* MARGOT, *shaking hands with her. As* MR. FRANK *comes back up the steps,* MRS. FRANK *questions him anxiously.*)

MRS. FRANK. What did he mean, about the noise?

MR. FRANK. First let us take off some of these clothes.

(*They all start to take off garment after garment. On each of their coats, sweaters, blouses, suits, dresses, is another yellow Star of David.* MR. *and* MRS. FRANK *are underdressed quite simply. The others wear several things—sweaters, extra dresses, bathrobes, aprons, nightgowns, etc.*)

MR. VAN DAAN. It's a wonder we weren't arrested, walking along the streets . . . Petronella with a fur coat in July . . . and that cat of Peter's crying all the way.

ANNE (*as she is removing a pair of panties*). A cat?

MRS. FRANK (*shocked*). Anne, please!

ANNE. It's all right. I've got on three more. (*She pulls off two more. Finally, as they have all removed their surplus clothes, they look to* MR. FRANK, *waiting for him to speak.*)

MR. FRANK. Now. About the noise. While the men are in the building below, we must have complete quiet. Every sound can be heard down there, not only in the workrooms, but in the offices too. The men come at about eight-thirty, and leave at about five-thirty. So, to be perfectly safe, from eight in the morning until six in the evening we must move only when it is necessary, and then in stockinged feet. We must not speak above a whisper. We must not run any water. We cannot use the sink, or even, forgive me, the w.c.[8] The pipes go down through the workrooms. It would be heard. No trash . . . (MR. FRANK *stops abruptly as he hears the sound of marching feet from the street below. Everyone is motionless, paralyzed with fear.* MR. FRANK *goes quietly into the room on the right to look down out of the window.* ANNE *runs after him, peering out with him. The tramping feet pass without stopping. The tension is relieved.* MR. FRANK, *followed by* ANNE, *returns to the main room and resumes his instructions to the group.*) . . . No trash must ever be thrown out which might reveal that someone is living up here . . . not even a potato paring. We must burn everything in the stove at night. This is the way we must live until it is over, if we are to survive.

(*There is silence for a second.*)

MRS. FRANK. Until it is over.

---

8. *w. c.*, water closet, the bathroom.

MR. FRANK (*reassuringly*). After six we can move about . . . we can talk and laugh and have our supper and read and play games . . . just as we would at home. (*He looks at his watch.*) And now I think it would be wise if we all went to our rooms, and were settled before eight o'clock. Mrs. Van Daan, you and your husband will be upstairs. I regret that there's no place up there for Peter. But he will be here, near us. This will be our common room, where we'll meet to talk and eat and read, like one family.

MR. VAN DAAN. And where do you and Mrs. Frank sleep?

MR. FRANK. This room is also our bedroom.

MRS. VAN DAAN. That isn't right.
We'll sleep here and you take the room upstairs. } (*Together*)

MR. VAN DAAN. It's your place.

MR. FRANK. Please. I've thought this out for weeks. It's the best arrangement. The only arrangement.

MRS. VAN DAAN (*to* MR. FRANK). Never, never can we thank you. (*Then to* MRS. FRANK) I don't know what would have happened to us, if it hadn't been for Mr. Frank.

MR. FRANK. You don't know how your husband helped me when I came to this country . . . knowing no one . . . not able to speak the language. I can never repay him for that. (*Going to* VAN DAAN) May I help you with your things?

MR. VAN DAAN. No. No. (*To* MRS. VAN DAAN) Come along, *liefje.*[9]

MRS. VAN DAAN. You'll be all right, Peter? You're not afraid?

PETER (*embarrassed*). Please, Mother.
(*They start up the stairs to the attic room above.* MR. FRANK *turns to* MRS. FRANK.)

MR. FRANK. You too must have some rest, Edith. You didn't close your eyes last night. Nor you, Margot.

ANNE. I slept, Father. Wasn't that funny? I knew it was the last night in my own bed, and yet I slept soundly.

MR. FRANK. I'm glad, Anne. Now you'll be able to help me straighten things in here. (*To* MRS. FRANK *and* MARGOT) Come with me . . . You and Margot rest in this room for the time being. (*He picks up their clothes, starting for the room on the right.*)

MRS. FRANK. You're sure . . . ? I could help . . . And Anne hasn't had her milk . . .

MR. FRANK. I'll give it to her. (*To* ANNE *and* PETER) Anne, Peter . . . it's best that you take off your shoes now, before you forget. (*He leads the way to the room, followed by* MARGOT.)

MRS. FRANK. You're sure you're not tired, Anne?

ANNE. I feel fine. I'm going to help Father.

MRS. FRANK. Peter, I'm glad you are to be with us.

PETER. Yes, Mrs. Frank.

(MRS. FRANK *goes to join* MR. FRANK *and* MARGOT.

During the following scene MR. FRANK *helps* MARGOT *and* MRS. FRANK *to hang up their clothes. Then he persuades them both to lie down and rest. The* VAN DAANS *in their room above settle themselves. In the main room* ANNE *and* PETER *remove their shoes.* PETER *takes his cat out of the carrier.*)

ANNE. What's your cat's name?

PETER. Mouschi.[10]

ANNE. Mouschi! Mouschi! Mouschi! (*She picks up the cat, walking away with it. To* PETER) I love cats. I have one . . . a darling little cat. But they made me leave her behind. I left some food and a note for

---

9. *liefje* (lēf′Hyə), darling.
10. *Mouschi* (müs′kē).

the neighbors to take care of her . . . I'm going to miss her terribly. What is yours? A him or a her?

PETER. He's a tom. He doesn't like strangers. *(He takes the cat from her, putting it back in its carrier.)*

ANNE *(unabashed).* Then I'll have to stop being a stranger, won't I? Is he fixed?

PETER *(startled).* Huh?

ANNE. Did you have him fixed?

PETER. No.

ANNE. Oh, you ought to have him fixed—to keep him from—you know, fighting. Where did you go to school?

PETER. Jewish Secondary.

ANNE. But that's where Margot and I go! I never saw you around.

PETER. I used to see you . . . sometimes . . .

ANNE. You did?

PETER. . . . in the school yard. You were always in the middle of a bunch of kids. *(He takes a penknife from his pocket.)*

ANNE. Why didn't you ever come over?

PETER. I'm sort of a lone wolf. *(He starts to rip off his Star of David.)*

ANNE. What are you doing?

PETER. Taking it off.

ANNE. But you can't do that. They'll arrest you if you go out without your star. *(He tosses his knife on the table.)*

PETER. Who's going out?

ANNE. Why, of course! You're right! Of course we don't need them any more. *(She picks up his knife and starts to take her star off.)* I wonder what our friends will think when we don't show up today?

PETER. I didn't have any dates with anyone.

ANNE. Oh, I did. I had a date with Jopie to go and play ping-pong at her house. Do you know Jopie deWaal?[11]

PETER. No.

ANNE. Jopie's my best friend. I wonder what she'll think when she telephones and there's no answer? . . . Probably she'll go over to the house . . . I wonder what she'll think . . . we left everything as if we'd suddenly been called away . . . breakfast dishes in the sink . . . beds not made . . . *(As she pulls off her star the cloth underneath shows clearly the color and form of the star.)* Look! It's still there! (PETER *goes over to the stove with his star.)* What're you going to do with yours?

PETER. Burn it.

ANNE. *(She starts to throw hers in, and cannot.)* It's funny, I can't throw mine away. I don't know why.

PETER. You can't throw . . . ? Something they branded you with . . . ? That they made you wear so they could spit on you?

ANNE. I know. I know. But after all, it *is* the Star of David, isn't it?

(In the bedroom, right, MARGOT *and* MRS. FRANK *are lying down.* MR. FRANK *starts quietly out.)*

PETER. Maybe it's different for a girl.

(MR. FRANK *comes into the main room.)*

MR. FRANK. Forgive me, Peter. Now let me see. We must find a bed for your cat. *(He goes to a cupboard.)* I'm glad you brought your cat. Anne was feeling so badly about hers. *(Getting a used small washtub.)* Here we are. Will it be comfortable in that?

PETER *(gathering up his things).* Thanks.

MR. FRANK *(opening the door of the room on the left).* And here is your room. But I warn you, Peter, you can't grow any more. Not an inch, or you'll have to sleep with your feet out of the skylight. Are you hungry?

---

11. *Jopie deWaal* (yoʹpē də välʹ).

PETER. No.

MR. FRANK. We have some bread and butter.

PETER. No, thank you.

MR. FRANK. You can have it for luncheon then. And tonight we will have a real supper . . . our first supper together.

PETER. Thanks. Thanks.

(*He goes into his room. During the following scene he arranges his possessions in his new room.*)

MR. FRANK. That's a nice boy, Peter.

ANNE. He's awfully shy, isn't he?

MR. FRANK. You'll like him, I know.

ANNE. I certainly hope so, since he's the only boy I'm likely to see for months and months.

(MR. FRANK *sits down, taking off his shoes.*)

MR. FRANK. Annele,[12] there's a box there. Will you open it?

(*He indicates a carton on the couch.* ANNE *brings it to the center table. In the street below there is the sound of children playing.*)

ANNE (*as she opens the carton*). You know the way I'm going to think of it here? I'm going to think of it as a boarding house. A very peculiar summer boarding house, like the one that we—(*She breaks off as she pulls out some photographs.*) Father! My movie stars! I was wondering where they were! I was looking for them this morning . . . and Queen Wilhelmina![13] How wonderful!

MR. FRANK. There's something more. Go on. Look further.

(*He goes over to the sink, pouring a glass of milk from a thermos bottle.*)

ANNE (*pulling out a pasteboard-bound book*). A diary! (*She throws her arms around her father.*) I've never had a diary. And I've always longed for one. (*She looks around the room.*) Pencil, pencil, pencil. (*She starts down the stairs.*) I'm going down to the office to get a pencil.

MR. FRANK. Anne! No!

(*He goes after her, catching her by the arm and pulling her back.*)

ANNE (*startled*). But there's no one in the building now.

MR. FRANK. It doesn't matter. I don't want you ever to go beyond that door.

ANNE (*sobered*). Never . . . ? Not even at night time, when everyone is gone? Or on Sundays? Can't I go down to listen to the radio?

MR. FRANK. Never. I am sorry, Anneke. It isn't safe. No, you must never go beyond that door.

(*For the first time* ANNE *realizes what "going into hiding" means.*)

ANNE. I see.

MR. FRANK. It'll be hard, I know. But always remember this, Anneke. There are no walls, there are no bolts, no locks that anyone can put on your mind. Miep will bring us books. We will read history, poetry, mythology. (*He gives her the glass of milk.*) Here's your milk. (*With his arm about her, they go over to the couch, sitting down side by side.*) As a matter of fact, between us, Anne, being here has certain advantages for you. For instance, you remember the battle you had with your mother the other day on the subject of overshoes? You said that you'd rather die than wear overshoes? But in the end you had to wear them? Well now, you see, for as long as we are here you will never have to wear overshoes! Isn't that good? And the coat that you inherited from Margot, you won't have to wear

---

12. *Annele* (än′ə lə), little Anne. *Anneke* (än′ə kə), used later, is a similar term of endearment.
13. *Queen Wilhelmina* (wil′hel mē′nə), queen of the Netherlands from 1890 to 1948.

that any more. And the piano! You won't have to practice on the piano. I tell you, this is going to be a fine life for you!

(ANNE'S *panic is gone.* PETER *appears in the doorway of his room, with a saucer in his hand. He is carrying his cat.*)

PETER. I . . . I . . . I thought I'd better get some water for Mouschi before . . .

MR. FRANK. Of course.

(*As he starts toward the sink the carillon begins to chime the hour of eight. He tiptoes to the window at the back and looks down at the street below. He turns to* PE-TER, *indicating in pantomime that it is too late.* PETER *starts back for his room. He steps on a creaking board. The three of them are frozen for a minute in fear. As* PETER *starts away again,* ANNE *tiptoes over to him and pours some of the milk from her glass into the saucer for the cat.* PETER *squats on the floor, putting the milk before the cat.* MR. FRANK *gives* ANNE *his fountain pen, and then goes into the room at the right. For a second* ANNE *watches the cat, then she goes over to the center table, and opens her diary.*

In the room at the right, MRS. FRANK *has sat up quickly at the sound of the carillon.* MR. FRANK *comes in and sits down beside her on the settee, his arm comfortingly around her.*

Upstairs, in the attic room, MR. *and* MRS. VAN DAAN *have hung their clothes in the closet and are now seated on the iron bed.* MRS. VAN DAAN *leans back exhausted.* MR. VAN DAAN *fans her with a newspaper.*

ANNE *starts to write in her diary. The lights dim out, the curtain falls.*

In the darkness ANNE'S VOICE *comes to us again, faintly at first, and then with growing strength.*)

ANNE'S VOICE. I expect I should be describing what it feels like to go into hiding. But I really don't know yet myself. I only know it's funny never to be able to go outdoors . . . never to breathe fresh air . . . never to run and shout and jump. It's the silence in the nights that frightens me most. Every time I hear a creak in the house, or a step on the street outside, I'm sure they're coming for us. The days aren't so bad. At least we know that Miep and Mr. Kraler are down there below us in the office. Our protectors, we call them. I asked Father what would happen to them if the Nazis found out they were hiding us. Pim[14] said that they would suffer the same fate that we would . . . Imagine! They know this, and yet when they come up here, they're always cheerful and gay as if there were nothing in the world to bother them . . . Friday, the twenty-first of August, nineteen forty-two. Today I'm going to tell you our general news. Mother is unbearable. She insists on treating me like a baby, which I loathe. Otherwise things are going better. The weather is . . .

(*As* ANNE'S VOICE *is fading out the curtain rises on the scene.*)

---

14. *Pim,* a nickname Anne gave to her father.

Discussion

1. (a) What is the time setting for this scene? **(b)** What difference is there in the appearance of the rooms?

2. The refugees speak of their apartment as the Secret Annex. **(a)** What advantages does the annex have as a hiding place? **(b)** What are its disadvantages? **(c)** Why does Mr. Kraler want a better bolt at the foot of the stairs?

3. (a) What are your impressions of the Van Daans? **(b)** Why has Mr. Frank invited the Van Daans to join his family in hiding?

4. (a) What are your impressions of Mr. Frank? **(b)** How does he show that he hopes to keep life in the annex as normal as possible? **(c)** How does he try to reconcile Anne to "going into hiding"?

5. (a) Why does Peter burn the Star of David? **(b)** Why can't Anne do the same? **(c)** Peter says, "Maybe it's different for a girl." How satisfactory is his explanation?

6. Peter has Mouschi and Anne has a new diary. How suitable do these things seem for Anne and Peter as you know them so far?

7. The scene ends as Anne starts to write in her diary. **(a)** What do the dimming lights and falling curtain signify? **(b)** What purpose is served by Anne's voice reading from her diary in this way?

Vocabulary
Combined Skills

Use your Glossary to answer the following questions:

1. Of what two words is the compound *blackout* formed?

2. Of what did a *carillon* originally consist?

3. Does the accented syllable in *mercurial* rhyme with *her, your,* or *tea*?

4. From what language does *rucksack* come? What does it mean?

5. Write the definition of *reserved* as it is used in this sentence: Her *reserved* manner in dealing with the unfair criticism won the admiration of all her friends.

Scene Three

It is a little after six o'clock in the evening, two months later.

MARGOT *is in the bedroom at the right, studying.* MR. VAN DAAN *is lying down in the attic room above.*

The rest of the "family" is in the main room. ANNE *and* PETER *sit opposite each other at the center table, where they have been doing their lessons.* MRS. FRANK *is on the couch.* MRS. VAN DAAN *is seated with her fur coat, on which she has been sewing, in her lap. None of them are wearing their shoes.*

Their eyes are on MR. FRANK, *waiting for him to give them the signal which will release them from their day-long quiet.* MR. FRANK, *his shoes in his hand, stands looking down out of the window at the back, watching to be sure that all of the workmen have left the building below.*

After a few seconds of motionless silence, MR. FRANK *turns from the window.*

MR. FRANK (*quietly to the group*). It's safe now. The last workman has left.

(*There is an immediate stir of relief.*)

ANNE. (*Her pent-up energy explodes.*) WHEE!

MRS. FRANK (*startled, amused*). Anne!

MRS. VAN DAAN. I'm first for the w.c.

(*She hurries off to the bathroom.* MRS. FRANK *puts on her shoes and starts up to the sink to prepare supper.* ANNE *sneaks* PETER'S *shoes from under the table and hides them behind her back.* MR. FRANK *goes into* MARGOT'S *room.*)

MR. FRANK (*to* MARGOT). Six o'clock. School's over.

(MARGOT *gets up, stretching.* MR. FRANK *sits down to put on his shoes. In the main room* PETER *tries to find his.*)

PETER (*to* ANNE). Have you seen my shoes?

ANNE (*innocently*). Your shoes?

PETER. You've taken them, haven't you?

ANNE. I don't know what you're talking about.

PETER. You're going to be sorry!

ANNE. Am I?

(PETER *goes after her.* ANNE, *with his shoes in her hand, runs from him, dodging behind her mother.*)

MRS. FRANK (*protesting*). Anne, dear!

PETER. Wait till I get you!

ANNE. I'm waiting! (PETER *makes a lunge for her. They both fall to the floor.* PETER *pins her down, wrestling with her to get the shoes.*) Don't! Don't! Peter, stop it. Ouch!

MRS. FRANK. Anne! . . . Peter!

(*Suddenly* PETER *becomes self-conscious. He grabs his shoes roughly and starts for his room.*)

ANNE (*following him*). Peter, where are you going? Come dance with me.

PETER. I tell you I don't know how.

ANNE. I'll teach you.

PETER. I'm going to give Mouschi his dinner.

ANNE. Can I watch?

PETER. He doesn't like people around while he eats.

ANNE. Peter, please.

PETER. No!

(*He goes into his room.* ANNE *slams his door after him.*)

MRS. FRANK. Anne, dear, I think you shouldn't play like that with Peter. It's not dignified.

ANNE. Who cares if it's dignified? I don't want to be dignified.

(MR. FRANK *and* MARGOT *come from the room on the right.* MARGOT *goes to help her mother.* MR. FRANK *starts for the center table to correct* MARGOT'S *school papers.*)

MRS. FRANK (*to* ANNE). You complain that I don't treat you like a grownup. But when I do, you resent it.

ANNE. I only want some fun . . . someone to laugh and clown with . . . After you've sat still all day and hardly moved, you've got to have some fun. I don't know what's the matter with that boy.

MR. FRANK. He isn't used to girls. Give him a little time.

ANNE. Time? Isn't two months time? I could cry. (*Catching hold of* MARGOT) Come on, Margot . . . dance with me. Come on, please.

MARGOT. I have to help with supper.

ANNE. You know we're going to forget how to dance . . . When we get out we won't remember a thing.

(*She starts to sing and dance by herself.* MR. FRANK *takes her in his arms, waltzing with her.* MRS. VAN DAAN *comes in from the bathroom.*)

MRS. VAN DAAN. Next? (*She looks around as she starts putting on her shoes.*) Where's Peter?

ANNE (*as they are dancing*). Where would he be!

MRS. VAN DAAN. He hasn't finished his lessons, has he? His father'll kill him if he catches him in there with that cat and his work not done. (MR. FRANK *and* ANNE *finish their dance. They bow to each other with extravagant formality.*) Anne, get him out of there, will you?

ANNE (*at* PETER'S *door*). Peter? Peter?

PETER (*opening the door a crack*). What is it?

ANNE. Your mother says to come out.

PETER. I'm giving Mouschi his dinner.

MRS. VAN DAAN. You know what your father says.

(*She sits on the couch, sewing on the lining of her fur coat.*)

PETER. For heaven's sake, I haven't even looked at him since lunch.

MRS. VAN DAAN. I'm just telling you, that's all.

ANNE. I'll feed him.

PETER. I don't want you in there.

MRS. VAN DAAN. Peter!

PETER (*to* ANNE). Then give him his dinner and come right out, you hear?

(*He comes back to the table.* ANNE *shuts the door of* PETER'S *room after her and disappears behind the curtain covering his closet.*)

MRS. VAN DAAN (*to* PETER). Now is that any way to talk to your little girl friend?

PETER. Mother . . . for heaven's sake . . . will you please stop saying that?

MRS. VAN DAAN. Look at him blush! Look at him!

PETER. Please! I'm not . . . anyway . . . let me alone, will you?

MRS. VAN DAAN. He acts like it was something to be ashamed of. It's nothing to be ashamed of, to have a little girl friend.

PETER. You're crazy. She's only thirteen.

MRS. VAN DAAN. So what? And you're sixteen. Just perfect. Your father's ten years older than I am. (*To* MR. FRANK) I warn you, Mr. Frank, if this war lasts much

longer, we're going to be related and then . . .

MR. FRANK. *Mazeltov!*[1]

MRS. FRANK (*deliberately changing the conversation*). I wonder where Miep is. She's usually so prompt.

(*Suddenly everything else is forgotten as they hear the sound of an automobile coming to a screeching stop in the street below. They are tense, motionless in their terror. The car starts away. A wave of relief sweeps over them. They pick up their occupations again.* ANNE *flings open the door of* PETER'S *room, making a dramatic entrance. She is dressed in* PETER'S *clothes.* PETER *looks at her in fury. The others are amused.*)

ANNE. Good evening, everyone. Forgive me if I don't stay. (*She jumps up on a chair.*) I have a friend waiting for me in there. My friend Tom. Tom Cat. Some people say that we look alike. But Tom has the most beautiful whiskers, and I have only a little fuzz. I am hoping . . . in time . . .

PETER. All right, Mrs. Quack Quack!

ANNE (*outraged—jumping down*). Peter!

PETER. I heard about you . . . How you talked so much in class they called you Mrs. Quack Quack. How Mr. Smitter made you write a composition . . . " 'Quack, quack,' said Mrs. Quack Quack."

ANNE. Well, go on. Tell them the rest. How it was so good he read it out loud to the class and then read it to all his other classes!

PETER. Quack! Quack! Quack . . . Quack . . . Quack . . .

(ANNE *pulls off the coat and trousers.*)

ANNE. You are the most intolerable, insufferable boy I've ever met!

---

1. *Mazeltov* (mä′zəl tof), an expression used among Jews to express congratulations or wish good luck.

(She throws the clothes down the stair-well. PETER *goes down after them.)*

PETER. Quack, quack, quack!

MRS. VAN DAAN *(to* ANNE*)*. That's right, Anneke! Give it to him!

ANNE. With all the boys in the world . . . Why I had to get locked up with one like you! . . .

PETER. Quack, quack, quack, and from now on stay out of my room!

(As PETER *passes her,* ANNE *puts out her foot, tripping him. He picks himself up, and goes on into his room.)*

MRS. FRANK *(quietly)*. Anne, dear . . . your hair. *(She feels* ANNE'S *forehead.)* You're warm. Are you feeling all right?

ANNE. Please, Mother.

(She goes over to the center table, slipping into her shoes.)

MRS. FRANK *(following her)*. You haven't a fever, have you?

ANNE *(pulling away)*. No. No.

MRS. FRANK. You know we can't call a doctor here, ever. There's only one thing to do . . . watch carefully. Prevent an illness before it comes. Let me see your tongue.

ANNE. Mother, this is perfectly absurd.

MRS. FRANK. Anne, dear, don't be such a baby. Let me see your tongue. *(As* ANNE *refuses,* MRS. FRANK *appeals to* MR. FRANK.*)* Otto . . . ?

MR. FRANK. You hear your mother, Anne.

*(ANNE *flicks out her tongue for a second, then turns away.)*

MRS. FRANK. Come on—open up! *(As* ANNE *opens her mouth very wide)* You seem all right . . . but perhaps an aspirin . . .

MRS. VAN DAAN. For heaven's sake, don't give that child any pills. I waited for fifteen minutes this morning for her to come out of the w.c.

ANNE. I was washing my hair!

MRS. FRANK. I think there's nothing the matter with our Anne that a ride on her bike, or a visit with her friend Jopie deWaal wouldn't cure. Isn't that so, Anne?

*(MR. VAN DAAN *comes down into the room. From outside we hear faint sounds of bombers going over and a burst of ack-ack.[2]*)*

MR. VAN DAAN. Miep not come yet?

MRS. VAN DAAN. The workmen just left, a little while ago.

MR. VAN DAAN. What's for dinner tonight?

MRS. VAN DAAN. Beans.

MR. VAN DAAN. Not again!

MRS. VAN DAAN. Poor Putti![3] I know. But what can we do? That's all that Miep brought us.

*(MR. VAN DAAN *starts to pace, his hands behind his back.* ANNE *follows behind him, imitating him.)*

ANNE. We are now in what is known as the "bean cycle." Beans boiled, beans *en casserole*,[4] beans with strings, beans without strings . . .

*(PETER *has come out of his room. He slides into his place at the table, becoming immediately absorbed in his studies.)*

MR. VAN DAAN *(to* PETER*)*. I saw you . . . in there, playing with your cat.

MRS. VAN DAAN. He just went in for a second, putting his coat away. He's been out here all the time, doing his lessons.

MR. FRANK *(looking up from the paper)*. Anne, you got an excellent in your history paper today . . . and very good in Latin.

ANNE *(sitting beside him)*. How about algebra?

MR. FRANK. I'll have to make a confession.

---

2. *ack-ack,* antiaircraft fire.

3. *Putti* (pŭt′ ē).

4. *en casserole* (ăn käs rŏl′), prepared and served in a covered baking dish.

Up until now I've managed to stay ahead of you in algebra. Today you caught up with me. We'll leave it to Margot to correct.

ANNE. Isn't algebra *vile*, Pim!

MR. FRANK. Vile!

MARGOT (*to* MR. FRANK). How did I do?

ANNE (*getting up*). Excellent, excellent, excellent, excellent!

MR. FRANK (*to* MARGOT). You should have used the subjunctive here . . .

MARGOT. Should I? . . . I thought . . . look here . . . I didn't use it here . . .

(*The two become absorbed in the papers.*)

ANNE. Mrs. Van Daan, may I try on your coat?

MRS. FRANK. No, Anne.

MRS. VAN DAAN (*giving it to* ANNE). It's all right . . . but careful with it. (ANNE *puts it on and struts with it.*) My father gave me that the year before he died. He always bought the best that money could buy.

ANNE. Mrs. Van Daan, did you have a lot of boy friends before you were married?

MRS. FRANK. Anne, that's a personal question. It's not courteous to ask personal questions.

MRS. VAN DAAN. Oh I don't mind. (*To* ANNE) Our house was always swarming with boys. When I was a girl we had . . .

MR. VAN DAAN. Oh, God. Not again!

MRS. VAN DAAN (*good-humored*). Shut up! (*Without a pause, to* ANNE. MR. VAN DAAN *mimics* MRS. VAN DAAN, *speaking the first few words in unison with her.*) One summer we had a big house in Hilversum.[5] The boys came buzzing round like bees around a jam pot. And when I was sixteen! . . . We were wearing our skirts very short those days and I had good-looking legs. (*She pulls up her skirt,*

going to MR. FRANK.) I still have 'em. I may not be as pretty as I used to be, but I still have my legs. How about it, Mr. Frank?

MR. VAN DAAN. All right. All right. We see them.

MRS. VAN DAAN. I'm not asking you. I'm asking Mr. Frank.

PETER. Mother, for heaven's sake.

MRS. VAN DAAN. Oh, I embarrass you, do I? Well, I just hope the girl you marry has as good. (*Then to* ANNE) My father used to worry about me, with so many boys hanging round. He told me, if any of them gets fresh, you say to him . . . "Remember, Mr. So-and-So, remember I'm a lady."

ANNE. "Remember, Mr. So-and-So, remember I'm a lady."

(*She gives* MRS. VAN DAAN *her coat.*)

MR. VAN DAAN. Look at you, talking that way in front of her! Don't you know she puts it all down in that diary?

MRS. VAN DAAN. So, if she does? I'm only telling the truth!

(ANNE *stretches out, putting her ear to the floor, listening to what is going on below. The sound of the bombers fades away.*)

MRS. FRANK (*setting the table*). Would you mind, Peter, if I moved you over to the couch?

ANNE (*listening*). Miep must have the radio on.

(PETER *picks up his papers, going over to the couch beside* MRS. VAN DAAN.)

MR. VAN DAAN (*accusingly, to* PETER). Haven't you finished yet?

PETER. No.

MR. VAN DAAN. You ought to be ashamed of yourself.

---

5. *Hilversum* (hil′vər səm), a health resort and residential area some miles from Amsterdam.

PETER. All right. All right. I'm a dunce. I'm a hopeless case. Why do I go on?

MRS. VAN DAAN. You're not hopeless. Don't talk that way. It's just that you haven't anyone to help you, like the girls have. *(To* MR. FRANK*)* Maybe you could help him, Mr. Frank?

MR. FRANK. I'm sure that his father . . . ?

MR. VAN DAAN. Not me. I can't do anything with him. He won't listen to me. You go ahead . . . if you want.

MR. FRANK *(going to* PETER*)*. What about it, Peter? Shall we make our school coeducational?

MRS. VAN DAAN *(kissing* MR. FRANK*)*. You're an angel, Mr. Frank. An angel. I don't know why I didn't meet you before I met that one there. Here, sit down, Mr. Frank . . . *(She forces him down on the couch beside* PETER.*)* Now, Peter, you listen to Mr. Frank.

MR. FRANK. It might be better for us to go into Peter's room.

*(*PETER *jumps up eagerly, leading the way.)*

MRS. VAN DAAN. That's right. You go in there, Peter. You listen to Mr. Frank. Mr. Frank is a highly educated man.

(As MR. FRANK *is about to follow* PETER *into his room,* MRS. FRANK *stops him and wipes the lipstick from his lips. Then she closes the door after them.)*

ANNE *(on the floor, listening)*. Shh! I can hear a man's voice talking.

MR. VAN DAAN *(to* ANNE*)*. Isn't it bad enough here without your sprawling all over the place?

*(*ANNE *sits up.)*

MRS. VAN DAAN *(to* MR. VAN DAAN*)*. If you didn't smoke so much, you wouldn't be so bad-tempered.

MR. VAN DAAN. Am I smoking? Do you see me smoking?

MRS. VAN DAAN. Don't tell me you've used up all those cigarettes.

MR. VAN DAAN. One package. Miep only brought me one package.

MRS. VAN DAAN. It's a filthy habit anyway. It's a good time to break yourself.

MR. VAN DAAN. Oh, stop it, please.

MRS. VAN DAAN. You're smoking up all our money. You know that, don't you?

MR. VAN DAAN. Will you shut up? *(During this,* MRS. FRANK *and* MARGOT *have studiously kept their eyes down. But* ANNE, *seated on the floor, has been following the discussion interestedly.* MR. VAN DAAN *turns to see her staring up at him.)* And what are you staring at?

ANNE. I never heard grownups quarrel before. I thought only children quarreled.

MR. VAN DAAN. This isn't a quarrel! It's a discussion. And I never heard children so rude before.

ANNE *(rising, indignantly)*. I, rude!

MR. VAN DAAN. Yes!

MRS. FRANK *(quickly)*. Anne, will you get me my knitting? *(*ANNE *goes to get it.)* I must remember, when Miep comes, to ask her to bring me some more wool.

MARGOT *(going to her room)*. I need some hairpins and some soap. I made a list. *(She goes into her bedroom to get the list.)*

MRS. FRANK *(to* ANNE*)*. Have you some library books for Miep when she comes?

ANNE. It's a wonder that Miep has a life of her own, the way we make her run errands for us. Please, Miep, get me some starch. Please take my hair out and have it cut. Tell me all the latest news, Miep. *(She goes over, kneeling on the couch beside* MRS. VAN DAAN.*)* Did you know she was engaged? His name is Dirk, and Miep's afraid the Nazis will ship him off to Germany to work in one of their war plants. That's what they're doing with some of the young Dutchmen . . . they pick them up off the streets—

MR. VAN DAAN (interrupting). Don't you ever get tired of talking? Suppose you try keeping still for five minutes. Just five minutes.

(He starts to pace again. Again ANNE follows him, mimicking him. MRS. FRANK jumps up and takes her by the arm up to the sink, and gives her a glass of milk.)

MRS. FRANK. Come here, Anne. It's time for your glass of milk.

MR. VAN DAAN. Talk, talk, talk. I never heard such a child. Where is my . . . ? Every evening it's the same, talk, talk, talk. (He looks around.) Where is my . . . ?

MRS. VAN DAAN. What're you looking for?

MR. VAN DAAN. My pipe. Have you seen my pipe?

MRS. VAN DAAN. What good's a pipe? You haven't got any tobacco.

MR. VAN DAAN. At least I'll have something to hold in my mouth! (Opening MARGOT'S bedroom door) Margot, have you seen my pipe?

MARGOT. It was on the table last night.

(ANNE puts her glass of milk on the table and picks up his pipe, hiding it behind her back.)

MR. VAN DAAN. I know. I know. Anne, did you see my pipe? . . . Anne!

MRS. FRANK. Anne, Mr. Van Daan is speaking to you.

ANNE. Am I allowed to talk now?

MR. VAN DAAN. You're the most aggravating . . . The trouble with you is, you've been spoiled. What you need is a good old-fashioned spanking.

ANNE (mimicking MRS. VAN DAAN). "Remember, Mr. So-and-So, remember I'm a lady."

(She thrusts the pipe into his mouth, then picks up her glass of milk.)

MR. VAN DAAN (restraining himself with difficulty). Why aren't you nice and quiet like your sister Margot? Why do you have to show off all the time? Let me give you a little advice, young lady. Men don't like that kind of thing in a girl. You know that? A man likes a girl who'll listen to him once in a while . . . a domestic girl, who'll keep her house shining for her husband . . . who loves to cook and sew and . . .

ANNE. I'd cut my throat first! I'd open my veins! I'm going to be remarkable! I'm going to Paris . . .

MR. VAN DAAN (scoffingly). Paris!

ANNE. . . . to study music and art.

MR. VAN DAAN. Yeah! Yeah!

ANNE. I'm going to be a famous dancer or singer . . . or something wonderful.

(She makes a wide gesture, spilling the glass of milk on the fur coat in MRS. VAN DAAN'S lap. MARGOT rushes quickly over with a towel. ANNE tries to brush the milk off with her skirt.)

MRS. VAN DAAN. Now look what you've done . . . you clumsy little fool! My beautiful fur coat my father gave me . . .

ANNE. I'm so sorry.

MRS. VAN DAAN. What do you care? It isn't yours . . . So go on, ruin it! Do you know what that coat cost? Do you? And now look at it! Look at it!

ANNE. I'm very, very sorry.

MRS. VAN DAAN. I could kill you for this. I could just kill you!

(MRS. VAN DAAN goes up the stairs, clutching the coat. MR. VAN DAAN starts after her.)

MR. VAN DAAN. Petronella . . . liefje! Liefje! . . . Come back . . . the supper . . . come back!

MRS. FRANK. Anne, you must not behave in that way.

ANNE. It was an accident. Anyone can have an accident.

MRS. FRANK. I don't mean that. I mean the answering back. You must not answer back. They are our guests. We must always show the greatest courtesy to them. We're all living under terrible tension. *(She stops as* MARGOT *indicates that* VAN DAAN *can hear. When he is gone, she continues.)* That's why we must control ourselves . . . You don't hear Margot getting into arguments with them, do you? Watch Margot. She's always courteous with them. Never familiar. She keeps her distance. And they respect her for it. Try to be like Margot.

ANNE. And have them walk all over me, the way they do her? No, thanks!

MRS. FRANK. I'm not afraid that anyone is going to walk all over you, Anne. I'm afraid for other people, that you'll walk on them. I don't know what happens to you, Anne. You are wild, self-willed. If I had ever talked to my mother as you talk to me . . .

ANNE. Things have changed. People aren't like that any more. "Yes, Mother." "No, Mother." "Anything you say, Mother." I've got to fight things out for myself! Make something of myself!

MRS. FRANK. It isn't necessary to fight to do it. Margot doesn't fight, and isn't she . . . ?

ANNE *(violently rebellious)*. Margot! Margot! Margot! That's all I hear from everyone . . . how wonderful Margot is . . . "Why aren't you like Margot?"

MARGOT *(protesting)*. Oh, come on, Anne, don't be so . . .

ANNE *(paying no attention)*. Everything she does is right, and everything I do is wrong! I'm the goat around here! . . . You're all against me! . . . And you worst of all!

(She rushes off into her room and throws herself down on the settee, stifling her sobs. MRS. FRANK *sighs and starts toward the stove.)*

MRS. FRANK *(to* MARGOT*)*. Let's put the soup on the stove . . . if there's anyone who cares to eat. Margot, will you take the bread out? *(*MARGOT *gets the bread from the cupboard.)* I don't know how we can go on living this way . . . I can't say a word to Anne . . . she flies at me . . .

MARGOT. You know Anne. In half an hour she'll be out here, laughing and joking.

MRS. FRANK. And . . . *(She makes a motion upwards, indicating the* VAN DAANS.*)* . . . I told your father it wouldn't work . . . but no . . . he had to ask them, he said . . . he owed it to him, he said. Well, he knows now that I was right! These quarrels! . . . This bickering!

MARGOT *(with a warning look)*. Shush. Shush.

(The buzzer for the door sounds. MRS. FRANK *gasps, startled.)*

MRS. FRANK. Every time I hear that sound, my heart stops!

MARGOT *(starting for* PETER'S *door)*. It's Miep. *(She knocks at the door.)* Father?

*(*MR. FRANK *comes quickly from* PETER'S *room.)*

MR. FRANK. Thank you, Margot. *(As he goes down the steps to open the outer door)* Has everyone his list?

MARGOT. I'll get my books. *(Giving her mother a list)* Here's your list. *(*MARGOT *goes into her and* ANNE'S *bedroom on the right.* ANNE *sits up, hiding her tears, as* MARGOT *comes in.)* Miep's here.

*(*MARGOT *picks up her books and goes*

back. ANNE *hurries over to the mirror, smoothing her hair.*)

MR. VAN DAAN (*coming down the stairs*). Is it Miep?

MARGOT. Yes. Father's gone down to let her in.

MR. VAN DAAN. At last I'll have some cigarettes!

MRS. FRANK (*to* MR. VAN DAAN). I can't tell you how unhappy I am about Mrs. Van Daan's coat. Anne should never have touched it.

MR. VAN DAAN. She'll be all right.

MRS. FRANK. Is there anything I can do?

MR. VAN DAAN. Don't worry.

(*He turns to meet* MIEP. *But it is not* MIEP *who comes up the steps. It is* MR. KRALER, *followed by* MR. FRANK. *Their faces are grave.* ANNE *comes from the bedroom.* PETER *comes from his room.*)

MRS. FRANK. Mr. Kraler!

MR. VAN DAAN. How are you, Mr. Kraler?

MARGOT. This is a surprise.

MRS. FRANK. When Mr. Kraler comes, the sun begins to shine.

MR. VAN DAAN. Miep is coming?

MR. KRALER. Not tonight.

(KRALER *goes to* MARGOT *and* MRS. FRANK *and* ANNE, *shaking hands with them.*)

MRS. FRANK. Wouldn't you like a cup of coffee? . . . Or, better still, will you have supper with us?

MR. FRANK. Mr. Kraler has something to talk over with us. Something has happened, he says, which demands an immediate decision.

MRS. FRANK (*fearful*). What is it?

(MR. KRALER *sits down on the couch. As he talks he takes bread, cabbages, milk, etc., from his briefcase, giving them to* MARGOT *and* ANNE *to put away.*)

MR. KRALER. Usually, when I come up here, I try to bring you some bit of good news.

What's the use of telling you the bad news when there's nothing that you can do about it? But today something has happened . . . Dirk . . . Miep's Dirk, you know, came to me just now. He tells me that he has a Jewish friend living near him. A dentist. He says he's in trouble. He begged me, could I do anything for this man? Could I find him a hiding place? . . . So I've come to you . . . I know it's a terrible thing to ask of you, living as you are, but would you take him in with you?

MR. FRANK. Of course we will.

MR. KRALER (*rising*). It'll be just for a night or two . . . until I find some other place. This happened so suddenly that I didn't know where to turn.

MR. FRANK. Where is he?

MR. KRALER. Downstairs in the office.

MR. FRANK. Good. Bring him up.

MR. KRALER. His name is Dussel . . . Jan Dussel.

MR. FRANK. Dussel . . . I think I know him.

MR. KRALER. I'll get him.

(*He goes quickly down the steps and out.* MR. FRANK *suddenly becomes conscious of the others.*)

MR. FRANK. Forgive me. I spoke without consulting you. But I knew you'd feel as I do.

MR. VAN DAAN. There's no reason for you to consult anyone. This is your place. You have a right to do exactly as you please. The only thing I feel . . . there's so little food as it is . . . and to take in another person . . .

(PETER *turns away, ashamed of his father.*)

MR. FRANK. We can stretch the food a little. It's only for a few days.

MR. VAN DAAN. You want to make a bet?

MRS. FRANK. I think it's fine to have him.

But, Otto, where are you going to put him? Where?

PETER. He can have my bed. I can sleep on the floor. I wouldn't mind.

MR. FRANK. That's good of you, Peter. But your room's too small . . . even for *you*.

ANNE. I have a much better idea. I'll come in here with you and Mother, and Margot can take Peter's room and Peter can go in our room with Mr. Dussel.

MARGOT. That's right. We could do that.

MR. FRANK. No, Margot. You mustn't sleep in that room . . . neither you nor Anne. Mouschi has caught some rats in there. Peter's brave. He doesn't mind.

ANNE. Then how about *this?* I'll come in here with you and Mother, and Mr. Dussel can have my bed.

MRS. FRANK. No. No. *No!* Margot will come in here with us and he can have her bed. It's the only way. Margot, bring your things in here. Help her, Anne.

(MARGOT *hurries into her room to get her things.*)

ANNE (*to her mother*). Why Margot? Why can't I come in here?

MRS. FRANK. Because it wouldn't be proper for Margot to sleep with a . . . Please, Anne. Don't argue. Please.

(ANNE *starts slowly away.*)

MR. FRANK (*to* ANNE). You don't mind sharing your room with Mr. Dussel, do you, Anne?

ANNE. No. No, of course not.

MR. FRANK. Good. (ANNE *goes off into her bedroom, helping* MARGOT. MR. FRANK *starts to search in the cupboards.*) Where's the cognac?

MRS. FRANK. It's there. But, Otto, I was saving it in case of illness.

MR. FRANK. I think we couldn't find a better time to use it. Peter, will you get five glasses for me?

(PETER *goes for the glasses.* MARGOT *comes out of her bedroom, carrying her possessions, which she hangs behind a curtain in the main room.* MR. FRANK *finds the cognac and pours it into the five glasses that* PETER *brings him.* MR. VAN DAAN *stands looking on sourly.* MRS. VAN DAAN *comes downstairs and looks around at all of the bustle.*)

MRS. VAN DAAN. What's happening? What's going on?

MR. VAN DAAN. Someone's moving in with us.

MRS. VAN DAAN. In here? You're joking.

MARGOT. It's only for a night or two . . . until Mr. Kraler finds him another place.

MR. VAN DAAN. Yeah! Yeah!

(MR. FRANK *hurries over as* MR. KRALER *and* DUSSEL *come up.* DUSSEL *is a man in his late fifties, meticulous, finicky . . . bewildered now. He wears a raincoat. He carries a briefcase, stuffed full, and a small medicine case.*)

MR. FRANK. Come in, Mr. Dussel.

MR. KRALER. This is Mr. Frank.

DUSSEL. Mr. Otto Frank?

MR. FRANK. Yes. Let me take your things. (*He takes the hat and briefcase, but* DUS- SEL *clings to his medicine case.*) This is my wife Edith . . . Mr. and Mrs. Van Daan . . . their son, Peter . . . and my daughters, Margot and Anne.

(DUSSEL *shakes hands with everyone.*)

MR. KRALER. Thank you, Mr. Frank. Thank you all. Mr. Dussel, I leave you in good hands. Oh . . . Dirk's coat.

(DUSSEL *hurriedly takes off the raincoat, giving it to* MR. KRALER. *Underneath is his white dentist's jacket, with a yellow Star of David on it.*)

DUSSEL (*to* MR. KRALER). What can I say to thank you . . . ?

MRS. FRANK (*to* DUSSEL). Mr. Kraler and Miep . . . They're our life line. Without them we couldn't live.

MR. KRALER. Please, please. You make us seem very heroic. It isn't that at all. We simply don't like the Nazis. (*To* MR. FRANK, *who offers him a drink*) No, thanks. (*Then going on*) We don't like their methods. We don't like . . .

MR. FRANK (*smiling*). I know. I know. "No one's going to tell us Dutchmen what to do with our damn Jews!"

MR. KRALER (*to* DUSSEL). Pay no attention to Mr. Frank. I'll be up tomorrow to see that they're treating you right. (*To* MR. FRANK) Don't trouble to come down again. Peter will bolt the door after me, won't you, Peter?

PETER. Yes, sir.

MR. FRANK. Thank you, Peter. I'll do it.

MR. KRALER. Good night. Good night.

GROUP. Good night, Mr. Kraler. We'll see you tomorrow, etc., etc.

(MR. KRALER *goes out with* MR. FRANK. MRS. FRANK *gives each one of the "grownups" a glass of cognac.*)

MRS. FRANK. Please, Mr. Dussel, sit down.

(MR. DUSSEL *sinks into a chair.* MRS. FRANK *gives him a glass of cognac.*)

DUSSEL. I'm dreaming. I know it. I don't believe my eyes. Mr. Otto Frank here! (*To* MRS. FRANK) You're not in Switzerland then? A woman told me . . . She said she'd gone to your house . . . the door was open, everything was in disorder, dishes in the sink. She said she found a piece of paper in the wastebasket with an address scribbled on it . . . an address in Zurich. She said you must have escaped to Zurich.

ANNE. Father put that there purposely . . . just so people would think that very thing!

DUSSEL. And you've been *here* all the time?

MRS. FRANK. All the time . . . ever since July.

(ANNE *speaks to her father as he comes back.*)

ANNE. It worked, Pim . . . the address you left! Mr. Dussel says that people believe we escaped to Switzerland.

MR. FRANK. I'm glad . . . And now let's have a little drink to welcome Mr. Dussel. (*Before they can drink,* MR. DUSSEL *bolts his drink.* MR. FRANK *smiles and raises his glass.*) To Mr. Dussel. Welcome. We're very honored to have you with us.

MRS. FRANK. To Mr. Dussel, welcome.

(*The* VAN DAANS *murmur a welcome. The "grownups" drink.*)

MRS. VAN DAAN. Um. That was good.

MR. VAN DAAN. Did Mr. Kraler warn you that you won't get much to eat here? You can imagine . . . three ration books among the seven of us . . . and now you make eight.

(PETER *walks away, humiliated. Outside a street organ is heard dimly.*)

DUSSEL (*rising*). Mr. Van Daan, you don't realize what is happening outside that you should warn me of a thing like that. You don't realize what's going on . . .

(*As* MR. VAN DAAN *starts his characteristic pacing,* DUSSEL *turns to speak to the others.*) Right here in Amsterdam every day hundreds of Jews disappear . . . They surround a block and search house by house. Children come home from school to find their parents gone. Hundreds are being deported . . . people that you and I know . . . the Hallensteins . . . the Wessels . . .

MRS. FRANK (*in tears*). Oh, no. No!

DUSSEL. They get their call-up notice . . . come to the Jewish theatre on such and such a day and hour . . . bring only what you can carry in a rucksack. And if you refuse the call-up notice, then they come and drag you from your home and ship you off to Mauthausen.[6] The death camp!

MRS. FRANK. We didn't know that things had got so much worse.

DUSSEL. Forgive me for speaking so.

ANNE (*coming to* DUSSEL). Do you know the deWaals? . . . What's become of them? Their daughter Jopie and I are in the same class. Jopie's my best friend.

DUSSEL. They are gone.

ANNE. Gone?

DUSSEL. With all the others.

ANNE. Oh, no. Not Jopie!

(*She turns away, in tears.* MRS. FRANK *motions to* MARGOT *to comfort her.* MARGOT *goes to* ANNE, *putting her arms comfortingly around her.*)

MRS. VAN DAAN. There were some people called Wagner. They lived near us . . . ?

MR. FRANK (*interrupting with a glance at* ANNE). I think we should put this off until later. We all have many questions we want to ask . . . But I'm sure that Mr. Dussel would like to get settled before supper.

DUSSEL. Thank you. I would. I brought very little with me.

MR. FRANK (*giving him his hat and briefcase*). I'm sorry we can't give you a room alone. But I hope you won't be too uncomfortable. We've had to make strict rules here . . . a schedule of hours . . . We'll tell you after supper. Anne, would you like to take Mr. Dussel to his room?

ANNE (*controlling her tears*). If you'll come with me, Mr. Dussel?

(*She starts for her room.*)

DUSSEL (*shaking hands with each in turn*).

---

6. *Mauthausen* (mout′houz ən), a Nazi concentration camp located in Austria.

Forgive me if I haven't really expressed my gratitude to all of you. This has been such a shock to me. I'd always thought of myself as Dutch. I was born in Holland. My father was born in Holland, and my grandfather. And now . . . after all these years . . . *(He breaks off.)* If you'll excuse me.

(DUSSEL gives a little bow and hurries off after ANNE. MR. FRANK *and the others are subdued.)*

ANNE *(turning on the light).* Well, here we are.

(DUSSEL looks around the room. In the main room MARGOT *speaks to her mother.)*

MARGOT. The news sounds pretty bad, doesn't it? It's so different from what Mr. Kraler tells us. Mr. Kraler says things are improving.

MR. VAN DAAN. I like it better the way Kraler tells it.

(They resume their occupations, quietiy. PETER *goes off into his room. In* ANNE'S *room,* ANNE *turns to* DUSSEL.)

ANNE. You're going to share the room with me.

DUSSEL. I'm a man who's always lived alone. I haven't had to adjust myself to others. I hope you'll bear with me until I learn.

ANNE. Let me help you. *(She takes his brief-case.)* Do you always live all alone? Have you no family at all?

DUSSEL. No one.

(He opens his medicine case and spreads his bottles on the dressing table.)

ANNE. How dreadful. You must be terribly lonely.

DUSSEL. I'm used to it.

ANNE. I don't think I could ever get used to it. Didn't you even have a pet? A cat, or a dog?

DUSSEL. I have an allergy for fur-bearing animals. They give me asthma.

ANNE. Oh, dear. Peter has a cat.

DUSSEL. Here? He has it here?

ANNE. Yes. But we hardly ever see it. He keeps it in his room all the time. I'm sure it will be all right.

DUSSEL. Let us hope so. *(He takes some pills to fortify himself.)*

ANNE. That's Margot's bed, where you're going to sleep. I sleep on the sofa there. *(Indicating the clothes hooks on the wall.)* We cleared these off for your things. *(She goes over to the window.)* The best part about this room . . . you can look down and see a bit of the street and the canal. There's a houseboat . . . you can see the end of it . . . a bargeman lives there with his family . . . They have a baby and he's just beginning to walk and I'm so afraid he's going to fall into the canal some day. I watch him . . .

DUSSEL *(interrupting).* Your father spoke of a schedule.

ANNE *(coming away from the window).* Oh, yes. It's mostly about the times we have to be quiet. And times for the w.c. You can use it now if you like.

DUSSEL *(stiffly).* No, thank you.

ANNE. I suppose you think it's awful, my talking about a thing like that. But you don't know how important it can get to be, especially when you're frightened . . . About this room, the way Margot and I did . . . she had it to herself in the afternoons for studying, reading . . . lessons, you know . . . and I took the mornings. Would that be all right with you?

DUSSEL. I'm not at my best in the morning.

ANNE. You stay here in the mornings then. I'll take the room in the afternoons.

DUSSEL. Tell me, when you're in here, what happens to me? Where am I spending my time? In there, with all the people?

ANNE. Yes.

DUSSEL. I see. I see.

ANNE. We have supper at half past six.

DUSSEL (going over to the sofa). Then, if you don't mind . . . I like to lie down quietly for ten minutes before eating. I find it helps the digestion.

ANNE. Of course. I hope I'm not going to be too much of a bother to you. I seem to be able to get everyone's back up.

(DUSSEL lies down on the sofa, curled up, his back to her.)

DUSSEL. I always get along very well with children. My patients all bring their children to me, because they know I get on well with them. So don't worry about that.

(ANNE leans over him, taking his hand and shaking it gratefully.)

ANNE. Thank you. Thank you, Mr. Dussel.

(The lights dim to darkness. The curtain falls on the scene. ANNE'S VOICE comes to us faintly at first, and then with increasing power.)

ANNE'S VOICE. . . . And yesterday I finished Cissy Van Marxvelt's latest book. I think she is a first-class writer. I shall definitely let my children read her. Monday the twenty-first of September, nineteen forty-two. Mr. Dussel and I had another battle yesterday. Yes, Mr. Dussel! According to him, nothing, I repeat . . . nothing, is right about me . . . my appearance, my character, my manners. While he was going on at me I thought . . . sometime I'll give you such a smack that you'll fly right up to the ceiling! Why is it that every grownup thinks he knows the way to bring up children? Particularly the grownups that never had any. I keep wishing that Peter was a girl instead of a boy. Then I would have someone to talk to. Margot's a darling, but she takes everything too seriously. To pause for a moment on the subject of Mrs. Van Daan. I must tell you that her attempts to flirt with Father are getting her nowhere. Pim, thank goodness, won't play.

(As she is saying the last lines, the curtain rises on the darkened scene. ANNE'S VOICE fades out.)

Discussion

1. Much of this scene is composed of incidents that provide a clearer picture of Anne. **(a)** What are some of her characteristics? Cite incidents to illustrate these character traits. **(b)** Does Anne seem to you a typical thirteen-year-old girl? Why or why not?

2. What does the behavior of Mr. Van Daan, Mrs. Van Daan, and Peter tell you about each?

3. **(a)** How are members of the audience suddenly reminded early in the scene, amidst the horseplay and teasing on stage, that they are not observing a normal household? **(b)** What effect does this reminder create?

4. **(a)** What effect does Mr. Dussel's arrival have upon arrangements in the household? **(b)** How do various members of the household react to his coming? **(c)** What information of the outside world does Mr. Dussel provide?

5. Why is Mr. Dussel shocked to discover that he, too, needs to go into hiding?

"This isn't a quarrel!" Mr. Van Daan tells Anne. "It's a discussion." Although synonyms have the same or nearly the same meaning, each may have a connotation or shade of meaning that makes it more appropriate in one context than in another.

For each of the following sentences, look up the word listed *first* in parentheses and read the synonym study following the entry. Decide which of the three words in parentheses is most appropriate in the sentence; write that word on your paper.

1. Coach Ridley reminded us that it is not good sportsmanship to *(scoff/jeer/sneer)* when an opposing player fumbles the ball.

2. Jeffrey's excuse for not showing up was some *(absurd/ridiculous/preposterous)* tale about being kidnaped by a flying saucer.

3. The judge decided to *(deport/banish/exile)* the foreign embassy employee who was caught spying and to send him back to his own country.

4. The diet and daily workout that Bonnie follows in her Olympic training are far more *(strict/rigid/rigorous)* than I'd care to try.

5. The scenes of cruelty and torture in that movie, according to the reviewer, were the most *(vile/base/low)* of anything she had ever seen.

Scene Four

It is the middle of the night, several months later. The stage is dark except for a little light which comes through the skylight in PETER'S *room.*

Everyone is in bed. MR. *and* MRS. FRANK *lie on the couch in the main room, which has been pulled out to serve as a makeshift double bed.*

MARGOT *is sleeping on a mattress on the floor in the main room, behind a curtain stretched across for privacy. The others are all in their accustomed rooms.*

From outside we hear two drunken soldiers singing "Lili Marlene." A girl's high giggle is heard. The sound of running feet is heard coming closer and then fading in the distance. Throughout the scene there is the distant sound of airplanes passing overhead.

A match suddenly flares up in the attic.

We dimly see MR. VAN DAAN. *He is getting his bearings. He comes quickly down the stairs, and goes to the cupboard where the food is stored. Again the match flares up, and is as quickly blown out. The dim figure is seen to steal back up the stairs.*

There is quiet for a second or two, broken only by the sound of airplanes, and running feet on the street below.

Suddenly, out of the silence and the dark, we hear ANNE *scream.*

ANNE *(screaming).* No! No! Don't . . . don't take me!

(She moans, tossing and crying in her sleep. The other people wake, terrified. DUSSEL *sits up in bed, furious.)*

DUSSEL. Shush! Anne! Anne, for God's sake, shush!

ANNE *(still in her nightmare).* Save me! Save me!

(She screams and screams. DUSSEL *gets*

out of bed, going over to her, trying to wake her.)

DUSSEL. For God's sake! Quiet! Quiet! You want someone to hear?

(In the main room MRS. FRANK *grabs a shawl and pulls it around her. She rushes in to* ANNE, *taking her in her arms.* MR. FRANK *hurriedly gets up, putting on his overcoat.* MARGOT *sits up, terrified.* PETER'S *light goes on his room.)*

MRS. FRANK *(to* ANNE, *in her room).* Hush, darling, hush. It's all right. It's all right. *(Over her shoulder to* DUSSEL) Will you be kind enough to turn on the light, Mr. Dussel? *(Back to* ANNE) It's nothing, my darling. It was just a dream.

*(*DUSSEL *turns on the light in the bedroom.* MRS. FRANK *holds* ANNE *in her arms. Gradually* ANNE *comes out of her nightmare, still trembling with horror.* MR. FRANK *comes into the room, and goes quickly to the window, looking out to be sure that no one outside has heard* ANNE'S *screams.* MRS. FRANK *holds* ANNE, *talking softly to her. In the main room* MARGOT *stands on a chair, turning on the center hanging lamp. A light goes on in the* VAN DAANS' *room overhead.* PETER *puts his robe on, coming out of his room.)*

DUSSEL *(to* MRS. FRANK, *blowing his nose).* Something must be done about that child, Mrs. Frank. Yelling like that! Who knows but there's somebody on the streets? She's endangering all our lives.

MRS. FRANK. Anne, darling.

DUSSEL. Every night she twists and turns. I don't sleep. I spend half my night shushing her. And now it's nightmares!

*(*MARGOT *comes to the door of* ANNE'S *room, followed by* PETER. MR. FRANK *goes to them, indicating that everything is all right.* PETER *takes* MARGOT *back.)*

MRS. FRANK *(to* ANNE).You're here, safe, you see? Nothing has happened. *(To* DUSSEL) Please, Mr. Dussel, go back to bed. She'll be herself in a minute or two. Won't you, Anne?

DUSSEL *(picking up a book and a pillow).* Thank you, but I'm going to the w.c. The one place where there's peace!

(He stalks out. MR. VAN DAAN, *in underwear and trousers, comes down the stairs.)*

MR. VAN DAAN *(to* DUSSEL). What is it? What happened?

DUSSEL. A nightmare. She was having a nightmare!

MR. VAN DAAN. I thought someone was murdering her.

DUSSEL. Unfortunately, no.

(He goes into the bathroom. MR. VAN DAAN *goes back up the stairs.* MR. FRANK, *in the main room, sends* PETER *back to his own bedroom.)*

MR. FRANK. Thank you, Peter. Go back to bed.

*(*PETER *goes back to his room.* MR. FRANK *follows him turning out the light and looking out the window. Then he goes back to the main room and gets up on a chair, turning out the center hanging lamp.)*

MRS. FRANK *(to* ANNE). Would you like some water? *(*ANNE *shakes her head.)* Was it a very bad dream? Perhaps if you told me . . . ?

ANNE. I'd rather not talk about it.

MRS. FRANK. Poor darling. Try to sleep then. I'll sit right here beside you until you fall asleep. *(She brings a stool over, sitting there.)*

ANNE. You don't have to.

MRS. FRANK. But I'd like to stay with you . . . very much. Really.

ANNE. I'd rather you didn't.

MRS. FRANK. Good night, then. *(She leans down to kiss* ANNE. ANNE *throws her arm*

up over her face, turning away. MRS. FRANK, *hiding her hurt, kisses* ANNE'S *arm.*) You'll be all right? There's nothing that you want?

ANNE. Will you please ask Father to come.

MRS. FRANK *(after a second).* Of course, Anne dear. *(She hurries out into the other room.* MR. FRANK *comes to her as she comes in.) Sie verlangt nach Dir!*[1]

MR. FRANK *(sensing her hurt).* Edith, *Liebe, schau . . .*[2]

MRS. FRANK. *Es macht nichts! Ich danke* *dem lieben Herrgott, dass sie sich wenigstens an Dich wendet, wenn sie Trost braucht! Geh hinein, Otto, sie ist ganz hysterisch vor Angst.*[3] *(As* MR. FRANK *hesitates) Geh zu ihr.*[4] *(He looks at her for a second and then goes to get a cup of water for* ANNE. MRS. FRANK *sinks*

---

1. *Sie verlangt nach Dir!* She wants to see you.
2. *Edith, Liebe, schau . . .* Edith, my dear, look . . .
3. *Es macht nichts! . . . vor Angst.* It doesn't matter. Thank God that she at least turns to you when she is in need of consolation. Go, Otto, she is hysterical with fear.
4. *Geh zu ihr.* Go to her.

down on the bed, her face in her hands, trying to keep from sobbing aloud. MARGOT *comes over to her, putting her arms around her.)* She wants nothing of me. She pulled away when I leaned down to kiss her.

MARGOT. It's a phase . . . You heard Father . . . Most girls go through it . . . they turn to their fathers at this age . . . they give all their love to their fathers.

MRS. FRANK. You weren't like this. You didn't shut me out.

MARGOT. She'll get over it . . .

(She smooths the bed for MRS. FRANK *and sits beside her a moment as* MRS. FRANK *lies down. In* ANNE'S *room* MR. FRANK *comes in, sitting down by* ANNE. ANNE *flings her arms around him, clinging to him. In the distance we hear the sound of ack-ack.)*

ANNE. Oh, Pim. I dreamed that they came to get us! The Green Police! They broke down the door and grabbed me and started to drag me out the way they did Jopie.

MR. FRANK. I want you to take this pill.

ANNE. What is it?

MR. FRANK. Something to quiet you.

(She takes it and drinks the water. In the main room MARGOT *turns out the light and goes back to her room.)*

MR. FRANK *(to* ANNE*).* Do you want me to read to you for a while?

ANNE. No. Just sit with me for a minute. Was I awful? Did I yell terribly loud? Do you think anyone outside could have heard?

MR. FRANK. No. No. Lie quietly now. Try to sleep.

ANNE. I'm a terrible coward. I'm so disappointed in myself. I think I've conquered my fear . . . I think I'm really grown-up . . . and then something happens . . .

and I run to you like a baby . . . I love you, Father. I don't love anyone but you.

MR. FRANK *(reproachfully).* Annele!

ANNE. It's true. I've been thinking about it for a long time. You're the only one I love.

MR. FRANK. It's fine to hear you tell me that you love me. But I'd be happier if you said you loved your mother as well . . . She needs your help so much . . . your love . . .

ANNE. We have nothing in common. She doesn't understand me. Whenever I try to explain my views on life to her she asks me if I'm constipated.

MR. FRANK. You hurt her very much now. She's crying. She's in there crying.

ANNE. I can't help it. I only told the truth. I didn't want her here . . . *(Then, with sudden change)* Oh, Pim, I was horrible, wasn't I? And the worst of it is, I can stand off and look at myself doing it and know it's cruel and yet I can't stop doing it. What's the matter with me? Tell me. Don't say it's just a phase! Help me.

MR. FRANK. There is so little that we parents can do to help our children. We can only try to set a good example . . . point the way. The rest you must do yourself. You must build your own character.

ANNE. I'm trying. Really I am. Every night I think back over all of the things I did that day that were wrong . . . like putting the wet mop in Mr. Dussel's bed . . . and this thing now with Mother. I say to myself, that was wrong. I make up my mind, I'm never going to do that again. Never! Of course I may do something worse . . . but at least I'll never do *that* again . . . I have a nicer side, Father . . . a sweeter, nicer side. But I'm scared to show it. I'm afraid that people are going to laugh at me if I'm serious. So the mean Anne comes to the outside and the good Anne stays on the inside, and I keep on trying to switch them around and have the good Anne outside and the bad Anne inside and be what I'd like to be . . . and might be . . . if only . . . only . . .

(She is asleep. MR. FRANK *watches her for a moment and then turns off the light, and starts out. The lights dim out. The curtain falls on the scene.* ANNE'S VOICE *is heard dimly at first, and then with growing strength.)*

ANNE'S VOICE. . . . The air raids are getting worse. They come over day and night. The noise is terrifying. Pim says it should be music to our ears. The more planes, the sooner will come the end of the war. Mrs. Van Daan pretends to be a fatalist. What will be, will be. But when the planes come over, who is the most frightened? No one else but Petronella! . . . Monday, the ninth of November, nineteen forty-two. Wonderful news! The Allies[5] have landed in Africa. Pim says that we can look for an early finish to the war. Just for fun he asked each of us what was the first thing we wanted to do when we got out of here. Mrs. Van Daan longs to be home with her own things, her needlepoint chairs, the Beckstein piano her father gave her . . . the best that money could buy. Peter would like to go to a movie. Mr. Dussel wants to get back to his dentist's drill. He's afraid he is losing his touch. For myself, there are so many things . . . to ride a bike again . . . to laugh till my belly aches . . . to have new clothes from the skin out . . . to have a hot tub filled to overflowing and wallow in it for hours . . . to be back in school with my friends . . .

(As the last lines are being said, the curtain rises on the scene. The lights dim on as ANNE'S VOICE *fades away.)*

---

5. *The Allies* (al′īz), the countries, including Britain and the United States, that fought against Germany, Italy, and Japan in World War II.

Discussion

1. Mr. Van Daan is seen just before Anne's nightmare. **(a)** What does he do? **(b)** Have any clues suggested this kind of action on his part? Explain.

2. **(a)** What does her nightmare reveal about Anne? **(b)** What do you think it may foreshadow?

3. What does the scene reveal about the feelings of **(a)** Mr. Dussel toward Anne; **(b)** Anne toward her mother; **(c)** her mother toward Anne? Find statements to support your answers.

4. Would these people be likely to express the same feelings toward each other if they were living in normal circumstances? Explain.

5. What signs are there that Anne is struggling for greater maturity?

6. **(a)** What do Mrs. Van Daan, Peter, Mr. Dussel, and Anne want to do when they get out of the annex? **(b)** How well do their wishes fit your impression of each person?

Scene Five

It is the first night of the Hanukkah[1] celebration. MR. FRANK *is standing at the. head of the table on which is the Menorah.[2] He lights the Shamos, or servant candle, and holds it as he says the blessing. Seated listening is all of the "family," dressed in their best. The men wear hats;* PETER *wears his cap.*

MR. FRANK *(reading from a prayer book).*"Praised be Thou, oh Lord our God, Ruler of the universe, who has sanctified us with Thy commandments and bidden us kindle the Hanukkah lights. Praised be Thou, oh Lord our God, Ruler of the universe, who has wrought wondrous deliverances for our fathers in days of old. Praised be Thou, oh Lord our God, Ruler of the universe, that Thou has given us life and sustenance and brought us to this happy season." (MR. FRANK *lights the one candle of the Menorah as he continues.)* "We kindle this Hanukkah light to celebrate the great and wonderful deeds wrought through the zeal with which God filled the hearts of the heroic Maccabees, two thousand years ago. They fought against indifference, against tyranny and oppression, and they restored our Temple to us. May these lights remind us that we should ever look to God, whence cometh our help." Amen. *(Pronounced O-mayn.)*

ALL. Amen.

*(*MR. FRANK *hands* MRS. FRANK *the prayer book.)*

MRS. FRANK *(reading).* "I lift up mine eyes unto the mountains, from whence cometh my help. My help cometh from the Lord who made heaven and earth. He will not suffer thy foot to be moved. He that keepeth thee will not slumber. He that keepeth Israel doth neither slumber nor sleep. The Lord is thy keeper. The Lord is thy shade upon thy right hand. The sun shall not smite thee by day, nor the moon by night. The Lord shall keep thee from all evil. He shall keep thy soul. The Lord shall guard thy going out and thy coming in, from this time forth and forevermore." Amen.

---

1. *Hanukkah* (hä′nə kə), a Jewish festival usually held in December. The festival commemorates the rededication of the temple in Jerusalem after the Maccabees (mak′ə bēz′), a family of Jewish patriots, led the Jews to victory over the Syrians in 165 B.C.
2. *Menorah* (mə nôr′ə), a candlestick with various numbers of branches used primarily in Jewish religious services. The *Shamos* (shäm′əs), or servant candle, is lit first, then used to light the Menorah.

ALL. Amen.

(MRS. FRANK *puts down the prayer book and goes to get the food and wine.* MARGOT *helps her.* MR. FRANK *takes the men's hats and puts them aside.*)

DUSSEL (*rising*). That was very moving.

ANNE (*pulling him back*). It isn't over yet!

MRS. VAN DAAN. Sit down! Sit down!

ANNE. There's a lot more, songs and presents.

DUSSEL. Presents?

MRS. FRANK. Not this year, unfortunately.

MRS. VAN DAAN. But always on Hanukkah everyone gives presents . . . everyone!

DUSSEL. Like our St. Nicholas' Day.[3]

(*There is a chorus of "no's" from the group.*)

MRS. VAN DAAN. No! Not like St. Nicholas! What kind of a Jew are you that you don't know Hanukkah?

MRS. FRANK (*as she brings the food*). I remember particularly the candles . . . First one, as we have tonight. Then the second night you light two candles, the next night three . . . and so on until you have eight candles burning. When there are eight candles it is truly beautiful.

MRS. VAN DAAN. And the potato pancakes.

MR. VAN DAAN. Don't talk about them!

MRS. VAN DAAN. I make the best *latkes*[4] you ever tasted!

MRS. FRANK. Invite us all next year . . . in your own home.

MR. FRANK. God willing!

MRS. VAN DAAN. God willing.

MARGOT. What I remember best is the presents we used to get when we were little . . . eight days of presents . . . and each day they got better and better.

MRS. FRANK (*sitting down*). We are all here, alive. That is present enough.

ANNE. No, it isn't. I've got something . . .

(*She rushes into her room, hurriedly puts on a little hat improvised from the lamp shade, grabs a satchel bulging with parcels and comes running back.*)

MRS. FRANK. What is it?

ANNE. Presents!

MRS. VAN DAAN. Presents!

DUSSEL. Look!

MRS. VAN DAAN. What's she got on her head?

PETER. A lamp shade!

ANNE. (*She picks out one at random.*) This is for Margot. (*She hands it to* MARGOT, *pulling her to her feet.*) Read it out loud.

MARGOT (*reading*).
"You have never lost your temper.
You never will, I fear,
You are so good.
But if you should,
Put all your cross words here."
(*She tears open the package.*) A new crossword puzzle book! Where did you get it?

ANNE. It isn't new. It's one that you've done. But I rubbed it all out, and if you wait a little and forget, you can do it all over again.

MARGOT (*sitting*). It's wonderful, Anne. Thank you. You'd never know it wasn't new.

(*From outside we hear the sound of a streetcar passing.*)

ANNE (*with another gift*). Mrs. Van Daan.

MRS. VAN DAAN (*taking it*). This is awful . . . I haven't anything for anyone . . . I never thought . . .

MR. FRANK. This is all Anne's idea.

MRS. VAN DAAN (*holding up a bottle*). What is it?

ANNE. It's hair shampoo. I took all the odds

---

3. *St. Nicholas' Day.* On December 6, the feast of St. Nicholas, Dutch children are given gifts. St. Nicholas, actually a fourth-century saint, is today a figure like Santa Claus. The feast has no real religious significance.
4. *latkes* (lät′kəs), potato pancakes.

and ends of soap and mixed them with the last of my toilet water.

MRS. VAN DAAN. Oh, Anneke!

ANNE. I wanted to write a poem for all of them, but I didn't have time. *(Offering a large box to* MR. VAN DAAN*)* Yours, Mr. Van Daan, is *really* something . . . something you want more than anything. *(As she waits for him to open it)* Look! Cigarettes!

MR. VAN DAAN. Cigarettes!

ANNE. Two of them! Pim found some old pipe tobacco in the pocket lining of his coat . . . and we made them . . . or rather, Pim did.

MRS. VAN DAAN. Let me see . . . Well, look at that! Light it, Putti! Light it.

*(*MR. VAN DAAN *hesitates.)*

ANNE. It's tobacco, really it is! There's a little fluff in it, but not much.

(Everyone watches as MR. VAN DAAN *cautiously lights it. The cigarette flares up. Everyone laughs.)*

PETER. It works!

MRS. VAN DAAN. Look at him.

MR. VAN DAAN *(spluttering)*. Thank you, Anne. Thank you.

*(*ANNE *rushes back to her satchel for another present.)*

ANNE *(handing her mother a piece of paper)*. For Mother, Hanukkah greeting.

(She pulls her mother to her feet.)

MRS. FRANK. *(She reads.)*
"Here's an I.O.U. that I promise to pay.
Ten hours of doing whatever you say.
Signed, Anne Frank."

*(*MRS. FRANK, *touched, takes* ANNE *in her arms, holding her close.)*

DUSSEL *(to* ANNE*)*. Ten hours of doing what you're told? *Anything* you're told?

ANNE. That's right.

DUSSEL. You wouldn't want to sell that, Mrs. Frank?

MRS. FRANK. Never! This is the most precious gift I've ever had!

(She sits, showing her present to the others. ANNE *hurries back to the satchel and pulls out a scarf, the scarf that* MR. FRANK *found in the first scene.)*

ANNE *(offering it to her father)*. For Pim.

MR. FRANK. Anneke . . . I wasn't supposed to have a present!

(He takes it, unfolding it and showing it to the others.)

ANNE. It's a muffler . . . to put round your neck . . . like an ascot, you know. I made it myself out of odds and ends . . . I knitted it in the dark each night, after I'd gone to bed. I'm afraid it looks better in the dark!

MR. FRANK *(putting it on)*. It's fine. It fits me perfectly. Thank you, Annele.

*(*ANNE *hands* PETER *a ball of paper, with a string attached to it.)*

ANNE. That's for Mouschi.

PETER *(rising to bow)*. On behalf of Mouschi, I thank you.

ANNE *(hesitant, handing him a gift)*. And . . . this is yours . . . from Mrs. Quack Quack. *(As he holds it gingerly in his hands)* Well . . . open it . . Aren't you going to open it?

PETER. I'm scared to. I know something's going to jump out and hit me.

ANNE. No. It's nothing like that, really.

MRS. VAN DAAN *(as he is opening it)*. What is it, Peter? Go on. Show it.

ANNE *(excitedly)*. It's a safety razor!

DUSSEL. A what?

ANNE. A razor!

MRS. VAN DAAN *(looking at it)*. You didn't make that out of odds and ends.

ANNE *(to* PETER*)*. Miep got it for me. It's not new. It's second-hand. But you really do need a razor now.

DUSSEL. For what?

ANNE. Look on his upper lip . . . you can see the beginning of a mustache.

DUSSEL. He wants to get rid of that? Put a little milk on it and let the cat lick it off.

PETER (starting for his room). Think you're funny, don't you.

DUSSEL. Look! He can't wait! He's going in to try it!

PETER. I'm going to give Mouschi his present!

(He goes into his room, slamming the door behind him.)

MR. VAN DAAN (disgustedly). Mouschi, Mouschi, Mouschi.

(In the distance we hear a dog persistently barking. ANNE brings a gift to DUSSEL.)

ANNE. And last but never least, my roommate, Mr. Dussel.

DUSSEL. For me? You have something for me? (He opens the small box she gives him.)

ANNE. I made them myself.

DUSSEL (puzzled). Capsules! Two capsules!

ANNE. They're ear-plugs!

DUSSEL. Ear-plugs?

ANNE. To put in your ears so you won't hear me when I thrash around at night. I saw them advertised in a magazine. They're not real ones . . . I made them out of cotton and candle wax. Try them . . . See if they don't work . . . see if you can hear me talk . . .

DUSSEL (putting them in his ears). Wait now until I get them in . . . so.

ANNE. Are you ready?

DUSSEL. Huh?

ANNE. Are you ready?

DUSSEL. Good God! They've gone inside! I can't get them out! (They laugh as MR. DUSSEL jumps about, trying to shake the plugs out of his ears. Finally he gets

them out. Putting them away.) Thank you, Anne! Thank you!

MR. VAN DAAN. A real Hanukkah! ⎫
MRS. VAN DAAN. Wasn't it cute of her? ⎬ (Together)

MRS. FRANK. I don't know when she did it.

MARGOT. I love my present.

ANNE (sitting at the table). And now let's have the song, Father . . . please . . . (To DUSSEL) Have you heard the Hanukkah song, Mr. Dussel? The song is the whole thing! (She sings) "Oh Hanukkah! Oh, Hanukkah! The sweet celebration . . ."

MR. FRANK (quieting her). I'm afraid, Anne, we shouldn't sing that song tonight. (To DUSSEL) It's a song of jubilation, of rejoicing. One is apt to become too enthusiastic.

ANNE. Oh, please, please. Let's sing the song. I promise not to shout!

MR. FRANK. Very well. But quietly now . . . I'll keep an eye on you and when . . .

(As ANNE starts to sing, she is interrupted by DUSSEL, who is snorting and wheezing.)

DUSSEL (pointing to PETER). You . . . You! (PETER is coming from his bedroom, ostentatiously holding a bulge in his coat as if he were holding his cat, and dangling ANNE'S present before it.) How many times . . . I told you . . . Out! Out!

MR. VAN DAAN (going to PETER). What's the matter with you? Haven't you any sense? Get that cat out of here.

PETER (innocently). Cat?

MR. VAN DAAN. You heard me. Get it out of here!

PETER. I have no cat. (Delighted with his joke, he opens his coat and pulls out a bath towel. The group at the table laugh, enjoying the joke.)

DUSSEL (*still wheezing*). It doesn't need to be the cat . . . his clothes are enough . . . when he comes out of that room . . .

MR. VAN DAAN. Don't worry. You won't be bothered any more. We're getting rid of it.

DUSSEL. At last you listen to me.

(*He goes off into his bedroom.*)

MR. VAN DAAN (*calling after him*). I'm not doing it for you. That's all in your mind . . . all of it! (*He starts back to his place at the table.*) I'm doing it because I'm sick of seeing that cat eat all our food.

PETER. That's not true! I only give him bones . . . scraps . . .

MR. VAN DAAN. Don't tell me! He gets fatter every day! Damn cat looks better than any of us. Out he goes tonight!

PETER. No! No!

ANNE. Mr. Van Daan, you can't do that! That's Peter's cat. Peter loves that cat.

MRS. FRANK (*quietly*). Anne.

PETER (*to MR. VAN DAAN*). If he goes, I go.

MR. VAN DAAN. Go! Go!

MRS. VAN DAAN. You're not going and the cat's not going! Now please . . . this is Hanukkah . . . Hanukkah . . . this is the time to celebrate . . . What's the matter with all of you? Come on, Anne. Let's have the song.

ANNE (*singing*).
"Oh, Hanukkah! Oh, Hanukkah!
The sweet celebration."

MR. FRANK (*rising*). I think we should first blow out the candle . . . then we'll have something for tomorrow night.

MARGOT. But, Father, you're supposed to let it burn itself out.

MR. FRANK. I'm sure that God understands shortages. (*Before blowing it out*) "Praised be Thou, oh Lord our God, who hast sustained us and permitted us to celebrate this joyous festival."

(*He is about to blow out the candle when suddenly there is a crash of something falling below. They all freeze in horror, motionless. For a few seconds there is complete silence.* MR. FRANK *slips off his shoes. The others noiselessly follow his example.* MR. FRANK *turns out a light near him. He motions to* PETER *to turn off the center lamp.* PETER *tries to reach it, realizes he cannot and gets up on a chair. Just as he is touching the lamp he loses his balance. The chair goes out from under him. He falls. The iron lamp shade crashes to the floor. There is a sound of feet below, running down the stairs.*)

MR. VAN DAAN (*under his breath*). God almighty! (*The only light left comes from the Hanukkah candle.* DUSSEL *comes from his room.* MR. FRANK *creeps over to the stairwell and stands listening. The dog is heard barking excitedly.*) Do you hear anything?

MR. FRANK (*in a whisper*). No. I think they've gone.

MRS. VAN DAAN. It's the Green Police. They've found us.

MR. FRANK. If they had, they wouldn't have left. They'd be up here by now.

MRS. VAN DAAN. I know it's the Green Police. They've gone to get help. That's all, they'll be back.

MR. VAN DAAN. Or it may have been the Gestapo[5] looking for papers . . .

MR. FRANK (*interrupting*). Or a thief, looking for money.

MRS. VAN DAAN. We've got to do something . . . Quick! Quick! Before they come back.

MR. VAN DAAN. There isn't anything to do. Just wait.

(MR. FRANK *holds up his hand for them to*

---

5. **Gestapo** (gə stä′pō), the Secret Police of Nazi Germany.

be quiet. He is listening intently. There is complete silence as they all strain to hear any sound from below. Suddenly ANNE *begins to sway. With a low cry she falls to the floor in a faint.* MRS. FRANK *goes to her quickly, sitting beside her on the floor and taking her in her arms.)*

MRS. FRANK. Get some water, please! Get some water!

*(*MARGOT *starts for the sink.)*

MR. VAN DAAN *(grabbing* MARGOT*)*. No! No! No one's going to run water!

MR. FRANK. If they've found us, they've found us. Get the water. *(*MARGOT *starts again for the sink.* MR. FRANK, *getting a flashlight)* I'm going down.

*(*MARGOT *rushes to him, clinging to him.* ANNE *struggles to consciousness.)*

MARGOT. No, Father, no! There may be someone there, waiting . . . It may be a trap!

MR. FRANK. This is Saturday. There is no way for us to know what has happened until Miep or Mr. Kraler comes on Monday morning. We cannot live with this uncertainty.

MARGOT. Don't go, Father!

MRS. FRANK. Hush, darling, hush. *(*MR. FRANK *slips quietly out, down the steps and out through the door below.)* Margot! Stay close to me.

*(*MARGOT *goes to her mother.)*

MR. VAN DAAN. Shush! Shush!

*(*MRS. FRANK *whispers to* MARGOT *to get the water.* MARGOT *goes for it.)*

MRS. VAN DAAN. Putti, where's our money? Get our money. I hear you can buy the Green Police off, so much a head. Go up-stairs quick! Get the money!

MR. VAN DAAN. Keep still!

MRS. VAN DAAN *(kneeling before him, pleading)*. Do you want to be dragged off to a concentration camp? Are you going to stand there and wait for them to come up and get you? Do something, I tell you!

MR. VAN DAAN *(pushing her aside)*. Will you keep still!

(He goes over to the stairwell to listen. PETER *goes to his mother, helping her up onto the sofa. There is a second of silence. Then* ANNE *can stand it no longer.)*

ANNE. Someone go after Father! Make Father come back!

PETER *(starting for the door)*. I'll go.

MR. VAN DAAN. Haven't you done enough?

(He pushes PETER *roughly away. In his anger against his father* PETER *grabs a chair as if to hit him with it, then puts it down, burying his face in his hands.* MRS. FRANK *begins to pray softly.)*

ANNE. Please, please, Mr. Van Daan. Get Father.

MR. VAN DAAN. Quiet! Quiet!

*(*ANNE *is shocked into silence.* MRS. FRANK *pulls her closer, holding her protectively in her arms.)*

MRS. FRANK *(softly, praying)*. "I lift up mine eyes unto the mountains, from whence cometh my help. My help cometh from the Lord who made heaven and earth. He will not suffer thy foot to be moved . . . He that keepeth thee will not slumber . . ."

(She stops as she hears someone coming. They all watch the door tensely. MR. FRANK *comes quietly in.* ANNE *rushes to him, holding him tight.)*

MR. FRANK. It was a thief. That noise must have scared him away.

MRS. VAN DAAN. Thank God.

MR. FRANK. He took the cash box. And the radio. He ran away in such a hurry that he didn't stop to shut the street door. It was swinging wide open. *(A breath of relief sweeps over them.)* I think it would be good to have some light.

MARGOT. Are you sure it's all right?

MR. FRANK. The danger has passed. *(MARGOT goes to light the small lamp.)* Don't be so terrified, Anne. We're safe.

DUSSEL. Who says the danger has passed? Don't you realize we are in greater danger than ever?

MR. FRANK. Mr. Dussel, will you be still! *(MR. FRANK takes ANNE back to the table, making her sit down with him, trying to calm her.)*

DUSSEL *(pointing to PETER)*. Thanks to this clumsy fool, there's someone now who knows we're up here! Someone now knows we're up here, hiding!

MRS. VAN DAAN *(going to DUSSEL)*. Someone knows we're here, yes. But who is the someone? A thief! A thief! You think a thief is going to go to the Green Police and say . . . I was robbing a place the other night and I heard a noise up over my head? You think a thief is going to do that?

DUSSEL. Yes. I think he will.

MRS. VAN DAAN *(hysterically)*. You're crazy! *(She stumbles back to her seat at the table. PETER follows protectively, pushing DUSSEL aside.)*

DUSSEL. I think some day he'll be caught and then he'll make a bargain with the Green Police . . . if they'll let him off, he'll tell them where some Jews are hiding! *(He goes off into the bedroom. There is a second of appalled silence.)*

MR. VAN DAAN. He's right.

ANNE. Father, let's get out of here! We can't stay here now . . . Let's go . . .

MR. VAN DAAN. Go! Where?

MRS. FRANK *(sinking into her chair at the table)*. Yes. Where?

MR. FRANK *(rising, to them all)*. Have we lost all faith? All courage? A moment ago we thought that they'd come for us. We were sure it was the end. But it wasn't the end. We're alive, safe. *(MR. VAN DAAN goes to the table and sits. MR. FRANK prays.)* "We thank Thee, oh Lord our God, that in Thy infinite mercy Thou hast again seen fit to spare us." *(He blows out the candle, then turns to ANNE.)* Come on, Anne. The song! Let's have the song! *(He starts to sing. ANNE finally starts falteringly to sing, as MR. FRANK urges her on. Her voice is hardly audible at first.)*

ANNE *(singing)*.

"Oh, Hanukkah! Oh, Hanukkah!
The sweet . . . celebration . . ."

(As she goes on singing, the others gradually join in, their voices still shaking with fear. MRS. VAN DAAN sobs as she sings.)

GROUP.

"Around the feast . . . we . . . gather
In complete . . . jubilation . . .
Happiest of sea . . . sons
Now is here.
Many are the reasons for good cheer."

(DUSSEL comes from the bedroom. He comes over to the table, standing beside MARGOT, listening to them as they sing.)

"Together
We'll weather
Whatever tomorrow may bring."

(As they sing on with growing courage, the lights start to dim.)

"So hear us rejoicing
And merrily voicing
The Hanukkah song that we sing.
Hoy!"

(The lights are out. The curtain starts slowly to fall.)

"Hear us rejoicing
And merrily voicing
The Hanukkah song that we sing."

(They are still singing, as the curtain falls.)

CURTAIN

Discussion

1. **(a)** How does this Hanukkah celebration differ from what the "family" members are used to? **(b)** Why do you think they hold the celebration under such circumstances?

2. Explain how the gifts Anne gives are appropriate for each person.

3. **(a)** What incident reveals Peter's sense of humor? **(b)** What effect does his behavior have on Mr. Dussel? on Mr. Van Daan?

4. **(a)** What event ends the celebration abruptly? **(b)** What possible significance do the characters see in this event? **(c)** What do you learn about each of the following from the way he or she reacts to the incident: Anne; Mr. Dussel; Mrs. Van Daan; Mr. Van Daan?

5. What decisions does Mr. Frank make throughout the scene that show him still to be the person in charge?

6. **(a)** Why at the end of the scene does Mr. Frank urge Anne to sing the Hanukkah song when earlier he had discouraged her? **(b)** What effect is created by concluding Act One with the singing of this song?

Composition

Throughout much of the play the characters are seen trying to live normal lives in an abnormal situation. Consider the kind of home life the Franks and the Van Daans must have had, based on remarks of various characters. What scenes in this play emphasize the characters' attempts to live their lives as usual? What scenes emphasize the changes they have been forced to make?

In a composition of one to two pages, explain the likenesses and differences of their lives "before" and their lives "now." Cite specific examples wherever possible.

(You may find the article "Finding Likenesses and Differences" in the Composition Guide helpful in writing this composition.)

Comment: Dramatic License

Since a drama is a series of events to be acted out rather than a narration, Frances Goodrich and Albert Hackett had to adapt Anne's diary entries to make them suitable for presentation on a stage. Making such changes, usually for the sake of the overall effect desired by the dramatists, is called using *dramatic license.*

From Anne's descriptions of events in the annex, the dramatists had to create dialogue for the persons involved. Too, they had to compress journal entries to provide necessary exposition, or background, for the play. For example, the first diary entry, which Mr. Frank begins to read aloud on stage, was drawn from parts of a number of entries. Finally, so as not to crowd the stage unduly with actors, in Miep and Mr. Kraler they created composite characters. The personalities of Miep Gies and Elli Vossen, both of whom worked in the warehouse building and were friends of Anne, merge on stage in Miep; Mr. Kraler and Mr. Koophuis, both business friends of Mr. Frank and both associated with Travis, Inc., become the single character of Mr. Kraler.

In reality, the people living in the Secret Annex had more freedom to move around than do the characters in the play. In the diary, Anne frequently mentions the trips to the "private office" on the first floor of the building where the inhabitants of the annex listened to news broadcasts, speeches, and concerts on the radio. The playwrights, however, realizing the difficulties in staging different settings, have confined the action and the characters to one set, the Secret Annex itself.

During the two years the Franks and the Van Daans occupied the Secret Annex, there were several burglaries in the office below. None of them occurred during the Hanukkah season. Again, the playwrights have used dramatic license in presenting only one of these burglaries. By having the burglary occur during the Hanukkah celebration, the playwrights have created an extremely dramatic situation; the hope and strength which the inhabitants receive from the religious ceremony contrast sharply with the ever present danger of discovery, brought into focus by the intrusion of the unknown thief.

Much of Anne's diary reveals her thoughts about herself, the special problems with which she, as a teenager, is faced. The following diary entry reveals an important aspect of Anne's personality:

Saturday, 15 July, 1944. . . . I have one outstanding trait in my character, which must strike anyone who knows me for any length of time and that is my knowledge of myself. I can watch myself and my actions, just like an outsider. The Anne of every day I can face entirely without prejudice, without making excuses for her, and watch what's good and what's bad about her. This "self-consciousness" haunts me, and every time I open my mouth I know as soon as I have spoken whether "that ought to have been different" or "that was right as it was." There are so many things about myself that I condemn; I couldn't begin to name them all. I understand more and more how true Daddy's words were when he said: "All children must look after their own upbringing." Parents can only give good advice or put them on the right paths, but the final forming of a person's character lies in their own hands.[1]

This is the type of personal, intimate revelation that Anne made only in her diary. To reveal this aspect of Anne's personality to the audience, the dramatists incorporated the entry into Scene Four in which Anne, still frightened and overwrought from her nightmare, confesses to her father things that in actuality she revealed to no one.

Frances Goodrich and Albert Hackett, through their careful selections and adaptations of diary entries, have succeeded in presenting vivid portraits of the inhabitants of the Secret Annex. At the same time, they have preserved the spirit of reality found in the historical source from which they had to work, the diary of a young girl.

---

1. From *Anne Frank: The Diary of a Young Girl*. Copyright 1952 by Otto H. Frank. Reprinted by permission of Doubleday & Company, Inc. and Vallentine, Mitchell & Co., Ltd.

Act Two

Scene One

In the darkness we hear ANNE'S VOICE, *again reading from the diary.*

ANNE'S VOICE. Saturday, the first of January, nineteen forty-four. Another new year has begun and we find ourselves still in our hiding place. We have been here now for one year, five months and twenty-five days. It seems that our life is at a standstill.

The curtain rises on the scene. It is afternoon. Everyone is bundled up against the cold. In the main room MRS. FRANK *is taking down the laundry, which is hung across the back.* MR. FRANK *sits in the chair down left, reading.* MARGOT *is lying on the couch with a blanket over her and the many-colored knitted scarf around her throat.* ANNE *is seated at the center table, writing in her diary.* PETER, MR. *and* MRS. VAN DAAN, *and* DUSSEL *are all in their own rooms, reading or lying down.*

As the lights dim on, ANNE'S VOICE *continues, without a break.*

ANNE'S VOICE. We are all a little thinner. The Van Daans' "discussions" are as violent as ever. Mother still does not understand me. But then I don't understand her either. There is one great change, however. A change in myself. I read somewhere that girls of my age don't feel quite certain of themselves.

(The buzzer of the door below suddenly sounds. Everyone is startled; MR. FRANK *tiptoes cautiously to the top of the steps and listens. Again the buzzer sounds, in* MIEP'S *V-for-Victory signal.[1])*

MR. FRANK. It's Miep! *(He goes quickly down the steps to unbolt the door.* MRS. FRANK *calls upstairs to the* VAN DAANS *and then to* PETER.*)*

MRS. FRANK. Wake up, everyone! Miep is here! *(*ANNE *quickly puts her diary away.* MARGOT *sits up, pulling the blanket around her shoulders.* MR. DUSSEL *sits on the edge of his bed, listening, disgruntled.* MIEP *comes up the steps, followed by* MR. KRALER. *They bring flowers, books, newspapers, etc.* ANNE *rushes to* MIEP, *throwing her arms affectionately around her.)* Miep . . . and Mr. Kraler . . . What a delightful surprise!

MR. KRALER. We came to bring you New Year's greetings.

MRS. FRANK. You shouldn't . . . you should have at least one day to yourselves. *(She goes quickly to the stove and brings down teacups and tea for all of them.)*

ANNE. Don't say that, it's so wonderful to see them! *(Sniffing at* MIEP'S *coat)* I can smell the wind and the cold on your clothes.

MIEP *(giving her the flowers)*. There you are. *(Then to* MARGOT, *feeling her forehead)* How are you, Margot? . . . Feeling any better?

MARGOT. I'm all right.

ANNE. We filled her full of every kind of pill so she won't cough and make a noise.

(She runs into her room to put the flowers in water. MR. *and* MRS. VAN DAAN *come from upstairs. Outside there is the sound of a band playing.)*

MRS. VAN DAAN. Well, hello, Miep. Mr. Kraler.

MR. KRALER *(giving a bouquet of flowers to* MRS. VAN DAAN*)*. With my hope for peace in the New Year.

PETER *(anxiously)*. Miep, have you seen Mouschi? Have you seen him anywhere around?

---

1. *V-for-Victory signal,* three short buzzes followed by a long one. In the Morse Code the letter V is transmitted by three dots and a dash. It was widely used as a victory symbol during World War II.

MIEP. I'm sorry, Peter. I asked everyone in the neighborhood had they seen a gray cat. But they said no.

(MRS. FRANK *gives* MIEP *a cup of tea.* MR. FRANK *comes up the steps, carrying a small cake on a plate.*)

MR. FRANK. Look what Miep's brought for us!

MRS. FRANK (*taking it*). A cake!

MR. VAN DAAN. A cake! (*He pinches* MIEP'S *cheeks gaily and hurries up to the cupboard.*) I'll get some plates.

(DUSSEL, *in his room, hastily puts a coat on and starts out to join the others.*)

MRS. FRANK. Thank you, Miepia.[2] You shouldn't have done it. You must have used all of your sugar ration for weeks. (*Giving it to* MRS. VAN DAAN) It's beautiful, isn't it?

MRS. VAN DAAN. It's been ages since I even saw a cake. Not since you brought us one last year. (*Without looking at the cake, to* MIEP) Remember? Don't you remember, you gave us one on New Year's Day? Just this time last year? I'll never forget it because you had "Peace in nineteen forty-three" on it. (*She looks at the cake and reads.*) "Peace in nineteen forty-four!"

MIEP. Well, it has to come sometime, you know. (*As* DUSSEL *comes from his room*) Hello, Mr. Dussel.

MR. KRALER. How are you?

MR. VAN DAAN (*bringing plates and a knife*). Here's the knife, *liefje*. Now, how many of us are there?

MIEP. None for me, thank you.

MR. FRANK. Oh, please. You must.

MIEP. I couldn't.

MR. VAN DAAN. Good! That leaves one . . . two . . . three . . . seven of us.

DUSSEL. Eight! Eight! It's the same number as it always is!

MR. VAN DAAN. I left Margot out. I take it for granted Margot won't eat any.

ANNE. Why wouldn't she!

MRS. FRANK. I think it won't harm her.

MR. VAN DAAN. All right! All right! I just didn't want her to start coughing again, that's all.

DUSSEL. And please, Mrs. Frank should cut the cake.

MR. VAN DAAN. What's the difference?

MRS. VAN DAAN. It's not Mrs. Frank's cake, is it, Miep? It's for all of us.
} (*Together*)

DUSSEL. Mrs. Frank divides things better.

MRS. VAN DAAN (*going to* DUSSEL). What are you trying to say?

MR. VAN DAAN. Oh, come on! Stop wasting time!
} (*Together*)

MRS. VAN DAAN (*to* DUSSEL). Don't I always give everybody exactly the same? Don't I?

MR. VAN DAAN. Forget it, Kerli.

MRS. VAN DAAN. No. I want an answer! Don't I?

DUSSEL. Yes. Yes. Everybody gets exactly the same . . . except Mr. Van Daan always gets a little bit more.

(VAN DAAN *advances on* DUSSEL, *the knife still in his hand.*)

MR. VAN DAAN. That's a lie!

(DUSSEL *retreats before the onslaught of the* VAN DAANS.)

MR. FRANK. Please, please! (*Then to* MIEP) You see what a little sugar cake does to us? It goes right to our heads!

MR. VAN DAAN (*handing* MRS. FRANK *the knife*). Here you are, Mrs. Frank.

MRS. FRANK. Thank you. (*Then to* MIEP *as she goes to the table to cut the cake*) Are you sure you won't have some?

---

2. *Miepia* (mēp′ʜyə).

MIEP (*drinking her tea*). No, really, I have to go in a minute.

(*The sound of the band fades out in the distance.*)

PETER (*to* MIEP). Maybe Mouschi went back to our house . . . they say that cats . . . Do you ever get over there . . . ? I mean . . . do you suppose you could . . . ?

MIEP. I'll try, Peter. The first minute I get I'll try. But I'm afraid, with him gone a week . . .

DUSSEL. Make up your mind, already someone has had a nice big dinner from that cat!

(PETER *is furious, inarticulate. He starts toward* DUSSEL *as if to hit him.* MR. FRANK *stops him.* MRS. FRANK *speaks quickly to ease the situation.*)

MRS. FRANK (*to* MIEP). This is delicious, Miep!

MRS. VAN DAAN (*eating hers*). Delicious!

MR. VAN DAAN (*finishing it in one gulp*). Dirk's in luck to get a girl who can bake like this!

MIEP (*putting down her empty teacup*). I have to run. Dirk's taking me to a party tonight.

ANNE. How heavenly! Remember now what everyone is wearing, and what you have to eat and everything, so you can tell us tomorrow.

MIEP. I'll give you a full report! Good-by, everyone!

MR. VAN DAAN (*to* MIEP). Just a minute. There's something I'd like you to do for me.

(*He hurries off up the stairs to his room.*)

MRS. VAN DAAN (*sharply*). Putti, where are you going? (*She rushes up the stairs after him, calling hysterically.*) What do you want? Putti, what are you going to do?

MIEP (*to* PETER). What's wrong?

PETER. (*His sympathy is with his mother.*) Father says he's going to sell her fur coat. She's crazy about that old fur coat.

DUSSEL. Is it possible? Is it possible that anyone is so silly as to worry about a fur coat in times like this?

PETER. It's none of your darn business. . . and if you say one more thing . . . I'll, I'll take you and I'll . . . I mean it . . . I'll . . .

(*There is a piercing scream from* MRS. VAN DAAN *above. She grabs at the fur coat as* MR. VAN DAAN *is starting downstairs with it.*)

MRS. VAN DAAN. No! No! No! Don't you dare take that! You hear? It's mine! (*Downstairs* PETER *turns away, embarrassed, miserable.*) My father gave me that! You didn't give it to me. You have no right. Let go of it . . . you hear?

(MR. VAN DAAN *pulls the coat from her hands and hurries downstairs.* MRS. VAN DAAN *sinks to the floor, sobbing. As* MR. VAN DAAN *comes into the main room the others look away, embarrassed for him.*)

MR. VAN DAAN (*to* MR. KRALER). Just a little— discussion over the advisability of selling this coat. As I have often reminded Mrs. Van Daan, it's very selfish of her to keep it when people outside are in such desperate need of clothing . . . (*He gives the coat to* MIEP.) So if you will please to sell it for us? It should fetch a good price. And by the way, will you get me cigarettes. I don't care what kind they are . . . get all you can.

MIEP. It's terribly difficult to get them, Mr. Van Daan. But I'll try. Good-by.

(*She goes.* MR. FRANK *follows her down the steps to bolt the door after her.* MRS. FRANK *gives* MR. KRALER *a cup of tea.*)

MRS. FRANK. Are you sure you won't have some cake, Mr. Kraler?

MR. KRALER. I'd better not.

MR. VAN DAAN. You're still feeling badly? What does your doctor say?

MR. KRALER. I haven't been to him.

MRS. FRANK. Now, Mr. Kraler! . . .

MR. KRALER (*sitting at the table*). Oh, I tried. But you can't get near a doctor these days . . . they're so busy. After weeks I finally managed to get one on the telephone. I told him I'd like an appointment . . . I wasn't feeling very well. You know what he answers . . . over the telephone . . . Stick out your tongue! (*They laugh. He turns to* MR. FRANK *as* MR. FRANK *comes back.*) I have some contracts here . . . I wonder if you'd look over them with me . . .

MR. FRANK (*putting out his hand*). Of course.

MR. KRALER. (*He rises.*) If we could go downstairs . . . (MR. FRANK *starts ahead,* MR. KRALER *speaks to the others.*) Will you forgive us? I won't keep him but a minute. (*He starts to follow* MR. FRANK *down the steps.*)

MARGOT (*with sudden foreboding*). What's happened? Something's happened! Hasn't it, Mr. Kraler?

(MR. KRALER *stops and comes back, trying to reassure* MARGOT *with a pretense of casualness.*)

MR. KRALER. No, really. I want your father's advice . . .

MARGOT. Something's gone wrong! I know it!

MR. FRANK (*coming back, to* MR. KRALER). If it's something that concerns us here, it's better that we all hear it.

MR. KRALER (*turning to him, quietly*). But . . . the children . . . ?

MR. FRANK. What they'd imagine would be worse than any reality.

(*As* MR. KRALER *speaks, they all listen with intense apprehension.* MRS. VAN

DAAN *comes down the stairs and sits on the bottom step.)*

MR. KRALER. It's a man in the storeroom . . . I don't know whether or not you remember him . . . Carl, about fifty, heavy-set, near-sighted . . . He came with us just before you left.

MR. FRANK. He was from Utrecht?

MR. KRALER. That's the man. A couple of weeks ago, when I was in the storeroom, he closed the door and asked me . . . how's Mr. Frank? What do you hear from Mr. Frank? I told him I only knew there was a rumor that you were in Switzerland. He said he'd heard that rumor too, but he thought I might know something more. I didn't pay any attention to it . . . but then a thing happened yesterday . . . He'd brought some invoices to the office for me to sign. As I was going through them, I looked up. He was standing staring at the bookcase . . . your bookcase. He said he thought he remembered a door there . . . Wasn't there a door there that used to go up to the loft? Then he told me he wanted more money. Twenty guilders[3] more a week.

MR. VAN DAAN. Blackmail!

MR. FRANK. Twenty guilders? Very modest blackmail.

MR. VAN DAAN. That's just the beginning.

DUSSEL *(coming to* MR. FRANK*).* You know what I think? He was the thief who was down there that night. That's how he knows we're here.

MR. FRANK *(to* MR. KRALER*).* How was it left? What did you tell him?

MR. KRALER. I said I had to think about it. What shall I do? Pay him the money? . . . Take a chance on firing him . . . or what? I don't know.

DUSSEL *(frantic).* For God's sake don't fire him! Pay him what he asks . . . keep him here where you can have your eye on him.

MR. FRANK. Is it so much that he's asking? What are they paying nowadays?

MR. KRALER. He could get it in a war plant. But this isn't a war plant. Mind you, I don't know if he really knows . . . or if he doesn't know.

MR. FRANK. Offer him half. Then we'll soon find out if it's blackmail or not.

DUSSEL. And if it is? We've got to pay it, haven't we? Anything he asks we've got to pay!

MR. FRANK. Let's decide that when the time comes.

MR. KRALER. This may be all imagination. You get to a point, these days, where you suspect everyone and everything. Again and again . . . on some simple look or word, I've found myself . . .

(The telephone rings in the office below.)

MRS. VAN DAAN *(hurrying to* MR. KRALER*).* There's the telephone! What does that mean, the telephone ringing on a holiday?

MR. KRALER. That's my wife. I told her I had to go over some papers in my office . . . to call me there when she got out of church. *(He starts out.)* I'll offer him half then. Good-by . . . we'll hope for the best! *(The group call their good-bys halfheartedly.* MR. FRANK *follows* MR. KRALER, *to bolt the door below. During the following scene,* MR. FRANK *comes back up and stands listening, disturbed.)*

DUSSEL *(to* MR. VAN DAAN*).* You can thank your son for this . . . smashing the light! I tell you, it's just a question of time now. *(He goes to the window at the back and stands looking out.)*

MARGOT. Sometimes I wish the end would come . . . whatever it is.

---

3. *Twenty guilders,* a little over $5.00 in American money. The guilder (gil′dər) is the monetary unit of the Netherlands.

MRS. FRANK (*shocked*). Margot!

(ANNE *goes to* MARGOT, *sitting beside her on the couch with her arms around her.*)

MARGOT. Then at least we'd know where we were.

MRS. FRANK. You should be ashamed of yourself! Talking that way! Think how lucky we are! Think of the thousands dying in the war, every day. Think of the people in concentration camps.

ANNE (*interrupting*). What's the good of that? What's the good of thinking of misery when you're already miserable? That's stupid!

MRS. FRANK. Anne!

(*As* ANNE *goes on raging at her mother,* MRS. FRANK *tries to break in, in an effort to quiet her.*)

ANNE. We're young. Margot and Peter and I! You grownups have had your chance! But look at us . . . If we begin thinking of all the horror in the world, we're lost! We're trying to hold onto some kind of ideals . . . when everything . . . ideals, hopes . . . everything, are being destroyed! It isn't our fault that the world is in such a mess! We weren't around when all this started! So don't try to take it out on us! (*She rushes off to her room, slamming the door after her. She picks up a brush from the chest and hurls it to the floor. Then she sits on the settee, trying to control her anger.*)

MR. VAN DAAN. She talks as if we started the war! Did we start the war?

(*He spots* ANNE'S *cake. As he starts to take it,* PETER *anticipates him.*)

PETER. She left her cake. (*He starts for* ANNE'S *room with the cake. There is silence in the main room.* MRS. VAN DAAN *goes up to her room, followed by* MR. VAN DAAN. DUSSEL *stays looking out the window.* MR. FRANK *brings* MRS. FRANK *her cake. She eats it slowly, without relish.* MR. FRANK *takes his cake to* MARGOT *and sits quietly on the sofa beside her.* PETER *stands in the doorway of* ANNE'S *darkened room, looking at her, then makes a little movement to let her know he is there.* ANNE *sits up, quickly, trying to hide the signs of her tears.* PETER *holds out the cake to her.*) You left this.

ANNE (*dully*). Thanks.

(PETER *starts to go out, then comes back.*)

PETER. I thought you were fine just now. You know just how to talk to them. You know just how to say it. I'm no good . . . I never can think . . . especially when I'm mad . . . That Dussel . . . when he said that about Mouschi . . . someone eating him . . . all I could think is . . . I wanted to hit him. I wanted to give him such a . . . a . . . that he'd . . . That's what I used to do when there was an argument at school . . . That's the way I . . . but here . . . And an old man like that . . . it wouldn't be so good.

ANNE. You're making a big mistake about me. I do it all wrong. I say too much. I go too far. I hurt people's feelings . . .

(DUSSEL *leaves the window, going to his room.*)

PETER. I think you're just fine . . . What I want to say . . . if it wasn't for you around here, I don't know. What I mean . . .

(PETER *is interrupted by* DUSSEL'S *turning on the light.* DUSSEL *stands in the doorway, startled to see* PETER. PETER *advances toward him forbiddingly.* DUSSEL *backs out of the room.* PETER *closes the door on him.*)

ANNE. Do you mean it, Peter? Do you really mean it?

PETER. I said it, didn't I?

ANNE. Thank you, Peter!

(In the main room MR. *and* MRS. FRANK *collect the dishes and take them to the sink, washing them.* MARGOT *lies down again on the couch.* DUSSEL, *lost, wanders into* PETER'S *room and takes up a book, starting to read.)*

PETER *(looking at the photographs on the wall).* You've got quite a collection.

ANNE. Wouldn't you like some in your room? I could give you some. Heaven knows you spend enough time in there . . . doing heaven knows what. . . .

PETER. It's easier. A fight starts, or an argument . . . I duck in there.

ANNE. You're lucky, having a room to go to. His lordship is always here . . . I hardly ever get a minute alone. When they start in on me, I can't duck away. I have to stand there and take it.

PETER. You gave some of it back just now.

ANNE. I get so mad. They've formed their opinions . . . about everything . . . but we . . . we're still trying to find out . . . We have problems here that no other people our age have ever had. And just as you think you've solved them, something comes along and bang! You have to start all over again.

PETER. At least you've got someone you can talk to.

ANNE. Not really. Mother . . . I never discuss anything serious with her. She doesn't understand. Father's all right. We can talk about everything . . . everything but one thing. Mother. He simply won't talk about her. I don't think you can be really intimate with anyone if he holds something back, do you?

PETER. I think your father's fine.

ANNE. Oh, he is, Peter! He is! He's the only one who's ever given me the feeling that I have any sense. But anyway, nothing

can take the place of school and play and friends of your own age . . . or near your age . . . can it?

PETER. I suppose you miss your friends and all.

ANNE. It isn't just . . . *(She breaks off, staring up at him for a second.)* Isn't it funny, you and I? Here we've been seeing each other every minute for almost a year and a half, and this is the first time we've ever really talked. It helps a lot to have someone to talk to, don't you think? It helps you to let off steam.

PETER *(going to the door).* Well, any time you want to let off steam, you can come into my room.

ANNE *(following him).* I can get up an awful lot of steam. You'll have to be careful how you say that.

PETER. It's all right with me.

ANNE. Do you really mean it?

PETER. I said it, didn't I?

(He goes out. ANNE *stands in her doorway looking after him. As* PETER *gets to his door he stands for a minute looking back at her. Then he goes into his room.* DUSSEL *rises as he comes in, and quickly passes him, going out. He starts across for his room.* ANNE *sees him coming, and pulls her door shut.* DUSSEL *turns back toward* PETER'S *room.* PETER *pulls his door shut.* DUSSEL *stands there, bewildered, forlorn.*

The scene slowly dims out. The curtain falls on the scene. ANNE'S VOICE *comes over in the darkness . . . faintly at first, and then with growing strength.)*

ANNE'S VOICE. We've had bad news. The people from whom Miep got our ration books have been arrested. So we have had to cut down on our food. Our stomachs are so empty that they rumble and make strange noises, all in different keys.

Mr. Van Daan's is deep and low, like a bass fiddle. Mine is high, whistling like a flute. As we all sit around waiting for supper, it's like an orchestra tuning up. It only needs Toscanini to raise his baton and we'd be off in the Ride of the Valkyries.[4] Monday, the sixth of March, nineteen forty-four. Mr. Kraler is in the hospital. It seems he has ulcers. Pim says we are his ulcers. Miep has to run the business and us too. The Americans have landed on the southern tip of Italy. Father looks for a quick finish to the war. Mr. Dussel is waiting every day for the warehouse man to demand more money. Have I been skipping too much from one subject to another? I can't help it. I feel that spring is coming. I feel it in my whole body and soul. I feel utterly confused. I am longing . . . so longing . . . for everything . . . for friends . . . for someone to talk to . . . someone who understands . . . someone young, who feels as I do . . .

(As these last lines are being said, the curtain rises on the scene. The lights dim on. ANNE'S VOICE *fades out.)*

---

4. ***Toscanini . . . Ride of the Valkyries.*** Toscanini (tos′kə-nē′nē), 1867–1957, was a world-famous Italian musical conductor. "Ride of the Valkyries" (val kir′ēz) is a vigorous musical composition by nineteenth-century German composer Richard Wagner (väg′nər).

Discussion

1. (a) Approximately how much time has passed between the end of Act One and the beginning of Act Two? **(b)** For how long have the Franks been in hiding? **(c)** How is the passing of time shown?

2. Describe incidents in this scene that make evident each of the following: **(a)** Mr. Dussel's disagreeable personality; **(b)** Miep's and Mr. Kraler's generosity; **(c)** Mr. Van Daan's greed; **(d)** Mrs. Van Daan's vanity; **(e)** Mr. Frank's levelheadedness.

3. (a) What new problem does Mr. Kraler present to the inhabitants of the annex? **(b)** What solution is decided upon?

4. (a) Explain the situation that causes Anne to flare up at her mother. **(b)** How does Anne's anger lead to greater understanding between herself and Peter?

5. (a) What does Anne mean when she says to Peter that in all the time in the annex "this is the first time we've ever really talked"? **(b)** In their private conversation what are some of the things they reveal about themselves?

6. (a) About how long after the rest of the scene is Anne's diary entry written? **(b)** What do you learn from this entry?

Scene Two

It is evening, after supper. From the outside we hear the sound of children playing. The "grownups," with the exception of MR. VAN DAAN, *are all in the main room.* MRS. FRANK *is doing some mending,* MRS. VAN DAAN *is reading a fashion magazine.* MR. FRANK *is going over business accounts.* DUSSEL, *in his dentist's jacket, is pacing up and down, impatient to get into his bedroom.* MR. VAN DAAN *is upstairs working on a piece of embroidery in an embroidery frame.*

In his room PETER *is sitting before the*

mirror, smoothing his hair. As the scene goes on, he puts on his tie, brushes his coat and puts it on preparing himself meticulously for a visit from ANNE. *On his wall are now hung some of* ANNE'S *motion picture stars.*

In her room ANNE *too is getting dressed. She stands before the mirror in her slip, trying various ways of dressing her hair.* MARGOT *is seated on the sofa, hemming a skirt for* ANNE *to wear.*

In the main room DUSSEL *can stand it no longer. He comes over, rapping sharply on the door of his and* ANNE'S *bedroom.*

ANNE *(calling to him).* No, no, Mr. Dussel! I am not dressed yet. (DUSSEL *walks away, furious, sitting down and burying his head in his hands.* ANNE *turns to* MARGOT.*)* How is that? How does that look?

MARGOT *(glancing at her briefly).* Fine.

ANNE. You didn't even look.

MARGOT. Of course I did. It's fine.

ANNE. Margot, tell me, am I terribly ugly?

MARGOT. Oh, stop fishing.

ANNE. No. No. Tell me.

MARGOT. Of course you're not. You've got nice eyes . . . and a lot of animation, and . . .

ANNE. A little vague, aren't you?

(She reaches over and takes a brassière out of MARGOT'S *sewing basket. She holds it up to herself, studying the effect in the mirror. Outside,* MRS. FRANK, *feeling sorry for* DUSSEL, *comes over, knocking at the girls' door.)*

MRS. FRANK *(outside).* May I come in?

MARGOT. Come in, Mother.

MRS. FRANK *(shutting the door behind her).* Mr. Dussel's impatient to get in here.

ANNE *(still with the brassière).* Heavens, he takes the room for himself the entire day.

MRS. FRANK *(gently).* Anne, dear, you're not going in again tonight to see Peter?

ANNE *(dignified).* That is my intention.

MRS. FRANK. But you've already spent a great deal of time in there today.

ANNE. I was in there exactly twice. Once to get the dictionary, and then three-quarters of an hour before supper.

MRS. FRANK. Aren't you afraid you're disturbing him?

ANNE. Mother, I have some intuition.

MRS. FRANK. Then may I ask you this much, Anne. Please don't shut the door when you go in.

ANNE. You sound like Mrs. Van Daan! *(She throws the brassière back in* MARGOT'S *sewing basket and picks up her blouse, putting it on.)*

MRS. FRANK. No. No. I don't mean to suggest anything wrong. I only wish that you wouldn't expose yourself to criticism . . . that you wouldn't give Mrs. Van Daan the opportunity to be unpleasant.

ANNE. Mrs. Van Daan doesn't need an opportunity to be unpleasant!

MRS. FRANK. Everyone's on edge, worried about Mr. Kraler. This is one more thing . . .

ANNE. I'm sorry, Mother. I'm going to Peter's room. I'm not going to let Petronella Van Daan spoil our friendship.

(MRS. FRANK hesitates for a second, then goes out, closing the door after her. She gets a pack of playing cards and sits at the center table, playing solitaire. In ANNE'S *room* MARGOT *hands the finished skirt to* ANNE. *As* ANNE *is putting it on,* MARGOT *takes off her high-heeled shoes and stuffs paper in the toes so that* ANNE *can wear them.)*

MARGOT *(to* ANNE*).* Why don't you two talk in the main room? It'd save a lot of trouble. It's hard on Mother, having to listen to those remarks from Mrs. Van Daan and not say a word.

ANNE. Why doesn't she say a word? I think it's ridiculous to take it and take it.

MARGOT. You don't understand Mother at all, do you? She can't talk back. She's not like you. It's just not in her nature to fight back.

ANNE. Anyway . . . the only one I worry about is you. I feel awfully guilty about you. (*She sits on the stool near* MARGOT, *putting on* MARGOT'S *high-heeled shoes.*)

MARGOT. What about?

ANNE. I mean, every time I go into Peter's room, I have a feeling I may be hurting you. (MARGOT *shakes her head.*) I know if it were me, I'd be wild. I'd be desperately jealous, if it were me.

MARGOT. Well, I'm not.

ANNE. You don't feel badly? Really? Truly? You're not jealous?

MARGOT. Of course I'm jealous . . . jealous that you've got something to get up in the morning for . . . But jealous of you and Peter? No.

(ANNE *goes back to the mirror.*)

ANNE. Maybe there's nothing to be jealous of. Maybe he doesn't really like me. Maybe I'm just taking the place of his cat . . . (*She picks up a pair of short, white gloves, putting them on.*) Wouldn't you like to come in with us?

MARGOT. I have a book.

(*The sound of the children playing outside fades out. In the main room* DUSSEL *can stand it no longer. He jumps up, going to the bedroom door and knocking sharply.*)

DUSSEL. Will you please let me in my room!

ANNE. Just a minute, dear, dear Mr. Dussel. (*She picks up her Mother's pink stole and adjusts it elegantly over her shoulder, then gives a last look in the mirror.*) Well, here I go . . . to run the gauntlet. (*She starts out, followed by* MARGOT.)

DUSSEL (*as she appears—sarcastic*). Thank you so much.

(DUSSEL *goes into his room.* ANNE *goes toward* PETER'S *room, passing* MRS. VAN DAAN *and her parents at the center table.*)

MRS. VAN DAAN. My God, look at her! (ANNE *pays no attention. She knocks at* PETER'S *door.*) I don't know what good it is to have a son. I never see him. He wouldn't care if I killed myself. (PETER *opens the door and stands aside for* ANNE *to come in.*) Just a minute, Anne. (*She goes to them at the door.*) I'd like to say a few words to my son. Do you mind? (PETER *and* ANNE *stand waiting.*) Peter, I don't want you staying up till all hours tonight. You've got to have your sleep. You're a growing boy. You hear?

MRS. FRANK. Anne won't stay late. She's going to bed promptly at nine. Aren't you, Anne?

ANNE. Yes, Mother . . . (*To* MRS. VAN DAAN) May we go now?

MRS. VAN DAAN. Are you asking me? I didn't know I had anything to say about it.

MRS. FRANK. Listen for the chimes, Anne dear.

(*The two young people go off into* PETER'S *room, shutting the door after them.*)

MRS. VAN DAAN (*to* MRS. FRANK). In my day it was the boys who called on the girls. Not the girls on the boys.

MRS. FRANK. You know how young people like to feel that they have secrets. Peter's room is the only place where they can talk.

MRS. VAN DAAN. Talk! That's not what they called it when I was young.

(MRS. VAN DAAN *goes off to the bathroom.* MARGOT *settles down to read her book.* MR. FRANK *puts his papers away*

and brings a chess game to the center table. He and MRS. FRANK *start to play. In* PETER'S *room,* ANNE *speaks to* PETER, *indignant, humiliated.)*

ANNE. Aren't they awful? Aren't they impossible? Treating us as if we were still in the nursery. *(She sits on the cot.* PETER *gets a bottle of pop and two glasses.)*

PETER. Don't let it bother you. It doesn't bother me.

ANNE. I suppose you can't really blame them . . . *they* think back to what they were like at our age. They don't realize how much more advanced we are . . . When you think what wonderful discussions we've had! . . . Oh, I forgot. I was going to bring you some more pictures.

PETER. Oh, these are fine, thanks.

ANNE. Don't you want some more? Miep just brought me some new ones.

PETER. Maybe later. *(He gives her a glass of pop and taking some for himself, sits down facing her.)*

ANNE *(looking up at one of the photographs).* I remember when I got that . . . I won it. I bet Jopie that I could eat five

ice-cream cones. We'd all been playing ping-pong . . . We used to have heavenly times . . . we'd finish up with ice cream at the Delphi, or the Oasis, where Jews were allowed . . . there'd always be a lot of boys . . . we'd laugh and joke . . . I'd like to go back to it for a few days or a week. But after that I know I'd be bored to death. I think more seriously about life now. I want to be a journalist . . . or something. I love to write. What do you want to do?

PETER. I thought I might go off some place . . . work on a farm or something . . . some job that doesn't take much brains.

ANNE. You shouldn't talk that way. You've got the most awful inferiority complex.

PETER. I know I'm not smart.

ANNE. That isn't true. You're much better than I am in dozens of things . . . arithmetic and algebra and . . . well, you're a million times better than I am in algebra. *(With sudden directness)* You like Margot, don't you? Right from the start you liked her, liked her much better than me.

PETER *(uncomfortably).* Oh, I don't know.

(In the main room MRS. VAN DAAN *comes from the bathroom and goes over to the sink, polishing a coffeepot.)*

ANNE. It's all right. Everyone feels that way. Margot's so good. She's sweet and bright and beautiful and I'm not.

PETER. I wouldn't say that.

ANNE. Oh, no, I'm not. I know that. I know quite well that I'm not a beauty. I never have been and never shall be.

PETER. I don't agree at all. I think you're pretty.

ANNE. That's not true!

PETER. And another thing. You've changed . . . from at first, I mean.

ANNE. I have?

PETER. I used to think you were awful noisy.

ANNE. And what do you think now, Peter? How have I changed?

PETER. Well . . . er . . . you're . . . quieter. *(In his room* DUSSEL *takes his pajamas and toilet articles and goes into the bathroom to change.)*

ANNE. I'm glad you don't just hate me.

PETER. I never said that.

ANNE. I bet when you get out of here you'll never think of me again.

PETER. That's crazy.

ANNE. When you get back with all of your friends, you're going to say . . . now what did I ever see in that Mrs. Quack Quack.

PETER. I haven't got any friends.

ANNE. Oh, Peter, of course you have. Everyone has friends.

PETER. Not me. I don't want any. I get along all right without them.

ANNE. Does that mean you can get along without me? I think of myself as your friend.

PETER. No. If they were all like you, it'd be different.

(He takes the glasses and the bottle and puts them away. There is a second's silence and then ANNE *speaks, hesitantly, shyly.)*

ANNE. Peter, did you ever kiss a girl?

PETER. Yes. Once.

ANNE *(to cover her feelings).* That picture's crooked. *(PETER goes over, straightening the photograph.)* Was she pretty?

PETER. Huh?

ANNE. The girl that you kissed.

PETER. I don't know. I was blindfolded. *(He comes back and sits down again.)* It was a party. One of those kissing games.

ANNE *(relieved).* Oh, I don't suppose that really counts, does it?

PETER. It didn't with me.

ANNE. I've been kissed twice. Once a man I'd never seen before kissed me on the cheek when he picked me up off the ice and I was crying. And the other was Mr. Koophuis,[1] a friend of Father's who kissed my hand. You wouldn't say those counted, would you?

PETER. I wouldn't say so.

ANNE. I know almost for certain that Margot would never kiss anyone unless she was engaged to them. And I'm sure too that Mother never touched a man before Pim. But I don't know . . . things are so different now. . . . What do you think? Do you think a girl shouldn't kiss anyone except if she's engaged or something? It's so hard to try to think what to do, when here we are with the whole world falling around our ears and you think . . . well . . . you don't know what's going to happen tomorrow and . . . What do you think?

PETER. I suppose it'd depend on the girl. Some girls, anything they do's wrong. But others . . . well . . . it wouldn't neces-

---

1. **Mr. Koophuis** (kōp′hous).

sarily be wrong with them. *(The carillon starts to strike nine o'clock.)* I've always thought that when two people . . .

ANNE. Nine o'clock. I have to go.

PETER. That's right.

ANNE *(without moving).* Good night.

(There is a second's pause, then PETER *gets up and moves toward the door.)*

PETER. You won't let them stop you coming?

ANNE. No. *(She rises and starts for the door.)* Sometime I might bring my diary. There are so many things in it that I want to talk over with you. There's a lot about you.

PETER. What kind of thing?

ANNE. I wouldn't want you to see some of it. I thought you were a nothing, just the way you thought about me.

PETER. Did you change your mind, the way I changed my mind about you?

ANNE. Well . . . You'll see . . .

(For a second ANNE *stands looking up at* PETER, *longing for him to kiss her. As he makes no move she turns away. Then suddenly* PETER *grabs her awkwardly in his arms, kissing her on the cheek.* ANNE *walks out dazed. She stands for a minute, her back to the people in the main room. As she regains her poise she goes to her mother and father and* MARGOT *silently kissing them. They murmur their good nights to her. As she is about to open her bedroom door, she catches sight of* MRS. VAN DAAN. *She goes quickly to her, taking her face in her hands and kissing her first on one cheek and then on the other. Then she hurries off into her room.* MRS. VAN DAAN *looks after her, and then looks over at* PETER'S *room. Her suspicions are confirmed.)*

MRS. VAN DAAN. *(She knows.)* Ah hah!

(The lights dim out. The curtain falls on the scene. In the darkness ANNE'S VOICE *comes faintly at first and then with growing strength.)*

ANNE'S VOICE. By this time we all know each other so well that if anyone starts to tell a story, the rest can finish it for him. We're having to cut down still further on our meals. What makes it worse, the rats have been at work again. They've carried off some of our precious food. Even Mr. Dussel wishes now that Mouschi was here. Thursday, the twentieth of April, nineteen forty-four. Invasion fever[2] is mounting every day. Miep tells us that people outside talk of nothing else. For myself, life has become much more pleasant. I often go to Peter's room after supper. Oh, don't think I'm in love, because I'm not. But it does make life more bearable to have someone with whom you can exchange views. No more tonight. P.S. . . . I must be honest. I must confess that I actually live for the next meeting. Is there anything lovelier than to sit under the skylight and feel the sun on your cheeks and have a darling boy in your arms? I admit now that I'm glad the Van Daans had a son and not a daughter. I've outgrown another dress. That's the third. I'm having to wear Margot's clothes after all. I'm working hard on my French and am now reading *La Belle Nivernaise.*[3]

(As she is saying the last lines, the curtain rises on the scene. The lights dim on, as ANNE'S VOICE *fades out.)*

---

2. *Invasion fever,* the expectation that the Allies would invade Europe to free it from German occupation. The invasion actually began on June 6, 1944, known as "D-Day."

3. *La Belle Nivernaise* (lä bel′ niv ər nez′), a tale by Alphonse Daudet, a nineteenth-century French novelist.

Discussion

1. **(a)** In what ways has Anne changed since the beginning of the previous scene? **(b)** What has contributed to this change? **(c)** Why is Mrs. Frank concerned about Anne's behavior?

2. **(a)** How do Anne and Margot differ? **(b)** In what ways does Margot show mature good sense when talking with Anne? **(c)** Does the relationship between the sisters seem natural? Explain.

3. **(a)** What feelings exist between the mother and each daughter? **(b)** How do you account for the closer relationship between Mrs. Frank and Margot?

4. **(a)** What are some of the things Peter and Anne are concerned about? **(b)** Discuss whether or not you think these concerns are typical for people their age.

5. **(a)** How and why does Anne dramatically alter her behavior to Mrs. Van Daan? **(b)** How does Mrs. Van Daan respond?

Vocabulary

Idioms

An *idiom* (id′ē əm) is a phrase or expression whose meaning cannot be understood from only the ordinary meanings of the words in it. For example, Anne tells Margot that she is going *to run the gauntlet.* Look up *gauntlet* in the Glossary. You will find the phrase *run the gauntlet* in dark type in the middle of the entry. Which of the two definitions that follow— *a* or *b*—fits the use of the word in the context of the play?

Locate each of the following italicized idioms in the Glossary by looking under the most important word. (You may have to try more than one word.) Look for the phrase in dark type in the middle of the entry or at the end. Then rewrite the sentence on your paper, substituting for the idiom a definition in your own words.

1. Anne refuses to let people *walk all over her,* the way they do Margot.

2. Mr. Dussel hopes Anne will *bear with him* because he has always lived alone.

3. Miep's sugar cake *goes right to their heads,* Mr. Frank claims.

4. Having someone to talk to, Anne tells Peter, helps her *let off steam.*

5. Mrs. Frank says that worry about Mr. Kraler has everyone *on edge.*

Scene Three

It is night, a few weeks later. Everyone is in bed. There is complete quiet. In the VAN DAANS' *room a match flares up for a moment and then is quickly put out.* MR. VAN DAAN, *in bare feet, dressed in underwear and trousers, is dimly seen coming stealthily down the stairs and into the main room, where* MR. *and* MRS. FRANK *and* MARGOT *are sleeping. He goes to the food safe and again lights a match. Then he cautiously opens the safe, taking out a half-loaf of bread. As he closes the safe, it creaks. He stands rigid.* MRS. FRANK *sits up in bed. She sees him.*

MRS. FRANK *(screaming).* Otto! Otto! *Komme schnell!*[1]

(The rest of the people wake, hurriedly getting up.)

MR. FRANK. *Was ist los? Was ist passiert?*[2]

---

1. *Komme schnell!* Hurry!
2. *Was ist los? Was ist passiert?* What's the matter? What happened?

(DUSSEL, *followed by* ANNE, *comes from his room.*)

MRS. FRANK (*as she rushes over to* MR. VAN DAAN). *Er stiehlt das Essen!*[3]

DUSSEL (*grabbing* MR. VAN DAAN). You! You! Give me that.

MRS. VAN DAAN (*coming down the stairs*). Putti . . . Putti . . . what is it?

DUSSEL (*his hands on* VAN DAAN'S *neck*). You dirty thief . . . stealing food . . . you good-for-nothing . . .

MR. FRANK. Mr. Dussel! For God's sake! Help me, Peter!

(PETER *comes over, trying, with* MR. FRANK, *to separate the two struggling men.*)

PETER. Let him go! Let go!

(DUSSEL *drops* MR. VAN DAAN, *pushing him away. He shows them the end of a loaf of bread that he has taken from* VAN DAAN.)

DUSSEL. You greedy, selfish . . . !

(MARGOT *turns on the lights.*)

MRS. VAN DAAN. Putti . . . what is it?

(*All of* MRS. FRANK'S *gentleness, her self-control, is gone. She is outraged, in a frenzy of indignation.*)

MRS. FRANK. The bread! He was stealing the bread!

DUSSEL. It was you, and all the time we thought it was the rats!

MR. FRANK. Mr. Van Daan, how could you!

MR. VAN DAAN. I'm hungry.

MRS. FRANK. We're all of us hungry! I see the children getting thinner and thinner. Your own son Peter . . . I've heard him moan in his sleep, he's so hungry. And you come in the night and steal food that should go to them . . . to the children!

MRS. VAN DAAN (*going to* MR. VAN DAAN *protectively*). He needs more food than the rest of us. He's used to more. He's a big man.

(MR. VAN DAAN *breaks away, going over and sitting on the couch.*)

MRS. FRANK (*turning on* MRS. VAN DAAN). And you . . . you're worse than he is! You're a mother, and yet you sacrifice your child to this man . . . this . . . this . . .

MR. FRANK. Edith! Edith!

(MARGOT *picks up the pink woolen stole, putting it over her mother's shoulders.*)

MRS. FRANK (*paying no attention, going on to* MRS. VAN DAAN). Don't think I haven't seen you! Always saving the choicest bits for him! I've watched you day after day and I've held my tongue. But not any longer! Not after this! Now I want him to go! I want him to get out of here!

MR. FRANK. Edith!

MR. VAN DAAN. Get out of here? } (*Together*)

MRS. VAN DAAN. What do you mean?

MRS. FRANK. Just that! Take your things and get out!

MR. FRANK (*to* MRS. FRANK). You're speaking in anger. You cannot mean what you are saying.

MRS. FRANK. I mean exactly that!

(MRS. VAN DAAN *takes a cover from the* FRANKS' *bed, pulling it about her.*)

MR. FRANK. For two long years we have lived here, side by side. We have respected each other's rights . . . we have managed to live in peace. Are we now going to throw it all away? I know this will never happen again, will it, Mr. Van Daan?

MR. VAN DAAN. No. No.

MRS. FRANK. He steals once! He'll steal again!

(MR. VAN DAAN, *holding his stomach, starts for the bathroom.* ANNE *puts her arms around him, helping him up the step.*)

MR. FRANK. Edith, please. Let us be calm.

---

3. *Er stiehlt das Essen!* He is stealing food.

We'll all go to our rooms . . . and afterwards we'll sit down quietly and talk this out . . . we'll find some way . . .

MRS. FRANK. No! No! No more talk! I want them to leave!

MRS. VAN DAAN. You'd put us out, on the streets?

MRS. FRANK. There are other hiding places.

MRS. VAN DAAN. A cellar . . . a closet. I know. And we have no money left even to pay for that.

MRS. FRANK. I'll give you money. Out of my own pocket I'll give it gladly.

(She gets her purse from a shelf and comes back with it.)

MRS. VAN DAAN. Mr. Frank, you told Putti you'd never forget what he'd done for you when you came to Amsterdam. You said you could never repay him, that you . . .

MRS. FRANK (counting out money). If my husband had any obligation to you, he's paid it, over and over.

MR. FRANK. Edith, I've never seen you like this before. I don't know you.

MRS. FRANK. I should have spoken out long ago.

DUSSEL. You can't be nice to some people.

MRS. VAN DAAN (turning on DUSSEL). There would have been plenty for all of us, if you hadn't come here!

MR. FRANK. We don't need the Nazis to destroy us. We're destroying ourselves.

(He sits down, with his head in his hands. MRS. FRANK goes to MRS. VAN DAAN.)

MRS. FRANK (giving MRS. VAN DAAN some money). Give this to Miep. She'll find you a place.

ANNE. Mother, you're not putting *Peter* out. Peter hasn't done anything.

MRS. FRANK. He'll stay, of course. When I say I must protect the children, I mean Peter too.

(PETER *rises from the steps where he has been sitting.*)

PETER. I'd have to go if Father goes.

(MR. VAN DAAN *comes from the bathroom.* MRS. VAN DAAN *hurries to him and takes him to the couch. Then she gets water from the sink to bathe his face.*)

MRS. FRANK (while this is going on). He's no father to you . . . that man! He doesn't know what it is to be a father!

PETER (starting for his room). I wouldn't feel right. I couldn't stay.

MRS. FRANK. Very well, then. I'm sorry.

ANNE (rushing over to PETER). No, Peter! No! (PETER *goes into his room, closing the door after him.* ANNE *turns back to her mother, crying.*) I don't care about the food. They can have mine! I don't want it! Only don't send them away. It'll be daylight soon. They'll be caught . . .

MARGOT (putting her arms comfortingly around ANNE). Please, Mother!

MRS. FRANK. They're not going now. They'll stay here until Miep finds them a place. (To MRS. VAN DAAN) But one thing I insist on! He must never come down here again! He must never come to this room where the food is stored! We'll divide what we have . . . an equal share for each! (DUSSEL *hurries over to get a sack of potatoes from the food safe.* MRS. FRANK *goes on, to* MRS. VAN DAAN.) You can cook it here and take it up to him.

(DUSSEL *brings the sack of potatoes back to the center table.*)

MARGOT. Oh, no. No. We haven't sunk so far that we're going to fight over a handful of rotten potatoes.

DUSSEL (dividing the potatoes into piles). Mrs. Frank, Mr. Frank, Margot, Anne, Peter, Mrs. Van Daan, Mr. Van Daan, myself . . . Mrs. Frank . . .

(The buzzer sounds in MIEP'S *signal.)*

MR. FRANK. It's Miep! *(He hurries over, getting his overcoat and putting it on.)*

MARGOT. At this hour?

MRS. FRANK. It is trouble.

MR. FRANK *(as he starts down to unbolt the door).* I beg you, don't let her see a thing like this!

DUSSEL *(counting without stopping).* . . . Anne, Peter, Mrs. Van Daan, Mr. Van Daan, myself . . .

MARGOT *(to* DUSSEL*).* Stop it! Stop it!

DUSSEL. . . . Mr. Frank, Margot, Anne, Peter, Mrs. Van Daan, Mr. Van Daan, myself, Mrs. Frank . . .

MRS. VAN DAAN. You're keeping the big ones for yourself! All the big ones . . . Look at the size of that! . . . And that!

(DUSSEL continues on with his dividing. PETER, with his shirt and trousers on, comes from his room.)

MARGOT. Stop it! Stop it!

(We hear MIEP'S *excited voice speaking to* MR. FRANK *below.)*

MIEP. Mr. Frank . . . the most wonderful news! . . . The invasion has begun.

MR. FRANK. Go on, tell them! Tell them!

(MIEP comes running up the steps, ahead of MR. FRANK. *She has a man's raincoat on over her nightclothes and a bunch of orange-colored flowers in her hand.)*

MIEP. Did you hear that, everybody? Did you hear what I said? The invasion has begun! The invasion!

(They all stare at MIEP, *unable to grasp what she is telling them.* PETER *is the first to recover his wits.)*

PETER. Where?

MRS. VAN DAAN. When? When, Miep?

MIEP. It began early this morning . . .

(As she talks on, the realization of what she has said begins to dawn on them. Everyone goes crazy. A wild demonstration

takes place. MRS. FRANK *hugs* MR. VAN DAAN.*)*

MRS. FRANK. Oh, Mr. Van Daan, did you hear that?

(DUSSEL embraces MRS. VAN DAAN. PETER *grabs a frying pan and parades around the room, beating on it, singing the Dutch National Anthem.* ANNE *and* MARGOT *follow him, singing, weaving in and out among the excited grownups.* MARGOT *breaks away to take the flowers from* MIEP *and distribute them to everyone. While this pandemonium is going on* MRS. FRANK *tries to make herself heard above the excitement.)*

MRS. FRANK *(to* MIEP*).* How do you know?

MIEP. The radio . . . The B.B.C.![4] They said they landed on the coast of Normandy!

PETER. The British?

MIEP. British, Americans, French, Dutch, Poles, Norwegians . . . all of them! More than four thousand ships! Churchill spoke, and General Eisenhower![5] D-Day they call it!

MR. FRANK. Thank God, it's come!

MRS. VAN DAAN. At last!

MIEP *(starting out).* I'm going to tell Mr. Kraler. This'll be better than any blood transfusion.

MR. FRANK *(stopping her).* What part of Normandy did they land, did they say?

MIEP. Normandy . . . that's all I know now . . . I'll be up the minute I hear some more! *(She goes hurriedly out.)*

MR. FRANK *(to* MRS. FRANK*).* What did I tell you? What did I tell you?

(MRS. FRANK indicates that he has forgotten to bolt the door after MIEP. *He hurries down the steps.* MR. VAN DAAN, *sitting on*

---

4. **B.B.C.**, the British Broadcasting Corporation.
5. **Churchill . . . Eisenhower.** Churchill was Prime Minister of England. Eisenhower was supreme commander of the Allied forces. He later became President of the U.S.

the couch, suddenly breaks into a convulsive sob. Everybody looks at him, bewildered.)

MRS. VAN DAAN *(hurrying to him)*. Putti! Putti! What is it? What happened?

MR. VAN DAAN. Please. I'm so ashamed.

(MR. FRANK comes back up the steps.)

DUSSEL. Oh, for God's sake!

MRS. VAN DAAN. Don't, Putti.

MARGOT. It doesn't matter now!

MR. FRANK *(going to MR. VAN DAAN)*. Didn't you hear what Miep said? The invasion has come! We're going to be liberated! This is a time to celebrate! *(He embraces MRS. FRANK and then hurries to the cupboard and gets the cognac and a glass.)*

MR. VAN DAAN. To steal bread from children!

MRS. FRANK. We've all done things that we're ashamed of.

ANNE. Look at me, the way I've treated Mother . . . so mean and horrid to her.

MRS. FRANK. No, Anneke, no.

(ANNE runs to her mother, putting her arms around her.)

ANNE. Oh, Mother, I was. I was awful.

MR. VAN DAAN. Not like me. No one is as bad as me!

DUSSEL *(to MR. VAN DAAN)*. Stop it now! Let's be happy!

MR. FRANK *(giving MR. VAN DAAN a glass of cognac)*. Here! Here! *Schnapps! Locheim!*[6]

(VAN DAAN takes the cognac. They all watch him. He gives them a feeble smile. ANNE puts up her fingers in a V-for-Victory sign. As VAN DAAN gives an answering V-sign, they are startled to hear a loud sob from behind them. It is MRS. FRANK, stricken with remorse. She is sitting on the other side of the room.)

MRS. FRANK *(through her sobs)*. When I think of the terrible things I said . . .

(MR. FRANK, ANNE, and MARGOT hurry to her, trying to comfort her. MR. VAN DAAN brings her his glass of cognac.)

MR. VAN DAAN. No! No! You were right!

MRS. FRANK. That I should speak that way to you! . . . Our friends! . . . Our guests! *(She starts to cry again.)*

DUSSEL. Stop it, you're spoiling the whole invasion!

(As they are comforting her, the lights dim out. The curtain falls.)

ANNE'S VOICE *(faintly at first and then with growing strength)*. We're all in much better spirits these days. There's still excellent news of the invasion. The best part about it is that I have a feeling that friends are coming. Who knows? Maybe I'll be back in school by fall. Ha, ha! The joke is on us! The warehouse man doesn't know a thing and we are paying him all that money! . . . Wednesday, the second of July, nineteen forty-four. The invasion seems temporarily to be bogged down. Mr. Kraler has to have an operation, which looks bad. The Gestapo have found the radio that was stolen. Mr. Drussel says they'll trace it back and back to the thief, and then, it's just a matter of time till they get to us. Everyone is low. Even poor Pim can't raise their spirits. I have often been downcast myself . . . but never in despair. I can shake off everything if I write. But . . . and that is the great question . . . will I ever be able to write well? I want to so much. I want to go on living even after my death. Another birthday has gone by, so now I am fifteen. Already I know what I want. I have a goal, an opinion.

(As this is being said—the curtain rises on the scene, the lights dim on, and ANNE'S VOICE fades out.)

---

6. *Schnapps!* (shnäps) *Locheim!* (lə Hī′əm). Mr. Frank is proposing a toast to life.

Discussion

1. (a) Why does Mrs. Frank become enraged for the first time? (b) Why do you think she reacts in a manner so unusual for her? (c) How has this episode been foreshadowed?

2. (a) What reason does Mrs. Van Daan give for her husband's behavior? (b) Is this an adequate defense for what he has done? Explain your answer.

3. (a) How does Peter display loyalty to his father? (b) Consider Peter's previous attitude toward his father. Why do you think he shows such loyalty now?

4. During this scene Mr. Frank says, "We don't need the Nazis to destroy us. We're destroying ourselves." (a) Point out the attitudes and actions of various characters that might lead Mr. Frank to make such a remark. (b) Do you think Mr. Frank's observation is accurate? Why or why not?

5. (a) What news does Miep bring? (b) How does this news lead to a general reconciliation? (c) If Miep hadn't come with her news, what do you think might have happened?

6. (a) What is Anne's mood in her closing diary entry? (b) What might this entry foreshadow?

Scene Four

It is an afternoon a few weeks later . . . Everyone but MARGOT *is in the main room. There is a sense of great tension.*

Both MRS. FRANK *and* MR. VAN DAAN *are nervously pacing back and forth,* DUSSEL *is standing at the window, looking down fixedly at the street below.* PETER *is at the center table, trying to do his lessons.* ANNE *sits opposite him, writing in her diary.* MRS. VAN DAAN *is seated on the couch, her eyes on* MR. FRANK *as he sits reading.*

The sound of a telephone ringing comes from the office below. They all are rigid, listening tensely. MR. DUSSEL *rushes down to* MR. FRANK.

DUSSEL. There it goes again, the telephone! Mr. Frank, do you hear?

MR. FRANK (*quietly*). Yes. I hear.

DUSSEL (*pleading, insistent*). But this is the third time, Mr. Frank! The third time in quick succession! It's a signal! I tell you it's Miep, trying to get us! For some reason she can't come to us and she's trying to warn us of something!

MR. FRANK. Please. Please.

MR. VAN DAAN (*to* DUSSEL). You're wasting your breath.

DUSSEL. Something has happened, Mr. Frank. For three days now Miep hasn't been to see us! And today not a man has come to work. There hasn't been a sound in the building!

MRS. FRANK. Perhaps it's Sunday. We may have lost track of the days.

MR. VAN DAAN (*to* ANNE). You with the diary there. What day is it?

DUSSEL (*going to* MRS. FRANK). I don't lose track of the days! I know exactly what day it is! It's Friday, the fourth of August. Friday, and not a man at work. (*He rushes back to* MR. FRANK, *pleading with him, almost in tears.*) I tell you Mr. Kraler's dead. That's the only explanation. He's dead and they've closed down the building, and Miep's trying to tell us!

MR. FRANK. She'd never telephone us.

DUSSEL *(frantic)*. Mr. Frank, answer that! I beg you, answer it!

MR. FRANK. No.

MR. VAN DAAN. Just pick it up and listen. You don't have to speak. Just listen and see if it's Miep.

DUSSEL *(speaking at the same time)*. For God's sake . . . I ask you.

MR. FRANK. No. I've told you, no. I'll do nothing that might let anyone know we're in the building.

PETER. Mr. Frank's right.

MR. VAN DAAN. There's no need to tell us what side you're on.

MR. FRANK. If we wait patiently, quietly, I believe that help will come.

(There is silence for a minute as they all listen to the telephone ringing.)

DUSSEL. I'm going down. *(He rushes down the steps.* MR. FRANK *tries ineffectually to hold him.* DUSSEL *runs to the lower door, unbolting it. The telephone stops ringing.* DUSSEL *bolts the door and comes slowly back up the steps.)* Too late. *(MR. FRANK goes to* MARGOT *in* ANNE'S *bedroom.)*

MR. VAN DAAN. So we just wait here until we die.

MRS. VAN DAAN *(hysterically)*. I can't stand it! I'll kill myself! I'll kill myself!

MR. VAN DAAN. For God's sake, stop it!

(In the distance, a German military band is heard playing a Viennese waltz.)

MRS. VAN DAAN. I think you'd be glad if I did! I think you want me to die!

MR. VAN DAAN. Whose fault is it we're here? *(MRS. VAN DAAN starts for her room. He follows, talking at her.)* We could've been safe somewhere . . . in America or Switzerland. But no! No! You wouldn't leave when I wanted to. You couldn't leave your things. You couldn't leave your precious furniture.

MRS. VAN DAAN. Don't touch me!

(She hurries up the stairs, followed by MR. VAN DAAN. PETER, *unable to bear it, goes to his room.* ANNE *looks after him, deeply concerned.* DUSSEL *returns to his post at the window.* MR. FRANK *comes back into the main room and takes a book, trying to read.* MRS. FRANK *sits near the sink, starting to peel some potatoes.* ANNE *quietly goes to* PETER'S *room, closing the door after her.* PETER *is lying face down on the cot.* ANNE *leans over him, holding him in her arms, trying to bring him out of his despair.)*

ANNE. Look, Peter, the sky. *(She looks up through the skylight.)* What a lovely, lovely day! Aren't the clouds beautiful? You know what I do when it seems as if I couldn't stand being cooped up for one more minute? I *think* myself out. I think myself on a walk in the park where I used to go with Pim. Where the jonquils and the crocus and violets grow down the slopes. You know the most wonderful part about *thinking* yourself out? You can have it any way you like. You can have roses and violets and chrysanthemums all blooming at the same time . . . It's funny . . . I used to take it all for granted . . . and now I've gone crazy about everything to do with nature. Haven't you?

PETER. I've just gone crazy. I think if something doesn't happen soon . . . if we don't get out of here . . . I can't stand much more of it!

ANNE *(softly)*. I wish you had a religion, Peter.

PETER. No thanks! Not me!

ANNE. Oh, I don't mean you have to be Orthodox[1] . . . or believe in heaven and

---

1. Orthodox, a follower of the branch of Judaism that keeps most closely to ancient ritual, customs, and traditions.

hell and purgatory and things . . . I just mean some religion . . . it doesn't matter what. Just to believe in something! When I think of all that's out there . . . the trees . . . and flowers . . . and sea gulls . . . when I think of the dearness of you, Peter, . . . and the goodness of the people we know . . . Mr. Kraler, Miep, Dirk, the vegetable man, all risking their lives for us every day . . . When I think of these good things, I'm not afraid any more . . . I find myself, and God, and I . . .

(PETER interrupts, getting up and walking away.)

PETER. That's fine! But when I begin to think, I get mad! Look at us, hiding out for two years. Not able to move! Caught here like . . . waiting for them to come and get us . . . and all for what?

ANNE. We're not the only people that've had to suffer. There've always been people that've had to . . . sometimes one race . . . sometimes another . . . and yet . . .

PETER. That doesn't make me feel any better!

ANNE *(going to him)*. I know it's terrible, trying to have any faith . . . when people are doing such horrible . . . But you know what I sometimes think? I think the world may be going through a phase, the way I was with Mother. It'll pass, maybe not for hundreds of years, but some day . . . I still believe, in spite of everything, that people are really good at heart.

PETER. I want to see something now . . . Not a thousand years from now!

(He goes over, sitting down again on the cot.)

ANNE. But, Peter, if you'd only look at it as part of a great pattern . . . that we're just a little minute in the life . . . *(She breaks off.)* Listen to us, going at each other like a couple of stupid grownups! Look at the sky now. Isn't it lovely? *(She holds out her hand to him. PETER takes it and rises, standing with her at the window looking out, his arms around her.)* Some day, when we're outside again, I'm going to . . .

(She breaks off as she hears the sound of a car, its brakes squealing as it comes to a sudden stop. The people in the other rooms also become aware of the sound. They listen tensely. Another car roars up to a screeching stop. ANNE and PETER come from PETER'S room. MR. and MRS. VAN DAAN creep down the stairs. DUSSEL comes out from his room. Everyone is listening, hardly breathing. A doorbell clangs again and again in the building below. MR. FRANK starts quietly down the steps to the door. DUSSEL and PETER follow him. The others stand rigid, waiting, terrified.

In a few seconds DUSSEL comes stumbling back up the steps. He shakes off PETER'S help and goes to his room. MR. FRANK bolts the door below, and comes slowly back up the steps. Their eyes are all on him as he stands there for a minute. They realize that what they feared has happened. MRS. VAN DAAN starts to whimper. MR. VAN DAAN puts her gently in a chair, and then hurries off up the stairs to their room to collect their things. PETER goes to comfort his mother. There is a sound of violent pounding on a door below.)

MR. FRANK *(quietly)*. For the past two years we have lived in fear. Now we can live in hope.

(The pounding below becomes more insistent. There are muffled sounds of voices, shouting commands.)

MEN'S VOICES. *Auf machen! Da drinnen! Auf machen! Schnell! Schnell! Schnell!*[2] *etc., etc.*

(The street door below is forced open. We hear the heavy tread of footsteps coming up. MR. FRANK *gets two school-bags from the shelves, and gives one to* ANNE *and the other to* MARGOT. *He goes to get a bag for* MRS. FRANK. *The sound of feet coming up grows louder.* PETER *comes to* ANNE, *kissing her good-by, then he goes to his room to collect his things. The buzzer of their door starts to ring.* MR. FRANK *brings* MRS. FRANK *a bag. They*

stand together, waiting. We hear the thud of gun butts on the door, trying to break it down.

ANNE *stands, holding her school satchel, looking over at her father and mother with a soft, reassuring smile. She is no longer a child, but a woman with courage to meet whatever lies ahead.*

The lights dim out. The curtain falls on the scene. We hear a mighty crash as the door is shattered. After a second ANNE'S VOICE *is heard.)*

---

2. **Auf machen . . . Schnell!** Open up in there! Hurry up!

ANNE'S VOICE. And so it seems our stay is over. They are waiting for us now. They've allowed us five minutes to get our things. We can each take a bag and whatever it will hold of clothing. Nothing else. So, dear Diary, that means I must leave you behind. Good-by for a while.

P.S. Please, please, Miep, or Mr. Kraler, or anyone else. If you should find this diary, will you please keep it safe for me, because some day I hope . . .
(*Her voice stops abruptly. There is silence. After a second the curtain rises.*)

Discussion

1. **(a)** Why does Mr. Dussel plead with Mr. Frank to answer the phone? **(b)** Why does Mr. Frank refuse to answer it? **(c)** Suppose you were in the theater audience watching this scene. What effect do you think the ringing telephone would have on you? Why?

2. How is tension between the Van Daans revealed?

3. **(a)** How does Anne attempt to cheer Peter up? **(b)** What does she say gives her faith? **(c)** How does Peter respond to Anne's ideas?

4. Mr. Frank says, "For the past two years we have lived in fear. Now we can live in hope." **(a)** What does he mean by this? **(b)** What does this statement show about him?

5. **(a)** How do the inhabitants behave upon the arrival of the police? **(b)** Do they behave as you would expect them to?

6. Anne's actual diary ends three days before her arrest. What, then, is the purpose of the diary entry in this scene?

Scene Five

It is again the afternoon in November, 1945. The rooms are as we saw them in the first scene. MR. KRALER *has joined* MIEP *and* MR. FRANK. *There are coffee cups on the table. We see a great change in* MR. FRANK. *He is calm now. His bitterness is gone. He slowly turns a few pages of the diary. They are blank.*

MR. FRANK. No more. (*He closes the diary and puts it down on the couch beside him.*)

MIEP. I'd gone to the country to find food. When I got back the block was surrounded by police . . .

MR. KRALER. We made it our business to learn how they knew. It was the thief . . . the thief who told them.

(MIEP *goes up to the gas burner, bringing back a pot of coffee.*)

MR. FRANK (*after a pause*). It seems strange to say this, that anyone could be happy in a concentration camp. But Anne was happy in the camp in Holland where they first took us. After two years of being shut up in these rooms, she could be out . . . out in the sunshine and the fresh air that she loved.

MIEP (*offering the coffee to* MR. FRANK). A little more?

MR. FRANK (*holding out his cup to her*). The news of the war was good. The British and Americans were sweeping through France. We felt sure that they would get to us in time. In September we were told that we were to be shipped to Poland

. . . The men to one camp. The women to another. I was sent to Auschwitz. They went to Belsen.[1] In January we were freed, the few of us who were left. The war wasn't yet over, so it took us a long time to get home. We'd be sent here and there behind the lines where we'd be safe. Each time our train would stop . . . at a siding, or a crossing . . . we'd all get out and go from group to group . . . Where were you? Were you at Belsen? At Buchenwald? At Mauthausen? Is it possible that you knew my wife? Did you ever see my husband? My son? My daughter? That's how I found out about my wife's death . . . of Margot, the Van Daans . . . Dussel. But Anne . . . I still hoped . . . . Yesterday I went to Rotterdam. I'd heard of a woman there. . . . She'd been in Belsen with Anne . . . I know now.

(*He picks up the diary again, and turns the pages back to find a certain passage. As he finds it we hear* ANNE'S VOICE.)

ANNE'S VOICE. In spite of everything, I still believe that people are really good at heart.

(MR. FRANK *slowly closes the diary.*)

MR. FRANK. She puts me to shame.

(*They are silent.*)

The CURTAIN *falls.*

---

1. **Auschwitz** (oush′vits) . . . **Belsen,** Nazi concentration camps in Poland and Germany, respectively. Buchenwald (bü′Hən vält′), mentioned later, was in Germany.

Discussion

1. (a) What is the time relationship between Act One, Scene One and Act Two, Scene Five? **(b)** What has Mr. Frank supposedly been doing for the entire time in between these scenes? **(c)** What device has been used throughout the play to build this illusion?

2. What information does Mr. Frank provide about what happened to the other characters?

3. Anne says, "In spite of everything, I still believe that people are really good at heart." **(a)** What is your reaction to this statement? **(b)** What are some possible consequences of believing the best or worst about people? Explain.

4. What is implied by Mr. Frank's reading Anne's diary entry, then saying, "She puts me to shame"?

Composition

People often reveal their true characters in the way they react to extreme situations, and in this play people are shown reacting to certain things in very different ways. Choose one of the following pairs of characters: (a) Anne and Peter; (b) Mr. Frank and Mr. Van Daan; (c) Mrs. Frank and Mrs. Van Daan. Consider how the two characters you have chosen react to being in hiding, to the shortages and inconveniencies they have to bear, to moments of fear, and to the behavior of other characters throughout the play.

Discuss the likenesses and differences of the reactions of the characters you have chosen in a composition of one to two pages. For each character, mention at least one specific example for each point listed above. Finally, you may wish to explain how their reactions to these things influence the way you feel about each character.

Comment: The Aftermath

After the inhabitants of the annex were captured on August 4, 1944, they were first sent to Westerbork, a concentration camp in Holland, about eighty miles from Amsterdam. On the morning of September 3, they began the long journey to Auschwitz, the infamous camp in Poland where 4,000,000 Jews died in the gas chambers. For three days they traveled, packed into freight cars. At the camp the men were separated from the women. Mrs. Frank died in the women's camp on January 6, 1945, after her daughters had been sent on to Bergen-Belsen.

It was October 30 when Anne and Margot began the journey to Bergen-Belsen in a cattle car. This camp, where 30,000 prisoners died, was located in Germany. In late 1944 it was in a disorganized state. The Allies were approaching. Food was scarce, and typhus was raging. Here Margot died at the end of February or the beginning of March, 1945, probably of a combination of typhus and starvation. Anne, already ill of typhus, died soon after. Three weeks later British troops liberated the camp.

Mrs. Van Daan also died during the typhus epidemic at Bergen-Belsen. Mr. Van Daan died in the gas chambers at Auschwitz. When the Nazis left Auschwitz in January, 1945, they took Peter Van Daan with them. Among other prisoners forced to march in freezing weather, he was not heard from again. Mr. Dussel was sent back to Germany and died in Neuengamme. Only Mr. Frank, who remained at Auschwitz until its liberation, survived.

A fuller record of the aftermath of the capture of Anne Frank can be found in Ernst Schnabel's book, *Anne Frank: A Portrait in Courage*.

Unit 8 Review: *The Diary of Anne Frank*

Content Review

1. In a true-to-life play such as this, it is especially important that the characters be seen clearly and in depth. **(a)** Which of Anne's feelings and concerns appear to you to be typical for a girl her age? **(b)** In what ways does she seem to be unusual? **(c)** If she had survived, what kind of person do you believe she would have become as an adult? Support your answer with evidence from the play.

2. Since Anne's diary supplied the source materials for the play, people and incidents are seen from her point of view. What different picture of the various inhabitants of the annex, including Anne, might be presented if the diary had been written by **(a)** Mr. Dussel; **(b)** Mrs. Frank; **(c)** Mrs. Van Daan?

3. Consider the following statement: *"The Diary of Anne Frank* is not dramatic enough. The last scene should show Anne's death in a concentration camp. Then we would really *feel* the tragedy." Explain why you agree or disagree with this viewpoint.

4. The Introduction to the unit speaks of the diary of Anne Frank as "a living tribute to the dignity, courage, and perseverance of the human spirit." Do these words seem an accurate description of the play you have just read? Defend your answer by referring to specific scenes and passages.

5. Do you believe that works such as Anne's diary and the play and motion picture based upon it can be influential in preventing future persecution of innocent people? Discuss.

Concept Review: Interpretation of New Material

The setting is a French country house; the time is a day during World War II. France, like the Netherlands and several other European countries, has been invaded and occupied by German troops. As the scene opens, Madame and her servant Si- mone have been watching out their window as two German soldiers escort a young stranger up to their door. Read this excerpt carefully and then answer the questions that follow it.

from The Pen of My Aunt · *Gordon Daviot*

STRANGER *(in a bright, confident, casual tone).* Ah, there you are, my dear Aunt. I am so glad. Come in, my friend, come in. My dear Aunt, this gentleman wants you to identify me.

MADAME. Identify you?

CORPORAL. We found this man wandering in the woods——

From "The Pen of My Aunt" by Gordon Daviot. Copyright 1954 by Gordon Daviot. Reprinted by permission of Watkins/Loomis Agency, Inc.

STRANGER. The Corporal found it inexplicable that anyone should wander in a wood.

CORPORAL. And he had no papers on him——

STRANGER. And I rightly pointed out that if I carry all the papers one is supposed to these days, I am no good to God or man. If I put them in a hip pocket, I can't bend forward; if I put them in a front pocket, I can't bend at all.

CORPORAL. He said that he was your nephew, Madame, but that did not seem to us very likely, so we brought him here.

(There is the slightest pause; just one moment of silence.)

MADAME. But of course this is my nephew.

CORPORAL. He is?

MADAME. Certainly.

CORPORAL. He lives here?

MADAME *(assenting)*. My nephew lives here.

CORPORAL. So! *(Recovering)* My apologies, Madame. But you will admit that appearances were against the young gentleman.

MADAME. Alas, Corporal, my nephew belongs to a generation who delight in flouting appearances. It is what they call "expressing their personality," I understand.

CORPORAL *(with contempt)*. No doubt, Madame.

MADAME. Convention is anathema to them,[1] and there is no sin like conformity. Even a collar is an offense against their liberty, and a discipline not to be borne by free necks.

CORPORAL. Ah yes, Madame. A little more discipline among your nephew's generation, and we might not be occupying your country today.

STRANGER. You think it was that collar of yours that conquered my country? You flatter yourself, Corporal. The only result of wearing a collar like that is varicose veins in the head.

MADAME *(repressive)*. Please! My dear boy. Let us not descend to personalities.

STRANGER. The matter is not personal, my good Aunt, but scientific. Wearing a collar like that retards the flow of fresh blood to the head, with the most disastrous consequences to the grey matter of the brain. The hypothetical grey matter. In fact, I have a theory——

CORPORAL. Monsieur, your theories do not interest me.

STRANGER. No? You do not find speculation interesting? . . .

CORPORAL. I have only one desire, Monsieur, and that is to see your papers.

STRANGER *(taken off-guard and filling in time)*. My papers?

MADAME. But is that necessary, Corporal? I have already told you that——

CORPORAL. I know that Madame is a very good collaborator[2] and in good standing——

MADAME. In that case——

CORPORAL. But when we begin an affair we like to finish it. I have asked to see Monsieur's papers, and the matter will not be finished until I have seen them.

MADAME. You acknowledge that I am in "good standing," Corporal?

CORPORAL. So I have heard, Madame.

MADAME. Then I must consider it a discourtesy on your part to demand my nephew's credentials.

CORPORAL. It is no reflection on Madame. It is a matter of routine, nothing more.

STRANGER *(murmuring)*. The great god Routine.

MADAME. To ask for his papers was routine; to insist on their production is discourtesy. I shall say so to your commanding officer.

---

1. *convention is anathema* (ə nath′ə mə) *to them.* Anything conventional, or customary, is intensely disliked by Madame's nephew and his generation.
2. *collaborator* (kə lab′ə rā′tər), person who gives help to or cooperates with an enemy, in this case the Nazis.

CORPORAL. Very good, Madame. In the meantime, I shall inspect your nephew's papers.

MADAME. And what if I——

STRANGER *(quietly)*. You may as well give it up, my dear. You could as easily turn a steamroller. They have only one idea at a time. If the Corporal's heart is set on seeing my papers, he shall see them. *(Moving towards the door)* I left them in the pocket of my coat.

SIMONE *(unexpectedly, from the background)*. Not in your *linen* coat?

STRANGER *(pausing)*. Yes. Why?

SIMONE *(with apparently growing anxiety)*. Your *cream* linen coat? The one you were wearing yesterday?

STRANGER. Certainly.

SIMONE. Merciful Heaven! I sent it to the laundry!

STRANGER. To the laundry!

SIMONE. Yes, monsieur; this morning; in the basket.

STRANGER *(in incredulous anger)*. You sent my coat, *with my papers in the pocket,* to the laundry!

SIMONE *(defensive and combatant)*. I didn't know Monsieur's papers were in the pocket.

STRANGER. You didn't know! You didn't know that a packet of documents weighing half a ton were in the pocket. An identity card, a *laisser passer*,[3] a food card, a drink card, an army discharge, a permission to wear civilian clothes, a permission to go farther than ten miles to the east, a permission to go more than ten miles to the west, a permission to——

SIMONE *(breaking in with spirit)*. How was I to know the coat was heavy! I picked it up with the rest of the bundle that was lying on the floor.

STRANGER *(snapping her head off)*. My coat was on the back of the chair.

SIMONE. It was on the floor.

STRANGER. On the back of the chair!

SIMONE. It was on the floor with your dirty shirt and your pajamas, and a towel and what not. I put my arms round the whole thing and then—woof! into the basket with them.

STRANGER. I tell you that coat was on the back of the chair. It was quite clean and was not going to the laundry for two weeks yet—if then. I hung it there myself, and——

MADAME. My dear boy, what does it matter? The damage is done now. In any case, they will find the papers when they unpack the basket, and return them tomorrow.

STRANGER. If someone doesn't steal them. There are a lot of people who would like to lay hold of a complete set of papers, believe me.

MADAME *(reassuring)*. Oh, no. Old Fleureau[4] is the soul of honesty. You have no need to worry about them. They will be back first thing tomorrow, you shall see; and then we shall have much pleasure in sending them to the Administration Office for the Corporal's inspection. Unless, of course, the Corporal insists on your personal appearance at the office.

CORPORAL *(cold and indignant)*. I have seen Monsieur. All that I want now is to see his papers.

STRANGER. You shall see them, Corporal, you shall see them. The whole half-ton of them. You may inspect them at your leisure. Provided, that is, that they come back from the laundry to which this idiot has consigned them.

MADAME *(again reassuring)*. They will come back, never fear. And you must not blame Simone. She is a good child and does her best.

---

3. *laisser passer* (les′ā pä sä′), a document that allows one to go past a military guard.
4. *Fleureau* (flėr ō′).

SIMONE *(with an air of belated virtue).* I am not one to pry into pockets.

MADAME. Simone, show the Corporal out, if you please.

SIMONE *(natural feeling overcoming her for a moment).* He knows the way out. *(Recovering)* Yes, Madame.

MADAME. And Corporal, try to take your duties a little less literally in future. My countrymen appreciate the spirit rather than the letter.[5]

---

5. *the spirit rather than the letter,* the spirit of the law rather than the letter of the law. Madame is advising the Corporal to interpret the law more flexibly.

CORPORAL. I have my instructions, Madame, and I obey them. Good day, Madame. Monsieur.

(He goes, followed by SIMONE—*door closes. There is a moment of silence.)*

STRANGER. For a good collaborator, that was a remarkably quick adoption.

MADAME. Sit down, young man. I will give you something to drink. I expect your knees are none too well.

STRANGER. My knees, Madame, are pure gelatine. As for my stomach, it seems to have disappeared.

MADAME *(offering him the drink she has poured out).* This will recall it, I hope.

STRANGER. You are not drinking, Madame.

MADAME. Thank you, no.

STRANGER. Not with strangers. It is certainly no time to drink with strangers. Nevertheless, I drink the health of a collaborator. *(He drinks.)* Tell me, Madame, what will happen tomorrow when they find that you have no nephew?

MADAME *(surprised).* But of course I have a nephew. I tell lies, my friend; but not *silly* lies. My charming nephew has gone to Bonneval[6] for the day. He finds country life dull.

STRANGER. Dull? This—this heaven?

MADAME *(dryly).* He likes to talk and here there is no audience. At Headquarters in Bonneval he finds the audience sympathetic.

STRANGER *(understanding the implication).* Ah.

MADAME. He believes in the Brotherhood of Man—if you can credit it.

STRANGER. After the last six months?

MADAME. His mother was American, so he has half the Balkans in his blood. To say nothing of Italy, Russia, and the Levant.[7]

STRANGER *(half-amused).* I see.

MADAME. A silly and worthless creature, but useful.

STRANGER. Useful?

MADAME. I—borrow his cloak.

STRANGER. I see.

MADAME. Tonight I shall borrow his identity papers, and tomorrow they will go to the office in St. Estephe.

STRANGER. But—he will have to know.

MADAME *(placidly).* Oh, yes, he will know, of course.

STRANGER. And how will you persuade such an enthusiastic collaborator to deceive his friends?

MADAME. Oh, that is easy. He is my heir.

---

6. *Bonneval* (bun väl′).
7. *His mother . . . the Levant.* Madame is referring to the fact that many Americans have ancestors of several different nationalities.

---

1. Where and when is this play set?

2. The Germans have brought the Stranger to Madame's house because **(a)** it is nearest to where they found him; **(b)** they have used her house for questioning before; **(c)** the Stranger has told them he lives there; **(d)** they found her address in his pocket.

3. What was the Stranger doing when the soldiers first spotted him?

4. By identifying the Stranger as her relative, Madame indicates to him that she will **(a)** protect him from the soldiers; **(b)** lend him some clothes; **(c)** take him on as a servant; **(d)** betray him.

5. When the Corporal asks to see the Stranger's identity papers, Madame responds by acting **(a)** kind and helpful; **(b)** confused and slow witted; **(c)** frightened and nervous; **(d)** haughty and insulted.

6. The Stranger talks so much about collars because **(a)** the Corporal has criticized his clothes; **(b)** he is trying to gain time;

(c) he has a theory about collars; (d) he dislikes the Corporal's uniform.

7. You can infer that the story about the coat being sent to the laundry is (a) true, as the Stranger told the soldiers; (b) a carefully planned lie; (c) a lie made up on the spot; (d) true, but the Stranger didn't know it.

8. When the Corporal calls Madame a "good collaborator" (519b, 8), he is characterizing her as someone who (a) goes along with what the Germans want; (b) is a hard worker; (c) is loyal only to her country; (d) is clever at telling lies.

9. Madame says that the identity papers will be (a) destroyed at the laundry; (b) sent to the Corporal at the Administration Office; (c) brought to Headquarters by the Stranger; (d) taken better care of in the future.

10. When Madame tells the Stranger that her nephew is her heir (522b, 14), she is implying that (a) she values family relationships; (b) his mother was his sister; (c) if he doesn't let her use the identity papers, she will not leave him her money; (d) anyone she leaves her money to must be a worthwhile person.

Composition Review

Choose one of the following assignments to write about. Assume you are writing for your classmates.

1. If the Stranger in *The Pen of My Aunt* is going to avoid being held by the Germans, he must have more than his share of good luck. Consider why each of the following things is lucky for the Stranger: he chooses to be taken to Madame's house in the first place; Madame has a real nephew who is not there; Madame and Simone are sympathetic and quick-witted.

In a few paragraphs, discuss how the Stranger's luck helps him in this excerpt. Mention the above points and any others you can think of. Do any of the characters seem to "help luck happen"? How do you think the Stranger's luck will hold up?

2. *The Diary of Anne Frank* presents clear pictures of several other characters besides Anne. Choose one scene from the play and choose one other character who interests you. Consider how that character thinks and reacts.

Write a diary entry a page or two long, describing the scene from this character's point of view. People remember things differently and report them in different ways, so your account of the same events might take on a completely different meaning or tone. (If you wish, you may write this assignment in the form of a play. Use *The Diary of Anne Frank* as a model for identifying characters, describing actions, etc.)

3. One of the most significant statements made by Anne Frank is: "In spite of everything, I still believe that people are really good at heart." How do the actions of Miep and Mr. Kraler help prove the truth of this statement? In *The Pen of My Aunt,* how do the actions of Madame and Simone provide further proof?

In a page or two, discuss how Anne's statement is proved by the four characters named. Do you think these people help others simply because they are "good at heart," or might they have other reasons as well? Does it matter, since they *do* help? Use specific speeches and actions from both plays to support your point.

Handbook of Literary Terms

alliteration

She sells seashells by the seashore.
Peter Piper picked a peck of pickled peppers.
Better buy better baby-buggy bumpers.

These old tongue twisters have always been enjoyed because people like to play with the sounds of language. We use repeated letter sounds in such everyday expressions as "busy as a bee," "down the drain," and "smooth as silk." Advertisers use them in slogans; poets use them in their writing.

The use of repeated consonant sounds is called *alliteration*. Usually, the repeated, or alliterative, sounds occur at the beginnings of words, as in these lines:

All *d*ay within the *d*reamy house,
The *d*oors upon their hinges creaked . . . .

> Alfred, Lord Tennyson, from "Mariana"

But sometimes they are found within words as well. Note the repetition of *l* in these lines:

The gray sea and the *l*ong b*l*ack *l*and;
And the ye*ll*ow half-moon *l*arge and *l*ow . . . .

> Robert Browning, from "Meeting at Night"

Alliteration in poetry helps create melody, sounds pleasant to hear. However, as Alexander Pope, an eighteenth–century English poet, said, "The sound must seem an echo to the sense." That is, the sounds should reflect the meaning—the sense—of a line. As you read the following lines, notice how the repeated *h, s,* and *sh* sounds echo the noise made by the scythes, or long-handled mowers, that are being swung through tall grass:

Hush, ah hush, the Scythes are saying,
Hush, and heed not, and fall asleep;
Hush, they say to the grasses swaying,
Hush, they sing to the clover deep!
5 *Hush—'tis the lullaby Time is singing—*
Hush, and heed not, for all things pass,
Hush, ah hush! and the Scythes are swinging
Over the clover, over the grass!

> Andrew Lang, from "Scythe Song"

The emphasis produced by alliteration can also be used to call attention to certain important words in a poem:

Like *trains* of cars on *tracks* of plush
I hear the level bee . . . .

> Emily Dickinson, from "The Bee"

Alliteration can point out contrasts:

Between the *d*ark and the *d*aylight,
When the night is beginning to lower . . . .

> Henry Wadsworth Longfellow,
> from "The Children's Hour"

Alliteration can link words that are similar in image, thought, and feeling:

We'll talk of *s*unshine and of *s*ong,
And *s*ummer days when we were young . . . .

> William Wordsworth, from "To a Butterfly"

Finally, the sounds produced by alliteration can affect the MOOD of a poem. Read the following lines and answer the questions that follow:

Sweet and low, sweet and low,
Wind of the western sea,
Low, low, breathe and blow,
Wind of the western sea!

> Alfred, Lord Tennyson,
> from "Sweet and Low"

In these lines, do the repeated *s, l, w,* and *b* sounds help create a calm and soothing effect or a tense and uneasy effect? In what ways are the sounds an "echo to the sense"?

alliteration (ə lit′ə rā′shən)

Repeated consonant sounds occurring at the beginning of words or within words. Alliteration is used to create melody, establish MOOD, call attention to important words, and point out similarities and contrasts.

Apply to **The Mewlips** on page 329

characterization

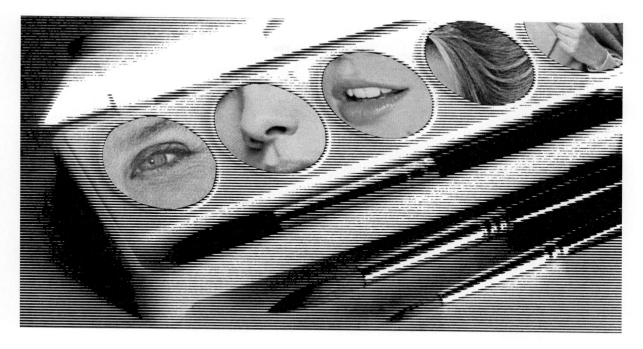

In order to create a fictitious character, the author may simply describe the character:

Karen was small for her age and inclined to plumpness. Her blue eyes viewed the people and events around her with a mixture of curiosity and amusement. She was not a woman, but she was past being a child; too sophisticated for toys, she might still, on impulse, turn a somersault on the living room rug.

1. Approximately how old is Karen?
2. What details help you visualize her?
3. What details reveal something about Karen's personality?

An author may reveal a character's personality through that character's speech and actions:

"But why can't I go?" Karen wailed. "Everyone else is going. You never let me go anywhere! You just don't want me to grow up and have fun!" Karen wheeled around and stormed out of the house, slamming the door behind her.

4. What does Karen reveal about her personality in this speech?

5. What do her actions contribute to your picture of her?

An author may give the reactions and opinions of other characters:

"I've known Karen a long time, ever since first grade. We've been best friends since last year. I like her because . . . well, I guess it's because she's always so happy and sure of herself and she's good at things like baseball and swimming and painting and stuff." Joanie paused, then added, "Everybody at school likes her."

6. What is Joanie's relationship to Karen?
7. What do you learn about Karen from Joanie's comments?

An author may show the character's inner thoughts and feelings:

The sunlight trickled between the slats of the bamboo blinds. Karen stretched luxuriously, pleasantly aware of the tingling sensation in her muscles.

She really ought to get up, she thought. Sally was coming over at eleven. Maybe she should make some sandwiches so they could eat out in the backyard. Mrs. Henley was taking them to the beach in the afternoon. She should also finish that letter to Peggy . . . maybe she would tonight . . . if she remembered . . . and if she had the time.

8. What is Karen thinking about?

9. What do her thoughts tell you about her personality?

Authors may use any one of the four methods of *characterization* illustrated above to bring to life the fictional people they create: (1) describing the character's appearance; (2) reporting the character's speech and behavior; (3) describing the reactions of other characters to the individual; and (4) revealing the character's thoughts and feelings. Most authors, however, use a combination of methods.

In the following novel excerpt, the author uses all four methods to characterize Meg, a teenaged girl who is visiting the principal of her former school. Charles Wallace is Meg's younger brother.

"I need to see you, please, Mr. Jenkins."

"Why aren't you in school?"

"I am. This school."

"Kindly don't be rude, Meg. I see you haven't changed any over the summer. I had hoped you would not be one of my problems this year. Have you informed anybody of your whereabouts?" The early morning light glinted off his spectacles, veiling his eyes. Meg pushed her own spectacles up her nose, but could not read his expression; as usual, she thought, he looked as though he smelled something unpleasant.

He sniffed. "I will have my secretary drive you to school. That will mean the loss of her services for a full half day."

"I'll hitchhike, thanks."

"Compounding one misdemeanor with another? In this state, hitchhiking happens to be against the law."

"Mr. Jenkins, I didn't come to talk to you about hitchhiking, I came to talk to you about Charles Wallace."

"I don't appreciate your interference, Margaret."

"The bigger boys are bullying him. They'll really hurt him if you don't stop them."

Madeleine L'Engle, from *A Wind in the Door*

Each of the following is a true statement about Meg. For each one point out lines from the excerpt which prove the statement and name the method or methods of characterization used.

1. Meg wears glasses.

2. Meg always finds that Mr. Jenkins looks sour.

3. Meg is concerned about Charles Wallace's safety.

4. Meg has caused problems for Mr. Jenkins in the past.

---

characterization

The methods an author uses to acquaint the reader with his or her characters. An author may describe the character's physical traits and personality, report the character's speech and behavior, give opinions and reactions of other characters toward this individual, or reveal the character's thoughts and feelings.

From *A Wind in the Door* by Madeleine L'Engle (Farrar, Straus and Giroux, 1980), pages 18-19.

Apply to "**Cress to the Rescue**" on page 78

connotation/denotation

Our new house just wasn't home until Dad's blue rocking chair arrived.

If you were to look up the words *house* and *home* in a dictionary, you would find that both words have approximately the same meaning—"a dwelling place." However, the speaker in the sentence above suggests that *home* has an additional meaning. Aside from the strict dictionary definition, or *denotation*, many people associate such things as comfort, love, security, or privacy with a home but do not necessarily make the same associations with a house. What is the first thing that comes to your mind when you think of a home? of a house? Why do you think that real-estate advertisers use the word *home* more frequently than *house?*

The various feelings, images, and memories that surround a word make up its *connotation.* Although both *house* and *home* have the same denotation, or dictionary meaning, *home* also has many connotations.

Read the following sentences and answer the questions that follow:

Annette was surprised.
Annette was amazed.
Annette was astonished.

1. What is the general meaning of each of the three sentences about Annette? Do the words *surprised, amazed,* and *astonished* have approximately the same denotation?

2. What additonal meanings are suggested by *astonished?* Would one be more likely to be *surprised* or *astonished* at seeing a ghost?

3. Which word in each pair below has the more favorable connotation to you?

thrifty—penny-pinching
pushy—aggressive
politician—statesman
chef—cook
slender—skinny

Since everyone reacts emotionally to certain words, writers often deliberately select words

that they think will influence your reactions and appeal to your emotions. Read the dictionary definition below:

cock roach (kok′rōch′), *n.* any of an order of nocturnal insects, usually brown with flattened oval bodies, some species of which are household pests inhabiting kitchens, areas around water pipes, etc. [Spanish *cucaracha*]

What does the word *cockroach* mean to you? Is a cockroach merely an insect or is it also a household nuisance and a disgusting creature? See what meanings poets Wild and Morley find in roaches in the following poems:

Roaches

Last night when I got up
to let the dog out I spied
a cockroach in the bathroom
crouched flat on the cool
5   porcelain,
           delicate
antennae probing the toothpaste cap
  and feasting himself on a gob
    of it in the bowl:
10 I killed him with one unprofessional
          blow,
  scattering arms and legs
  and half his body in the sink . . .

I would have no truck with roaches,
15 crouched like lions in the ledges of sewers

(Continued)

"Roaches" by Peter Wild from *Poetry of the Desert Southwest* published by The Baleen Press, 1973. Reprinted by permission of the author.

their black eyes in the darkness
        alert for tasty slime,
breeding quickly and without design,
laboring up drainpipes through filth
20   to the light;
  I read once they are among
    the most antediluvian[1] of creatures,
    surviving everything,
    and in more primitive times
25 thrived to the size of your hand . . .

  yet when sinking asleep
    or craning at the stars,
  I can feel their light feet
    probing in my veins,
30 their whiskers nibbling
    the insides of my toes;
  and neck arched,
    feel their patient scrambling
up the dark tubes of my throat.

Peter Wild

from **Nursery Rhymes for the Tender-hearted**
(dedicated to Don Marquis)

Scuttle, scuttle, little roach—
How you run when I approach:
Up above the pantry shelf
Hastening to secrete yourself.

5 Most adventurous of vermin,
How I wish I could determine
How you spend your hours of ease,
Perhaps reclining on the cheese.

Cook has gone, and all is dark—
10 Then the kitchen is your park;
In the garbage heap that she leaves
Do you browse among the tea leaves?

How delightful to suspect
All the places you have trekked:
15 Does your long antenna whisk its
Gentle tip across the biscuits?

Do you linger, little soul,
Drowsing in our sugar bowl?
Or, abandonment most utter,
20 Shake a shimmy on the butter?

Do you chant your simple tunes
Swimming in the baby's prunes?
Then, when dawn comes, do you slink
Homeward to the kitchen sink?

25 Timid roach, why be so shy?
We are brothers, thou and I.
In the midnight, like yourself,
I explore the pantry shelf!

Christopher Morley

Reread the dictionary definition. Which of the denotative characteristics of a cockroach do both poets include in their poems? What characteristics does Wild give to roaches that are not in the dictionary definition? What additional characteristics does Morley give to roaches?

In each poem, the insect acquires meanings beyond its dictionary definition. Both poets lead us away from a literal view of roaches to a non-literal one. Which poet succeeds in giving roaches favorable connotations? Which poet comes closer to expressing your own feelings about roaches?

connotation

The emotional, imaginative, cultural, or traditional associations surrounding a word, as opposed to its strict, literal dictionary meaning.

denotation

The strict dictionary meaning of a word, presented objectively and without emotional associations.

1. *antediluvian* (an′ti də lü′vē ən), very old.

"Nursery Rhymes for the Tender-hearted" from *Chimneysmoke* by Christopher Morley (J.B. Lippincott). Copyright 1921, renewed 1949 by Christopher Morley. Reprinted by permission of Harper & Row, Publishers, Inc.

Apply to "**The Peaceable Tree**" on page 180

figurative language

The Eagle

He clasps the crag with crooked hands;
Close to the sun in lonely lands,
Ringed with the azure world, he stands.

The wrinkled sea beneath him crawls;
5 He watches from his mountain walls,
And like a thunderbolt he falls.

Alfred, Lord Tennyson

1. Explain the meaning of each of the following phrases in the context of the poem:

    a. crooked hands

    b. close to the sun in lonely lands

    c. wrinkled sea beneath him crawls

    d. his mountain walls

    e. like a thunderbolt he falls

2. This poem is a description of an eagle, yet it differs greatly from the ordinary dictionary definition of *eagle:* "a large, strong bird of prey that has keen eyes and powerful wings." How does the above poem suggest the eagle's strength? Which lines emphasize his keen vision? Which presents a more colorful description of the eagle, the poem or the dictionary? Explain your answer.

To make his description of the eagle especially clear and appealing, Tennyson uses *figurative language* instead of literal language. In literal language, words are used in their ordinary meaning, without exaggeration or inventiveness. (The dictionary definition of *eagle* is written in literal terms.) Figurative language goes beyond the ordinary meanings of words in order to emphasize ideas or emotions. Whenever you use a *figure of speech* such as "you're eating like a pig" or "he runs like the wind" you are comparing two different things in order to emphasize a similarity. Some of the most common figures of speech are SIMILE, METAPHOR, and HYPERBOLE.

Read the poem below and answer the questions that follow:

Companions

A leaf ran at my heels
Halfway across the dusk.
It rattled like a cough.
It was as curled as an old man's
    hand around a hoe.
5 It was as brown as the apes.
In a gust we parted,
the leaf stumbling one way
and I another.
It was not a decision;
10 we merely went on separate journeys.
The wind rose behind me
and I carried it on my shoulders
    all the way
like a raving corner of the sea.

Adrien Stoutenburg

1. To what things is the leaf compared?

2. How do the words that describe the leaf's movements make it seem human?

3. In what ways do the leaf and the wind both act as "companions"?

Effective figurative language has several characteristics: it makes its point by being both forceful and brief; it has a quality of freshness about it; it fits the situation; the things being compared must be alike in some recognizable way so that the general effect of the comparison is consistent and appropriate:

> But the cruel rocks, they gored her side,
> Like the horns of an angry bull.
>
> Henry Wadsworth Longfellow, from
> "The Wreck of the Hesperus"

Look at the cartoon below. Has the cartoonist illustrated the literal or the figurative meaning of the expression "work for peanuts"?

Reprinted by permission of Lawrence Lariar.

"I'm awful tired of working for peanuts!"

figurative language

Any language that goes beyond the literal meaning of words in order to furnish new effects or fresh insights into an idea or a subject. The most common figures of speech are SIMILE, METAPHOR, and HYPERBOLE.

Apply to "**Music Inside My Head**" on page 24

It was a perfect day for a picnic. The morning was bright and clear with a few scattered clouds of the white, fluffy variety that kids find pictures in. Roses were in bloom, and birds sang outside my window. Nothing could go wrong on such a perfect day. Or so I, in my childlike innocence, thought.

1. Where is the first suggestion that something is going to happen to spoil the narrator's perfect day?

2. At this point, do you have any definite idea of what may go wrong?

Sometimes an author gives the reader clues or suggestions about events that will happen later. This technique is called *foreshadowing*. In the paragraph above, you know that something will happen to mar the "perfect day," but you don't know whether it will be a humorous incident, such as a cow eating the picnic lunch, or a tragic event, such as a drowning or an automobile accident.

Not all foreshadowing is as obvious as that in the example above. Frequently, future events are merely hinted at through dialogue, description, or the attitudes and reactions of the characters.

In the following novel excerpt the main character, David Copperfield, recounts an event from his childhood. His mother, a young, attractive woman, had been widowed shortly before David was born. Peggotty is a trusted and devoted servant of the Copperfield family. As you read, notice clues that might foreshadow future events:

Peggotty and I were sitting one night by the parlor fire, alone. I had been reading to Peggotty about crocodiles. I remember she had a cloudy impression, after I had done, that they were a sort of vegetable. I was tired of reading, and dead sleepy; but having leave, as a high treat, to sit up until my mother came home from spending the evening at a neighbor's, I would rather have died upon my post (of course) than have gone off to bed. . . .

"Peggotty," says I suddenly, "were you ever married?"

"Lord, Master Davy," replied Peggotty, "what's put marriage in your head?"

She answered with such a start that it quite woke me. And then she stopped in her work, and looked at me, with her needle drawn out to its thread's length.

"But were you ever married, Peggotty?" says I. "You are a very handsome woman, an't you?"

"Me handsome, Davy!" said Peggotty. "Lawk no, my dear! But what put marriage in your head?"

"I don't know! You mustn't marry more than one person at a time, may you, Peggotty?"

"Certainly not," says Peggotty, with the promptest decision.

"But if you marry a person, and the person dies, why then you may marry another person, mayn't you, Peggotty?"

"You may," says Peggotty, "if you choose."

"You an't cross, I suppose, Peggotty, are you?" said I, after sitting quiet for a minute.

I really thought she was, she had been so short with me. But I was quite mistaken; for she laid aside her work (which was a stocking of her own), and opening her arms wide, took my curly head within them, and gave it a good squeeze. I know it was a good squeeze, because, being very plump, whenever she made any little exertion after she was dressed, some of the buttons on the back of her gown flew off. And I recollect two bursting while she was hugging me.

"Now let me hear some more about the crorkindills," said Peggotty, "for I an't heard half enough."

I couldn't quite understand why Peggotty looked so queer, or why she was so ready to go back to the crocodiles. However, we returned to those monsters, with fresh interest on my part; but I had my doubts of Peggotty, who was thoughtfully sticking her needle into various parts of her face and arms all the time.

We had exhausted the crocodiles, and begun with the alligators, when the garden bell rang. We went to the door, and there was my mother, looking unusually pretty, I thought, and with her a gentleman with beautiful black hair and whiskers, who had walked home with us from church last Sunday.

As my mother stepped down on the threshold to take me in her arms and kiss me, the gentleman said I was a more highly privileged little fellow than a monarch.

"What does that mean?" I asked him.

He patted me on the head; but somehow I didn't like him or his deep voice, and I was jealous that his hand should touch my mother's in touching me—which it did. I put it away as well as I could.

"Oh, Davy!" remonstrated my mother.

"Dear boy!" said the gentleman. "I cannot wonder at his devotion. Come, let us shake hands!"

My right hand was in my mother's left, so I gave him the other.

"Why, that's the wrong hand, Davy!" laughed the gentleman.

My mother drew my right hand forward; but I resolved, for my former reason, not to give it to him, and I did not. I gave him the other, and he shook it heartily, and said I was a brave fellow, and went away.

At this minute I see him turn around in the garden, and give us a last look with his ill-omened black eyes, before the door was shut.

Peggotty, who had not said a word or moved a finger, secured the fastenings instantly, and we all went into the parlor. My mother, contrary to her usual habit, instead of coming to the elbow-chair by the fire, remained at the other end of the room, and sat singing to herself.

"Hope you have had a pleasant evening, ma'am," said Peggotty, standing as stiff as a barrel in the center of the room, with a candlestick in her hand.

"Much obliged to you, Peggotty," returned my mother in a cheerful voice, "I have had a very pleasant evening."

"A stranger or so makes an agreeable change," suggested Peggotty.

"A very agreeable change, indeed," returned my mother.

Peggotty continuing to stand motionless in the middle of the room, and my mother resuming her singing, I fell asleep. . . .

Charles Dickens, from David Copperfield

1. How does Peggotty's attitude suggest that David's mother is about to remarry? When do you learn whom she will probably marry?

2. Which of Mrs. Copperfield's actions lead you to expect the marriage?

3. What hints are there in the man's attitude that foreshadow the marriage?

4. Find the clues that suggest the man is not as kind and generous as he tries to appear.

Foreshadowing frequently serves two purposes. It builds suspense by raising questions that encourage the reader to go on and find out more about the event that is being foreshadowed. The preceding passage, for example, foretells Mrs. Copperfield's marriage to the blackhaired gentleman. It does not, however, explain how David will fit into this marriage, or what will happen to Peggotty, who obviously does not approve of the marriage.

Foreshadowing is also a means of adding plausibility to a narrative by partially preparing the reader for events to follow. In this passage, the gentleman appears to like David even though the boy dislikes him immediately. The "last look" the gentleman gives them "with his ill-omened black eyes" also suggests that the man is not so kind and generous as he appears to be and that he may be the cause of much future unhappiness for the Copperfields.

foreshadowing

An author's use of hints or clues to suggest events that will occur later in a narrative.

Apply to "**To Build a Fire**" on page 295

hyperbole

So fair art thou, my bonnie lass,
   So deep in love am I:
And I will love thee still, my dear,
   Till all the seas go dry.

Robert Burns, from
"A Red, Red Rose"

According to the last line, how long will the speaker's love last? Do you think the last line is intended to be taken literally or figuratively? What is the effect of the last line?

Hyperbole is an exaggerated statement used to increase or heighten effect. When you say, "I could eat a horse," you are deliberately exaggerating in order to let your listener know that you are extremely hungry.

Read the limerick below and answer the questions that follow:

There was a young lady from Lynn
Who was so exceedingly thin
   That when she essayed
   To drink lemonade
She slid down the straw and fell in.

Author Unknown

1. What is the exaggerated statement in this limerick?

2. What is the purpose of the hyperbole?

hyperbole (hī pėr′bə lē)

An exaggerated statement used especially as a figure of speech to heighten effect.

Apply to "**takes talent**" on page 167

imagery

The hot July sun beat relentlessly down, casting an orange glare over the farm buildings, the fields, the pond. Even the usually cool green willows bordering the pond hung wilting and dry. Our sun-baked backs ached for relief. We quickly pulled off our sweaty clothes and plunged into the pond, but the tepid water only stifled us and we soon climbed back onto the brown, dusty bank. Our parched throats longed for something cool—a strawberry ice, a tall frosted glass of lemonade.

We pulled on our clothes and headed through the dense, crackling underbrush, the sharp briars pulling at our damp jeans, until we reached the watermelon patch. As we began to cut open the nearest melon, we could smell the pungent skin mingling with the dusty odor of dry earth. Suddenly the melon gave way with a crack, revealing the deep, pink sweetness inside.

1. From the paragraph above pick out words and phrases that appeal to your sense of **(a)** sight; **(b)** sound; **(c)** smell; **(d)** taste; **(e)** touch and feeling.

2. Which sense impression is strongest?

To make descriptions of people, places, events, and the like seem real, writers often use words and phrases that appeal to the senses. These words and phrases, called *images,* help a reader mentally experience what the characters in the literary selection are actually experiencing.

Well-chosen images arouse a particular response or emotion in the reader's imagination, as in the poem in the next column.

Horse

A
quarter horse, no rider
canters through the pasture

thistles raise soft purple burrs
5 her flanks are shiny in the sun

I whistle and she runs
almost sideways toward me

the oats in my hand are sweets to her:

dun mane furling in its breeze,
10 her neck
corseted with muscle,
wet teeth friendly against my hand—
how can I believe
you ran under a low maple limb
15 to knock me off?

Jim Harrison

To what senses does the poet appeal in this poem? Pick out the sensory images which seem most vivid to you.

imagery

Concrete details that appeal to the senses. By using specific images, authors establish MOOD and arouse emotion in their readers.

Apply to "**A Christmas Memory**" on page 238

inference

Help Wanted:
Young person to work at Sox ballpark. Some sales experience helpful but not necessary. Uniform provided. Apply at concession stand, corner Addison and 14th.

1. The person who takes this job will probably be **(a)** a major-league baseball player; **(b)** an usher; **(c)** a hot-dog vendor.

2. What details tell you what kind of job this is?

Study carefully the following cartoon:

Reprinted by permission of Lawrence Lariar.

"Miss Feiner. Yoo-hoo."

1. Why is the skier calling to Miss Feiner?
2. What do you think happened to Miss Feiner?

A correct conclusion that you draw from just a few hints is called an *inference.*

Many writers do not tell a reader everything outright. Instead they rely on a reader's ability to "read between the lines" and make reasonable inferences from the information presented.

A reader can make inferences from an author's description of a scene or character, from a character's conversation and actions, from the way in which other characters react to a particular individual, and even from an author's choice of words.

In the following novel excerpt the author describes Jo, a young writer, on the day she first takes a manuscript to a publisher:

"There, I've done my best! If this won't suit I shall have to wait till I can do better."

Lying back on the sofa, Jo read the manuscript carefully through, making dashes here and there, and putting in many exclamation points; then she tied it up with a smart red ribbon, and sat a minute looking at it with a sober, wistful expression, which plainly showed how earnest her work had been. Then Jo produced another manuscript; and, putting both in her pocket, crept quietly down the stairs.

She put on her hat and jacket as noiselessly as possible, and, going to the back entry window, got out upon the roof of a low porch, swung herself down to the grassy bank, and took a roundabout way to the road.

If anyone had been watching her, he would have thought her movements decidedly peculiar; for she went off at a great pace till she reached a certain number in a certain busy street. She went into the doorway, looked up the dirty stairs, and, after standing stock still a minute, suddenly dived into the street, and walked away as rapidly as she came. This maneuver she repeated several times, to the great amusement of a black-eyed young gentleman lounging in the window of a building opposite. On returning for the third time, Jo gave herself a shake, pulled her hat over her eyes, and walked up the stairs, looking as if she were going to have all her teeth out.

There was a dentist's sign, among others, which adorned the entrance, and, after staring a moment at the pair of artificial jaws which slowly opened and shut to draw attention to a fine set of teeth, the

young gentleman put on his coat, took his hat, and went down to post himself in the opposite doorway, saying, with a smile and a shiver, "It's like her to come alone, but if she has a bad time she'll need someone to help her home."

Louisa May Alcott, from *Little Women*

1. How can you tell that Jo doesn't want anyone to see her leave the house?

2. How do Jo's actions reveal her nervousness?

3. Where does the "black-eyed gentleman" assume that Jo is going?

4. Does the "black-eyed gentleman" know Jo? How do you know?

inference

A reasonable and intelligent conclusion drawn from hints or other information provided by an author.

Apply to "Charles" on page 192

inversion

```
SUBJECT   VERB   COMPLEMENT
    ↙        ↓          ↘
The February sky   is       pale.
```

The sentence above illustrates the normal pattern of an English sentence: subject, followed by verb, followed by complement. Notice how the normal pattern is changed in the lines that follow:

> Pale is the February sky,
>   And brief the midday's sunny hours;
> The wind-swept forest seems to sigh
>   For the sweet time of leaves and flowers. . . .
>
> William Cullen Bryant, from
> "The Twenty-Second of February"

The parts of the sentences in lines 1 and 2 of the verse are not in normal order—the complement comes before the verb, followed by the subject. Are the parts of the third line in normal order? Would this verse rhyme if Bryant had written the first line in normal order?

> These lessons he learned from his past. . . .
>
> Rudolfo A. Anaya, from
> "A Celebration of Grandfathers"

The parts of this line are not in normal order either. They are *inverted*. When the sentence is rewritten in normal order, it reads:

> He learned these lessons from his past. . . .

What main idea does the first sentence seem to stress? What idea is emphasized in the rewritten sentence?

Writers often use *inversion* for emphasis or to achieve a certain poetic effect. Sometimes only the normal order of noun and modifier is reversed, as in "It came upon a midnight clear" instead of "It came upon a clear midnight." At other times the normal order of noun, verb, and modifiers may be reversed, as in the lines on the next page.

Slowly and smoothly went the ship,
Moved onward from beneath.

Samuel Taylor Coleridge, from
"The Rime of the Ancient Mariner"

An inverted line may seem difficult at first, but it should not cause you problems if you concentrate on the meaning instead of the form.

A Fine Day

Clear had the day been from the dawn,
All checkered was the sky,
Thin clouds like scarfs of cobweb lawn
Veil'd heaven's most glorious eye.
5 The wind had no more strength than this,
That leisurely it blew,
To make one leaf the next to kiss
That closely by it grew.

Michael Drayton

Read the poem aloud. What idea is emphasized in the first two lines? Now put these two lines in normal order, beginning with the subjects, "the day" and "the sky." Then read the rest of the poem as it is written. Is the meaning of the first two lines altered when you change the order? Is the effect of the poem changed? How does rewriting the first two lines affect the rhyme scheme of the poem? Explain.

inversion

The reversal of the usual order of words in a sentence to create a special effect or for emphasis.

Apply to "**Still Life: Lady with Birds**" on page 176.

irony

Verbal irony

It was one of those days! The alarm clock failed to go off, John ripped the sleeve of his new shirt, spilled orange juice on his math paper, and missed his ride to school. When he finally climbed on a city bus after a thirty-minute wait in the rain, he told the driver, "This is certainly going to be a great day!"

1. What does John mean by his statement?
2. Does he actually believe it *is* going to be a great day? That is, does he want his statement to be taken literally?

John is using *verbal irony* when he says the opposite of what he really means or feels. Can you recall a situation in which you used verbal irony? Describe it.

Irony of situation

Read the following synopsis of a short story by O. Henry entitled "The Cop and the Anthem":

It is late autumn in New York, and Soapy, a bum, decides that it is time for him to make his usual arrangements for the winter months: he will get himself arrested and sentenced to prison. There he will have food and lodging, at least. To achieve this goal, Soapy plans to eat a large and expensive meal, and then leave without paying for it. However, when he goes into a fashionable restaurant, he is turned away because of his shabby clothes. Next he smashes a store window and immediately confesses his deed to a policeman. But the policeman refuses to believe him. He does get his meal in a not-so-fashionable restaurant, but instead of being arrested when he can't pay, he is merely thrown out onto the street.

Soapy makes several more attempts to be arrested, including stealing an umbrella. But it turns out that the man with the umbrella had himself stolen it earlier. Soapy gives up in despair and heads for the park and his accustomed bench, but on the way he stops before a church. As he stands there listening to the music from within, he is reminded of his happy childhood and the depths to which he has now fallen. He resolves to reform his life, find a job, and to become successful. But as he stands there lost in thought, he is finally arrested—for vagrancy!

1. What does Soapy at first hope will happen to him?

2. Why doesn't it happen?

3. When does the result he hoped for actually occur?

4. Why is the outcome a surprise?

This story, in which things turn out contrary to what is expected, is an example of *irony of situation.* The ironic situation occurs because Soapy does not get arrested when he actually commits crimes but does get arrested when he loiters in front of a church making the decision to alter his life for the better.

Dramatic irony

Below is part of a synopsis of a detective mystery. Read it and answer the questions that follow:

Scene One: The play begins in the dimly lighted library of a huge, old house. A tall man wearing gloves enters and crosses to a painting which hangs above a sofa. He removes the painting, revealing a wall safe behind it. With the skill of a professional burglar, he carefully begins twirling the lock until after a few moments he succeeds in opening the safe. Greedily he grabs the jewels he finds within and makes a speedy exit.

Scene Two: The library is now ablaze with light. The wall safe is open as we left it at the close of the last scene. A famous detective has just arrived and has assembled in the library the owners of the house, guests, and various servants. Among those seated on the sofa beneath the safe is the tall man. He appears to be completely calm and collected. One by one, the detective questions each of the servants. The tall man is next. . . .

1. At this point in the action, what do you know that none of the characters in the play (except the tall man) know?

2. Why might the tall man's answers to the detective's questions mean more to you than to the other characters in the play?

Dramatic irony occurs in fiction or drama when the reader or spectator knows more about the true state of affairs than the characters do. Authors often employ dramatic irony to create suspense. For example, dramatic irony is used by Edgar Allan Poe in ''The Tell-Tale Heart.'' When the police arrive, you know that the narrator has just killed and hidden the old man. By allowing you to know more than the police know, the author helps increase your feelings of suspense as the narrator becomes more and more uncomfortable.

irony

The contrast between what is expected, or what appears to be, and what actually is.

Verbal irony is the contrast between what is said and what is actually meant.

Irony of situation refers to a happening that is the opposite of what is expected or intended.

Dramatic irony occurs when the audience or reader knows more than the characters do.

Apply to ''**Back There**'' on page 341

metaphor

Night

Night is a cavalier dauntless and bold;
Riding through clouds on a steed strapped
    with gold,
Sapphires flash from his cloak's sable folds
And each silken pocket a star-baby holds.

Christine Wood Bullwinkle

1. The speaker in the poem above makes a comparison between two essentially different things, night and a cavalier, or horseman. What does this comparison suggest about night?

2. In line 3 what are the sapphires being compared to? In what ways are the two things the same? What is the sable cloak being compared to? What similarities exist between these things?

3. Consider each of the following literal descriptions of night: "the time between evening and morning," "dark," "evening." Which is a more vivid description of night—the poem, or any of the literal descriptions?

In literature and, particularly, in poetry, a writer often expresses one thing in terms of another (night as a cavalier). This use of FIGURATIVE LANGUAGE helps the reader see unexpected, but valid, connections between things that are basically different. When things that are basically unlike are related through implied comparison, these comparisons are called *metaphors*.

In a metaphor there is never a connective such as *like* or *as* to signal that a comparison is being made. (See SIMILE.) As a result, metaphors are not always easy to spot. Explain what makes the following sentence a metaphor: "The tumbleweeds are the children of the desert."

Look for the metaphor in this poem:

For a Hopi Silversmith

he has gathered the windstrength
from the third mesa
into his hand
and cast it into silver

5 i have wanted to see
the motion of wind
for a long time

thank you
for showing me

Joy Harjo

1. What does a silversmith do?

2. What has the silversmith done, according to the speaker, that is so special?

3. How might designing and working a piece of silver remind the speaker of gathering and casting the strength and motion of the wind?

metaphor

A figure of speech that involves an implied comparison between two relatively unlike things.

Christine Wood Bullwinkle, "Night" from *Poems for the Children's Hour* by Josephine Bouton, ed. (Springfield, Mass.: Milton Bradley Co.), 1927.

"For a Hopi Silversmith" from *The First Skin Around Me* published by Territorial Press. Copyright © 1976 by Joy Harjo. Reprinted by permission.

Apply to "**Sky Diver**" on page 157

mood

The Harbor

Passing through huddled and ugly walls
By doorways where women
Looked from their hunger-deep eyes,
Haunted with shadows of hunger-hands,
5 Out from the huddled and ugly walls,
I came sudden, at the city's edge,
On a blue burst of lake—
Long lake waves breaking under the sun
On a spray-flung curve of shore;
10 And a fluttering storm of gulls,
Masses of great gray wings
And flying white bellies
Veering and wheeling free in the open.

                         Carl Sandburg

1. What is the setting in lines 1 through 5? Is the setting a pleasant one?

2. What is the effect of the poet's use of words such as *huddled, ugly, hunger–deep, haunted, shadows,* and *hunger–hands?* What feelings do these words create?

3. In the last eight lines of the poem, what words and images help create feelings of freedom and optimism?

4. What sort of statement about the lake does Sandburg seem to be making?

In this poem, as in any piece of writing, the author selects such elements as setting, specific details, and images to convey the desired *mood*—in this case one that moves from an atmosphere of ugliness and hopelessness to an atmosphere of beauty, openness, and optimism. Another poet might have treated either or both scenes in an entirely different way, depending on his or her purpose. In any case, specific words, details, and setting communicate that mood.

As you read the following poem, pay particular attention to the mood being created:

Running–I

What were we playing? Was it prisoner's base?
I ran with whacking keds
Down the cart-road past Rickard's place,
And where it dropped beside the tractor-sheds

5 Leapt out into the air above a blurred
Terrain, through jolted light,

Took two hard lopes, and at the third
Spanked off a hummock-side exactly right,

And made the turn, and with delighted strain
10 Sprinted across the flat
By the bull-pen, and up the lane.
Thinking of happiness, I think of that.

                         Richard Wilbur

1. What mood does the poem communicate to you—happiness, excitement, exhaustion, or what?

2. What details in the poem help create this mood?

mood

The total feeling in a literary work. The choice of setting, objects, details, images, and words all contribute to create a specific mood.

Apply to "**The Tell-Tale Heart**" on page 256

plot

The material following the story "If Cornered, Scream" deals with *conflict, details, pattern of events, climax,* and *conclusion.* These are all important elements of *plot.*

If Cornered, Scream

On the night it happened she hurried across the hospital parking lot, unlocked her car door, and got in. She started the car, waved to her co-workers, honked to the security guard, and drove the half block to the freeway entrance. The late hour meant light traffic, and though she was a good driver, she was always relieved whenever she had negotiated an entrance ramp. That done, she settled back, driving easily.

Then in the dim dashboard light she saw the gas gauge indicating empty and remembered with annoyance that she hadn't had time to stop for gas. Working a late shift at the hospital was not an ideal situation, but it meant more money and allowed her to attend graduate classes during the days.

As she drove, she found herself gripping the steering wheel and made a conscious effort to relax and think pleasant thoughts. Each night during the drive home, she relived the safety lectures given to the nurses—make sure someone on the ward knows where you are at all times; leave the grounds in groups; avoid isolated places in the hospital; if cornered, scream.

Again she deliberately relaxed her grip on the wheel and took a deep breath.

Funny, she thought, she didn't know why, but she was even more uptight than usual. She was tired and looked forward to a long soak in the tub and her new magazine which had lain unread the last three days.

The gas gauge again caught her attention. She could probably make it home on what was still left in the tank, but she would have to fill up before class in the morning. If she stopped tonight at the station that Gabriel ran on Imperial Highway, she'd have a few extra minutes in the morning and wouldn't have to rush.

She approached Imperial Highway, flicked on the right blinker, headed down the off-ramp, waited at the stoplight, and then made a left turn. She pulled into the station at a pump and rolled down the window as Gabriel walked to the car.

Since he always spoke pleasantly on the nights she stopped for gas, she had automatically discounted the few disturbing rumors that accompanied his sudden appearance in the area.

"Hi, Florence Nightingale. Fill 'er up?"

"Hi, Gabriel. Yes, fill it up, please."

As she handed him the gas-tank key, he asked, "Any more ping-pong playing under the hood?"

"No, no more noise. It stopped when you did whatever you did."

Gabriel filled the tank, cleaned the windows and mirrors, and gave her the change from a twenty. When he finished he said offhandedly, "By the way, my birthday was Sunday. Why don't you step inside the office and see what my sister gave me? You won't believe your eyes!"

"Oh, Gabriel, I'm in a really big hurry. I just can't stop tonight. But I will next time. I promise."

"Aw, come on. It won't be new any more by then. Besides, this is something extra-special. Come on. Only take a second."

As she and Gabriel talked back and forth, she realized she was wasting more time than if she went in and saw the silly gift.

Looking more agreeable than she felt, she said, "Okay, you win, Gabriel. Remember, this better be good!"

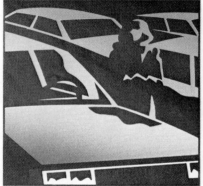  

"It is. You'll see. Oh, before you get out, angle the car over this way—just in case anyone wants to pull in." Watching his gestures, she parked the car and followed him to the station office.

Once inside, Gabriel locked the door and quickly took a gun out of the drawer. Through the roar of her heartbeat in her ears she heard him say that there was no birthday and no present. Her fingers tingled. Nausea pitched and rolled through her body like seasickness. Each time the nausea crested, her legs felt like loosened moorings.

Her nose and toes were cold and she knew clinically, almost like an observer, that she was experiencing the symptoms of shock. She was unable to make a self-protective move, or even to scream. She tried to prepare to die, but didn't know how. Crazily, in the midst of her silent hysteria, the absurdity of it struck her, and she had a demented desire to laugh. Gabriel's lips were moving but she still couldn't hear above the roar in her ears.

Finally she heard sounds coming from his mouth. The sounds became words as her head cleared, and the words began to make sense.

". . . sorry I had to scare you by telling you that. But don't feel bad, I was scared myself when I saw that dude on the floor in the back of your car. I had you angle the car that way so that I can see both doors from here. And if he tries to get out, he belongs to me. I'll call the cops now. It's okay. Good thing you stopped for gas tonight."

In a few minutes she was aware of the sirens, the flashing lights of the squad cars, and the bellow of the bullhorn.

Patricia J. Thurmond

Conflict

1. When does the main character first think that her life is in danger? Is she able to make any move to prevent this danger? Is her conflict with Gabriel real or imagined?

2. Has this "danger" been foreshadowed earlier in the story? If so, where?

Every story, novel, or play develops around a struggle or *conflict*. Sometimes there may be only one main conflict. Sometimes, characters may be involved in several conflicts.

Conflicts in literature are of two general types: (1) *external conflict,* in which the character or main figure (sometimes an animal or group) struggles against another character, nature, or society; and (2) *internal conflict,* in which two elements of a character's personality struggle against one another. What is the internal conflict in this story? Is there an external conflict? Explain.

Details

Many details that an author chooses are helpful in developing plot. Why is each of the following details important to the story?

1. the late hour
2. the empty gas gauge
3. the main character's early-morning class

Pattern of Events

1. What purpose does each of the following incidents serve?

    a. The main character drives out of a hospital parking lot.
    b. She looks at her gas gauge.
    c. She turns off the freeway.
    d. Gabriel cleans the windows and mirrors.
    e. Gabriel asks her to look at his birthday present.
    f. The main character finally agrees.
    g. Gabriel tells her to angle the car out of the way of the gas pumps.
    h. He takes a gun out of a drawer.
    i. He tells her there's a man on the floor in the back of her car.

2. Could any of these incidents be eliminated without damaging the story? Explain.

3. Could the order of these incidents be rearranged without lessening the impact of the story?

4. What is the outcome of the story?

An author writes a story with a specific outcome in mind. Therefore, those incidents that are important to the ending are arranged in a cause-effect relationship. Each incident should logically follow the preceding ones since each is a necessary link to the outcome. In a well-planned story no one incident can be moved or eliminated without damaging or even ruining the effect the writer is trying to achieve.

Climax and Conclusion

In your opinion, where in the story is the highest point of interest or emotional intensity? Does the course of events or the main character's course of action change at this point? Explain.

The *climax* of a story takes place when the reader experiences the greatest emotional response to a character's problem, when the situation is such that the conflict must be resolved one way or another, or when a character starts to take a decisive action to end the conflict.

The climax of "If Cornered, Scream" begins when the main character suffers shock at seeing Gabriel's gun and continues until she starts listening to what he is telling her and realizes that the gun is only meant to protect her. Not every story contains a climax in this sense; sometimes the problem is left unresolved.

The *conclusion* of a story includes the resolution of the conflict and any events following it. Sometimes the conclusion contains a direct or implied comment on the conflict.

What events follow the resolution of the conflict or the climax in this story?

---

plot

A series of related events selected by the author to present and bring about the resolution of some *internal* or *external conflict.* In a carefully constructed plot, *details* and incidents are selected and arranged in a cause-effect relationship so that each is a necessary link leading to the outcome of the story. The events usually follow a pattern: a situation is established; a conflict or problem arises; certain events bring about a *climax,* or a character takes a decisive action; the conflict is resolved.

Apply to "The Inspiration of Mr. Budd" on page 32

On Friday, September 13, 1965, I was born to JoAnn and Bob Cheever.

Robert H. Cheever, Jr., was born to JoAnn and Bob Cheever on Friday, September 13, 1965.

What is the only important difference between the two sentences above?

Before beginning to write, an author must decide who the narrator will be; that is, who will tell the story. A story may be told by one of the characters, as in the first sentence, or by an outsider, as in the second sentence. The relationship between the narrator and the story he or she tells is called *point of view*.

The four passages that follow tell the same incident from different points of view. Notice how the amount of information given about each character depends upon the point of view used.

1. As I placed the carefully wrapped package on the park bench, I looked up and saw Molly walking across the street. I hoped that she hadn't seen me.

a. Is the narrator a character in the incident or an outsider?

b. Do you know what the narrator is doing?

c. Do you know what Molly is doing? what she is thinking?

2. As George placed the carefully wrapped package on the park bench, he looked up and saw Molly walking across the street.

a. Is the narrator a character in the incident or an outsider?

b. Do you know what George is doing? what he is thinking?

c. Do you know what Molly is doing? what she is thinking?

3. George, anxiously hoping that no one was watching him, placed a carefully wrapped package on an empty park bench. But when he looked around, he saw Molly watching him from across the street.

a. Is the narrator a character in the incident or an outsider?

b. Do you know what George is doing? what he is thinking?

c. Do you know what Molly is doing? what she is thinking?

4. George, anxiously hoping that no one was watching him, placed a carefully wrapped package on an empty park bench. But Molly, who was walking home, saw him and couldn't help thinking that he was acting strangely.

a. Is the narrator a character in the incident or an outsider?

b. Do you know what George is doing? what he is thinking?

c. Do you know what Molly is doing? what she is thinking?

An author uses a narrator much as a movie director uses a camera. Through choice of point of view (who the narrator is), the author can focus sharply on some details and characters while showing others less clearly.

First-Person Point of View

In example number 1, the narrator is George, a character in the story. In telling the story from his personal point of view, the narrator ("I," or first person) can tell us his own thoughts, but he cannot tell us the thoughts of other characters. Just as you can report what you see others doing, the narrator can tell us only what he sees other characters doing or what he is told by other characters; and just as you cannot enter the minds of other people, the narrator cannot enter the minds of characters other than himself. (For examples of the first-person point of view see "Top Man" and "Not Poor, Just Broke.")

Third-Person-Objective Point of View

In example number 2 the narrator is not a character in the story but is an outsider, or third person. This narrator can tell us what is happening, but does not tell us the thoughts of any of the characters. Like a newspaper reporter, this narrator can give only the facts as they occur; he or she cannot enter into the characters' minds. Example 2 is written from the third-person-objective point of view.

This point of view is also called the third-person-dramatic point of view because it is the point of view a playwright uses. (Since this point of view greatly limits the amount of information an author can give, it is seldom used except in plays and in mystery or detective stories.)

Third-Person-Limited Point of View

In the third example the narrator sees into the mind of only one character, George. This is known as the third-person-limited point of view. (For examples of the third-person-limited point of view see ''The Inspiration of Mr. Budd'' and ''The Treasure of Lemon Brown.'')

Omniscient (om nish′ənt) Point of View

In the fourth example, the narrator again is an outsider, a third person. But here the narrator has the ability to see into the minds and record the thoughts of both characters. Like a superhuman being, this narrator is *omniscient* (all-knowing). (For examples of the use of the omniscient point of view see ''Cress to the Rescue'' and ''To Build a Fire.'')

---

point of view

The relationship between the narrator and the story he or she tells. The author's choice of narrator for a story determines the amount of information a reader will be given. The four major points of view are:

1. *First Person:* The narrator (''I'') is a character in the story who can reveal only personal thoughts and feelings and what he or she sees and is told by other characters.

2. *Third-Person Objective:* The narrator is an outsider who can report only what he or she sees and hears.

3. *Third-Person Limited:* The narrator is an outsider who sees into the mind of one of the characters.

4. *Omniscient:* The narrator is an all-knowing outsider who can enter the minds of more than one of the characters.

Apply to **''Mr. Mendelsohn''** on page 198

---

rhyme

Rough
tough
Mad
bad

Lone Dog

I'm a lean dog, a keen dog, a wild dog and lone;
I'm a rough dog, a tough dog, hunting on my own;
I'm a bad dog, a mad dog, teasing silly sheep;
I love to sit and bay the moon, to keep fat souls
    from sleep.

5 I'll never be a lap dog, licking dirty feet,
A sleek dog, a meek dog, cringing for my meat;
Not for me the fireside, the well-filled plate,
But shut door, and sharp stone, and cuff and kick
    and hate.

Not for me the other dogs, running by my side,
10 Some have run a short while, but none of
    them would bide.
Oh, mine is still the lone trail, the hard trail, the
    best,
Wide wind and wild stars, and hunger of the
    quest.

Irene Rutherford McLeod

In the first stanza of ''Lone Dog,'' which words at the ends of lines rhyme? Which words rhyme in the second stanza? the third?

In poetry, this device of ending two or more lines with words that sound alike is called *end rhyming;* end words that share a particular sound are *end rhymes.*

When used in a poem, end rhymes set up a definite pattern of sounds, or a *rhyme scheme.* You can chart a rhyme scheme with letters of the alphabet by using the same letter for end words that rhyme. Consider, for example, the following limerick:

There was an old man from Peru	*a*
Who dreamed he was eating his shoe.	*a*
He awoke in the night	*b*
And turned on the light	*b*
And found out it was perfectly true.	*a*

Author Unknown

The rhyme scheme for this limerick is *a* (the sound ending line 1); *a* (a sound rhyming with line 1); *b* (a new, or second rhyming sound); *b* (a sound rhyming with the second sound); *a* (a rhyme for the first sound).

If the limerick had a third rhyming sound, it would be designated by the letter *c.* A fourth rhyme would be labeled *d,* and so on. By using this method, you can chart the rhyme scheme of any poem that uses end rhymes.

1. Make a chart of the rhyme scheme for a stanza of McLeod's "Lone Dog."

2. Reread the first line of "Lone Dog." Which words *within* the line rhyme?

Rhyming words within a line are called *internal rhymes.* Find at least three examples of internal rhyme in "Lone Dog."

In a second type of internal rhyme, a word within a line rhymes with the end word:

For the moon never *beams* without bringing me
    dreams
  Of the beautiful Annabel Lee . . . .

Edgar Allan Poe, from "Annabel Lee"

Can you find any internal rhymes of this type in "Lone Dog"?

---

rhyme

The repetition of syllable sounds. End words that share a particular sound are called *end rhymes.* Rhyming words within a line of poetry are called *internal rhymes.*

Apply to **"The Walrus and the Carpenter"** on page 145

I Never Saw a Purple Cow

I never saw a purple cow,
I never hope to see one.
But I can tell you anyhow,
I'd rather see than be one.

Gelett Burgess

Read the above verse aloud. Notice that its author has arranged words in a way that automatically causes you to place greater stress on some words or syllables than on others. This combination of stressed and unstressed words or syllables creates a pattern that gives the line a definite flow, or *rhythm.* In the case of this nonsense rhyme, the rhythm is very regular (capital letters indicate stressed words or syllables):

    i NEVer SAW a PURple COW,
    i NEVer HOPE to SEE one.
    but I can TELL you ANyHOW,
    i'd RATHer SEE than BE one.

The *ti TUM ti TUM ti TUM* rhythm gives the verse a singsong effect. Also, each line of the verse is *end-stopped;* that is, the words are so arranged that a pause, designated by a punctuation mark, is necessary at the end of each line. These pauses, which call attention to the verse's rhymes, strengthen its singsong effect.

In a nonsense verse like "I Never Saw a Purple Cow," the regular rhythm heightens its humorous effect. In most other types of poetry, however, such absolute rhythmic regularity is uncommon. Pay special attention to rhythm as you read the following lines:

The splendor falls on castle walls
  And snowy summits old in story;
The long light shakes across the lakes,
  And the wild cataract leaps in glory.
5 Blow, bugle, blow, set the wild echoes flying,
Blow, bugle; answer, echoes, dying, dying, dying.

Alfred, Lord Tennyson, from *The Princess*

1. On which words or syllables in the first line do accents fall? in the second line? the third?

aLONG CAME the DOCtor!
aLONG CAME the NURSE!
aLONG CAME the LAdy
with the BIG, FAT PURSE!

Second, rhythm allows the poet to fit the movement of the poem to the MOOD he or she is trying to create:

WORK—WORK—WORK
  Till the BRAIN beGINS to SWIM!
WORK—WORK—WORK
  Till the EYES are HEAVy and DIM!
SEAM, and GUSset, and BAND,
  BAND, and GUSset, and SEAM,
Till Over the BUTtons I FALL aSLEEP,
  And SEW them ON in a DREAM!

> Thomas Hood, from
> "The Song of the Shirt"

Would you describe the mood of these lines as light and cheerful or heavy and weary? Is the rhythm in keeping with the mood of the lines? Explain.

Third, the poet can use rhythm to emphasize important words. Read these lines aloud:

Hang a lantern aloft in the belfry arch
Of the North Church tower as a signal light,—
One, if by land, or two, if by sea;
And I on the opposite shore will be. . . .

> Henry Wadsworth Longfellow,
> from "Paul Revere's Ride"

1. What words are significant to the meaning of these lines?

2. Which syllables do you naturally emphasize? Do some or all of these syllables appear in significant words?

---

rhythm

A series of stressed and unstressed sounds in a group of words. Rhythm may be regular or it may be varied.

Apply to "The Circus; Or One View of It" on page 164

the fourth? (Notice how the rhythm changes in the last two lines.)

2. Where is the first pause in the stanza? the second pause?

Line 1 of this stanza overflows into the second line; it is a *run-on* line. Because you do not pause at the end of a run-on line, you do not emphasize the rhyme, thus increasing the poem's rhythmical variety. The variety of the rhythm causes the reader to stress the poem's meaning rather than its rhythm.

Rhythm is everywhere; it is inescapable. Even the most CASual EVeryday SPEECH FALLS into RHYTHmic PHRASes. But poets do not use rhythm simply because it exists. In poetry—as in well-written prose—rhythm has definite purposes.

First, rhythm is used because it is enjoyable for its own sake. Think of the pleasure young children get from nursery rhymes. And on all the sidewalks of America children jump rope to chants such as the one in the next column.

satire

"I remember when you could crawl through this desert and feel safe even at three o'clock in the morning. . . ."

1. According to the cartoon, why is it no longer safe to crawl through the desert?

2. Do you think the cartoonist intended this cartoon to be taken literally? Why or why not?

3. What social problem is the cartoonist commenting on?

The author of the poem below is commenting on a different kind of social problem:

The Ingredients of Expedience

There's a new recipe for water
That's caught on to such a degree
I now pass it on to others
The way it was passed on to me:
5 Into an ocean of fluids
    Add a roentgen of fallout or two,
    Aluminum cans, detergents
    (With the phosphates most pleasing to you).
    Stir in ground glass, melted plastics,
10 Any leftovers, sewage, rough waste.
    Thicken with chemical acids
    And mix to a pliable paste:
    Mercury, mustard or nerve gas
    Well blended with plenty of oil,
15 Insecticides, powdered or liquid,
    Then slowly bring all to a boil.
    That's it. Oh, yes, one reminder—
    And forgive me for throwing a curve—
    Fish die, but children prefer it
20 If you cool before you serve.

                      Henry Gibson

1. According to the poem, what is the "new recipe for water"?

2. What is the poet's attitude toward this new kind of water?

3. *Expedience* means "personal advantage" or "self-interest." Who might benefit by having water like that described in the poem?

A literary work in which the author makes fun of the vices or follies of society is called a *satire*. A satire can deal with almost any subject, from minor human absurdity (the existence of a particular clothing fad, for example) to major social and political problems (crime, pollution, the futility of war). But all satire has one thing in common: it uses humor, which may range from light-hearted to bitter, to comment on the weakness of people and society.

The purpose of much satire is to draw people's attention to serious social problems and to encourage people to think or act in a certain way. What is the author of "The Ingredients of Expedience" satirizing? How is he trying to influence readers' ideas about the state of our water supply?

Sometimes the language, style, or ideas of a literary work are mimicked for satiric or comic effect. This is called *parody* (par′ə dē).

Read the following parody of a Greek myth and answer the questions that come after:

Endremia and Liason
(From the Greek Mythology)

Endremia was the daughter of Polygaminous, the God of Ensilage, and Reba, the Goddess of Licorice. She was the child of a most unhappy union, it later turned out, for when she was a tiny child her father struck her mother with an anvil and turned himself into a lily pad to avoid the vengeance of Jove. But Jove was too sly for Polygaminous and struck him with a bolt of lightning the size of the Merchants Bank Building which threw him completely off his balance so that he toppled over into a chasm and was dashed to death.

In the meantime, Little Endremia found herself alone in the world with nobody but Endrocine, the Goddess of Lettuce, and her son Bilax, the God of Gum Arabic, to look after her. But, as Polygaminous (her father; have you forgotten so soon, you dope?) had turned Endremia into a mushroom before he turned himself into a lily pad, neither of her guardians knew who she was, so their protection did her no good.

But Jove had not so soon forgotten the daughter of his favorite (Reba), and appeared to her one night in the shape of a mushroom gatherer. He asked her how she would like to get off that tree (she was one of those mushrooms which grow on trees) and get into his basket. Endremia, not knowing that it was Jove who was asking her, said not much. Whereupon Jove unloosed his mighty wrath and struck down the whole tree with a bolt of lightning which he had brought with him in case Endremia wouldn't listen to reason.

This is why it is never safe to eat the mushrooms which grow on trees, or to refuse to get into Jove's basket.

Robert Benchley

1. Compare ''Endremia and Liason'' to other Greek myths you have read. Is the style similar? the characters? the plot? How is it different?

2. In your opinion, what purpose did the author have in mind in writing ''Endremia and Liason''?

satire

A literary work in which the author ridicules the vices or follies of people and society, usually for the purpose of producing some change in attitude or action. In *parody,* the language, style, or ideas of another literary work are mimicked for comic or satiric effect.

Apply to "**Phaëthon**" on page 444

setting

Below is the first paragraph of a short story. Read it and answer the questions that follow:

One sunny afternoon in the autumn of the year 1861 a soldier lay in a clump of laurel by the side of a road in western Virginia. He lay at full length upon his stomach, his feet resting upon the toes, his head upon the left forearm. His extended right hand loosely grasped his rifle. But for . . . a slight rhythmic movement of the cartridge box at the back of his belt he might have been thought to be dead. He was asleep at his post of duty . . . if detected he would be dead shortly afterward, death being the just and legal penalty of his crime.

Ambrose Bierce, from ''A Horseman in the Sky''

1. Where does the story take place? What details tell you this?

2. When do the events of this story take place? What clues indicate that the Civil War is going on?

The time and place in which the events of a narrative occur form what is called the *setting.* The place may be a region, a city or town, or even a house or room. The time may be a period in history, a particular time of year, or a certain time of day. In some narratives, the setting is specific and detailed, as in the paragraph above, but in others, it may be intentionally obscure:

The stranger rode slowly into the dusty town. His wide-brimmed Stetson was pulled forward on his head, casting a shadow over his gaunt face. The sunlight sparkled on his spurs and on the handle of his gun which hung casually by his right side. He headed straight for the stagecoach office and reined his horse.

1. Where does this event take place? What details tell you this?

2. In approximately what period of history does this event occur? How do you know?

Soon after the successful lift-off, Mission Control received its first communication from the spacecraft *Encounter.* ''All systems are GO,'' reported Astronaut Jake Lewis, whose voice came in loud and clear. ''Next stop—the planet Mars!''

1. Where does this take place? How do you know?

2. In approximately what period does it take place? What details tell you this?

"Land ho!" shouted the lookout to the other Vikings. "To the starboard beam, about three miles off!"

1. Where does this take place? How do you know?

2. Is there any indication of time of day? of time in history? Explain.

In some narratives the description of setting is either brief or merely suggested through the use of details scattered throughout the story. An author can suggest the setting by references to articles of clothing, famous historical figures, well-known landmarks, or through the dialect and speech patterns of the characters. Not all stories have a setting in which both the time and place are identifiable.

Frequently a setting which is presented in detail forms an important part of the narrative. It may have an effect on the events of the PLOT; it may reveal character; or it may create a certain MOOD or atmosphere, as in the following example:

At Santa Ysabel del Mar the season was at one of those moments when the air rests quiet over land and sea. The old breezes were gone; the new ones were not yet risen. The flowers in the mission garden opened wide; no wind came by day or night to shake the loose petals from their stems. Along the basking, silent, many-colored shore gathered and lingered the crisp odors of the mountains. The dust hung golden and motionless long after the rider was behind the hill, and the Pacific lay like a floor of sapphire, whereon to walk beyond the setting sun into the East.[1] One white sail shone there. Instead of an hour, it had been from dawn till afternoon in sight between the short headlands; and the Padre[2] had hoped that it might be the ship his homesick heart awaited. But it had slowly passed. From an arch in his garden cloisters he was now watching the last of it. Presently it was gone, and the great ocean lay empty.

Owen Wister, from "Padre Ignacio"

1. What is the setting of this excerpt?

2. How does setting affect the Padre?

3. What effect does the author create in this paragraph?

4. What specific words and phrases help to create this effect?

setting

The time and place in which the events of a narrative occur. The setting may be specific and detailed and introduced at the very beginning of the story, or it may be merely suggested through the use of details scattered throughout the story. In some stories the setting is vital to the narrative: it may have an effect on the events of the PLOT, reveal character, or create a certain atmosphere. In other stories the setting is relatively unimportant: the story could happen almost anywhere or at any time.

1. *East,* here, the Orient.
2. *Padre* (päʹ drā), father. It is used as a name for a priest, especially in regions where Spanish is spoken.

Apply to "**Top Man**" on page 54

simile

My heart is like an apple-tree
    Whose boughs are bent with thick-set fruit. . . .

           Christina Rossetti, from ''A Birthday''

And the muscles of his brawny arms
    Are strong as iron bands.

        Henry Wadsworth Longfellow,
        from ''The Village Blacksmith''

In both examples above, comparisons are made. What things are being compared in each? What word in each example tells you that a comparison is being made?

A *simile,* one type of FIGURATIVE LANGUAGE, is a stated comparison between two things that are really very different but that share some common quality. To create a vivid picture, a writer points out the quality they share. Similes are introduced by the use of *like* or *as.* If you were to say ''Jason runs *like* the wind and is *as* strong as an ox,'' you would be using similes. You would be indicating comparisons between Jason's speed and the speed of the wind, and Jason's strength and the strength of an ox.

One important thing to remember is that statements comparing things that are essentially alike are not similes. Ordinary statements such as ''She looks like her mother'' or ''She skates as well as I do'' are not similes. A simile reveals a similar quality in two elements that are otherwise different. Is ''They came dressed like their favorite literary characters'' a simile? Why or why not?

simile (sim′ə lē)

A figure of speech that involves a direct comparison between two unlike things, usually with the words *like* or *as.*

Apply to ''**The Base Stealer**'' on page 52

stereotype

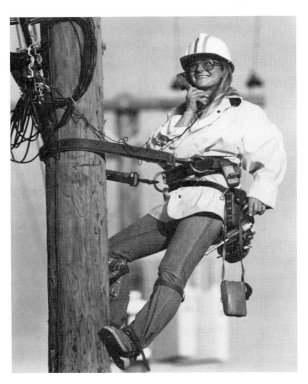

Does anything surprise you about this photograph? Although it has become more and more common to see women working at jobs that traditionally have been done by men, it still may be unusual to see women working at physically demanding jobs like this one. Perhaps some people expect to see instead a strong-looking man with a tough manner. These people have a fixed idea, or *stereotype,* in their minds of what a typical repairperson looks and acts like.

Stereotypes are helpful to the cartoonist who wants to make us laugh through a simple sketch, to the author who wishes to create a character in as few words as possible, and to the television or film writer who has only a limited time to spend on characterization. Each relies upon commonly held generalizations to characterize a person, group, issue, etc. Always remember, however, that stereotyped characters lack individuality and that they have no distinguishing traits except those expected of the larger group to which they belong. For example, in fairy tales, the courageous, handsome, and charming prince is a stereotype. You have probably been exposed so often to this stereotype that every time you encounter a prince in your reading you may still *expect* him to be handsome, courageous, and charming, unless the author specifically tells you differently.

Read the following descriptions of stereotyped characters. Then from the choices listed, choose the one that fits the stereotype:

1. wears white hat; rides the range; seldom talks; best friend is horse. **(a)** farmer; **(b)** cowboy; **(c)** gambler; **(d)** rancher's daughter.

2. young and attractive; wears frilly clothes; reacts to a mouse or crawling insect by screaming or fainting. **(a)** model; **(b)** gangster's girlfriend; **(c)** child; **(d)** maiden in distress.

3. rides in a limousine; wears a lot of jewelry; throws large, elegant parties. **(a)** nurse; **(b)** airline pilot; **(c)** movie star; **(d)** judge.

PLOTS or situations may also be stereotyped. While watching television you may have had the feeling at some time that you have seen a program before, although the names and characters have been changed. Stereotyped situations or plots include those that have become trite or uninteresting from overuse, such as the disabled airplane with at least one ill passenger or the widow who fights to save the ranch. Can you name other stereotyped plots?

Stereotypes can be misleading and potentially damaging if they lead a reader to accept certain highly generalized views about *real* people and situations. In real life, people and situations are much more complicated.

---

stereotype (ster′ē ə tīp′)

A fixed, generalized idea about a character or situation. An example of a stereotyped character might be the wicked stepmother in fairy tales; a stereotyped situation might be a plot about a small boy and his brave dog.

Apply to "**The Ugly Duckling**" on page 98

What does this picture of an eagle suggest to you? If your answer is the United States or perhaps a quality such as courage, strength, or independence, you recognize the eagle as a *symbol.* A symbol may be an object, a person, an action, a situation—anything that suggests a meaning beyond its obvious meaning.

While some symbols suggest the same thing to most people (the heart is a universal symbol of love), other symbols have different meanings for different people. What might a gun symbolize to a hunter? a thief? a soldier?

Characters in literature often have personal symbols. You can recognize them by noting the objects, persons, or situations for which a character shows strong feelings. Watch for the repetition of an object or an action. In "Fifteen," for example, the motorcycle seems to be a symbol to the speaker of challenge and discovery; in "Top Man," Osborn places the ice ax on the mountain's summit as a symbol of his respect for Nace.

Look for the symbols in the two poems that follow:

I Saw a Man Pursuing the Horizon

I saw a man pursuing the horizon;
Round and round they sped.
I was disturbed at this;
I accosted the man.
5 "It is futile," I said.
"You can never——"
"You lie," he cried,
And ran on.

Stephen Crane

1. Explain how the horizon in "I Saw a Man. . ." symbolizes a goal.

2. In what ways might pursuing the horizon symbolize trying to achieve an impossible goal? In what ways might pursuing the horizon symbolize industriousness and persistence?

In the poem that follows, the road is more than just a road. Read the poem carefully and answer the questions that come after:

Uphill

Does the road wind uphill all the way?
    Yes, to the very end.
Will the day's journey take the whole long day?
    From morn to night, my friend.

But is there for the night a resting place?
5   A roof for when the slow dark hours begin.
May not the darkness hide it from my face?
    You cannot miss that inn.

Shall I meet other wayfarers at night?
10   Those who have gone before.
Then must I knock, or call when just in sight?
    They will not keep you standing at that door.

Shall I find comfort, travel-sore and weak?
    Of labor you shall find the sum.
15 Will there be beds for me and all who seek?
    Yea, beds for all who come.

Christina Rossetti

1. What kind of "journey" do you think is being discussed?

2. What does each of the following elements represent: **(a)** the road; **(b)** the uphill climb; **(c)** the day; **(d)** the night; **(e)** the journey's end; **(f)** the inn; **(g)** the other wayfarers?

symbol

A person, place, event, or object that has a meaning in itself but suggests other meanings as well.

Apply to "**Caged Bird**" on page 119

theme

About Crows

The old crow is getting slow.
    The young crow is not.
Of what the young crow does not know
    The old crow knows a lot.

5 At knowing things the old crow
    Is still the young crow's master.
What does the slow old crow not know?
    How to go faster.

The young crow flies above, below,
10   And rings around the slow old crow.
What does the fast young crow not know?
    Where to go.

John Ciardi

1. What is the chief characteristic of the young crow in this poem? What is the chief characteristic of the old crow?

2. What accounts for the differences between the two crows?

3. Is this poem only about birds? Could the comment the speaker makes about youth and age be applied to people as well? Explain.

4. Which of the following statements best expresses the main idea of the poem? **(a)** Youthful enthusiasm is often a poor substitute for the wisdom of experience. **(b)** Don't expend too much energy without having a destination in mind. **(c)** Although the young crow can fly much faster than the old crow, the young crow does not know in which direction to go.

The main idea of a literary work is called the *theme*. The theme, or main idea, of the poem above is best expressed in statement **a.**

Statement **b** presents a moral: it tells the reader how to act. It is not the theme because the poem does not tell the reader how to act or behave.

Statement **c** gives the PLOT of the poem, not the theme. A plot is the pattern of events—the "what specifically happens"—in a poem or narrative. For example, the plot of a story might concern a young soldier during his first battle. The events of the plot might include the man's thoughts before the battle; the battle itself and what the young man thinks, feels, and does during the battle; and the outcome of the battle and the young man's new impressions of war.

The theme of such a story might be the idea that fighting solves nothing. This theme might not be stated anywhere in the story but it will be suggested through the events of the plot and the attitudes of the characters.

It is important also to recognize the difference between the *theme* of a literary work and the *subject* of a literary work. The subject is the topic on which an author has chosen to write. The theme, however, makes some statement about or expresses some opinion on that topic. For instance, in the above example the subject of the story might be war while the theme of the story might be the idea that war is futile.

Not every literary work has a theme. Some are written purely to entertain the reader. A mystery story, for example, written primarily to keep the reader in suspense, may not have a theme.

theme

The main idea or underlying meaning of a literary work. A theme may be stated or implied. Theme differs from the *subject,* or topic, of a literary work in that it involves a statement or opinion about the topic. Not every literary work has a theme.

Apply to "**The Greatest Gift**" on page 318

Afoot and light-hearted I take to the open road,
Healthy, free, the world before me,
The long, brown path before me leading wherever
   I choose.
Henceforth I ask not good-fortune, I myself
   am good-fortune.
5 Henceforth I whimper no more, postpone no
   more, need nothing,
Done with indoor complaints, libraries,
   querulous criticisms.
Strong and content I travel the open road.

    Walt Whitman, from "Song of the Open Road"

1. Does the speaker regret leaving the indoors? Explain.

2. What is this poem about? What might the "open road" represent?

3. What is the speaker's attitude as he sets forth? What words and phrases convey his attitude?

To achieve a complete understanding of most literary works, you must determine how the author feels about the subject. An author's attitude toward the subject is called *tone*. The tone of a literary work serves the same basic purpose as a tone of voice; it helps to indicate the speaker's attitude, whether it is one of anger, sadness, amusement, joy, defiance, or some other emotion. The tone may, in fact, reflect a combination of several different emotions.

Sometimes an author will state directly how he or she feels about a character, a situation, or an idea. The speaker in the poem, for example, states that he feels "light-hearted," "healthy," "free," "strong," and "content." The attitude, or tone, of Whitman's poem is one of enthusiasm and joyful optimism. Read the following novel excerpt to see whether you can determine the author's attitude toward the subject:

It was Miss Murdstone who was arrived, and a gloomy-looking lady she was; dark, like her brother, whom she greatly resembled in face and voice, and with very heavy eyebrows, nearly meeting over her large nose. She brought with her two uncompromising hard black boxes, with her initials on the lids

in hard brass nails. When she paid the coachman she took her money out of a hard steel purse, and she kept the purse in a very jail of a bag which hung upon her arm by a heavy chain, and shut up like a bite. It seemed that there had never been such a metallic lady altogether as Miss Murdstone was.

Charles Dickens, from David Copperfield

1. (a) What sort of woman is being described in this paragraph? Cite specific words that the author uses to describe her. **(b)** How do her possessions contribute to the picture of this woman?

2. (a) What is the author's attitude toward the woman? How do you know? **(b)** Is this attitude stated or implied?

In most literary works the author's attitude will not be stated directly, as it is in the excerpt from Whitman's "Song of the Open Road," but will be suggested through the author's choice of words and details. In the paragraph above, for example, Charles Dickens never states that this character is not likable. However, by describing her and her possessions as "gloomy-looking," "dark," "uncompromising," and "metallic," he implies his opinion of her and draws the reader into sharing his attitude.

tone

The author's attitude, stated or implied, toward a subject. Some possible attitudes are earnestness, seriousness, bitterness, humor, sympathy, indignation, whimsicality, joy, mockery, cynicism, and irony. An author's tone can be revealed through choice of words and details. Tone should not be confused with MOOD, which is the climate of feeling within a literary work. For example, an author may create a mood of mystery around a character or setting but may treat that character or setting in an ironic, serious, or humorous tone.

Apply to "The Ransom of Red Chief" on page 274

Composition Guide

How can you become a better writer? It takes practice. It also takes the awareness that the process of writing begins long before you sit down to write, and that it does not end until you have revised, edited, and proofread your composition. This Guide offers practical advice for writing many of the composition assignments in this book. It is not meant as a complete course in how to write. But the articles do provide useful tips and techniques you can apply to the kinds of composition assignments that accompany selections in this text. You will find that the general approach—as well as many of the specific suggestions—apply to other kinds of writing as well.

This Guide includes the following articles:

Getting Started

If you are like many others, you may think that the hardest part of writing is getting started in the first place. Perhaps you have in mind all the things you know you must do— come up with ideas, organize them, and get them down on paper. And you know that at the same time you must think about spelling, punctuation, and writing readable sentences. You may find yourself staring for many minutes at a blank piece of paper before you get up enough courage to write that first word—only to cross it out and start again. The solution is simple. Try not to think of your composition as one enormous job, but as a collection of little jobs—each one small enough that you know you can handle it. Here are some steps that you can take one at a time:

1. Understand the assignment. Ask questions if you don't. Pay particular attention to what the assignment calls for you to do. If, for example, you are supposed to discuss the figurative language in a selection, be sure you understand what the different types of figurative language are and how they operate. A "character sketch" calls for more than just a physical description; you will want to include character traits as well—and perhaps some speeches and actions that reveal those traits. If the assignment suggests a topic sentence for you to agree or disagree with, be sure you understand the meaning of that sentence. The other articles in this Guide contain suggestions on how to approach different types of assignments.

2. Think it over. If your composition isn't due for several days, take one or two of those days to think about what you're going to write. This doesn't mean one or two days of putting it off, but of thinking about your assignment from as many different angles as you can. If the assignment asks you to take a position or form a conclusion, do so now—but with the idea that you may need to change your mind later as you write or revise. Use this time also to become thoroughly familiar with your subject. Most of the assignments in this book are based in some way on selections you have read. Don't be misled into believing that since you have read through a selection once, you know it. Reread it—carefully. And maybe reread it again. You will find yourself reading in a different way and responding to different things. You will probably find yourself understanding more now that you have a specific goal.

3. Jot down ideas. Anything that occurs to you while thinking about your assignment or talking it over in class discussions or with friends may be useful. Jot it down. Also write down any new things you notice about a selection as you reread it. Don't try for any order in these notes; don't even worry about complete sentences. Just be sure you can understand what you had in mind.

4. Plan ahead. Organize your paper—at least in your head. An outline of sorts does help. Your outline doesn't have to be formal. For a short paper, a list of three or four main points may be just enough. Such a list not only helps you make sure to cover all the points you

want to cover, but it helps you decide how to organize them as well.

5. Consider your audience. You vary your speaking style as you talk to a friend, a child, a parent. Your tone of voice varies as you borrow a pen, explain how to get to the post office, or tell a joke. The same is true of your writing. Is your composition meant to be read by your teacher, by other students, or perhaps by some imaginary person? Your audience will influence your tone, vocabulary, choice of details, and a great deal more.

6. Write a rough draft. Plan from the start that you will *not* hand in your first version. This will free you from worry about neatness, correctness, and trying to be brilliant, all at once. And the feeling of freedom will help you get your ideas down on paper. If you can't think of a first sentence, start with the second sentence—or with the second paragraph. Above all, save a title for the last. Try to write as quickly as you can to keep a flow of words going. Refer to your plan from time to time to be sure you're including important points. Since no one else will see your first draft, you can start sentences over, insert things or move things around, even write notes to yourself on how you will fix things later.

Looking It Over

You have now gotten down on paper your ideas in sentence form, and you have been helped in this process by not worrying about grammar, usage, mechanics, or how well you were expressing yourself. Now, however, is the time to deal with these equally important parts of composition.

One very helpful trick is to let your composition rest for a while. Put it away for a day or so if you can—or even overnight. That

way you can come back to it with fresh eyes. Furthermore, the more "distance" you can put between yourself and your writing, the less sensitive you will be about cutting and rewriting.

1. Give your paper a critical "once-over." First, quickly read through your paper. If possible, read it aloud to get a sense of the flow of language and ideas. Then, go back

through it in more detail. As you examine your rough draft, consider the following points:
- Is the main idea of the paper clearly stated (probably in the first paragraph)?
- Does the paper have a definite sense of moving from one thing to another and ending with the most important ideas?
- Are the opening and closing paragraphs forceful and interesting? Is the last paragraph a conclusion to what has gone before, or is it merely a restatement of the first paragraph or a summary of points?
- Has each paragraph been given its appropriate weight and developed in sufficient detail? Generally speaking, your paragraphs should be approximately the same length, although an occasional short paragraph may provide dramatic contrast.
- Are your examples and details clear? Do they all relate directly to your purpose? Is each one necessary?
- Have you used transition words (*first, next, on the other hand, as a result*) to show how your ideas are related?
- Does your composition completely fulfill the assignment? (Reread your original assignment to make sure.)

2. Revise. Writers tend to fall in love with their own words and hesitate to change them. Try to be objective—ruthless, if necessary. Be prepared to cut words or phrases that are repetitious or wordy (*at this point in time* instead of *now; due to the fact that* instead of *because*). Cut also details and examples that may be interesting but that are not to the point.

As you revise and rewrite, you can change the position of sentences or even paragraphs by drawing arrows. You can "flesh out" sentences that seem weak and paragraphs that seem incomplete. Keep in mind your purpose, which is to fulfill your assignment to the best of your ability. If necessary, write a second draft.

3. Edit. Now concern yourself with sentence structure, grammar, punctuation, and the like.

Go over your paper once again sentence by sentence. Consider the following points:
- Is each sentence clear and complete? Will each word and phrase be understandable to your readers?
- Have you used strong verbs and precise nouns wherever possible? Have you used a string of descriptive words where one or two carefully chosen words would be more effective?
- Have you used too many *and*'s? Have you repeated sentence patterns over and over, so that they become monotonous? Consider what sentences could be combined to reduce choppiness or better show relationships. Consider what sentences could be varied in structure so that they don't always follow the subject-verb pattern. Here are some other possible patterns:
- "Cautiously she opened the door . . ."
- "Sparkling and delicate, the snowflake . . ."
- "Down the stairs thumped the dog . . ."

4. Proofread. After you have copied your paper in its final form, your last task before handing it in is to proofread to catch any errors that remain or that might have slipped in. Again, letting the paper rest a bit will give you a fresher view of it and make you a more efficient proofreader.

Read slowly, word by word. You may find it helpful to use a ruler or a card with a narrow slot cut in it to help you focus on only one line or a few words at a time. Check carefully for errors in grammar, mechanics, and usage.
- Are all words spelled correctly? Be sure you haven't switched any letters around. (Use a dictionary if you're not sure.)
- Is your punctuation logical and helpful in making meaning clear? Have you used quotation marks correctly?
- Have you checked pronouns and verbs for common errors, such as faulty agreement, incorrect pronoun form or reference, or incorrect form of the verb?
- Can you spot any errors in word choice or usage?

Describing a Person or a Place

You have probably described hundreds of things in your life: what you wanted for your birthday; how beautiful your vacation spot was; what kind of person your new neighbor is. But now you have an assignment to *write* a description. Where should you begin, and what should you say?

A written description is meant to create a picture in a reader's mind, and that reader will probably be more interested in the person or place you are describing if your description gives some sort of main impression. Here are some guidelines to help you create that picture and make that impression:

1. Form a picture in your mind. Try to visualize the person or place in as much detail as you can. Put yourself in the picture as well: where are you in relation to what you are going to describe? Imagine yourself moving through the place or relating in some way to the person.

2. Get a general impression. No two people and no two things are exactly alike—what makes *this* one special? What in particular do you want your reader to see and feel? What sort of mood do you want to create?

If you are describing a place such as a house, consider what makes that house unlike every other house in the neighborhood. Perhaps it is dilapidated and falling to ruin; perhaps it has some odd architectural feature. Does it make you feel sad, happy, mysterious, or what? The mood it puts you in *could* be the main impression that you create with your description.

If you are describing a person, your main impression might have to do with how you react to that person—whether a real person or a character in a story. Or, if you are writing about a character, your main impression might reflect the key point of the story: "In many ways Emma Hu is a typical high-school senior, but her actions are nevertheless influenced by her Chinese background''; ''Although Lemon Brown looks and acts like an old derelict, his secret 'treasure' gives him a sense of dignity and worth.''

3. List details from your picture. Now start listing details, those bits and pieces of your mental picture that stand out the most. As you list them, group details that seem to have something in common. Keep in mind that you want to *show* what your subject is like. Don't simply tell that a fairground is lively and fun, for example; demonstrate that it is by including details from all five senses:
• The *sight* of the hundreds of flickering lights and the Ferris wheel going round and round
• The *sound* of music playing and barkers calling
• The *smell* of cotton candy, hot dogs, and popcorn
• The *taste* of an ice-cold cola
• The *feel* of the warm night air, the sawdust underfoot, and people jostling each other

If you had trouble before in deciding on a main impression, just start listing as many details about your subject as you can. Then take a look at what you have. Does any certain kind of detail seem to stand out? If so, then that aspect of your subject that you are already paying most attention to might very well be your main impression.

4. Choose a method of presentation. Even though you already have a main impression and details that contribute to it, you still have some choice in how you will ''frame'' your picture. (If you were filming a movie, this would be similar to choosing a camera angle.) Suppose you are writing about an old house. You might group your details in time order, describing the house when it is new and then when it is old and falling apart. Or, you might describe it from front to back, as your eye takes it in. Or, you might describe it first from a distance and then gradually move closer and closer, revealing more and more details as you approach. Jot down a brief description of your method of presentation to use as an outline for writing.

5. Create the picture. No matter whether your subject is one that seems complex ("my uncle, a very funny person") or one that seems simple and straightforward ("my hall locker, a garbage dump"), you will not be able to include every detail in your composition. As you write, choose especially those details that will contribute to the main impression you want your reader to get. In "Cress to the Rescue" the narrator gives only a brief physical description of Edwin Kibbler, Jr. Yet the reader receives a strong impression of the kind of person he is from how he acts, what little he says, and how others react to him.

Choose your descriptive words carefully, as well. Most is not necessarily best. "It was a cold, wet, gusty, bleak, dark, overcast morning" may seem thorough, but one or two well-chosen words will often make your point much better: "It was a wet, nasty morning." Comparisons and figurative language can be very useful here. For example, "The plowed fields formed a checkerboard across the land" may tell a reader more about their appearance than several paragraphs of description. And "The harsh wind sandpapered his skin" suggests not only what is happening but how the character feels about it. You might also personalize objects or places to seem like human beings: "Laughing, the sunlight danced on the water"; "the branches of the tree waved goodbye to us . . ." Try to use new and original combinations and to avoid old, worn-out expressions. If you have heard a comparison used often before, try to avoid it in your writing.

6. Don't just stop—finish. Round off your description with a sentence or two that give a sense of completion, such as one of the following:
• Summary: "Everything about him suggested anger."
• Opinion: "The sheer variety of scenery in our area is astonishing."
• Question: "Who wouldn't have fallen in love with such an endearing kitten?"
• Memory: "To this day, in my mind and heart, she is waving after us gently and sadly."

If you haven't before stated in words your main impression, do it here.

Telling About an Event or an Experience

". . . And then what happened?" We tell each other stories every day: a joke, something that happened at school, the plot of a movie. These stories are made up of connected events or experiences—one thing which leads to another which leads to another. You must know some people who seem to have the knack of telling stories in a way to make you want to listen. Here are some suggestions to help you improve your story-telling abilities:

1. Decide on an event or experience. This may sound simple enough, but before you decide, ask yourself: "Why am I telling this story?" Perhaps you simply want to amuse or entertain your reader. Fine—a lot of stories do no more than that. Ask yourself further, though: "Will my audience care about what happened?" It is up to you to make them care.

If you are writing about literature, your purpose is especially important. You may need to summarize events that lead up to a certain point in a selection you have read. To demonstrate your understanding of a character, you may need to describe the experience that influenced that character's life the most; for example: "Larry's involvement with the hawk, Joey, had a great effect on him." Or, you may need to tell about an event or experience of your own that is similar to something you just read about. In any event, the reasons you have for telling the story will influence the way you tell it.

2. Arrange events in order. Make a list of the key events or high points that ought to be mentioned. Put them in the proper chronological (time) order so that you can keep them straight in your mind. For the most part, you should tell the events in the order that they happened to avoid confusing your reader (and yourself).

3. Decide on a "time frame." Charles Dickens began his novel *David Copperfield* with a chapter entitled, "I Am Born." In most of your writing, however, you will not be telling everything that happened in your life or in a character's life. Think for a moment about short stories and novels you have read. Although the connected events may go back for years, writers very often choose to begin their stories somewhere in the middle so that they can include the major events—those most meaningful to the characters—without wasting too much time getting to the "action." Decide how far back you need to go in order to include all the events that are necessary to your narrative.

4. Make your characters and actions clear. As you begin telling your story, establish as

quickly as possible who your characters are and what their relationships are to each other. If the setting is important to what happens, establish that quickly, too. Be sure to make clear what the characters are doing and why they are doing these things. If events that happened earlier are important to understanding, decide when you will mention them and in how much detail. Often a simple summary will be quite enough. For events that need more elaboration, many writers use flashbacks. If you use a flashback, be sure to signal it clearly: "He thought back to when he was seven years old, to the incident that first kindled his love for music." Your writing should sound as if you are in control of what you are relating, not as if you are saying, "Oh, I forgot to mention that before she went to the airport . . ."

Don't feel you need to tell every single thing that happens. "Jean drove to work" or even "Later, at work, Jean . . ." may be more effective than "Jean went to the garage, got out her car, got in it, and drove off, heading for work . . ." On the other hand, important events may not necessarily be just big events. Does it matter that a character in a story has bacon and eggs for breakfast? Maybe it does. Maybe every other day that character had only a glass of juice, so this new breakfast may signal some change in the character's life. Remembering your purpose for writing will help you decide if an event is meaningful enough to include.

5. Keep up the interest level. One way to do this is to use a variety of techniques:
• Help the reader visualize characters and setting through description. But if the events are more important than the scene, keep descriptions brief.
• Show the reactions of other people. Did they react the same way you or your character reacted? Why or why not?
• Use some dialogue. Instead of telling about all the events as a narrator, let your characters

show their emotions, reactions, etc. through their speech. You can even use dialogue to suggest action: "Oops! Well, don't worry—catsup doesn't stain *too* badly, and anyway, that color goes well with your shirt." If you are writing about literature, dialogue can help you prove your point; for example: "The narrator in 'My Teacher, the Hawk' confesses, 'To say he never forgave me is one thing. To say I've never forgiven myself is another.' That one line proves that Larry will never forget the hawk." And your use of that quote helps prove that you understood the story.

• Use lively verbs and exact nouns. "He said" can get boring after a while. Try "He answered . . . shouted . . . whispered . . . sighed . . . mumbled . . . ," etc.

• Keep subjects active where possible. "I painted the steps," not "The steps were painted by me." "Susan received the package," not "The package was received by Susan."

• Use connecting words of time and movement. *At the same time, afterwards, immediately, then, suddenly, while* are all connecting words that can give the reader a sense of movement.

• Vary sentence length and construction. But avoid short, choppy sentences as well as long sentences that string too many events together at once.

6. Conclude your story. A successful narrative builds to some sort of climax—a peak of interest or excitement. You can just stop there, of course, but some sort of conclusion will help round out the story, give you a chance to comment upon it, and remind the reader why you're telling the story in the first place. Here are some possible conclusions:

• A summary of the experience: "We all agreed we'd had enough fudge to last us for the rest of our lives."

• An ironic comment: "On the whole, after experiencing that wild roller-coaster ride down the mountainside with our faulty brakes, I prefer the merry-go-round."

• A statement of determination for the future: " 'Remind me,' said Bruce, heading out the door, 'never to ask you for a favor again!' "

• An appropriate saying, quotation, or proverb: "It was all further proof of the old saying, 'People who live in glass houses shouldn't throw stones.' "

• Your own reaction to the story: "If I had been Cress Delahanty, I wouldn't have offered to pay for Edwin's teeth."

Supporting a Point

Certain kinds of composition assignments ask you to express an opinion and to defend it: "What causes the downfall of the man in 'To Build a Fire'? Is it fate, bad luck, inexperience, cold weather, foolishness, or something else? Support your opinion with details from the story." In compositions of this sort, your main job is to persuade your reader that your opinion is right. Here are some suggestions on how to go about it:

1. Go to the source. In most cases, the source will be the literary selection itself. Don't

form any opinions or come to any conclusions until you have reread the story, poem, or play in question and have carefully considered your reaction to it.

2. State your point. Often you can make use of words or phrases in the assignment itself to put your conclusion into sentence form. State your opinion clearly and forcefully: "The downfall of the man was caused not by fate or cold or accident, but by his own foolishness." (Not: "It seems to me that maybe the man's downfall . . .") This statement may eventually serve as your opening or closing sentence, but for now it will help you focus on your evidence.

3. List your evidence. List everything you can find or think of that supports, or "proves," your statement. Include facts, details, reasons, inferences, opinions, and quotations. Don't fuss with how they are worded (except that facts should be accurate and quotations should be exact), and don't try to organize them at this point. Just get them down on paper. Often this process is called *brainstorming*.

4. Sift your evidence. Select the strongest and most convincing items from your list. You will find that your best evidence will be clear details from the selection:
• Man "without imagination"
• "Not given much to thinking"
• "This man did not know cold"
• Ignored advice of old timer at Sulphur Creek
• "It was his own fault or, rather, his mistake"

Your weakest evidence will be unsupported opinions: "The man failed because he was inexperienced. Greenhorns are always careless and overconfident." This opinion is itself rather careless. Not only can it be dismissed rather easily (many inexperienced people are overly cautious), but it draws you and your reader away from, rather than into, the selection.

5. Take a look at the other side. Before you begin your first draft ask yourself: "What's the best evidence *against* my viewpoint? Why doesn't this evidence change my mind?" (It's always possible that you *will* change your mind. No harm done. Go back to the evidence and rethink your position.)

If your composition is to be several paragraphs or longer, it's an excellent idea to include some discussion of opposing evidence early in your own argument: "It is true that an accident—breaking through the ice—starts the death struggle for the man. But by that time he has ignored so many danger signs that disaster

is sure to happen. He has an 'accident' in the same sense that a blindfolded driver speeding through rush-hour traffic would have an 'accident.' "

By openly dealing with opposing evidence, you show your reader you're smart enough to see other sides to a question, fair enough to consider them, and confident enough to overcome them. Keep such a discussion short and to the point, however: state it, deal with it, and then forget it.

6. Arrange your evidence. Present your evidence in order of importance, saving the best for last. This allows your argument to build momentum and guarantees a strong conclusion.

7. Explain your evidence. A quotation or other reference to a selection is not proof until you make it so. Make sure your reader understands how your evidence relates to your point. Asking yourself, "So what?" about each supporting detail is better than having your reader ask, "So what?" later.

Avoid the common mistake of focusing on details that may be interesting but that are not important ("The man grew a 'beard' of tobacco-stained ice"). Avoid also the mistake of lapsing into a pointless summary of the plot ("The man built a fire and ate, and then he . . ."). When you tell part of the story, you should have a definite purpose in doing so. (See "Describing an Event or an Experience" in this Guide.) In case of either mistake, a "So what?" will help get you back on the track.

8. Finish with a clincher. After you've made your best point, quickly bring your paper to a close. Summarize your evidence and restate your conclusion (but *don't* just repeat your first paragraph word for word). This may be the place to add—briefly—your own reaction to the selection: "Because the man, through his foolishness, does bring about his own downfall,

it is difficult to feel very sorry for him'';
''Although I may never travel on foot through
the frozen North, I shall certainly try to avoid
similar foolishness in the things I do.'' Your
last paragraph is *not* the place, however, to
introduce a last-minute bit of evidence or an
''I-just-thought-of-this'' point. Leave your
reader with a sense of completeness.

Finding Likenesses and Differences

''How are they alike? How are they
different?'' These two simple questions are the
ones you must answer when your writing
assignment is to find likenesses and differences
between two or more characters, incidents,
objects, ideas—or even whole selections. Other
terms that may be used are *compare* (find
likenesses) and *contrast* (find differences).
Simply finding and mentioning such points may
not be enough, however. The way you organize
your materials can have much to do with the
effectiveness of your composition. Here are
some steps you can follow in planning your
paper:

1. Examine the assignment. Be sure you
understand what is being called for. Writing
assignments may be general (''Compare Cress
Delahanty with Edwin Kibbler''), or they may
be more specific (''Compare Larry's attitude
toward wild animals and his treatment of them
with Janice Allack's in 'My Teacher, the
Hawk' ''). An assignment may ask you to
discuss only likenesses or only differences—
or both. Your composition should fulfill the
assignment exactly; it should include the
likenesses and differences called for and no
others.

2. Find points of comparison. Think of the
most important issues or categories that apply
to your subjects. For example, suppose your
assignment reads, ''Discuss the likenesses and
differences of Martin Nace and Paul Osborn as
mountaineers in 'Top Man.' '' In planning your
composition, you will have to decide whether
certain background details (where they come
from) or certain character traits (one talks a
lot, and one keeps to himself) are relevant to
their abilities *as mountaineers*. Physical
description would probably not be very
relevant, since both men must be in superb
physical condition to make such a climb in the
first place. On the other hand, age might be
relevant, since Osborn makes a point of it.
After some consideration, you might come up
with points of comparison like these:
• Background and experience
• Attitude toward climbing
• Methods
• Judgments
If the assignment were to compare two
appearances, settings, patterns of behavior,
etc., you would start with a totally different
list. You may find later that you need to drop
some points of comparison and add others, but
starting with such points will help you get
organized and keep you from comparing your
subjects in unrelated categories.

3. List details. Use your list of points of
comparison as heads for separate columns.
Then go back through the selection carefully,
listing in their appropriate columns whatever
details you think may be useful. A partial list
might look like the one on the next page.

MARTIN NACE	PAUL OSBORN

Background and experience

MARTIN NACE	PAUL OSBORN
Official in Indian Civil Service	1 year out of college
Explored & climbed in Himalayas for 20 yrs.	Many spectacular ascents in Alps & Rockies
Member of 5 British expeditions to K3	Reputation as "most skilled & audacious" of younger American climbers

Attitude

Matter of fact, cautious, slow	Overwhelming desire to act, to conquer
"The apostle of trial-and-error & watchful waiting"	Wants to take short, straight line
Utter concentration on problem at hand	Becomes irked over difference of opinion
Spirit deep inside him—patient, indomitable	Given to temper
	Thinks Nace is "through"

Methods ("utterly dissimilar")

Slow, methodical	Magnificent—peerless mountaineer
Unspectacular	Attacks mountain head on
Studies mountain, spars with it, wears it down	Always discovering new routes & short cuts

Judgments

His instant decision saves lives of men	Rashly eager
Careful approach	Doesn't want to wait & test
Saves Osborn's life	Puts his own life in danger

4. Form an opinion. Some assignments ask for your opinion; for example: "Do you think Nace or Osborn is the better mountaineer?" Now—and not before—is the time to form such an opinion, based as much as possible on the evidence you have gathered. If it is not called for in the assignment, form an opinion anyway. You might be able to use your opinion as the opening or closing of your paper. Even if you do not use it in your composition, forming your own opinion will help you sift through your details and shape your paper.

5. Pick a pattern. There are a number of ways to organize a paper of likenesses and differences. You can compare the subjects point by point, writing a sentence or two for each. For example: "In their methods the men are completely different: Osborn 'attacked the mountain, head on,' but Nace 'studied it, sparred with it, wore it down.'"

A second method is to discuss completely one of your subjects first, and then turn to the other subject. Be sure to give your subjects "equal time"; that is, use about the same amount of space for each and cover the same points of comparison.

A third method is to discuss all the likenesses of your subjects in one part of your paper and all the differences in another. No matter which pattern you choose, be aware that the material coming last in your paper will seem to have the greatest emphasis. Therefore, if you wish to emphasize the differences between your subjects, discuss the differences last.

6. Watch your balance. A paper of likenesses and differences should leave the reader with the impression that you have been fair to all the people or things you are comparing. One way to do this is to say approximately the same *number* of things about each subject. And any opinion you express should seem to be a fair one, based on the evidence. But beware of letting this balance take over your style, as well. Sentence after sentence all constructed with *but* or *on the other hand* will become boring to read. Make a particular effort to vary sentence construction and the length of sentences and paragraphs.

7. Add a conclusion. Don't just stop after you have presented all the likenesses and differences. At the very least, your conclusion should remind your reader of your purpose— why the comparison has been made. This may be the best place, also, to state your own opinion or what you have learned from the comparison.

Being Someone Else

Children do it for fun ("Now you be the bad guys, and we'll be the good guys"). Actors and actresses do it as part of their jobs. Many people do it while telling jokes ("Did you hear about the kangaroo who went up to the zoo-keeper and said . . .") or just in daily conversation. Most of us have a chance, at one time or another, to play at being someone else.

How do you go about being someone else in writing, however? To take on another personality—and do it convincingly—involves much more than just identifying the character whose speech you will deliver next ("So the kangaroo said . . . and the zoo-keeper replied . . ."). It involves making an effort to put yourself in that character's place, to think as that character would think, to react as that character would react, and to speak as that character would speak.

1. Put yourself in someone's place. The more you know about someone, the easier it is to understand how that person thinks and reacts to situations—and to predict how that person would react in a new situation. This holds true for fictional characters as well as real people. Spend some time thinking about what you know of the character's background: age, sex, education, the part of the country he or she was raised in, and so on. Make a list of these things.

Next consider what you know of the character's motivation—what makes the character do what he or she does? It may be something from inside, such as a desire to succeed or to impress others, or a wish for revenge. It may be something from outside, such as having been forbidden to leave or ordered to do a job. (In cases like this, how does your character *feel* about obeying orders?) Add to your list brief descriptions of any such motivations.

Finally, consider the situation your character is in *at this moment*. People express themselves differently in different situations. For example, what would you say if you were hanging by your hands outside the window of a burning building? What would you say later, after you had been rescued and were relaxing over a cup of soup?

2. Plan what you will say. *What* you say in your character's place may be based on an assignment ("Assume that you are Jean Fritz, writing a letter to your grandmother back in the United States and telling her about the incident at school"). In this case, you should reread the selection and make notes on exactly what did happen. Or, you may have free choice in what you say ("What do you think Princess Camilla talked about with Great-Aunt Malkin when they met in the forest? Assume that you are Great-Aunt Malkin . . ."). In this case, you will have to make up the incidents and speeches. But be sure that what you make up fits the characters and the situation. (What sorts of things do you suppose Princess Camilla and Great-Aunt Malkin *would* discuss?)

3. Plan how you will say it. Now your knowledge of the character's background comes into play. People from different backgrounds say things in different ways. If your character has speeches in the selection, study them. Does your character customarily use sentences that are long and involved or short and to the point? Does he or she use common, everyday words or unusual words? (For example, Bill in "The Ransom of Red Chief" is fond of big words but frequently misuses them.) Does your character have any peculiar speech patterns that you can copy? (For example, the Chancellor in "The Ugly Duckling" tends to ramble on and on without getting to the point.) Does your character tend to express emotions while speaking, or hide them?

Consider also the specific situation your character is in. Is he or she undergoing emotional or physical stress, or relaxing?

Actors and actresses on stage have a kind of trick to make their entrances convincing: they concentrate on where they are supposed to be coming from (not the dressing room, but the great hall of the castle) and what they were supposed to be doing (not sitting and waiting for their cues, but fighting a duel). Concentrating on the situation and what has supposedly gone on before will help you speak more convincingly for your character.

If you still have trouble thinking of what to say, you might try role-playing with a friend. Act out your character and situation, and then write down the words or speeches you used spontaneously.

4. Compare with the original. After you have completed your composition, read aloud at least part of the selection in which your character appears, and then read aloud your own words. Ask yourself these questions:
• Have you managed to capture the feeling and flow of the original?
• Do the words you have given your character resemble other words by that character?
• Are the ideas or emotions expressed consistent with what you know about that character?
• Do they seem reasonable for the specific situation?

Glossary

The pronunciation of each word is shown just after the word, in this way: **ab bre vi ate** (ə brē′vē āt). The letters and signs used are pronounced as in the words below. The mark ′ is placed after a syllable with primary or heavy accent, as in the example above. The mark ′ after a syllable shows a secondary or lighter accent, as in **ab bre vi a tion** (ə brē′vē ā′shən).

Some words, taken from foreign languages, are spoken with sounds that do not otherwise occur in English. Symbols for these sounds are given in the key as "foreign sounds."

	Full pronunciation key				

a	hat, cap	j	jam, enjoy	u	cup, butter
ā	age, face	k	kind, seek	u̇	full, put
ä	father, far	l	land, coal	ü	rule, move
		m	me, am		
b	bad, rob	n	no, in		
ch	child, much	ng	long, bring	v	very, save
d	did, red			w	will, woman
		o	hot, rock	y	young, yet
e	let, best	ō	open, go	z	zero, breeze
ē	equal, be	ô	order, all	zh	measure, seizure
ėr	term, learn	oi	oil, voice		
		ou	house, out		
f	fat, if			ə	represents:
g	go, bag	p	paper, cup		a in about
h	he, how	r	run, try		e in taken
		s	say, yes		i in pencil
i	it, pin	sh	she, rush		o in lemon
ī	ice, five	t	tell, it		u in circus
		th	thin, both		
		ᴛʜ	then, smooth		

foreign sounds

ʏ as in French *du.* Pronounce (ē) with the lips rounded as for (ü).

à as in French *ami.* Pronounce (ä) with the lips spread and held tense.

œ as in French *peu.* Pronounce (ā) with the lips rounded as for (ō).

ɴ as in French *bon.* The ɴ is not pronounced, but shows that the vowel before it is nasal.

ʜ as in German *ach.* Pronounce (k) without closing the breath passage.

	Grammatical key			

adj.	adjective	*prep.*	preposition
adv.	adverb	*pron.*	pronoun
conj.	conjunction	*v.*	verb
interj.	interjection	*v.i.*	intransitive verb
n.	noun	*v.t.*	transitive verb
sing.	singular	*pl.*	plural

-able, *suffix forming adjectives from verbs and nouns.* that can be
____ed: *Enjoyable* = that can be enjoyed.

a bode (ə bōd′), *n.* place of residence; dwelling; house or home.
—*v.* a pt. and a pp. of **abide.**

a bom i na ble (ə bom′ə nə bəl), *adj.* **1** arousing disgust and
hatred; detestable; loathsome: *Kidnapping is an abominable crime.*
2 very unpleasant; disagreeable: *abominable manners.*

a brupt (ə brupt′), *adj.* **1** characterized by sudden change;
unexpected: *an abrupt turn.* **2** very steep. **3** short or sudden in
speech or manner; blunt. [< Latin *abruptum* broken off < *ab-* off
+ *rumpere* to break] —**a brupt′ly,** *adv.*

ab scond (ab skond′), *v.i.* go away hurriedly and secretly,
especially to avoid punishment; go off and hide.

ab stract (*adj.* ab′strakt, ab strakt′; *v.* ab strakt′), *adj.* **1** thought
of apart from any particular object or actual instance; not concrete:
Sweetness is an abstract quality. **2** not representing any actual
object; having little or no resemblance to real or material things:
abstract paintings. —*v.t.* **1** take away; remove; extract: *Iron is
abstracted from ore.* **2** take away secretly, slyly, or dishonestly.
—**ab′stract ly,** *adv.*

ab surd (ab sèrd′, ab zèrd′), *adj.* plainly not true, logical, or
sensible; ridiculous. See synonym study below. [< Latin *absurdus*
out of tune, senseless] —**ab surd′ly,** *adv.* —**ab surd′ness,** *n.*
Syn. Ridiculous, absurd, preposterous mean not sensible or
reasonable. **Ridiculous** emphasizes the laughable effect produced
by something out of keeping with good sense: *Her attempts to be the
life of the party were ridiculous.* **Absurd** emphasizes inconsistency
with what is true or sensible: *His belief that he was too clever to be
caught in his crime was absurd.* **Preposterous** suggests extreme
absurdity and, often, the idea of being contrary to nature: *The child
drew a preposterous man with arms growing from his head.*

a bys mal (ə biz′məl), *adj.* **1** too deep or great to be measured;
bottomless. **2** INFORMAL. extremely bad; of very low quality.
—**a bys′mal ly,** *adv.*

a byss (ə bis′), *n.* **1** a bottomless or very great depth. **2** anything
too deep or great to be measured; lowest depth. [< Late Latin
abyssus < Greek *abyssos* < *a-* without + *byssos* bottom]

ac cede (ak sēd′), *v.i.,* -**ced ed,** -**ced ing.** **1** give in; agree;
consent *(to)*: *Please accede to my request.* **2** become a party *(to)*:
Our government acceded to the treaty.

ac claim (ə klām′), *v.t.* **1** welcome with shouts or other signs of
approval: *The crowd acclaimed the winning team.* **2** proclaim or
announce with approval: *The newspapers acclaimed the results of
the election.* [< Latin *acclamare* < *ad-* to + *clamare* cry out]

ac cli mate (ə klī′mit, ak′lə māt), *v.t., v.i.,* -**mat ed,** -**mat ing.**
accustom or become accustomed to a new climate, surroundings, or
conditions. —**ac cli ma tion** (ak′lə mā′shən), *n.*

ac cord ance (ə kôrd′ns), *n.* agreement; harmony: *in accordance with the rules.*

ac cord ing ly (ə kôr′ding lē), *adv.* in agreement with what is
expected or stated; correspondingly: *These are the rules; you can act
accordingly or leave the club.*

ac cus tomed (ə kus′təmd), *adj.* **1** usual; customary.
2 accustomed to, used to; in the habit of: *The farmer was
accustomed to hard work. She is accustomed to jogging daily.*

ac rid (ak′rid), *adj.* **1** sharp, bitter, or stinging to the mouth, eyes,
skin, or nose. **2** irritating in manner. [< Latin *acris* sharp]

ac tive (ak′tiv), *adj.* **1** moving or capable of moving rather quickly
much of the time; nimble: *as active as a kitten.* **2** showing much or
constant action; brisk: *an active market, active trade.* —**ac′tive ly,**
adv. —**ac′tive ness,** *n.*

a cute (ə kyüt′), *adj.* **1** acting keenly on the senses; sharp; intense:
acute pain. **2** crucial; critical: *an acute shortage of water.* **3** quick in
perceiving and responding
to impressions; keen: *an
acute sense of smell.*

ad journ (ə jèrn′), *v.t.*
put off until a later time;
postpone. —*v.i.* **1** stop
business or proceedings for
a time; recess: *The court
adjourned from Friday
until Monday.* **2** INFORMAL.
go *(to* another place*)*, especially for conversation.

a do be (ə dō′bē), *n.*
1 brick made of sun-dried

adobe building and oven

clay. **2** building made of such bricks or of sun-dried clay. —*adj.*
built or made of adobe. [< Spanish < Arabic *at-tub* the brick]

aes thet ic (es thet′ik), *adj.* **1** based on or determined by beauty
rather than by practically useful, scientific, or moral considerations.
2 having or showing an appreciation of beauty in nature or art.

af fec ta tion (af′ek tā′shən), *n.* behavior that is not natural,
but assumed to impress others; pretense.

af firm (ə fèrm′), *v.t.* **1** declare positively to be true: *I affirmed the
report to be true.* **2** confirm or ratify.

a fore (ə fôr′), *adv., prep., conj.* ARCHAIC or DIALECT. before.

a fore men tioned (ə fôr′men′shənd), *adj.* spoken of before;
mentioned earlier.

aft (aft), *adv.* at or toward the stern of a ship, boat, or aircraft.

af ter math (af′tər math), *n.* result or consequence, especially of something destructive.

ag ile (aj′əl), *adj.* **1** moving with speed, ease, and elegance;
lively; nimble: *as agile as a kitten.* **2** mentally alert; quick-
witted. [< Latin *agilis* < *agere* to move] —**ag′ile ly,** *adv.*
—**ag′ile ness,** *n.*

a gil i ty (ə jil′ə tē), *n.* **1** liveliness; nimbleness. **2** alertness.

ag i tate (aj′ə tāt), *v.t.,* -**tat ed,** -**tat ing.** **1** move or shake violently: *A sudden wind agitated the surface of the river.* **2** disturb or
upset very much. [< Latin *agitatum* moved to and fro < *agere* to
move] —**ag′i tat′ed ly,** *adv.* —**ag i ta′tion,** *n.*

air (er, ar), *n.* **1** the odorless, tasteless, and invisible mixture of
gases that surrounds the earth. **2** space overhead; sky: *Birds fly in
the air.* **3** a simple melody or tune.

a jar (ə jär′), *adj.* slightly open: *Please leave the door ajar.*

al ien ate (ā′lyə nāt, ā′lē ə nāt), *v.t.,* -**at ed,** -**at ing.** **1** turn away
the normal feelings, fondness, or devotion of anyone. **2** transfer
(property, a property right, etc.) to the ownership of another.

al le giance (ə lē′jəns), *n.* **1** the loyalty owed to one's country or
government. **2** faithfulness to a person, cause, etc.; loyalty.

al li ance (ə lī′əns), *n.* **1** union formed by mutual agreement,
especially to protect or further mutual interests. **2** a joining of
independent nations by treaty. **3** any joining of efforts or interests
by persons, families, states, or organizations. [< Old French
aliance < *alier* unite]

al lure (ə lür′), *v.t.,* -**lured,** -**lur ing.** tempt or attract very
strongly; fascinate; charm.

a mass (ə mas′), *v.t.* heap together; pile up, especially for
oneself; accumulate.

am ber (am′bər), *n.* **1** a hard, translucent, yellow or yellowish-
brown fossil resin, easily polished and used for jewelry, in making
pipe stems, etc. **2** the color of amber; yellow or yellowish brown.

am ble (am′bəl), *n., v.,* -**bled,** -**bling.** —*n.* gait of a horse or
mule when it lifts first the two legs on one side and then the two on
the other. —*v.i.* **1** (of a horse or mule) go with such a gait. **2** walk
at an easy, slow pace.

am ne sia (am nē′zhə), *n.* partial or entire loss of memory caused
by injury to the brain, or by disease, shock, etc. [< Greek *amnēsia*
forgetfulness < *a-* not + *mimnēskesthai* remember]

am phi the a ter (am′fə thē′ə tər), *n.* **1** a circular or oval
building with tiers of seats around a central open space. **2** place of
public contest; arena.

-an, *suffix forming adjectives and nouns, especially from proper
nouns.* **1** of or having to do with ____: *Mohammedan* = *of or
having to do with Mohammed.* **2** native or inhabitant of ____:
American = *native or inhabitant of America.* **3** person who knows
much about or is skilled in ____: *Magician* = *person skilled in
magic. Historian* = *person who knows much about history.* Also,
-ian, -ean.

a nach ro nism (ə nak′rə niz′əm), *n.* **1** error in fixing a date or
dates. **2** anything out of keeping with a specified time, especially
something proper to a former age but not to the present. [< Greek
anachronismos < *ana-* back + *chronos* time]

an ec dote (an′ik dōt), *n.* a short account of some interesting
incident, especially one in the life of a person.

an es thet ic (an′əs thet′ik), *n.* substance that causes anethesia,
or the loss of the feeling of pain, touch, cold, etc.

an guish (ang′gwish), *n.* **1** severe physical pain; great suffering.
2 extreme mental pain or suffering: *the anguish of despair.* —**an′-
guished,** *adj.*

an tag o nist (an tag′ə nist), *n.* person who fights, struggles, or
contends against another; adversary; opponent.

an thro po log i cal (an′thrə pə loj′ə kəl), *adj.* of anthropology, the science or study of human beings, dealing especially with
their fossil remains, physical characteristics, cultures, customs, and
beliefs.

ap a thet ic (ap/ə thet/ik), *adj.* **1** lacking interest or desire for action; indifferent. **2** lacking in feeling; unemotional. —**ap/ a thet/i cal ly,** *adv.*

a pos tle or **A pos tle** (ə pos/əl), *n.* **1** one of the twelve disciples, **the Apostles,** chosen by Christ to preach the gospel to all the world. **2** leader of any reform movement or new belief who displays great vigor in seeking to popularize it.

ap pall ing (ə pô/ling), *adj.* causing horror; dismaying; terrifying. —**ap pall/ing ly,** *adv.*

ap pa ra tus (ap/ə rā/təs, ap/ə rat/əs), *n., pl.* **-tus** or **-tus es. 1** the tools, machines, or other equipment necessary to carry out a purpose or for a particular use: *apparatus for an experiment in chemistry, gardening apparatus.* **2** a mechanism or piece of machinery: *An automobile is a complicated apparatus.*

ap pease (ə pēz/), *v.t.,* **-peased, -peas ing. 1** put an end to by satisfying (an appetite or desire): *A good dinner will appease your hunger.* **2** make calm or quiet; pacify. —**ap peas/ing ly,** *adv.*

ap pend age (ə pen/dij), *n.* thing attached to something larger or more important; addition.

ap pen dix (ə pen/diks), *n., pl.* **-dix es** or **-di ces.** addition at the end of a book or document.

ap pli ca bil i ty (ap/lə kə bil/ə tē), *n.* quality of being applicable or appropriate for use.

ap praise (ə prāz/), *v.t.,* **-praised, -prais ing.** estimate the quality or merit of; judge: *Few can properly appraise the work of a new artist.* —**ap prais/ing ly,** *adv.*

ap pre hen sion (ap/ri hen/shən), *n.* **1** expectation of misfortune; dread of impending danger; fear. **2** arrest. **3** understanding.

ap pre hen sive (ap/ri hen/siv), *adj.* afraid that some misfortune is about to occur; anxious about the future; fearful. —**ap/ pre hen/sive ly,** *adv.* —**ap/pre hen/sive ness,** *n.*

ap pro ba tion (ap/rə bā/shən), *n.* **1** favorable opinion; approval. **2** act of formally and authoritatively approving; sanction.

ar bor (är/bər), *n.* a shady place formed by trees, shrubs, or by vines growing on a lattice.

ar dent (ärd/nt), *adj.* **1** glowing with passion; passionate; impassioned: *ardent love.* **2** very enthusiastic; eager. [< Latin *ardentem* burning] —**ar/dent ly,** *adv.*

ar dor (är/dər), *n.* **1** warmth of emotion; passion. **2** great enthusiasm; eagerness; zeal: *patriotic ardor.*

ar du ous (är/jü əs), *adj.* **1** hard to do; requiring much effort; difficult: *an arduous lesson.* **2** using up much energy; strenuous: *an arduous climb* [< Latin *arduus* steep] —**ar/du ous ly,** *adv.*

a ri a (är/ē ə, er/ē ə, ar/ē ə), *n.* **1** song for a voice or instrument; air; melody. **2** (in operas) a vocal solo.

ar ma da (är mä/də), *n.* **1** a large fleet of warships. **2 the Armada,** the Spanish fleet that was sent to attack England in 1588 but was defeated in the English Channel. **3** any large group of military vehicles. [< Spanish < Medieval Latin *armata* armed force. Doublet of ARMY.]

ar mour y (är/mər ē), *n., pl.* **-mour ies. 1** place where weapons are kept; arsenal. **2** place where weapons are manufactured. Also, **armory.**

ar ro gant (ar/ə gənt), *adj.* excessively proud and contemptuous of others. —**ar/ro gant ly,** *adv.*

art ful (ärt/fəl), *adj.* **1** slyly clever; crafty; deceitful: *a swindler's artful tricks.* **2** skillful; clever. —**art/ful ly,** *adv.* —**art/fulness,** *n.*

as cend (ə send/), *v.i.* go up; rise; move upward: *He watched the airplane ascend.* —*v.t.* go to or toward the top of: *A small party is planning to ascend Mount Everest.*

as cent (ə sent/), *n.* **1** act of going up; upward movement; rising: *early balloon ascents.* **2** act of climbing a ladder, mountain, etc.

as cot (as/kət, as/kot), *n.* necktie with broad ends, resembling a scarf, tied so that the ends may be laid flat, one across the other. [< *Ascot,* English race track]

as pect (as/pekt), *n.* **1** way in which a subject or situation appears to the mind: *The whole aspect of the situation is changing.* **2** way in which an object appears to the eye; appearance. **3** facial expression; countenance: *the solemn aspect of the judge.* [< Latin *aspectus* < *ad-* at + *specere* look]

as pire (ə spīr/), *v.i.,* **-pired, -pir ing. 1** have an ambition for something; desire earnestly; seek: *I aspired to be captain of the team.* **2** rise high. —**as pir/ing ly,** *adv.*

as sert (ə sèrt/), *v.t.* **1** state positively; declare firmly; affirm: *She asserts that she will go whether we do or not.* **2** maintain (a right, a claim, etc.); insist upon: *Assert your independence.* **3 assert oneself,** insist on one's rights; demand recognition: *If you feel you've been treated unfairly, you should assert yourself.*

a hat	i it	oi oil	ch child		a in about
ā age	ī ice	ou out	ng long		e in taken
ä far	o hot	u cup	sh she	ə =	i in pencil
e let	ō open	u̇ put	th thin		o in lemon
ē equal	ô order	ü rule	ŦH then		u in circus
ėr term			zh measure		< = derived from

as sume (ə süm/), *v.t.,* **-sumed, -sum ing. 1** take for granted without actual proof; suppose: *She assumed that the train would be on time.* **2** take upon oneself formally; undertake (an office or responsibility): *assume leadership.* **3** take on; put on: *The problem had assumed a new form.*

as sur ance (ə shur/əns), *n.* **1** a making sure or certain. **2** statement intended to make a person more sure or certain. **3** security, certainty, or confidence.

a sun der (ə sun/dər), *adv.* in pieces; into separate parts: *Lightning split the tree asunder.*

at tain (ə tān/), *v.t.* **1** reach (a state or condition) by living, growing, or developing: *attain the age of 80.* **2** win or acquire by effort: *attain a goal.* **3** reach (a place); arrive at; gain: *attain the top of a hill.* —*v.i.* succeed in coming or getting *(to):* *attain to a position of great influence.*

at ten tive (ə ten/tiv), *adj.* **1** paying attention; observant. **2** courteous; polite: *an attentive host.* —**at ten/tive ly,** *adv.*

at tire (ə tīr/), *n.* clothing or dress: *wear rich attire.*

at ti tude (at/ə tüd, at/ə tyüd), *n.* **1** way of thinking, feeling, or acting; feeling or behavior of a person toward a situation: *My attitude toward school has changed.* **2** position of the body appropriate to an action, purpose, emotion, etc.; posture; pose.

at trib ute (*v.* ə trib/yüt; *n.* at/rə byüt), *v.,* **-ut ed, -ut ing,** *n.* —*v.t.* regard as an effect or product of; think of as caused by: *She attributes her great age to a carefully planned diet.* —*n.* a quality considered as belonging to a person or thing; characteristic: *Patience is an attribute of a good teacher.*

au da cious (ô dā/shəs), *adj.* **1** having the courage to take risks; recklessly daring; bold: *an audacious pilot.* **2** rudely bold; impudent. —**au da/cious ly,** *adv.* —**au da/cious ness,** *n.*

au dac i ty (ô das/ə tē), *n.* **1** reckless daring; boldness. **2** rude boldness [< Latin *audacia* < *audax* bold < *audere* to dare]

au di ble (ô/də bəl), *adj.* that can be heard; loud enough to be heard. [< Latin *audire* hear] —**au/di bly,** *adv.*

au di ence (ô/dē əns), *n.* **1** people gathered in a place to hear or see: *a theater audience.* **2** a formal interview with a person of high rank: *The queen granted an audience to the ambassador.*

au thor i ta tive (ə thôr/ə tā/tiv), *adj.* **1** proceeding from a recognized authority; official: *The president issued an authoritative declaration of policy.* **2** of or characterized by authority; commanding: *In authoritative tones the policeman shouted, "Keep back."*

a venge (ə venj/), *v.t.,* **a venged, a veng ing.** take revenge for or on behalf of: *Hamlet avenged his father's murder.*

av id (av/id), *adj.* extremely eager or enthusiastic. [< Latin *avidus* < *avere* desire eagerly] —**av/id ly,** *adv.* —**av/id ness,** *n.*

awe (ô), *n., v.,* **awed, aw ing.** —*n.* **1** a feeling of wonder and reverence inspired by anything of great beauty, majesty, or power: *The young girl stood in awe before the queen.* **2** dread mingled with reverence. —*v.t.* cause to feel awe; fill with awe: *The majesty of the mountains awed us.*

bade (bad, bād), *v.t.,* a pt. of **bid.**
➤ **Bade** is used chiefly in formal and literary English: *The king bade her remain.*

bar bar ic (bär bar/ik), *adj.* **1** like barbarians; suited to an uncivilized people; rough and rude. **2** crudely rich or splendid.

bar ba rism (bär/bə riz/əm), *n.* **1** condition of uncivilized people. **2** a barbarous act, custom, or trait.

bar rage (bə räzh/), *n.* barrier of artillery fire to check the enemy or to protect one's own soldiers when advancing or retreating.

barrel organ, hand organ, or large, portable music box that is made to play tunes by turning a crank.

bas-re lief (bä/ri lēf/), *n.* carving or sculpture in which the figures stand out only slightly from the background. [< French]

bat tal ion (bə tal/yən), *n.* **1** a military unit of infantry, etc. **2** a large division of an army in battle array. **3 battalions,** *pl.* armies; military forces.

bat ter y (bat′ər ē), *n., pl.* **-ter ies.** **1** a single electric cell: *a flashlight battery.* **2** a military unit of artillery, usually commanded by a captain.

bay o net (bā′ə nit, bā′ə net′), *n.* a heavy, daggerlike blade for piercing or stabbing, made to be attached to the muzzle of a rifle.

bea con (bē′kən), *n.* **1** fire or light used as a signal to guide or warn. **2** a tall tower for a signal; lighthouse. **3** any thing or person that is a guiding or warning signal.

bear (ber, bar), *v.t.,* **bore, borne, bear ing.** **1** take from one place to another; carry. **2** hold up; support. **3** put up with; abide: *She can't bear the noise.*

bear out, confirm; prove.

bear up, keep one's courage; not lose hope or faith.

bear with, put up with; be patient with.

beck on (bek′ən), *v.i., v.t.* to signal by a motion of the head or hand: *He beckoned me to follow him. The tall man beckoned to her.* [Old English *bēcnan < bēacen* sign, beacon]

be get (bi get′), *v.t.,* **be got, be got ten, be get ting.** **1** become the father of. **2** cause to be; produce.

be lea guer (bi lē′gər), *v.t.* **1** surround with troops. **2** surround. **—be lea′guered,** *adj.*

bel lig er ent (bə lij′ər ənt), *adj.* **1** waging or carrying on regular recognized war; at war; fighting. **2** fond of fighting; warlike. **—bel lig′er ent ly,** *adv.*

ben e dic tion (ben′ə dik′shən), *n.* **1** the asking of God's blessing, as at the end of a church service. **2** blessing.

ben e fac tor (ben′ə fak′tər, ben′ə fak′tər), *n.* person who has helped others, either by gifts of money or by some kind act.

be reft (bi reft′), *adj.* deprived; left alone and desolate.

be seech (bi sēch′), *v.t.,* **-sought** or **-seeched, -seech ing.** ask earnestly; beg; implore.

be set ting (bi set′ing), *adj.* regularly attacking: *a besetting sin.*

bes tial (bes′chəl), *adj.* like a beast or animal; beastly. [< Latin *bestialis < bestia* beast] **—bes′tial ly,** *adv.*

bes tial ize (bes′chə līz), *v.t.* make bestial or beastly.

be stow (bi stō′), *v.t.* **1** give (something) as a gift; give; confer. **2** make use of; apply.

be troth al (bi trō′FHəl, bi trô′thəl), *n.* a promise in marriage; engagement.

bid (bid), *v.t.,* **bade, bid, bid ding.** **1** tell (someone) what to do, where to go, etc.; command; order: *Do as I bid you. You bade me forget what is unforgettable.* **2** say or tell (a greeting, etc.); wish: *My friends came to bid me good-by.*

bil low (bil′ō), *n.* **1** a great, swelling wave or surge of the sea. **2** a great rolling or swelling mass of smoke, flame, air, etc. **—v.i.** **1** rise or roll in big waves; surge. **2** swell out; bulge.

bin dle (bin′dl), *n., v.,* **-dled, -dling.** **—n.** a bundle; bedroll. **—v.i.** wrap in a bundle or bedroll.

black out (blak′out′), *n.* the extinguishing or concealing of all the lights of a city, district, etc., as a protection against an air raid. [< *black + out*]

blanch (blanch), *v.t.* make white or pale: *Old age blanched his hair.* **—v.i.** turn white or pale: *blanch with fear.* [< Old French *blanchir < blanc* white]

bland (bland), *adj.* **1** gentle or soothing; balmy: *a bland summer breeze.* **2** smoothly agreeable and polite: *a bland smile.* [< Latin *blandus* soft] **—bland′ly,** *adv.* **—bland′ness,** *n.*

bois ter ous (boi′stər əs), *adj.* **1** noisily cheerful; exuberant: *a boisterous game.* **2** rough and stormy; turbulent: *a boisterous wind.* **3** rough and noisy; clamorous: *a boisterous child.* [Middle English *boistrous*] **—bois′ter ous ly,** *adv.* **—bois′ter ous ness,** *n.*

borne (bôrn, bōrn), *v.* a pp. of **bear.** *I have borne it as long as I can.*

➤ **borne. Borne** is the past participle of *bear* in most of its meanings: *The ship was borne along by the breeze. The men had borne these burdens without complaint.*

bound (bound), *adj.* **1** under some obligation; tied down by circumstance, duty, etc.; obliged: *I feel bound by my promise.* **2** certain; sure: *It is bound to get dark soon.* **3** tied fast; fastened: *bound hands.* [Middle English *bounden*]

boun ty (boun′tē), *n., pl.* **-ties.** a generous gift.

brake (brāk), *n.* thicket, or clump of small trees growing close together.

bran dish (bran′dish), *v.t.* wave or shake threateningly; flourish. **—n.** a threatening shake; flourish. [< Old French *brandiss-,* a form of *brandir* to brand < *brand* sword]

bra va do (brə vä′dō), *n., pl.* **-does** or **-dos.** a show of courage or boldness without much real courage; defiant or blustering behavior. [< Spanish *bravada,* ultimately < *bravo*]

brave (brāv), *adj.* **brav er, brav est.** **1** without fear; having or showing courage in the face of danger. **2** making a fine appearance; showy; splendid: *a brave display of flags.* **3** ARCHAIC. fine; excellent. **—brave′ly,** *adv.* **—brave′ness,** *n.*

bra zen (brā′zn), *adj.* **1** having no shame; bold; impudent. **2** loud and harsh; brassy. **3** made of brass. **4** like brass in color or strength.

breach (brēch), *n.* an opening made by breaking down something solid, as a gap made in a wall. **—v.t.** break through; make an opening in: *The wall had been breached in several places.* [Old English *brǣc* a break]

breech (brēch), *n.* **1** the part of a gun behind the barrel. **2** the lower part; back part. [< *breeches*]

brev i ty (brev′ə tē), *n., pl.* **-ties.** **1** shortness in time. **2** shortness in speech or writing; conciseness.

brig and (brig′ənd), *n.* person who robs travelers on the road, especially one of a gang of robbers in mountain or forest regions.

brim stone (brim′stōn′), *n.* sulfur, a highly flammable, nonmetallic element used in making matches and gunpowder.

brin y (brī′nē), *adj.,* **brin i er, brin i est.** of or like brine, or salty water; very salty: *a briny taste.* **—brin′i ness,** *n.*

brook (brúk), *v.t.* put up with; endure; tolerate.

Bud dha (bü′də, bùd′ə), *n.* 563?-483? B.C., a religious teacher of northern India and the founder of Buddhism.

buoy ant (boi′ənt, bü′yənt), *adj.* **1** able to float. **2** hopeful; cheerful; lighthearted **—buoy′an cy,** *n.* **—buoy′ant ly,** *adv.*

bur gle (bėr′gəl), *v.t.,* **-gled, -gling.** INFORMAL. burglarize; rob. [back-formation < *burglar*]

bur nish (bėr′nish), *v.t.* **1** make (metal) smooth and bright; polish (a surface) by rubbing until shiny: *burnish brass.* **2** make bright and glossy. **—bur′nished,** *adj.*

cache (kash), *n.* a hiding place, especially of goods, treasure, food, etc. [< French *cacher* to hide]

ca coph o ny (kə kof′ə nē), *n., pl.* **-nies.** succession of harsh, clashing sounds; dissonance; discord. [< Greek *kakophōnia < kakos* bad + *phōnē* sound]

cal cu lus (kal′kyə ləs), *n., pl.* **-li** (-lī), **-lus es.** system of calculation in advanced mathematics.

cal li o pe (kə lī′ə pē, kal′ē ōp), *n.* a musical instrument having a series of steam whistles played by pushing keys.

can dor (kan′dər), *n.* **1** a saying openly what one really thinks; honesty in giving one's opinion. **2** fairness; impartiality.

can non ade (kan′ə nād′), *n., v.,* **-ad ed, -ad ing.** **—n.** a continued firing of cannons; barrage. **—v.t.** attack with cannons.

cap i tal (kap′ə təl), *n.* **1** city where the government of a country, state, or province is located. **2** capital letter. **3** amount of money or property that companies or individuals use to increase their wealth: *The Smith Company has capital amounting to $300,000.* **4** source of power or advantage; resources.

ca pit u late (kə pich′ə lāt), *v.i.,* **-lat ed, -lat ing.** surrender on certain terms or conditions: *The men in the fort capitulated on condition that they be allowed to go away unharmed.* **—ca pit′ u la′tor,** *n.* **—ca pit′u la′tion,** *n.*

ca price (kə prēs′), *n.* **1** a sudden change of mind without reason; whim. **2** tendency to change suddenly and without reason.

car il lon (kar′ə lon, kə ril′yən), *n.* **1** set of bells arranged for playing melodies. **2** melody played on such bells. [< French, ultimately < Latin *quattuor* four (because it originally consisted of four bells)]

car nage (kär′nij), *n.* slaughter of a great number of people.

cas cade (ka skād′), *n.* **1** a small waterfall. **2** anything like this: *Her dress had a cascade of ruffles down the front.*

case ment (kās′mənt), *n.* **1** window or part of a window which opens on hinges like a door. **2** any window.

Cau ca sian (kô kā′zhən, kô kā′shən), *n.* member of the division of the human race that includes the original inhabitants of Europe, southwestern Asia, and northern Africa, and their descendants throughout the world.

cau ter ize (kô′tə rīz), *v.t.,* **-ized, -iz ing.** burn with a hot iron or a caustic substance. Doctors sometimes cauterize wounds to prevent bleeding or infection. **—cau′ter i za′tion,** *n.*

ca vort (kə vôrt′), *v.* prance about; jump around.

ce les tial (sə les′chəl), *adj.* **1** of the sky; having to do with the heavens: *The sun, moon, planets, and stars are celestial bodies.* **2** of or belonging to heaven as the place of God and the angels.

cen trif u gal (sen trif′yə gəl, sen trif′ə gəl), *adj.* moving or tending to move away from a center. —**cen trif′u gal ly,** *adv.*

char ac ter (kar′ik tər), *n.* **1** all the qualities or features possessed; sort; nature: *He dislikes people of that character.* **2** moral strength or weakness: *a person of shallow, changeable character.* **3** person or animal in a play, poem, story, or book. **4** letter, mark, or sign used in writing or printing. **5** writing or printing of a certain style: *books in Gothic character.* [< Latin < Greek *charaktēr* instrument for marking, distinctive mark < *charassein* engrave]

chasm (kaz′əm), *n.* a deep opening or crack in the earth; gap.

chas tise (cha stīz′), *v.t.,* **-tised, -tis ing.** **1** inflict punishment or suffering on to improve; punish. **2** criticize severely; rebuke.

chid den (chid′n), *v.* pp. of **chide.**

chide (chīd), *v.,* **chid ed, chid** or **chid den, chid ing.** —*v.t.* find fault with; reproach or blame; scold: *She chided the little girl for soiling her dress.* —*v.i.* find fault; speak in rebuke.

cho ris ter (kôr′ə stər, kor′ə stər), *n.* **1** singer in a choir or chorus. **2** leader of a choir.

chron ic (kron′ik), *adj.* **1** lasting a long time. **2** never stopping; constant; habitual: *a chronic liar.*

chrys o lite (kris′ə līt), *n.* a green or yellow semiprecious stone.

cir cum spect (sèr′kəm spekt), *adj.* watchful on all sides; cautious or prudent; careful. [< Latin *circumspectum* < *circum* around + *specere* look] —**cir′cum spect′ly,** *adv.*

cit ron (sit′rən), *n.* **1** a pale-yellow citrus fruit somewhat like a lemon. **2** its rind, candied and used in fruit cakes, candies, etc. [< Middle French < Italian *citrone* < Latin *citrus* citrus tree]

clair voy ant (kler voi′ənt, klar voi′ənt), *adj.* supposedly having the power of seeing or knowing things that are out of sight.

clar et (klar′ət), *n.* **1** kind of red wine. **2** a dark purplish red. —*adj.* dark purplish-red.

cleave (klēv), *v.t.,* **cleft** or **cleaved, cleav ing.** **1** cut, divide, or split open. **2** pass through; pierce: *The airplane cleft the clouds.*

co her ent (kō hir′ənt), *adj.* **1** logically connected; consistent: *A sentence that is not coherent is hard to understand.* **2** sticking together; holding together. —**co her′ent ly,** *adv.*

coiffe (kwäf), *n.* style of arranging the hair. —*v.t.* to dress (the hair) by arranging or styling. [< French]

col lab o rate (kə lab′ə rāt′), *v.i.,* **-rat ed, -rat ing.** **1** work together. **2** aid or cooperate traitorously. —**col lab′o ra′tor,** *n.*

col lec tive (kə lek′tiv), *adj.* **1** of a group; as a group; taken all together: *collective revenues of the government.* **2** of or derived from a number of persons taken or acting together.

com mence (kə mens′), *v.,* **-menced, -menc ing.** —*v.i.* make a start; begin. —*v.t.* begin (an action); enter upon.

com mend (kə mend′), *v.t.* **1** speak well of; praise. **2** recommend. **3** hand over for safekeeping; entrust: *She commended the child to his care.*

com mon place (kom′ən plās′), *adj.* not new or interesting; everyday; ordinary. —**com′mon place′ness,** *n.*

com mon wealth (kom′ən welth′), *n.* **1** the people who make up a nation; citizens of a state. **2** a democratic state; republic.

com mune (*v.* kə myün′; *n.* kom′yün), *v.,* **-muned, -mun ing,** *n.* —*v.i.* talk intimately. —*n.* intimate talk; communion.

com pas sion ate (kəm pash′ə nit), *adj.* desiring to relieve another's suffering; sympathetic. —**com pas′sion ate ly,** *adv.*

com pel (kəm pel′), *v.t.,* **-pelled, -pel ling.** **1** drive or urge with force; force: *Rain compelled them to stop.* **2** cause or get by force: *A police officer can compel obedience to the law.* —**com pel′ling ly,** *adv.*

com pen sa tion (kom′pən sā′shən), *n.* **1** something given as an equivalent; something given to make up for a loss, injury, etc. **2** pay: *Equal compensation should be given for equal work.* **3** a balancing by equal power, weight, etc.

com pe tent (kom′pə tənt), *adj.* **1** properly qualified; able; fit: *a competent bookkeeper.* **2** legally qualified. —**com′pe tent ly,** *adv.*

com ply (kəm plī′), *v.i.,* **-plied, -ply ing.** act in agreement with a request or command: *I will comply with the doctor's request.*

com po sure (kəm pō′zhər), *n.* calmness; quietness; self-control.

com pro mise (kom′prə mīz′), *v.,* **-mised, -mis ing,** *n.* —*v.t.* settle (a dispute) by agreeing that each will give up a part of what he or she demands. —*v.i.* make a compromise. —*n.* **1** settlement of a dispute by a partial yielding on both sides. **2** result of such a settlement. [< Old French *compromis* a compromise < Latin *compromissum* < *compromittere* promise together < *com-* together + *promittere* promise] —**com′pro mis′er,** *n.*

a hat	i it	oi oil	ch child		a in about
ā age	ī ice	ou out	ng long		e in taken
ä far	o hot	u cup	sh she	ə =	i in pencil
e let	ō open	ù put	th thin		o in lemon
ē equal	ô order	ü rule	ᴛH then		u in circus
èr term			zh measure		< = derived from

con ceive (kən sēv′), *v.,* **-ceived, -ceiv ing.** —*v.t.* **1** form in the mind; think up: *The Wright brothers conceived the design of the first successful motor-driven airplane.* **2** have (an idea or feeling). —*v.i.* have an idea or feeling; think; imagine: *We cannot conceive of such a thing happening.*

con cep tion (kən sep′shən), *n.* **1** thought; idea; impression: *Your conception of the problem is different from mine.* **2** act or power of conceiving.

con ces sion (kən sesh′ən), *n.* **1** a conceding; granting; yielding. **2** something conceded or granted by a government or controlling authority; grant. Land or privileges given by a government to a business company are called concessions. **3** privilege or space leased for a particular use: *the hot-dog concession at the ballpark.*

con coct (kon kokt′, kən kokt′), *v.t.* **1** prepare by mixing with a variety of ingredients: *concoct a drink.* **2** make up; devise: *concoct an excuse.*

con cus sion (kən kush′ən), *n.* **1** a sudden, violent shaking; shock. **2** injury to a soft part of the body, especially the brain, caused by a blow, fall, or other physical shock.

con dense (kən dens′), *v.,* **-densed, -dens ing.** —*v.t.* **1** make denser or more compact; compress. **2** put into fewer words; express briefly. —*v.i.* become denser or more compact.

con de scend ing (kon′di sen′ding), *adj.* **1** stooping to the level of one's inferiors. **2** scornful; patronizing.

con fer (kən fèr′), *v.,* **-ferred, -fer ring.** —*v.i.* consult together; exchange ideas; talk things over: *The President often confers with advisers.* —*v.t.* give; award; bestow: *to confer a medal on a hero.* [< Latin *conferre* < *com-* together + *ferre* bring]

con fla gra tion (kon′flə grā′shən), *n.* a great and destructive fire: *A conflagration destroyed most of the city.*

con found (kon found′, kən found′), *v.t.* **1** confuse; mix up: *The shock confounded me.* **2** surprise and puzzle. **3** ARCHAIC. make uneasy and ashamed. **4** ARCHAIC. defeat; overthrow. [< Old French *confondre* < Latin *confundere* pour together, mix up, confuse]

con front (kən frunt′), *v.t.* **1** meet face to face; stand facing. **2** face boldly; oppose. **3** bring face to face; place before: *The prosecuting attorney confronted the accused with the forged check.* —**con′fron ta′tion,** *n.*

con jec tur al (kən jek′chər əl), *adj.* involving conjecture or guesswork. —**con jec′tur al ly,** *adv.*

con science (kon′shəns), *n.* sense of right and wrong; ideas and feelings within a person that warn of what is wrong. —**con′science less,** *adj.*

con scious ness (kon′shəs nis), *n.* condition of being conscious; awareness. People and animals have consciousness; plants and stones do not.

con se quence (kon′sə kwens, kon′sə kwəns), *n.* **1** result or effect; outcome: *The consequence of my fall was a broken leg.* **2** a logical result; deduction; inference.

con sign (kən sīn′), *v.t.* **1** hand over; deliver: *The dog was consigned to the pound.* **2** send: *We will consign the goods to you by express.* **3** set apart; assign.

con sole (kən sōl′), *v.t.,* **-soled, -sol ing.** ease the grief or sorrow of; comfort. [< Middle French *consoler* < Latin *consolari* < *com-* + *solari* soothe] —**con sol′a ble,** *adj.*

con spic u ous (kən spik′yü əs), *adj.* **1** easily seen; clearly visible: *A traffic sign should be conspicuous.* **2** worthy of notice; remarkable. —**con spic′u ous ly,** *adv.*

con spir a cy (kən spir′ə sē), *n., pl.* **-cies.** **1** act of conspiring; secret planning with others to do something unlawful or wrong, especially against a government, public personage, etc. **2** a plot or intrigue.

con sta ble (kon′stə bəl, kun′stə bəl), *n.* a police officer, especially in a township, district, or rural area of the United States.

con strue (kən strü′), *v.t.,* **-strued, -stru ing.** show the meaning of; explain; interpret: *Different judges may construe the same law differently.*

con sum mate (*v.* kon′sə māt; *adj.* kən sum′it), *v.,* **-mat ed,**

573

-mat ing, *adj.* —*v.t.* bring to completion; realize; fulfill. —*adj.* in the highest degree; complete; perfect.

con tend (kən tend′), *v.i.* **1** work hard against difficulties; fight; struggle: *The first settlers in America had to contend with sickness and lack of food.* **2** take part in a contest; compete. **3** argue; dispute. —**con tend′er,** *n.*

con tig u ous (kən tig′yü əs), *adj.* **1** in actual contact; touching. **2** adjoining; near. [< Latin < *contingere* touch closely]

con triv ance (kən trī′vəns), *n.* **1** thing invented; mechanical device. **2** act or manner of contriving. **3** plan; scheme.

con trive (kən trīv′), *v.t.,* **-trived, -triv ing. 1** plan with cleverness or skill; invent; design: *contrive a new kind of engine.* **2** plan; scheme; plot: *contrive a robbery.*

con va les cence (kon′və les′ns), *n.* the gradual recovery of health and strength after illness.

con ven tion al (kən ven′shə nəl), *adj.* **1** depending on conventions; customary: *"Good morning" is a conventional greeting.* **2** of the usual type or design; commonly used or seen: *conventional furniture.* **3** (in the arts) following custom and traditional models; formal.

con vic tion (kən vik′shən), *n.* **1** act of proving or declaring guilty. **2** a being convinced. **3** firm belief; certainty.

con vul sive (kən vul′siv), *adj.* **1** violently disturbing. **2** having or producing convulsions or violent spasms. —**con vul′sive ly,** *adv.*

cor dial (kôr′jəl), *adj.* warm and friendly in manner; hearty; sincere: *a cordial welcome.* [< Medieval Latin *cordialem* < Latin *cordis* heart] —**cor′dial ly,** *adv.*

cor don (kôrd′n), *n.* line or circle of soldiers, policemen, forts, etc., enclosing or guarding a place. [< French]

cor nice (kôr′nis), *n.* an ornamental, horizontal molding along the top of a wall, pillar, building, etc.

coun sel (koun′səl), *n., v.,* **-seled, -sel ing** or **-selled, -sel ling.** —*n.* **1** act of exchanging ideas; talking things over; consultation. **2** carefully considered advice: *The lawyer's counsel was that we avoid a lawsuit.* —*v.t.* give advice to; advise.

coun te nance (koun′tə nəns), *n., v.,* **-nanced, -nanc ing.** —*n.* **1** expression of the face: *an angry countenance.* **2** face; features: *a noble countenance.* —*v.t.* approve or encourage; sanction: *I won't countenance such a plan.*

counter-, *prefix.* **1** in opposition to; against: *Counteract = act against.* **2** in return: *Counterattack = attack in return.* **3** corresponding: *Counterpart = corresponding part.*

coun ter bal ance (*n.* koun′tər bal′əns; *v.* koun′tər bal′əns), *n., v.,* **-anced, -anc ing.** —*n.* weight balancing another weight. —*v.t.,* act as a counterbalance to; offset.

coun ter plot (koun′tər plot′), *n., v.,* **-plot ted, -plot ting.** —*n.* a plot to defeat another plot. —*v.i.* plot in opposition. —*v.t.* plot against (another plot or plotter).

cour i er (kėr′ē ər, kur′ē ər), *n.* **1** messenger sent in haste: *Government dispatches were sent by couriers.* **2** a secret agent who transfers information to and from other agents.

cour ti er (kôr′tē ər), *n.* **1** person often present at a royal court. **2** person who tries to win the favor of another by flattery.

couth (küth), *adj.* cultured; graceful; sophisticated. —*n.* culture; grace; sophistication: *Have you no couth?* [back-formation < *uncouth*] —**couth′ly,** *adv.* —**couth′ness,** *n.*

cre scen do (krə shen′dō), *adj., adv., n., pl.* **-dos.** —*adj., adv.* (in music) with a gradual increase in force or loudness. —*n.* a gradual increase in force or loudness, especially in music.

cre vasse (krə vas′), *n.* a deep crack or crevice in the ice of a glacier, or in the ground after an earthquake. [< French < Old French *crevace.* Doublet of CREVICE.]

crevasse

crev ice (krev′is), *n.* a narrow split or crack; fissure.

crotch et y (kroch′ə tē), *adj.* full of odd notions or unreasonable whims. —**crotch′et i ness,** *n.*

crypt (kript), *n.* an underground room or vault.

cryp tic (krip′tik), *adj.* having a hidden meaning; secret; mysterious: *a cryptic message.* —**cryp′ti cal ly,** *adv.*

cub (kub), *n.* **1** a young bear, fox, lion, etc. **2** a young or inexperienced person. **3** cub scout. [origin uncertain]

cudg el (kuj′əl), *n., v.,* **-eled, -el ing** or **-elled, -el ling.** —*n.* a short, thick stick used as a weapon; club. —*v.t.* beat with a cudgel. —**cudg′el er,** *n.*

cue (kyü), *n., v.,* **cued, cue ing** or **cu ing.** —*n.* action, speech, or word which gives the signal for an actor, singer, musician, etc., to enter or to begin. —*v.t.* provide (a person) with a cue or hint.

cun ning (kun′ing), *adj.* **1** clever in deceiving; sly: *a cunning fox, a cunning thief.* **2** skillful; clever: *The old watch was a fine example of cunning workmanship.* [Old English *cunnung* < *cunnan* know (how)] —**cun′ning ly,** *adv.*

cur (kėr), *n.* a dog of mixed breed; mongrel.

curt (kėrt), *adj.* rudely brief; short; abrupt: *a curt way of talking.* [< Latin *curtus* cut short] —**curt′ly,** *adv.*

cus to dy (kus′tə dē), *n., pl.* **-dies. 1** watchful keeping; charge; care: *Parents have the custody of their young children.* **2** a being confined or detained; imprisonment. **3 in custody,** in the care of the police; under arrest.

cy cle (sī′kəl), *n., v.,* **-cled, -cling.** —*n.* **1** period of time or complete process of growth or action that repeats itself in the same order. The seasons of the year—spring, summer, autumn, and winter—make a cycle. **2** bicycle, tricycle, or motorcycle. —*v.i.* pass through a cycle; occur over and over again in the same order. [< Late Latin *cyclus* < Greek *kyklos* wheel, circle, ring]

cyn i cal (sin′ə kəl), *adj.* **1** doubting the sincerity and goodness of others. **2** sneering; sarcastic. —**cyn′i cal ly,** *adv.*

dan de li on (dan′dl ī′ən), *n.* a common weed with deeply notched leaves and bright-yellow flowers. [< Middle French *dent de lion* lion's tooth; from its toothed leaves]

das tard ly (das′tərd lē), *adj.* like a dastard; mean and cowardly.

deb o nair or **deb o naire** (deb′ə ner′, deb′ə nar′), *adj.* pleasant, courteous, and cheerful. [< Old French *debonaire* < *de bon aire* of good disposition] —**deb′o nair′ly,** *adv.*

de cease (di sēs′), *n., v.,* **-ceased, -ceas ing.** —*n.* act or fact of dying; death. —*v.i.* die. [< Latin *decessus* < *decedere* depart < *de-* away *cedere* go]

de cor (dā kôr′), *n.* **1** decoration. **2** the decoration and furnishings of a room, house, store, office, etc.

de cree (di krē′), *n., v.,* **-creed, -cree ing.** —*n.* something ordered or settled by authority; official decision. —*v.t.* order or settle by authority: *Fate decreed that Ulysses should travel long and far.* —*v.i.* decide; determine.

de cry (di krī′), *v.t.,* **-cried, -cry ing. 1** express strong disapproval of; condemn. **2** make little of.

deem (dēm), *v.t., v.i.* form or have an opinion; think, believe, or consider. [Old English *dēman* < *dōm* judgment]

def er ence (def′ər əns), *n.* **1** respect for the judgment, opinion, wishes, etc., of another. **2** great respect.

de flect (di flekt′), *v.t., v.i.* bend or turn aside; change direction. [< Latin *deflectere* < *de-* away + *flectere* to bend]

de lir i ous (di lir′ē əs), *adj.* **1** temporarily out of one's senses. **2** wildly enthusiastic. —**de lir′i ous ly,** *adv.*

de ment ed (di men′tid), *adj.* mentally ill; insane; crazy.

de mure (di myúr′), *adj.,* **-mur er, -mur est. 1** artifically proper; assuming an air of modesty; coy: *a demure smile.* **2** reserved or composed in demeanor; serious and sober.

den ti frice (den′tə fris), *n.* paste, powder, or liquid for cleaning the teeth. [< Latin *dentifricium* < *dentem* tooth + *fricare* to rub]

de ploy (di ploi′), *v.t.* **1** spread out (troops, military units, etc.) from a column into a long battle line. **2** spread out, extend, or place, especially in a planned or strategic position: *deploy offensive missiles, deploy actors on a stage.* **3** use: *deploy one's talents to the best advantage.* —*v.i.* (of troops, military units, etc.) spread out strategically or so as to form a more extended front or line.

de port (di pôrt′, di pōrt′), *v.t.* **1** force to leave a country; banish; expel. See synonym study below. **2** behave or conduct (oneself) in a particular manner. [< Latin *deportare* < *de-* away + *portare* carry] —**de port′a ble,** *adj.*

Syn. 1 Banish, exile, deport mean cause to leave a country. **Banish** means to force a person, by order of authority, to leave his or her own or a foreign country, permanently or for a stated time: *Napoleon was banished to Elba.* **Exile** means either to compel another to leave his or her own country or home or voluntarily to remove oneself from either for a protracted period: *The kaiser was exiled from Germany after World War I. She exiled herself abroad because of her dissatisfaction with the government.* **Deport** usually means to banish a person from a country of which he or she is not a citizen: *Aliens who have entered the United States illegally may be deported.*

de pose (di pōz′), *v.t.*, **-posed, -pos ing.** put out of office or a position of authority, especially a high one like that of king.

de pute (di pyüt′), *v.t.*, **-put ed, -put ing.** appoint to act on one's behalf; appoint as one's substitute or agent; delegate.

de ri sion (di rizh′ən), *n.* scornful laughter; ridicule.

de scry (di skrī′), *v.t.*, **-scried, -scry ing. 1** catch sight of; be able to see; make out: *descry an island on the horizon.* **2** discover by observation; detect.

des o late (des′ə lit), *adj.* **1** laid waste; devastated; barren: *desolate land.* **2** not lived in; deserted: *a desolate house.* **3** unhappy; forlorn; wretched. **4** dreary; dismal: *a desolate life.* [< Latin *desolatum* < *de-* + *solus* alone] **—des′o late ly,** *adv.* **—des′o late ness,** *n.* **—des′o la′tion,** *n.*

de ter (di tėr′), *v.t.*, **-terred, -ter ring.** discourage or prevent from acting or proceeding by fear or consideration of danger or trouble; hinder: *The extreme heat deterred us from going downtown.* [< Latin *deterrere* < *de-* from + *terrere* frighten]

de te ri o rate (di tir′ē ə rāt′), *v.*, **-rat ed, -rat ing.** —*v.i.* become lower in quality or value; depreciate: *Machinery deteriorates rapidly if it is not taken care of.* —*v.t.* make lower in quality or value. [< Latin *deterioratum* worsened < *deterior* worse] **—de ter′i o ra′tion,** *n.* **—de ter′i o ra′tive,** *adj.*

de ter mi nate (di tėr′mə nit), *adj.* **1** with exact limits; fixed; definite. **2** settled; positive. **3** determined; resolute.

de vi ous (dē′vē əs), *adj.* **1** out of the direct way; winding. **2** straying from the right course; not straightforward: *a devious scheme, a devious nature.* **—de′vi ous ly,** *adv.*

de vise (di vīz′), *v.t.*, **-vised, -vis ing.** think out; plan or contrive; invent: *I devised a way of raising boards up to my tree house by using a pulley.*

de vout (di vout′), *adj.* **1** active in worship and prayer; religious. **2** earnest; sincere: *devout thanks.* **—de vout′ly,** *adv.*

dex ter i ty (dek ster′ə tē), *n.* **1** skill in using the hands or body. **2** skill in using the mind; cleverness.

di a tribe (dī′ə trīb), *n.* speech or discussion bitterly and violently directed against some person or thing; denunciation.

die sel or **Die sel** (dē′zəl, dē′səl), *n.* **1** diesel engine. **2** a truck, locomotive, train, etc., with a diesel engine. —*adj.* **1** equipped with or run by a diesel engine: *a diesel tractor.* **2** of or for a diesel engine: *diesel fuel.* [< Rudolf *Diesel*, 1858-1913, German engineer who invented the diesel engine]

di lap i dat ed (di lap′ə dā′tid), *adj.* fallen into ruin or disrepair; decayed through neglect. [< Latin *dilapidatum* scattered; ruined (as by hailstones) < *dis-* + *lapis* stone]

dil i gence (dil′ə jəns), *n.* constant and earnest effort to accomplish what is undertaken; industry.

di min ish (də min′ish), *v.t.* **1** make smaller; lessen; reduce. **2** lessen the importance, power, or reputation of; degrade. —*v.i.* become smaller; lessen; decrease. [ultimately < Latin *dis-* apart + *minus* less] **—di min′ish a ble,** *adj.*

dire (dīr), *adj.*, **dir er, dir est.** causing great fear or suffering; dreadful. [< Latin *dirus*] **—dire′ly,** *adv.* **—dire′ness,** *n.*

dis arm (dis ärm′), *v.t.* **1** take weapons away from: *The police disarmed the robbers.* **2** remove anger or suspicion from; make friendly: *The speaker's honesty disarmed the angry crowd.*

dis con so late (dis kon′sə lit), *adj.* **1** without hope; forlorn; unhappy. **2** causing discomfort; cheerless.

dis creet (dis krēt′), *adj.* very careful and sensible in speech and action; having or showing good judgment; wisely cautious. **—dis creet′ly,** *adv.* **—dis creet′ness,** *n.*

dis cre tion (dis kresh′ən), *n.* **1** quality of being discreet; great carefulness in speech or action; good judgment; wise caution: *Use your own discretion.* **2** freedom to decide or choose: *It is within the principal's discretion to punish a pupil.*

dis dain ful (dis dān′fəl), *adj.* feeling or showing disdain; scornful. **—dis dain′ful ly,** *adv.* **—dis dain′ful ness,** *n.*

dis em bark (dis′em bärk′), *v.i.*, *v.t.* go or put ashore from a ship; land from a ship. **—dis′em bar ka′tion,** *n.*

dis en gage (dis′en gāj′), *v.t.*, **-gaged, -gag ing. 1** free or release from anything that holds; detach; loosen. **2** free from an

a hat	i it	oi oil	ch child		a in about
ā age	ī ice	ou out	ng long		e in taken
ä far	o hot	u cup	sh she	ə =	i in pencil
e let	ō open	ù put	th thin		o in lemon
ē equal	ô order	ü rule	ᴛʜ then		u in circus
ėr term			zh measure		< = derived from

engagement, pledge, or obligation; stop taking part. **3** (in military use) withdraw from combat or contact with (an enemy).

dis en tan gle (dis′en tang′gəl), *v.t.*, *v.i.* **-gled, -gling.** free from tangles or complications; untangle.

dis grun tled (dis grun′tld), *adj.* in bad humor; discontented. [< *dis-* + obsolete *gruntle* to grunt, grumble]

dis heart en (dis härt′n), *v.t.* cause to lose hope; discourage; depress. **—dis heart′en ing ly,** *adv.* **—dis heart′en ment,** *n.*

di shev eled or **di shev elled** (də shev′əld), *adj.* not neat; rumpled; mussed; disordered: *disheveled appearance.*

dis mem ber (dis mem′bər), *v.t.* **1** separate or divide into parts: *After the war the defeated country was dismembered.* **2** cut or tear the limbs from; divide limb from limb. **—dis mem′ber ment,** *n.*

dis po si tion (dis′pə zish′ən), *n.* **1** one's habitual ways of acting toward others or of thinking about things; nature: *a cheerful disposition.* **2** tendency; inclination: *a disposition to argue.* **3** a settlement: *What disposition did the court make of the case?*

dis pute (dis pyüt′), *v.*, **-put ed, -put ing,** *n.* —*v.i.* **1** give reasons or facts for or against something; argue; debate; discuss. **2** wrangle; quarrel. —*v.t.* argue about; debate; discuss. —*n.* **1** argument; debate. **2** a quarrel.

dis qui et (dis kwī′ət), *v.t.* make uneasy or anxious; disturb. —*n.* uneasy feelings; anxiety. **—dis qui′et ing ly,** *adv.*

dis sec tion (di sek′shən, dī sek′shən), *n.* act of cutting apart an animal, plant, etc., in order to examine or study the structure.

dis sem ble (di sem′bəl), *v.*, **-bled, -bling.** —*v.t.* **1** hide (one's real feelings, thoughts, plans, etc.); disguise. **2** pretend; feign. —*v.i.* conceal one's opinions, motives, etc.

dis sim i lar (di sim′ə lər), *adj.* not similar; unlike; different.

dis sim u late (di sim′yə lāt), *v.*, **-lat ed, -lat ing.** —*v.t.* disguise or hide under a pretense; dissemble. —*v.i.* hide the truth; dissemble. **—dis sim′u la′tion,** *n.* **—dis sim′u la′tor,** *n.*

dis suade (di swād′), *v.t.*, **-suad ed, -suad ing. 1** persuade not to do something. **2** advise against. [< Latin *dissuadere* < *dis-* against + *suadere* to urge]

dis tem per (dis tem′pər), *n.* an infectious viral disease of dogs and other animals, accompanied by fever, a short, dry cough, and a loss of strength.

di ver si ty (də vėr′sə tē, dī vėr′sə tē), *n.*, *pl.* **-ties. 1** complete difference; unlikeness. **2** point of unlikeness. **3** variety: *a diversity of food on the table.*

di vert (də vėrt′, dī vėrt′), *v.t.* **1** turn aside: *A ditch diverted water from the stream into the fields.* **2** amuse; entertain: *Listening to music diverted me after a hard day's work.*

di vine (də vīn′), *adj.* **1** of God or a god: *a divine act.* **2** like God or a god; heavenly. **3** INFORMAL. excellent or delightful; unusually good or great. **—di vine′ly,** *adv.* **—di vine′ness,** *n.*

dog ged (dô′gid, dog′id), *adj.* not giving up; stubborn: *dogged determination.* [< *dog*] **—dog′ged ness,** *n.*

dog ma tism (dôg′mə tiz′əm, dog′mə tiz′əm), *n.* positive and emphatic assertion of opinion.

dole ful (dōl′fəl), *adj.* very sad or dreary; mournful; dismal. **—dole′ful ly,** *adv.* **—dole′ful ness,** *n.*

do main (dō mān′), *n.* **1** territory under the control of one ruler or government. **2** land owned by one person; estate. [< Middle French *domaine* < Latin *dominium* < *dominum* lord, master]

do mes tic (də mes′tik), *adj.* **1** of the home, household, or family affairs: *domestic problems, a domestic scene.* **2** attached to home; devoted to family life. —*n.* servant in a household.

do min ion (də min′yən), *n.* **1** power or right of governing and controlling; rule; control. **2** territory under the control of one ruler or government.

dor mant (dôr′mənt), *adj.* **1** lying asleep; sleeping or apparently sleeping. **2** in a state of rest or inactivity; not in motion.

dote (dōt), *v.i.*, **dot ed, dot ing. 1** be weak-minded and childish because of old age. **2 dote on** or **dote upon,** be foolishly fond of; be too fond of. [Middle English *doten*] **—dot′er,** *n.*

dow dy (dou′dē), *adj.*, **-di er, -di est.** poorly dressed; not neat; not stylish; shabby. [origin uncertain] **—dow′di ly,** *adv.*

575

drowse (drouz), v., **drowsed, drows ing,** n. —v.i. be sleepy; be half asleep. —v.t. **1** make sleepy. **2** pass (time) in drowsing. —n. a being half asleep; sleepiness. [Old English *drūsian* to sink]

du bi ous (dü′bē əs, dyü′bē əs), adj. **1** filled with or being in doubt; doubtful; uncertain. **2** feeling doubt; hesitating. [< Latin *dubiosus* < *dubius* doubtful] —**du′bi ous ly,** adv.

du ly (dü′lē, dyü′lē), adv. **1** according to what is due; as due; rightly; suitably: *The documents were duly signed before a lawyer.* **2** when due; at the proper time: *The debt will be duly paid.*

dun (dun), adj. dull, grayish-brown. —n. a dull, grayish brown.

dwin dle (dwin′dl), v.t., v.i., **-dled, -dling.** make or become smaller and smaller; shrink; diminish. [ultimately Old English *dwīnan* waste away]

dys pep tic (dis pep′tik), adj. **1** having to do with dyspepsia, or indigestion. **2** suffering from dyspepsia. **3** gloomy; pessimistic.

ebb (eb), n. a flowing of the tide away from the shore; fall of the tide. —v.i. **1** flow out; fall: *The tide ebbed.* **2** grow less or weaker; decline: *My courage ebbed as I neared the haunted house.*

ec sta sy (ek′stə sē), n., pl. **-sies. 1** condition of very great joy; thrilling or overwhelming delight. **2** any strong feeling that completely absorbs the mind; uncontrollable emotion.

ec stat ic (ek stat′ik), adj. **1** full of ecstasy: *an ecstatic look of pleasure.* **2** caused by ecstasy: *an ecstatic mood.*

ed dy (ed′ē), n., pl. **-dies,** v., **-died, -dy ing.** —n. water, air, smoke, etc., moving against the main current, especially when having a whirling motion. —v.i., v.t. move against the main current in a whirling motion; whirl.

edge (ej), n., v., **edged, edg ing.** —n. **1** line or place where something ends or begins; part farthest from the middle; side. **2** the extreme border or margin of anything; rim; brink. **3 on edge, a** disturbed; irritated; tense. **b** eager; anxious. **4 take the edge off,** take away the force, strength, or pleasure of. —v.t. **1** put an edge on; form an edge on: *edge a path with flowers.* **2** move little by little. —v.i. move sideways.

e go tism (ē′gə tiz′əm, eg′ə tiz′əm), n. **1** habit of thinking, talking, or writing too much of oneself; conceit. **2** selfishness.

eke (ēk), v.t., **eked, ek ing. 1 eke out, a** add to; increase. **b** barely manage to make (a living, a profit, etc.). **c** make (something) last longer by careful or economic use. **2** ARCHAIC and DIALECT. increase.

el e va tion (el′ə vā′shən), n. **1** a raised place: high place: *A hill is an elevation.* **2** height above the earth's surface: *The airplane cruised at an elevation of 35,000 feet.* **3** height above sea level: *The elevation of Denver is 5300 feet.*

e lic it (i lis′it), v.t. draw forth; bring out: *elicit the truth by discussion.* [< Latin *elicitum* lured out < *ex-* out + *lacere* entice]

e lude (i lüd′), v.t., **e lud ed, e lud ing. 1** avoid or escape by cleverness, quickness, etc.: *The sly fox eluded the dogs.* **2** baffle: *The cause of cancer has eluded scientists.*

e lu sive (i lü′siv), adj. **1** hard to describe or understand; baffling: *an elusive idea.* **2** tending to elude or escape: *an elusive enemy.*

em a nate (em ə nāt′), v., **-nat ed, -nat ing.** —v.i. originate from a person or thing as a source; come forth; spread out: *The rumor emanated from Chicago.* —v.t. send out; emit.

em bed (em bed′), v.t., **-bed ded, -bed ding. 1** fix or enclose in a surrounding mass; fasten firmly: *Precious stones are often found embedded in rock.* **2** plant in a bed: *He embedded the bulbs in a box of sand.* Also, **imbed.**

em i grate (em′ə grāt), v.i., **-grat ed, -grat ing.** leave one's own country or region to settle in another. [< Latin *emigratum* moved out < *ex-* out + *migrare* to move]

➔ **emigrate, immigrate.** *Emigrate* means to move out of a country or region, *immigrate* to move into a country. One who *emigrates* from Norway might *immigrate* to the United States.

e mit (i mit′), v.t., **e mit ted, e mit ting. 1** give off; send out; discharge: *The sun emits light and heat.* **2** put into circulation; issue. **3** utter; express. [< Latin *emittere* < *ex-* out + *mittere* send]

em phat ic (em fat′ik), adj. **1** said or done with force or stress; strongly expressed. **2** speaking with force or stress; expressing oneself strongly. —**em phat′i cal ly,** adv.

en core (äng′kôr, äng′kōr; än′kôr, än′kōr), interj., n. —interj. once more; again. —n. **1** a demand by the audience for the repetition of a song, etc., or for another appearance of a performer,

2 the repetition of a song, etc., or the reappearance of a performer in response to such a demand. [< French]

en deav or (en dev′ər), v.i., v.t. make an effort; try hard; attempt earnestly; strive: *A runner endeavors to win a race.* —n. an earnest attempt; hard try; effort.

en gulf (en gulf′), v.t. swallow up; overwhelm: *A wave engulfed the small boat.* —**en gulf′ment,** n.

en sem ble (än säm′bəl), n. **1** all the parts of a thing considered together. **2** a united performance of the full number of singers, musicians, etc. **3** group of musicians or musical instruments.

en sue (en sü′), v.i., **-sued, -su ing. 1** come after; follow. **2** happen as a result.

en tan gle (en tang′gəl), v.t., **-gled, -gling. 1** get twisted up and caught; tangle: *I entangled my feet in the coil of rope and fell down.* **2** get into difficulty; involve: *Don't get entangled in their scheme.* **3** perplex; confuse. —**en tan′gle ment,** n.

en ter prise (en′tər prīz), n. **1** an important, difficult, or dangerous plan to be tried; great or bold undertaking. **2** any undertaking; project; venture: *a business enterprise.*

en thuse (en thüz′), v., **-thused, -thus ing.** INFORMAL. —v.i. show enthusiasm. —v.t. fill with enthusiasm. [back-formation < *enthusiasm*]

en treat (en trēt′), v.t. ask or keep asking earnestly; beg and pray: *The prisoners entreated their captors to let them go.* [< Old French *entraitier* < *en-* in + *traitier* to treat] —**en treat′y,** n.

en vel op (en vel′əp), v.t. **1** wrap or cover; enfold. **2** hide; conceal: *Fog enveloped the village.* **3** surround; encircle: *envelop the enemy.* [< Old French *enveloper* < *en-* in + *voloper* to wrap]

ep i logue or **ep i log** (ep′ə lôg, ep′ə log), n. **1** a concluding section added to a novel, poem, etc., that rounds out or interprets the work. **2** any concluding act or event.

ep i tha la mic (ep′ə thə lā′mik), adj. honoring a bride, bridegroom, or newly married couple.

ep i thet (ep′ə thet), n. **1** a descriptive expression; word or phrase expressing some quality or attribute. **2** an insulting or contemptuous word or phrase used in place of a person's name.

ere (er, ar), ARCHAIC. —prep. before.

er mine (ér′mən), n., pl. **-mines** or **-mine.** any of several kinds of weasel of northern regions which are brown in summer but white with a black-tipped tail in winter.

ermine—about 11 in. (28 cm.) long with tail

Esq. or **Esqr.,** Esquire, a title of respect.

eu ca lyp tus (yü′kə lip′təs), n., pl. **-tus es, -ti** (-tī). any of a genus of tall evergreen trees of the myrtle family, found mainly in Australia and neighboring islands; gum tree.

e vac u ate (i vak′yü āt), v.t., **-at ed, -at ing. 1** leave empty; withdraw from: *The tenants evacuated the building.* **2** withdraw; remove: *evacuate civilians from a war zone.* [< Latin *evacuatum* emptied out < *ex-* out + *vacuus* empty] —**e vac′u a′tion,** n.

e voke (i vōk′), v.t., **e voked, e vok ing.** call forth; bring out: elicit: *A good joke evokes a laugh.*

ex ceed ing ly (ek sē′ding lē), adv. very greatly; extremely.

ex cru ci at ing (ek skrü′shē ā′ting), adj. causing great suffering; very painful; torturing. —**ex cru′ci at′ing ly,** adv.

ex e cute (ek′sə kyüt), v.t., **-cut ed, -cut ing. 1** carry out; do. **2** make according to a plan or design: *The same artist executed that painting and that statue.*

ex hil a rate (eg zil′ə rāt′), v.t., **-rat ed, -rat ing.** make merry or lively; put into high spirits; cheer.

ex hort (eg zôrt′), v.t. urge strongly; advise or warn earnestly. [< Latin *exhortari* < *ex-* + *hortari* urge strongly]

ex pec ta tion (ek′spek tā′shən), n. **1** an expecting; anticipation. **2** a being expected. **3** something expected.

ex pel (ek spel′), v.t., **-pelled, -pel ling. 1** drive out with much force; force out. **2** put (a person) out; dismiss permanently.

ex trac tion (ek strak′shən), n. **1** an extracting or removing: *the extraction of a tooth.* **2** origin; descent: *Miss Del Rio is of Spanish extraction.*

ex trav a gant (ek strav′ə gənt), adj. spending carelessly and lavishly; wasteful. —**ex trav′a gant ly,** adv.

ex trem i ty (ek strem′ə tē), n., pl. **-ties. 1** the very end; farthest possible place; last part or point. **2 extremities,** pl. the hands and feet. **3** an extreme degree: *Joy is the extremity of happiness.*

ex u ber ant (eg zü′bər ənt), adj. **1** very abundant; overflowing; lavish: *exuberant joy.* **2** abounding in health and spirits; overflowing with good cheer. [< Latin *exuberantem* growing luxuriantly < *ex-* thoroughly + *uber* fertile] —**ex u′ber ant ly,** *adv.*

a hat	i it	oi oil	ch child		a in about
ā age	ī ice	ou out	ng long		e in taken
ä far	o hot	u cup	sh she	ə =	i in pencil
e let	ō open	u̇ put	th thin		o in lemon
ē equal	ô order	ü rule	ᵀH then		u in circus
ėr term			zh measure	<	= derived from

fal ter (fôl′tər), *v.i.* 1 hesitate in action from lack of courage. 2 move unsteadily; stumble; totter. 3 come forth in hesitating, broken sounds: *My voice faltered as I stood up to speak.* —**fal′- ter er,** *n.* —**fal′ter ing ly,** *adv.*

fa nat ic (fə nat′ik), *n.* person who is carried away beyond reason because of feelings or beliefs, especially in religion or politics. —*adj.* unreasonably enthusiastic or zealous.

fan ci er (fan′sē ər), *n.* person who has a liking for or is especially interested in something: *a dog fancier.*

fan cy (fan′sē), *v.,* **-cied, -cy ing,** *n., pl.* **-cies.** —*v.t.* 1 picture to oneself; imagine; conceive: *Can you fancy yourself on the moon?* 2 have an idea or belief; suppose: *I fancy that is right, but I am not sure.* 3 be fond of; like: *I fancy the idea of having a picnic.* —*n.* 1 power to imagine; imagination; fantasy: *Dragons and giants are creatures of fancy.* 2 a liking; fondness: *They took a great fancy to each other.* [contraction of *fantasy*]

fan fare (fan′fer, fan′far), *n.* 1 a short tune or call played on trumpets, bugles, hunting horns, or the like. 2 a loud show of activity, talk, etc.; showy flourish. [< French, back-formation < *fanfarer,* to blow a fanfare]

fast ness (fast′nis), *n.* 1 a strong, safe place; stronghold. 2 a being fast or firm; firmness. 3 a being quick or rapid; swiftness.

fa tal ist (fā′tl ist), *n.* believer in fatalism, the belief that fate controls everything that happens.

fa tigue (fə tēg′), *n.* 1 weariness caused by hard work or effort. 2 task or exertion producing weariness.

fa tu i ty (fə tü′ə tē, fə tyü′ə tē), *n., pl.* **-ties.** self-satisfied stupidity; idiotic folly; silliness.

fe ro cious (fə rō′shəs), *adj.* 1 savagely cruel or destructive; fierce. 2 INFORMAL. extremely intense: *a ferocious headache.* [< Latin *ferocem* fierce] —**fe ro′cious ly,** *adv.*

fer vent (fėr′vənt), *adj.* showing great warmth of feeling; very earnest; ardent: *fervent devotion.* —**fer′vent ly,** *adv.*

fer vid (fėr′vid), *adj.* 1 full of strong feeling; intensely emotional; ardent; spirited. 2 intensely hot. —**fer′vid ly,** *adv.*

fes toon (fe stün′), *n.* a string or chain of flowers, leaves, ribbons, etc., hanging in a curve between two points. —*v.t.* decorate with festoons.

fi as co (fē as′kō), *n., pl.* **-cos** or **-coes.** a complete or ridiculous failure; humiliating breakdown. [< Italian, literally, flask]

fi na le (fə nä′lē, fi nal′ē), *n.* 1 the concluding part of a piece of music or a play. 2 the last part; end. [< Italian]

fis sure (fish′ər), *n., v.,* **-sured, -sur ing.** —*n.* 1 a long, narrow opening; split; crack: *a fissure in a rock.* 2 a splitting apart; division into parts. —*v.t.* split apart; divide into parts. —*v.i.* become split or cleft. [< Latin *fissura* < *findere* cleave]

fix (fiks), *v.t.,* **fixed, fix ing.** 1 make firm; fasten tightly. 2 make stiff or rigid: *eyes fixed in death.*

flail (flāl), *n.* instrument for threshing grain by hand, consisting of a wooden handle at the end of which a stouter and shorter pole or club is fastened so as to swing freely. —*v.t.* 1 strike with a flail. 2 beat; thrash. [< Old French *flaiel* < Latin *flagellum* whip]

fla min go (flə ming′gō), *n., pl.* **-gos** or **-goes.** any of a family of large, web-footed, aquatic tropical birds with feathers that vary from pink to scarlet. [< Portuguese < Spanish *flamenco,* literally, Flemish (from comparing the ruddy complexion of Flemings to the bird's color)]

flat (flat), *adj.,* **flat ter, flat test,** *n.* —*adj.* 1 smooth and level; even; plane: *flat land.* 2 at full length; horizontal: *The storm left the trees flat on the ground.* 3 not very deep or thick: *A plate is flat.* 4 with little air in it; deflated: *a flat tire.* 5 not to be changed; positive; absolute: *a flat refusal.* 6 in music: below the true pitch; too low in pitch. —*n.* 1 something flat. 2 flatboat. 3 land that is flat and level. 4 swamp.

flaw less (flô′lis), *adj.* without a flaw; perfect. —**flaw′less ly,** *adv.* —**flaw′less ness,** *n.*

fledg ling or **fledge ling** (flej′ling), *n.* 1 a young bird that has just grown feathers needed for flying. 2 a young, inexperienced person.

fling (fling), *v.t.,* **flung, fling ing.** 1 throw with force; throw: *fling a stone.* 2 throw aside; discard; abandon.

flo rid (flôr′id, flor′id), *adj.* 1 reddish; ruddy: *a florid complexion.* 2 elaborately ornamented; showy; ornate: *florid language.*

floss (flôs, flos), *n.* 1 short, loose, silk fibers. 2 a shiny, untwisted silk thread made from such fibers. It is used for embroidery. 3 soft, silky fluff or fibers. Milkweed pods contain white floss. —*v.i.* use dental floss: *Did you floss this morning?*

flot sam (flot′səm), *n.* 1 wreckage of a ship or its cargo found floating on the sea. 2 **flotsam and jetsam, a** wreckage or cargo found floating on the sea or washed ashore. **b** odds and ends.

flour ish (flėr′ish), *v.i.* 1 grow or develop with vigor; do well; thrive. 2 be in the best time of life or activity: *Our business is flourishing.* 3 make a showy display. —*v.t.* wave in the air; brandish: *He flourished the letter when he saw us.* —*n.* a waving about: *remove one's hat with a flourish.* [< Old French *floriss-,* a form of *florir* to flourish < Latin *florere* to bloom < *florem* flower] —**flour′ish ing ly,** *adv.*

flu ent (flü′ənt), *adj.* 1 flowing smoothly or easily. 2 speaking or writing easily and rapidly. —**flu′ent ly,** *adv.*

flung (flung), *v.* pt. and pp. of **fling.**

foil (foil), *v.t.* 1 prevent from carrying out plans, attempts, etc.; get the better of; outwit or defeat: *The hero foiled the villain.* 2 prevent (a scheme, plan, etc.) from being carried out.

fore bod ing (fôr bō′ding, fōr bō′ding), *n.* 1 prediction; warning. 2 a feeling that something bad is going to happen.

fore close (fôr klōz′, fōr klōz′), *v.,* **-closed, -clos ing.** —*v.t.* 1 shut out; prevent; exclude. 2 take away the right to redeem (a mortgage). When the conditions of a mortgage are not met, the holder can foreclose and have the property sold to satisfy his or her claim. —**fore clos′er,** *n.*

fore sight (fôr′sīt′, fōr′sīt′), *n.* 1 power to see or know beforehand what is likely to happen. 2 careful thought for the future.

fore stall (fôr stôl′, fōr stôl′), *v.t.* 1 prevent by acting first. 2 act sooner than; get ahead of. [Middle English *forstallen* < Old English *foresteall* prevention]

for lorn (fôr lôrn′), *adj.* 1 left alone and neglected. 2 wretched in feeling or looks; unhappy. 3 hopeless; desperate. —**for lorn′ly,** *adv.*

for ti tude (fôr′tə tüd, fôr′tə tyüd), *n.* courage in facing pain, danger, or trouble; firmness of spirit. [< Latin *fortitudo* strength < *fortis* strong]

foy er (foi′ər, foi′ā), *n.* an entrance hall used as a lounging room in a theater, apartment house, or hotel; lobby.

frail ty (frāl′tē), *n., pl.* **-ties.** 1 a being frail; weakness. 2 moral weakness; liability to yield to temptation.

frank furt er (frangk′fər tər), *n.* a reddish smoked sausage made of beef and pork, or of beef alone; wiener. [< German *Frankfurter* of or from Frankfurt]

fraud u lent (frô′jə lənt, frô′dyə lənt), *adj.* 1 guilty of fraud; cheating; dishonest. 2 intended to deceive: *a fraudulent offer.* 3 done by fraud; obtained by trickery. —**fraud′u lent ly,** *adv.*

freight (frāt), *n.* 1 load of goods carried on a train, truck, ship, or aircraft. 2 train for carrying goods. 3 load; burden. —*v.t.* 1 load with freight. 2 load; burden; oppress.

frog (frog, frôg), *n.* 1 any of various small, tailless amphibians, having a smooth skin and powerful web-footed hind legs. 2 an ornamental fastener on a garment, consisting of a loop and a button which passes through it. 3 **frog in the throat,** slight hoarseness caused by soreness or swelling in the throat. [Old English *frogga*]

frog (def. 2)—three frogs on a dress

froth y (frô′thē, froth′ē), *adj.,* **froth i er, froth i est.** 1 foamy. 2 light or trifling; unimportant: *frothy conversation.*

fruit less (früt′lis), *adj.* 1 having no results; of no use; unsuccessful. 2 producing no fruit. —**fruit′less ly,** *adv.*

fugue (fyüg), *n.* (in psychiatry), a period during which a patient suffers from loss of memory, often begins a new life, and, upon recovery, remembers nothing of the amnesic period.

fu tur i ty (fyü tür′ə tē, fyü tyür′ə tē), *n., pl.* **-ties.** 1 future. 2 a future state or event. 3 quality, condition, or fact of being future.

gait (gāt), *n.* 1 the manner of walking or running: *He has a lame gait because of an injured foot.* 2 (of horses) any one of various manners of stepping or running, as the gallop, trot, pace, etc.

gal le on (gal′ē ən, gal′yən), *n.* a large, high ship with three or four decks, used especially in the 1400s and 1500s. [< Spanish *galeón* < *galea* galley]

gar goyle (gär′goil), *n.* figure in the shape of a grotesque animal or human being, often for draining water from the gutter of a building. [< Middle French *gargouille* throat, waterspout]

gar ish (ger′ish, gar′ish), *adj.* 1 excessively bright; glaring: *a garish yellow.* 2 obtrusively bright in color; gaudy: *a garish suit.*

gar land (gär′lənd), *n.* wreath or string of flowers, leaves, etc. —*v.t.* 1 decorate with garlands. 2 form into garlands. [< Old French *garlande*]

gar ru lous (gar′ə ləs, gar′yə ləs), *adj.* 1 talking too much; talkative. 2 using too many words; wordy. [< Latin *garrulus* < *garrire* to chatter] —**gar′ru lous ly,** *adv.*

gargoyle

gaunt let (gônt′lit, gänt′lit), *n.* 1 a former punishment or torture in which the offender had to run between two rows of people who struck him or her with clubs or other weapons. 2 **run the gauntlet, a** pass between two rows of people each of whom strikes the runner as he or she passes. **b** be exposed to unfriendly attacks or severe criticism. Also, **gantlet.** [< Swedish *gatlopp* a running through a lane]

gen ial (jē′nyəl), *adj.* smiling and pleasant; cheerful and friendly; kindly: *a genial welcome.*

ges tic u late (je stik′yə lāt), *v.i.,* **-lat ed, -lat ing.** make or use gestures to show ideas or feelings. [< Latin *gesticulatum* gesticulated, ultimately < *gestus* gesture] —**ges tic′u la′tion,** *n.*

gild (gild), *v.t.,* **gild ed** or **gilt, gild ing.** 1 cover with a thin layer of gold or similar material; make golden. 2 make (something) look bright and pleasing. 3 make (something) seem better than it is. [Old English *-gyldan* < *gold* gold] —**gild′er,** *n.*

gin ger ly (gin′jər lē), *adv.* with extreme care or caution. —*adj.* extremely cautious or wary. —**gin′ger li ness,** *n.*

gird (gėrd), *v.t.,* **gird ed** or **girt, gird ing.** 1 put a belt, cord, etc., around. 2 fasten with a belt, cord, etc.: *gird on one's sword.*

gir dle (gėr′dl), *n.* 1 belt, sash, cord, etc., worn around the waist. 2 anything that surrounds: *a girdle of trees around the pond.* 3 a light corset worn about the hips or waist.

glance (glans), *n., v.,* **glanced, glanc ing.** —*n.* 1 a quick look directed at someone or something. 2 swift, slanting movement or impact. —*v.i.* 1 look quickly: *glance at a page, glance out the window.* 2 hit and go off at a slant: *The spear glanced against the wall and missed the target.*

glan du lar (glan′jə lər, glan′dyə lər), *adj.* of the glands, bodily organs such as the liver, the kidneys, etc.

glow er (glou′ər), *v.i.* stare angrily; scowl fiercely: *The rivals glowered at each other.* —*n.* an angry stare; fierce scowl.

gnarled (närld), *adj.* containing gnarls; knotted; twisted.

gnash (nash), *v.t.* strike or grind together: *gnash one's teeth.*

goad (gōd), *n.* 1 a sharp-pointed stick for driving cattle; gad. 2 anything which drives or urges one on. —*v.t.* drive or urge on; act as a goad to: *Hunger can goad a person to steal.* [Old English *gād*]

gor crow (gôr′krō), *n.* carrion crow, or common European crow that feeds on dead and decaying flesh.

gorge (gôrj), *n.* 1 a deep, narrow valley, usually steep and rocky, especially one with a stream. 2 mass stopping up a narrow passage: *An ice gorge blocked the river.*

graft (graft), *n.* 1 unlawful profits made by a person in and through an official position, especially in connection with politics or government business. 2 money dishonestly taken.

grap pling hook (grap′ling hük), *n.* a large iron hook used to seize and hold fast any large, heavy item.

grave (grāv), *adj.,* **grav er, grav est.** 1 earnest; thoughtful; serious: *People are grave in church.* 2 threatening to life; dangerous. 3 important; weighty; momentous: *a grave decision.* [< Middle French < Latin *gravis* heavy, serious] —**grave′ly,** *adv.*

griev ous (grē′vəs), *adj.* 1 hard to bear; causing great pain or suffering. 2 very evil or offensive; outrageous.

gro tesque (grō tesk′), *adj.* 1 odd or unnatural in shape, appearance, manner, etc.; fantastic; odd: *a grotesque monster.* 2 ridiculous; absurd: *The monkey's grotesque antics made the children laugh.*

grotesque (def. 1)

gru el ing or **gru el ling** (grü′ə ling), *adj.* very tiring; exhausting: *The marathon is a grueling contest.* —*n.* an exhausting or very tiring experience. —**gru′el ing ly, gru′el ling ly,** *adv.*

guer ril la (gə ril′ə), *n.* member of a band of fighters who harass the enemy by sudden raids, ambushes, etc. Guerrillas are not part of a regular army. —*adj.* of or by guerrillas: *a guerrilla attack.*

guild (gild), *n.* association or society formed by people having the same interests, work, etc., for some useful or common purpose: *the hospital guild of a church.* Also, **gild.**

guise (gīz), *n.* 1 style of dress. 2 outward appearance. 3 assumed appearance: *Under the guise of friendship he plotted treachery.*

haft (haft), *n.* handle, especially that of a knife, sword, etc.

hap (hap), *n., v.,* **happed, hap ping.** ARCHAIC. —*n.* chance; luck. —*v.i.* happen. [< Scandinavian (Old Icelandic) *happ*]

har ry (har′ē), *v.t.,* **-ried, -ry ing.** 1 raid and rob with violence; lay waste; pillage. 2 keep troubling; worry; torment.

haugh ty (hô′tē), *adj.,* **-ti er, -ti est.** too proud and scornful of others. —**haugh′ti ly,** *adv.* —**haugh′ti ness,** *n.*

head (hed), *n.* 1 the top part of the human body containing the brain, eyes, nose, ears, and mouth. 2 the top part of anything: *the head of a pin.* 3 the front part of anything: *the head of a procession.* 4 the chief person; leader; commander; director.

go to one's head, a affect one's mind. **b** make one dizzy. **c** make one conceited.

hang one's head, be ashamed and show that one is.

head and shoulders above, considerably better than; much superior to.

heark en (här′kən), *v.i.* pay attention to what is said; listen attentively; listen. Also, **harken.** [Old English *heorcnian*]

hence (hens), *adv.* 1 as a result of this; therefore: *The king died, and hence his son became king.* 2 from now: *years hence.*

her ald (her′əld), *n.* person who carries messages and makes announcements; messenger.

he red i tar y (hə red′ə ter′ē), *adj.* 1 passing by inheritance from generation to generation: *"Prince" and "princess" are hereditary titles.* 2 transmitted or being transmitted by means of genes from parents to offspring: *Color blindness is hereditary.* 3 derived from one's parents or ancestors: *a hereditary custom, a hereditary enemy to a country.*

here in af ter (hir′in af′tər), *adv.* afterward in this document, statement, etc.

hi ber nate (hī′bər nāt), *v.i.,* **-nat ed, -nat ing.** spend the winter in a state like sleep or in an inactive condition, as woodchucks, prairie dogs, and some other wild animals do. [< Latin *hibernatum* wintered < *hibernus* wintry] —**hi′ber na′tion,** *n.*

hilt (hilt), *n.* handle of a sword, dagger, or tool.

hist (hist), *interj.* be still! listen!

hith er (hiᴛʜ′ər), *adv.* to this place; here.

hith er to (hiᴛʜ′ər tü′), *adv.* until now: *a fact hitherto unknown.*

hoard (hôrd, hōrd), *v.t., v.i.* save and store away (money, goods, etc.) for preservation or future use: *A squirrel hoards nuts for the winter.*

hom age (hom′ij, om′ij), *n.* dutiful respect; reverence: *Everyone paid homage to the great leader.*

hov el (huv′əl, hov′əl), *n.* house that is small, crude, and unpleasant to live in. [Middle English]

hu mane (hyü mān′), *adj.* not cruel or brutal; kind; merciful. —**hu mane′ly,** *adv.* —**hu mane′ness,** *n.*

hu mil i ate (hyü mil′ē āt), *v.t.,* **-at ed, -at ing.** lower the pride, dignity, or self-respect of; make ashamed. [< Latin *humiliare* < *humilis* low] —**hu mil′i at′ing ly,** *adv.*

hy gien ic (hī jē′nik, hī jen′ik, hī′jē en′ik), *adj.* 1 favorable to health; healthful; sanitary. 2 having to do with health or hygiene.

hyp o crit i cal (hip′ə krit′ə kəl), *adj.* of or like a hypocrite, a person who pretends to be what he or she is not; insincere.

hy poth e sis (hī poth′ə sis), *n., pl.* **-ses** (-sēz′). 1 something assumed because it seems likely to be a true explanation. 2 proposition assumed as a basis for reasoning.

-ian, *suffix.* a form of **-an,** as in *mammalian, Italian.*

i de al ism (ī dē′ə liz′əm), *n.* 1 an acting according to one's ideals of what ought to be, regardless of circumstances or of the approval or disapproval of others. 2 a neglecting practical matters in following ideals; not being practical.

i dle (ī′dl), *adj.,* **i dler, i dlest.** 1 doing nothing; not busy; not working: *idle hands.* 2 fond of doing nothing; lazy. —**i′dle ness,** *n.* —**i′dly,** *adv.*

il lit er a cy (i lit′ər ə sē), *n., pl.* **-cies.** 1 inability to read and write. 2 lack of education; lack of cultural knowledge. 3 error in speaking or writing, caused by a lack of education or knowledge.

im mac u late (i mak′yə lit), *adj.* without a spot or stain; absolutely clean. —**im mac′u late ly,** *adv.*

im mi nent (im′ə nənt), *adj.* likely to happen soon; about to occur: *Black clouds show rain is imminent.* [< Latin *imminentem* overhanging, threatening] —**im′mi nent ly,** *adv.*

im mod er ate (i mod′ər it), *adj.* not moderate; extreme or excessive: *loud and immoderate laughter.* —**im mod′er ate ly,** *adv.* —**im mod′er ate ness,** *n.* —**im mod′e ra′tion,** *n.*

im mor tal (i môr′tl), *adj.* 1 living forever; never dying; everlasting. 2 remembered or famous forever. —*n.* 1 an immortal being. 2 **immortals,** *pl.* the gods of ancient Greece and Rome.

im mor tal i ty (im′ôr tal′ə tē), *n.* 1 life without death; a living forever. 2 fame that lasts forever.

im pair (im per′, im par′), *v.t.* make worse; damage; harm; weaken: *Poor eating habits impaired her health.*

im par tial (im pär′shəl), *adj.* showing no more favor to one side than to the other; fair; just. —**im par′tial ly,** *adv.*

im pen e tra ble (im pen′ə trə bəl), *adj.* 1 that cannot be penetrated, pierced, or passed: *The thorny branches made a thick, impenetrable hedge.* 2 impossible to explain or understand.

im per a tive (im per′ə tiv), *adj.* not to be avoided; that must be done; urgent; necessary: *It is imperative that this very sick child should stay in bed.* [< Latin *imperativus* < *imperare* to command]

im per cep ti ble (im′pər sep′tə bəl), *adj.* that cannot be perceived or felt; very slight, gradual, subtle, or indistinct.

im pe ri ous (im pir′ē əs), *adj.* 1 haughty or arrogant; domineering; overbearing. 2 not to be avoided; necessary; urgent. —**im pe′ri ous ly,** *adv.* —**im pe′ri ous ness,** *n.*

im promp tu (im promp′tü, im promp′tyü), *adj.* without previous thought or preparation; offhand: *a speech made impromptu.* —*adj.* made or done without previous thought or preparation: *an impromptu speech, an impromptu party.*

im pro vise (im′prə vīz), *v.,* **-vised, -vis ing.** 1 make up (music, poetry, etc.) on the spur of the moment; sing, recite, speak, etc., without preparation. 2 provide offhand; make for the occasion: *The stranded motorists improvised a tent out of two blankets and some long poles.* —**im′pro vis′er,** *n.*

im pu dent (im′pyə dənt), *adj.* shamelessly bold; very rude and insolent. [< Latin *impudentem* < *in-* not + *pudere* be modest]

im pulse (im′puls), *n.* 1 a sudden, driving force or influence; push: *the impulse of a wave, the impulse of hunger.* 2 a sudden inclination or tendency to act: *I had a strong impulse to contact my old friend.* —**im pul′sive,** *adj.*

in-, *prefix.* not; the opposite of; the absence of: *Inexpensive = not expensive. Inattention = the absence of attention.* Also, **i-, il-, im-,** and **ir-.** [< Latin]

in ac tiv i ty (in′ak tiv′ə tē), *n.* absence of activity; idleness; slowness.

in ad e quate (in ad′ə kwit), *adj.* not adequate; not enough; not as much as is needed: *inadequate preparation for an examination.* —**in ad′e quate ly,** *adv.* —**in ad′e quate ness,** *n.*

a hat	i it	oi oil	ch child		a in about
ā age	ī ice	ou out	ng long		e in taken
ä far	o hot	u cup	sh she	ə =	i in pencil
e let	ō open	u̇ put	th thin		o in lemon
ē equal	ô order	ü rule	ŦH then		u in circus
ėr term			zh measure	< = derived from

in ar tic u late (in′är tik′yə lit), *adj.* 1 not uttered in distinct syllables or words: *an inarticulate mutter.* 2 unable to speak in words; dumb: *inarticulate with grief. Cats and dogs are inarticulate.* 3 not able to put one's thoughts or feelings into words easily and clearly. —**in′ar tic′u late ly,** *adv.*

in au gu rate (in ô′gyə rāt′), *v.t.,* **-rat ed, -rat ing.** 1 install in office with formal ceremonies: *A President of the United States is inaugurated every four years.* 2 make a formal beginning of; begin.

in cal cu la ble (in kal′kyə lə bəl), *adj.* 1 too great in number to be counted; innumerable. 2 impossible to foretell or reckon beforehand. 3 that cannot be relied on; uncertain.

in car ce rate (in kär′sə rāt′), *v.t.,* **-rat ed, -rat ing.** imprison.

in cen di ar y (in sen′dē er′ē), *adj.* 1 having to do with the crime of setting property on fire intentionally. 2 deliberately stirring up strife, violence, or rebellion: *incendiary speeches.*

in ci sor (in sī′zər), *n.* tooth having a sharp edge adapted for cutting; one of the front teeth in mammals between the canine teeth in either jaw. Human beings have eight incisors.

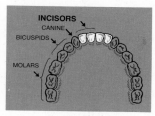

incisors of a human being

in con ti nent (in kon′tə nənt), *adj.* without self-control. —**in con′ti nent ly,** *adv.*

in cor rupt i ble (in′kə rup′tə bəl), *adj.* 1 not to be corrupted; honest: *The incorruptible judge could not be bribed.* 2 not subject to decay; lasting forever: *Diamonds are incorruptible.*

in cre du li ty (in′krə dü′lə tē, in′krə dyü′lə tē), *n.* lack of belief; doubt.

in cred u lous (in krej′ə ləs), *adj.* 1 not ready to believe; doubting; skeptical. 2 showing a lack of belief: *an incredulous smile.* —**in cred′u lous ly,** *adv.*

in dent (*v.* in dent′; *n.* in′dent, in dent′), *v.t.* 1 make notches or jags in (an edge, line, border, etc.): *an indented coastline.* 2 begin (a line) farther from the left margin than the other lines: *The first line of a paragraph is usually indented.* —*v.i.* form a notch or recess. —*n.* a notch; indentation. [< Old French *endenter* < Late Latin *indentare* to crunch on < Latin *in-* + *dentem* tooth]

in dig nant (in dig′nənt), *adj.* angry at something unworthy, unjust, unfair, or mean. [< Latin *indignantem* < *indignus* unworthy < *in-* not + *dignus* worthy] —**in dig′nant ly,** *adv.*

in dig na tion (in′dig nā′shən), *n.* anger at something unworthy, unjust, unfair, or mean; anger mixed with scorn; righteous anger: *Cruelty to animals aroused our indignation.*

in dom i ta ble (in dom′ə tə bəl), *adj.* that cannot be discouraged, beaten, or conquered; unyielding. [< Latin *indomitus* untamed < *in-* not + *domare* to tame]

in duce (in düs′, in dyüs′), *v.t.,* **-duced, -duc ing.** 1 lead on; influence; persuade: *Advertisements induce people to buy.* 2 bring about; cause: *Some drugs induce sleep.*

in duce ment (in düs′mənt, in dyüs′mənt), *n.* 1 something that influences or persuades. 2 act of influencing or persuading.

in dulge (in dulj′), *v.,* **-dulged, -dulg ing.** —*v.i.* give in to one's pleasure; let oneself have, use, or do what one wants: *A smoker indulges in tobacco.* —*v.t.* 1 give in to; let oneself have, use, or do: *She indulged her fondness for candy by eating a whole box.* 2 give in to the wishes or whims of; humor: *We often indulge a sick person.*

in ef fa ble (in ef′ə bəl), *adj.* not to be expressed in words; too great to be described in words. —**in ef′fa ble ness,** *n.*

in ef fec tu al (in′ə fek′chü əl), *adj.* 1 without effect; useless. 2 not able to produce the effect wanted; powerless. —**in′ef fec′-tu al ly,** *adv.*

in ert (in ėrt′), *adj.* 1 having no power to move or act; lifeless: *A stone is an inert mass of matter.* 2 inactive; slow; sluggish.

579

in ev i ta ble (in ev′ə tə bəl), *adj.* not to be avoided; sure to happen; certain to come: *Death is inevitable.* [< Latin *inevitabilis* < *in-* not + *evitare* avoid < *ex-* out + *vitare* shun]

in ex haust i ble (in′ig zô′stə bəl), *adj.* 1 that cannot be exhausted; very abundant. 2 that cannot be wearied; tireless.

inferiority complex, an abnormal feeling of being inferior to, or not as good as, other people, sometimes made up for by overly aggressive behavior.

in fest (in fest′), *v.t.* trouble or disturb frequently or in large numbers: *a swamp infested with mosquitoes. The national park was infested with tourists.* [< Latin *infestare* to attack < *infestus* hostile] —**in′fes ta′tion,** *n* —**in fest′er,** *n.*

in fir mar y (in fèr′mər ē), *n., pl.* **-mar ies.** 1 place for the care of the infirm, sick, or injured. 2 any hospital.

in fu ri ate (in fyur′ē āt), *v.t.,* **-at ed, -at ing.** fill with wild, fierce anger; make furious; enrage. —**in fur′i at′ing ly,** *adv.*

in gen ious (in jē′nyəs), *adj.* 1 skillful in making; good at inventing. 2 cleverly planned or made: *This mousetrap is an ingenious device.* [< Latin *ingeniosus* < *ingenium* natural talent < *in-* in + *gignere* beget, be born]

in graft (in graft′), *v.t.* 1 graft (a shoot, etc.) from one tree or plant into another. 2 fix in; implant. Also, **engraft.**

in grat i tude (in grat′ə tüd, in grat′ə tyüd), *n.* lack of gratitude or thankfulness; being ungrateful.

in jec tion (in jek′shən), *n.* 1 act or process of injecting or forcing (liquid, medicine, etc.) into a chamber or passage: *Drugs are often given by injection.* 2 liquid injected: *an injection of penicillin.*

in so lent (in′sə lənt), *adj.* boldly rude; intentionally disregarding the feelings of others; insulting. [< Latin *insolentem* arrogant, contrary to custom < *in-* not + *solere* be accustomed] —**in′so lent ly,** *adv.*

inst., 1 instant (of the present month). "The 10th inst." means "the tenth day of the present month."

in sta bil i ty (in′stə bil′ə tē), *n.* lack of firmness; being unstable; unsteadiness.

in sub stan tial (in′səb stan′shəl), *adj.* 1 frail; flimsy: *A cobweb is very insubstantial.* 2 unreal; not actual; imaginary: *Dreams and ghosts are insubstantial.* —**in′sub stan′tial ly,** *adv.*

in suf fer a ble (in suf′ər ə bəl), *adj.* intolerable; unbearable: *insufferable rudeness.* —**in suf′fer a ble ness,** *n.*

in su per a ble (in sü′pər ə bəl), *adj.* that cannot be passed over or overcome; insurmountable: *an insuperable barrier.*

in tan gi ble (in tan′jə bəl), *adj.* 1 not capable of being touched or felt: *Sound and light are intangible.* 2 not easily grasped by the mind; vague: *Charm is an intangible quality.*

in tel li gence (in tel′ə jəns), *n.* 1 ability to learn and know; mind. 2 knowledge, news, or information: *intelligence of a person's whereabouts.* 3 secret information, especially about an enemy.

in tel li gi ble (in tel′ə jə bəl), *adj.* capable of being understood; clear; comprehensible. —**in tel′li gi bly,** *adv.*

in ten si fy (in ten′sə fī), *v.t., v.i.,* **-fied, -fy ing.** make or become intense or more intense; strengthen; increase. —**in ten′si fi ca′tion,** *n.*

in ter im (in′tər im), *n.* time between; the meantime. —*adj.* for the meantime; temporary. [< Latin, in the meantime < *inter* between]

in ter lace (in′tər lās′), *v.,* **-laced, -lac ing.** —*v.t.* arrange (threads, strips, or branches) so that they go over and under each other; weave together; intertwine: *Baskets are made by interlacing reeds or fibers.* —*v.i.* cross each other over and under; mingle together in an intricate manner: *interlacing roads and streams.*

in ter mi na ble (in tèr′mə nə bəl), *adj.* 1 never stopping; unceasing; endless. 2 so long as to seem endless; very long and tiring. —**in ter′mi na bly,** *adv.*

in tern (in tèrn′), *v.t.* confine within a country or place; force to stay in a certain place, especially during wartime.

in ter ro gate (in ter′ə gāt), *v.,* **-gat ed, -gat ing.** —*v.t.* ask questions of; examine or get information from by asking questions.

in ter vene (in′tər vēn′), *v.i.,* **-vened, -ven ing.** 1 come between; be between: *A week intervenes between my sister's birthday and mine.* 2 come between persons or groups to help settle a dispute; act as an intermediary: *The President was asked to intervene in the coal strike.* [< Latin *intervenire* < *inter-* between + *venire* come] —**in′ter ven′er, in′ter ve′nor,** *n.*

in ti ma cy (in′tə mə sē), *n., pl.* **-cies.** 1 being intimate; close acquaintance; closeness. 2 a familiar or intimate act.

in tro spec tive (in′trə spek′tiv), *adj.* characterized by intro-

spection, or examination of one's own thoughts and feelings. —**in′tro spec′tive ly,** *adv.*

in trude (in trüd′), *v.,* **-trud ed, -trud ing.** —*v.i.* force oneself in; come unasked and unwanted. —*v.t.* give unasked and unwanted; force in: *intrude one's opinions upon others.* [< Latin *intrudere* < *in-* in + *trudere* to thrust] —**in trud′er,** *n.*

in tu i tion (in′tü ish′ən, in′tyü ish′ən), *n.* immediate perception or understanding of truths, facts, etc., without reasoning: *By experience with many kinds of people the doctor had developed great powers of intuition.*

in var i a ble (in ver′ē ə bəl, in var′ē ə bəl), *adj.* always the same; unchanging; unchangeable; constant: *an invariable habit.* —**in var′i a ble ness,** *n.* —**in var′i a bly,** *adv.*

in ven to ry (in′vən tôr′ē, in′vən tōr′ē), *n., pl.* **-ries, *v.,*** **-ried, -ry ing.** —*n.* a complete and detailed list of articles with their estimated value. —*v.t.* make a complete and detailed list of.

in voice (in′vois), *n.* list of goods sent to a purchaser showing prices, amounts, shipping charges, etc.

in vol un tar y (in vol′ən ter′ē), *adj.* 1 not voluntary; not done of one's own free will; unwilling: *involuntary consent.* 2 not done on purpose; not intended: *an involuntary injury.*

ir re place a ble (ir′i plā′sə bəl), *adj.* not replaceable; impossible to replace with another.

ir ri gate (ir′ə gāt), *v.t.,* **-gat ed, -gat ing.** supply (land) with water by using ditches, by sprinkling, etc. [< Latin *irrigatum* watered, irrigated < *in-* + *rigare* to water, wet] —**ir′ri ga′tion,** *n.*

i tin er ant (ī tin′ər ənt, i tin′ər ənt), *adj.* traveling from place to place, especially in connection with some employment or vocation.

-ity, *suffix forming nouns from adjectives.* quality, condition, or fact of being _____: *Sincerity = quality or condition of being sincere.* Also, **-ty.** [< Old French *-ité* < Latin *-itatem*]

ja pon i ca (jə pon′ə kə), *n.* camellia, a variety of shrub with glossy leaves and white, red, or pink flowers.

jaun ty (jôn′tē, jän′tē), *adj.,* **-ti er, -ti est.** 1 easy and lively; sprightly; carefree: *The happy children walked with jaunty steps.* 2 smart; stylish: *She wore a jaunty little hat.*

jell (jel), *v.i.* 1 become jelly; thicken or congeal. 2 INFORMAL. take definite form; become fixed: *Her hunch soon jelled into a plan.* —*v.t.* cause to jell. —*n.* jelly. [back-formation < *jelly*]

jour ney man (jèr′nē mən), *n., pl.* **-men.** 1 worker who knows a trade. 2 worker who has served an apprenticeship.

ju bi lant (jü′bə lənt), *adj.* expressing or showing joy; rejoicing. [< Latin *jubilantem* < *jubilum* wild shout] —**ju′bi lant ly,** *adv.* —**ju′bi la′tion,** *n.*

jus ti fy (jus′tə fī), *v.t.,* **-fied, -fy ing.** 1 show to be just or right; give a good reason for; defend: *The fine quality of the cloth justifies its high price.* 2 show to be just or right.

kin dle (kin′dl), *v.,* **-dled, -dling.** —*v.t.* 1 set on fire; light. 2 stir up; arouse: *kindle enthusiasm.* —*v.i.* 1 catch fire; begin to burn: *This damp wood will never kindle.* 2 become stirred up or aroused. 3 light up; brighten: *The girl's face kindled as she told about the airplane ride.*

la bo ri ous (lə bôr′ē əs, lə bōr′ē əs), *adj.* requiring much work; requiring hard work. —**la bo′ri ous ly,** *adv.*

lab y rinth (lab′ə rinth′), *n.* 1 number of connecting passages so arranged that it is hard to find one's way from point to point; maze. 2 **Labyrinth** (in Greek legends) the maze built by Daedalus for King Minos of Crete to imprison the Minotaur. 3 any confusing, complicated arrangement: *a labyrinth of dark and narrow streets.* [< Greek *labyrinthos*]

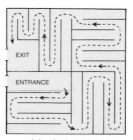

labyrinth (def. 1)

lack a dai si cal (lak′ə dā′zə kəl), *adj.* lacking interest or enthusiasm; languid; listless; dreamy. [< *lackaday* alas, variant of *alack a day!*] —**lack′a dai′si cal ly,** *adv.*

la ment (lə ment′), *v.t.* **1** express grief for; mourn for. **2** regret: *We lamented his absence.* —*v.i.* express grief; mourn; weep: *Why does she lament?* [< Latin *lamentari* < *lamentum* a wailing] —**la ment′ing ly,** *adv.*

lam en ta tion (lam′ən tā′shən), *n.* loud grief; cries of sorrow.

lapse (laps), *n., v.,* **lapsed, laps ing.** —*n.* **1** a slight mistake or error. **2** a falling into disuse: *the lapse of a custom.* —*v.i.* **1** make a slight mistake or error. **2** slip by; pass away: *Our interest in the dull story soon lapsed.* **3** fall into disuse. [< Latin *lapsus* fall < *labi* to slip]

ledg er book (lej′ər bùk′), *n.* book of accounts in which a business keeps a final record of all transactions.

le o tard (lē′ə tärd), *n.* Usually, **leotards,** *pl.* a tight-fitting one-piece garment worn by dancers, acrobats, etc. [< French *léotard* < Jules *Léotard*, French aerialist of the 1800s]

-less, *suffix forming adjectives from verbs and nouns.* without a ____; that has no ____: *Homeless = without a home.*

lest (lest), *conj.* for fear that: *Be careful lest you fall.*

leth ar gy (leth′ər jē), *n., pl.* **-gies.** drowsy dullness; lack of energy; sluggish inactivity. [< Greek *lēthargia* < *lēthē* forgetfulness + *argos* lazy < *a-* not + *ergon* work]

lib e rate (lib′ə rāt′), *v.t.,* **-rat ed, -rat ing.** set free; free or release from slavery, prison, confinement, etc.

lithe (līтн), *adj.* bending easily; supple: *lithe of body, a lithe willow.* [Old English *līthe* mild] —**lithe′ly,** *adv.* —**lithe′-ness,** *n.*

lo (lō), *interj.* Often, **lo and behold.** look! see! behold! [Old English *lā*]

loath (lōth, lōтн), *adj.* unwilling or reluctant; averse: *The little girl was loath to leave her mother.* [Old English *lāth* hostile]

➤ **loath, loathe.** These two forms are quite close in appearance, and are ultimately related to each other, but are distinct in function and meaning. *Loath* is always an adjective, and means "reluctant, unwilling": *They were loath to eat any more cake. Loathe,* a verb, means "hate, despise": *She loathed the thought of getting up early.*

loathe (lōтн), *v.t.,* **loathed, loath ing.** feel strong dislike and disgust for; abhor; hate; detest: *loathe cockroaches.* [Old English *lāthian* to hate < *lāth* hostile] ➤ See **loath** for usage note.

lodging house, house in which rooms are rented.

lo qua cious (lō kwā′shəs), *adj.* talking much; fond of talking. —**lo qua′cious ly,** *adv.* —**lo qua′cious ness,** *n.*

lu mi nous (lü′mə nəs), *adj.* **1** shining by its own light. **2** full of light; shining; bright. **3** easily understood; clear; enlightening.

mack i naw (mak′ə nô), *n.* **1** kind of short coat made of heavy woolen cloth, often in a plaid pattern. **2** a large, heavy, flat-bottomed boat with a sharp prow and square stern, formerly used on the Great Lakes. [< *Mackinaw* City, town in northern Michigan]

maes tro (mī′strō; *Italian* mä es′trō), *n., pl.* **-tros,** ITALIAN **ma es tri** (mä es′trē). **1** a great composer, teacher, or conductor of music. **2** master of any art. [< Italian < Latin *magister* master]

magic lantern, an early type of projector for showing photographic slides on a screen.

make shift (māk′shift′), *adj.* used for a time instead of the right thing; temporarily substituted.

mal a prop ism (mal′ə prop′iz′əm), *n.* **1** a ridiculous misuse of words, especially a confusion of two words somewhat similar in sound but different in meaning, as a musical *progeny* for a musical *prodigy.* Malapropisms are often used for humorous effect. **2** instance of this; a misused word. [< Mrs. *Malaprop,* character in Richard Sheridan's play *The Rivals,* noted for her absurd misuse of words < *malapropos*]

ma lig nant (mə lig′nənt), *adj.* **1** very evil, hateful, or malicious. **2** having an evil influence; very harmful.

ma neu ver (mə nü′vər), *n.* **1** a planned movement of troops, ships, etc., especially for tactical purposes. **2** an agile or skillful movement made to elude or deceive. —*v.i.* plan skillfully; use clever tricks; scheme: *maneuver for some advantage.*

man i fest (man′ə fest), *adj.* apparent to the eye or to the mind; plain; clear: *a manifest error.* —**man′i fest′ly,** *adv.*

man tle (man′tl), *n.* **1** a long, loose cloak without sleeves.

---

a hat	i it	oi oil	ch child		a in about
ā age	ī ice	ou out	ng long		e in taken
ä far	o hot	u cup	sh she	ə =	i in pencil
e let	ō open	ù put	th thin		o in lemon
ē equal	ô order	ü rule	ŦH then		u in circus
ėr term			zh measure	< = derived from

2 anything that covers like a mantle: *The ground had a mantle of snow.*

mark (märk), *n.* **1** trace or impression, such as a line, dot, spot, stain, or scar, made by some object on the surface of another. **2** grade or rating. **3** something aimed at; target; goal. —*v.t.* **1** give grades to; rate. **2** show clearly; indicate: *A frown marked her disapproval.* **3** pay attention to; notice; observe: *Mark well my words.* **4** keep (the score); record.

mar row (mar′ō), *n.* **1** the soft tissue that fills the cavities of most bones and is the source of red blood cells and many white blood cells. **2** the inmost or essential part.

mar shal (mär′shəl), *n., v.,* **-shaled, -shal ing** or **-shalled, -shal ling.** —*n.* officer of various kinds, especially a police officer. —*v.t.* **1** arrange in proper order: *marshal facts for a debate.* **2** conduct with ceremony: *We were marshaled before the queen.*

mar tyr (mär′tər), *n.* **1** person who chooses to die or suffer rather than renounce a religious faith. **2** person who is put to death or made to suffer greatly because of a belief, cause, or principle.

mas tiff (mas′tif), *n.* any of a breed of large, powerful dogs having a short, thick coat, drooping ears, and hanging lips. [< Old French *mastin;* influenced by Old French *mestif* mongrel]

mat ri mo ni al (mat′rə mō′nē əl), *adj.* of or having to do with marriage. —**mat′ri mo′ni al ly,** *adv.*

mean¹ (mēn), *v.t.,* **meant, mean ing. 1** have as its thought: *What does this word mean?* **2** have as a purpose; have in mind; intend: *I do not mean to go.* [Old English *mǣnan* to mean, tell, say]

mastiff—about 30 in. (76 cm.) high at the shoulder

mean² (mēn), *adj.* **1** of a petty, unkind, small-minded nature: *mean thoughts.* **2** low in quality or grade; poor: *the meanest of gifts.* **3** of little importance or value: *the meanest flower.* **4** SLANG. excellent; clever; skillful: *to play a mean game of tennis.* [Old English *(ge)mǣne* common]

mean³ (mēn), *adj.* **1** halfway between two extremes: *the mean annual air temperature.* **2** intermediate in kind, quality, or degree; average. [< Old French *meien* < Latin *medianus* of the middle < *medius* middle of]

med i tate (med′ə tāt), *v.,* **-tat ed, -tat ing.** —*v.i.* engage in deep and serious thought; think quietly; reflect. —*v.t.* think about; consider; plan; intend. —**med′i ta′tion,** *n.* —**med′i ta′tor,** *n.*

me lo di ous (mə lō′dē əs), *adj.* **1** sweet-sounding; pleasing to the ear; musical. **2** producing melody: *melodious birds.*

men ace (men′is), *n., v.,* **-aced, -ac ing.** —*n.* something that threatens; threat. —*v.t.* offer a menace to; threaten: *Floods menaced the valley towns with destruction.* —*v.i.* be threatening. —**men′ac ing ly,** *adv.*

mer cu ri al (mər kyùr′ē əl), *adj.* **1** sprightly and animated; quick. **2** changeable; fickle. **3** containing mercury.

merge (mėrj), *v.,* **merged, merg ing.** —*v.t.* cause to be swallowed up or absorbed so as to lose its own character or identity; combine or consolidate: *The steel trusts merged various small businesses.* —*v.i.* become swallowed up or absorbed so as to lose its own character or identity: *The twilight merges into darkness.*

mes quite (me skēt′), *n.* a deep-rooted tree or shrub of the pea family, common in the southwestern United States and in Mexico.

me te or ol o gy (mē′tē ə rol′ə jē), *n.* science dealing with the atmosphere and atmospheric conditions or phenomena, especially as they relate to weather. —**me′te or ol′o gist,** *n.*

me tic u lous (mə tik′yə ləs), *adj.* extremely or excessively careful about details. —**me tic′u lous ly,** *adv.*

met ro nome (met′rə nōm), *n.* device that can be adjusted to make loud ticking sounds at different speeds, used especially to mark time for persons practicing on musical instruments.

met ro pol i tan (met′rə pol′ə tən), *adj.* of a metropolis; belonging to a large city or cities: *metropolitan newspapers.* —*n.* person who lives in a large city and has metropolitan ideas or manners.

met tle (met′l), *n.* **1** quality of disposition or temperament. **2** spirit; courage. **3 on one's mettle,** ready to do one's best.

minc ing (min′sing), *adj.* **1** putting on a dainty and refined manner: *a mincing voice.* **2** walking with short steps. —**minc′ing ly,** *adv.*

min i mal (min′ə məl), *adj.* least possible; very small; having to do with a minimum. —**min′i mal ly,** *adv.*

mi rac u lous (mə rak′yə ləs), *adj.* **1** constituting a miracle; supernatural. **2** marvelous; wonderful: *miraculous good fortune.* —**mi rac′u lous ly,** *adv.* —**mi rac′u lous ness,** *n.*

mis cre ant (mis′krē ənt), *adj.* having very bad morals; wicked; base. —*n.* a base or wicked person; villain.

mod er ate (mod′ər it), *adj.* **1** kept or keeping within proper bounds; not extreme: *moderate expenses, moderate styles.* **2** not very large or good; fair; medium: *a moderate profit.* [< Latin *moderatum* regulated < *modus* measure]

moi e ty (moi′ə tē), *n., pl.* **-ties.** **1** half. **2** part.

mo men tar i ly (mō′mən ter′ə lē, mō′mən ter′ə lē), *adv.* **1** for a moment: *hesitate momentarily.* **2** at every moment; from moment to moment: *The danger was increasing momentarily.*

mo men tum (mō men′təm), *n., pl.* **-tums, -ta** (-tə). **1** force with which a body moves: *A falling object gains momentum as it falls.* **2** impetus resulting from movement: *The runner's momentum carried him far beyond the finish line.*

mon arch (mon′ərk), *n.* king, queen, emperor, empress, etc.; ruler. [< Greek *monarchos* < *monos* alone + *archein* to rule]

mo not o nous (mə not′n əs), *adj.* **1** continuing in the same tone or pitch: *a monotonous voice.* **2** not varying; without change; uniform. **3** wearying because of its sameness; tedious: *monotonous work.* —**mo not′o nous ly,** *adv.* —**mo not′o nous ness,** *n.*

moor (mùr), *n.* an open wasteland, usually covered with heather.

mo rose (mə rōs′), *adj.* gloomy; sullen; ill-humored: *a morose person.* [< Latin *morosus,* originally, set in one's ways < *morem* custom, habit] —**mo rose′ly,** *adv.* —**mo rose′ness,** *n.*

mor tal (môr′tl), *adj.* **1** sure to die sometime. **2** of human beings; of mortals: *Mortal bodies feel pain.* **3** very great; deadly: *mortal terror.* —*n.* a being that is sure to die sometime. [< Latin *mortalis* < *mortem* death]

mo ti va tion (mō′tə vā′shən), *n.* stimulus; cause or reason for action. —**mo′ti va′tion al,** *adj.*

mo tor (mō′tər), *n.* engine that makes a machine go: *an electric motor.* —*adj.* **1** run by a motor: *a motor vehicle.* **2** causing or having to do with motion or action. **3** (of muscles, impulses, centers, etc.) concerned with or involving motion or activity. **4** of, having to do with, or involving muscular or glandular activity: *a motor response.* [< Latin, mover < *movere* to move]

mul ti tude (mul′tə tüd, mul′tə tyüd), *n.* **1** a great many; crowd; host: *a multitude of enemies.* **2 the multitude,** the common people. [< Latin *multitudo* < *multus* much]

mute (myüt), *adj., n., v.,* **mut ed, mut ing.** —*adj.* **1** not making any sound; silent: *The little girl stood mute with embarrassment.* **2** unable to speak; dumb. —*n.* **1** person who cannot speak. **2** clip, pad, or other device, used to soften, deaden, or muffle the sound of a musical instrument. —*v.t.* deaden or soften the sound of (a tone, voice, a musical instrument, etc.) with or as if with a mute. —**mute′ly,** *adv.* —**mute′ness,** *n.*

mu tu al (myü′chü əl), *adj.* done, said, felt, etc., by each toward the other; given and received: *mutual promises, mutual dislike.* —**mu′tu al ly,** *adv.*

na ï ve té or **na i ve te** (nä ē′və tā′), *n.* quality of being naïve or childlike; unspoiled freshness; artlessness.

nar y (ner′ē, nar′ē), *adv.* DIALECT. not: *nary a one.* [< *ne'er a*]

nec tar (nek′tər), *n.* **1** (in Greek and Roman myths) the drink of the gods. **2** any delicious drink. [< Latin < Greek *nektar*]

ne go ti ate (ni gō′shē āt), *v.,* **-at ed, -at ing.** —*v.i.* talk over and arrange terms; confer; consult: *Both countries negotiated for peace.* —*v.t.* **1** arrange for: *They finally negotiated a peace treaty.* **2** get past or over: *The car negotiated the sharp curve easily.*

neur o sur geon (nùr′ō sèr′jən), *n.* physician who specializes in neurosurgery, surgery involving the brain or other parts of the nervous system.

noi some (noi′səm), *adj.* **1** that disgusts; offensive, especially to the smell: *a noisome odor.* **2** harmful; injurious: *a noisome pestilence.* [Middle English *noy,* variant of *annoy* + *-some*]

non cha lant (non′shə lənt, non′shə länt′), *adj.* without enthusiasm; coolly unconcerned; indifferent. [< French < *non-* not + *chaloir* care about] —**non′cha lant ly,** *adv.*

non com mit tal (non′kə mit′l), *adj.* not committing oneself; not saying yes or no: *"I will think it over" is a noncommittal answer.*

no ta tion (nō tā′shən), *n.* **1** set of signs or symbols used to represent numbers, quantities, or other values. **2** the representing of numbers, quantities, or other values by symbols or signs: *Music has a special system of notation.*

note wor thy (nōt′wèr′ŦHē), *adj.* worthy of notice; remarkable.

no to ri ous (nō tôr′ē əs, nō tōr′ē əs), *adj.* **1** well-known, especially because of something bad; having a bad reputation: *a notorious gambler.* **2** well-known; celebrated.

nov el (nov′əl), *adj.* of a new kind or nature; strange; new; unfamiliar: *a novel idea.* —*n.* long story with characters and a plot. [< Latin *novellus,* diminutive of *novus* new]

nu cle us (nü′klē əs, nyü′klē əs), *n., pl.* **-cle i** or **-cle us es.** **1** a central part or thing around which other parts or things are collected. **2** a beginning to which additions are to be made. **3** the central part of an atom.

nur ture (nèr′chər), *v.,* **-tured, -tur ing,** *n.* —*v.t.* bring up; care for; foster; rear; train: *They nurtured the child as if he had been their own.* —*n.* a bringing up; rearing; training; education: *The two sisters had received very different nurture.*

o blique (ə blēk′), *adj.* **1** neither perpendicular to nor parallel with a given line or surface; slanting. **2** not straightforward; indirect. —**o blique′ly,** *adv.*

ob scure (əb skyùr′), *adj.,* **-scur er, -scur est,** *v.,* **-scured, -scur ing.** —*adj.* **1** not clearly expressed; hard to understand. **2** not well known; attracting no notice: *an obscure little village, an obscure poet.* **3** not distinct; not clear: *an obscure shape, obscure sounds.* **4** dark; dim: *an obscure corner.* —*v.t.* **1** hide from view; make obscure; darken: *Clouds obscure the sun.* **2** make dim or vague to the understanding.

ob se qui ous (əb sē′kwē əs), *adj.* polite or obedient from hope of gain or from fear: *Obsequious courtiers greeted the royal couple.* [< Latin *obsequiosus* < *obsequium* dutiful service < *ob-* after + *sequi* follow] —**ob se′qui ous ly,** *adv.*

ob sti na cy (ob′stə nə sē), *n., pl.* **-cies.** **1** a refusal to give in; stubbornness. **2** an obstinate act.

oc tave (ok′tiv, ok′tāv), *n.* **1** interval between a musical tone and another tone having twice or half as many vibrations. From middle C to the C above it is an octave. **2** the eighth tone above or below a given tone. [< Latin *octavus* eighth < *octo* eight]

o gre (ō′gər), *n.* **1** (in folklore and fairy tales) giant or monster that supposedly eats people. **2** person like such a monster.

o men (ō′mən), *n.* **1** sign of what is to happen; object or event that is believed to mean good or bad fortune: *Spilling salt is said to be an omen of bad luck.* **2** prophetic meaning; foreboding: *Some people consider a black cat a creature of ill omen.* [< Latin *omen, ominis*]

om i nous (om′ə nəs), *adj.* unfavorable; threatening: *ominous clouds.* —**om′i nous ly,** *adv.* —**om′i nous ness,** *n.*

on slaught (ôn′slôt′, on′slôt′), *n.* a vigorous attack. [probably < Dutch *aanslag* an attempt, stroke]

op por tun ist (op′ər tü′nist, op′ər tyü′nist), *n.* person who uses every opportunity to gain advantage, regardless of right or wrong.

op pres sive (ə pres′iv), *adj.* **1** hard to bear; burdensome: *The intense heat was oppressive.* **2** harsh; unjust.

o ra tor i cal (ôr′ə tôr′ə kəl), *adj.* **1** of oratory, or skill in public speaking. **2** characteristic of orators or oratory: *He has an oratori-*

cal manner even in conversation. —**o′ra tor′i cal ly,** *adv.*

orb (ôrb), *n.* **1** anything round like a ball; sphere; globe. **2** sun, moon, planet, or star. **3** the eyeball or eye. [< Latin *orbis* circle]

or ches trate (ôr′kə strāt), *v.t.,* **-trat ed, -trat ing.** compose or arrange (music) for performance by an orchestra. —**or′ches trat′er, or′ches tra′tor,** *n.* —**or′ches tra′tion,** *n.*

ord nance (ôrd′nəns), *n.* **1** cannon or artillery. **2** military apparatus or supplies of all kinds.

os ten ta tious (os′ten tā′shəs), *adj.* **1** done for display; intended to attract notice. **2** showing off; liking to attract notice. —**os′ten ta′tious ly,** *adv.* —**os′ten ta′tious ness,** *n.*

ost ler (os′lər), *n.* person who takes care of horses at an inn or stable.

o va tion (ō vā′shən), *n.* an enthusiastic public welcome; burst of loud clapping or cheering. [< Latin *ovationem* < *ovare* rejoice]

pac i fy (pas′ə fī), *v.t.,* **-fied, -fy ing.** **1** make peaceful; quiet down: *pacify angry demonstrators, pacify a crying baby.* **2** bring under control; subdue: *pacify a rebellious region.*

pa go da (pə gō′də), *n.* temple or other sacred building having many stories, with a roof curving upward from each story, found in India, China, Japan, and other Asian countries. [< Portuguese *pagode* < Tamil *pagavadi* < Sanskrit *bhagavatī* goddess]

pal at a ble (pal′ə tə bəl), *adj.* **1** agreeable to the taste; pleasing. **2** agreeable to the mind or feelings; acceptable.

pa lav er (pə lav′ər), *n.* **1** unnecessary or idle words; mere talk. **2** smooth, persuading talk; fluent talk; flattery.

pall (pôl), *n.* **1** a heavy cloth of black, purple, or white velvet, spread over a coffin. **2** a dark, gloomy covering: *A pall of smoke shut out the sun from the city.* [Old English *pæll* < Latin *pallium* cloak]

pagoda

pal try (pôl′trē), *adj.,* **-tri er, -tri est.** **1** almost worthless; trifling; petty; mean. **2** of no worth; despicable; contemptible.

par a pet (par′ə pet, par′ə pit), *n.* **1** a low wall or mound of stone, earth, etc., in front of a walk or platform at the top of a fort, trench, etc., to protect soldiers; rampart. **2** a low wall or barrier at the edge of a balcony, roof, bridge, etc.

par a pher nal ia (par′ə fər nā′lyə), *n., pl. or sing.* **1** personal belongings. **2** equipment; outfit.

par ent age (per′ən tij, par′ən tij), *n.* **1** descent from parents; family line; ancestry. **2** parenthood.

pa ren tal (pə ren′tl), *adj.* of or having to do with a parent or parents; like a parent's. —**pa ren′tal ly,** *adv.*

par ox ysm (par′ək siz′əm), *n.* **1** a sudden, severe attack of the symptoms of a disease, usually recurring periodically: *a paroxysm of coughing.* **2** a sudden outburst of emotion or activity.

par ry (par′ē), *v.t.,* **-ried, -ry ing.** ward off or block (a thrust, stroke, weapon, etc.) in fencing, boxing, etc.

pa ter nal (pə tèr′nl), *adj.* **1** of or like a father; fatherly. **2** related on the father's side of the family: *a paternal aunt, paternal grandparents.* [< Latin *paternus* < *pater* father]

pa tron age (pā′trə nij, pat′rə nij), *n.* regular business given to a store, hotel, etc., by customers.

peak ed (pē′kid), *adj.* sickly in appearance; wan; thin. [< earlier *peak* look sick; origin uncertain] —**peak′ed ness,** *n.*

peer less (pir′lis), *adj.* without an equal; matchless.

pee vish (pē′vish), *adj.* **1** feeling cross; fretful; complaining: *a peevish child.* **2** showing annoyance or irritation. [Middle English *pevysh*] —**pee′vish ly,** *adv.* —**pee′vish ness,** *n.*

pen non (pen′ən), *n.* **1** a long, narrow flag originally carried on the lance of a knight. **2** any flag or banner.

per ceive (pər sēv′), *v.t.,* **-ceived, -ceiv ing.** **1** be aware of through the senses; see, hear, taste, smell, or feel. **2** take in with the mind; observe; understand. [< Old French *perceivre* < Latin *percipere* < *per-* thoroughly + *capere* to grasp]

a hat	**i** it	**oi** oil	**ch** child		a in about
ā age	**ī** ice	**ou** out	**ng** long		e in taken
ä far	**o** hot	**u** cup	**sh** she	**ə** =	i in pencil
e let	**ō** open	**u̇** put	**th** thin		o in lemon
ē equal	**ô** order	**ü** rule	**ᵺ** then		u in circus
ėr term			**zh** measure		< = derived from

per cep tion (pər sep′shən), *n.* **1** act of perceiving, seeing, or understanding: *His perception of the change came in a flash.* **2** power of perceiving: *a keen perception.* **3** understanding: *I now have a clear perception of what went wrong.*

per cus sion ist (pər kush′ə nist), *n.* person who plays a percussion instrument, a musical instrument played by striking it, such as a drum, cymbal, or piano.

pe remp tor y (pə remp′tər ē, per′əmp tôr′ē), *adj.* **1** leaving no choice; decisive; final; absolute. **2** allowing no denial or refusal: *a peremptory command.* —**pe remp′tor i ly,** *adv.*

per me ate (pèr′mē āt), *v.t.,* **-at ed, -at ing.** spread through the whole of; pass through; pervade: *Smoke permeated the house.*

per pen dic u lar (pèr′pən dik′yə lər), *adj.* **1** standing straight up; vertical; upright. **2** very steep; precipitous. **3** at right angles to a given line, plane, or surface. —**per′pen dic′u lar ly,** *adv.*

per pet u al (pər pech′ü əl), *adj.* **1** lasting forever; eternal: *the perpetual hills.* **2** never ceasing; continuous; constant: *a perpetual stream of visitors.* —**per pet′u al ly,** *adv.*

per sist (pər sist′, pər zist′), *v.i.* **1** continue firmly; refuse to stop or be changed. **2** remain in existence; stay: *On the tops of very high mountains snow persists throughout the year.* **3** say again and again. [< Latin *persistere* < *per-* to the end + *sistere* to stand]

per sist ent (pər sis′tənt, pər zis′tənt), *adj.* **1** not giving up, especially in the face of dislike, disapproval, or difficulties; persisting. **2** going on; continuing; lasting. —**per sist′ent ly,** *adv.*

per son i fy (pər son′ə fī), *v.t.,* **-fied, -fy ing.** **1** be a type of: *Satan personifies evil.* **2** regard or represent as a person. We personify time when we refer to *Father Time.*

per vade (pər vād′), *v.t.,* **-vad ed, -vad ing.** go or spread throughout; be throughout: *The odor of pines pervades the air.* [< Latin *pervadere* < *per-* through + *vadere* go] —**per vad′er,** *n.*

pe ti tion (pə tish′ən), *n.* **1** a formal request to a superior or to one in authority for some privilege, right, benefit, etc.: *Many people signed a petition asking the city council for a new library.* **2** that which is requested or prayed for.

pin ion (pin′yən), *n.* **1** the last joint of a bird's wing. **2** wing. **3** any one of the stiff flying feathers of the wing; quill.

pin na cle (pin′ə kəl), *n.* **1** a high peak or point of rock, ice, etc. **2** the highest point: *at the pinnacle of one's fame.*

pis ton (pis′tən), *n.* a short cylinder, or a flat, round piece of wood or metal, fitting closely inside a tube in which it is moved back and forth, often by the force of vapor combustion or steam. Pistons are used in pumps, engines, compressors, etc. [< French < Italian *pistone* < *pistare* to pound]

piv ot (piv′ət), *n.* **1** shaft, pin, or point on which something turns. **2** a turn on or as if on a pivot. —*v.i.* turn on or as if on a pivot.

plain tive (plān′tiv), *adj.* expressive of sorrow; mournful; sad. [< Old French *plaintif* < *plaint* plaint] —**plain′tive ly,** *adv.*

plait (plāt, plat *for 1;* plāt, plēt *for 2*), *n., v.t.* **1** braid. **2** pleat. [< Old French *pleit,* ultimately < Latin *plicare* to fold]

pla teau (pla tō′), *n., pl.* **-teaus** or **-teaux** (-tōz′). **1** large, high plain; tableland. **2** a level, especially the level at which something is unchanged for a period.

po di um (pō′dē əm), *n., pl.* **-di ums, -di a** (-dē ə). a raised platform, especially one used by a public speaker or an orchestra conductor. [< Latin < Greek *podion* < *podos* foot]

poetic justice, ideal justice, with goodness being suitably rewarded and wrongdoing properly punished, as shown often in poetry, drama, and fiction.

poign ant (poi′nyənt), *adj.* **1** very painful; piercing. **2** stimulating to the mind, feelings, or passions; keen; intense: *a subject of poignant interest.*

poise (poiz), *n., v.,* **poised, pois ing.** —*n.* mental balance, composure, or self-possession: *She has perfect poise and never seems embarrassed.* —*v.t.* balance: *poise yourself on your toes.* —*v.i.* **1** be balanced. **2** hang supported or suspended. **3** hover, as a bird in the air.

pome gran ate (pom′gran′it), *n.* a reddish-yellow fruit with a thick skin and many seeds, each enveloped in a juicy red pulp which has a pleasant, slightly sour taste. [< Old French *pome grenate* apple with grains]

pom pa dour (pom′pə dôr, pom′pə dōr), *n.* **1** arrangement of a woman's hair in which it is puffed high over the forehead or brushed straight up and back from the forehead. **2** hair so arranged. [< the Marquise de *Pompadour*]

pompadour (def. 1)

por tal (pôr′tl, pōr′tl), *n.* door, gate, or entrance, usually an imposing one. [< Medieval Latin *portale* < Latin *porta* gate]

pos ter i ty (po ster′ə tē), *n.* generations of the future. [< Latin *posteritatem* < *posterus* coming after]

po tent (pōt′nt), *adj.* having great power; powerful; strong.

po ten tial (pə ten′shəl), *adj.* possible as opposed to actual; capable of coming into being or action: *There is a potential danger of being bitten when one plays with a strange dog.* —**po ten′tial ly,** *adv.*

pre-, *prefix.* **1** before in time, rank, etc.: *Prewar = before a war.* **2** before in position, space, etc.; in front of: *Premolar = in front of the molars.* **3** beforehand; in advance: *Prepay = pay in advance.* [< Latin *prae-, pre-*]

pre am ble (prē′am′bəl), *n.* **1** introduction to a speech or a writing. **2** a preliminary or introductory fact or circumstance, especially one showing what is to follow.

pre ar range (prē′ə rānj′), *v.t.,* **-ranged, -rang ing.** arrange beforehand. —**pre′ar range′ment,** *n.*

pre car i ous (pri ker′ē əs, pri kar′ē əs), *adj.* **1** not safe or secure; uncertain; dangerous; risky. **2** dependent on chance or circumstance. —**pre car′i ous ly,** *adv.*

pre cau tion ar y (pri kô′shə ner′ē), *adj.* of or using precaution, or care taken beforehand.

prec i pice (pres′ə pis), *n.* **1** a very steep or almost vertical face of rock; cliff or steep mountainside. **2** situation of great peril.

pre cip i tate (*v.* pri sip′ə tāt; *adj.* pri sip′ə tit, pri sip′ə tāt), *v.,* **-tat ed, -tat ing,** *adj.* —*v.t.* **1** hasten the beginning of; bring about suddenly: *precipitate an argument.* **2** throw headlong; hurl. —*adj.* very hurried; sudden. —**pre cip′i tate ly,** *adv.*

pre cip i tous (pri sip′ə təs), *adj.* **1** like a precipice; very steep: *precipitous cliffs.* **2** hasty; rash. **3** rushing headlong; very rapid. —**pre cip′i tous ly,** *adv.*

pred a tor (pred′ə tər), *n.* animal or person that lives by preying upon other animals. [< Latin *praedatorius* < *praedari* prey upon, plunder < *praeda* prey]

pred e ces sor (pred′ə ses′ər), *n.* person holding a position or office before another.

pre dom i nance (pri dom′ə nəns), *n.* a being predominant, or having more power or authority than others.

pre em i nent or **pre-em i nent** (prē em′ə nənt), *adj.* standing out above all others; superior. —**pre em′i nent ly,** *adv.*

preen (prēn), *v.t.* **1** smooth or arrange (the feathers) with the beak. **2** dress or groom (oneself) carefully; primp.

prem ise (prem′is), *n.* **1** (in logic) a statement assumed to be true and used to draw a conclusion. **2 premises,** *pl.* **a** house or building with its grounds. **b** (in law) things mentioned previously, such as the names of the parties concerned, a description of the property, the price, grounds for complaint, etc.

pre mo ni tion (prē′mə nish′ən, prem′ə nish′ən), *n.* notification or warning of what is to come; forewarning.

pre sume (pri züm′), *v.,* **-sumed, -sum ing.** —*v.t.* **1** take for granted without proving; suppose: *The law presumes innocence until guilt is proved.* **2** take upon oneself; venture; dare: *May I presume to tell you you are wrong?* —*v.i.* act with improper boldness; take liberties.

pre tense (prē′tens, pri tens′), *n.* **1** make-believe; pretending. **2** a showing off; display; ostentation: *a manner free from pretense.*

prime (prīm), *v.t.,* **primed, prim ing.** **1** prepare by putting something in or on. **2** supply (a gun) with powder.

pri or (prī′ər), *adj.* coming before; earlier: *I can't go with you because I have a prior engagement.* [< Latin]

pro cliv i ty (prō kliv′ə tē), *n., pl.* **-ties.** tendency; inclination.

pro cure (prə kyùr′), *v.t.,* **-cured, -cur ing.** **1** obtain by care or effort; secure: *procure a job.* **2** bring about; cause.

prof fer (prof′ər), *v.t.* offer for acceptance; present: *We proffered regrets at having to leave so early.* —*n.* an offer made. [< Anglo-French *proffrir* < Old French *pro-* forth + *offrir* to offer]

pro found (prə found′), *adj.* **1** very deep: *a profound sigh, a profound sleep.* **2** deeply felt; very great. **3** having or showing great knowledge or understanding: *a profound book, a profound thinker, a profound thought.*

pro gres sion (prə gresh′ən), *n.* a progressing; a moving forward; going ahead: *Creeping is a slow method of progression.*

pro gres sive (prə gres′iv), *adj.* **1** making progress; advancing to something better; improving: *a progressive nation.* **2** favoring progress; wanting improvement or reform in government, business, etc. **3** moving forward; developing: *a progressive disease.* —**pro gres′sive ly,** *adv.* —**pro gres′sive ness,** *n.*

prom e nade (prom′ə nād′, prom′ə näd′), *n., v.,* **-nad ed, -nad ing.** —*n.* **1** walk for pleasure or display: *a promenade in the park.* **2** a public place for such a walk: *Atlantic City has a promenade along the beach.* **3** dance or ball. **4** march of all the guests at the opening of a formal dance. —*v.i.* walk about or up and down for pleasure or for display: *promenade on a ship's deck.* —*v.t.* **1** walk through. **2** take on a promenade. [< French < *promener* take for a walk < Latin *prominare* drive on < *pro-* forward + *minare* to drive] —**prom′e nad′er,** *n.*

prom i nent (prom′ə nənt), *adj.* **1** well-known or important; distinguished: *a prominent citizen.* **2** that catches the eye; easy to see: *A single tree in a field is prominent.* **3** standing out; projecting: *Some insects have prominent eyes.* [< Latin *prominentem* projecting < *pro-* forward + *minere* to jut] —**prom′i nent ly,** *adv.*

prompt (prompt), *adj.* **1** ready and willing; on time; quick; punctual: *Be prompt to obey.* **2** done at once; made without delay. —*v.t.* **1** cause (someone) to do something: *Curiosity prompted me to ask the question.* **2** give rise to; suggest; inspire: *A kind thought prompted the gift.* —**prompt′ly,** *adv.* —**prompt′ness,** *n.*

proph e cy (prof′ə sē), *n., pl.* **-cies.** **1** a telling what will happen; foretelling future events. **2** thing told about the future. **3** a divinely inspired utterance, revelation, writing, etc.

proph e sy (prof′ə sī), *v.,* **-sied, -sy ing.** —*v.i.* **1** tell what will happen. **2** speak when or as if divinely inspired. —*v.t.* **1** foretell; predict: *The sailor prophesied a severe storm.* **2** utter in prophecy.

prop o si tion (prop′ə zish′ən), *n.* **1** what is offered to be considered; proposal: *The corporation made a proposition to buy out the small business.* **2** INFORMAL. a business enterprise; an undertaking: *a paying proposition.*

pro pound (prə pound′), *v.t.* put forward; propose: *propound a theory, propound a riddle.* [earlier *propone* < Latin *proponere* < *pro-* forth + *ponere* to put] —**pro pound′er,** *n.*

pro sa ic (prō zā′ik), *adj.* matter-of-fact; ordinary; not exciting.

pro trude (prō trüd′), *v.,* **-trud ed, -trud ing.** —*v.t.* thrust forth; stick out: *The saucy child protruded her tongue.* —*v.i.* be thrust forth; project: *Her teeth protrude too far.* [< Latin *protrudere* < *pro-* forward + *trudere* to thrust]

prov i dence (prov′ə dəns), *n.* **1** God's care and help. **2 Providence,** God. **3** instance of God's care and help.

prov i den tial (prov′ə den′shəl), *adj.* **1** happening by or as if by God's intervention; fortunate. **2** of or proceeding from divine power or influence. —**prov′i den′tial ly,** *adv.*

prow (prou), *n.* the front part of a ship or boat; bow.

psy cho-ex per i men tal ist (sī′kō ek sper′ə men′tə list), *n.* one who does experiments on or about the mind.

psy chol o gy (sī kol′ə jē), *n., pl.* **-gies. 1** science or study of the mind. **2** the mental states and processes of a person or persons; mental nature and behavior.

pul sa tion (pul sā′shən), *n.* **1** a beating; throbbing. **2** a beat; throb. **3** vibration; quiver.

pulse (puls), *n., v.,* **pulsed, puls ing.** —*n.* **1** the regular beating of the arteries caused by the rush of blood into them after each contraction of the heart. **2** any regular, measured beat: *the pulse in music, the pulse of an engine.* **3** feeling; sentiment: *the pulse of the nation.* —*v.i.* beat; throb; vibrate: *My heart pulsed with excitement.* [< Latin *pulsus* < *pellere* to beat]

pum mel (pum′əl), *v.t., v.i.,* **-meled, -mel ing** or **-melled, -mel ling.** strike or beat; beat with the fists. Also, **pommel.**

pur ga to ry (pėr′gə tôr′ē, pėr′gə tōr′ē), *n., pl.* **-ries. 1** (in Roman Catholic belief) a place in which the souls of those who have died penitent are purified from sin. 2 any condition or place of temporary suffering or punishment.

pur loin (pər loin′), *v.t., v.i.* steal. [< Anglo-French *purloigner* to remove] —**pur loin′er,** *n.*

quay side (kē′sīd′), *n.* beside a quay, the dock or landing place where ships load and unload.

queue (kyü), *n., v.,* **queued, queu ing** or **queue ing.** —*n.* 1 braid of hair hanging down from the back of the head. 2 a line of people, automobiles, etc. —*v.i.* 1 form or stand in a long line. 2 **queue up,** line up. Also, *cue.*

quiv er[1] (kwiv′ər), *v.i.* shake with a slight but rapid motion; shiver; tremble: *The dog quivered with excitement.* —*n.* act of quivering; tremble. [Old English *cwifer* nimble] —**quiv′er er,** *n.* —**quiv′er ing ly,** *adv.*

quiv er[2] (kwiv′ər), *n.* case to hold arrows. [< Old French *cuivre*]

quoth (kwōth), *v.t.* ARCHAIC. said. [Old English *cwæth,* past tense of *cwethan* say]

ra di ant (rā′dē ənt), *adj.* 1 shining; bright; beaming: *a radiant smile.* 2 sending out rays of light or heat: *The sun is a radiant body.* —**ra′di ant ly,** *adv.*

ral ly (ral′ē), *v.,* **-lied, -ly ing,** *n., pl.* **-lies.** —*v.t.* bring together, especially to get in order again: *The commander was able to rally the fleeing troops.* —*v.i.* 1 come together in a body for a common purpose or action. 2 come to help a person, party, or cause: *She rallied to the side of her injured friend.* —*n.* 1 a rallying; recovery. 2 a mass meeting or assembly for a common purpose or action: *a political rally.*

ram rod (ram′rod′), *n.* rod for ramming down the charge in a gun that is loaded from the muzzle. —*adj.* stiff; rigid; unbending.

rant (rant), *v.i.* speak wildly, extravagantly, violently, or noisily. —*n.* extravagant, violent, or noisy speech.

ra pi er (rā′pē ər), *n.* a long and light sword used for thrusting.

rapt (rapt), *adj.* 1 lost in delight. 2 so busy thinking of or enjoying one thing that one does not know what else is happening. 3 showing a rapt condition; caused by a rapt condition: *a rapt smile.*

rap tur ous (rap′chər əs), *adj.* full of rapture, delight, or great joy. —**rap′tur ous ly,** *adv.* —**rap′tur ous ness,** *n.*

rar e fy (rer′ə fī, rar′ə fī), *v.t.,* **-fied, -fy ing.** 1 make less dense: *The air on high mountains is rarefied.* 2 refine; purify.

ra tion al (rash′ə nəl), *adj.* 1 reasoned out; sensible; reasonable: *When very angry, people seldom act in a rational way.* 2 able to think and reason clearly: *Human beings are rational animals.*

ra tion ale (rash′ə nal′, rash′ə nä′lē), *n.* the basic reason. [< Latin, neuter of *rationalis* rational]

rau cous (rô′kəs), *adj.* hoarse; harsh-sounding: *the raucous caw of a crow.* [< Latin *raucus*] —**rau′cous ly,** *adv.*

realm (relm), *n.* 1 kingdom. 2 region or sphere in which something rules or prevails.

rea son (rē′zn), *n.* 1 cause or motive for an action, feeling, etc.: *I have my own reasons for doing this.* 2 ability or power to think and draw conclusions. 3 right thinking; good sense.

re coil (ri koil′), *v.i.* 1 draw back; shrink back: *Most people would recoil at seeing a snake in the path.* 2 spring back: *The gun recoiled after I fired.* 3 react.

re con nais sance (ri kon′ə səns), *n.* examination or survey, especially for military purposes. [< French]

rec on noi ter (rek′ə noi′tər, rē′kə noi′tər), *v.t.* approach and examine or observe in order to learn something. —*v.i.* approach a place and make a first survey of it.

red coat (red′kōt′), *n.* (in former times) a British soldier.

re flect (ri flekt′), *v.t.* 1 turn back or throw back (light, heat, sound, etc.): *The sidewalks reflect heat on a hot day.* 2 give back a likeness or image of: *The sky was reflected in the still pond.* —*v.i.* 1 cast back light, heat, sound, etc. 2 think carefully; ponder; deliberate: *Take time to reflect before making a decision.*

ref or ma tion (ref′ər mā′shən), *n.* a reforming or a being reformed; change for the better; improvement.

re frain[1] (ri frān′), *v.i.* hold oneself back, especially from satisfying a momentary impulse: *Refrain from talking in the library.*

a hat	i it	oi oil	ch child		a in about
ā age	ī ice	ou out	ng long		e in taken
ä far	o hot	u cup	sh she	ə =	i in pencil
e let	ō open	ù put	th thin		o in lemon
ē equal	ô order	ü rule	ᴛʜ then		u in circus
ėr term			zh measure	< = derived from

[< Old French *refrener* < Latin *refrenare* furnish with a bridle, refrain < *re-* back + *frenum* bridle] —**re frain′ment,** *n.*

re frain[2] (ri frān′), *n.* phrase or verse recurring regularly in a song or poem, especially at the end of each stanza; chorus.

re fute (ri fyüt′), *v.t.,* **-fut ed, -fut ing.** show (a claim, opinion, or argument) to be false or incorrect; prove wrong; disprove.

re gal (rē′gəl), *adj.* 1 belonging to a king or queen; royal. 2 fit for a king or queen; stately.

re gard (ri gärd′), *v.t.* 1 think of; consider or look on. 2 look at; look closely at; watch. —*n.* 1 a steady look; gaze. 2 good opinion; esteem; favor.

re gress (ri gres′), *v.i.* 1 go back; move in a backward direction. 2 return to an earlier or less advanced state.

re it e rate (rē it′ə rāt′), *v.t.,* **-rat ed, -rat ing.** say or do several times; repeat (an action, demand, etc.) again and again.

re lent (ri lent′), *v.i.* become less harsh or cruel; be more tender and merciful. [ultimately < Latin *re-* again + *lentus* slow]

re lent less (ri lent′lis), *adj.* without pity; not relenting; unyielding. —**re lent′less ly,** *adv.* —**re lent′less ness,** *n.*

re mand (ri mand′), *v.t.* 1 send back. 2 send back (a prisoner or an accused person) into custody.

re morse (ri môrs′), *n.* deep, painful regret for having done wrong.

rend (rend), *v.t.,* **rent, rend ing.** 1 pull apart violently; tear: *Wolves will rend a lamb.* 2 split: *Lightning rent the tree.*

ren der (ren′dər), *v.t.* 1 cause to become; make: *Fright rendered me speechless.* 2 give; do: *render a service, render judgment.* 3 offer for consideration, approval, payment, etc.; hand in; report: *render a bill.* 4 give in return: *render thanks.*

ren e gade (ren′ə gād), *n., adj., v.,* **-gad ed, -gad ing.** —*n.* deserter from a religious faith, a political party, etc.; traitor. —*adj.* like a traitor; deserting; disloyal. —*v.i.* turn renegade.

re nounce (ri nouns′), *v.t.,* **-nounced, -nounc ing.** 1 declare that one gives up; give up entirely; give up: *He renounces his claim to the money.* 2 cast off; refuse to recognize as one's own; repudiate; disown. [< Middle French *renoncer* < Latin *renuntiare* < *re-* back + *nuntius* message] —**re nounce′ment,** *n.*

re pent ant (ri pen′tənt), *adj.* feeling repentance or regret; sorry for wrongdoing; repenting. —**re pent′ant ly,** *adv.*

re pose (ri pōz′), *n., v.,* **-posed, -pos ing.** —*n.* 1 rest or sleep: *Do not disturb her repose.* 2 quietness; ease: *repose of manner.* 3 peace; calmness. —*v.i.* 1 lie at rest: *The cat reposed upon the cushion.* 2 lie in a grave.

rep ro bate (rep′rə bāt), *n., adj.* —*n.* a very wicked or unprincipled person; scoundrel. —*adj.* very wicked; unprincipled.

re served (ri zėrvd′), *adj.* 1 kept in reserve; kept by special arrangement: *a reserved seat.* 2 set apart: *a reserved section at the stadium.* 3 self-restrained in action or speech. 4 disposed to keep to oneself. —**re serv′ed ly,** *adv.* —**re serv′ed ness,** *n.*

res ig na tion (rez′ig nā′shən), *n.* 1 act of resigning. 2 a written statement giving notice that one resigns. 3 patient acceptance.

res o lute (rez′ə lüt), *adj.* 1 having a fixed resolve; determined; firm. 2 constant in pursuing a purpose; bold.

re sound (ri zound′), *v.i.* 1 give back sound; echo. 2 sound loudly. 3 be filled with sound.

re source ful (ri sôrs′fəl, ri sōrs′fəl), *adj.* good at thinking of ways to do things; quick-witted. —**re source′ful ly,** *adv.*

res pite (res′pit), *n.* 1 time of relief and rest; lull: *a respite from the heat.* 2 a putting off; delay.

re splend ent (ri splen′dənt), *adj.* very bright; shining; splendid: *the resplendent sun, a face resplendent with joy.* [< Latin *resplendentem* < *re-* back + *splendere* to shine] —**re splend′ent ly,** *adv.*

re tain (ri tān′), *v.t.* 1 continue to have or hold; keep.

re tort (ri tôrt′), *v.i.* reply quickly or sharply. —*v.t.* 1 say in sharp reply. 2 return in kind; turn back on: *retort insult for insult.*

ret ri bu tion (ret′rə byü′shən), *n.* a deserved punishment;

return for wrongdoing. [< Latin *retributionem*, ultimately < *re-* back + *tribuere* assign]

re veil le (rev′ə lē), *n.* a signal on a bugle or drum to waken soldiers or sailors in the morning. [< French *réveillez(-vous)* awaken!]

re ver be rate (ri ver′bə rāt′), *v.i.,* **-rat ed, -rat ing. 1** echo back: *His voice reverberates from the high ceiling.* **2** be cast back; be reflected a number of times, as light or heat.

rev er ent (rev′ər ənt), *adj.* feeling or showing reverence, or a feeling of deep respect, awe, and love. —**rev′er ent ly,** *adv.*

rev er ie (rev′ər ē), *n.* **1** dreamy thoughts; dreamy thinking of pleasant things. **2** condition of being lost in dreamy thoughts. Also, **revery.** [< French *rêverie* < *rêver* to dream]

rhap so dy (rap′sə dē), *n., pl.* **-dies. 1** extravagant enthusiasm in speech or writing: *go into rhapsodies over a gift.* **2** (in music) an instrumental composition resembling an improvisation. **3** a kind of poem suitable for recitation at one time. [< Greek *rhapsōidia* verse composition < *rhaptein* to stitch + *ōidē* song, ode]

rheu mat ic (rü mat′ik), *adj.* **1** of or having to do with rheumatism. **2** having to do with rheumatic fever, a disease that often causes swelling of the heart which results in harmful aftereffects.

rime (rīm), *n.,* white frost; hoarfrost.

roil (roil), *v.t.* **1** make (water, etc.) muddy by stirring up sediment. **2** rile. [< Old French *rouiller*]

ro man ti cize (rō man′tə sīz), *v.t.,* **-cized, -ciz ing.** make romantic, or imaginary and unrealistic.

ruck sack (ruk′sak′, rûk′sak′), *n.* knapsack. [< German *Rucksack*]

ru in a tion (rü′ə nā′shən), *n.* ruin; destruction; downfall.

ruse (rüz, rüs), *n.* scheme or device to mislead others; trick. [< French < *ruser* to dodge < Old French]

sac ri le gious (sak′rə lij′əs, sak′rə lē′jəs), *adj.* injurious or insulting to sacred persons or things.

sac ris ty (sak′ri stē), *n., pl.* **-ties.** place where the sacred vessels, robes, etc., of a church are kept; vestry.

sa gac i ty (sə gas′ə tē), *n.* keen, sound judgment; mental acuteness; shrewdness.

sa hib (sä′ib, sä′hib), *n.* sir; master (in colonial India, a term of respect used to or about Europeans). [< Hindi *sāhib* < Arabic *sāhib* lord]

sa lon (sə lon′), *n.* **1** a large room for receiving or entertaining guests. **2** assembly of guests in such a room, especially the regular gathering of famous artists, writers, politicians, etc., as guests of a well-known host or hostess. **3** place used to exhibit works of art. **4** exhibition of works of art. **5** a fashionable or stylish shop. [< French < Italian *salone* < *sala* hall; of Germanic origin]

sa loon (sə lün′), *n.* **1** place where alcoholic drinks are sold and drunk; tavern. **2** salon. [< French *salon.* See SALON.]

sal u tar y (sal′yə ter′ē), *adj.* **1** beneficial: *give someone salutary advice.* **2** good for the health; wholesome.

sal vage (sal′vij), *n., v.,* **-vaged, -vag ing.** —*n.* act of saving a ship or its cargo from wreck, capture, etc. —*v.t.* save from fire, flood, shipwreck, etc. [< French, ultimately < Latin *salvus* safe]

sat u rate (sach′ə rāt′), *v.t.,* **-rat ed, -rat ing.** soak thoroughly; fill full: *During the fog, the air was saturated with moisture.* [< Latin *saturatum* filled < *satur* full]

saun ter (sôn′tər, sän′tər), *v.i.* walk along slowly and happily; stroll: *saunter in the park.* —*n.* **1** a leisurely or careless gait. **2** a stroll. [origin uncertain] —**saun′ter er,** *n.*

sav age (sav′ij), *adj.* **1** not civilized; barbarous: *savage customs.* **2** violently aggressive; fiercely cruel or brutal: *a savage dog.* **3** wild or rugged: *savage mountain scenery.* **4** undomesticated; untamed. **5** furiously angry; enraged. —**sav′age ly,** *adv.*

sa vor (sā′vər), *n.* a taste or smell; flavor: *The soup has a savor of onion.* —*v.t.* **1** enjoy the savor of; perceive or appreciate by taste or smell: *We savored the soup.* **2** think about with great delight; relish: *I wanted to savor my victory.*

scab bard (skab′ərd), *n.* sheath or case for the blade of a sword.

scant ling (skant′ling), *n.* **1** a small beam or piece of timber, often used as an upright piece in the frame of a building. **2** small beams or timbers collectively.

scoff (skôf, skof), *v.i.* make fun to show one does not believe something; mock. See synonym study below. —*v.t.* jeer at; deride.

—*n.* **1** mocking words or acts. **2** something ridiculed or mocked.

[< Scandinavian (Danish) *skuffe* deceive] —**scoff′ing ly,** *adv.*

Syn. *v.i.* **Scoff, jeer, sneer** mean to show scorn or contempt for someone or something. **Scoff** implies scornful irreverence or cynicism: *scoff at religion.* **Jeer** implies mocking laughter: *The mob jeered when the speaker got up to talk.* **Sneer** means to express ill-natured contempt or disparagement by look, tone, or manner of speech: *sneer at everything sentimental.*

scorn (skôrn), *v.t.* look down upon; think of as mean or low; despise: *scorn sneaks and liars.* —*n.* **1** a feeling that a person, animal, or act is mean or low; contempt. See synonym study below. **2** person, animal, or thing that is scorned or despised.

Syn. *n.* **1 Scorn, contempt, disdain** mean a strong feeling that someone or something is unworthy of respect. **Scorn** implies angry dislike or disapproval of what is considered worthless or evil: *He attacked their proposals in words of bitter scorn.* **Contempt** implies disgust combined with strong disapproval: *We feel contempt for a coward.* **Disdain** implies feeling oneself above a person or thing considered mean or low: *We feel disdain for a person who cheats.*

scorn ful (skôrn′fəl), *adj.* showing contempt; full of scorn; mocking. —**scorn′ful ly,** *adv.* —**scorn′ful ness,** *n.*

scru ti ny (skrüt′n ē), *n., pl.* **-nies. 1** close examination; careful inspection. **2** a looking searchingly at something.

scut tle (skut′l), *n., v.,* **-tled, -tling.** —*n.* **1** an opening in the deck or side of a ship, with a lid or cover. **2** an opening in a wall or roof, with a lid or cover. —*v.t.* cut a hole or holes through the bottom or sides of (a ship) to sink it.

scythe (sīᴙH), *n., v.,* **scythed, scyth ing.** —*n.* a long, thin, slightly curved blade on a long handle, for cutting grass, etc. —*v.t.* cut or mow with a scythe. [Old English *sithe;* spelling influenced by Latin *scindere* to cut]

se cur i ty (si kyúr′ə tē), *n., pl.* **-ties. 1** freedom from danger, care, or fear; feeling or condition of being safe. **2** something that secures or makes safe: *Rubber soles are a security against slipping.* **3** Usually, **securities,** *pl.* bond or stock certificates.

se date (si dāt′), *adj.* quiet; calm; serious. [< Latin *sedatum,* related to *sedere* sit] —**se date′ly,** *adv.*

sed i men tar y (sed′ə men′tər ē), *adj.* (in geology) formed by the depositing of sediment, or earth, stones, etc., deposited by water, wind, or ice.

self same (self′sām′), *adj.* very same; identical.

se man tic (sə man′tik), *adj.* having to do with the meaning of words. —**se man′ti cal ly,** *adv.*

sem blance (sem′bləns), *n.* **1** outward appearance: *Their story had the semblance of truth, but was really false.* **2** likeness: *These clouds have the semblance of a huge head.* [< Old French < *sembler* seem < Latin *similare* make similar < *similis* similar]

semi-, *prefix.* **1** half: *Semicircle = half a circle.* **2** partly; incompletely: *Semicivilized = partly civilized.*

se nil i ty (sə nil′ə tē), *n.* **1** old age. **2** the mental and physical deterioration often characteristic of old age.

sen si bil i ty (sen′sə bil′ə tē), *n., pl.* **-ties. 1** ability to feel or perceive: *Some drugs lessen a person's sensibilities.* **2** sensitiveness. **3** fineness of feeling: *She has an unusual sensibility for colors.*

sen ti nel (sen′tə nəl), *n.* person stationed to keep watch and guard against surprise attacks.

se rene (sə rēn′), *adj.* **1** peaceful; calm: *a serene smile.* **2** not cloudy; clear; bright: *a serene sky.* —**se rene′ly,** *adv.*

sev er (sev′ər), *v.t.* **1** cut apart; cut off: *sever a rope.* **2** break off: *The two countries severed friendly relations.* [< Old French *sevrer,* ultimately < Latin *separare* to separate]

shack le (shak′əl), *n.* a metal band fastened around the ankle or wrist of a prisoner, slave, etc. Shackles are usually fastened to each other, the wall, the floor, etc., by chains. **2 shackles,** *pl.* chains; fetters.

sheath ing (shē′ᴙHing, shē′thing), *n.* casing; covering.

shied (shīd), *v.* a pt. and a pp. of **shy.** started back or aside suddenly: *The horse shied at the newspaper blowing along the ground.*

shil ling (shil′ing), *n.* **1** a former coin of Great Britain, which was equal to 12 pence or ¹⁄₂₀th of a pound. **2** unit of money of colonial America corresponding to the British shilling. [Old English *scilling*]

shorn (shôrn, shōrn), *v.* a pp. of **shear.** —*adj.* sheared, or cut with shears or scissors.

show down (shō′doun′), *n.* a meeting face to face in order to settle an issue or dispute: *The showdown between the mayor and the council over the new budget resulted in a welcome compromise.*

shut tle (shut′l), *n., v.,* **-tled, -tling.** —*n.* device that carries the thread from one side of the web to the other in weaving.

si dle (sī′dl), *v.,* **-dled, -dling,** *n.* —*v.i.* **1** move sideways.

2 move sideways slowly so as not to attract attention: *The little boy shyly sidled up to the visitor.* —*n.* movement sideways.

si es ta (sē es′tə), *n.* a nap or rest taken at noon or in the afternoon. [< Spanish < Latin *sexta (hora)* sixth (hour) of the Roman day, noon]

si mul ta ne ous (sī′məl tā′nē əs, sim′əl tā′nē əs), *adj.* existing, done, or happening at the same time: *The two simultaneous shots sounded like one.* —**si′mul ta′ne ous ly,** *adv.*

sin gu lar (sing′gyə lər), *adj.* 1 extraordinary; unusual: *a person of singular ability, a story of singular interest.* 2 strange; odd; peculiar. 3 being the only one of its kind.

sin is ter (sin′ə stər), *adj.* 1 showing ill will; threatening: *a sinister rumor, a sinister look.* 2 bad; evil; dishonest. 3 disastrous; unfortunate. 4 on the left; left. [< Latin, left; the left side being considered unlucky] —**sin′is ter ly,** *adv.*

skein (skān), *n.* 1 a small, coiled bundle of yarn or thread. There are 120 yards in a skein of cotton yarn. 2 a confused tangle.

skulk (skulk), *v.i.* 1 keep out of sight to avoid danger, work, duty, etc.; hide or lurk in a cowardly way. 2 move in a stealthy, sneaking way. —*n.* person who skulks. —**skulk′er,** *n.*

slav er (slav′ər), *v.i.* let saliva run from the mouth; drool. —*v.t.* wet with saliva; slobber. —*n.* saliva running from the mouth.

slew (slü), *v.* a pt. of **slay.** killed violently.

slough (slou *for 1;* slü *for 2*), *n.* 1 a soft, deep, muddy place. 2 a swampy place; marshy inlet. —*v.i.* to travel through a slough.

smite (smīt), *v.,* **smote, smit ten** or **smote, smit ing.** —*v.t.* 1 give a hard blow to (a person, etc.) with the hand, a stick, or the like; strike. 2 attack with a sudden pain, disease, etc.

smor gas bord (smôr′gəs bôrd, smôr′gəs bōrd), *n.* a buffet luncheon or supper consisting of a large variety of meats, salads, hors d'oeuvres, etc. [< Swedish *smörgåsbord* < *smörgås* bread and butter, sandwich + *bord* table]

smote (smōt), *v.* pt. and a pp. of **smite.**

snuff (snuf), *v.t.* draw in through the nose; draw up into the nose. —*n.* powdered tobacco, often scented, taken into the nose.

sol emn (sol′əm), *adj.* 1 of a serious, grave, or earnest character: *a solemn face.* 2 causing serious or grave thoughts: *The organ played solemn music.* 3 done with form and ceremony: *a solemn procession.* 4 gloomy; dark; somber in color. [< Latin *sollemnis*] —**sol′emn ly,** *adv.* —**sol′emn ness,** *n.*

sol em nize (sol′əm nīz), *v.t.,* **-nized, -niz ing.** 1 hold or perform (a ceremony or service): *The marriage was solemnized in the cathedral.* 2 make serious or grave.

som ber (som′bər), *adj.* 1 having deep shadows; dark; gloomy: *A cloudy winter day is somber.* 2 sad; dismal: *His losses made him very somber.*

som no lent (som′nə lənt), *adj.* 1 sleepy; drowsy. 2 tending to produce sleep. [< Latin *somnolentus* < *somnus* sleep] —**som′no lent ly,** *adv.*

sore (sôr, sōr), *adj.,* **sor er, sor est.** 1 causing sharp or continuous pain. 2 sad; distressed: *The suffering of the poor makes her heart sore.* 3 severe; distressing: *Your going away is a sore grief to us.* —**sore′ly,** *adv.* —**sore′ness,** *n.*

sou sa phone (sü′zə fōn′), *n.* a wind instrument similar to the tuba, with a flaring bell that faces forward. [< John Philip *Sousa,* who designed it]

sown (sōn), *v.* a pp. of **sow.** planted; seeded.

spar (spär), *v.i.,* **sparred, spar ring.** 1 make motions of attack and defense with the arms and fists; box. 2 dispute.

spas mod ic (spaz mod′ik), *adj.* having to do with a spasm, or sudden tightening of the muscles: *a spasmodic cough.*

spat (spat), *v.* a pt. and a pp. of **spit.**

spec tre (spek′tər), *n.* 1 phantom or ghost, especially one of a terrifying nature or appearance. 2 thing causing terror or dread. Also, **specter.** [< Latin *spectrum* appearance]

spec u la tion (spek′yə lā′shən), *n.* 1 careful thought; reflection. 2 a guessing; conjecture.

spec u la tive (spek′yə lā′tiv, spek′yə lə tiv), *adj.* carefully thoughtful; reflective. —**spec′u la′tive ly,** *adv.*

splat (splat), *n.* 1 a sound like that of something splashing, spattering, or slapping. 2 a spot. —*interj.* the making of such a sound. —*adv.* with such a sound. [back-formation < *splatter*]

sousaphone

a hat	i it	oi oil	ch child	⎧ a in about
ā age	ī ice	ou out	ng long	⎪ e in taken
ä far	o hot	u cup	sh she	ə = ⎨ i in pencil
e let	ō open	ù put	th thin	⎪ o in lemon
ē equal	ô order	ü rule	ᴛʜ then	⎩ u in circus
ėr term			zh measure	< = derived from

splay (splā), *v.t.* 1 spread out; expand; extend. 2 make slanting; bevel. —*v.i.* 1 have or lie in a slanting direction; slope. 2 spread out; flare. —*adj.* wide and flat; turned outward. [Middle English *splayen,* short for *displayen* display]

spright ly (sprīt′lē), *adj.,* **-li er, -li est,** *adv.* —*adj.* lively; gay. —*adv.* in a lively manner. Also, **spritely.**

squan der (skwon′dər), *v.t.* spend foolishly; waste: *squander one's money in gambling.* [origin uncertain] —**squan′der er,** *n.*

stac ca to (stə kä′tō), *adj.* 1 (in music) with breaks between the successive tones; disconnected; detached. 2 abrupt: *a staccato manner.* [< Italian, literally, detached]

stalk (stôk), *v.t.* approach or pursue without being seen or heard: *The hunters stalked the lion.* —*v.i.* 1 spread silently and steadily: *Disease stalked through the land.* 2 walk with slow, stiff, or haughty strides. —*n.* 1 a haughty gait. 2 act of stalking. [Old English *(be)stealcian* steal along] —**stalk′a ble,** *adj.* —**stalk′er,** *n.*

sta tion (stā′shən), *n.* 1 place which a person is appointed to occupy in the performance of some duty; assigned post: *The guard took his station at the door of the bank.* 2 a regular stopping place: *a bus station, a railroad station.* 3 social position; rank: *A serf was a person of humble station in life.*

sta tus (stā′təs, stat′əs), *n.* social or professional standing; position; rank: *lose status. What is her status in the government?*

stealth y (stel′thē), *adj.,* **stealth i er, stealth i est.** done in a secret manner; secret; sly: *The cat crept in a stealthy way toward the bird.* —**stealth′i ly,** *adv.* —**stealth′i ness,** *n.*

steam (stēm), *n.* 1 the invisible vapor or gas formed when water is heated to the boiling point. 2 the white cloud or mist formed by the condensation, when cooled, of this vapor or gas. 3 INFORMAL. power; energy; force. 4 **let off steam,** INFORMAL. **a** get rid of excess energy. **b** relieve one's feelings.

steel (stēl), *n.* 1 an alloy of iron and varying amounts of carbon. 2 steellike hardness or strength: *nerves of steel.* —*v.t.* 1 point, edge, or cover with steel. 2 make hard or strong like steel: *steel oneself against possible failure.* [Old English *stēle*]

ster e op ti con (ster′ē op′tə kən, stir′ē op′tə kən), *n.* projector arranged to combine two images on a screen so that they gradually become one image with three-dimensional effect.

sti fle (stī′fəl), *v.t.,* **-fled, -fling.** 1 stop the breath of; smother. 2 keep back; stop: *stifle a cry, stifle a yawn.*

stim u lus (stim′yə ləs), *n., pl.* **-li.** 1 something that stirs to action or effort; incentive: *Ambition is a great stimulus.* 2 something that excites an organ or part of the body to a specific activity or function; something that produces a response. [< Latin, originally, goad]

stip u la tion (stip′yə lā′shən), *n.* 1 a definite arrangement; agreement. 2 condition in an agreement.

stren u ous (stren′yü əs), *adj.* 1 very active: *We had a strenuous day moving into our new house.* 2 full of energy: *a strenuous worker.* 3 requiring much energy: *strenuous exercise.*

strict (strikt), *adj.* 1 very careful in following a rule or in making others follow it: *The teacher was strict but fair.* 2 harsh; severe: *a strict parent.* See synonym study below. —**strict′ly,** *adv.*

Syn. 1,2 **Strict, rigid, rigorous** mean severe and unyielding or harsh and stern. **Strict** emphasizes showing or demanding a very careful and close following of a rule, standard, or requirement: *Our teacher is strict and insists that we follow instructions to the letter.* **Rigid** emphasizes being firm and unyielding, not changing or relaxing for anyone or under any conditions: *They maintain a rigid working schedule.* **Rigorous** emphasizes the severity, harshness, or sternness of the demands made, conditions imposed, etc.: *We believe in rigorous enforcement of the laws.*

stride (strīd), *v.,* **strode, strid den, strid ing,** *n.* —*v.i.* walk with long steps: *stride rapidly down the street.* —*n.* a long step.

strive (strīv), *v.i.,* **strove** or **strived, striv en, striv ing.** 1 try hard; work hard: *strive for self-control.* 2 struggle; fight: *The swimmer strove against the tide.*

strode (strōd), *v.* pt. of **stride.**

strove (strōv), *v.* a pt. of **strive.**

stul ti fy (stul′tə fī), *v.t.,* **-fied, -fy ing.** 1 make futile; frustrate:

stultify a person's efforts. **2** cause to appear foolish or absurd.

stu pe fy (stü′pə fī, styü′pə fī), *v.t.*, **-fied, -fy ing.** **1** make stupid, dull, or senseless. **2** overwhelm with shock or amazement; astound: *They were stupefied by the calamity.*

stu por (stü′pər, styü′pər), *n.* **1** a dazed condition; loss or lessening of the power to feel: *He lay in a stupor, unable to tell what had happened to him.* **2** intellectual or moral numbness.

sua vi ty (swä′və tē, swav′ə tē), *n., pl.* **-ties.** smoothly agreeable quality or behavior; smooth politeness; blandness.

sub con scious (sub kon′shəs), *adj.* not wholly conscious; existing in the mind but not fully perceived or recognized: *a subconscious fear.* —*n.* thoughts, feelings, etc., that are present in the mind but not fully perceived or recognized.

sub due (səb dü′, səb dyü′), *v.t.*, **-dued, -du ing.** **1** overcome by force; conquer. **2** keep down; hold back; suppress: *We subdued a desire to laugh.* **3** tone down; soften.

sub ject (*n.* sub′jikt, sub′jekt; *v.* səb jekt′), *n.* **1** something thought about, discussed, investigated, etc. **2** something learned or taught; course of study in some branch of learning. **3** person under the power, control, or influence of another: *the subjects of a monarch.* **4** person or thing that undergoes or experiences something: *Rabbits and mice are often subjects for medical experiments.* —*v.t.* **1** bring under some power or influence: *Rome subjected all Italy to its rule.* **2** cause to undergo or experience something: *The lawyer subjected the witness to grueling cross-examination.*

sub mis sion (səb mish′ən), *n.* **1** a yielding to the power, control, or authority of another; giving in: *The defeated general showed his submission by giving up his sword.* **2** obedience; humbleness: *They bowed in submission to the queen's order.*

sub or di nate (*adj., n.* sə bôrd′n it; *v.* sə bôrd′n āt), *adj., n., v.,* **-nat ed, -nat ing.** —*adj.* **1** lower in rank: *In the army, lieutenants are subordinate to captains.* **2** lower in importance; secondary. **3** under the control or influence of something else; dependent. —*n.* a subordinate person or thing. —*v.t.* make subordinate: *He subordinated his wishes to those of his guests.* [< Medieval Latin *subordinatum* lowered in rank < Latin *sub-* under + *ordinem* order] —**sub or′di nate ly,** *adv.*

sub side (səb sīd′), *v.i.*, **-sid ed, -sid ing.** grow less; die down; become less active; abate: *The storm finally subsided.*

suc ces sion (sək sesh′ən), *n.* **1** group of persons or things coming one after another; series. **2** the coming of one person or thing after another.

suck er (suk′ər), *n.* shoot growing from an underground stem or root. —*v.t.* to remove these shoots.

suf fuse (sə fyüz′), *v.t.*, **-fused, -fus ing.** overspread (with a liquid, dye, etc.): *eyes suffused with tears. At twilight the sky was suffused with color.*

suit or (sü′tər), *n.* man who is courting a woman.

sulk y (sul′kē), *adj.*, **sulk i er, sulk i est.** silent and bad-humored because of resentment; sullen: *Some children become sulky when they cannot have their own way.* —**sulk′i ly,** *adv.* —**sulk′i ness,** *n.*

sul len (sul′ən), *adj.* **1** silent because of bad humor or anger. **2** showing bad humor or anger. **3** gloomy; dismal. [Middle English *soleine*, ultimately < Latin *solus* alone] —**sul′len ly,** *adv.*

sump tu ous (sump′chü əs), *adj.* lavish and costly; magnificent; rich: *a sumptuous banquet.* —**sump′tu ous ly,** *adv.*

su per nat ur al (sü′pər nach′ər əl), *adj.* above or beyond what is natural: *supernatural voices. Ghosts are supernatural beings.* —*n.* **the supernatural,** supernatural influences or phenomena.

sup ple ment (*n.* sup′lə mənt; *v.* sup′lə ment), *n.* **1** something added to complete a thing, or to make it larger or better. **2** something added to supply a deficiency: *a diet supplement.* —*v.t.* supply something additional to.

sup po si tion (sup′ə zish′ən), *n.* **1** act of supposing. **2** thing supposed; belief; opinion.

surge (sèrj), *v.*, **surged, surg ing,** *n.* —*v.i.* **1** rise and fall; move like waves: *A great wave surged over us. The crowd surged through the streets.* **2** rise or swell (up) violently or excitedly, as feelings, thoughts, etc. —*n.* a swelling wave; sweep or rush of waves.

sur mise (sər mīz′), *v.t., v.i.*, **-mised, -mis ing.** infer or guess: *We surmised that the delay was caused by some accident.*

sur pass (sər pas′), *v.t.* do better than; be more than; excel.

sur rep ti tious (sèr′əp tish′əs), *adj.* **1** stealthy; secret: *a surreptitious glance.* **2** secret and unauthorized: *surreptitious meetings.* —**sur′rep ti′tious ly,** *adv.*

sus tain (sə stān′), *v.t.* **1** keep up; keep going: *Hope sustains him*

in his misery. **2** supply with food, provisions, etc.: *sustain a family.* **3** hold up; support: *Arches sustain the weight of the roof.*

sus te nance (sus′tə nəns), *n.* **1** food; nourishment. **2** means of living; support: *give money for the sustenance of the poor.*

sway (swā), *n.* influence, control, or rule: *a country under the sway of a dictator.*

swoon (swün), *v.i.* **1** faint: *swoon at the sight of blood.* **2** fade or die away gradually. —*n.* a faint.

syl van (sil′vən), *adj.* of, in, or having woods: *live in a sylvan retreat.* Also, **silvan.** [< Latin *sylvanus, silvanus* < *silva* forest]

sym met ri cal (si met′rə kəl), *adj.* having symmetry; well-proportioned. —**sym met′ri cal ly,** *adv.*

syn co pate (sing′kə pāt), *v.t.*, **-pat ed, -pat ing.** in music: **a** begin (a tone) on an unaccented beat and hold it into an accented one. **b** introduce syncopation into (a passage, etc.). —**syn′co pa′tion,** *n.* —**syn′co pa′tor,** *n.*

syn drome (sin′drōm), *n.* **1** group of signs and symptoms that are characteristic of a particular disease. **2** any signs that are characteristic of a certain condition, quality, behavior, or type.

tab leau (tab′lō), *n., pl.* **-leaux** (-lōz), **-leaus.** **1** a striking scene; picture. **2** representation of a picture, statue, scene, etc., by a person or group posing in appropriate costume.

tac i turn (tas′ə tèrn′), *adj.* speaking very little; not fond of talking. —**tac′i turn′ly,** *adv.*

tack ward (tak′wərd), *adv.* in a zigzag course.

tal on (tal′ən), *n.* **1** claw of an animal, especially a bird of prey. **2** a clawlike, grasping finger. **3 talons,** *pl.* clawlike fingers; grasping hands. [< Old French, heel, ultimately < Latin *talus* ankle]

tan gi ble (tan′jə bəl), *adj.* **1** that can be touched or felt by touch: *A chair is a tangible object.* **2** real; actual; definite: *a tangible improvement, tangible evidence.* —**tan′gi bil′i ty,** *n.*

tap es try (tap′ə strē), *n., pl.* **-tries.** **1** fabric with pictures or designs woven in it, used to hang on walls, cover furniture, etc. **2** a picture in tapestry.

tat too (ta tü′), *n., pl.* **-toos.** **1** signal on a bugle, drum, etc., calling soldiers or sailors to their quarters at night. **2** series of raps, taps, etc.: *The hail beat a loud tattoo on the windowpane.* [< Dutch *taptoe* < *tap* taproom + *toe* pull to, shut]

taunt (tônt, tänt), *v.t.* **1** jeer at; mock; reproach; deride. **2** get or drive by taunts; provoke: *taunt someone into taking a dare.* —*n.* a bitter or insulting remark; mocking; jeering. [origin uncertain]

taut (tôt), *adj.* tightly drawn; tense: *a taut rope.*

tech ni cian (tek nish′ən), *n.* **1** an expert in the technicalities of a subject. **2** an expert in the technique of an art.

tem per (tem′pər), *n.* **1** state of mind; mood. **2** calm state of mind: *He became angry and lost his temper.* **3** the degree of hardness, toughness, flexibility, etc., of a substance: *The temper of the clay was right for shaping.*

tem per a ment (tem′pər ə mənt), *n.* a person's nature or disposition: *a nervous temperament.*

tem per a men tal (tem′pər ə men′tl), *adj.* **1** subject to moods and whims; easily irritated; sensitive. **2** due to temperament; constitutional.

ten don (ten′dən), *n.* a tough, strong band of fibrous tissue that joins a muscle to a bone or some other part. [< Medieval Latin *tendonem* < Greek *tenōn;* influenced by Latin *tendere* to stretch]

ten et (ten′it), *n.* doctrine, principle, belief, or opinion held as true by a school, sect, party, or person. [< Latin, he holds]

ten ta tive (ten′tə tiv), *adj.* **1** done as a trial or experiment. **2** hesitating. —**ten′ta tive ly,** *adv.* —**ten′ta tive ness,** *n.*

Ter ti ar y (tèr′shē er′ē, tèr′shər ē), *n., pl.* **-ar ies,** *adj.* —*n.* **1** the period of time from 70 million to 2 million years ago, during which the great mountain systems, such as the Alps, Himalayas, Rocky Mountains, and Andes, appeared, and rapid development of mammals occurred. **2** rocks formed in this period. —*adj.* of or having to do with the Tertiary or its rocks.

thence (ᴛʜens, thens), *adv.* **1** from that place; from there: *A few miles thence is a river.* **2** for that reason; therefore. **3** from that.

the o ret i cal (thē′ə ret′ə kəl), *adj.* **1** planned or worked out in the mind, not from experience; based on theory, not on fact. **2** dealing with theory only; not practical.

the sis (thē′sis), *n., pl.* **-ses** (-sēz). proposition or statement to be proved or to be maintained against objections.

thith er (thiᴛʜ′ər, ᴛʜiᴛʜ′ər), *adv.* to that place; there. —*adj.* on that side; farther. [Old English *thider*]

throt tle (throt′l), *n., v.,* **-tled, -tling.** —*n.* valve regulating the flow of gasoline vapor, steam, etc., to an engine. —*v.t.* stop the breath of by pressure on the throat; choke; strangle. [Middle English *throtel* < *throte* throat]

tier (tir), *n.* one of a series of rows arranged one above another: *tiers of seats in a stadium.* —*v.t., v.i.* arrange, or be arranged, in tiers. [< Middle French *tire,* originally, order < *tirer* to draw]

ti rade (tī′rād, tə rād′), *n.* **1** a long speech showing strong feeling. **2** a long, scolding speech.

tol er a ble (tol′ər ə bəl), *adj.* **1** able to be borne or endured; bearable. **2** fairly good; passable: *She is in tolerable health.*

tol e rate (tol′ə rāt′), *v.t.,* **-rat ed, -rat ing. 1** allow or permit: *The teacher would not tolerate any disorder.* **2** bear; endure; put up with: *I cannot tolerate loud noises.*

top o graph i cal (top′ə graf′ə kəl), *adj.* of or having to do with the surface features of a place or region. A topographical map shows mountains, rivers, etc.

tor rent (tôr′ənt, tor′ənt), *n.* **1** a violent, rushing stream of water. **2** a heavy downpour: *The rain came down in torrents.* **3** any violent, rushing stream; flood: *a torrent of abuse.*

touch stone (tuch′stōn′), *n.* **1** a black stone used to test the purity of gold or silver. **2** any means of testing; a test.

trans fix (tran sfiks′), *v.t.* **1** pierce through: *The hunter transfixed the lion with a spear.* **2** make motionless or helpless (with amazement, terror, grief, etc.). —**trans fix′ion,** *n.*

trans for ma tion (tran′sfər mā′shən), *n.* a transforming, or a changing of the appearance, shape, or nature of a thing or person.

trans pose (tran spōz′), *v.t.,* **-posed, -pos ing.** change the position or order of; interchange.

tra verse (trə vėrs′, trav′ərs), *v.i.,* **-versed, -vers ing. 1** walk or move in a crosswise direction; move back and forth: *That horse traverses.* **2** ski in a diagonal course.

treach er ous (trech′ər əs), *adj.* **1** not to be trusted; not faithful; disloyal. **2** having a false appearance of strength, security, etc.; not reliable; deceiving: *Thin ice is treacherous.*

treach er y (trech′ər ē), *n., pl.* **-er ies.** a breaking of faith; treacherous behavior; deceit. [< Old French *trecherie* < *trechier* to cheat]

tread (tred), *v.,* **trod, trod den** or **trod, tread ing,** *n.* —*v.i.* **1** set the foot down; walk; step: *tread through the meadow.* **2** step heavily; trample: *Don't tread on the flower beds.* —*v.t.* **1** set the feet on; walk on or through; step on: *tread the streets.* **2** follow; pursue; step according to: *tread the path of virtue.* —*n.* **1** act or sound of treading: *the tread of marching feet.* **2** way of walking: *walk with a heavy tread.*

tri bu nal (tri byü′nl, trī byü′-nl), *n.* **1** court of justice; place of judgment. **2** place where judges sit in a court of law.

trib ute (trib′yüt), *n.* **1** money paid by one nation or ruler to another for peace or protection, in acknowledgment of submission, or because of some agreement. **2** any forced payment. **3** an acknowledgment of thanks or respect.

tri dent (trīd′nt), *n.* a three-pronged spear. —*adj.* three-pronged. [< Latin *tridentem* < *tri-* three + *dentem* tooth]

trident

tri fle (trī′fəl), *n., v.,* **-fled, -fling.** —*n.* **1** thing having little value or importance. **2** a small amount; little bit: *I was a trifle late.* —*v.i.* talk or act lightly, not seriously: *Don't trifle with serious matters.* [< Old French *trufle* mockery, diminutive of *truffe* deception]

tri lin gual (trī ling′gwəl), *adj.* **1** able to speak three languages. **2** using three languages: *Switzerland is a trilingual country.* **3** written or expressed in three languages: *a trilingual text.*

tri syl lab ic (tris′ə lab′ik, trī′sə lab′ik), *adj.* having three syllables. —**tri syl′lab′i cal ly,** *adv.*

trod (trod), *v.* pt. and a pp. of **tread.**

trod den (trod′n), *v.* a pp. of **tread.**

tu mult (tü′mult, tyü′mult), *n.* **1** noise or uproar; commotion: *the tumult of the storm.* **2** a violent disturbance or disorder: *The cry of "Fire!" caused a tumult in the theater.* **3** a violent disturbance of mind or feeling; confusion or excitement. [< Latin *tumultus*]

a hat	i it	oi oil	ch child		a in about
ā age	ī ice	ou out	ng long		e in taken
ä far	o hot	u cup	sh she	ə = {	i in pencil
e let	ō open	u̇ put	th thin		o in lemon
ē equal	ô order	ü rule	ŦH then		u in circus
ėr term			zh measure	< = derived from

tu mul tu ous (tu mul′chü əs, tyü mul′chü əs), *adj.* **1** characterized by tumult; very noisy or disorderly; violent. **2** greatly disturbed. **3** rough; stormy. —**tu mul′tu ous ly,** *adv.*

tur ban (tėr′bən), *n.* **1** scarf wound around the head or around a cap, worn by men in parts of India and in some other countries. **2** any hat or headdress like this. [< Middle French *turbant* < Turkish *tülbend.* Doublet of TULIP.]

tym pa ni (tim′pə nē), *n. pl.* kettledrums. [< Italian, plural of *timpano* < Latin *tympanum*] Also, **timpani.** —**tym′pa nist,** *n.*

ty rant (tī′rənt), *n.* **1** person who uses power cruelly or unjustly. **2** a cruel or unjust ruler. **3** an absolute ruler, as in ancient Greece, who gained office by seizing it. [< Old French < Latin *tyrannus* < Greek *tyrannos*]

turban (def. 1)

un-, *prefix.* not ____; the opposite of ____: *Unequal = not equal; the opposite of equal. Unchanged = not changed. Unjust = not just.*

un a bashed (un′ə basht′), *adj.* not embarrassed, ashamed, or awed. —**un′a bash′ed ly,** *adv.*

un bri dled (un brī′dld), *adj.* **1** not having a bridle on. **2** not controlled; not restrained: *unbridled anger.*

un doubt ed ly (un dou′tid lē), *adv.* beyond doubt; certainly.

un du la tion (un′jə lā′shən, un′dyə lā′shən), *n.* **1** a wavelike motion; an undulating. **2** a wavy form. **3** one of a series of wavelike bends, curves, swellings, etc.

un eas y (un ē′zē), *adj.,* **-eas i er, -eas i est. 1** restless; disturbed; anxious: *an uneasy sleep, be uneasy about a decision.* **2** not comfortable. **3** not easy in manner; awkward. —**un eas′i ly,** *adv.*

un fore seen (un′fôr sēn′, un′fōr sēn′), *adj.* not known beforehand; unexpected.

u ni son (yü′nə sən, yü′nə zən), *n.* **1** harmonious combination or union; agreement: *The feet of marching soldiers move in unison. They spoke in unison.* **2** identity in pitch of two or more sounds, tones, etc. [< Medieval Latin *unisonus* sounding the same < Latin *unus* one + *sonus* sound]

un tram meled or **un tram melled** (un tram′əld), *adj.* not hindered; not restrained; free.

va cate (vā′kāt), *v.,* **-cat ed, -cat ing.** —*v.t.* **1** go away from and leave empty or unoccupied; make vacant: *They will vacate the house at the end of the month.* **2** make void; annul; cancel. —*v.i.* go away; leave. [< Latin *vacatum* emptied]

vac u ous (vak′yü əs), *adj.* showing no thought or intelligence; foolish; stupid: *a vacuous smile.* —**vac′u ous ly,** *adv.*

vag a bond (vag′ə bond), *n.* **1** an idle wanderer; tramp; vagrant. **2** a disreputable person; rascal. [< Old French < Latin *vagabundus* < *vagari* wander < *vagus* rambling]

val et (val′it, val′ā), *n.* **1** servant who takes care of a man's clothes and gives him personal service. **2** worker in a hotel who cleans or presses clothes. —*v.t., v.i.* serve as a valet.

val or (val′ər), *n.* bravery; courage.

var i ance (ver′ē əns, var′ē əns), *n.* **1** difference; disagreement: *variances in the spelling of proper names.* **2** a disagreeing or falling out; discord; quarrel. **3** a varying; change.

ve he ment (vē′ə mənt), *adj.* **1** having or showing strong feeling; caused by strong feeling; eager; passionate. **2** forceful; violent.

589

[< Latin *vehementem* being carried away < *vehere* carry] —**ve′-he ment ly**, *adv.*

venge ance (ven′jəns), *n.* **1** punishment in return for a wrong; revenge: *swear vengeance against an enemy.* **2 with a vengeance, a** with great force or violence. **b** extremely.

ven om ous (ven′ə məs), *adj.* **1** poisonous: *a venomous bite, a venomous snake.* **2** spiteful; malicious. —**ven′om ous ly**, *adv.*

ven ture (ven′chər), *n.*, *v.*, **-tured, -tur ing.** —*n.* **1** a risky or daring undertaking: *courage equal to any venture.* **2** thing risked; stake. —*v.t.* **1** expose to risk or danger: *Men venture their lives in war.* **2** dare when embarrassment, rejection, or rebuff might follow: *No one ventured to interrupt the speaker.* —*v.i.* dare to come, go, or proceed: *They ventured out on the thin ice and fell through.* [short for *aventure*, an earlier form of *adventure*]

verge (vèrj), *n.* **1** the point at which something begins or happens; brink: *business on the verge of ruin.* **2** a limiting edge, margin, or bound of something; border: *the verge of a cliff.*

ver i fy (ver′ə fī), *v.t.,* **-fied, -fy ing. 1** prove to be true; confirm. **2** test the correctness of; check for accuracy.

vex (veks), *v.t.* **1** anger by trifles; annoy; provoke. **2** worry; trouble; harass. **3** disturb by commotion; agitate.

vi cin i ty (və sin′ə tē), *n., pl.* **-ties. 1** region near or about a place; surrounding district; neighborhood: *know many people in New York and its vicinity.* **2** nearness in place; being close.

vig il (vij′əl), *n.* a staying awake for some purpose; a watching; watch. [< Latin *vigilia* < *vigil* watchful]

vile (vīl), *adj.,* **vil er, vil est. 1** very bad: *vile weather.* **2** foul; disgusting; obnoxious: *a vile smell.* **3** evil; low; immoral: *vile habits.* See synonym study below. [< Latin *vilis* cheap]
Syn. 3 Base, vile, low mean morally inferior and contemptible. **Base** means reduced to a low moral state, without honor or without moral standards, usually by selfishness or cowardice: *Betraying a friend for a reward is base.* **Vile** means evil and without moral standards or decency: *Ill-treatment and torture of helpless prisoners is a vile outrage.* **Low** means without a sense of decency or of what is honorable: *To steal from the collection plate in church is low.*

vin di cate (vin′də kāt), *v.t.,* **-cat ed, -cat ing. 1** clear from suspicion, dishonor, a hint or charge of wrongdoing, etc. **2** defend successfully against opposition; uphold; justify.

vir ile (vir′əl), *adj.* **1** of, belonging to, or characteristic of a man; manly; masculine. **2** vigorous; forceful.

vir tue (vėr′chü), *n.* moral excellence; goodness.

vis age (viz′ij), *n.* **1** face. **2** appearance or aspect. [< Old French < *vis* face < Latin *visus* sight < *videre* to see]

vis i bil i ty (viz′ə bil′ə tē), *n., pl.* **-ties.** condition or quality of being visible, or able to be seen.

vol ley (vol′ē), *n., pl.* **-leys. 1** shower of stones, bullets, arrows, etc. **2** the discharge of a number of guns or other weapons firing missiles at once. **3** a rapid outpouring or burst of words, oaths, shouts, cheers, etc.

vo lu mi nous (və lü′mə nəs), *adj.* **1** forming or filling a large book or many books: *a voluminous report.* **2** writing much: *a voluminous author.* **3** of great size; very bulky; large: *A voluminous cloak covered him from head to foot.*

vo lup tu ous (və lup′chü əs), *adj.* **1** caring much for the pleasures of the senses. **2** giving pleasure to the senses: *voluptuous music, voluptuous beauty.* [< Latin *voluptuosus* < *voluptas* pleasure]

vouch safe (vouch sāf′), *v.t.,* **-safed, -saf ing.** be willing to grant, do, or give: *The proud man vouchsafed no reply when we spoke to him.*

waft (waft, wäft), *v.t.* carry over water or through air: *The waves wafted the boat to shore.* —*v.i.* float. —*n.* **1** a breath or puff of air,

wind, scent, etc. **2** a waving movement; wave. **3** act of wafting.

walk (wôk), *v.i.* **1** go on foot. **2** roam: *The ghost will walk tonight.* **3** (in baseball) go to first base after the pitcher has thrown four balls. —*v.t.* **1** go over, on, or through: *The captain walked the deck.* **2** (in baseball) allow (a batter) to reach first base by pitching four balls.
walk out, a go on strike. **b** leave suddenly.
walk out on, INFORMAL. desert.
walk over, a defeat easily and by a wide margin. **b** act without regard for; trample on; override.

wane (wān), *v.i.,* **waned, wan ing. 1** lose size; become smaller gradually. **2** decline in power, influence, or importance. **3** decline in strength or intensity: *The light of day wanes in the evening.* **4** draw to a close.

war y (wer′ē, war′ē), *adj.,* **war i er, war i est. 1** on one's guard against danger, deception, etc.: *a wary fox.* **2** cautious or careful. **3 wary of,** cautious or careful about: *be wary of driving in heavy traffic.* —**war′i ly,** *adv.*

wel ter weight (wel′tər wāt′), *n.* boxer who weighs more than 135 pounds and less than 147 pounds.

wend (wend), *v.,* **wend ed** or **went, wend ing.** —*v.t.* direct (one's way): *We wended our way home.* —*v.i.* go.

whence (hwens), *adv.* from what place; from where: *Whence do you come?* —*conj.* **1** from what place, source, or cause: *She told whence she came.* **2** from which: *Let them return to the country whence they came.*

wick et (wik′it), *n.* **1** a small door or gate: *The big door has a wicket in it.* **2** a small window or opening, often having a grate or grill over it: *Buy your tickets at this wicket.*

wield (wēld), *v.t.* hold and use; manage; control: *wield a hammer.*

wings (wingz), *n. pl.* the spaces to the right or left of the stage of a theater, out of sight of the audience.

wist ful (wist′fəl), *adj.* longing; yearning: *A child stood looking with wistful eyes at the toys in the window.* —**wist′ful ly,** *adv.* —**wist′ful ness,** *n.*

wit (wit), *v.t., v.i.,* **wist, wit ting. 1** ARCHAIC. know. **2 to wit,** that is to say; namely: *To my daughter I leave all I own—to wit: my house, what is in it, and the land on which it stands.*

with al (wi ŦHôl′, wi thôl′), *adv.* **1** with it all; as well; besides; also: *I am tired and hungry and hurt withal.* **2** ARCHAIC. **a** in spite of all; nevertheless. **b** therewith. —*prep.* ARCHAIC. with. [Middle English < *with* + *all*]

wont (wunt, wōnt, wônt), *adj.* accustomed: *He was wont to read the paper at breakfast.* —*n.* custom; habit: *She rose early, as was her wont.* [originally past participle of Old English *wunian* be accustomed]

wrath ful (rath′fəl), *adj.* feeling or showing wrath; very angry. —**wrath′ful ly,** *adv.* —**wrath′ful ness,** *n.*

writhe (rīŦH), *v.,* **writhed, writh ing.** —*v.i.* **1** twist and turn; twist about. **2** suffer mentally; be very uncomfortable. —*v.t.* twist or bend (something). [Old English *wrīthan*]

wrought (rôt), *v.* ARCHAIC. a pt. and a pp. of **work.** worked; brought about.

ye (yē; *unstressed* yi), *pron. pl.* ARCHAIC. you. [Old English *gē*]

yeo man ry (yō′mən rē), *n.* yeomen, or (formerly) in Great Britain, people who owned land and farmed it themselves.

yon (yon), *adj., adv.* ARCHAIC. yonder; within sight but not near.

zeal (zēl), *n.* eager desire or effort; earnest enthusiasm; fervor: *religious zeal, work with zeal for pollution control.*

ze nith (zē′nith), *n.* **1** the point in the heavens directly overhead. **2** the highest point; apex: *At the zenith of its power Rome ruled all of civilized Europe.*

Glossary Illustration Acknowledgments

570—© Hap Stewart/Jeroboam Inc.; 574—National Film Board of Canada Phototheque; 581—Walter Chandoha; 583—Courtesy of the Consulate General of Japan, New York; 584—Courtesy of Istituto Geografico de Agostini-Novara; 589—(trident) Culver Pictures, Inc.; (turban) F.A.O.

Index of Reading and Literature Skills

Index of Vocabulary Exercises

Combined Skills Exercises

Index of Composition Assignments

Personal

Explanatory

Describe a character, using appropriate details, 139
Explain why someone is newsworthy, 139
Support a point about a character, 210
Explain why a character is most admired, 253
Support a statement about fantasy, 270
Explain why a character's plan fails, 313
Explain what historical figure's fate should be changed, 353
Explain what a character would consider "the greatest gift," 385
Explain a preference for becoming a character, 385
Support a statement about parental guidance, 445
Explain how immortals show human characteristics, 451
Describe a typical Greek hero, using examples, 451
Explain the term *poetic justice,* using an example, 451
Explain the likenesses and differences of characters' previous and present lives, 491
Explain how a statement is proven true, 523

Creative

Write a script for a scene, 75
Describe a character, 75
Write dialogue for an offstage scene, 113

Write a dialogue, 159
Write a fable, 189
Describe events from a certain point of view, 261
Write a newspaper article from a character's point of view, 313
Write a diary entry from a character's point of view, 313
Write a continuation of a selection, 327
Describe another world, 337
Write a progress report from a character's point of view, 379
Describe an imaginary experience, 385
Write a nature myth, 396
Recount events from a character's point of view, 400
Describe a monster, 413
Write a diary entry from a character's point of view, 523

Critical

Compare and contrast characters' feelings, 139
Compare and contrast two characters, 231
Discuss a character in light of a given topic, 253
Explain how a character generates certain attitudes in others, 253
Discuss likenesses and differences of characters' reactions, 516
Discuss how a character is helped by luck, 523

Index of Authors and Titles

Illustration Acknowledgments

Illustrations not credited are from Scott, Foresman and Company.

Unit 1   1—Robert McQuilkin Photography; 3—*Red-Tailed Hawk Mantling* by George McLean/Mill Pond Press, Inc., Venice, FL 33595; 7—From *The Art of Robert Bateman*, copyright © 1981 by Madison Press Books. Artwork copyright © 1983 by Boshkung Inc.; 12—Robert Wahlgren; 19—Yoshi Miyake; 25—Chuck Mitchell; 37, 40—Ben Othero; 47—Howard Simmons; 52—Wide World Photos; 55—Galen Rowell/High & Wild Photo; 59—Chris Bonington/Woodfin Camp & Associates; 63—Bob & Ira Spring; 73—Courtesy Chicago Historical Society.

Unit 2   76, 77—© BEELDRECHT, Amsterdam/V.A.G.A., New York, Collection Haags Gemeentemusem-The Hague, 1981; 79—Michael Conway; 88—Courtesy Gene Moore, Tiffany and Company; 91—Robert Korta; 97—Nina Leen, LIFE Magazine © Time, Inc.; 102 through 112—From Katherine Briggs: *ABBEY LUBBERS, BANSHEES & BOGGARTS* (Kestrel Books) pp. 33, 77. Illustrations copyright © 1979 by Yvonne Gilbert. Reprinted by permission of Penguin Books, Ltd.; 114, 115—From *Black Pilgrimage* by Tom Feelings. Published by Lothrop, Lee & Shepard Co., New York. Copyright © 1972 by Tom Feelings. All rights reserved. Reproduced by permission; 119—The Phillips Collection; 121, 127—Mike Muir; 137—UPI.

Unit 3   140, 141, 143—Robert Amft; 145, 147—John Tenniel illustration; 149—Robert Wahlgren; 152—*Passengers* by Nancy Ekholm Burkert, courtesy Mr. & Mrs. T. VanAlyea, Jr.; 154—Dan Morrill; 157—Charlotte Newfeld; 159—From *Jukebox: The Golden Age*, Lancaster, Miller & Schnobrich Publishers, Berkeley. Photo by Kaz Tsuruta; 162—Robert Llewellyn; 164, 165—Library of Congress; 167—From *archy and mehitabel* by Don Marquis. Illustration by George Herriman. Copyright 1930, 33 by Doubleday Company, Inc. Reproduced by permission; 169—Bert Williams Photography; 172, 173—Phil Renaud; 177—*Mexican* painted by Dwight D. Eisenhower/Private Collection; 180—From *Creative American Quilting* by Suzzy Payne and Susan Murwin. Copyright © 1983 by Suzzy Payne and Susan Murwin. Published by Fleming H. Revell Co. Used by permission; 182—Robert Amft; 184—© 1981 Don Dixon; 187—Robert Amft.

Unit 4   190, 191—Robert Amft; 193—Photographs: Sharon Downie Cooper; 199—© 1983 by Rodney Smith from *In the Land of Light: Israel, a Portrait of Its People*. Houghton, Mifflin Company; 215—Courtesy The New York Philharmonic Orchestra/Photo: Don Hunstein; 232—Brown Brothers; 235—Tony Kelly; 239–245—Franz Altschuler; 251—Courtesy Institute for Intercultural Studies, NY.

Unit 5   254, 255—Leo and Diane Dillon; 257—Robert Amft; 263—Photo by Simon Marsden from *In Ruins* by Duncan McLaren, a Borzoi Book published by Alfred A. Knopf, Inc. All rights reserved. Reproduced by permission; 266, 267—Judith Cheng; 275, 281—John Slobodnik; 285—© Bill Binzen; 291—Donald Fiorino; 297—Paul Fusco/MAGNUM Photos; 305—Lisa Ebright; 310—Robert Amft.

Unit 6   314, 315—© Toby Richards; 316—*Amusement Park* by Vestie Davis/Collection of Rebecca and Sarah Bahm; 319, 324, 328—Museum of Modern Art/Film Stills Archive; 329—From *The Pictures of J. R. R. Tolkien* by J. R. R. Tolkein. Copyright © 1979 by George Allen and Unwin (Publishers) Ltd. Reprinted by permission of Houghton, Mifflin Company; 333—Andy Zito; 339—*Medicine Man* by Oscar Howe. Photograph courtesy Patricia Janis Broder, *American Indian Painting and Sculpture*, Abbeville Press, N.Y.; 342—Reprinted from *Holiday* Magazine, courtesy Travel-Holiday Magazine Inc., Travel Building, Floral Park, N.Y.; 349—© Bill Binzen; 359 through 375—Allen Davis; 382, 383—Courtesy Mme. Rene Magritte.

Unit 7   386, 387—Don Nibbelink; 391 through 405, also 416, 438, 441—Reprinted by permission of Schocken Books Inc. from *Gods, Men & Monsters from the Greek Myths* by Michael Gibson, illustrated by Giovanni Caselli. Copyright © 1977 by Eurobook Limited; 410 (t,l)—Illustration of Medusa from p. 104 by Wayne Anderson in *THE FLIGHT OF DRAGONS* by Peter Dickinson. Illustration copyright © 1979 by Wayne Anderson. Reprinted by permission of Harper & Row, Publishers, Inc.; 410 (t,r and b,l)—Scala, Florence; 410 (b,r)—Uffizi Gallery; 419—Robert Amft; 423, 426, 427—Don Nibbelink; 433 (t)—Courtesy of the Trustees of the British Museum; 433 (b)—Museum of Fine Arts, Boston.

Unit 8   452 through 514—Herb Danska; 517—Loomis Dean, courtesy Otto Frank. LIFE magazine © Time, Inc.; 521—Ben Othero.

Handbook   531—From the collection of Cynthia Zilliac; 537—Illustration by Louis Jambor from *Little Women* by Louisa May Alcott. Illustrated Junior Library edition, copyright 1947. Copyright renewed © 1974 by Grosset & Dunlap, Inc.; 540—*Awatovi Snake Society* (detail) by Neil David, Sr. Photograph courtesy Patricia Janis Broder, *American Indian Painting and Sculpture*, Abbeville Press, N.Y.; 541—Robert Amft; 551—Mark Daniels; 552—Courtesy A. T. & T. Co. Photo Center; 553—Sternboard Eagle, Index of American Design, National Gallery of Art, Washington, D.C.; 556—Shelley Canton.